EU LAW IN POPULIST TIMES

The rise of Euroskepticism and populism poses a dramatic challenge to the EU and highlights the EU's growing legal powers over core areas of state sovereignty. Authored by leading academics and policymakers, this book provides a comprehensive and cutting-edge analysis of the fields of EU law at the heart of contemporary political debates – economic policy, human migration, internal security, and constitutional fundamentals at the national level. Following the specialist contributions, the conclusion draws out critical lessons for improving legitimacy and advancing the rule of law, rights, and democracy in sovereignty-sensitive areas of EU law. Accessible to students, this volume is an invaluable resource for researchers and scholars of EU law and politics.

FRANCESCA BIGNAMI is Leroy Sorenson Merrifield Research Professor of Law at George Washington University. Among her recent publications is the volume *Comparative Law and Regulation: Understanding the Global Regulatory Process* (2016).

EU Law in Populist Times

CRISES AND PROSPECTS

Edited by
FRANCESCA BIGNAMI
George Washington University

CAMBRIDGE
UNIVERSITY PRESS

University Printing House, Cambridge CB2 8BS, United Kingdom

One Liberty Plaza, 20th Floor, New York, NY 10006, USA

477 Williamstown Road, Port Melbourne, VIC 3207, Australia

314–321, 3rd Floor, Plot 3, Splendor Forum, Jasola District Centre, New Delhi – 110025, India

79 Anson Road, #06–04/06, Singapore 079906

Cambridge University Press is part of the University of Cambridge.

It furthers the University's mission by disseminating knowledge in the pursuit of education, learning, and research at the highest international levels of excellence.

www.cambridge.org
Information on this title: www.cambridge.org/9781108485081
DOI: 10.1017/9781108755641

© Francesca Bignami 2020

This publication is in copyright. Subject to statutory exception and to the provisions of relevant collective licensing agreements, no reproduction of any part may take place without the written permission of Cambridge University Press.

First published 2020

Printed in the United Kingdom by TJ International Ltd, Padstow Cornwall

A catalogue record for this publication is available from the British Library.

Library of Congress Cataloging-in-Publication Data
NAMES: Bignami, Francesca, editor.
TITLE: EU law in populist times : crises and prospects / edited by Francesca Bignami, George Washington University, Washington DC
OTHER TITLES: European Union law in populist times
DESCRIPTION: Cambridge, United Kingdom ; New York, NY, USA ; Cambridge University Press, 2019. | "I am grateful to The George Washington University Law School, Queen Mary University of London, the FREE Group, and the Electronic Privacy Information Center (EPIC) for providing the funding for the conference held on March 23-24, 2018, at which initial drafts of the chapters were presented."–ECIP preface. | Includes bibliographical references and index.
IDENTIFIERS: LCCN 2019036039 (print) | LCCN 2019036040 (ebook) | ISBN 9781108485081 (hardback) | ISBN 9781108719179 (paperback) | ISBN 9781108755641 (epub)
SUBJECTS: LCSH: Law–European Union countries–Congresses. | Populism–European Union countries–Congresses. | European Union countries–Politics and government–21st century–Congresses.
CLASSIFICATION: LCC KJE935 .E9 2019 (print) | LCC KJE935 (ebook) | DDC 341.242/2–dc23
LC record available at https://lccn.loc.gov/2019036039
LC ebook record available at https://lccn.loc.gov/2019036040

ISBN 978-1-108-48508-1 Hardback

Cambridge University Press has no responsibility for the persistence or accuracy of URLs for external or third-party internet websites referred to in this publication and does not guarantee that any content on such websites is, or will remain, accurate or appropriate.

Contents

Notes on Contributors	*page* ix
Preface	xvii
INTRODUCTION	1

1   **Introduction: EU Law, Sovereignty, and Populism**   3
Francesca Bignami

PART I   ECONOMIC POLICY   31

2   **The Future of the European Economic and Monetary Union: Issues of Constitutional Law**   33
Matthias Ruffert

3   **Post-Crisis Economic and Social Policy: Some Thoughts on Structural Reforms 2.0**   67
Philomila Tsoukala

4   **Politicized Integration: The Case of the Eurozone Crisis**   91
Nicolas Jabko

5   **EU Financial Regulation after the Neoliberal Moment**   110
Elliot Posner

6   **The Euro Crisis and the Transformation of the European Political System**   135
Renaud Dehousse

vi *Contents*

PART II HUMAN MIGRATION 155

7   On Equal Treatment, Social Justice and the Introduction of
    Parliamentarism in the European Union 157
    Ulf Öberg and Nathalie Leyns

8   The Emerging Architecture of EU Asylum Policy: Insights into
    the Administrative Governance of the Common European
    Asylum System 191
    Evangelia (Lilian) Tsourdi

9   Databases for Non-EU Nationals and the Right to Private Life:
    Towards a System of Generalised Surveillance of Movement? 227
    Niovi Vavoula

PART III INTERNAL SECURITY 267

10 The EU and International Terrorism: Promoting Free
    Movement of Persons, the Right to Privacy and Security 269
    Gilles de Kerchove and Christiane Höhn

11 The Preventive Turn in European Security Policy: Towards a
    Rule of Law Crisis? 301
    Valsamis Mitsilegas

12 The Opening Salvo: The CLOUD Act, e-Evidence Proposals,
    and EU–US Discussions Regarding Law Enforcement Access
    to Data across Borders 319
    Jennifer Daskal

13 Preserving Article 8 in Times of Crisis: Constraining
    Derogations from the European Convention on
    Human Rights 342
    Marc Rotenberg and Eleni Kyriakides

14 Progress and Failure in the Area of Freedom, Security,
    and Justice 375
    Emilio De Capitani

Contents

vii

PART IV CONSTITUTIONAL FUNDAMENTALS
411

15 Defending Democracy in EU Member States: Beyond Article
7 TEU
Kim Lane Scheppele and R. Daniel Kelemen
413

16 The Politics of Resentment and First Principles in the
European Court of Justice
Tomasz Tadeusz Koncewicz
457

17 The Populist Backlash against Europe: Why Only Alternative
Economic and Social Policies Can Stop the Rise of Populism
in Europe
Bojan Bugarič
477

18 The Democratic Disconnect, the Power-Legitimacy Nexus,
and the Future of EU Governance
Peter L. Lindseth
505

CONCLUSION
531

19 Conclusion: The Rule of Law, Rights, and Democracy in
Sovereignty-Sensitive Domains
Francesca Bignami
533

Index
577

Notes on Contributors

Francesca Bignami
Francesca Bignami is Leroy Sorenson Merrifield Research Professor of Law at George Washington University. Her research interests include EU and US administrative law, regulatory law, and privacy law. Among her recent publications is the volume *Comparative Law and Regulation: Understanding the Global Regulatory Process* (2016). She is an elected member of the International Academy of Comparative Law and a member of the editorial board of the American Journal of Comparative Law. Until 2008, she was Full Professor of Law at Duke Law School, where she also served as the Director of Duke University's Center for European Studies. She received her AB from Harvard University and her JD from Yale Law School.

Bojan Bugarič
Bojan Bugarič is Professor of Law at the University of Sheffield. Previously, he was Professor of Law at the University of Ljubljana, Slovenia. He was a Fulbright Visiting Professor at the University of California, Los Angeles (UCLA). His research interests include constitutional and comparative constitutional law, EU law, law and democracy, and law and development, broadly conceived. Among his most recent publications are "Central Europe's Descent into Autocracy: A Constitutional Analysis of Authoritarian Populism," *International Journal of Constitutional Law* (2019); "The Right to Democracy in a Populist Era," *American Journal of International Law* (2018). He has a SJD from Wisconsin Law School, a master's degree from UCLA, and a LLB from University of Ljubljana.

Jennifer Daskal
Jennifer Daskal is an Associate Professor of Law at American University Washington College of Law, where she teaches and writes in the fields of

criminal, national security, and constitutional law. From 2009–2011, she was counsel to the Assistant Attorney General for National Security at the Department of Justice. From 2016–2017, she was an Open Society Institute Fellow working on issues related to privacy and law enforcement access to data across borders. Her recent publications include "Borders and Bits," *Vanderbilt Law Review* (2018) and "The Un-Territoriality of Data," *Yale Law Journal* (2015). She is an executive editor of and regular contributor to the Just Security blog.

Emilio De Capitani

Emilio De Capitani is Visiting Professor at the Department of Law, Queen Mary University of London, where he teaches on issues linked with the European Area of Freedom Security and Justice and the institutional dynamics of the European Parliament. He is a former member of the European Parliament's civil service where he served as Secretary of the European Parliament Civil Liberties Committee (LIBE, 1998–2011) and was responsible for the European Parliament's interinstitutional relations and the "legislative backbone" (1985–1998). He has been a teaching fellow at the Scuola Superiore S. Anna (Pisa) and Visiting Professor at Università degli Studi di Napoli "L'Orientale".

Renaud Dehousse

Renaud Dehousse is President of the European University Institute (EUI), a position held since September 1, 2016. Before coming to the EUI, he was Professor and Jean Monnet Chair in EU law and European Policy Studies at Sciences Po Paris, where he founded and directed the Centre d'études européennes (2005–2016). He chaired Sciences Po Paris's executive board from 2013 to 2016. Before joining Sciences Po in 1999, he taught at the EUI, where he directed the European Law Academy, and at the University of Pisa. Among his policy activities, he was a scientific advisor at Notre Europe, a study and research center founded by Jacques Delors.

Gilles de Kerchove

Gilles de Kerchove was appointed EU Counter-Terrorism Coordinator on September 19, 2007. In this position, he coordinates the work of the European Union in the field of counter-terrorism, closely monitors the implementation of the EU's counter-terrorism strategy and fosters better communication between the EU and third countries to ensure that the Union plays an active role in the fight against terrorism. He previously was Director for Justice and Home Affairs at the Council Secretariat and Deputy Secretary of the Convention responsible for drafting the EU Charter of Fundamental Rights (1999–2000). He has published a number of books on European law.

Christiane Höhn

Christiane Höhn is the Principal Adviser to the EU Counter-Terrorism Coordinator, Brussels, a position she has held since 2010. Her previous assignments at the EU were transatlantic relations and nonproliferation and disarmament. Prior to joining the Council of the EU in 2004, she was a researcher at the Max Planck Institute for International Law in Heidelberg and an affiliate at the Center for Public Leadership, Harvard Kennedy School of Government. She holds a PhD in international law from Heidelberg University, an LLM from Harvard Law School and the two German State examinations in law. She has published a book and several articles on international law and international affairs.

Nicolas Jabko

Nicolas Jabko is Associate Professor of Political Science at Johns Hopkins University. He received his PhD from UC Berkeley in 2001 and was a member of the research faculty at Sciences Po-Paris for nine years before coming to Johns Hopkins. His current research interests include neoliberalism, economic crisis, and constructivist and pragmatist approaches to political economy. He is the author of *L'Europe par le Marché: Histoire d'une stratégie improbable* (2009) and *Playing the Market: A Political Strategy for Uniting Europe, 1985–2005* (2006), and co-editor of the eighth volume of the *State of the European Union* series (2005).

R. Daniel Kelemen

R. Daniel Kelemen is Professor of Political Science and Jean Monnet Chair in European Union Politics at Rutgers University. Kelemen's research interests include the politics of the European Union, law and politics, comparative political economy, and comparative public policy. His most recent book, *Eurolegalism: The Transformation of Law and Regulation in the European Union* (2011), won the Best Book Award from the European Union Studies Association. Kelemen previously served as the Director of the Center for European Studies at Rutgers University. Prior to Rutgers, Kelemen was Fellow in Politics, Lincoln College, University of Oxford. He was educated at Berkeley (AB in Sociology) and Stanford (MA and PhD in Political Science).

Tomasz Tadeusz Koncewicz

Tomasz Tadeusz Koncewicz is Professor of Law and Director of the Department of European and Comparative Law at the University of Gdańsk. In 2017–2018 he was LAPA Crane Fellow at Princeton University. Currently, he is 2019 Fernand Braudel Senior Fellow at the Department Law of the European University Institute in Florence. His extensive experience in European law includes serving as référendaire at the Court of Justice of the EU in Luxembourg, and as the legal adviser to the Office of the Polish Constitutional Court. He is an attorney specializing in strategic litigation before supranational courts. Professor Koncewicz received law degrees from the Universities of Wroclaw and Edinburgh.

Eleni Kyriakides

Eleni Kyriakides is International Counsel at the Electronic Privacy Information Center (EPIC) and oversees EPIC's International Program. She has contributed to EPIC's amicus submissions on global privacy issues, including the Microsoft case (US Supreme Court) and the "Schrems II" case (CJEU). Ms. Kyriakides has spoken before the European Parliament on cross-border access to data by law enforcement, represented EPIC at international data protection conferences, and organized NGO panels in Brussels and Hong Kong in cooperation with the Public Voice coalition. She is a graduate of Columbia Law School, where she was a Harlan Fiske Stone Scholar.

Nathalie Leyns

Nathalie Leyns is Legal Secretary (référendaire) at the General Court of the European Union. Previously, she was admitted to the Luxembourg bar (2013) and worked as a lawyer for two leading European and international law firms, where she specialized in corporate law, banking law, and investment funds. She earned her law degree in 2010 from the Université Libre de Bruxelles, received a diploma from the European Inter-University Center in 2011, and graduated from the University of Cambridge in 2012 with a specialization in European Union law.

Peter L. Lindseth

Peter Lindseth is Olimpiad S. Ioffe Professor of International and Comparative Law at the University of Connecticut Law School (UConn). Peter Lindseth's research and teaching focus on administrative law in comparative perspective, along with compliance, European integration, and legal history. His books include a reinterpretation of the history of European integration, *Power and Legitimacy: Reconciling Europe and the Nation-State*, as well as two co-edited volumes on *Comparative Administrative Law*, which have redefined that field. In addition to his work at UConn, Professor Lindseth is a regular Visiting Professor at Queen Mary University of London and a Research Associate at the Centre for International Studies at the University of Oxford.

Valsamis Mitsilegas

Valsamis Mitsilegas is Professor of European Criminal Law and Global Security, Academic Lead for Internationalization and, since 2012, Head of the Department of Law at Queen Mary University of London (QMUL). He served as Dean for Research for the Humanities and Social Sciences and Inaugural Director of the Queen Mary Institute for the Humanities and Social Sciences (IHSS) from January to December 2017 and has been the Director of the Queen Mary Criminal Justice Centre since 2011. From 2001 to 2005 he served as legal adviser to the House of Lords European Union Committee.

Ulf Öberg

Ulf Öberg has been a judge at the General Court of the European Union since September 19, 2016. Admitted to the Swedish bar in 2006, he was the founder and managing partner of the boutique law firm Advokatfirman Öberg & Associés AB and has pleaded extensively before Swedish courts and the EU Courts in matters involving, among others, European competition law, state aid law, constitutional law, as well as employment and labor law. As well as being a lecturer at the University of Stockholm for sixteen years, Mr. Öberg has written and lectured on legal topics relating primarily to competition law and constitutional law. He was a clerk for the late Justice Hans Ragnemalm at the Court of Justice of the European Union from 1995 to 2000.

Elliot Posner

Elliot Posner is a Professor of Political Science at Case Western Reserve University. His research focuses on international cooperation, regulatory power, bureaucracy, new market formation, and international order. He has written on the politics of finance in the European Union, the internal sources of the polity's external power, the changing terms of transatlantic regulatory cooperation, and the political relevance of transnational soft law in Brussels' rulemaking. He and Abraham Newman are the authors of *Voluntary Disruptions: International Soft Law, Finance and Power* (2018). In 2018–2019 he was a fellow at IMÉRA Institute for Advanced Study, Aix-Marseille Université.

Marc Rotenberg

Marc Rotenberg is President and Executive Director of the Electronic Privacy Information Center (EPIC) in Washington, DC. He teaches information privacy and open government law at Georgetown University Law Center and frequently testifies before Congress on emerging privacy and civil liberties issues. He is a founding board member and former Chair of the Public Interest Registry, which manages the .ORG domain. He currently serves on expert panels for the National Academies of Science and the OECD

Directorate for Science, Technology, and Innovation. He is a graduate of Harvard College and Stanford Law School, and received an LLM in International and Comparative Law.

Matthias Ruffert

Matthias Ruffert is Professor of Public Law and European Law at the Law Faculty of the Humboldt University Berlin and Director of the Walter Hallstein-Institute for European Constitutional Law since April 2016. From 2002–2016, he was Professor of Public Law, European Law and Public International Law at the Friedrich-Schiller-University Jena, Germany. He has also served as Judge at the Administrative Court of Appeal of Thuringia (2006–2016), Member of the Thuringian Constitutional Court (2010–2015), and Member of the Review Board "Jurisprudence" of the Deutsche Forschungsgemeinschaft/German National Science Foundation (2008–2016, since 2010 as spokesperson).

Kim Lane Scheppele

Kim Lane Scheppele is the Laurance S. Rockefeller Professor of Sociology and International Affairs in the Woodrow Wilson School and the University Center for Human Values at Princeton University. From 2005–2015, she was Director of the Program in Law and Public Affairs at Princeton, after ten years on the faculty of the University of Pennsylvania Law School. Scheppele's work focuses on the intersection of constitutional and international law, particularly in constitutional systems under stress. Scheppele is an elected member of the American Academy of Arts and Sciences and the International Academy of Comparative Law. In 2014, she received the Law and Society Association's Kalven Prize for influential scholarship.

Philomila Tsoukala

Philomila Tsoukala is a Professor of Law at Georgetown Law. Her research interests focus on the position of family law in the political economy of Western liberal states, with a special emphasis on the gendered character of family and market regulation. Her 2015 article "Household Regulation and European Integration: The Family Portrait of a Crisis" won the Yntema Prize from the American Society of Comparative Law. She is coeditor, along with Professors Areen and Spindelman, of a major Family Law casebook. She has a SJD from Harvard Law School, a master's degree from Paris II, Panthéon-Assas, and a LLB from Aristotle University of Thessaloniki.

Evangelia (Lilian) Tsourdi

Evangelia (Lilian) Tsourdi is an Assistant Professor and Dutch Research Council grantee at the Law Faculty of Maastricht University, as well as a visiting professor at Sciences Po Paris. She is a member of the coordination team of the Odysseus Academic Network for Legal Studies on Immigration and Asylum in Europe. She holds a PhD from the Université libre de Bruxelles (ULB), and was previously a Max Weber Fellow at the European University Institute (EUI) and a Departmental Lecturer at the Refugee Studies Centre of the University of Oxford. She has coedited two books: *Exploring the Boundaries of Refugee Law: Current Protection Challenges* (2015) and *Research Handbook on EU Migration and Asylum Law* (with P. De Bruycker, 2020).

Niovi Vavoula

Niovi Vavoula is Lecturer in Migration and Security at Queen Mary, University of London and an editorial assistant of the *New Journal of European Criminal Law*. Prior to her appointment, she was a part-time teacher at the London School of Economics and Political Science (LSE) and Post-Doctoral Research Assistant at Queen Mary, University of London. She holds a PhD (2017) and LLM in European Law (2011) from Queen Mary, University of London and an LLB from the University of Athens (2008). Her monograph on the privacy challenges stemming from the establishment of pan-European immigration databases will be published in early 2020.

Preface

The impetus for this book is the disjuncture between the canon of EU law, especially as the subject is taught in US law schools, and the new legal and political realities of populism and growing Euroskepticism. Both the traditional focus on the substantive law of the single market and the conventional narrative of European integration as a technocratic and apolitical project are woefully inadequate for understanding EU law's current place in European politics and society. Although this shift is recognized by virtually all EU law scholars and is reflected in the breadth of research agendas, the scholarship remains fragmented and there is no single text that presents the range of EU law that has become salient in today's political environment. Neither is there a single text that engages in sustained theoretical and normative reflection on the evolution of EU law in each of the important new policy areas and that draws out the analytical and theoretical connections across the myriad domains.

This book aims to fill both the teaching and scholarly gaps. It presents the law of economic policy, human migration, internal security, and constitutional fundamentals (designed to counter democratic backsliding) with a law or public policy student in mind. Although the book assumes familiarity with the legal and institutional structure of the EU, it narrates the development of the law in the specific policy domains from scratch. At the same time, the chapters expose the reader to the cutting-edge theoretical and policy debates that mark the individual areas of legal inquiry and that stretch across the subject areas. By taking stock of the new dimensions of the increasingly sprawling field of EU law, the book speaks to upper-level students, as well as to researchers and policymakers specialized in one subfield of EU law who wish to understand the connections with other subfields. The conviction underlying the book is that it is necessary to have a solid grasp of the EU xviii *Preface*

law at the heart of today's polarized debates if one is to engage with those debates and to understand the constructive possibilities for the EU's future.

A project of this breadth required the generous collaboration and support of a great number of individuals and institutions. I am grateful to The George Washington University Law School, Queen Mary University of London, the FREE Group, and the Electronic Privacy Information Center (EPIC) for providing the funding for the conference held on March 23–24, 2018, at which initial drafts of the chapters were presented. At the conference, the authors received valuable feedback from colleagues, including Fernanda Nicola, Dimitry Kochenov, Abe Newman, Anna Gelpern, and Philippe De Bruycker. Herb Somers, Foreign and International Law Librarian at the Burns Law Library, provided valuable assistance at multiple stages of the project. I thank the anonymous reviewers for their helpful comments. To Catalina Milos, an advanced researcher and doctoral student at GW Law, I extend my deep gratitude for her extraordinarily professional, knowledgeable, and dedicated work on the project, from its inception to the completion of the manuscript. JonZachary Forbes assisted with the final stages of the manuscript. Daniela Caruso and Dmitry Kochenov read the introduction and conclusion to the book and gave me invaluable suggestions and insights. Most of all, I thank the authors for their commitment to the project, their patience in tailoring their contributions to the overall ambition of the book, and the superb chapters that follow.

Introduction

1

Introduction

EU Law, Sovereignty, and Populism

FRANCESCA BIGNAMI

Over the past decade, the European Union has been shaken to the core by the rise of populist parties and movements. The watershed moment was the global financial crisis of 2008, which, for Europe, quickly escalated into a sovereign debt crisis. In southern debtor countries, populist left-wing parties have risen to prominence on anti-austerity platforms. They have either been in government, as in the case of Greece's Syriza party and Italy's Five Star Movement, or have come close to entering government, as with Spain's Podemos party, which won 21 percent of the vote in the 2015 parliamentary elections.

Although the economic crisis was not as dramatic in Eastern Europe, there it has served as fodder for the rise of authoritarian populism, beginning with Hungary, where Fidesz won a parliamentary supermajority in 2010.[1] At the same time, parties on the extreme right in Western Europe have mutated from fringe to mainstream political players. Although not openly authoritarian, as some of their East European counterparts, they are both ethnonationalist and anti-immigrant. To take the most salient examples, in France, the Front National's candidate came second in the last presidential election; in the Netherlands, the Party for Freedom became the second-largest party in the last parliamentary elections; the Sweden Democrats won 17 percent of the vote in the most recent elections; and, representing an extraordinary moment for German postwar politics, in 2017 the Alternative für Deutschland entered the Bundestag with over 12 percent of the vote. Perhaps the most striking, and certainly the most consequential, example of the populist turn to date was the British referendum of June 2016, in which the majority voted to leave the European Union, and which has triggered the painful and protracted Brexit process. The most recent test of strength for populist parties was the May

---

[1] For purposes of brevity, the term "Eastern Europe" is used in this chapter to refer to the countries in the former Eastern Bloc that joined the EU in 2004 and in later years.

2019 vote for the 2019–2024 European Parliament. The results confirmed the decline of the mainstream parties of the left and the right and the growing strength of newer forces across the political spectrum, including, but not limited to, the extreme right.

The national parties and movements behind the populist turn are radically different in many respects, but they all share a common hostility to the EU political establishment. In Western Europe, these parties typically oppose the political forces that have governed their countries throughout the postwar era and that have generally been proponents of European integration. In Eastern Europe, due to the volatile character of party systems, certain populist parties such as Fidesz (in Hungary) and Law and Justice (in Poland) have had significant experience in government in recent years. In these cases, anti-establishment sentiment is directed almost entirely outwards, at mainstream politics in Western Europe and at the EU level.

In populist discourse, the European Union is shorthand for a variety of evils – from greedy bankers, to austerity-imposing technocrats, social dumping, uncontrolled immigration, and enforced pluralism and multi-culturalism.[2] On the left, the EU is blamed for dismantling the welfare state and undermining social rights through its management of the euro crisis. On the right, the principal rallying cry is the ethnic and cultural identity of the nation state. European integration is, by definition, a cosmopolitan political project that seeks to overcome parochial nationalisms and it has proven an easy target for right-wing populists. In particular, the ire of the right has been fueled by EU policies aimed at promoting the migration of persons among the Member States, as well as managing the migration of certain categories of individuals from outside the EU.

As this string of complaints highlights, at the heart of the populist critique is not simply an amorphous establishment, but a concrete set of EU laws and policies. Populist leaders take aim at the elements of the EU agenda that go to the heart of national sovereignty: economic policy, human migration, internal security, and fundamental constitutional precepts connected with the rule of law, rights, and democracy. These are all relatively new areas of EU govern-ance linked to the EU's switch in *raison d'être* in the Maastricht Treaty signed in 1992. Until then, the EU had been primarily a market-making and market-regulating entity. In the Maastricht Treaty, the foundations of an ambitious

---

[2] Throughout this introductory chapter, and reflecting the nomenclature that has applied since the Lisbon Treaty, which was signed in 2007 and entered into force in late 2009, the term "European Union" is used to refer to the political entity that was previously named the European Economic Community and, later, the European Community.

political union were laid down. The Member States committed to economic and monetary union (EMU) and cooperation on justice and home affairs (now renamed the Area of Freedom, Security, and Justice or AFSJ), which refers to border control, immigration from third countries, and law enforcement and criminal justice.[3] These AFSJ competences were added to an already substantial body of law facilitating the intra-European migration of Member State nationals for economic purposes, known as the law of free movement of persons. The preamble to the Maastricht Treaty also prominently stated the common attachment of all the signatory states in their own constitutional law to the "principles of liberty, democracy and respect for human rights and fundamental freedoms and of the rule of law." In the years since Maastricht, cooperation on EMU, AFSJ, and free movement of persons has been extensive, and there have also been efforts to improve human rights and rule-of-law monitoring. As a result, the EU has come to exercise authority over core areas of state sovereignty. The classic economic, territorial control, security, and constitutional functions of the nation state are performed today not by Member States alone, but in conjunction with the EU.

This book affords a detailed and comprehensive analysis of the sovereignty-sensitive areas of EU law that have become extraordinarily salient with the populist surge and that have taken on extreme urgency for the future of Europe – *economic policy*; *human migration*, defined in this book as both intra-European migration and third-country immigration (economic immigration and asylum seekers), as well as border control of the EU external border; *internal security*, which refers to both police and judicial cooperation; and *constitutional fundamentals*, a long list of values, but which can be boiled down to the rule of law, rights, and democracy. With the growing importance and politicization of these areas of EU governance, it has become critical to understand their basic legal contours, their fundamental challenges, and their future prospects. The contributors to this volume, all recognized authorities in their respective subfields, provide a state-of-the-art account of the law, debates, and future reform possibilities in each of these hot-button areas. At the same time, the authors employ a variety of theoretical frameworks, drawn from both the law and political science, to illuminate and assess the current trajectories of EU law.

By providing a cross-cutting perspective on the subjects, this volume fills an important gap in the legal literature, both didactic and scholarly. Didactic

---

[3] The Maastricht Treaty also included cooperation on foreign and defense policy, called the Common Foreign and Security Policy, but this continues to be the least developed area of European integration and is not taken up in this volume.

efforts at the systematic exposition of EU law continue to focus on the single market as the substantive core of the field and to treat economic policy, human migration, internal security, and constitutional fundamentals as peripheral, and unrelated, topics.[4] Although this approach is faithful to the historical development of European integration, it is out of touch with the current realities of EU law and politics. Today, with the exception of intelligence agencies, defense, and foreign policy, EU law squarely occupies every sovereignty-sensitive area of public policymaking and this book provides an essential guide to that law. In doing so, it equips the reader with the basic knowledge necessary to engage in the highly charged debates that have swept European politics. The claims thrown around about the EU and its law contain a mixture of truth, over-simplification, and falsehood. This book lays the groundwork for a more level-headed understanding of how the EU intervenes in core areas of state sovereignty.

From a scholarly perspective, by affording a cross-cutting look at what are generally siloed areas of legal scholarship, this volume creates important theoretical and normative opportunities. It serves as the basis for drawing out analytical frames and theoretical dynamics that can improve our understanding of EU law and inform the future development of the law.[5] In these areas, the EU exerts legal authority over issues that are central to the symbolic politics, the organizational and policy backbone, and the public law of the nation state. Because of the national sensitivities of economic policy, human migration, internal security, and constitutional fundamentals, the EU's legal authority was not announced in a grand act of political union, but rather has accrued piecemeal through spillover – inter-state cooperation on relatively low-hanging fruit has expanded to cooperation in more controversial policy areas. In the concluding chapter of this volume, I argue that there are three critical implications of these shared roots that have not been adequately

---

[4] See, e.g., Roger J. Goebel et al., *Cases and Materials on European Law*, 4th ed. (Saint Paul, MN: West Academic Publishing, 2015); Anthony Arnull, *European Union Law* (Oxford: Oxford University Press, 2017); Stephen Weatherill, *Cases & Materials on EU Law*, 12th ed. (Oxford: Oxford University Press, 2016).

[5] The proposition that a cross-cutting analysis of EU governance outside the single market domain can lead to fruitful theoretical insights has been explored in political science, see Philipp Genschel and Markus Jachtenfuchs, eds., *Beyond the Regulatory Polity? The European Integration of Core State Powers* (Oxford: Oxford University Press, 2014) and Gerda Falkner, ed., *EU Policies in Times of Crisis* (Abingdon: Routledge, 2017). Legal scholarship so far has examined the far-ranging legal and constitutional consequences of the euro crisis, e.g., Damian Chalmers, Markus Jachtenfuchs, and Christian Joerges, eds., *The End of the Eurocrats' Dream: Adjusting to European Diversity* (Cambridge: Cambridge University Press, 2016), but has not included developments in other areas of sovereignty-sensitive EU law in the analysis.

Introduction: EU Law, Sovereignty, and Populism

appreciated in the subject-specific legal scholarship – implications for the quality of law, the protection of rights, and the operation of democracy.

The remainder of this introduction proceeds as follows. The next section explains the historical spillover trajectory through which EU law has come to occupy sovereignty-sensitive areas and thus serve as fodder for populist parties and political movements. I then preview the individual chapters by subject area, focusing on the unique theoretical and analytical contribution of each. Last, I sketch the cross-cutting legal challenges and reform proposals that are set out in depth in my concluding chapter to this book.

I SPILLOVER INTO ECONOMIC POLICY, HUMAN MIGRATION, INTERNAL SECURITY, AND CONSTITUTIONAL FUNDAMENTALS

How has the EU been catapulted from a free trade organization to a quasi-federal entity with power over economic policy, the territorial belonging and safety of people, and the essential aspects of liberal democratic political morality? The answer is spillover. That is, the Member States have pooled sovereignty in relatively well-delimited areas that benefit from a high degree of consensus and then, based on the experience with such cooperation, have proceeded to share sovereignty in other, related areas. This logic, associated with the positive and normative theory of neo-functionalism, was originally conceived as a process of gradually expanding supranational governance by jumping from one successful cooperative endeavor to another to maximize the common gains to be had from European integration.[6] In many respects, the gradual expansion of free movement of persons in the 1980s and 1990s can be said to have followed this trajectory. In the past decade or so, the political incentives underpinning spillover have been cast more in the

---

[6] Jean Monnet, *Memoirs*, trans. Richard Mayne (London: Third Millennium Publishing, 2015), 300, 393–394 (first published in Great Britain in 1978 by William Collins Sons & Co. Ltd); Ernst Haas, *The Uniting of Europe* (Stanford, CA: Stanford University Press, 1968), xxxi–xxxvii. Although spillover is associated with the broader theory of neo-functionalism, this discussion is not meant to take sides in the long-running debate between neo-functionalists and intergovernmentalists in political science. See Liesbet Hooghe and Gary Marks, "A Postfunctionalist Theory: From Permissive Consensus to Constraining Dissensus," *British Journal of Political Science* 39, no. 1 (2009): 3–5. The concept of spillover is used only to capture the sequencing of the policies that have come to occupy the EU agenda, and not to address the question of which actors (national governments or supranational institutions) and interest groups (national or transnational) are responsible for putting those policies on the EU agenda.

8   *Francesca Bignami*

negative vein – new policy prerogatives being necessary to stave off disaster.[7] The prime example of this negative logic is the euro crisis and the leap from monetary union to economic and fiscal policy. Regardless of the precise nature of the incentives, the undeniable centrality of spillover to European integration has come with the absence of a grand plan for a federal union. What has generally come first for nation states has come piece-by-piece and last, if at all, for the European Union.

1 Economic Policy

To turn to the spillover specifics: As hinted previously, in the case of economic policy, it was tight cooperation on monetary policy that gave rise to economic interdependence and intense pressure to integrate fiscal and budgetary matters during the euro crisis. The Maastricht Treaty introduced the goal of monetary union and a single currency, and the process was completed on January 1, 2002, when the euro entered into circulation in the twelve original members of the Eurozone.[8] To the extent that there was a Eurozone economic policy it was fiscal discipline, to be imposed by legal rules and financial markets. To avoid inflationary pressures and promote the overall economic stability of the Eurozone, Member States signed up to the Stability and Growth Pact in 1997, which set a 3 percent GDP limit for budget deficits and a 60 percent GDP limit for state debt. There were so-called preventive and corrective arms, designed to ensure that Member States complied with the budgetary limits. At the same time, there was the Treaty "no-bail out clause," which prohibited the assumption of national debt by either the EU or the Member States and therefore made debtor countries reliant on markets to finance their budgets – and hence, the theory went, subject to the discipline of financial-market demand for their debt.

As was obvious to anyone who witnessed the unfolding of events after 2008, fiscal discipline as the EU's lone economic policy tool failed miserably.[9] After the euro was introduced, financial markets for sovereign debt failed to price in different risk premiums for countries with different debt prospects and economic outlooks – say, Germany and Italy. Moreover, as demonstrated by the

---

[7] Erik Jones, R. Daniel Kelemen, and Sophie Meunier, "Failing Forward? The Euro Crisis and the Incomplete Nature of European Integration," *Comparative Political Studies* 49, no. 7 (2016): 1010–1034.

[8] For a brief overview of this early EMU history, see Chapter 2 and literature cited therein.

[9] For description and analysis of the euro crisis from a political economy perspective, see Matthias Matthijs and Mark Blyth, eds., *The Future of the Euro* (Oxford: Oxford University Press, 2015).

failed effort to enforce the deficit limit against France and Germany in 2004, it was politically impossible to enforce the EU rules limiting budget spending. When the global financial crisis hit in 2008, the EU was woefully unprepared. First came the banking crisis. Particularly hard-hit were smaller economies such as Ireland that had experienced large inflows of private capital during the heady first days of monetary union. Then, by 2010, the banking crisis had escalated into a sovereign debt crisis, as countries were forced to underwrite their banks' debts and as their own access to credit dried up. Propelled by the fear of contagion and financial and economic collapse – and as many have noted, solicitous of the economic interests of the French and German banks that were some of the biggest lenders in the crisis-hit countries – Eurozone leaders acted in fits and starts to prop up the system.

The end result is a radically transformed EMU that contains both a more robust economic dimension and a more interventionist monetary policy. The European Central Bank (ECB) has assumed an increasingly important role in crisis prevention and management.[10] To avoid a recurrence of the financial crisis, there is now centralized ECB licensing and supervision of large banks (Single Supervisory Mechanism) and a mechanism for winding up failing banks, including an EU fund to compensate partially the shareholders and creditors of failed banks (Single Resolution Mechanism). Moreover, during and after the euro crisis, the ECB intervened with economic stimulus through a massive quantitative easing program involving the purchase of sovereign debt and other types of securities on secondary markets.

Beyond the financial markets dimension, there is also now a more extensive EU economic policy.[11] This is the change that has generated the most political controversy and has been responsible for fueling many strands of populist discontent – both in southern debtor countries, where anti-establishment parties have accused EU-imposed austerity of dismantling the public sector and welfare programs, and in northern creditor states, where parties on the center-right, including populist ones, have resisted fiscal transfers to sinking southern economies.[12] There now is a permanent organization, the European Stability Mechanism (ESM), with the capacity to undertake large-scale fiscal transfers to Eurozone states in grave financial difficulty. These transfers are structured as loans subject to strict conditionality. Although program

---

[10] On EU banking and economic law, see Antonio Estella, *Legal Foundations of EU Economic Governance* (Cambridge: Cambridge University Press, 2018).

[11] On all of what follows in this section and for extensive citations to the scholarly literature, see the contributions in Part I of this volume.

[12] See Hanspeter Kriesi and Takis S. Pappas, eds., *European Populism in the Shadow of the Great Recession* (Colchester: ECPR Press, 2016).

countries, i.e. those receiving ESM loans, are subject to particularly tight constraints on their public spending, all Eurozone countries now take part in a heightened system of economic surveillance and sanctioning. The Fiscal Compact requires that the signatory countries adhere to a balanced budget rule and introduce mechanisms domestically to enforce the rule. EU legislation known as the Six Pack and the Two Pack has put into place an elaborate monitoring system: Each year, as part of the European Semester, all Member States submit their economic and budgetary plans for review by the European Commission (and Council); in addition, Eurozone countries submit their draft annual budgets before those budgets can be voted on by their national parliaments. There is surveillance for budget deficits in excess of the target imposed by the Stability and Growth Pact (Excessive Deficit Procedure) and for macroeconomic imbalances (Macroeconomic Imbalance Procedure), which comprise a broad range of macroeconomic indicators linked to economic stability. Eurozone Member States that breach these targets and indicators can be required to put down deposits or pay fines or their payments from the European Structural and Investment Funds can be suspended.[13]

2 Human Migration

Turning to human migration, the spillover story begins with the renewed impetus for market integration in the Single European Act of 1986. That treaty contained an important provision declaring that "[t]he internal market shall comprise an area without internal frontiers in which the free movement of goods, services, persons and capital is ensured in accordance with the provisions of this Treaty."[14] The commitment to remove borders for persons soon ran into political difficulty because logically speaking the freedom to travel without having to stop at the border and produce papers would have to extend to all individuals crossing national borders, not only to persons with the right to move to seek employment or engage in other forms of economic activity under the existing law on free movement of persons.[15] Although this law has been in considerable flux over the past decades, it was the case in 1986, and it

[13] The Structural and Investment Funds represent the largest part of the EU budget and are directed at the agricultural and fishing industries and promoting territorial cohesion by funding projects in less prosperous regions. See European Commission, *European Structural and Investment Funds 2014–2020: Official Texts and Commentaries* (Luxembourg: Publications Office of the European Union, 2015).

[14] Article 8a Treaty Establishing the European Economic Community.

[15] On this early history of the Schengen Convention and Justice and Home Affairs, see Steve Peers, *EU Justice and Home Affairs Law* (Harlow: Longman, 1999), 63–76.

still is, that the travel and residence rights that are conferred under the law of free movement of persons are tethered to the activity of an economically active person who is a citizen of one Member State and moves to another Member State, either alone or with the rest of the family unit.[16] The person moving must generally be a citizen of another Member State and must move for a *bona fide* economic reason – in the case of travel for short periods, receiving services such as those connected with the tourist or healthcare industries, and in the case of longer periods of residence, participating in the labor market or attending an educational establishment. The Single European Act's market "without internal frontiers" would facilitate the movement not only of individuals with rights under the existing free movement law, but also everyone else – most notably third-country nationals and individuals engaged in criminal activity.

In light of the ramifications of the removal of border controls, the Member States divided early on into two groups – the skeptics, comprising the United Kingdom, Ireland, and Denmark, and the integrationists, comprising the original core of continental Member States. Because of these and other divisions, a subset of Member States moved forward with the project under international law and outside the EU framework, with the Schengen Agreement in 1985 and then the Schengen Convention in 1990. The Schengen Convention, which came into force in 1993 in seven Member States but was only applied in 1995, removed border checks among the participating Member States and created a single, common external border around the so-called Schengen Area. At the same time, as hinted previously, it was widely recognized that this policy would not only facilitate intra-European migration of EU nationals but would also have spillover effects for the movement of third-country nationals. Therefore, the removal of border controls was accompanied by cooperation on immigration, asylum, and visa policy (collectively referred to here as the immigration aspects of human migration).[17] The centerpiece of so-called Schengen flanking measures was, and continues to be, the Schengen Information System (SIS), a centralized database of information on undesirable persons.[18] Especially in the early years, the SIS was

---

[16] For a general discussion of the law of free movement of persons through the Treaty of Lisbon, see Koen Lenaerts, Piet Van Nuffel, and Robert Bray, *Constitutional Law of the European Union*, 2nd ed. (London: Sweet & Maxwell, 2005).

[17] Because of the focus of this volume, this chapter does not address cooperation on civil matters such as contracts enforcement, which is historically connected to cooperation on immigration and law enforcement and in many texts is discussed in conjunction with the latter two policies.

[18] See generally Chapter 9 and the literature cited therein. The original SIS has been replaced by a second-generation database called SIS II, but the basic contours remain the same.

dominated by entries on third-country nationals who were to be refused entry or stay in the Schengen Area. In parallel, there was cooperation on asylum policy through a separate international agreement – the Dublin Convention, which was signed in 1990 and entered into force in 1997.[19] This was designed to address the problem of "refugees in orbit," namely the prospect that no Schengen Area country would take responsibility for examining a particular asylum claim, and the problem of using the borderless travel area to file asylum claims in multiple jurisdictions.

Although spillover from borders to immigration has not been entirely even across the specific issue areas, cooperation today is robust. This is reflected in both the formal and the substantive dimensions of EU policymaking. Since the Amsterdam Treaty, which was signed in 1997 and entered into force in 1999, the authority to make and implement policy on border controls and immigration are squarely EU competences under what is now called the Treaty on the Functioning of the European Union (TFEU). Moreover, there has been significant EU output in most of the issue areas, with the notable exception of long-term economic immigration.[20] There is extensive law and administrative policy on managing the common external border; on visa policy, i.e. whether and under what conditions third-country nationals must obtain a visa to come into the Schengen Area for short stays of three months or less, as well as the requirements for entry and exit of citizens of visa-free countries; and on asylum seekers and the system for processing individuals who qualify for refugee protection under international law.

Parallel to the development of the Schengen Area was the emergence of an increasingly robust law of free movement of persons.[21] In the 1970s and early 1980s most of the impetus came from the European Court of Justice, which issued a string of important judgments on the rights of workers, their family members, and students under the Treaty and secondary legislation. By 1990, however, the legislative branch had begun to take the lead, with a series of measures that extended certain free movement rights to non-economically active

---

[19] See generally Chapter 8.

[20] See generally Steve Peers, *EU Immigration and Asylum Law*, vol. I of *EU Justice and Home Affairs Law*, 4th ed. (Oxford: Oxford University Press, 2016); for a comprehensive overview of developments since 2009, see Chapter 14.

[21] For a brief overview of this historical trajectory, see Chapter 7. See also Dimitry Kochenov and Richard Plender, "EU Citizenship: From an Incipient Form to an Incipient Substance? The Discovery of the Treaty Text," *European Law Review* 37, no. 4 (2012): 369–396; Dimitry Kochenov, ed., *EU Citizenship and Federalism: The Role of Rights* (Cambridge: Cambridge University Press, 2017); Martijn van den Brink, "EU Citizenship and (Fundamental) Rights: Empirical, Normative, and Conceptual Problems," *European Law Journal* 25, no. 1 (2019): 21–36.

Introduction: EU Law, Sovereignty, and Populism 13

persons. Then, in the Maastricht Treaty, the Member States introduced the status of EU citizenship. Although the rights conferred by EU citizenship were notoriously ambiguous, supranational citizenship in conjunction with the existing market freedoms combined to expand the free movement rights of Member State nationals. The adoption of the Citizenship Directive in 2004,[22] which codified much of the Court of Justice's case law and which coincided with East European accession, set the stage for the current era of intra-EU migration.

The remarkable internal migration that has resulted from the law of free movement of persons, in combination with the Schengen system, has been a source of political backlash in the Member States. Right-wing populist parties have drawn much of their strength from the fear of migration within the Schengen Area and the perceived threat to economic well-being and, even more so, to national and ethnic identity.[23] The campaigning on the Brexit referendum illustrates vividly the variety of anxieties that human migration has triggered.[24] On the one hand, the finger was pointed at low-skill workers from Member States in Eastern Europe who were accused of dragging down working conditions and wage levels and undermining British national identity. On the other hand, even though the United Kingdom never joined the Schengen Area and therefore was never at risk of so-called secondary movements of refugees from frontline countries like Greece and Italy to other Schengen states, images of Syrian refugees lining up at the Hungarian and Austrian borders went viral during the Brexit campaign. The not-so-subtle message was that the United Kingdom risked being overwhelmed by people from the Middle East belonging to an entirely different ethnic, racial, cultural, and religious tradition. Strands of this economic and identitarian political rhetoric can be found in virtually every Member State.

3 *Internal Security*

As mentioned in the last section, the removal of internal border controls and the creation of the Schengen Area raised the prospect of both illegitimate

---

[22] European Parliament and Council, Directive 2004/58/EC, 2004 O.J. (L 229) 35.

[23] Hooghe and Marks, "A Postfunctionalist Theory of European Integration," 13; Liesbet Hooghe and Gary Marks, "Re-engaging Grand Theory: European Integration in the 21st Century," EUI Working Papers, RSCAS 2018/43, 2018, 9–12.

[24] See Simon Deakin, "Brexit, Labour Rights and Migration: Why Wisbech Matters to Brussels," *German Law Journal, Brexit Supplement* 17 (2016): 13–20; Jonathan Faull, "European Law in the United Kingdom," *European Law Review* 43, no. 5 (2018): 785–786; Neil Nugent, "Brexit: Yet Another Crisis for the EU," in *Brexit and Beyond: Rethinking the Futures of Europe*, eds. Benjamin Martill and Uta Staiger (London: UCL Press, 2018), 59.

migration by third-country nationals *and* the exploitation of border-free travel by criminal actors, to avoid detection by their national police authorities. Therefore, the Schengen Convention also contained a law enforcement component. Most importantly, the Schengen Information System (SIS) included data on individuals wanted for arrest and extradition, witnesses or persons summoned by judicial authorities, and objects such as stolen vehicles connected to police investigations and criminal proceedings. The SIS was designed to be accessed not only by national border control officers and immigration officials but also by police and customs enforcement authorities when investigating individuals on their national territory or at their external borders.

Spillover from borders to policing and criminal justice, what this book refers to collectively as internal security policy, has developed more slowly than immigration policy.[25] Although internal security was included in the Maastricht Treaty, it remained in the Treaty on European Union for almost two decades. (The Treaty on European Union [TEU] is the Treaty that, together with the TFEU, comprises the legal foundation of the EU and that historically was more intergovernmental and less supranational than the TFEU.[26]) In the Lisbon Treaty, however, competences for internal security were transferred to the TFEU. This change included qualified majority voting in the Council for most types of internal security measures, which has accelerated considerably the policy output in the domain. The result today is a fairly developed body of EU law that covers everything from the early stages of police investigations up through criminal prosecution and conviction.

---

[25] See generally Steve Peers, *EU Criminal Law, Policing, and Civil Law*, vol. II of *EU Justice and Home Affairs Law*, 4th ed. (Oxford: Oxford University Press, 2016); for a comprehensive overview of developments since 2009, see Chapter 14.

[26] The distinction between intergovernmentalism and supranationalism appears at a number of points in this introductory chapter and the rest of the volume. For most purposes, the distinguishing characteristic concerns the institutions and processes through which decisions are to be made and enforced. In the supranational, "Community method" the European Commission, European Parliament, and the European Court of Justice are fully empowered, and Member State voting in the Council is by qualified majority. In intergovernmentalism, most of the power rests with the Member States, with no or little role for the other institutions, and the voting rule is unanimity. Historically, the procedures contained in the TEU were of the intergovernmental variety, while those in the predecessor treaties to the TFEU were of the supranational variety. The situation has changed since the Lisbon Treaty, since the TEU was revamped to incorporate the EU's constitutional and institutional framework. Still today, however, policy areas over which the Member States seek to retain control, most notably the Common Foreign and Security Policy, remain in the TEU.

The connection between internal security policy and populism is less direct than with respect to economic policy and human migration and, if anything, operates in the inverse sense. In certain populist discourse, human migration in the Schengen Area has been linked to terrorism, serious crime, and other types of social disorder. The threat to economic well-being and national identity from the influx of foreign nationals is coupled with the perception of risk to physical safety and public order. In political rhetoric, the association between violence and the loss of control over borders is particularly evident with respect to terrorist acts by Islamic extremists; however, it also extends to less dramatic forms of criminal violence and to other types of immigrant populations. In limited respects, the EU's growing body of internal security law and policy can be said to be directed at these fears. The Schengen system has been implicated in certain highly visible security failures such as the Paris terrorist attack of fall 2015, involving Islamic extremists that moved between Belgium and France,[27] and European policymakers have sought to improve counter-terrorism coordination among the Member States.[28] The law enforcement aspects of the numerous EU databases on third-country nationals have been enhanced, playing to the characterization of third-country nationals as potential threats to physical safety and public order.[29] Overall, however, there is strong continuity between the original purposes of Schengen flanking measures and the evolution of EU law and policy in the internal security domain. The Schengen Area of borderless travel and Europe's increasingly integrated social space have created significant challenges for police and judicial authorities, still organized along national lines, and therefore policymakers have sought to enhance the tools available to these authorities in pursuing cross-border criminal activity.

4 Constitutional Fundamentals

In the case of constitutional fundamentals, the spillover trajectory is still in its incipiency. In the aftermath of World War Two, European cooperation split into two different international systems: the Council of Europe, headquartered in Strasbourg, was dedicated to fundamental rights and democracy; the

---

[27] See, e.g., *Rapport fait au nom de la commission d'enquête relative aux moyens mis en œuvre par l'État pour lutter contre le terrorisme depuis le 7 janvier 2015*, Rapport No. 3922, Assemblé nationale, Quatorzième Législature (July 5, 2016).

[28] See Chapters 10 and 11.

[29] See Chapter 9.

European Economic Community, headquartered in Brussels, had responsibility for markets.[30] Over time, this division of labor has broken down. Most notably, since the 1960s, the European Court of Justice has developed a jurisprudence of rights and values under the rubric of *principes généraux du droit*, applicable to the EU's own institutions and scheme of government; with the Charter of Fundamental Rights of the European Union, proclaimed in 2000 and officially adopted in 2009, the EU also acquired a formal catalogue of rights.[31] Still today, however, the Member States are reluctant to cede control over their internal democratic and human rights practices to EU scrutiny. Compared to the Council of Europe system, the EU is significantly more powerful and therefore giving it full-fledged prerogatives would represent a far greater loss of state control and sovereignty over the essential blueprint of how national government works and domestic affairs are conducted.

The question of giving the EU a role in monitoring internal affairs cropped up with prospect of enlargement to the East after the fall of the Berlin Wall. At the Copenhagen European Council of 1993, when the official green light was given to the eventual membership of countries in the former East, the accession criteria were crafted to include, among other things, respect for the rule of law, rights, and democracy.[32] The European Commission was tasked with monitoring the progress of the candidate countries toward fulfillment of these criteria, one of the prerequisites for becoming a Member State. However, there was concern that even if the applicant states met the Copenhagen criteria before accession, afterwards, as post-Communist states with a recent history of authoritarianism, they would be tempted to backtrack on fundamental values. Therefore, with the Amsterdam Treaty of 1997, the TEU was amended to include the principles of the rule of law, rights, and

---

[30] For an analysis of the early EU choice to side step the issue of fundamental rights, see Gráinne de Búrca, "The Road Not Taken: The European Union as a Global Human Rights Actor," *American Journal of International Law* 105, no. 4 (2011): 649–693.

[31] On the early history of this constitutional transformation, see Bill Davies, *Resisting the European Court of Justice: West Germany's Confrontation with European Law, 1949–1979* (New York: Cambridge University Press, 2012); on developments after the Maastricht Treaty, see Jean-Claude Piris, *The Lisbon Treaty: A Legal and Political Analysis* (Cambridge: Cambridge University Press, 2010).

[32] For a detailed discussion of this pre-accession history, see Milada Anna Vachudova, *Europe Undivided: Democracy, Leverage, and Integration after Communism* (Oxford: Oxford University Press, 2005); Dmitry Kochenov, *EU Enlargement and the Failure of Conditionality: Pre-Accession Conditionality in the Fields of Democracy and the Rule of Law* (The Hague: Kluwer Law International, 2008).

democracy (Article 6) and a procedure for sanctioning Member States for "a serious and persistent breach" of those principles (Article 7).[33]

What are now numbered Articles 2 and 7 of the TEU remain the EU's main policy tool for overseeing the rule of law, rights, and democracy at the national level. Notwithstanding the many tweaks to the procedure that have been made since 1997, it remains a weak policy instrument. The list of liberal democratic principles, now called values, has gotten longer, but the values themselves remain vague and undefined: "respect for human dignity, freedom, democracy, equality, the rule of law and respect for human rights, including the rights of persons belonging to minorities."[34] As a result, the Council of Europe system continues to operate as the primary reference point for the flesh and bones of the values and the EU institutions have relied heavily on European Court of Human Rights (ECtHR) case law and Venice Commission opinions.[35] Moreover, the Article 7 TEU procedure remains highly intergovernmental and the determination of a "serious and persistent breach" is subject to unanimity among the Member States (with the exception of the Member State being sanctioned); even though Article 7 TEU has been formally triggered against Poland, and now Hungary, the process has been excruciatingly slow and most doubt that it will ever be brought to completion and sanctions imposed.[36]

Although EU powers over the rule of law, rights, and democracy are less substantial than in any of the other policy areas covered in this volume, there is evidence that here too spillover is pushing in the direction of greater European integration. In this domain, the spillover comes from the administrative and judicial architecture essential to virtually every field of EU law. The EU has a very small administrative and judicial apparatus. For the most part, it relies on the bureaucracies and judiciaries of the Member States to implement EU law through a system known as integrated administration:

---

[33] On the post-Amsterdam legal trajectory of the rule of law, democracy, and rights, see Chapter 15 and literature cited therein.

[34] Article 2 TEU.

[35] The Venice Commission is an advisory body of the Council of Europe. It authors reports and studies in the areas of the rule of law, democracy, and rights, see, e.g., Venice Commission, Rule of Law Checklist, Study No. 711/2013. CDL-AD(2016)007 (March 18, 2016), and issues opinions on the constitutional situation in Member States, including many recent ones on Poland and Hungary. See Venice Commission, "Documents by Opinions and Studies," www.venice.coe.int/WebForms/documents/by_opinion.aspx?lang=EN.

[36] *Reasoned Proposal in Accordance with Article 7(1) of the Treaty on European Union Regarding the Rule of Law in Poland*, COM (2017) 835 final (December 20, 2017); European Parliament, *Report on a Proposal Calling on the Council to Determine, Pursuant to Article 7(1) of the Treaty on European Union, the Existence of a Clear Risk of a Serious Breach by Hungary of the Values on Which the Union Is Founded*, A8–0250/2018 (July 4, 2018).

National authorities implement the law on their territories in cooperation with other national authorities and coordinated by EU-level authorities.[37] As is essential in rule-of-law systems, these national authorities are subject to the jurisdiction of their national courts, which in turn participate in the EU court system by making preliminary references on EU law to the European Court of Justice (ECJ). In the single market days, the national authorities responsible for implementation were mostly the bureaucratic actors responsible for regulating markets, under the supervision of their courts; now that the EU exercises competences in civil and criminal justice, these authorities are also courts directly, which are responsible for deciding civil and criminal cases. A certain degree of civil service independence from executive branch politics has always been important for Member State administrative authorities to faithfully perform their tasks under EU law, resist inevitable national biases, and cooperate with their counterparts at the EU level and in the Member States. For all of the obvious rule-of-law reasons, the independence of courts is even more critical. It is because of the centrality of national courts, especially in the implementation of EU criminal law, that it has been possible to mount challenges before the ECJ against authoritarian moves to curb judicial independence in Hungary and Poland, outside the throttled Article 7 TEU framework, and inside the powerful judicial architecture of the TFEU.[38]

The emerging jurisprudence on independence of courts and, in some cases, administrative actors has the potential to unravel the EU's system of integrated administration because, as a matter of law and not simply practice,[39] Member State actors can refuse to cooperate with their counterparts in other Member States if there are reasons to suspect their rule-of-law bona fides. The most prominent illustration of this point comes from the liberty-impinging area of criminal law – the *Celmer* preliminary reference in which the Irish court maintained that it did not have a duty to execute a European

---

[37] See Francesca Bignami, "Foreword: The Administrative Law of the European Union," *Law and Contemporary Problems* 68, no. 1 (2004): 10–16; Giacinto Della Cananea, "The European Union's Mixed Administrative Proceedings," *Law and Contemporary Problems* 68, no. 1 (2004): 197–218; Herwig C. H. Hofmann, Gerard C. Rowe, and Alexander H. Türk, *Administrative Law and Policy of the European Union* (Oxford: Oxford University Press, 2012).

[38] For a discussion of this jurisprudence, see Chapter 15.

[39] On the importance of cooperation and trust in the practice of EU integrated administration, with particular attention to East–West relations, see Francesca Bignami, "The Challenge of Cooperative Regulatory Relations after Enlargement," in *Law and Governance in an Enlarged European Union*, eds. George A. Bermann and Katharina Pistor (Portland and Oxford: Hart Publishing, 2004), 97–140.

arrest warrant originating in Poland and return the suspect to Poland to face trial.[40] Even matters of less consequence for liberal rights can be affected by a lack of trust in the independence and integrity of the cooperating authorities. For instance, short-stay visas and long-term residence permits give foreign nationals the right to travel anywhere within the Schengen Area;[41] social security certificates give the recipient the right to avoid paying into the social security system of the host state where he or she is temporarily working (because the certificate warrants that the worker is paying into the system of the home state).[42] If there are doubts as to the structural independence and operational good faith of the issuing authorities, why should other Member States recognize those visas, residence permits, and social security certificates as valid, along with all the benefits they confer within the single market and the Schengen Area? As with the euro crisis, where the need to save the single currency spurred the development of economic policy, the threat of unraveling policies that European political leaders are highly invested in, for instance the preservation of the Schengen Area, might prompt more vigorous legislative action, such as making access to European Structural and Investment Funds conditional on the domestic rule of law.[43] It goes without saying that these incentives are especially strong for the ECJ, which bears direct responsibility for the EU's implementation architecture, and which is coming under pressure to develop a role in monitoring respect for liberal democratic values at the national level.

In the case of constitutional fundamentals, there is a two-way relationship between EU law and populism. On the one hand, Article 7 TEU and the Court of Justice's jurisprudence are targeted directly at the authoritarian strand of populism that seeks to take over liberal democratic institutions and undo checks and balances in the name of "the people."[44] On the other hand, like economic policy and human migration, the conflict generated by the EU's intervention plays to an important element of populism's political base. In the rhetoric of authoritarian populists, the genuine representatives of the people

---

[40] Case C-216/18 PPU, *Minister for Justice and Equality* v. *LM*, ECLI:EU:C:2018:586. For an analysis of the relationship between judicial independence and judicial cooperation in the context of the European Arrest Warrant, see Petra Bárd and Wouter van Ballengooij, "Judicial Independence as a Precondition for Mutual Trust? The CJEU in *Minister for Justice and Equality* v. *LM*," *New Journal of European Criminal Law*, 9, no. 3 (2018): 353–365.

[41] For a general discussion of this aspect of immigration law, see Chapter 14.

[42] For a discussion of EU social security law and emerging cracks in the judicial and administrative architecture of that law due to lack of trust among certain national authorities, see Chapter 7.

[43] Kim Lane Scheppele and R. Daniel Kelemen discuss the possible development of conditionality in Chapter 15.

[44] On authoritarian populism, see Chapter 17 and the literature cited therein.

(themselves) are pitted against independent courts and supranational bodies, which are cast as elite bodies that thwart the will of the people and that serve other, external masters.[45] Resisting the EU, and in particular the law of the EU, is an important component of this ideology. There are many examples of outright noncompliance with EU law. For instance, Hungary and Poland, along with the Czech Republic and Slovakia, refused to take their refugee quotas under the emergency EU relocation decisions adopted during the height of the Syrian refugee crisis.[46] The Polish government initially resisted attempts to require Poland to comply with EU law on nature conservation and continued logging notwithstanding an ECJ interim order.[47] Article 7 TEU and the European Court of Justice's case law on judicial independence is yet another arena for this populist–supranational conflict to play out, but an extraordinarily visible one where the payoffs for authoritarian leaders are potentially high.

In the preamble to the Treaty of Rome, signed in 1957, the political leaders of the original six Member States declared that they were "determined to lay the foundations of an ever closer union among the peoples of Europe." This historical discussion of the spillover process by which the EU has come to exercise legal authority in classic areas of state sovereignty shows that Europe's founding fathers were actually quite prescient. At the same time, as also highlighted by the discussion, this law has been highly salient and has served as a rallying cry for populist political forces, many of which directly oppose ever closer union. This is the general state of affairs in sovereignty-sensitive domains. It is now time to take each field in turn and preview the individual contributions.

II SURVEY OF THE VOLUME

The book's consideration of the individual subjects begins with *economic policy* and the legal and institutional landscape of post-crisis Eurozone governance. In Chapter 2, Matthias Ruffert briefly narrates the historical development of EMU, with special attention to the role of constitutional courts, and then turns to a presentation of the most salient reform proposals that have been put forward by a variety of stakeholders. He unpacks the proposals by

---

[45] For a discussion of what is often referred to as "the politics of resentment," see Chapter 16 and the literature cited therein.

[46] See Bruno De Witte and Evangelia (Lilian) Tsourdi, "Confrontation on Relocation: The Court of Justice Endorses the Emergency Scheme for Compulsory Relocation of Asylum Seekers within the European Union: *Slovak Republic and Hungary* v. *Council*," *Common Market Law Review* 55, no. 5 (2018): 1457–1494.

[47] See Chapter 16 for a detailed discussion of the Polish Białowieża Forest saga.

focusing on three elements that are common to virtually all of them: an expanded budget for the Eurozone; more flexible surveillance of national budgetary discipline; and a revised institutional framework including, most prominently, more parliamentary accountability. Ruffert argues that as a matter of intergovernmental and party politics, and possibly also as a matter of constitutional law, more budgetary spending will have to be coupled with a robust commitment to fiscal stability if the proposals are to move forward. With respect to parliamentary accountability, Ruffert takes the view that it is largely satisfied through the ESM's consensus rule for granting loans, since the governments on the Board of Governors answer to their national parliaments. In the future, however, as EMU governance becomes more politically driven, he argues that accountability to the European Parliament may have to be enhanced; at the same time, the constitutional framework should be flexible, to allow for political debate and change.

Chapter 3 turns specifically to the fiscal and economic surveillance aspect of EMU governance. As Philomila Tsoukala explains, in the course of the European Semester, the European Commission reviews the budgetary and economic policies of the Member States and formulates country-specific recommendations (CSRs) designed to improve growth and fiscal stability. Based on its experience in administering conditionality in country bailouts, the Commission has developed CSRs into a far-reaching set of structural reforms and best practices for public administration and labor, welfare, tax, and social security policy. There can be powerful incentives to adopt the recommended reforms, especially for Member States at risk of being sanctioned under the corrective limb of the Macroeconomic Imbalance Procedure. As analyzed by Tsoukala, CSRs are largely aimed at liberalizing markets and creating export-based economies. Although some commentators have argued that the recent inclusion of social indicators for evaluating national economic policy represents a change of direction, Tsoukala is skeptical. She argues that EMU's continued emphasis on budgetary discipline and the low capacity for redistribution in the Eurozone will most likely produce pressure to converge on a minimalist version of the welfare state – flexible labor markets and welfare for the neediest. Overall, Tsoukala questions the legitimacy of CSRs given that the European Commission is a technocratic body cut off from genuine democratic debate.

Nicolas Jabko, in Chapter 4, takes a step back from the specifics of economic governance and situates the post-2008 developments in the political science literature on European integration and international relations. He asks the question of why, contrary to general expectations, the politically charged issue of bailouts, with their highly visible consequences for state sovereignty, gave way to more European integration rather than disintegration. The answer, Jabko argues, requires a more fluid concept of sovereignty than is generally presumed in political science theories. In Jabko's theoretical account, European political leaders responded to the flaws in EMU revealed by the euro crisis by searching for solutions that were both transformational and that took on board sovereignty concerns. They proposed greater solidarity through loans, but at the same time only as a "last resort" to preserve the Eurozone; they required considerable discipline of recipient countries, but framed as a temporary, *quid pro quo* for loan financing. European leaders built political coalitions in support of these new sovereignty practices – both at the international level and among their domestic electorates. The last step, in this account, was to progressively institutionalize the new sovereignty practices in EU economic governance.

Before the sovereign debt crisis, there was the banking crisis, and Chapter 5 by Elliot Posner analyzes its impact on EU financial regulation. Since financial regulation is one of the most globalized of all policy areas, Posner considers both its internal and the external dimensions. He demonstrates that the integration of European financial markets that occurred in the 1990s rested on an internal political bargain that gave a central role to the United Kingdom, the region's leading financial center, and on a regulatory harmonization strategy that drew from the (often neoliberal) standards of transnational regulatory bodies, widely seen as technocratic and neutral. This both accelerated integration internally and elevated the EU externally, making it an important player in global standard-setting. After the crisis, the internal political bargain suffered: the EU ratcheted up regulation through Banking Union and other reforms and, in the process, London was often isolated or part of the losing coalition. Posner argues that these internal divisions have, in combination with other factors, diminished the EU's international bargaining heft. The likely upshot, especially in view of Brexit, is a London–New York alliance in transnational standard-setting bodies that will set the regulatory terms for global financial markets and that will sideline the EU.

The part on economic policy concludes with Renaud Dehousse's analysis of the impact of the euro crisis on the wider European political system. In Chapter 6, he uncovers two important trends. On the one hand, the response of European leaders to the euro crisis was to seek to depoliticize macroeconomic policy, by empowering the European Commission in the surveillance procedure and by giving the ECB authority over the banking system. On the other hand, politicization has been occurring at both the national and the EU levels. Largely because of austerity, domestic political parties have come to mobilize around EU issues, either rejecting the idea of integration entirely or opposing specific EU policies. At the same time, at the EU level, there is a trend toward parliamentary government and an effort to enhance the importance of European elections, with the development of the so-called *Spitzenkandidaten* system: in elections for the European Parliament, European political parties each select a candidate for president of the European Commission, and the candidate of the winning party or coalition of parties becomes president. This resembles the confidence relationship between parliament and government in a domestic parliamentary system and has contributed to a more political role for the Commission president. (This system, however, is still in flux, as demonstrated by the recent elections for the 2019–2024 European Parliament, which led to the appointment of a *Spitzenkandidaten* outsider as Commission president.) Dehousse demonstrates that there are fundamental contradictions between the de-politicized "trusteeship" model and the parliamentary government model, evident for instance in the Commission's ambiguous role in enforcing the Eurozone budget-deficit targets. Dehousse argues that these contradictions will have to be addressed, although he underscores that this will be difficult in the current environment of widespread opposition to Brussels and growing polarization among the Member States.

The book then moves to *human migration*. Chapter 7, by Ulf Öberg and Nathalie Leyns, focuses on intra-EU migration and the historical evolution of the law of free movement of persons. They argue that through to the 1990s, the principle of non-discrimination in the context of free movement of workers (for long-term employment) and services (for short-term labor movements) was interpreted as protecting both foreign and domestic workers: On the one hand, Member State nationals were guaranteed access to employment in other Member States but at the same time, through the application of the principle of equality and equal pay for equal work, the nationals of host Member States were guaranteed that their wages and working conditions would not be undercut. This was largely also the case for the ECJ's interpretation of the Posting of Workers Directive, which was adopted in 1996 and which was designed to facilitate the cross-border provision of services and ensure a minimum level of social protection for posted workers. However, in their account, the Court's approach changed after the 2004 accession: in the *Laval*, *Ruffert*, and *Viking* line of cases, what had previously been viewed as legitimate social demands for non-discrimination in line with the labor law principle of *lex loci laboris* came to be seen as xenophobic and protectionist, and the minimum labor standards contained in the Directive were interpreted as a ceiling that prevented the imposition of higher standards, such as average pay rates. This jurisprudence, together with other developments, has generated political backlash, and Öberg and Leyns trace a number of EU legislative and jurisprudential developments favorable to labor and social rights that lead them to be optimistic about the future prospects of EU democracy.

In Chapter 8, Evangelia (Lilian) Tsourdi turns to migration from outside the EU, and one of the most developed and salient areas of EU policy involving third-country nationals – the Common European Asylum System. After exploring the foundational legal principles that govern in this area, Tsourdi focuses on the administrative component, which she argues is under-developed and bears a large part of the blame for the mishandling of the 2015–2016 refugee crisis. She identifies three key elements of asylum imple-mentation – the Dublin System of assigning responsibility for asylum seekers to the Member State of first irregular entry; practical cooperation among national authorities under the umbrella of an EU agency (EASO); and EU funding. Tsourdi argues that on each dimension there has been change, driven by attempts at fairer burden-sharing in the asylum system – relocation of asylum applicants from the state of first entry to other Member States, a greater role for EASO in managing migration hotspots, and more EU funding.

In Chapter 9, Niovi Vavoula tackles the proliferation of EU databases on third-country nationals. Vavoula traces three waves of databases: (1) those connected with the early Schengen and Dublin Conventions (SIS and Euro-dac); (2) those fueled by the tendency post-9/11 to view immigration as a potential security risk, including the database for short-stay visa applicants (VIS), the second-generation SIS (SIS II), and the revamped Eurodac; (3) those prompted by the Paris and Brussels terrorist attacks of 2015 and 2016, including two databases designed to cover visa-free travelers (EES and ETIAS) and legislation designed to make all of the existing databases interoperable. The chapter then conducts an evaluation of the databases from the perspective of personal data protection and privacy. Among the numerous concerns, one of the most basic is how travel and the everyday exercise of personal freedoms by third-country nationals are viewed as inherently suspicious and operate as a trigger for state surveillance.

The next part of the book covers *internal security*, i.e. police and judicial cooperation. In light of the highly salient Paris and Brussels terrorist attacks of 2015 and 2016, this section opens with internal security policy focused specif-ically on counter-terrorism. In Chapter 10, Gilles de Kerchove and Christiane Höhn give essential background on the historical evolution, legal framework, and institutional architecture for EU counter-terrorism policy. As they explain, the EU's competences in the field are significant, but they are largely centered on law enforcement cooperation, and exclude cooperation between (domestic) security services and (foreign) intelligence services. These fall under the umbrella of "national security" and remain the sole responsibility of the Member States. The chapter then analyzes in depth one of the most important elements of EU counter-terrorism strategy – the use of information and EU databases to detect planned terrorist attacks and apprehend suspected terrorists.

Valsamis Mitsilegas follows with a critical perspective on some of the policy developments in the counter-terrorism field, as well as internal security more generally. In Chapter 11, he argues that the blurring of the boundaries between police and criminal law and other areas of law has led to a general shift from the classic repressive model of state coercive action to a paradigm of preventive justice. One of the key elements of this shift has been the mobilization of data collected for a variety of purposes – as described in the previous two chapters of the book – to prevent future criminal acts. Another aspect has been the use of external affairs competences to target internal security risks. In light of the implications of the preventive paradigm for the rule of law and fundamental rights, Mitsilegas argues that the EU should drop the "security crisis" mentality that has produced the preventive paradigm and should adopt a more reflective approach, aimed at managing security within a solid framework of human rights and the rule of law.

As de Kerchove and Höhn underscore, EU–US cooperation on counter-terrorism and combating other types of serious crime is essential. In Chapter 12, the book turns to a recent effort to bolster law enforcement investigations that has an important transatlantic dimension – the CLOUD Act in the United States and the e-Evidence proposals in the EU. As Jennifer Daskal explains, the rise of a globally connected Internet and cloud storage have led to ever-increasing amounts of digital evidence being held by private service providers located outside the territory of the investigating nation. The traditional mutual legal assistance process, which requires the use of official inter-state channels to obtain the evidence, has proven cumbersome in this new context. In response, the United States has recently enacted the CLOUD Act, which clarifies that US warrant authority reaches all data under the control of US service providers, without regard to the location of the data; the EU has proposed legislation that would allow Member State authorities to directly compel the production of stored data held by service providers located in another Member State. Daskal assesses the potential for international cooperation under these legislative schemes and argues that they represent an important first step in addressing the problem of evidence gathering in the contemporary, globalized data environment.

Chapter 13, by Marc Rotenberg and Eleni Kyriakides, considers the role of the European Convention on Human Rights (ECHR) in safeguarding fundamental rights. As explained earlier in this introduction, the Council of Europe system, including the ECHR and the ECtHR, has traditionally had primary responsibility for overseeing Member State respect for liberal democratic rights, rights which come under great pressure when states respond to international terrorism. Rotenberg and Kyriakides describe how France used Article 15 ECHR ("Derogation in Time of Emergency") to derogate from important Article 8 ECHR privacy rights in the aftermath of the Paris terrorist attacks; Turkey did the same after the failed coup attempt in the summer of 2016. They argue that neither France nor Turkey satisfied the requirements for derogations under the ECtHR's jurisprudence, and they propose new institutional mechanisms that would give NGOs an important role in identifying and publicizing excessive derogations from Article 8 rights.

As explained in the spillover section of this introduction, border control, immigration, and internal security policy have common political and legal origins and today are all part of the Area of Freedom Security and Justice (AFSJ). In Chapter 14, Emilio De Capitani concludes this part of the book with a holistic analysis of recent developments in the AFSJ. After analyzing the full range of legal innovations that were introduced in the Lisbon Treaty, he canvasses the legislative track record in the AFSJ. He points to a number of significant flaws with how the Lisbon governance model has worked in practice, in particular from the perspective of the European Parliament. These include the failure of national police authorities to communicate the statistics and data necessary for good policymaking; and the empowerment of EU agencies at the expense of the Commission and Parliament. The chapter ends with a list of pragmatic recommendations for the 2019–2024 legislature.

Moving to *constitutional fundamentals*, the book takes up the problem of democratic backsliding in the Member States and the response in EU law. Chapter 15 by Kim Lane Scheppele and R. Daniel Kelemen gives the historical and legal background of Articles 2 and 7 TEU and explains why partisan politics in a multi-level, federal-type system like the EU make it unlikely that Article 7 will ever be deployed against Hungary, Poland, or other cases of democratic backsliding. The chapter puts forward a series of more promising legal alternatives for enforcing liberal democratic values: systemic infringement actions under Article 258 TFEU; suspension of payments of European Structural and Investment Funds (ESIF) to Hungary and Poland under the existing ESIF rules requiring effective judicial oversight in recipient countries; and allowing courts of one Member State to stop cooperating with courts of another Member State under EU criminal and civil justice schemes based on a legitimate concern for judicial independence in that Member State.

In Chapter 16, Tomasz Tadeusz Koncewicz shifts our attention specifically to Poland. He explores the role of resentment – anxiety about the "other," anger at the liberal establishment, fear of exclusion – in driving the current illiberal turn and a switch in constitutional doctrine from rule *of* law to rule *by* law. The chapter then analyzes how the politics of resentment has played out on the EU stage with the *Białowieża Forest* case. Brought in 2017, this was an infringement action against Poland for logging in the ancient Białowieża Forest in violation of EU nature conservation directives. On the one hand, the case vindicated the rule of law, as it resulted in two interim orders and a judgment against Poland, as well as a novel legal doctrine of periodic penalty payments being available for noncompliance with interim measures. On the other hand, Koncewicz argues that the ultimate result was disappointing, since the Commission lacked the political resolve to apply the periodic penalty payments against Poland.

Chapter 17 offers a complementary diagnosis of authoritarian populism in Poland and Hungary. Bojan Bugarič argues that populism in general, and the illiberal variety in Poland and Hungary in particular, can be explained in large part by austerity and the neoliberal structural reforms of the past decades. After considering the legal and economic sanctions in the EU toolkit and explaining why they are unlikely to work, the chapter focuses on economic and social policies. Bugarič argues that populist leaders have built their following by promising better material conditions and that European political leaders should counter by articulating an alternative to austerity and offering progressive economic policies that promote growth, better jobs, high-quality social services, and high environmental standards.

The last chapter in this part rounds out the discussion of constitutional fundamentals by shining the spotlight on EU governance and the perennial problem of the democratic deficit. In Chapter 18, Peter L. Lindseth argues that even as extensive regulatory power has been delegated to supranational EU institutions, the experience of legitimate, democratic self-government has remained stubbornly national. This is a historical-sociological problem, not one of institutional architecture as suggested by the term "democratic deficit," and therefore Lindseth calls it the "democratic disconnect." The democratic disconnect is used as an analytical frame for understanding the developments in economic policy, migration, and internal security over the past decade: in all of these areas, the EU has been called upon to do more, but it has relied almost exclusively on autonomous national fiscal and human capacity to do so, since only the state has the legitimacy and hence the power to mobilize resources. Looking forward, Lindseth argues that even as the ECJ takes on a more important role in monitoring constitutional fundamentals at the national level, as advocated by Scheppele, Kelemen, and Koncewicz, it should avoid erecting a quasi-federalist constitution for the EU that is out of sync with the sociological experience of democratic self-government.

III ASSESSING THE OVERALL LEGAL ARCHITECTURE OF SOVEREIGNTY-SENSITIVE DOMAINS

The book's concluding chapter takes stock of the policy areas covered in the volume and brings to light three important legal and normative challenges that cut across all of them. As discussed earlier, it is commonplace that the rule of law, rights, and democracy are the bedrock of the European constitutional tradition. Like Member State law, EU law is expected to abide by these elements of the European constitutional tradition, and the concluding chapter assesses how it measures up. By tracing the development of EU law in sovereignty-sensitive areas, both the formal legal powers and how those powers have been used over the past decade, the concluding chapter reveals a number of common characteristics and shortcomings on the three dimensions. At the same time, by understanding the shortcomings, it is possible to make proposals for advancing the rule of law, rights, and democracy across the spectrum of policy areas.

First, the rule of law: As chronicled earlier, the EU has come to exercise powers over economic policy, human migration, internal security, and constitutional fundamentals not by grand design but through spillover, and in seeking to accommodate sovereignty concerns, European leaders have constructed a highly complex legal order. To govern in these controversial areas, they have used two very different types of legal norms, what I call international and supranational, and over time the norms in the international category have migrated into the supranational category. This process of migration, in turn, has generated confusion, undermining what in legal scholarship and doctrine is referred to as legal certainty. *Variety* in the type of norm and *change* in the status of the norms over time, have generated extreme legal complexity and have undermined the knowability of law – a central element of the rule of law. The chapter argues that legal simplification can be advanced by integrating economic and internal security law into the core TFEU and, within the TFEU, by limiting the doctrine of direct effect as a pre-condition for domestic litigation based on EU law.

Second, with respect to rights, the concluding chapter highlights the inadequacies of access to justice and the procedure for testing EU law. The preliminary reference system is the primary vehicle by which EU citizens can challenge the validity of EU law based on the higher law of fundamental rights.[48] In sovereignty-sensitive areas, however, it is more difficult to use the system, since Member States tend to retain considerable discretion in implementing EU legislation, which for a variety of reasons complicates making the validity claim in the preliminary reference procedure. At the same time, it is more important to get cases heard in areas such as economic policy, immigration, and internal security. There, unlike single market regulation where the economic rights of relatively sophisticated market actors are at stake, the fundamental rights of ordinary citizens come under pressure – the civil, political, and social rights that are central to the liberal and social democratic identity kit. Because of these deficiencies, the chapter takes up two proposals that would expand direct access for individuals to the European Court of Justice.

The third and final element of the European constitutional tradition considered in the concluding chapter is democracy, taking the institutional template contained in the Lisbon Treaty as the baseline. Lawmaking across the different policy areas, even those like immigration and internal security which are now formally governed through the supranational Community method, has tended to veer toward intergovernmentalism because of their sovereignty stakes. Intergovernmentalism is a process in which the asymmetric interdependence and bargaining power of states determine outcomes and democratic politics operate between domestic electorates and their political leaders. It is a political fact. Intergovernmental politics, however, both at the European and the domestic levels, avoid the moral dilemmas of Europe-wide governance and short circuit the construction of a Europe-wide identity. Therefore, this chapter argues for greater accountability to the European Parliament, even though decisional powers for the Parliament might not yet be politically feasible. Although the European Parliament undoubtedly has its flaws, which the chapter discusses, it is the one forum where Europe-wide debates and politics can be conducted and it offers an important arena for developing a European perspective on sovereignty-sensitive policy areas.

Independently, when seen in isolation from the perspective of any of the legal sub-fields, the problems of legal complexity, access to justice, and retreat

---

[48] For a general description of the preliminary reference system, see Court of Justice of the European Union, Recommendations to National Courts and Tribunals, in Relation to the Initiation of Preliminary Ruling Proceedings, 2016 O.J. (C 439) 1.

to intergovernmentalism may not be perceived as particularly grave. Lawyers, with enough training, can always decipher the complexities of their fields of specialization; there are alternatives to the ECJ for assessing fundamental rights compliance in the various policy areas; intergovernmentalism can produce the action necessary for successful policy outputs. However, when these shortcomings exist across the entire gamut, it is hard to avoid the conclusion that they compromise the legal system as a whole and that they can and should be addressed through common forms of legal innovation. These are the cross-cutting theoretical and normative lessons that I draw in my conclusion to this volume. But before delving further into these general lessons, it is time now to turn to the details of how law and governance have evolved in each of the policy domains.

I
Economic Policy

2

The Future of the European Economic and Monetary Union

Issues of Constitutional Law

MATTHIAS RUFFERT[*]

I SOME DISTURBING DATA BY WAY OF INTRODUCTION

The state debt crisis is not over in Europe. To give the most extreme example, the Greek debt currently owed to the European Stability Mechanism (ESM) is €45.9 billion and the debt owed to the ESM's predecessor, the European Financial Stability Facility (EFSF), is €130.9 billion, for an average term of thirty years. This enormous debt burden is shouldered by a country with eleven million inhabitants and with a Gross National Product (GNP) per capita that ranks around fortieth place worldwide.[1] State debt in the Eurozone in general is around 90 percent of GNP, and in Italy it is above 130 percent.[2] Growth in both Greece and Italy is below the Eurozone average (2.5 percent). There is nearly full employment in Germany, i.e. unemployment is near 4 percent, but the unemployment rate is at 8.5 percent in the whole Eurozone, 11.0 percent in Italy, 8.8 percent in France, and a dismal 16.1 percent in Spain.[3]

Some compare these debt, growth, and unemployment figures with those from before the euro crisis. Such comparisons are not necessarily very

---

[*] I am grateful toward Martin Junker for his excellent research assistance.

[1] These data are provided by the ESM, www.esm.europa.eu/assistance/greece#bringing_greece _back_to_growth. The GDP is ranked according to the International Monetary Fund, www.imf.org/external/datamapper/NGDPDPC@WEO/OEMDC/ADVEC/WEOWORLD.

[2] All data are taken from Eurostat, http://ec.europa.eu/eurostat/tgm/table.do?tab=table&init=1& language=en&pcode=teina225&plugin=1.

[3] Data for the EU from Eurostat, http://ec.europa.eu/eurostat/tgm/table.do?tab=table&init=1& language=de&pcode=teilm020&plugin=1. The discrepancy is even better illustrated if we compare the Italian or Spanish figures with the few East German regions, which are still poorly developed economically. None of them has a comparable unemployment rate today, according to data from the *Bundesagentur für Arbeit* (Federal Employment Agency), https:// statistik.arbeitsagentur.de/Navigation/Statistik/Statistik-nach-Regionen/Politische-Gebietsstruktur-Nav.html.

revealing, since those data contained the very distortions that led to the breakdown of the system. There are many possible causes and exacerbators of the euro crisis: while some pin the blame on the common currency, it is equally possible that Member States with weaker economic performance failed to invest their surpluses from entering the Eurozone into fiscal responsibility and competitiveness. But even though it is difficult, particularly in a piece of legal scholarship, to come to any conclusions as to the reasons for the present state of affairs, these figures alone point to an undeniable need for reform.

In the light of the reform imperatives, the following chapter will first give a very brief introduction to the current state of the Economic and Monetary Union (EMU) and will outline the current proposals for the reconstruction of the Eurozone.[4] This picture will include a sketch of the main stakeholders and the operating political forces as well as of the role of courts (Section II). The proposals will then be analyzed in the light of European constitutional law – understood as a combination of complementary supranational and national rules and principles (*Verfassungsverbund*).[5] Three main aspects will be considered: budget reform, control powers, and institutional rearrangement (Section III). Finally, some perspectives will be developed from this analysis (Section IV).

II THE POLITICAL SCENERY

1 *The Development of the Eurozone: An Overview*

The debate on the future of the Eurozone is often dominated by the argument that the construction of the European currency was bound to fail from the beginning because of the asymmetry between, on the one hand, a single currency and the concomitant exclusive competence of the Union for monetary policy and, on the other hand, continued Member State autonomy over

---

[4] Part of this has been elaborated by the author in German in: Matthias Ruffert, "Verfassungsrechtliche Zukunftsfragen der Europäischen Wirtschafts- und Währungsunion," in *Festschrift für Matthias Schmidt-Preuß zum 70*, ed. Markus Ludwigs (Berlin: Duncker & Humblot, 2018).

[5] The term has been coined in Germany by Ingolf Pernice. See Ingolf Pernice, "Bestandssicherung der Verfassungen: Verfassungsrechtliche Mechanismen zur Wahrung der Verfassungsordnung," in *Der europäische Verfassungsraum*, eds. Roland Bieber and Pierre Widmer (Zürich: Schulthess Juristische Medien, 1995), 235. Further developed in Ingolf Pernice, "The Treaty of Lisbon. Multilevel Constitutionalism in Action," *Columbia Journal of European Law* 15, no. 3 (2009): 349–407.

economic policy.[6] This narrative is flawed. The creation of the euro in the Treaty of Maastricht in 1993 is better read as a continuation of the achievements of the Single Market in the 1980s. Although the power over economic policy remained with the Member States, co-ordination of these powers was (and, according to the letter of the Treaties, still is) driven by "the principle of an open market economy with free competition" (today Articles 119 and 120 of the Treaty on the Functioning of the European Union or TFEU). Member States were expected to pursue solid budgetary and economic policies and to preserve, by this means, the stability of the common currency. A series of provisions was inserted into the Treaty of Maastricht for this purpose, most prominently the no-bail-out clause in (following today's numbering) Article 125(1) TFEU, and the prohibition of monetary funding of public budgets in Article 123(1) TFEU. This steering of monetary, i.e. price, stability by market forces was complemented by an administrative procedure, the deficit procedure in Article 126 TFEU.[7] Thus there was a form of common economic policy: the economic policies of the Member States were bound by the same market and fiscal responsibility principles. It was also a viable economic policy, since other aims and instruments might have been too ambitious, at least at the time of the Maastricht Treaty, and perhaps even still today.[8]

The original understanding of Economic and Monetary Union is best described in the Maastricht judgment of the German Bundesverfassungsgericht (Federal Constitutional Court or FCC). As the Court said in October 1993:

> The Maastricht Treaty governs the monetary union as a community committed to long-term stability, in particular to monetary stability. It is true that it is not possible to foresee whether it will actually be possible, using as a basis the provisions contained within the Maastricht Treaty, to maintain long-term stability for the ECU currency. The fear that the efforts to achieve stability will fail, which could then result in further concessions in terms of monetary policy on the part of the Member States, is, however, too intangible a basis upon which to claim that the Maastricht Treaty is legally vague. The

---

[6] For a good summary, see Ingolf Pernice, "Domestic Courts, Constitutional Constraints and European Democracy: What Solution for the Crisis?" in *The Constitutionalization of European Budgetary Constraints,* eds. Maurice Adams, Federico Fabbrini, and Pierre Larouche (Oxford: Hart Publishing, 2016), 310.

[7] Matthias Ruffert, "Mehr Europa: Eine rechtswissenschaftliche Perspektive," *Zeitschrift für Gesetzgebung* 28, no. 1 (2013): 1–20.

[8] See the seminal article by Päivi Leino and Tuomas Saarenheimo, "Sovereignty and Subordination: On the Limits of EU Economic Policy Coordination," *European Law Review* 42, no. 2 (April 2017): 166–189.

Maastricht Treaty sets long-term standards which establish the goal of stability as the yardstick by which the monetary union is to be measured, which endeavour, by institutional provisions, to ensure that these objectives are fulfilled, and which finally do not stand in the way of withdrawal from the Community as a last resort if it proves impossible to achieve the stability sought.

The FCC then enumerated the well-known Treaty provisions oriented toward monetary stability and continued: "This concept of the monetary union as a community of stability is the basis and object of the German Act of Consent."[9] This orientation of the EMU was further strengthened by the Stability and Growth Pact, which was adopted in 1997 just before the third stage of implementation of the euro, and which most notably imposed a ceiling of 3 percent GDP for state deficits and 60 percent GDP for state debt.[10]

Today, we know that the Eurozone took a very different path. As early as in 2004, the deficit control procedure under Article 126 TFEU lost its teeth when the strongest Member States, Germany and France, were given leeway to raise their deficits above the 3 percent GDP threshold without facing the sanctions foreseen in that provision.[11] With the collapse of the Greek budget in spring 2010, the need to save the system through guarantees and loans outweighed the imperatives of the no-bail-out clause, culminating in Christine Lagarde's famous statement "[w]e violated all the rules because we wanted to close ranks and really rescue the euro zone."[12] To bring politics back into the realm of law, a system of conditional bailouts was established, initially in the (still quite

---

[9] 89 *Entscheidungen des Bundesverfassungsgerichts*, 204ff. (Maastricht). English translation available at Manfred Brunner and Others v. The European Union Treaty, *Common Market Law Review* 31, no. 2 (1994): 235, paras. 89–90.

[10] The Stability and Growth Pact is composed of a declaration and two regulations: Resolution of the European Council on the Stability and Growth Pact, 1997 O.J. (C 236) 1; Council Regulation (EC) 1466/97, On the Strengthening of the Surveillance of Budgetary Positions and the Surveillance and Coordination of Economic Policies, 1997 O.J. (L 209) 1; Council Regulation (EC) 1467/97, On Speeding Up and Clarifying the Implementation of the Excessive Deficit Procedure, 1997 O.J. (L 209) 6.

[11] This was in summer 2004, and a few months later Germany triggered the internal reform process that, according to many, laid the foundation for its current economic success. In France, it took until late 2017 for the new President Emmanuel Macron to begin a comparable reform process. For a less critical view of the re-interpretation of the procedure under Article 126, see Ulrich Häde, "Vertrag zur Gründung der Europäischen Union und Vertrag über die Arbeitsweise der Europäischen Union: Kommentar," in *EUV/AEUV*, eds. Christian Calliess and Matthias Ruffert (Munich: Verlag C.H. Beck, 2016), Article 126 AEUV, paras. 12ff.

[12] Available at Reuters Staff, "France's Lagarde: EU Recues 'Violated' Rules: Report," *Reuters*, December 18, 2010, www.reuters.com/article/2010/12/18/us-france-lagarde-idUSTRE6BH0V020101218.

dubious in legal terms) first Greek rescue package (€110 billion in total), then in the (even more dubious[13]) European Financial Stability Facility, which was created as a private law vehicle and which pooled together guarantees from the Member States, the EU, and the International Monetary Fund (IMF) for a total lending capacity of €750 billion. Later, the European Stability Mechanism[14] was created to accomplish the same functions as the EFSF, but through a public international law instrument with a sound legal basis in Article 136(3) TFEU (added to the Treaty using the simplified revision procedure).[15] Alongside these developments, it became clear that the fiscal stability rules had to be strengthened.[16] The "Six Pack"[17] was elaborated early

---

[13] Compare in particular Rainer Palmstorfer, "To Bail Out or Not to Bail Out? The Current Framework of Financial Assistance for Euro-Area Member States Measured against the Requirements of EU Primary Law," *European Law Review* 37, no. 6 (2012): 771–784. For the opposite opinion see in particular Martin Selmayr, "Die 'Euro-Rettung' und das Unionsprimärrecht: Von putativen, unnötigen und bisher versäumten Vertragsänderungen zur Stabilisierung der Wirtschafts- und Währungsunion," *Zeitschrift für Öffentliches Recht* 68 (2013): 259–318.

[14] See European Stability Mechanism, www.esm.europa.eu/. For an explanation: Alberto de Gregorio Morino, "Legal Developments in the Economic and Monetary Union during the Debt Crisis: The Mechanisms of Financial Assistance," *Common Market Law Review* 49, no. 5 (2012): 1613–1646.

[15] European Council Decision 2011/199/EU, Amending Article 136 of the Treaty on the Functioning of the European Union with Regard to a Stability Mechanism for Member States whose Currency is the Euro, 2011 O.J. (L 91) 1. In force since May 1, 2013.

[16] For the state of the art, see Fabian Amtenbrink and René Repasi, "Compliance and Enforcement in Economic Policy Coordination in EMU," in *The Enforcement of EU Law and Values*, eds. András Jakab and Dimitry Kochenov (Oxford: Oxford University Press, 2017), 145–181. See also the illustrative table in: Alexandre de Streel, "EU Fiscal Governance and the Effectiveness of its Reform," in *The Constitutionalization of European Budgetary Constraints*, eds. Maurice Adams, Federico Fabbrini, and Pierre Larouche (Oxford: Hart Publishing, 2016), 100.

[17] European Parliament and Council Regulation (EU) 1173/2011, On the Effective Enforcement of Budgetary Surveillance in the Euro Area, 2011 O.J. (L 306) 1; European Parliament and Council Regulation (EU) 1174/2011, On Enforcement Measures to Correct Excessive Macroeconomic Imbalances in the Euro Area, 2011 O.J. (L 306) 8; European Parliament and Council Regulation (EU) 1175/2011, Amending Council Regulation (EC) No 1466/97 on the Strengthening of the Surveillance of Budgetary Positions and the Surveillance and Coordination of Economic Policies, 2011 O.J. (L 306) 12; European Parliament and Council Regulation (EU) 1176/2011, On the Prevention and Correction of Macroeconomic Imbalances, 2011 O.J. (L 306) 25; Council Regulation (EU) 1177/2011, Amending Regulation (EC) No 1467/97 on Speeding up and Clarifying the Implementation of the Excessive Deficit Procedure, 2011 O.J. (L 306) 33; Council Directive 2011/85/EU, On Requirements for Budgetary Frameworks of the Member States, 2011 O.J. (L 306) 41. Frédéric Allemand and Francesco Martucci, "La Nouvelle Gouvernance Économique Européenne," *Cahiers de Droit Européen* 48, no. 1/2 (2012): 17–99, 409–457.

on and was complemented by the "Two Pack"[18] for program countries; both sets of rules were designed to enhance the surveillance of Member States' economic policies and to foster budgetary discipline. Fiscal responsibility was also enhanced through the so-called Fiscal Compact, an international treaty that provides for balanced budgets and that requires the Member States to implement constitutional-level "debt brakes" into their national law.[19]

The bailout and fiscal stability developments were complemented by the asset-buying programs of the European Central Bank (ECB). First was the Securities Market Programme (SMP), which saved Berlusconi's government in Italy from collapse in summer 2011. Second came the program called Outright Monetary Transactions (OMT), which was never applied. Finally, the current asset-purchasing programs were introduced, summed up under the heading of "quantitative easing." Under quantitative easing, the ECB has acquired government and corporate debt and other securities amounting to over €2,000 billion since 2015.[20]

Last but not least, the EU established the foundations of a Banking Union to break the vicious circle of interdependence between banks and the states whose debt is held by banks.[21] Banking Union includes a Single Supervisory

---

[18] European Parliament and Council Regulation (EU) 472/2013, On the Strengthening of Economic and Budgetary Surveillance of Member States in the Euro Area Experiencing or Threatened with Serious Difficulties with Respect to their Financial Stability, 2013 O.J. (L 140) 1; European Parliament and Council Regulation (EU) 473/2013, On Common Provisions for Monitoring and Assessing Draft Budgetary Plans and Ensuring the Correction of Excessive Deficit of the Member States in the Euro Area, 2013 O.J. (L 140) 11. Kenneth A. Armstrong, "The New Governance of EU Fiscal Discipline," *European Law Review* 38, no. 5 (2013): 601–617; Alicia Hinarejos, "Fiscal Federalism in the European Union: Evolution and Future Choices for EMU," *Common Market Law Review* 50, no. 6 (2013): 1621–1642; Alexandre de Streel, "La gouvernance économique européenne réformée," *Revue Trimestrielle de Droit Européen*, no. 3 (2013): 455–481.

[19] The official title is the "Treaty on Stability, Coordination and Governance" (TSCG), signed in 2012, effective in 2013, available at www.consilium.europa.eu/media/20399/stootscg26_en12.pdf. On this Treaty see Paul Craig, "The Stability, Coordination and Governance Treaty: Principle, Politics and Pragmatism," *European Law Review* 37, no. 3 (2012): 231–248; Steve Peers, "The Stability Treaty: Permanent Austerity or Gesture Politics," *European Constitutional Law Review* 8, no. 3 (2012): 404–441; Gianni Lo Schiavo, *The Role of Financial Stability in EU Law and Policy* (Alphen aan den Rijn: Wolters Kluwer, 2017), 99ff.; Alexander Thiele, "The 'German Way' of Curbing Public Debt," *European Constitutional Law Review* 11, no. 1 (2015): 30–54.

[20] This figure is drawn from the latest preliminary reference of the FCC, *Bundesverfassungsgericht*, Beschluss des Zweiten Senats vom 18. Juli 2017, 2 BvR 859/15- Rn. (1-137), paras 8ff., 18ff., www.bverfg.de/e/rs20170718_2bvr085915.html. This is further explained at note 42.

[21] Ann-Katrin Kaufhold, "Die Europäische Bankenunion: vollendet unvollendet? Eine Zwischenbilanz," *Zeitschrift für Gesetzgebung* 32, no. 1 (2017): 18–37; Niamh Moloney,

Mechanism (SSM), which shifts significant supervisory competences to the ECB,[22] a Single Resolution Mechanism (SRM) with a Single Resolution Board to supervise the resolution of banks in the Eurozone if necessary, and a Single Resolution Fund. This Fund is financed by the Eurozone Member States, according to the scheme set down in an international treaty (Intergovernmental Agreement or IGA) and by 2024 is set to be capitalized by 1 percent of all covered assets held by Member State banks, i.e. €55 billion.[23]

2 Active Courts

It is perhaps not surprising that a development of this depth and scale – and it is doubtful that such rapid and deep change could have been achieved by any other community of states, let alone any state of the same economic weight – has been the object of legal challenges on a number of fronts. This activity has been so extensive that it is no exaggeration to conclude that the courts have become full-fledged stakeholders in the governance of the Eurozone.[24] Today there is a rich European jurisprudence on EMU: The European Court of Justice (ECJ) issued two very important judgments in *Pringle* and *Gauweiler*.[25] The Irish Supreme Court made the first reference on EMU issues during the crisis (which led to the *Pringle* judgment).[26] The French Constitutional

"European Banking Union: Assessing Its Risks and Resilience," *Common Market Law Review* 51, no. 6 (2014): 1609–1670. See also Sabino Cassese, "A New Framework of Administrative Arrangements for the Protection of Individual Rights." Paper presented at the ECB Legal Conference, September 4–5 2017, 239–255. www.rwi.uzh.ch/dam/jcr:9bebb762-d2d1-46d0-914b-852bb5a77ef6/ECB%20Legal%20Conference%202017.pdf.

[22] Council Regulation (EU) 1024/2013, Conferring Specific Tasks on the European Central Bank Concerning Policies Relating to the Prudential Supervision of Credit Institutions, 2013 O.J. (L 287) 63.

[23] European Parliament and Council Regulation (EU) 806/2014, Establishing Uniform Rules and a Uniform Procedure for the Resolution of Credit Institutions and Certain Investment Firms in the Framework of a Single Resolution Mechanism and a Single Resolution Fund and Amending Regulation (EU) No 1093/2010, 2014 O.J. (L 225) 1. The text of the IGA is available at Council Doc. 8457/14 of May 14, 2014.

[24] Samo Bardutzky and Elaine Fahey, "Who Got to Adjudicate the EU's Financial Crisis and Why? Judicial Review of the Legal Instruments in the Eurozone," in *The Constitutionalization of European Budgetary Constraints*, eds. Maurice Adams, Federico Fabbrini, and Pierre Larouche (Oxford: Hart Publishing, 2016), 341–358.

[25] Case C-370/12, *Thomas Pringle v. Government of Ireland*, ECLI:EU:C:2012:756 (European Stability Mechanism or ESM case); Case C-62/14, *Peter Gauweiler v. Deutscher Bundestag*, ECLI:EU:C:2015:400 (Outright Monetary Transactions or OMT case). On *Gauweiler*, see the special issue of the *Maastricht Journal of European and Comparative Law* 23 (2016): 1, edited by Federico Fabbrini.

[26] Supreme Court of Ireland, *Pringle v. Government of Ireland*, IESC 47 (2012).

Council and the Supreme Court of Estonia scrutinized the ESM (in the case of Estonia, parts of it) and the Fiscal Compact.[27] The Greek Council of State and the Portuguese Constitutional Court handed down judgments on the conditionality measures negotiated by their governments with the EU and the IMF;[28] in Portugal, certain of these measures were held to be unconstitutional.[29]

It may appear somewhat counterintuitive to bill the courts, whether supra-national or national, as stakeholders in the political process and as actors on the crisis management scene, but their active role cannot be denied.[30] Although their judgments are thoroughly grounded in law, and rely on methodologically sound arguments, the courts have played a political role in the unfolding of the euro crisis and the construction of Eurozone governance. This is particularly true for the German FCC.[31] There is no doubt that the German federal government used the possibility of negative rulings by the FCC as a bargaining chip to resist calls for more rescue funds; and that the FCC was aware of its role and deliberately sought to increase its leverage.

---

[27] Conseil Constitutionnel [French Constitutional Council], Decision 2012-653DC of August 9, 2012, www.conseil-constitutionnel.fr/conseil-constitutionnel/english/case-law/decision/decision-no-2012-653-dc-of-9-august-2012.115501.html; Riigikohus [Supreme Court of Estonia], Judgment 3-4-1-6-12 of July 12, 2012, www.riigikohus.ee/en/constitutional-judgment-3-4-1-6-12.

[28] Simvoulio tis Epikratias [Greek Council of State], Case 668/2012 of February 20, 2012. The case is explained by Dimitris Triantafyllou, "Die asymmetrische Demokratie," *Europarecht* 49, no. 4 (2014): 458–468, and (short) by Lina Papadopoulou, "Can Constitutional Rules, Even if 'Golden,' Tame Greek Public Debt?" in *The Constitutionalization of European Budgetary Constraints*, eds. Maurice Adams, Federico Fabbrini, and Pierre Larouche (Oxford: Hart Publishing, 2016): 231.

[29] Tribunal Constitucional [Portuguese Constitutional Court], Decision 399/2010 (Surtax on Personal Income Tax 2010); Decision 396/2011 (State Budget 2011); Decision 353/2012 (State Budget 2012); Decision 187/2013 (State Budget 2013); Decision 474/2013 (Public Workers Requalification); Decision 602/2013 (Labour Code); Decision 794/2013 (40-Hour Work Week); Decision 862/2013 (Pensions Convergence); Decision 413/2014 (State Budget 2014); Decision 572/2014 (Special Solidarity Contribution 2014); Decision 574/2014 (Pay Cuts 2014–2018); Decision 575/2014 (Special Sustainability Contribution). Summaries of the decisions are available at www.tribunalconstitucional.pt/tc/en/acordaos/. From scholarship: Mariana Canotilho, Teresa Violante, and Rui Lanceiro, "Austerity Measures under Judicial Scrutiny: The Portuguese Constitutional Case-Law," *European Constitutional Law Review* 11, no. 1 (2015): 155–183; Roberto Cisotta and Daniele Gallo, "The Portuguese Constitutional Court Case-Law on Austerity Measures: A Reappraisal." Working Paper 4/2014, LUISS Guido Carli, Dipartimento di Giurisprudenza, 2014.

[30] Matthias Ruffert, "Das Bundesverfassungsgericht als Akteur im Prozess der europäischen Integration," *Europäische Grundrechte Zeitschrift* 44 (2017): 241–249.

[31] On the following, Matthias Ruffert, "The EMU in the ECJ: A New Dimension of Dispute Resolution in the Process of European Integration," in *Democracy in the EMU in the Aftermath of the Crisis*, eds. Luigi Daniele, Pierluigi Simone, and Roberto Cisotta (Cham: Springer International Publishing, 2017), 340–342.

The Future of the European Economic and Monetary Union

To understand this interplay between courts and intergovernmental bargaining, it is important to bear in mind that it was by no means self-evident that German constitutional law would apply in a significant way to EMU. It was only in mid-2009, just six months before Greece's de facto-insolvency, that the FCC set down, for the first time, limits on the transfer of budgetary powers to the EU. The legal theory that served as the basis for these limits was dubious and has been called into question by scholars.[32] In the Lisbon Treaty judgment, the FCC said: "The German Bundestag must decide, in an accountable manner *vis-à-vis* the people, on the total amount of the burdens placed on citizens. The same applies correspondingly to essential state expenditure."[33] The Court held that the core of the taxing and spending power cannot be transferred to the EU – not even by an amendment to the *Grundgesetz* – because the EU is structurally incapable of providing the necessary level of democratic legitimacy. The Court concluded that the only way in which Germany could surrender such powers would be through the adoption of a new constitution by a vote of the German people, as provided for under Article 146 of the *Grundgesetz*.[34]

The FCC soon applied this jurisprudence to the Greek rescue package and then to the ESM Treaty. Initially, it sought to establish objective limits on Germany's budgetary involvement, to protect the Bundestag's constitutional powers over the budget in future cases.[35] This line of reasoning, however, was abandoned and the Court now seeks to achieve long-term preservation of the democratic principle, an objective that can be applied to the Bundestag's role in budgetary decisions generally speaking, not only in the EU context. As the Court has stated: "Article 79 (3) of the Basic Law does not guarantee the unchanged further existence of the law in force but those structures and

---

[32] One of the best examples of the extensive scholarship on this judgment is, Matthias Jestaedt, "Warum in die Ferne schweifen, wenn der Maßstab liegt so nah?" *Der Staat* 48 (2009): 497–516.

[33] Bundesverfassungsgericht, Judgment 2BvE 2/08 of June 30, 2009, para. 256. A translation is available at www.bundesverfassungsgericht.de/SharedDocs/Entscheidungen/EN/2009/06/es20090630_2bve000208en.html;jsessionid=57638495472D1C3F681DB1D1DEE5267F.2_cid370.

[34] Judgment 2BvE 2/08, paras. 244ff.

[35] Bundesverfassungsgericht, Judgment 2BvR 987/10 of September 7, 2011, para. 131. A translation is available at www.bundesverfassungsgericht.de/SharedDocs/Entscheidungen/EN/2011/09/rs20110907_2bvr098710en.html. The Bundesverfassungsgericht is not the only national court to have issued judgments on the rescue measures; compare the overview given by Francette Fines, "À Propos de Quelques Limites Constitutionnelles au Fédéralisme Économique Européen," in *L'Union Européenne et le Fédéralisme Économique*, eds. Stéphane de la Rosa, Francesco Martucci, and Edouard Dubout (Brussels: Bruylant Edition, 2015), 213–232.

procedures which keep the democratic process open and, in this context, safeguard parliament's overall budgetary responsibility."[36]

A bold construction of constitutional law thus strongly influenced European politics. Nonetheless, on the substance, the grounds on which the FCC has reviewed economic and monetary policy is relatively firm, in particular since the Court clarified its relationship toward the ECJ and declared that a preliminary reference was a necessary precondition to the assessment of an EU act as *ultra vires*.[37] The preliminary reference procedure was used in the later OMT case (*Gauweiler*), and produced the excellent analysis of the OMT program in the ECJ's judgment of January 14, 2014.[38] The judgment is of great political importance: without it, there would be no limitation on the purchase of assets, which in the ECJ's reasoning is based on the principle of proportionality and the necessary temporal distance between the issuance of government debt and the purchase of such debt on the secondary market.[39]

In the German judgment that followed the ECJ's preliminary ruling, the FCC refined its principle of "national identity lock" (*Identitätskontrolle*), set down in the earlier Lisbon Treaty judgment, and clarified the consequences of holding an EU measure to be *ultra vires* or in breach of the principles at the heart of German constitutional identity: It is above all Germany's political institutions that are responsible for avoiding the effects of such "unconstitutional" EU acts in the German legal sphere.[40] The FCC, however, did not forbear its harsh (and not unjustified) criticism of the ECJ's preliminary ruling.[41] It had three main objections: (i) the ECJ, in accepting that the

---

[36] Bundesverfassungsgericht, Judgment 2BvR 1390/12 of September 12, 2012, para. 222. A translation is available at www.bundesverfassungsgericht.de/SharedDocs/Entscheidungen/EN/2012/09/rs20120912_2bvr139012en.html.

[37] Bundesverfassungsgericht, Order 2BvR 2661/06 of July 6, 2010. A translation is available at www.bundesverfassungsgericht.de/SharedDocs/Entscheidungen/EN/2010/07/rs20100706_2bvr266106en.html. Angela Schwerdtfeger, "Europäisches Unionsrecht in der Rechtsprechung des Bundesverfassungsgerichts –Grundrechts-, ultra-vires- und Identitätskontrolle im gewaltenteiligen Mehrebenensystem," *Europarecht* (2015): 301ff. Still critical, Markus Ludwigs, "Der Ultra-vires-Vorbehalt des BVerfG –Judikative Kompetenzanmaßung oder legitimes Korrektiv?" *Neue Zeitschrift für Verwaltungsrecht* (2015): 537–543.

[38] Bundesverfassungsgericht, Order 2BvR 2728/13 of January 14, 2014, paras. 84ff. A translation is available at www.bundesverfassungsgericht.de/SharedDocs/Entscheidungen/EN/2014/01/rs20140114_2bvr272813en.html.

[39] Case C-62/14, *Peter Gauweiler v. Deutscher Bundestag*, ECLI:EU:C:2015:400, paras. 66ff.,106.

[40] Bundesverfassungsgericht, Judgment 2BvR 2728/13 of June 21, 2016, paras.153ff., 163ff. A translation is available at www.bverfg.de/e/rs20160621_2bvr272813en.html.

[41] Judgment 2BvR 2728/13, paras. 181ff. The chief legal officer of the ECB has made the case for judicial restraint: Chiara Zilioli, "'Justiciability of Central Banks' Decisions and the Imperative to Respect Fundamental Rights." Paper presented at the ECB Legal Conference, September 4–5 2017, 91–103. www.rwi.uzh.ch/dam/jcr:9bebb762-d2d1-46d0-914b-852bb5a77ef6/ECB%

The Future of the European Economic and Monetary Union 43

OMT program was a matter of monetary policy and thus within the ambit of the ECB's competence might not have sufficiently scrutinized "the underlying factual assumptions," in particular with respect to indications such as the selectivity of the purchases "that evidently argue against a character of monetary policy"; (ii) in view of the principle of conferral (Article 5(1) TEU), which strictly limits the EU to the powers conferred by the Treaty, the ECJ was too lenient in accepting the ECB's own assessment of its power to undertake the program; (iii) the ECJ failed to address the central issue of the preliminary reference, *viz.* whether "the independence granted to the European Central Bank (Article 130 TFEU) leads to a noticeable reduction in the level of democratic legitimation of its actions" and therefore requires that the Bank's mandate be interpreted restrictively and be subject to strict judicial review.

On July 18, 2017, the FCC took up these objections in a new reference to the ECJ and called into question the legality of certain of the ECB's quantitative easing measures.[42] The preliminary reference applied the legal standard established by the ECJ in *Gauweiler* to assess the legality of the ECB's purchase of state assets, relying in particular on the language of Article 123(1) TFEU.[43]

The ECJ rejected the FCC's objections in its judgment of December 11, 2018.[44] It did not find an intrusion by the ECB into the Member States' economic policy competences, nor did it consider the ECB's Public Sector Purchasing Programme to be an instrument of monetary funding of public budgets. It remains an open question whether the FCC will accept this assessment in the subsequent proceedings.[45] It also remains to be seen how the FCC will handle the ECJ's provocative finding that one of the questions referred (about the distribution of losses in case of default of a debtor State)

20Legal%20Conference%202017.pdf (84 and 96ff. in particular against the opinion of the FCC). See further Juliane Kokott and Christop Sobotta, "Judicial Review and Institutional Balance with Regard to European Monetary Policy." Paper presented at the ECB Legal Conference, September 4–5 2017, 104–111; Matthias Lehmann, "Varying Standards of Judicial Scrutiny over Central Bank Actions." Paper presented at the ECB Legal Conference, September 4–5 2017, 112–132.

[42] There is little scholarship on this issue. One of the few examples is Jan-Willem van den End, Jakob de Haan, and Ide Kearney, "Quantitative Easing (QE) in the Euro Area: An Exposition," *Zeitschrift für Staats- und Europarecht* 13 (2015): 87–98.

[43] Bundesverfassungsgericht, Judgment 2BvR 859/15 of July 18, 2017, www.bverfg.de/e/rs20170718_2bvr085915.html (there is no official translation of the decision into English). See, however, Bundesverfassungsgericht, Press Release no. 70/2017 of August 15, 2017, www.bundesverfassungsgericht.de/SharedDocs/Pressemitteilungen/EN/2017/bvg17-070.html; Questions of the FCC to the ECJ in the Case C-493/17, 2017 O.J. (C 402) 9–11.

[44] Case C-493/17, *Weiss and Others*, ECLI:EU:C:2018:1000.

[45] The oral hearing is scheduled for the end of July 2019.

was inadmissible because it was hypothetical – inadmissibility findings are rare, and certainly remarkable with respect to questions referred by a constitutional court.

Although this FCC jurisprudence is solid in substance, the procedural route by which the cases were litigated is problematic. In taking these cases, the FCC expanded dramatically traditional standing doctrine. Standing to oppose EU initiatives based on lack of competence and constitutional limits was accorded to every citizen, based on the principles of democratic election of the Bundestag (Article 38 *Grundgesetz*) together with the inviolability of the principle of democracy (Articles 20(1), 79(3) and 146 *Grundgesetz*).[46] Indeed, the FCC speaks of a "right to democracy" (*Recht auf Demokratie*). This permissive concept of standing applies even if the claimant is a member of parliament – and these cases have been brought by the very same member of parliament for many years now.[47] The dissenting opinions to the preliminary reference in the OMT case have impressively shown the consequences of such a liberal standing doctrine.[48] There is an obvious discrepancy between the FCC's precise analysis on the merits, which has had a significant political impact, and its construction of standing, which is near absurd.

In sum, the FCC and other courts have played an important role in shaping the political response to the euro crisis. In assessing the possible reforms, canvassed in the following section, it will be important to take into account the extensive jurisprudence that has been developed on EMU and to anticipate the possible reactions of the courts.

3 *Stakeholders and Proposals*

In light of the objective need for reform, laid out in the first section, there is no scarcity of reform proposals. Among the most active participants in the debate on the EMU's future have been the EU institutions themselves. On the institutional front, two lines of development are converging: first, throughout

---

[46] Judgment 2BvE 2/08. See, in particular, para. 179: "Article 146 of the Basic Law creates a right of participation of the citizen entitled to vote. Article 146 of the Basic Law confirms the pre-constitutional right to give oneself a constitution from which constitutional authority emanates and by which it is bound." See the criticism in Matthias Ruffert, "Die europäische Schuldenkrise vor dem Bundesverfassungsgericht–Anmerkung zum Urteil vom 7. September 2011," *Europarecht* (2011): 842–855.

[47] Bundesverfassungsgericht, Judgment 2BvE 2/08, para. 199.

[48] Dissenting opinions of Judges Gerhardt and Lübbe-Wolff to Order 2BvR 2728/13. Christoph Ohler, "Rechtliche Maßstäbe der Geldpolitik nach dem Gauweiler-Urteil des EuGH," *Neue Zeitschrift für Verwaltungsrecht* (2015):1006.

the crisis, there was close cooperation between the main organs of the EU.[49] In 2015, this culminated in the Five Presidents' Report entitled *Completing Europe's Economic and Monetary Union*. The five Presidents of the European Commission, the European Council, the European Parliament, the Eurogroup (the informal Council body comprising euro area Member States), and the European Central Bank proposed completing the EMU in two steps: the first phase was to be completed by 2017 (a date already in the past) and the second phase, during which the pace of institutional reform was to be accelerated, by 2025.[50] The second line of development has been propelled by the European Commission and began with the Commission's *White Paper on the Future of Europe* published in spring 2017.[51] It was subsequently advanced by a *Reflection Paper on the Deepening of the Economic and Monetary Union* in May 2017[52] and by the "State-of-the-Union" address of Jean-Claude Juncker in September 2017.[53] The speed with which the Commission has sought to shape the future of the Eurozone is quite remarkable: from the five possible scenarios in the *White Paper*, to the specific proposals put forward in Juncker's address, to the formal proposals issued by the Commission of December 6, 2017 (which will be scrutinized in Section III).[54]

[49] Herman Van Rompuy, President of the European Council, *Towards a Genuine Economic and Monetary Union*, EUCO 120/12 (June 26, 2012); Herman Van Rompuy, President of the European Council, in close cooperation with José Manuel Barroso, Jean-Claude Juncker, and Mario Draghi, *Towards a Genuine Economic and Monetary Policy* (December 5, 2012), www.consilium.europa.eu/uedocs/cms_Data/docs/pressdata/en/ec/134069.pdf; European Council Conclusions, EUCO 205/12 (December 13–14, 2012), sec. I.; *Final Report of the Future of Europe Group of the Foreign Ministers of Austria, Belgium, Denmark, France, Italy, Germany, Luxembourg, the Netherlands, Poland, Portugal and Spain*, September 17, 2012, www.cer.eu/sites/default/files/westerwelle_report_sept12.pdf.
[50] *The Five President's Report: Completing Europe's Economic and Monetary Union*, June 22, 2015, https://ec.europa.eu/commission/sites/beta-political/files/5-presidents-report_en.pdf.
[51] *Commission White Paper on the Future of Europe. Reflections and Scenarios for the EU27 by 2025*, COM (2017) 2025 (March 1, 2017).
[52] *Commission Reflection Paper on the Deepening of the Economic and Monetary Union*, COM (2017) 291 (May 31, 2017).
[53] Jean-Claude Juncker, President European Commission, State of the Union Address 2017, September 13, 2017, http://europa.eu/rapid/press-release_SPEECH-17-3165_en.htm.
[54] There is a comprehensive presentation in Communication from the Commission, *Further Steps Towards Completing Europe's Economic and Monetary Union: A Roadmap*, COM (2017) 821 final (December 6, 2017). The whole package including a roadmap is available at https://ec.europa.eu/commission/publications/completing-europes-economic-and-monetary-union-factsheets_de.

National politicians have also taken initiatives, most prominently French President Emmanuel Macron in his Sorbonne speech of September 26, 2017.[55] (In fact, it bears noting that these ideas appeared even earlier, in his speech at Humboldt University Berlin on January 10, 2017.[56]) Although Macron's speech also covered a number of other policy areas, it focused extensively on the EMU. For a long time, there was no reply from the German side given the extensive period that was required to form a new German government after the general elections of September 24, 2017. The 177-page coalition agreement that was signed on the morning of February 7, 2018 after more than 24 hours of final negotiation starts with a chapter entitled *Ein neuer Aufbruch für Europa – A New Start for Europe*.[57] It contains a series of reform ambitions for the Eurozone that closely mirror the language of the Commission and Macron. Indeed, the parallels are so close in places that there were rumors that the then-leader of the German social democrats, Martin Schulz, had involved Commission President Juncker in the drafting process.

This anecdotal remark hints at a very important point when describing the different proposals. The current debates on the future of the Eurozone would be dramatically over-simplified if characterized as simply a political conflict between different national interests – French and German, German and Greek, and others – or between Members States and the EU. Some of the most vociferous disagreements are between leaders from different parts of the political spectrum. Macron is a French president and politician with socialist roots who proposes more or less what he promised in his electoral campaign. The German social democrats are marketing the coalition agreement, including the key chapter on Europe, as their success, and that chapter would not be the same without Martin Schulz, despite his departure from the Social Democratic Party of Germany (SPD) leadership after the agreement was concluded. Even the Commission, since the introduction of the *Spitzenkandidaten* process in 2014, has become more politicized. In the 2014 European Parliament elections, the main European political groups campaigned on their candidates for the presidency of the Commission,

---

[55] Initiative pour l'Europe- Discours d'Emmanuel Macron pour une Europe souveraine, unie, démocratique, September 26, 2017, www.elysee.fr/declarations/article/initiative-pour-l-europe-discours-d-emmanuel-macron-pour-une-europe-souveraine-unie-democratique/ (in French).

[56] Speech Emmanuel Macron, Humboldt University-EM, January 10, 2017, www.rewi.hu-berlin.de/de/lf/oe/whi/FCE/2017/rede-macron (in English).

[57] *Ein neuer Aufbruch für Europa. Eine neue Dynamik für Deutschland. Ein neuer Zusammenhalt für unser Land*, February 7, 2018, www.cdu.de/system/tdf/media/dokumente/koalitionsvertrag_2018.pdf?file=1.

The Future of the European Economic and Monetary Union 47

respectively the Christian Democrat Juncker and the Social Democrat Schulz, and Juncker's subsequent appointment as President has cast the Commission in a more political mold. The same political fissures are also visible in the proposals that have been made by expert and civil society groups.

This discussion of the politics behind the EMU debate leads naturally to the third set of proposals – those that have been generated by scholars and civil society actors. The French economist and bestselling author Thomas Piketty, together with three academic collaborators (all of whom are close to the French *Parti Socialiste* and its presidential candidate Bénoît Hamon), have published a *Treaty on the Democratisation of the Governance of the Euro-Area (T-Dem)*. They propose that T-Dem be a separate treaty and temporarily provide for better and more democratic governance of the Eurozone until the next treaty reform.[58] The various translations of their publication hint at a total reform of Europe, and the banderole around the German edition says: "Take back control over Europe!" (*Holt Euch die Kontrolle über Europa zurück!*).[59] The title expressly alludes to the Brexiteers' slogan, but given that the French socialist candidate only won 6.4 percent of the votes in the 2017 French presidential election, the proposal is unlikely to gain political support.

There are other initiatives that are less clearly politically aligned and are more balanced. The *Glienicker Group*, composed of eleven independent economists, lawyers, and political scientists, came forward with suggested changes to the Eurozone as early as 2013.[60] A number of individual researchers have also engaged with the reform debate, including the Italian author Federico Fabbrini[61] and those included in the collection that appeared in the Luxembourgian online-journal *Revue de l'euro*.[62]

III MEASURES

The following section systematically canvasses the reform proposals that have been made by examining three components that are common to almost all:

---

[58] *Draft Treaty on the Democratization of the Governance of Euro Area (T-DEM)*, 2017, http://piketty.pse.ens.fr/fr/files/T-DEM%20-%20Final%20english%20version%209march2017.pdf.

[59] Stéphanie Hennette, Thomas Piketty, Guillaume Sacriste, and Antoine Vauchez, *Pour un traité de démocratisation de l'Europe* (Paris: Éditions du Seuil, 2017).

[60] Glienicker Gruppe, *Aufbruch in die Euro-Union*, October 17, 2013, http://glienickergruppe.eu/de/aufbruch-in-die-euro-union/ (nicht paginiert).

[61] Federico Fabbrini, *Economic Governance in Europe* (New York: Oxford University Press, 2016), 151–180, 233–270.

[62] See their website here: https://resume.uni.lu/publications/revue-ecu-euro.

new EU budgetary powers, modification of the system of fiscal control and fiscal responsibility, and reforms to the institutional framework. The analysis pays special attention to the legal aspects of each of these possible Eurozone innovations and examines their viability under EU and domestic constitutional law.

1 A New Budget?

1.1 Budgetary Developments

Initially, the EMU had no budget. Conceptually, it was not needed, since the EMU's original design relied on markets to impose budgetary discipline and price stability, backed up by the no bail-out clause in Article 125(1) TFEU (see Section II.1). Today, however, after all the events narrated earlier in this chapter, there is a rescue fund in the form of the European Stability Mechanism. The potential budget for state support, subject to strict conditionality, is €700 billion. The ESM pools assets and guarantees of the Member States, using the EU's institutions (the Commission and ECB) for executive purposes.[63] In addition to this amount, there is €55 billion allocated to the Single Resolution Fund (SRF), in the context of the Banking Union and the funds to be available in the event of failed banks.[64] Again, as with the ESM, financing of the SRF is not part of the EU budget but is provided for separately by the Member States.

In the spending context, the activity of the ECB must also be mentioned. Under the current quantitative easing programs, the ECB has purchased around €2,000 billion in Member State debt, and its balance sheet quadrupled between the introduction of the euro and 2017.[65] The official reasoning for these programs is to combat deflation, and it is likely that at least some forms of quantitative easing are within the economic policy discretion of the ECB. However, the budgetary effects of its policies are obvious. Member States in fiscal difficulty use the extremely low interest rates to refinance their debt, and economically stronger Member States use the same low interest rates to consolidate their budgets. This indirect budgetary effect of monetary policy is entirely under the control of the ECB and is not institutionally steered by the Commission, Parliament, and Council.

---

[63] Official information available at www.esm.europa.eu/about-us.
[64] See Section II.1.
[65] These numbers are drawn from the latest preliminary reference of the FCC, Judgment 2BvR 859/15, paras. 8*ff.*, 18*ff.*

1.2 A Consensus in Favor of Expanding the EU Budget?

Most of the current reform proposals continue with this budgetary trend and propose either a special budget for the Eurozone or the expansion of the existing EU budget, with the aim, among others, of loosening the exclusive control of the Member States and the ECB and increasing the clout of the EU institutions. As early as 2015, the Five Presidents' Report proposed a "macro-economic stabilisation function" for the euro – a fund or part of the budget to intervene in cases of so-called asymmetric shocks.[66] Some of the civil society and expert stakeholders support the establishment of a Eurozone budget and have dedicated most of their efforts to reflecting on the institutional design of such a budget.[67] One interesting proposal is for the introduction of a common European unemployment insurance.[68] There are also proposals for how to finance the budget. Among the various candidates are a tax on financial transactions and a harmonized company tax, the latter possibility a favorite of President Macron.[69]

The current proposals of the Commission take up these ideas. In its Communication *New Budgetary Instruments for a Stable Euro Area within the Union Framework*, the Commission formally envisages a stabilization function that could be designed, alternatively, as a European Investment Protection Scheme, as a European Unemployment Reinsurance Scheme ("reinsurance fund"), or as "a rainy day fund [that] could accumulate funds from Member States on a regular basis" and from which "disbursements would be triggered on a pre-defined basis."[70] The Commission further proposes a European Monetary Fund (EMF) that would operate as an agency of the Union and bring the ESM budget closer to the EU institutions.[71] Beyond these suggestions, however, the Commission proposal on a new budget line is fairly vague, in particular with respect to the stabilization function. Budget spending should be "[n]eutral over the medium-term and not lead to permanent transfers between Member States." The fine line that the Commission is

---

[66] See *The Five President's Report*, 14.

[67] See, in particular, *Draft Treaty on the Democratization of the Governance of Euro Area (T-DEM)*.

[68] Cf. the proposal of the Glienicker Gruppe, available at www.glienickergruppe.de/english.html.

[69] Initiative pour l'Europe- Discours d'Emmanuel Macron.

[70] Communication from the Commission, *New Budgetary Instruments for a Stable Euro Area within the Union Framework*, COM (2017) 822 final (December 6, 2017), 14. For further information: *Commission Proposal for a Regulation of the European Parliament and of the Council*, COM (2017) 826 final (December 6, 2017).

[71] *Commission Proposal for a Council Regulation on the Establishment of the European Monetary Fund*, COM (2017) 827 final (December 12, 2017).

walking between austerity and stimulus is particularly evident in the following passage from the proposal:

> [The budget should c]ontribute to sound fiscal policy and minimise moral hazard. There would be no conditionality attached to the support but there would be strict, pre-defined eligibility criteria based on sound macroeconomic policies in order to access the stabilisation function. As a general principle, only Member States that comply with the EU surveillance framework during the period preceding the large asymmetric shock should be eligible for access. This will avoid moral hazard and create an additional incentive for compliance with sound fiscal and structural policies.[72]

In the end, the outcome will be determined by intergovernmental and domestic politics. The Member States with the least interest in expanding the EU's budgetary capacity are, naturally, the ones that contribute the most to the budget.[73] The core issue is how important the continued existence of the Eurozone weighs in their domestic politics. If elements of the political spectrum are willing to contemplate the dissolution of the Eurozone, then it will be more difficult for such Member States to support budgetary expansion. It is also beyond doubt that different views on economic policy play a role in this political assessment. A more liberal or even monetarist position is not necessarily a more nationalist perspective than an interventionist, economic stimulus perspective. The German coalition agreement signed in February 2018 is particularly revealing on this score. Both of the political parties in the agreement support a Franco-German initiative on corporate taxation as well as a tax on financial transactions. By contrast, the passage affirming the deployment of specific budgetary means for economic stabilization, social convergence, and structural reforms within the Eurozone, leading to a future investment budget for the Eurozone, bears the clear mark of Martin Shultz and the SPD. It comes very close to what Macron and the Commission are

---

[72] Communication from the Commission, COM (2017) 822 final, 14.

[73] Speech by the Prime Minister of the Netherlands, Mark Rutte, at the Bertelsmann Stiftung, Berlin, March 2, 2018, www.government.nl/documents/speeches/2018/03/02/speech-by-the-prime-minister-of-the-netherlands-mark-rutte-at-the-bertelsmann-stiftung-berlin. "The promise that a common currency will bring us all more prosperity and not a redistribution of existing prosperity. Because that will be the net effect if we continue to allow some countries to run high deficits for years, to build up high levels of debt, and to abstain from modernising their economies. Then the currency union will end up as a transfer union, and that is not the way to make the euro stronger. Let alone to win more public support." See also the initiative of eight Ministers of Finance (Denmark, Estonia, Finland, Ireland, Latvia, Lithuania, the Netherlands, Sweden), reported in the Media: Von Werner Mussler, "Nord-Allianz Stellt Sich Gegen Euroideen," *Frankfurter Allgemeine*, March 7, 2018, www.faz.net/aktuell/wirtschaft/deutsche-europa-politik-schuert-misstrauen-anderer-staaten-15481094.html.

The Future of the European Economic and Monetary Union   51

proposing, and makes a strong commitment to increased German spending: "Wir sind zu höheren Beiträgen Deutschlands zum EU-Haushalt bereit." ("We are ready for higher contributions of Germany to the EU budget.")[74] It remains to be seen what will be left of this commitment after Martin Schulz' disappearance from the political scene. There is, to be sure, no objective truth, but a political process.

1.3 Constitutional Issues: A Differentiated View

The development of new budgetary instruments may change the face of the European Union. On one hand, the risk that European funding could be used in some Member States to avoid necessary reforms cannot be denied;[75] on the other hand, it has been empirically shown that the temporary deployment of considerable funds can successfully restructure an economy, as happened in the Irish case. The political challenge of producing extensive and successful economic reforms therefore lies in balancing the quest for stability with the useful deployment of funding.

Constitutional law poses no insurmountable obstacles. As the Commission observed in its proposal, it might be necessary to raise the ceiling on the amount of funding that can be directly raised by the EU (the EU's so-called own resources)[76] but doing so only requires the consensus of the Member States, not a treaty amendment. In the *Pringle* judgment, the ECJ found that EU financial assistance to Member States would not violate the no-bailout clause in Article 125(1) TFEU if it was indispensable for guaranteeing the financial stability of the Eurozone and subject to strict conditions. Since there is no suggestion that conditionality will be removed, the proposed budget appears to satisfy these criteria. Similarly, Article 136(3), second sentence TFEU stipulates that "[t]he granting of any required financial assistance under the [stability] mechanism will be made subject to strict conditionality" and again, there is no suggestion that the contemplated budget would contravene this requirement. The *Pringle* judgment also made clear that a fund for the repayment of pre-crisis state debts or the introduction of so-called Eurobonds – common bonds of economically stronger and weaker Eurozone countries – would require a formal treaty amendment.[77] Such measures, however, have

---

[74] Speech Emmanuel Macron, Humboldt University-EM, 8, lines 233–234.

[75] On this risk (moral hazard), see Alicia Hinarejos, *The Euro Area Crisis in Constitutional Perspective* (New York: Oxford University Press, 2015), 170.

[76] Communication from the Commission, COM (2017) 822 final, 15n28.

[77] Franz Mayer and Christian Heidfeld, "Verfassungs- und europarechtliche Aspekte der Einführung von Eurobonds," *Neue Juristische Wochenschrift* (2012): 424–425; Franz Mayer and

not been proposed by the Commission.[78] Even the German FCC would have little reason to intervene: If the Bundestag maintains its overall budgetary responsibility there would be no breach of the German constitutional requirement "to keep the democratic process open." The decision-making process outlined in the proposed EMF Regulation requires the Bundestag's assent for the allocation of the necessary funds.

The constitutional assessment of the ECB's lenient monetary policies (quantitative easing), which in certain respects mimic fiscal policy, is more problematic. In its reference of July 18, 2017, the FCC analyzed the ECB's core program, the Public Sector Purchase Programme, under the requirements of Article 123 TFEU.[79] Although the text of Article 123(1) TFEU only prohibits the direct purchase of Member State bonds, the ECJ ruled in *Gauweiler* that this prohibition may not be informally circumvented and gave some indications of what would constitute such circumvention. The FCC develops this line of reasoning and postulates a violation of Article 123 TFEU because: (i) there is *de facto* certainty on the markets that government bonds will eventually be purchased by the Eurosystem; (ii) it is not possible to verify that certain minimum time periods are respected between the issuance of government debt on the primary market and the purchase of the debt on the secondary market, contributing to the blurring of sovereign responsibility and the Eurosystem; (iii) all purchased bonds were – without exception – held by the ECB until maturity; and (iv) even bonds with a negative yield when they were first issued were purchased. More generally speaking, the FCC questions

---

Christian Heidfeld, "Eurobonds, Schuldentilgungsfonds und Projektbonds: Eine dunkle Bedrohung?" *Zeitschrift für Rechtspolitik* (2012): 131–132; Alberto de Gregorio Merino, "Legal Developments in the Economic and Monetary Union during the Debt Crisis: The Mechanisms of Financial Assistance," *Common Market Law Review* 49, no. 5 (2012): 1631; Frédéric Allemand, "La faisabilité juridique des projets d'euro-obligations," *Revue Trimestrielle de Droit Européen* 48, no. 3 (2012): 553–593; Werner Heun and Alexander Thiele, "Verfassungs- und europarechtliche Zulässigkeit von Eurobonds," *Juristenzeitung* (2012): 980–982. A divergent view is taken by Sebastian Piecha, "Die Europäische Gemeinschaftsanleihe–Vorbild für EFSF, ESM und Euro-Bonds?" *Europäische Zeitschrift für Wirtschaftsrecht* (2012): 532; Lo Schiavo, *The Role of Financial Stability*, 115ff., 123 (but see page 142). On the fund-solution with a divergent result, see Frank Schorkopf, "Verfassungsrechtliche Grenzen und Möglichkeiten für eine Umsetzung des Schuldentilgungspaktes des Sachverständigenrates, Gutachten," 2012, www.sachverstaendigenrat-wirtschaft.de/fileadmin/dateiablage/download/publikationen/rechtsgutachten_schuldentilgungspakt.pdf.

[78] One of the most far-fetched claims is that the Greek debt was "odious" in the sense of public international law and should consequently be struck down. See Ilias Bantekas and Renoud Vivien, "On the Odiousness of Greek Debt," *European Law Journal* 22, no. 4 (2016): 539–565.

[79] Judgment 2BvR 859/15.

The role that the ECB has assumed in economic policy, given that the Treaty primarily assigns it monetary policy responsibilities. The FCC also reiterates its concern about the preservation of the Bundestag's budgetary powers, given the uncertainty of how ECB losses are dealt with when the bonds mature. In its judgment of December 11, 2018, the ECJ rejected the FCC's objections. It did not find an intrusion by the ECB into the Member States' economic policy competences, nor did it consider the ECB's Public Sector Purchasing Programme to be an instrument of monetary funding of public budgets. It remains an open question whether the FCC will accept this assessment in the subsequent proceedings.

The preliminary ruling is a welcome addition to the legal analysis of the ECB's asset-buying programs: The first, the Securities Market Programme, was probably in breach of EU law, at least in summer 2011 with respect to Italy, but no court will ever decide the issue since the program was terminated before it had a chance to be litigated; the second, OMT, came under extensive scrutiny in both national courts and the ECJ, but it was never implemented by the ECB; the third, Quantitative Easing (QE), is the most dramatic of the ECB's programs, but did not draw legal opposition until the FCC's preliminary reference.[80]

2 A Recalibration of Control Powers?

2.1 Fiscal Stability and Control in the Eurozone

In the EMU's original design, stability of the common currency (price stability) was to be achieved by requiring fiscal and budgetary responsibility in the Member States – imposed through a combination of market forces (the prohibition on bailouts and monetary funding) and administrative control (Section II.1).[81] Subsequently, this control was first weakened – recall the "unpunished" German-French infringement of 2004 – and then strengthened in reaction to the state debt crisis – recall the Fiscal Compact and the Six Pack and the Two Pack rules. Whether the euro crisis was caused by the banking crisis of 2007/2008[82] or lax budgetary policies, encouraged by the failure to sanction Franco-German infringement of the rules, is a matter of extensive

---

[80] See again Ruffert, "The EMU in the ECJ," 344–345.
[81] Ruffert, "Mehr Europa: Eine rechtswissenschaftliche Perspektive."
[82] On the causes of the euro crisis, see Rosa Lastra and Geoffrey Wood, "The Crisis of 2007-09: Nature, Causes, and Reactions," *Journal of International Economic Law* 13, no. 3 (2010): 539.

debate. The answer is probably different for each country. What is clear, however, is that most political actors take the view that a common currency without a mutual commitment to fiscal responsibility is untenable. The legal control tools that are currently available, including the Fiscal Compact and the surveillance framework in Article 121 TFEU are too feeble when binding duties in economic matters are at stake. Any future reform should provide for further fiscal stability.

2.2 From Rigidity to Flexibility?

Many of the proposals currently on the table do not seek primarily to improve the EU's instruments of fiscal control. The Commission proposes to transform the Fiscal Compact into a Council Directive laying down provisions for strengthening fiscal responsibility and the medium-term budgetary orientation in the Member States.[83] Formally, this follows from Article 16 of the Fiscal Compact, according to which five years after its entry into force "on the basis of an assessment of the experience with its implementation" the necessary steps will be taken to incorporate its substance into the legal framework of the EU.[84] The purpose of this clause, however, was to integrate the Fiscal Compact into the Treaty on the Functioning of the European Union – not to pass a mere directive. After the United Kingdom and the Czech Republic blocked the inclusion of the Fiscal Compact in the Lisbon Treaty, it became necessary to resort to an international treaty, but the intent was to eventually incorporate the Compact into EU primary law. The choice of a directive, which by definition allows room for maneuver at the national level, is also questionable in light of the experience of the Member States under the Fiscal Compact. The Commission's assessment has shown Member State implementation to not be entirely satisfactory:[85] Even though the Commission

[83] *Commission Proposal for a Council Directive Laying Down Provisions for Strengthening Fiscal Responsibility and the Medium-Term Budgetary Orientation in the Member States*, COM (2017) 824 final (December 6, 2017).

[84] For another view of the Fiscal Compact, see Chapter 17.

[85] *Report from the Commission Presented Under Article 8 of the Treaty on Stability, Coordination and Governance in the Economic and Monetary Union*, C (2017) 1201 final (February 22, 2017). Independent assessments are to be found in: Giacomo Delledonne, "A Legalization of Financial Constitutions in the EU? Reflections on the German, Spanish, Italian and French Experiences," in *The Constitutionalization of European Budgetary Constraints*, eds. Maurice Adams, Federico Fabbrini, and Pierre Larouche (Oxford: Hart Publishing, 2016), 181–204; Marek Antoš, "Fiscal Stability Rules in Central European Constitutions," in *The Constitutionalization of European Budgetary Constraints*, eds. Maurice Adams, Federico Fabbrini, and Pierre Larouche (Oxford: Hart Publishing, 2016), 205–222.

The Future of the European Economic and Monetary Union 55

found that all legal systems are in compliance with the provisions of the Compact, in certain important cases, that compliance was conditional upon a particular interpretation of national law, a formal commitment by the national government, and/or actions to be taken by the national government (e.g. the nomination of board members of the supervisory institution).[86]

The proposed Directive replaces the idea of a debt brake with "a framework of binding and permanent numerical fiscal rules which are specific to [the Member States]" and which shall be oriented toward "a medium-term objective in terms of structural balance" (Article 3(1)). There is no fixed debt limit but rather flexible, political targets, and allowing the Member States such flexibility is the clear intent of the Directive. Control of whether the Member States effectively pursue the fiscal targets is the responsibility of independent bodies within the Member States – not the Commission, an EU agency, or, as under the Fiscal Compact, the European Court of Justice. The reasons given by the Commission for the transfer of oversight responsibility from the EU to the national level are to promote "an enhanced sense of national ownership of fiscal policy" and to respect "Member States' sovereign specificities." All in all, the Directive seeks to introduce political oversight of the Member States' budgetary performance – not, as in the past, administrative control based on clear benchmarks and automatic triggers or market-based discipline. This may be fine-tuning of the Fiscal Compact, which will remain in force,[87] but it may also be a lot less.

2.3 Constitutional Issues: No Progress without Stability

By partly shifting fiscal control powers from central authorities to national authorities that are not even part of an EU network (and not in a contractual

---

[86] See the formulation for France: "The national provisions adopted by FR are compliant with the requirements set in Article 3(2) of the TSCG and in the common principles in light of the formal commitment provided by national authorities to interpret the organic law consistently with Article 3(2) of the TSCG together with the compliant set-up of the monitoring institution, the clarifications provided by national authorities on the substance of the correction mechanism, and the formal commitment provided by national authorities to apply the comply-or-explain principle in line with the common principles." *Report from the Commission,* C (2017) 1201 final, 12.

[87] Johannes Graf von Luckner, "How to Bring It Home: The EU's Options for Incorporating the Fiscal Compact into EU Law," *Europeanlawblog.eu,* April 9, 2018, https://europeanlawblog .eu/2018/04/09/how-to-bring-it-home-the-eus-options-for-incorporating-the-fiscal-compact-into-eu-law/; Diane Fromage and Bruno de Witte, "The Treaty on Stability, Coordination and Governance: Should it be Incorporated in EU Law?" *VerfBlog,* November 6, 2017, https:// verfassungsblog.de/the-treaty-on-stability-coordination-and-governance-should-it-be-incorporated-in-eu-law/.

relationship with any Union institution[88]), the Commission responds to attacks on rule-based fiscal governance by flying the white flag. This is not the lesson that should have been learned from the series of events that began in 2004. Neither is the Commission's response particularly savvy: Member States with an interest in fiscal responsibility will not consent to the proposed Directive, which requires unanimity, and the failure of the proposal risks compromising the entire legislative package, which includes a number of other components. Beyond political skillfulness, constitutionality under national law is at stake, especially in light of the German FCC's Maastricht Treaty judgment from 1993. An overly lenient system of fiscal control risks triggering constitutional scrutiny of whether the "basis and object of the German Act of Consent" are still in place.

Fiscal stability measures have also been called into question from the other side of the political spectrum. The buzzword "austerity" has become popular. It is obvious that if European policies are perceived as economically destructive, and are blamed for unemployment, in particular youth unemployment, then the EU's future is not a very bright future. In the current debate, however, this criticism has moved from the realm of politics to human rights.[89]

Fundamental rights are not new to the EMU debate. They have been used to contest bailout conditionality in a number of Eurozone States. Early on, the

[88] It appears that the earlier proposal to link future support for Member States to conditions that are negotiated in a contractual relationship has been abandoned. See the earlier communications: Communication from the Commission, *Towards a Deep and Genuine EMU: The Introduction of a Convergence and Competitiveness Instrument*, COM (2013) 165 final (March 20, 2013); Communication from the Commission, *Towards a Deep and Genuine EMU: Ex Ante Coordination of Plans for Major Economic Policy Reforms*, COM (2013) 166 final (March 20, 2013). On this, see Paul Craig, "Economic Governance and the Euro Crisis: Constitutional Architecture and Constitutional Implications," in *The Constitutionalization of European Budgetary Constraints*, eds. Maurice Adams, Federico Fabbrini, and Pierre Larouche (Oxford: Hart Publishing, 2016), 28*ff.*

[89] For a most extensive discussion, see Anastasia Poulou, "Financial Assistance Conditionality and Human Rights Protection: What Is the Role of the EU Charter of Human Rights," *Common Market Law Review* 54, no. 4 (2017): 994 (with further references in footnote 10, as well as at pages 1013–1014); Anastasia Poulou, "Austerity and European Social Rights: How Can Courts Protect Europe's Lost Generation?" *German Law Journal* 15, no. 6 (2014): 1145–1176; Andreas Fischer-Lescano, "Troika in der Austerität: Rechtsbindungen der Unionsorgane beim Abschluß von Memoranda of Understanding," *Kritische Justiz* 47 (2014): 2–25; Alicia Hinarejos, "A Missed Opportunity: The Fundamental Rights Agency and the Euro Area Crisis," *European Law Journal* 22, no. 1 (2016): 61–73; Margot E. Salomon, "Of Austerity, Human Rights and International Institutions," *European Law Journal* 21, no. 4 (2015): 521–545.

The Future of the European Economic and Monetary Union 57

Social Committee of the Council of Europe evaluated the situation in Greece;[90] certain Portuguese measures were declared unconstitutional by the Portuguese Constitutional Court.[91] What is new, however, is the claim that the Commission and the ECB are infringing fundamental rights enshrined in the Charter of Fundamental Rights of the EU (Charter), in particular property, the right of collective action, and social rights. The matter reached the ECJ in the case of *Ledra Advertising*. The Court held that there could be non-contractual liability of the EU institutions for violations of economic and social rights, under Article 340(2) TFEU, but such liability was denied in the case at bar.[92]

In light of the importance of the case, it is worthwhile exploring the matter a bit further. In *Ledra Advertising*, private creditors of Cypriot banks that had suffered extensive financial losses following the bank restructuring in Cyprus brought an action against the Commission and the ECB. The restructuring was required by the Memorandum of Understanding (MoU) issued under Article 13(3) and (4) ESM, imposing conditions on stability support for Cyprus. The Court held that both institutions were bound by the Charter insofar as they had been involved in establishing the restructuring measures in the MoU and – contrary to what had been stated by the Advocate General and held by the General Court[93] – could consequently be held liable for any breach of fundamental rights caused by these measures.[94] In the specific facts of the cases, however, the Court held that there had been no fundamental rights breach, since the interference with the claimants' property was not disproportionate or intolerable in "view of the objective of ensuring the stability of the banking system in the euro area."[95]

The fundamental rights argument as developed in the judgment of the ECJ (and in some of the legal literature) is not convincing, insofar as the reasoning of the judgment is concerned, albeit not the outcome. To begin with, there is no doubt that all EU institutions and bodies are bound by the rights in the Charter in whatever context – including activities in program countries and

---

[90] Reported in Poulou, "Financial Assistance Conditionality and Human Rights Protection," 1015, 1021.

[91] Poulou, 1018–1019.

[92] Joined Cases C-8/15 P to C-10/15 P, *Ledra Advertising v. Commission & ECB*, ECLI:EU:C:2016:701.

[93] Case T-289/13, Order *Ledra Advertising*, ECLI:EU:T:2014:981, paras. 44-47; Opinion Advocate General Wahl, Conclusions, April 21, 2016, ECLI:EU:C:2016:290, paras. 85*ff*.

[94] *Ledra Advertising*, paras. 57*ff*.

[95] *Ledra Advertising*, para. 74. See also the argument in Case C-258/14, *Florescu and Others v. Casa Judeteana*, ECLI:EU:C:2017:448, paras. 49*ff*. On this issue, see Menelaos Markakis and Paul Dermine, "Bailouts, the Legal Status of the Memoranda of Understanding, and the Scope of Application of the EU Charter: Florescu," *Common Market Law Review* 55, no. 2 (2018): 643–672.

policies of budgetary control. Furthermore, they can be held liable for breaches of fundamental rights caused by them. Article 51(1) of the Charter is clear on the matter. Their responsibility may be triggered by their activities within the framework of the ESM, a conclusion that is also plausible in the light of the *Pringle* judgment. So far, the reasoning in *Ledra Advertising* is perfectly in line with the governing law and jurisprudence. The part that fails to convince is that which imputes the entire content of a Memorandum of Understanding to the EU institutions. The negotiation of MoUs is confidential, so we cannot know which actors were responsible for which parts of the MoU – the Commission, the ECB, the Member State, or, if it was still on board, the IMF.[96] Joint responsibility for any mistake in the terms of the MoU, including those on bank restructuring, would be a novelty under public international and EU law, and does not have a sound basis in law.[97]

More broadly speaking, the large margin of appreciation afforded to the EU institutions in economic matters strongly suggests that there will rarely, if ever, be a violation of the Charter. In most, if not all, cases the interference with human rights will probably be held to be justified and the relevant regulation found to be proportionate. Furthermore, it is doubtful that many of the specific entitlements to social rights that are invoked are actually contained in the Charter. And looking beyond the particularities of the EU legal order, entitlements to social rights and positive action by the state are, as a matter of theory and practice, rarely effective in attenuating the hardship caused by economic policies. In sum, responsibility for restructuring measures lies in the political sphere, not the legal one. The Member States are responsible for their social and economic policies, including the deliberate assumption of enormous public debt in some countries, and they should continue to be held politically accountable for their policies.

3 New Institutions?

3.1 The Institutional Framework of the Eurozone

Formally, the institutional framework of the EU remained unchanged throughout the crisis. The only institutional development lay in the activation of Article 136(1) and (2) TFEU for the decision-making of the Eurozone

---

[96] Elena Mönning, *Internationales Staatensanierungsverwaltungsrecht* (Tübingen: Mohr Siebeck, 2018):109–120.

[97] See also Poulou, "Financial Assistance Conditionality and Human Rights Protection," 1013, who says that the ECJ's solution is "not thoroughly explained." She also gives a critical view in: Anastasia Poulou, "The Liability of the EU in the ESM framework," *Maastricht Journal of European and Comparative Law* 24, no. 1 (2017): 133ff.

The Future of the European Economic and Monetary Union 59

European Council and Eurozone Council. (Article 136(1) and (2) stipulate that the adoption of fiscal surveillance and economic policy measures is by a vote of the Eurozone Member States only, not all Member States.) During the most critical moments of the euro crisis, each European Council or ECOFIN-Council was preceded by a Eurozone (European) Council, and there were numerous meetings of the Eurozone Member States only. Not least because a crisis is always the "hour of the executive," these bodies emerged as the strongest players. Thus, the interplay of Commission, Council, and Parliament in the Community method was replaced by intergovernmental bargaining and steering, and in the beginning was even dubbed a separate "Union method."[98] This intergovernmental turn was often criticized. The ESM and the predecessor rescue frameworks (the first Greek rescue package and the EFSF) were established as creatures of the governments of the Eurozone, with a very limited role of the European Parliament and the Commission. Indeed, at many important junctures, the European Council's conclusions resembled EU legislation, contrary to the institutional set up under Article 15(1) TEU, which confers upon the European Council the power to "provide the Union with the necessary impetus for its development and [shall] define the general political directions and priorities thereof" but expressly says that the European Council "shall not exercise legislative functions."[99]

In the euro crisis, the only supranational actor that emerged as powerful was the ECB.[100] But the ECB is also out of reach of the European Parliament.[101] Rather, parliamentary accountability occurs at Member State level, because Member State financial contributions to stability support require that national parliaments exercise their budgetary powers. The only element of Eurozone

---

[98] Speech by Federal Chancellor Angela Merkel at the Opening Ceremony of the 61st Academic Year of the College of Europe in Bruges, November 2, 2010, 7–11, www.coleurope.eu/content/news/Speeches/Europakolleg%20Brugge%20Mitschrift%20englisch.pdf.

[99] Matthias Ruffert, "The Many Faces of Rule-Making in the EU," in *The Actors of Postnational Rule-Making*, ed. Elaine Fahey (Oxford: Routledge, 2016), 52–53 referring to the relevant "legislation." Also see, for a general perspective, Henri de Waele, "Strained Actorness: The 'New' European Council in Theory and Practice," in *The Actors of Postnational Rule-Making*, ed. Elaine Fahey (Oxford: Routledge, 2016), 91–112.

[100] For another analysis of the institutional effects of the euro crisis, see Chapter 6.

[101] On the issue of ECB accountability see Yves Mersch, "Aligning Accountability with Sovereignty in the European Union: The ECB's Experience. Keynote Speech." Paper presented at the ECB Legal Conference, September 4–5, 2017, 13–21. www.rwi.uzh.ch/dam/jcr:9bebb762-d2d1-46d0-914b-852bb5a77ef6/ECB%20Legal%20Conference%202017.pdf. See as well the following articles in the same volume. Generally, on the new role of the ECB, see Thomas Beukers, "The New ECB and its Relationship with the Eurozone Member States: Between Central Bank Independence and Central Bank Intervention," *Common Market Law Review* 50, no. 6 (2013): 1579–1620.

governance over which the European Parliament exercises some influence is in the so-called economic dialogue, which occurs as part of the coordination of Member States' economies in the European Semester.[102] Even there, however, the strongest supranational player is the Commission, which in turn is subordinate to the intergovernmental bargaining in the Council, as laid out in Article 121 TFEU.

3.2 A Consensus for New Institutions?

Many observers consider this framework to be undemocratic due to the limited powers of the European Parliament. Although they acknowledge the involvement of national parliaments, they think it is inadequate since this form of democratic accountability is potentially asymmetric: because the stability function relies on contributions from creditor states, their parliaments can exercise significant clout, whereas debtor-state parliaments are in a relatively weak position.[103]

To address this concern, one of the most far-reaching proposals has been advanced by the group of socialist-leaning French scholars behind T-DEM, the reform project discussed earlier. The central plank of T-DEM is a Eurozone Assembly composed of four-fifths of members from national parliaments of the Eurozone, and one-fifth of members from the European Parliament. This assembly would manage a genuine Eurozone budget to provide stability support and other types of funding.[104] Other proposals also have recourse to a Eurozone assembly, mainly to guarantee the democratic control of a European treasury.[105] The EU institutions are more cautious. The Five Presidents' Report proposed better cooperation between the European Parliament and

---

[102] European Parliament and Council Regulation (EU) 1175/2011, Amending Council Regulation (EC) No 1466/97 on the Strengthening of the Surveillance of Budgetary Positions and the Surveillance and Coordination of Economic Policies, 2011 O.J. (L 306) 12, Article 2–ab. See the rather skeptical assessment by Cristina Fasone, "European Economic Governance and Parliamentary Representation: What Place for the European Parliament?" *European Law Journal* 20, no. 2 (2014): 184; see further Christopher Schoenfleisch, *Integration Durch Koordinierung?* (Tübingen: Mohr Siebeck, 2018), 119–118.

[103] The statement is made prominently by Dimitris Triantafyllou, "Die Asymmetrische Demokratie," *Europarecht* 49, no. 4 (2014): 458–467. See also Mark Dawson and Floris de Witte, "From Balance to Conflict: A New Constitution for the EU," *European Law Journal* 22, no. 2 (2016): 220; Pavlos Elefhteriadis, "Democracy in the Eurozone," in *Legal Challenges in the Global Financial Crisis*, eds. Wolf-Georg Ringe and Peter M. Huber (Oxford: Hart, 2014), 42–43.

[104] *Draft Treaty on the Democratization*, Articles 12(2) and 14–16 of the proposal.

[105] See also the summary in French, available at www.elysee.fr/assets/Initiative-pour-lEurope-une-Europe-souveraine-unie-et-democratique-Emmanuel-Macron.pdf.

The Future of the European Economic and Monetary Union 61

national parliaments and the establishment of a euro area treasury.[106] It also called for an independent European Fiscal Board that would issue independent advisory assessments of the Member States' budgets, and a network of authorities ("euro area system of Competitiveness Authorities") that would make proposals for improving competitiveness.[107] By way of contrast, suggestions that the European Council be strengthened have fallen out of favor.[108]

More recently, in December 2017, the Commission proposed a European Minister of Economy and Finance, but without any changes to parliamentary accountability. The new position would be a very modest development and would simply entail a new "double-hat" for the president of the Eurozone and a member of the Commission.[109] In the same set of proposals, the Commission advocated transforming the ESM into an EU agency, to be called the European Monetary Fund.[110]

3.3 Constitutional Issues: Less Is More

The constitutional question is whether these proposed institutional arrangements are compatible with the EU's multi-level constitutional construction or whether, indeed, any change at all is required in the current governance structure. Contrary to the oft-repeated assertion, the principle of representative democratic rule (Article 10(2) TEU) is not, as a general matter, infringed by the current design of the ESM. The discrepancy between creditor and debtor states and the powers of their national parliaments in the budgetary realm cannot fairly be attributed to the EU, the Member States, or the Eurozone Member State signatories of the ESM.[111] It is true that the state debt crisis prompted substantial financial support for program countries, as early as May 2010 in the Greek case, notwithstanding the legal obstacle in the no-bailout clause in Article 125(1) TFEU.[112] The Greek rescue package contained extensive conditionality, which significantly limited the scope of action of future Greek parliaments. Yet the alternatives to the rescue package were

---

[106] *The Five President's Report*, 18.

[107] *The Five President's Report*, 7, 14, and 23.

[108] Fabbrini, *Economic Governance in Europe*.

[109] Communication from the Commission, *A European Minister of Economy and Finance*, COM (2017) 823 final (December 6, 2017).

[110] *Commission Proposal for a Council Regulation*, COM (2017) 827 final, 5.

[111] This line of argument is taken from Matthias Ruffert, "Europäische Demokratie in der Krise?" in *Privatrecht, Wirtschaftsrecht, Verfassungsrecht*, eds. Cordula Stumpf, Friedemann Kainer, and Christian Baldus (Baden-Baden: Nomos, 2015), 710–717.

[112] See Note 13.

arguably worse, and any other course of events would have had as great, or even greater, impact on the Greek budget and the freedom of maneuver of Greek political institutions.[113] In short, there is no causal link between the current limitations on Greece's freedom of political action and the conditionality imposed on that country.[114]

Nonetheless, the question of parliamentary accountability in the ESM Treaty is more complex, as there is no direct participation of the European Parliament and national parliaments, in particular in the procedure used to grant states stability support under Article 13(2). Such parliamentary involvement, however, may be necessary under national constitutional law (for instance, German constitutional law) and under EU constitutional law. Moreover, the lower the legitimacy provided by the European Parliament, the greater the need for participation by national parliaments. As Christian Calliess has argued, the EU is a construct of communicating pipes.[115] Today, this democratic equilibrium is satisfied since the decision to grant stability support requires the consensus of the ESM members, i.e. a unanimous decision of the Board of Governors.[116] Therefore, each Member State has the power to veto stability support, and if governments answer to their parliaments, each national parliament participates, at least in theory, in the stability support decision. This institutional configuration has not been changed in the Commission's proposed European Monetary Fund.[117] The only exception is the ESM's emergency voting procedure under Article 4(4), where a qualified majority of 85 percent of the votes cast is sufficient, allocated according to the contribution key in Annex I.

In the future, parliamentary accountability at the supranational level may very well have to be enhanced. Further, it cannot be denied that – beyond strong constitutional arguments – the regulation of stability support through

[113] Kaarlo Tuori and Klaus Tuori, *The Eurozone Crisis* (New York: Cambridge University Press, 2014), 76. "Whether a timely Greek default would actually have reduced uncertainty and helped to sort out the crisis quickly or whether it would have led to a catastrophe, such as the crash of the euro, will probably remain an unresolved question."

[114] See the differentiated assessment of the Greek development in Papadopoulou, "Can Constitutional Rules, Even if 'Golden,' Tame Greek Public Debt?" 223–248.

[115] See (in German: 'kommunizierende Röhren') Christian Calliess, "Der Kampf um den Euro: Eine 'Angelegenheit der Europäischen Union' zwischen Regierung, Parlament und Volk," *Neue Zeitschrift für Verwaltungsrecht* 31 (2012): 2.

[116] European Stability Mechanism Treaty, Article 13(2), Article 4(2), first sentence, and Article 5 (6)(f).

[117] *Commission Proposal for a Council Regulation*, COM (2017) 827 final.

The Future of the European Economic and Monetary Union   63

international law external to EU law (the German term *Ersatzunionsrecht*[118] is most revealing) is flawed in political terms. It is also politically inappropriate in a union of equal states to oppose creditors and debtors, those who give and those who take. The political shape of the Union is influenced by a structure of negotiations between both sides. This is the political basis for supranational parliamentary backup of a European *gouvernement économique*, and indeed Article 5 of the proposed EMF Regulation contains the nucleus of such backup.[119]

Some of the proposals argue against entrusting the European Parliament with this function, since doing so would empower Members of Parliament (MPs) from countries outside the Eurozone to vote on Eurozone matters and therefore would exacerbate the democratic deficit.[120] Thence, the proposed mixed chambers of national MPs and Members of the European Parliament (MEPs). This, however, is not convincing. The proposal runs the risk of repeating all the flaws of the European Parliament when it was composed of delegated members, before direct elections were introduced in 1979: MPs not acting as parliamentarians (in parliamentary groups) but as state representatives, and MPs with an unbearable workload, as members of two parliaments.[121] But above all, the core assumption of this line of thought is wrong in constitutional terms. The euro is the currency of the whole Union (Article 3(4) TEU). Certain Member States are granted an exception before they fulfil the convergence criteria (Articles 139 and 140 TFEU), and one Member State (Sweden) is in breach of EU law for not introducing the euro. The United Kingdom aside, only Denmark can deviate from Article 3(4) TEU. This, however, does not change the legitimacy of the European Parliament as the

---

[118] Term developed by Ralph Alexander Lorz and Heiko Sauer, "Ersatzunionsrecht und Grundgesetz: Verfassungsrechtliche Zustimmungsgrundlagen für den Fiskalpakt, den ESM-Vertrag und die Änderung des AEUV," *Die öffentliche Verwaltung* 65 (2012): 573–582.
[119] *Commission Proposal for a Council Regulation*, COM (2017) 827 final. See the proposed Article 6 on accountability toward national parliaments.
[120] See, e.g., Herman Van Rompuy, President of the European Council, *Towards a Genuine Economic and Monetary Union*, EUCO 120/12, 2. See also Stefan Kadelbach, "Lehren aus der Finanzkrise: Ein Vorschlag zur Reform der Politischen Institutionen der Europäischen Union," *Europarecht* 48 (2013): 499; Nicolai von Ondarza, "Auf dem Weg zur Union in der Union: Institutionelle Auswirkungen der differenzierten Integration in der Eurozone auf die EU," *Integration* 36 (2013): 30–33. These reflections are developed in Matthias Ruffert, "Politische Gestaltung durch das Europäische Parlament," in *Politische Gestaltung durch Repräsentativorgane*, eds. David Capitant, Matthias Jestaedt, Johannes Masing, and Armel Le Divellec (Tübingen: Mohr Siebeck, 2017).
[121] Matthias Ruffert, "Parlamentarisierung von Herrschaft im Mehrebenensystem," in *Parlamentsrecht*, eds. Martin Morlok, Utz Schliesky, and Dieter Wiefelspütz (Baden-Baden: Nomos, 2016), paras. 42, 34*ff*.

representative of *all* citizens of the Union.[122] Consequently, the transitional procedures (Article 139(4) TFEU) only suspend the voting rights of non-Eurozone members in the Council, not in the European Parliament. In light of these premises, the Commission's current reform package does not propose institutional modifications for the European Parliament and does not vest the European Minister of Economy and Finance with special competences, but only aims at better institutional coordination between the Eurogroup and the Commission.[123]

As long as the main responsibility for taxing and spending lies with the Member States, their parliaments must retain primary responsibility for ensuring democratic accountability. As the EMU evolves from a market-based structure to a more complicated arrangement, still to be determined, but undoubtedly involving a more significant redistributive and supervisory component, the legitimacy and accountability issues multiply. This is one of the fundamental weaknesses of the EMU, and is one of the great challenges for future institutional design.[124]

IV PERSPECTIVES

To conclude, it is important to go beyond a legal assessment of the existing proposals, and take a closer look at the future of the EMU, again from a legal scholar's perspective. Very important decisions lie ahead for the EMU.[125] The need for action is perhaps less visible than in the heyday of the euro crisis, because of the current strength of the global economy, but is still crucial, as underscored by the economic data presented earlier in this chapter. What lessons can be learned for the future from this chapter's reflections on the current proposals? Three aspects shall be highlighted.

---

[122] Andreas Maurer reaches a similar result, but following a questionable line of argument, in Andreas Maurer, "Mehrebenenparlamentarismus und Interparlamentarische Zusammenarbeit in der Europäischen Union," in *Modelle des Parlamentarismus im 21: Jahrhundert*, eds. Claudio Franzius, Franz C. Mayer, and Jürgen Neyer (Baden-Baden: Nomos, 2015), 374ff.

[123] Graphic presentation in the Communication from the Commission, COM (2017) 821 final, 3.

[124] See again Leino and Saarenheimo, "Sovereignty and subordination." See also Federico Lupo Pasini, "Economic Stability and Economic Governance in the Euro Area," *Journal of International Economic Law* 16, no. 1 (2013): 221; Hinarejos, *The Euro Area Crisis in Constitutional Perspective*, 159–166; and more skeptical, Jukka Snell, "The Trilemma of European Economic and Monetary Integration, and its Consequences," *European Law Journal* 22, no. 2 (2016): 164.

[125] Since the December 2018 and June 2019 European Council meetings, it has become clear that the initial proposals have all been pared back significantly; it appears that there will be a rather reduced Eurozone budget and that the ESM will provide the common backstop to the Single Resolution Fund (SRF). The process is still ongoing.

The first is political rather than legal. In a context determined by intergovernmental negotiations, only proposals that balance stronger budgetary commitment, on the one hand, with improved fiscal stability measures on the other hand have any prospect of being adopted. There are stakeholders on both sides, in favor of responsible fiscal governance *and* more government spending. In this respect, the Commission proposal is one-sided.[126] The impetus to strengthen the EU budget and the Eurozone's potential for monetary intervention should be matched by an equally robust system of fiscal responsibility and stability control. There appears to be a political desire to end "austerity." But can we really talk about austerity when we observe a monetary framework of unprecedented public asset purchases by the ECB?

The second concluding observation is motivated by politics too, but has ramifications for designing a constitutional (and therefore legal) EMU. It is obvious that in the debate on the future of Eurozone governance, there are divergent political interests at play. The interests, views, and attitudes underpinning the reform proposals analyzed in this chapter are attributable not only to Member States but also to competing elements of the political spectrum. What if François Fillon had won the election in France instead of Emmanuel Macron (Marine Le Pen set aside)? What if in Germany the so-called Jamaica-coalition of the Christian Democrat, Liberal, and Green parties had succeeded, with a Liberal finance minister, instead of today's grand-coalition between Christian and Social Democrats, with a Social Democrat finance minister? The challenge of populism notwithstanding, it is a platitude that modern democracies thrive from the competition and alternation in power of political families, and this dynamic should be equally central in the EU, in particular in economic matters. Too lenient budgetary policies might be counterbalanced by a more stability-oriented vote in subsequent elections; exaggerated fiscal stability requirements that suffocate investment and growth might be followed by more Keynesian-oriented policies. It is unclear whether the ongoing negotiations in the Eurozone Councils will be able to counterbalance the handwriting of the French socialist Commissioner for Economic and Financial Affairs, Pierre Moscovici, in the Commission's proposals. However, to the extent that future arrangements come to rely more on political steering than market discipline, they should allow for political change, debate, and compromise. This flexibility is essential for a democratic economic constitution of the EU.

---

[126] It might be submitted that the Editorial Comments in *Common Market Law Review* 55, no. 3 (2018): 709–718 reflect the same unbalanced position.

Such a constitution also needs – third and final remark – a sound basis in economics. Here our competence as legal scholars reaches its limits. In the legal literature, writers far too often draw from economic scholarship selectively, according to their own political standpoints. The fact that the interest of independent economics in the questions we are addressing appears to be rather limited contributes to this phenomenon. Legal scholarship, though, can make a strong contribution to the debate: elaborating and advancing general principles and rules that are able to uphold the rule of law in the context of economic governance; emphasizing procedural fairness and the openness of the democratic process; and knowing that there is no predetermined truth in the matters at stake.

3

Post-Crisis Economic and Social Policy
Some Thoughts on Structural Reforms 2.0

PHILOMILA TSOUKALA

Managing the euro crisis has been a process of institutional transformation for the EU. The European Semester has emerged as a powerful tool for economic policy coordination between the Member States. Beyond the new enforcement tools that the Semester affords the Commission and Council in case of noncompliance with country-specific recommendations, the management of the crisis has given the Commission experience in structural reforms. The Commission now regularly uses this experience in formulating its yearly country-specific recommendations to Member States. Far from a stalwart of untethered neoliberalism, the Commission has been fashioning itself as the manager with a human face, the institution that understands both the structural reform requirements for a global economy and the special need for strong social institutions that could shield European citizens from the worst of the shocks provoked by globalized markets. Hence the name, "Structural Reforms 2.0," per the Juncker Commission.[1]

In this chapter, I review the Commission's emerging structural reform "know-how," as represented in its latest reflection papers and European Semester documents. The European Commission seems to have drawn from its experience in managing loan conditionality for debtor countries like Greece, Portugal, and Ireland, in order to come up with the set of structural reforms that it considers necessary for any country to thrive within the context of the euro. At the same time, it has taken on board the critiques of structural reforms that point to the potentially negative short-term effects of structural adjustment. Thus, the Commission seems to have fully embraced the idea of the EU as a soft alternative to unfettered globalization and has taken it upon itself to monitor certain aspects of the welfare state in Member States.

---

[1] Pierre Moscovici, Commissioner European Commission, Speech Structural Reforms 2.0: For a Stronger and More Inclusive Recovery, SPEECH/16/2124 (June 9, 2016).

The Commission's recommendations, however, while presented in the mode of technocratic expertise, entail deeply political choices in almost every imaginable regulatory field. Despite constant assurances that there is no "one-size fits all" model for structural reforms, what is shaping up through the European Semester is effectively a list of desirable reforms – a set menu of options – which the Commission now openly characterizes as "EU best practices." If applied, they would provoke deep restructurings and adjustments of national political economies with winners and losers to boot. These demands for deep restructurings are couched in a language of technical adjustment and fine-tuning that does not do justice to the qualitative reform required of the Member States or to the substantive trade-offs between market efficiency and social fairness that only a democratic process can legitimize. Contrary to some observers, I conclude that the inclusion of social policy goals into the European Semester can be an indication of both the success of socially minded actors in influencing the content of macroeconomic governance, and of the success of market-minded actors in adapting to demands for "social fairness" in macroeconomic governance without ceding much space in terms of the kinds of reforms required. Much of this "socialization" of the European Semester will depend on how the rest of the management of the common currency evolves.

I BACKGROUND TO THE COORDINATION OF MEMBER STATE ECONOMIC POLICIES

The Maastricht Treaty infamously introduced the idea of the common currency without establishing a common EU-wide economic policy. At the insistence of Germany, Member States adopted the Stability and Growth Pact (SGP), which was meant to commit Member States to budgetary and fiscal restraint.[2] More specifically, Member States agreed to maintain their budget

---

[2] The legal basis for the SGP can be found in the Treaties (now Articles 121 and 126 of the Consolidated Version of the Treaty on the Functioning of the European Union, October 26, 2012, 2012 O.J. (C 326) 47 [hereinafter TFEU]). Its content was specified in two Regulations and one Council Resolution. See Council Regulation (EC) 1466/97, On the Strengthening of the Surveillance of Budgetary Positions and the Surveillance and Coordination of Economic Policies, 1997 O.J. (L 209) 1; Council Regulation (EC) 1467/97, On Speeding Up and Clarifying the Implementation of the Excessive Deficit Procedure, 1997 O.J. (L 209) 6; Resolution of the European Council on the Stability and Growth Pact, 1997 O.J. (C 236) 1. For the particularly important role that the governments of Germany and the Netherlands played in the adoption of the SGP see Martin Heipertz and Amy Verdun, "The Dog that Would Never Bite? What We Can Learn from the Origins of the Stability and Growth Pact," *Journal of European Public Policy* 11, no. 5 (2004): 756–780.

deficit to less than 3 percent of their GDP and their debt to less than 60 percent of their GDP. The Treaties specified a mechanism of multilateral surveillance of state economic policies, aimed at ensuring respect of the SGP, the so-called preventive arm of the SGP. More specifically, the Council, on the basis of a Commission proposal would set broad guidelines on economic policy that the Member States should respect. It would then monitor Member State adherence to those guidelines based on reports submitted by the Commission. The Council could address specific recommendations to Member States if it thought that the Member State's economic policy deviated from the broad guidelines.[3]

In addition to the "preventive arm" of this process of multilateral surveillance, the Treaties provided for a "corrective arm," which was meant to induce compliance with budgetary and debt limits. The Commission would decide whether a specific Member State was in violation of the budget and debt limit criteria of the SGP. In other words, it would decide whether there was an excessive deficit or a Member State was close to running an excessive deficit and make a relevant recommendation to the Council. The Council would then address recommendations to the Member State in question, suggesting measures to bring the deficit situation under control. The specific efforts of the Member State to correct the deficit would be monitored. If the Member State failed to respond to Council recommendations, the Council could resort to a number of more coercive strategies such as requiring the Member State to make a non–interest-bearing deposit with the Union until the problem was corrected, or, in the last resort, impose fines of an "appropriate size."[4]

The SGP and its preventive and corrective arms were fiercely debated in the relevant literature with critics arguing both that the pact was too "inflexible" in imposing a numerically fixed limit to budget and debt deficits, and that it was too "soft" or "ineffective."[5] The implementation of the multilateral surveillance seemed to vindicate the latter critique. Between 2001 and 2003, several Member States were found to be in violation of the SGP; however, no sanctions were imposed, and after a vote from a divided Council, the excessive deficit procedure was put in abeyance for France and Germany, despite the

---

[3] Article 121 TFEU.

[4] Article 126 TFEU.

[5] See generally Heipertz and Verdun, "The Dog that Would Never Bite?"; Jakob de Haan et al., "Why Has the Stability and Growth Pact Failed?" *International Finance* 7, no. 3 (2004): 235–260; Jürgen von Hagen, "Fiscal Discipline and Growth in Euroland: Experiences with the Stability and Growth Pact." Working Paper no. B 06-2003, ZEI, Center for European Integrations, 2003, 1–35.

fact that neither state had complied.[6] The SGP Regulations were reformed in 2005, introducing further flexibility in the application of the excessive deficit procedure.[7]

The ideological tides started changing against flexibility and in favor of stricter enforcement after the Greek crisis, which transformed into a euro crisis, starting in 2010. Whatever one may think about the origins and causes of the crisis, there was little doubt that Greece's debt burden had exposed it to the pressures of international markets, which in turn had affected other Eurozone Member States. This reinforced the consensus around the need for stricter oversight of Member State economic policy by the EU. This translated into a series of measures embodied in the so-called Six Pack and Two Pack, adopted between 2011 and 2013.[8] In addition, twenty-five Member States adopted the Treaty on Stability, Coordination, and Governance in 2012, which commits them to a balanced budget.[9]

Perhaps the most important change brought about by the post-2010 package of new measures is the creation of the European Semester, described by the Council as "a cycle of economic and fiscal policy coordination" aimed at ensuring "convergence and stability in the EU," "sound public finances," and fostering of economic growth.[10] Each year in December, the Commission analyzes the economic situation and publishes an "Annual Growth Survey" (AGS) in preparation for the upcoming European Semester. Between January and July, the Council reviews the AGS and after obtaining the opinion of the European Parliament adopts its conclusions on the AGS. The European Council then proposes guidelines based on this process. The second phase of the European Semester includes a review of the specific policies of individual Member States. Each Member State submits a report on its proposed policies and budget. The Commission then publishes country-specific

---

[6] See generally Heipertz and Verdun, "The Dog that Would Never Bite?" 765.

[7] Jean-Victor Louis, "The Review of the Stability and Growth Pact," *Common Market Law Review* 43, no. 1 (2006): 85–106.

[8] The Six Pack consisted of five Regulations and one Directive, while the Two Pack included two Regulations. The most important reforms included an intensification of the ex-ante surveillance of economic policy and the introduction of the potential for the imposition of ex-post fines in cases of violation. See Council of the EU, "European Semester: A Guide to the Main Rules and Documents," November 10, 2017, www.consilium.europa.eu/en/policies/european-semester/european-semester-key-rules-and-documents/.

[9] Daniel Gros, "The Treaty on Stability, Coordination and Governance in the Economic and Monetary Union (aka Fiscal Compact)." Working Document, Centre for European Political Studies, March 8, 2012.

[10] Council of the EU, "European Semester: Overview," March 14, 2018, www.consilium.europa.eu/en/policies/european-semester/.

recommendations on the basis its own review, which are then adopted by the Council. Member States then take these recommendations into consideration before discussing their national budgets.

Running parallel to the review of economic policies, the European Semester also includes a review of each Member State's macroeconomic position. This process is the heir to the preventive and corrective arms of the SGP. A review of a certain number of macroeconomic indicators results in a judgment about whether a Member State is in macroeconomic imbalance. The Commission incorporates the macroeconomic imbalance analysis in its country-specific recommendations and the Council in turn adopts them. Member States are expected to comply with those recommendations in deciding their national budgets. The barrage of measures included in the Six Pack and Two Pack after the 2010 crisis include the possibility of the automatic imposition of fines in cases of Member State noncompliance with the country-specific recommendations. Thus far, this possibility has only been mobilized once, against Spain, on the rather technical basis that the statistics provided by one of its provinces were inaccurate.[11]

The European Semester has imposed a certain European "timing" to national budgetary processes that would otherwise differ widely from one another. As Nicolas Jabko observes in his contribution to this volume, this shift in timing is of symbolic importance, signaling a new, "practice of sovereignty," and one that accepts more intrusion on national budgets from the EU level.[12] The European Semester has also brought about a renewed emphasis on structural reforms, imagined as the main way in which Member States can alter basic features of their economic performance with the goal of achieving better growth and "convergence" at the EU level. The structural reform recommendations of the Council, as proposed by the Commission, can give us a picture of the kind of economy imagined as ideal by EU experts. A careful reading of the latest round of such recommendations allows us to observe the emergence of certain types of structural reforms as desirable for most Member States, as well as a certain degree of carry-over from the "know-how" the Commission developed in managing the bail-out agreements of Greece, Ireland, and Portugal.

While the effectiveness of the European Semester has been highly doubted in the relevant literature, I believe it still carries a great deal of weight, especially since it seems to have solidified the Commission's claimed expertise in structural reforms, which in turn is shaping what the Commission has

[11] See discussion in this chapter.
[12] See Chapter 4.

referred to as "European best practices."[13] The acceptance of these proposed structural reforms may differ from Member State to Member State depending on many factors, the most important of which perhaps is the Member State's fiscal and economic position.[14] The other important innovation post-crisis is the creation of the European Stability Mechanism (ESM), whose funds could potentially be accessed by Member States in distress. However, this would be only on condition of compliance with proposed reforms, which are designed by the European Commission, in coordination with the European Central Bank and, where needed, the International Monetary Fund.[15] Thus, Member States that may feel more exposed to the vagaries of international markets because of their fiscal positions will experience more pressure to comply with proposed structural reform recommendations. Unsurprisingly, Germany has felt no impulse to comply with the European Semester recommendations on its persistent surplus, which is thought to impede the adjustment of debtor Member States.[16]

Finally, the corpus of Commission-endorsed structural reforms is currently one of the most important sites of discursive contestation between those who would like to see the EU take a more "social" turn and those who believe that European welfarism lies at the heart of the EU's current economic woes. The twists and turns of the "social," therefore, within the European Semester are worth following and analyzing.

---

[13] Memorandum of Understanding Between the European Commission Acting on Behalf of the European Stability Mechanism and the Hellenic Republic and the Bank of Greece (August 2015), 5, https://ec.europa.eu/info/sites/info/files/01_mou_20150811_en1.pdf ("Greece will design and implement a wide range of reforms in labour markets and product markets (including energy) that not only ensure full compliance with EU requirements, but which also aim at achieving European best practices").

[14] Mark Hallerberg et al., "How Effective and Legitimate is the European Semester? Increasing the Role of the European Parliament." Bruegel Working Paper no. 2011/09, September 2011, 23 ("As to its effectiveness, the preliminary evidence is that countries have adapted differently to the new procedures depending on whether they are 'old' or 'new' Member States; if their economic interests lie exclusively with the EU or not; and if they have strong or weak national fiscal frameworks.")

[15] "Lending toolkit," European Stability Mechanism website, last visited October 24, 2018, www.esm.europa.eu/assistance/lending-toolkit. For scholarly treatment of the European Commission's role in the ESM see Michael W. Bauer and Stefan Becker, "The Unexpected Winner of the Crisis: The European Commission's Strengthened Role in Economic Governance," *Journal of European Integration* 36, no. 3 (2014): 213–229.

[16] European Commission Staff Working Document: Country Report Germany 2017, SWD (2017) 71 final (February 22, 2017), 1–2.

II FROM ONE-SIZE-FITS-ALL TO ADAPTABLE CONVERGENCE?

The European Commission has produced a voluminous literature in the last eight years in the course of managing the euro crisis and the loan agreements between Eurozone members and debtor countries.[17] In addition, it now has several years of European Semester coordination under its belt.[18] The country-specific recommendations for the European Semester allow us to draw conclusions about the kinds of reforms the Commission believes are needed for successful economic governance within the EMU. Tracing the evolution of recommended reforms to their latest iteration suggests that far from treating Greece and other bailout countries as an extreme and rare case of macroeconomic instability, the Commission is drawing conclusions about desirable reforms for potentially every member of the Eurozone from its experience as a manager of bailout conditionality.[19]

---

[17] Greece has received financial assistance on three different occasions. The first bailout agreement in 2010 was between Greece, Eurozone Member States, and the International Monetary Fund, as was the second one in 2012. In 2015 Greece received a financial assistance package from the recently created European Stability Mechanism. The European Commission has been in charge of supervising implementation of all these programs on behalf of the Eurozone creditors. Besides the basic agreement on the conditionality of these programs, which was encapsulated in Memoranda of Understanding (MoU), each one of these programs had several rounds of review with voluminous reports on compliance. For a comprehensive list of all the major publications produced in the process of this supervision, see "Financial Assistance to Greece," European Commission website, last visited July 6, 2018, https://ec .europa.eu/info/business-economy-euro/economic-and-fiscal-policy-coordination/eu-financial-assistance/which-eu-countries-have-received-assistance/financial-assistance-greece_ en#financial-assistance-programmes. For the documents generated in the case of the Irish bailout, see "Financial Assistance to Ireland," European Commission website, last visited July 6, 2018, https://ec.europa.eu/info/business-economy-euro/economic-and-fiscal-policy-coordination/eu-financial-assistance/which-eu-countries-have-received-assistance/financial-assistance-ireland_en; for Portugal, see "Financial Assistance to Portugal," European Commission website, last visited July 6, 2018, https://ec.europa.eu/info/business-economy-euro/ economic-and-fiscal-policy-coordination/eu-financial-assistance/which-eu-countries-have-received-assistance/financial-assistance-portugal_en; for the case of Cyprus's bailout see "Financial Assistance to Cyprus," European Commission website, last visited July 6, 2018, https://ec.europa.eu/info/business-economy-euro/economic-and-fiscal-policy-coordination/eu-financial-assistance/which-eu-countries-have-received-assistance/financial-assistance-cyprus_en.

[18] The first round of the European Semester took place in 2011. See European Commission Memorandum MEMO/11/14, European Semester: A New Architecture for the New EU Economic Governance–Q&A (January 12, 2011).

[19] Institutionally, this is also exemplified in the transformation of the initially country-specific "Task Force for Greece" into the "Structural Reform Support Program." The Task Force for Greece, staffed by a mix of Commission employees and Greek civil servants, was meant to provide technical assistance to the Greek state in its structural reform efforts and expedite the

74   *Philomila Tsoukala*

The first thing to note is that the Commission has fully embraced the idea that there were structural defects in the design of the euro that led to a patchwork institutional response in the panicked, emergency follow-up to the crisis.[20] In fact, the Commission goes as far as to acknowledge theories of sudden stoppage of liquidity in an incomplete monetary union, that is in a union without a lender of last resort.[21] However, it steers clear of blaming the joining together of really disparate economies under one currency as a culprit, which is what theories of the Eurozone as a nonoptimal currency area have tended to do.[22] Instead, the Commission points a finger to a combination of "pre-crisis imbalances" in Member States and a faulty institutional set-up in the Economic and Monetary Union (EMU), especially as regards supervision of the banking sector and guarantees that could function as a backstop in a liquidity crisis.[23] This story of co-production of the crisis then allows the Commission to emphasize that the reforms necessary for fixing the institutional gaps at EU level are well underway, but since they are incomplete, Member States should hurry to undergo the necessary reforms in order to avoid the production of further imbalances.

During the first years of crisis management, the Commission insisted on competitiveness gaps between Member States as a causal factor in the production of the crisis, and therefore insisted on recommending reducing labor costs

channeling and use of EU structural funds in the country. See José Manuel Durão Barroso, President of the European Commission, European Renewal – State of the Union Address 2011, SPEECH/11/607 (September 28, 2011). It seems to have inspired the newly established "Structural Reform Support Service" designed "to support Member States in the preparation, design and implementation of institutional, structural and administrative reforms." See European Commission Press Release IP/18/4143, Commission Provides Support for a Further 32 Reform Projects in Greece (June 13, 2018). The new service places special emphasis on projects that improve governance, such as judicial reform and anti-corruption. See "Structural Reform Support Service," European Commission website, last visited July 6, 2018, https://ec .europa.eu/info/funding-tenders/funding-opportunities/funding-programmes/overview-funding-programmes/structural-reform-support-programme-srsp_en.

[20] *Commission Reflection Paper on the Deepening of the Economic and Monetary Union*, COM (2017) 291 (May 31, 2017), 9 ("shortcomings in the way the EMU responds to major shocks"); *Commission Reflection Paper*, COM (2017) 291, 17 ("the institutional architecture of the EMU is a mixed system ... many new rules or bodies were established in an ad hoc manner over time, often in response to emergencies").

[21] *Commission Reflection Paper*, COM (2017) 291, 9 ("sudden stop in capital flows exposed the unsustainable debt and competitiveness gaps that had accumulated over time"). For an overview of the way in which a sudden stop in the flow of credit can transform a liquidity crisis into a solvency crisis, see Paul De Grauwe, "Managing a Fragile Eurozone," *CESifo Forum* 2 (Summer 2011): 40.

[22] Paul De Grauwe, *Economics of Monetary Union* 12th ed. (Oxford: Oxford University Press, 2018), 24–54.

[23] *Commission Reflection Paper*, COM (2017) 291, 9.

to improve competitiveness.[24] This strategy may very well have been one of the few tools available for inducing an adjustment in indebted Member States without the availability of a devaluation, but competitiveness in and of itself figured prominently as a goal in the first few years of the post-crisis European Semester.[25] While competitiveness still figures in many of its country-specific recommendations, there seems to be new emphasis on the existence of persistent divergences between Member States in the post-crisis recovery and an appreciation of the negative effects of such divergences beyond the economy:

> wide gaps in growth ... opened between a group of more vulnerable countries and the others, with significant social and political costs.[26]

The Commission attributes these divergences to preexisting country-specific weaknesses, which were hidden through the pre-crisis credit bubble – and this is as close as the Commission comes to acknowledging a contribution of the currency itself to the crisis.[27] Despite the fact that the Commission recognizes the pre-crisis economic convergence to be partly an artifact of the credit bubble illusion, its plans are geared toward producing the institutional conditions that will lead to "re-convergence."[28] Thus, it considers divergence between European economies bad for the overall project of European integration, especially in the current conditions of an institutional halfway house, where monetary policy has been devolved upward to the EU, while economic policy remains under national control subject to European Semester coordination.[29]

This brings us to the Commission's idea of what needs to be done by every Eurozone Member State – not just the debtor states. The general idea is

[24] *Commission Annual Growth Survey: Advancing the EU's Comprehensive Response to the Crisis*, COM (2011) 11 final (January 12, 2011), 2 ("price and cost competitiveness remain problematic ... the EU needs to use this crisis to address decisively the issue of its global competitiveness").

[25] *Commission Annual Growth Survey*, COM (2011) 11 final; *Commission Annual Growth Survey 2012*, COM (2011) 815 final (November 23, 2011), 3; *Commission Annual Growth Survey 2013*, COM (2012) 750 final (November 28, 2012), 3; *Commission Annual Growth Survey 2014*, COM (2013) 800 final (November 13, 2013), 3.

[26] *Commission Reflection Paper*, COM (2017) 291, 10.

[27] *Commission Reflection Paper*, 9, 12.

[28] *Commission Reflection Paper*, 12.

[29] *Commission Reflection Paper*, 7 ("As robust as it is today, the EMU remains incomplete. The 'Monetary' pillar of the EMU is well developed, as illustrated by the role of the European Central Bank (ECB). However, the 'Economic' component is lagging behind, with less integration at EU level hampering its ability to support fully the monetary policy and national economic policies").

"structural reforms to modernise economies and make them more resilient to shocks."[30] This is judged necessary, as despite institutional progress the structure of the EMU remains incomplete and it is therefore crucially important for each Member State to have strong capacity to adapt to a potential future external shock. Thus, in the Commission's view converging toward "more resilient economic and social structures" should be the goal for everyone.[31]

Reaffirming its belief in the idea that the Single Market is a strong engine for convergence between European economies, the Commission prioritizes a deepening of the Single Market as the first step in the direction of re-convergence.[32] The second step in the same process is a stronger economic coordination through the European Semester. There, the Commission envisages a more "binding convergence process"[33] that would focus substantively on:

> quality of public spending; investment in education and training; embracing more open and more competitive products and services markets, and creating fair and efficient tax and benefit systems.[34]

A minimum of social standards should also be included in this convergence process and the entire enterprise should be reinforced with tighter surveillance mechanisms, according to the Commission.[35] The real bite behind the monitoring of the convergence process seems to be the newly created link between progress on structural reforms and access to EU structural funds. More specifically, in order to access the funds for projects co-financed by the European Structural and Investment Funds (ESIFs), national governments need to address the country-specific recommendations addressed to them at the end of the European Semester.[36] In its proposals on how to further deepen the EMU, the Commission proposes an outright shift toward imposing reforms as conditionality for accessing ESI funds in the future.[37]

From a substantive perspective, the Commission has been working on better defining the scope of desirable structural reforms over the past eight years. In his speech on structural reforms, Commissioner Moscovici recently provided some more details as to the elements of structural reforms now

---

[30] *Commission Reflection Paper*, 13.
[31] *Commission Reflection Paper*, 23.
[32] *Commission Reflection Paper*, 24.
[33] *Commission Reflection Paper*, 24.
[34] *Commission Reflection Paper*, 24.
[35] *Commission Reflection Paper*, 24.
[36] *Commission Reflection Paper*, 25.
[37] *Commission Reflection Paper*, 25.

Post-Crisis Economic and Social Policy

77

considered necessary for all Member States.[38] According to Moscovici, the "key word for structural reforms 2.0 is productivity." This implies deep restructuring of education and vocational training systems and it also requires continued emphasis on reforms of welfare regimes toward "flexicurity."[39]

Specific examples of how the Commission has operationalized these broad ideas about structural reform can be found in the country-specific recommendations (CSRs) for each country in the last several years. A list of recommended reforms was helpfully summarized by Vice-President Dombrovskis:

> At national level, structural reform encompasses a broad set of measures, such as labour market reform; upskilling and re-skilling working people of all ages so that their profiles fit the jobs on offer; shifting the tax burden away from labour, especially low paid labour; ensuring long term sustainability of social and pension systems; boosting investment in R&D, with an eye on both the quantity and quality; and improving the governance and effectiveness of our public services.[40]

Many elements on this list were present even before the crisis. Labor market reform still figures in many of the CSRs, and often focuses on reducing protections for permanent workers, which is thought to create labor market segmentation, in other words a sharp division between workers with permanent and precarious contracts. Increased protections for workers are also believed to be problematic from the perspective of job creation.[41] The Commission often still uses the language of "rigidities" in the labor markets to

---

[38] Moscovici, SPEECH/16/2124.

[39] Moscovici, SPEECH/16/2124. Flexicurity combines the concepts of security and flexibility and has been long considered by the Commission as the ideal model for European welfarism. The idea is to treat the labor market as the main engine of both growth for the country and income security for workers. A country that adopts a flexicurity model of welfare would invest money in re-training and re-skilling unemployed workers so that they can return to the labor market as soon as possible. The flexicurity model is thought to stand in contrast with other models of welfarism that seek to simply provide a safe floor for workers' incomes and that are increasingly believed to discourage return to labor markets. See Ton Wilthagen and Frank Tros, "The Concept of 'Flexicurity': A New Approach to Regulating Employment and Labour Markets," *European Review of Labour and Research* 10, no. 2 (2004): 166–186.

[40] Valdis Dombrovskis, European Commission Vice-President, Speech at the Conference on Structural Reforms to Encourage Investment and Growth (March 3, 2017), https://ec.europa .eu/commission/commissioners/2014-2019/dombrovskis/announcements/vp-dombrovskis-speech-conference-structural-reforms-encourage-investment-and-growth_en.

[41] *Commission Annual Growth Survey 2017*, COM (2016) 725 final (November 16, 2016), 10 ("Those Member States that pursued comprehensive labour market and social protection reforms prior to the crisis have been better able to support employment and preserve fairness during the economic downturn. Such reforms encompass flexible and reliable contractual arrangements that promote labour market transitions and avoid a two-tier labour market").

describe labor protections.[42] It also continues to look suspiciously at minimum wage regulations, as potentially increasing workers' reservation wages and therefore their willingness to take up new jobs.[43]

Other elements such as the improvement of governance have made an appearance after the crisis and now regularly include items that fall well beyond the EU's competences such as taxation and judicial reform. The evaluation of governance now reads like an International Monetary Fund assessment in that it leaves out very little outside of the scope of desirable reform. While there is very little that can be done at EU level to induce countries to comply with recommendations that fall beyond the macroeconomic imbalance procedure, the Commission has created a new "carrot" for countries undertaking such reforms in the provision of technical support through the newly created Structural Reforms Support Service.[44]

III PRELIMINARY OBSERVATIONS ON "STRUCTURAL REFORMS 2.0"

The Commission's recommendations for the types of reforms needed by Member States suggest that it has moved away from the emergency emphasis on quick adjustments via labor cost cuts and toward a broader idea about what kinds of reforms would be conducive to growth. Despite the Commission's repeated declarations about how there is no such thing as a "one-size-fits-all" model, what emerges from the post-crisis literature it has produced is a very consistent emphasis on transforming every European country into an outward-looking, export-based economy. In addition, the Commission has a checklist of reforms that will be needed to achieve this result. That checklist continues to revolve around items that were already in the Commission's recommendations even before the crisis struck, namely, the deepening of the single market through liberalization of labor, service, and product markets, along with the

---

[42] *Commission Recommendation for a Council Recommendation on the 2017 National Reform Programme of Portugal and Delivering a Council Opinion on the 2017 Stability Programme of Portugal*, COM (2017) 521 final (May 22, 2017), 3–5.

[43] *Commission Recommendation for a Council Recommendation*, COM (2017) 521 final, 6 (acknowledging the benefits of the minimum wage for the purposes of avoiding in-work poverty, but emphasizing the risks entailed for the low-skilled); *Commission Recommendation for a Council Recommendation on the 2017 National Reform Programme of France and Delivering a Council Opinion on the 2017 Stability Programme of France*, COM (2017) 509 final (May 22, 2017), 6 ("in the current context of high unemployment, there are risks that the cost of labour at the minimum wage hampers employment opportunities for low skilled people").

[44] See Note 19.

transformation of European welfare regimes from factors of labor inactivity, to factors of labor activation.

In other words, a belief in liberalizing markets as an engine of growth in and of itself is still very much present in the Commission's recommendations, despite acknowledgment that said processes did not produce the desired upward "convergence" of European economies, except briefly through the operation of the credit bubble. A newly acquired emphasis on turning countries into globally competitive export engines begs the question of how exactly this will be achieved, given the truly gaping chasms in productive capacities between the different Member States and the traditional reliance of debtor and creditor states within the EU on trade between themselves as an engine for growth.

What seems to have changed through the crisis years is the list of areas that can be included in the broad category of structural reforms. The experience of crisis management seems to have expanded the checklist of reforms considerably. The Commission now regularly delves deeply into tax and social security regimes in its yearly recommendations, as well as into the catch-all category of the efficiency of public administration, which includes anything from judicial reform to using generic drugs to cut expenses in public health systems to improving the connections between educational systems and industry. This might be why the Commission insists that there is no one-size-fits-all model in its recommendations. Every country has a different mix of items on the checklist that need urgent action so each CSR includes different actionable items. It is still true, however, that the big picture is one of the Commission pushing Member States to adopt reforms that it thinks will allow them to become export-based economies, hopefully of high-tech product and services.

The other big difference between early post-crisis recommendations and more recent ones is the increased emphasis on the social aspects of the economy. The Juncker Commission prominently advertises the inclusion of social fairness as a goal of the economic convergence process, talking more broadly about "economic and social divergence" as a problem.[45] It also touts the inclusion of social indicators in the yearly monitoring process of the European Semester as an indication that the EU now puts economic considerations on par with social ones.[46] Some academic observers have taken these developments as an indication of the flexibility of the European Semester as an economic governance tool that is able to accommodate goals of economic

---

[45] *Commission Reflection Paper*, COM (2017) 291, 12.
[46] *Commission Reflection Paper*, 33.

adjustment and growth with more social goals of ensuring social fairness in growth (or in crisis).[47]

This warrants a few preliminary observations. The first one is that the flexibility of the European Semester can go both directions and it is still quite early to make a judgment about whether the inclusion of "social" language is, in fact, a step forward, a step backward, or none of the above for those who care about the concept of a Social Europe. This is partly because much depends on what will happen next in the rest of the governance structure of the EMU. It may very well be that the Commission aspires to a deepening of the EMU that includes redistribution at EU level – some proto EU-level welfare state. However, the politics of the Member States currently make this a highly unlikely event in the short to middle term. If it turns out to be true that all we can see in the next several years is management of an incomplete EMU, which by definition necessitates fiscal prudence and a switch to export-led growth for all Member States, without the capacity for more EU-level redistribution, then the emphasis on the "social" in the European Semester is likely to serve the purpose of merely ensuring that "economic and social priorities are sustainable and work hand in hand."[48] In other words, the emphasis here is on the sustainability of the welfare regimes given the need for fiscal prudence in the face of structural adjustment of productive models.

This emphasis on sustainability in turn will mean countries will be pressured to converge toward flexible welfare models that emphasize adaptability of workers to changing circumstances and the provision of minimum standards to the neediest. While these may very well be worthy goals for a welfare regime to achieve, they entail highly contested political values, which cannot merely be adopted under the guise of technical necessity but need to be negotiated between the stakeholders at national level. One could argue that since Member States have already agreed to the euro, what its management necessitates should also be considered democratically legitimate. However, that would be a highly formalist and counterproductive approach to the problem, risking even worse backlash from various populist movements around the EU. While the European Semester has produced very mixed results on Member State compliance, the Commission is working diligently to develop not only the substantive ideas about what constitutes desirable

[47] Amy Verdun and Jonathan Zeitlin, "Introduction: The European Semester as a New Architecture of EU Socioeconomic Governance in Theory and Practice," *Journal of European Public Policy* 25, no. 2 (2018): 144 ("Semester provides a workable, if still imperfect framework for integrating EU social and economic policy co-ordination, without sacrificing the objectives of either process").

[48] *Commission Reflection Paper*, COM (2017) 291, 10.

reform in these fields but also the tools necessary to gradually increase its capacity for enforcement.

The Commission's emphasis on what it considers an appropriate tax regime for properties is just one example of this newly acquired substantive "know-how" on structural reforms. Since the crisis, the Commission has been recommending a switch from transaction taxes on property to recurrent property taxes. This made a first appearance in the Greek program, where the Troika, i.e. the Commission, the European Central Bank, and the International Monetary Fund, noted that the transaction tax on property affected labor mobility. The link is as follows: one-time transaction taxes on property make property more affordable; indeed Greece has one of the highest home ownership rates in Europe even after the crisis. People who own property are less likely to pick up and leave in order to go look for a new job elsewhere. In other words, owning property increases the reservation wage for the unemployed and decreases labor mobility. Therefore less home ownership is a worthy goal for reform in the case of Greece because it would improve labor mobility and therefore decrease unemployment rates. This is an astonishing proposal on the part of the institutions formerly known as the Troika, especially since at the time, Greece's welfare regime had very little capacity to deal with the negative effects of the crisis and home ownership functioned as a social stabilizer in the absence of welfare rights.[49]

The Commission's theoretical commitment to recurrent property taxes as a more efficient tool is recently evident in the Commission's Staff Working Paper on Spain's 2017 Country Report. The authors once again emphasize that recurrent property taxes "allow a more efficient allocation of assets, as well as higher labour mobility."[50] The same recommendation can be found in Sweden's 2017 CSRs, with the purpose of decreasing the levels of household indebtedness, presumably because fewer people would even try to buy with recurrent property taxes.[51] One can find the same recommendation in

---

[49] Georgios Symeonidis et al., "Comparative Analysis of Poverty in Greece Versus Richer European Countries in the Debt-Crisis Era." Working Paper no. 712, Luxembourg Income Study, August 2017, 15 ("higher owned housing percentages for pensioners in Greece versus [other] countries seems to be one of the few alleviating factors in the lives of this group in the current crisis").

[50] Commission Staff Working Document: Country Report Spain 2017, SWD (2017) 74 final (February 22, 2017), 24.

[51] Commission Recommendation for a Council Recommendation on the 2017 National Reform Programme of Sweden and Delivering a Council Opinion on the 2017 Convergence Programme of Sweden, COM (2017) 526 final (May 22, 2017), 5.

Austria's and Ireland's CSRs as well, this time with the reasoning that it is a good way to increase tax revenue.[52]

The point here is not that recurrent property taxes are wrong, or inefficient or undesirable. Rather the point is that they have now started to figure in the Commission's recommendations regularly, and regardless of the country's type of welfare regime. In the case of Greece, which belongs to the Mediterranean style of welfarism, in which the family internalizes much of the cost of unemployment and other forms of economic dependency, high levels of debt-free home ownership allowed the country to weather a dramatic drop in its GDP with less homelessness than would otherwise have been possible. The road through which recurrent property taxes lead to more labor mobility per the creditors' plans is through the eventual loss of home ownership by people who can no longer foot the tax bill, which in turn will naturally lead to better takeup of available low-paying jobs. In an economic environment that is still dire, moving forward with the recurrent property tax without jobs waiting for the newly dispossessed is a risky gamble. In the case of Sweden, the recurrent property tax is suggested as a means of disincentivizing people from taking up mortgages. It is an entirely different context, in which the measure does not risk causing social harm, because the economic conditions are entirely different and the background welfare regime is Scandinavian-style welfarism that provides more than the minimum to more than the neediest. In the cases of Austria and Ireland, the measure is recommended as a better way to raise tax revenue, without any discussion at all of the potential unintended social consequences. In all cases, these measures, with huge distributional consequences for different groups of stakeholders are proposed as merely technical improvements on "governance," without much consideration for the kind of democratic legitimation necessary for their adoption.

Other examples include the Commission's ideas about how to incentivize female labor participation. Those include providing full-day daycares and affordable childcare options, which are regularly included in the recommendations for countries showing low levels of female participation.[53] But they also include more contested measures such as undoing the tax disincentives for the second wage earner to take up a job, when, for example, the tax code

---

[52] *Commission Recommendation for a Council Recommendation on the 2017 National Reform Programme of Austria and Delivering a Council Opinion on the 2017 Stability Programme of Austria*, COM (2017) 519 final (May 22, 2017), 5; *Commission Recommendation for a Council Recommendation on the 2017 National Reform Programme of Ireland and Delivering a Council Opinion on the 2017 Stability Programme of Ireland*, COM (2017) 507 final (May 22, 2017), 5 [hereinafter *Recommendation for Ireland*].

[53] *Recommendation for Ireland*, COM (2017) 507 final, 6.

provides for free health care insurance of a homemaker. In its 2017 recommendations to Germany, the Commission notes that free health care for a homemaker discourages her from taking up a job or increasing her hours worked in a part-time job.[54] This is another example of a structural reform that is suggested on the basis of its importance for labor market participation, but it entails a very deep restructuring of the Member State's welfare regime under the guise of a technical recommendation from an institution that now declares it cares equally about economic and social goals of convergence, and is taking steps to supervise both equally.

It is worth mentioning that the 2015 Greek Memorandum of Understanding (MoU) repeatedly refers to reforming the Greek labor regime and welfare system according to "EU best practices." This is further indication that the elaboration of the conditionality for indebted countries has served as a kind of laboratory in which the Commission has worked out its ideas about what counts as an EU best practice. In its section on a Greek "growth strategy" the MoU refers to structural reforms according to "European best practices" right before it describes how major assets should be privatized for more efficient use of resources.[55] Does the Commission as part of the institutions managing the Greek loan conditionality ascribe to privatization of public assets as a European best practice? It is unclear perhaps, but worrisome nonetheless in its presentation as a merely technocratic measure for better fiscal governance. If Greece achieves a restructuring of this magnitude in the midst of dire economic circumstances and without extra funding for the achievement of this goal, that is probably good news for the Commission, which will most likely have to push for similar reforms everywhere else, without the kind of spending capacity at EU level that would allow a sweetening of the pill.

As far as Greece's reform of its welfare regime goes, the MoU is unequivocal. There needs to be a fair sharing of the burdens of adjustment and that means creating a true safety net, which is in turn defined as attending to the

---

[54] *Commission Recommendation for a Council Recommendation on the 2017 National Reform Programme of Germany and Delivering a Council Opinion on the 2017 Stability Programme of Germany*, COM (2017) 505 final (May 22, 2017), 6.

[55] Memorandum of Understanding Between the European Commission Acting on Behalf of the European Stability Mechanism and the Hellenic Republic and the Bank of Greece, 2 ("Greece will design and implement a wide range of structural reforms that not only ensure full compliance with EU requirements, but which also aim at achieving European best practices. The authorities will continue to implement an ambitious privatisation programme, and a new independent Privatisation and Investment Fund (HCAP) has been established supporting a more efficient use of resources").

needs of the poorest and the neediest.[56] The MoU specifically mentions that this type of welfare regime would be in line with EU best practices. If the idea is that a welfare regime that attends to the needs only of the neediest is the goal for everyone, then we are again talking about a deep transformation of many welfare regimes around Europe, whether those are of the universalist or continental variant, both of which typically have included a certain level of de-commodification as their goal.[57] In other words, the welfare regime encapsulated in the MoU is, following Esping-Andersen's categorization, in the liberal mold, which requires citizens to turn to the market and commodify their labor in order to satisfy their basic needs, unless they fall in specific categories of extreme need or incapacity. A transformation of the Greek regime from the familialist provision of welfare to a minimum state-provided safety net for the neediest might prove to be a good thing – even though that's also subject to debate – or at the very least something that many citizens will experience as an improvement over their prior situation. The de-commodification push in Scandinavian and continental regimes, however, is a different story, and probably not a move that is going to be well received. In all cases, we are talking about deep, extremely political transformations that are presented as a "best practice" through a process in which the European Commission is an important actor. Even a cursory review of the CSRs shows that the Commission has put its years of managing debtor conditionality to use in developing a substantive body of reforms it considers desirable for every Member State.

This seems to be true even in domains that would seem to fall well outside of the European institutions' purview such as the functioning of a Member State's judicial regime. During the process of monitoring the conditionality of Greece's latest loan – from the ESM this time – the Commission required Greece to create a "monitoring mechanism" for financial crimes, "including notably corruption and money laundering cases, with the objective to build a

---

[56] Memorandum of Understanding, 18 ("A fairer society will require that Greece improves the design of its welfare system in line with EU best practices, so that there is a genuine social safety net which targets scarce resources to those in most need").

[57] Esping-Andersen famously categorized welfare regimes into three ideal types: the universalist (like Sweden and other Scandinavian countries), the corporatist (like Germany), and the liberal (like the United States). Each regime entails different degrees of de-commodification and de-familialization. The concept of de-commodification measures how much a state allows its citizens to be free from the pressure to sell their labor in the market in order to satisfy basic needs. De-familialization measures the degree to which a welfare regime allows individuals to be free from personal care obligations to other members of their family. See generally Gøsta Esping-Anderson, *The Three Worlds of Welfare Capitalism* (Cambridge: Polity Press, 1990).

credible track-record of prosecuting and sanctioning such crimes."[58] While any state might want to improve its record on corruption, a framework of European governance in which the national executive branch is urged to put pressure on its judiciary in order to satisfy the conditions that will lead to the disbursement of money from its European creditors is politically problematic regardless what one may think of the substance. Lest someone think that this is Greek exceptionalism again, in Portugal's 2017 CSRs, the Commission commends the country's efforts in the direction of fighting corruption through the judicial system.[59] Nonetheless, it notes that "it remains to be seen whether [the improvements in numbers of prosecutions in corruption cases] will be reflected by improvements in final conviction rates."[60] In other words, the Commission is seen as taking a position on the substantive outcomes of judicial cases pending in front of the independent judiciary of a sovereign Member State. Tone deafness to political sensibilities is arguably another part of the Commission know-how that sometimes seems to carry over to the regular European Semester process from bailout program management.

IV WHY DO CSRS MATTER ANYWAY?

A plausible objection to these preliminary observations is that none of this really matters given that the preliminary empirical research on the effectiveness of the European Semester shows mixed results at best, and depends largely on the uptake of the proposed reforms by national actors.[61] In other words, none of these critiques are really significant, if Member States can refuse to comply and if, in the end, it all boils down to national-level actors making decisions about which reforms they are or are not going to push through.

First, one should note that the empirical evidence so far mostly comes from a study of the situation before the financial penalty against non-compliance had ever been used by the Commission. Second, the data on effectiveness pre-

---

[58] Greece: Technical Memorandum of Understanding Accompanying the MoU of the ESM Programme (March 2018), 45, https://ec.europa.eu/info/sites/info/files/economy-finance/tmu_3rd_review.pdf.

[59] See *Commission Recommendation for a Council Recommendation*, COM (2017) 521 final, 8.

[60] *Commission Recommendation for a Council Recommendation*, 8.

[61] Zsolt Darvas and Álvaro Leandro, "The Limitations of Policy Coordination in the Euro Area Under the European Semester," Bruegel Policy Contribution 2015/19, November 2015; Hallerberg et al., "How Effective and Legitimate is the European Semester?" For an overview of the relevant literature see Verdun and Zeitlin, "Introduction: The European Semester as a New Architecture."

dates the adoption of Regulation 1303/2013, which gives the Commission the possibility of conditioning the disbursement of structural funds to Member States on their compliance with CSRs.

With respect to the first point, on the Commission's recommendation, the Council adopted a financial penalty against Spain for a misrepresentation of regional statistics by Valencia in July 2015 as part of the Excessive Deficit Procedure (EDP).[62] The fine was imposed on a country for a misrepresentation by one of its regions so it was not a penalty based on the Macroeconomic Imbalance Procedure (MIP), but it does set a precedent. Despite the fact that this fine was set in the EDP rather than the MIP process, research shows that some of the actors involved in the European Semester, namely Commission officials and state representatives in the Council, may see the imposition of this fine as a precedent for the MIP as well.[63] This seems to be why state officials through the Council then proceeded to object to the Commission's proposal to include a number of "social" indicators in the regular scoreboard that serves as the baseline for assessing macroeconomic imbalances in the European Semester.[64] State actors did not want the intrusive process of multilateral surveillance to go too deeply into employment and labor policy.[65] The Commission, however, proceeded to do it, "because it is our choice" as one official apparently put it.[66] In the mind of the actors

[62] European Council Press Release 581/15, Deficit Data in Valencia: Spain Fined for Misreporting (July 13, 2015).

[63] See James D. Savage, "Enforcing the European Semester: The Politics of Asymmetric Information in the Excessive Deficit and Macroeconomic Imbalance Procedure," Draft paper, 24, https://ecpr.eu/Filestore/PaperProposal/ob987b53–9c28–493a-acb1–8018badb6e48.pdf.

[64] Savage, "Enforcing the European Semester," 24 ("The Council, meanwhile, rejected the promotion of social indicators because they potentially exposed the member states' economic and social policies to Commission programmatic intervention and fines").

[65] Savage, "Enforcing the European Semester," 21–22 ("What they don't want is to take the risk to be fined for social issues"). The version of this draft paper that was published does not include the story of how the social indicators were adopted by the Commission. See James D. Savage and David Howarth, "Enforcing the European Semester: The Politics of Asymmetric Information in the Excessive Deficit and Macroeconomic Imbalance Procedures," *Journal of European Public Policy* 25, no. 2 (2018): 212–230.

[66] Savage, "Enforcing the European Semester," 22. The European Parliament recently published a study about the mainstreaming of employment and social indicators into macroeconomic surveillance. The trade unions and anti-poverty NGOs consulted expressed reservations about the process. They underlined that the role of social indicators in the Semester is "ambiguous" and complained that their consultation was very limited. See European Parliament, Directorate-General for Internal Policies, Mainstreaming Employment and Social Indicators into Macroeconomic Surveillance, IP/A/EMPL/2014-18 (February 2016), 44. The European Trade Union Confederation went as far as to say that the structural reforms promoted through the European Semester have undermined the European social model. See European Trade Union Confederation, "The ETUC Position on the Annual Growth Survey 2016–for a Europe

directly involved then, the possibility of a fine to enforce CSRs even in areas such as employment and social indicators is not science fiction but a real possibility.

On the second point, Regulation 1303/2013 gives the Commission the possibility to condition disbursement of structural funds on compliance with CSRs.[67] In other words, this Regulation created a possibility for inserting a process of conditionality much like the one creditor countries were subject to as part of the loan agreements. The Commission refers to this possibility in its papers somewhat euphemistically ("closer linkage between national reforms and existing EU funding") but since 2016 CSRs all include a separate article that reminds Member States that Article 23 of Regulation 1303/2013 gives the Commission this prerogative. Admittedly, it is politically hard to envisage such an imposition even though a partial precedent has been set on the specific issue of misreported statistics. The literature so far cautions that ex-post conditionality, that is the proposal to suspend funding until a fiscal or macroeconomic imbalance has been corrected, will be almost impossible to properly monitor and enforce, while it will also cause tensions between Member States.[68] However, another reason to think that cohesion fund conditionality might someday become reality is that its biggest proponent seems to be the German government, which is the biggest creditor in the context of an incomplete monetary union.[69]

In summary, the objection that weak country-compliance renders some of the policy reforms in the CSRs irrelevant is becoming less sustainable in the face of the new enforcement mechanisms in place and the suggestion that they could be used. The probability of their use becomes even greater in a

---

that Works for Workers and Citizens," October 28-29, 2015, www.etuc.org/sites/default/files/document/files/en-etuc-position-ags.pdf /.

[67] European Parliament and Council Regulation (EU) 1303/2013, Laying Down Common Provisions on the European Regional Development Fund, the European Social Fund, the Cohesion Fund, the European Agricultural Fund for Rural Development and the European Maritime and Fisheries Fund and Laying Down General Provisions on the European Regional Development Fund, the European Social Fund, the Cohesion Fund and the European Maritime and Fisheries Fund and repealing Council Regulation (EC) No. 1083/2006, 2013 O.J. (L 347) 320.

[68] Cinzia Alcidi and Daniel Gros, "How to Strengthen the European Semester?," Centre for European Political Studies Research Report no. 2017/15, December 2017, 18–20; Robin Huguenot-Noël et al., "Can the EU Structural Funds Reconcile Growth, Solidarity and Stability Objectives? A Study on the Role of Conditionalities in Spurring Structural Reforms and Reducing Macroeconomic Imbalances," Issue Paper no. 83, European Policy Centre, October 2017, 16.

[69] Alcidi and Gros, "How to Strengthen the European Semester?" 18–20; Huguenot-Noël et al., "Can the EU Structural Funds Reconcile Growth, Solidarity and Stability Objectives?" 16.

scenario where the EMU continues to lack the necessary tools to avert another crisis, such as a full banking union. Should another big crisis come along, the disbursement of ESM funds to Member States will surely be conditioned on compliance with suggested reforms; the content of these reforms will surely be influenced by the prior stages of crisis management.

It is interesting to compare with developments in the area of rule-of-law conditionality. As Kim Scheppele and Daniel Kelemen's contribution to this book highlights, various proposals for imposing rule-of-law conditionality on structural fund access have been put forth in the cases of Hungary and Poland, but without success.[70] Both of these countries have adopted a number of reforms that reinforce autocratic power in the executive arm. The Commission seems to be split on the desirability of such conditionality with President Juncker opposing it as "poison for the European continent."[71] From the perspective of the perceived legitimacy of the Union, a situation in which structural reforms can be imposed as conditionality for the purposes of macroeconomic and budgetary discipline but without the equivalent conditionality in the case of human rights violations would be very problematic.

This chapter's analysis of developments in the European Semester as potentially negative for Social Europe stands somewhat at odds with recent research by Jonathan Zeitlin and Bart Vanhercke.[72] Zeitlin and Vanhercke observe that developments over the last several years have, if anything, "socialized" the European Semester at the initiative of actors who are working on behalf of Social Europe. Their extensive surveys document the impressive expansion of CSRs to include social objectives and further show that this outcome was the result of collaborative processes of different actors within the Commission and different committees in the Council. In this respect, it is worth noting that there is at least some indication that there was a certain degree of conflict in the process of "socializing" the European Semester; resistance came from Member State reluctance to allow the Commission to intrusively monitor the employment and social fields.[73]

---

[70] See Chapter 15.

[71] Chapter 15, 446.

[72] Jonathan Zeitlin and Bart Vanhercke, "Socializing the European Semester: EU Social and Economic Policy Co-ordination in Crisis and Beyond," *Journal of European Public Policy* 25, no. 2 (2018): 149–174.

[73] Savage, "Enforcing the European Semester."

Moreover, even though the process might have become somewhat more inclusive, it is still true that the model of Social Europe that seems to predominate in the European Semester is one where the market is understood as the main motor for growth and prosperity and where social policy reforms are geared toward creating adaptable, employable workers who will turn to employment for meeting even their basic needs. As Mark Dawson observes, even social officials in the EU institutional structure seem to subscribe to a version of social policy as first and foremost a production factor rather than a tool for creating lives that are not entirely market dependent – an astonishing development that narrows the scope of Social Europe as previously understood.[74]

This potential narrowing of the meaning of Social Europe reflects a broader EU institutional trend and comes about through a process mostly concentrated in the EU executive arm. As noted in Renaud Dehousse's chapter, one of the hallmarks of the EU's recent crises has been the empowerment of technocratic actors in the process of norm production.[75] Even if the executive itself is now subject to constraints coming from a multilateral surveillance process of relevant experts at national and EU level, it is not a process that seriously engages democratic deliberation. Verdun and Zeitlin document the increased participation of national representatives in the Council in the formulation of the CSRs and note that "much of the real debate" about the recommendations takes place in the dialogue between the Commission and the Council's committees.[76] They then take this development as an indication that "peer review by expert officials enhances rather than restricts the scope for democratic debate."[77] Beyond the problems with equating the dialogue between national and supranational experts with democratic deliberation, this position overlooks the potential for the process of multilateral deliberation to become more coercive. Note that when the moment came for deciding whether social indicators were going to be included in the European Semester, national representatives in the Council opposed it, and the Commission proceeded to include them anyway, knowing very well that national representatives opposed it because they did not want close surveillance or potential fines imposed in the process.[78]

---

[74] Mark Dawson, "New Governance and the Displacement of Social Europe: The Case of the European Semester," *European Constitutional Law Review* 14, no. 1 (2018): 206–207.

[75] See Chapter 6.

[76] Verdun and Zeitlin, "Introduction: The European Semester as a New Architecture," 145.

[77] Verdun and Zeitlin, "Introduction: The European Semester as a New Architecture," 145–146.

[78] Savage, "Enforcing the European Semester."

A last reason one might downplay the potentially negative effect of "the social" in CSRs is the launching of a "European Pillar of Social Rights" by the Commission in April 2017.[79] However, on this topic, I am in agreement with Sacha Garben's estimation that while there are many promising aspects to the Social Pillar, it does not address the fundamental issue of the "displacement of the national and European legislative process in the two areas where the most important social decisions have been made in the EU during the past decade: the internal market and European economic governance."[80] Yet another illustration of the displacement of legislative politics in the social domain can be found in this chapter. The carryover of expertise from the loan agreements to the European Semester, with the identification of "EU best practices," demonstrates how policy reforms with deep implications for welfare states are elaborated in the domain of economic governance, through the input of economic expertise. At the current stage, the multilateral surveillance mechanism incorporating a dialogue between national and supranational experts on the contested issues seems to have produced a renewed emphasis on Social Europe. In the process, however, the very concept has been redefined in a way that excludes options, a choice with profound consequences that instead should be decided through a genuine democratic engagement at the national and supranational levels.

[79] *Commission Recommendation on the European Pillar of Social Rights*, C (2017) 2600 final (April 26, 2017); Communication from the Commission, *Establishing a European Pillar of Social Rights*, COM (2017) 250 final (April 26, 2017); European Parliament, European Commission, and Council of the European Union, *European Pillar of Social Rights*, November 17, 2017, https://ec.europa.eu/commission/sites/beta-political/files/social-summit-european-pillar-social-rights-booklet_en.pdf.

[80] Sacha Garben, "The Constitutional (Im)balance Between 'the Market' and 'the Social' in the European Union," *European Constitutional Law Review* 13, no. 1 (2017): 23–61.

4

Politicized Integration
The Case of the Eurozone Crisis

NICOLAS JABKO

The EU crises of the 2010s blindsided Europe's political leaders and high-lighted the EU's shortcomings and deep unpopularity. By politicizing the EU, the crises threw into disarray the normally rather depoliticized, technocratic environment of EU policymaking. There is now a consensus among scholars that European integration has become increasingly politicized.[1] However politicization is defined and measured, the Eurozone crisis has finally driven home the fact that decisions made at the EU level are not merely technical and that they have major political repercussions. Yet this intense politicization may appear dangerous for the EU, insofar as the European Union embodies "a system of multi-level governance which facilitates social interaction across national boundaries, increases immigration and undermines national sover-eignty."[2] As politicization engages touchy issues of national sovereignty, anti-EU backlashes become more likely. And indeed, in view of increasingly strident conflict, observers often diagnosed near-paralysis and even a danger of outright collapse for the European Union. The politicization of the Euro-zone crisis seemed especially threatening because it reflected deep conflicts among Member States.[3] The increasing recourse to a rhetoric of sovereignty manifested sharply divergent state goals. The states in need of EU financing claimed a sovereign right to decide on their economic policies, whereas creditor states and EU officials have insisted that loan recipients should accept

---

[1] Pieter De Wilde, Anna Leupold, and Henning Schmidtke, "The Differentiated Politicisation of European Governance," *West European Politics* 39, no. 1 (2016): 3–22.

[2] Liesbet Hooghe and Gary Marks, "A Postfunctionalist Theory of European Integration: From Permissive Consensus to Constraining Dissensus," *British Journal of Political Science* 39, no. 1 (2009):11.

[3] Philipp Genschel and Markus Jachtenfuchs, "From Market Integration to Core State Powers: The Eurozone Crisis, the Refugee Crisis, and Integration Theory," *Journal of Common Market Studies* 56, no. 1 (2018): 178–196.

temporary limitations to their sovereignty as the price to pay for better Eurozone governance.

Although such conflicts certainly underscored the seriousness of EU troubles, there was also something deeper at stake here – namely, the very logic of European integration in times of crisis. Invocations of sovereignty were more than disingenuous rhetoric. Yet politicization, as it turned out, did not prevent significant integration from taking place. To make sense of member governments' re-assertion of their sovereignty in the reform process, scholars have offered diagnoses of "executive federalism"[4] or "new intergovernmentalism."[5] And partly because of this overbearing presence of national governments, recent advances in Eurozone integration have often been portrayed, at best, as pyrrhic victories for the EU. For example, Jones, Kelemen, and Meunier have analyzed European integration as a process of "failing forward" in the face of successive crises, with the EU adopting reforms that are "self-undermining" in the long run.[6] It remains to be seen whether this pessimism is ultimately justified, however. Thus far, the more striking fact is that the Eurozone has come a remarkably long way from the relatively hands-off approach of the Maastricht Treaty to the institutional framework that has emerged from the Eurozone crisis – an elaborate set of new economic monitoring procedures, a European Stability Mechanism, an assertive new role of the European Central Bank (ECB), and a Banking Union. Insofar as all these reforms bolstered the EU's authority in the face of crisis, they epitomize the European Union's "dynamic order."[7] EU officials have taken national sovereignty claims seriously, without, however, reversing the process of European integration. They have stitched together reforms that aimed at strengthening EU governance while addressing various national concerns with sovereignty.

Building on recent scholarship on sovereignty practices in the field of international relations, I present an explanation of how politicized integration defied conventional expectations of disintegration. Overall, the Eurozone's

---

[4] Jürgen Habermas, *The Crisis of the European Union: A Response* (Cambridge: Polity Press, 2012).

[5] Christopher J. Bickerton, Dermot Hodson, and Uwe Puetter, "The New Intergovernmentalism: European Integration in the Post-Maastricht Era," *Journal of Common Market Studies* 53, no. 4 (2015): 703–722.

[6] Erik Jones, R. Daniel Kelemen, and Sophie Meunier, "Failing Forward? The Euro Crisis and the Incomplete Nature of European Integration," *Comparative Political Studies* 49, no. 7 (2016): 1–25.

[7] Nicolas Jabko and Adam Sheingate, "Practices of Dynamic Order," *Perspectives in Politics* 16, no. 2 (2018): 312–327.

Politicized Integration

shift from an outright prohibition to a conditional acceptance of bailouts amounts to a fundamental reconstitution of sovereignty. To explain this outcome, I argue that crises represent opportunities for actors to recombine ideational repertoires of national sovereignty and EU governance in novel ways. Integrationist steps that were long rejected as anathema to national sovereignty were adopted not only for the sake of better EU governance but also in the name of modernizing the exercise of Member States' sovereignty. Although the post-crisis institutional framework is more elaborate, Member States still enjoy considerable flexibility under the new regime, which they only forgo when they seek financial assistance. This solution, which both upgraded EU powers and reaffirmed national sovereignty in a different form, has been criticized as weak and belated. To be sure, it is not a comprehensive and permanent solution – and it certainly did not stem the anti-EU mood among European voters. Yet it offers crucial insights into how the EU responds to and ultimately defuses crisis. Instead of classic interstate bargaining among sharply constraining national interests, we can observe dynamic and open policymaking processes in which *ad hoc* coalitions actively reconstitute sovereignty practices. Before reviewing how this logic operated in the case of the Eurozone crisis, this chapter begins by elaborating the analytic logic of re-constituting sovereignty against the backdrop of recent international relations and EU literature on sovereignty.

I CRISIS AND RECONSTITUTION OF SOVEREIGNTY

The conventional way of considering sovereignty in the European Union is to define it as a constitutional question, through the lens of a contractual perspective. As Genschel and Jachtenfuchs remark, there is a "tacit consensus" among many scholars to characterize the EU as a relatively self-contained authority structure within a broader constitutional arrangement of powers. This consensus can in turn be traced back to a widely accepted solution to scholarly interrogations about what the EU means for sovereignty. When Europe was "re-launched" in the late 1980s, international relations scholars coined the concept of "pooled sovereignty."[8] They viewed Europe's integration as a series of discrete decisions to "pool" sovereignty to the EU level. Such decisions involve cost–benefit calculations, which in turn hinge on the rational pursuit of state preferences rather than on narrowly construed

---

[8] Robert O. Keohane and Stanley Hoffmann, "Introduction," in *The New European Community*, eds. Robert O. Keohane and Stanley Hoffmann (Boulder, CO: Westview, 1991), 1–40.

sovereignty considerations.[9] In this respect, European integration is viewed as consistent with "the central insight of regime theory: the decision to delegate or pool sovereignty in international regimes is analytically separate from (and subordinate to) bargaining over substantive cooperation."[10] Sovereignty is conceived as an essentially national authority that can be contracted out in certain conditions.

This contractual perspective on the EU depicts a system of powers that is both orderly and dispassionate, in line with rationalist understandings of sovereignty in international relations. In a seminal volume on international regimes, Krasner referred to sovereignty as a "constitutive principle" that "designates states as the only actors with unlimited rights to act in the international system."[11] To be sure, international relations scholars also recognize that international regimes have become quite deep and widespread. Keohane has thus described the EU as a beneficial outcome for states that accept "gradations in sovereignty."[12] Yet such encroachments on state sovereignty by international regimes are usually conceptualized as the results of rational decisions by governments to contract out circumscribed sovereign powers to international institutions. The authority that is exercised at the EU level pertains to the "regulatory state"[13] and is essentially non-majoritarian, nonpolitical, and administrative. Only the details of policies remain to be worked out, and European institutions act as the agents of Member State principals. Although the existence of a principal–agent relationship implies well-known risks of "agency loss," these risks are not sufficiently high to disturb the calculus of interest that leads states to "pool" or "delegate" their sovereignty in the first place.

Recent scholarship in comparative politics as well as in international relations has begun to chip away at this conception of the EU as an orderly and dispassionate equilibrium of powers, however. In the contractual characterization of sovereignty, powers are allocated in orderly fashion at any point in time. Yet Cooley and Spruyt note that this is not the case because the EU

---

[9] Robert O. Keohane, "Ironies of Sovereignty: The European Union and the United States," *Journal of Common Market Studies* 40, no. 4 (2002): 743–765.

[10] Andrew Moravcsik, *The Choice for Europe: Social Purpose and State Power from Messina to Maastricht* (Ithaca, NY: Cornell University Press, 1998), 21.

[11] Stephen D. Krasner, ed., *International Regimes* (Ithaca, NY: Cornell University Press, 1983), 18.

[12] Keohane, "Ironies of Sovereignty," 756.

[13] Giandomenico Majone, "The Rise of the Regulatory State in Europe," *West European Politics* 17, no. 3 (1994): 77–101.

entails "incomplete contracting."[14] Through international treaties, Member States have empowered European institutions to build an autonomous power structure at the European level. In this light, EU institutions are not merely the agents of Member State principals. "Agency loss" is pervasive, not exceptional. "Incomplete" EU institutions sustain momentum for further European integration – a point also explicit in Jones, Kelemen, and Meunier's concept of "failing forward." In a similar vein, a recent volume edited by Genschel and Jachtenfuchs has focused on the EU's accretion of "core state powers," defined as characteristic "functions of sovereign government."[15] It enumerates conditions under which the EU is more likely to gain such powers, especially as a result of processes of "integration by stealth" or (more rarely) "integration by publicity."

These critiques are useful to understand the dynamic nature of sovereignty in the EU. Concepts of "incomplete contracting," "integration by stealth," and "failing forward" have the merit of highlighting an agentic role for EU officials and the relative fluidity of power relations in policy areas that are progressively integrated at the EU level. Yet they do not explain why political leaders would raise the stakes in times of crisis, for example by touting sovereignty or the risk of EU collapse. From this perspective, sovereignty appears both more open-ended and more passionate than in the contractual conception. Sovereignty itself becomes politicized in response to events, which can in turn push forward, rather than impede, the integration process. This goes against the widespread expectation that politicization leads to a "constraining dissensus,"[16] whereas European integration is expected to take place incrementally and below the political radar. Increasingly strident invocations of sovereignty manifest the ever-present precariousness of the EU political order but also the fragility of states' claims to sovereignty in moments of crisis. Invocations of sovereignty and criticisms of existing delegations of sovereignty to the EU can themselves reframe policy and constitutional debates, paradoxically leading to major changes in the exercise of sovereignty.

To explain these changes, I build on recent international relations scholarship that views sovereignty as an evolving nexus of practices. New sovereignty practices typically come about as a result of tacit incremental adjustment and reflexive deliberation. From this perspective, state sovereignty is much more

---

[14] Alexander Cooley and Hendrik Spruyt, *Contracting States: Sovereign Transfers in International Relations* (Princeton, NJ: Princeton University Press, 2009).

[15] Philipp Genschel and Markus Jachtenfuchs, eds., *Beyond the Regulatory Polity? The European Integration of Core State Powers* (Oxford: Oxford University Press, 2014), 1.

[16] Hooghe and Marks, "A Postfunctionalist Theory of European Integration."

fluid than the rationalist/contractualist scholarship implies. For example, Schmidt has analyzed sovereignty as a practical norm, i.e. an "entrenched habit" that changes in response to real-world challenges.[17] Schmidt explores how, in response to a new military and geopolitical context, the unprecedented practice of establishing military bases in other sovereign countries took root after 1945. In this case, the "habit" of sovereignty changed through processes of deliberative innovation as policymakers "defined workable courses of action, set more specific aims, and came to terms with new situations."[18] This is very relevant to the process of European integration, which can be analyzed as a powerful stimulus for the constant re-definition of Member States' sovereignty practices. In adjusting to changed circumstances, Member States may alter their definitions and practices of sovereignty to allow for more EU institution-building and policymaking. From a critical international relations perspective, "the meanings attached to sovereignty and the practices which follow from them are historically and geographically variable"[19] – a point also made by constructivist scholars.[20]

International relations scholars themselves have begun to fruitfully apply this practical understanding of sovereignty to the EU. In the EU context, extensive areas of "delegated" sovereignty have accrued at the EU level in the form of EU competences. Yet these delegations of sovereignty and the ensuing new sovereignty practices remain relatively fragile. The "pooling" or "delegation" of sovereignty to the EU level does not indicate that Member State claims to sovereignty are no longer relevant, or that the EU constitutional order is "stable" in a meaningful sense. Sovereignty is never really a stable equilibrium. When national politicians perceive undue encroachments of the EU on national sovereignty, they are quick to denounce them in the name of what Werner and de Wilde call "sovereignty claims."[21] Member States retain their capacity to make sovereignty claims because the Member States are still recognized as sovereign within the European Union as well as in international

---

[17] Sebastian Schmidt, "Foreign Military Presence and the Changing Practice of Sovereignty: A Pragmatist Explanation of Norm Change," *American Political Science Review* 108, no. 4 (2014): 817–829.

[18] Schmidt, "Foreign Military Presence and the Changing Practice of Sovereignty," 824.

[19] Cynthia Weber, *Simulating Sovereignty: Intervention, the State, and Symbolic Exchange* (Cambridge: Cambridge University Press, 1995), 16.

[20] Friedrich V. Kratochwil, *Rules, Norms, and Decisions: On the Conditions of Practical and Legal Reasoning in International Relations and Domestic Affairs* (Cambridge: Cambridge University Press, 1991); John Gerard Ruggie, "Territoriality and Beyond: Problematizing Modernity in International Relations," *International Organization* 47, no. 1 (1993): 139–174.

[21] Wouter G. Werner and Jaap H. De Wilde, "The Endurance of Sovereignty," *European Journal of International Relations* 7, no. 3 (2001): 283–313.

society. European integration is therefore suffused with what Adler-Nissen and Gammeltoft-Hansen have called "sovereignty games," in which "states engage in new practices and modify their understandings of their own sovereignty."[22] This can lead member governments either to push for the renationalization of EU competences, or else for a strengthening of EU governance as an avenue for sovereign control – all in the name of reasserting state sovereignty.

1 How Sovereignty is Reconstituted in the Course of EU Crises

My intervention in this literature on sovereignty practices starts from the observation that politicization plays an unusually important role in the EU, especially in times of crisis. This is unlike many other international contexts, where national sovereignty is a matter of course and where, precisely for that reason, it can evolve more quietly and pragmatically. Practices of sovereignty in international relations typically evolve as a result of incremental habitual change, reflection, and deliberation over the shortcomings of established practices among elite circles of policymakers. These actors see that, in a changed international context, existing practices of sovereignty create problems, and they begin to discuss, renegotiate, and reconstruct new sovereignty practices as much as possible to avoid running into crisis. In the EU context, however, the fact that existing sovereignty practices are problematic is not in itself sufficient ground for incremental change. Because the EU is already the beneficiary of major delegations of sovereignty, suspicion of EU "technocrats" and sensitivity about further "losses" of sovereignty are unusually high. Pressures in the EU political system therefore tend to accumulate without being resolved, ultimately leading to a breaking point, a.k.a. "crisis." Significant change in sovereignty practices becomes possible, however, when a crisis erupts, its stakes become highly politicized, and it becomes evident well beyond the usual EU policymaking circles that established practices cannot continue.

My main claim is that politicization in situations of crisis can actually accelerate the reconstitution of sovereignty practices that become more evidently fragile. I agree with most EU scholars that politicization can easily turn into a "constraining dissensus."[23] Yet a key tenet underlying the diagnosis of a "constraining" politicization does not hold, namely that the EU "undermines

---

[22] Rebecca Adler-Nissen and Thomas Gammeltoft-Hansen, *Sovereignty Games: Instrumentalizing State Sovereignty in Europe and Beyond* (New York: Palgrave Macmillan, 2008), 15.

[23] Hooghe and Marks, "A Postfunctionalist Theory of European Integration."

national sovereignty."[24] Instead, I highlight an alternative path for the evolution of sovereignty practices that *can* ultimately lead to more integration, rather than paralysis and disintegration. The evolution of sovereignty practices provided the backdrop against which European crisis management played itself out. National concerns with sovereignty were never out of sight, but they did not prevent the reform of the Eurozone. Member States accepted reforms that were inconceivable before the crisis because the EU attended to their sovereignty concerns. In the wake of the 2016 debate on Greece's exit from the Eurozone and protracted Brexit negotiations after the UK referendum to leave the EU, it also became increasingly apparent that calls for a clean and costless withdrawal from the Eurozone were not credible. In the end, the concerns about sovereignty that emerged in full sight with the Eurozone crisis became ingredients in the reforms that European leaders crafted.

II RECONSTITUTING SOVEREIGNTY IN THE EUROZONE CRISIS

In 2009–2010, the Eurozone was caught in a debt spiral in which massively indebted states and failing banks could not be rescued by EU institutions because of a "no bailout" principle entrenched in the Treaty. Many observers at the time forecast the end of the euro and the return to national currencies.[25] As it turned out, these predictions were overdrawn. Yet it took a long time to defuse the Eurozone crisis, and transfers of powers and resources to the EU were limited by Member States' desire to retain as much control as possible over their own economic policies. Despite the creation of highly conditional and largely indirect financial assistance mechanisms, the "no bailout" provisions of the Treaty remain in effect and the EU still does not have a fiscal union.

In view of such limitations, most scholarship on the Eurozone crisis has stressed elements of continuity with the status quo ante. Some have emphasized enduring national economic interests and the sunk costs of interdependence.[26] Others have identified preexisting neoliberal ideas and institutions as

---

[24] Hooghe and Marks, "A Postfunctionalist Theory of European Integration," 11.

[25] See, e.g., Paul Krugman, "Killing the Euro," *The New York Times*, December 1, 2011, www.nytimes.com/2011/12/02/opinion/krugman-killing-the-euro.html.

[26] See, e.g., Frank Schimmelfennig, "Liberal Intergovernmentalism and the Euro Area Crisis," *Journal of European Public Policy* 22, no. 2 (2015): 177–195; Frank Schimmelfennig, "European Integration (Theory) in Times of Crisis," Paper prepared for EUSA Conference, Miami, May 4–6, 2017.

key constraints on institutional change.[27] In return for a relaxing of the "no bailout" principle, struggling Member States had to agree to draconian economic reform conditions as *sine qua non* for financial assistance. The increasing dominance of Germany's Chancellor Angela Merkel seemed to embody that continuity. She acted as the spokesperson for Northern European states that refused to pay for Southern "sinners"[28] and strove to impose German solutions.[29] To be sure, Germany had a stake in preserving existing Eurozone institutions that favored fiscal self-discipline. By insisting on strong rules, Merkel was also defending ordoliberal economic ideas that held the higher ground in German policy circles.

Continuity with the status quo ante and its defense by Germany are only one side of the coin, however – and arguably not the most significant one in the EU's crisis response. What is missing from many scholarly accounts is an appreciation of how brinksmanship altered settled notions of sovereignty and governance in the Eurozone. The Eurozone crisis was arguably the first "real crisis" of the European integration process.[30] The EU introduced significant institutional innovations that conventional lines of scholarly explanation in terms of incremental change have trouble explaining. There is now a permanent institution in charge of issuing loans to struggling states, the European Stability Mechanism; the European Central Bank has become considerably more activist than at the outset of the crisis; a new Banking Union has been established, supervised by the European Union and aimed at breaking the "doom loop" between Member States and national banks, which would be a "radical" step in the direction of a seamlessly integrated Eurozone financial area.[31] All these reforms imply a much greater collective and individual liability of the Member States for the preservation of the Eurozone, and a shift of the Economic and Monetary Union in the direction of a collective

---

[27] See, e.g., Peter A. Hall, "The Economics and Politics of the Euro Crisis," *German Politics* 21, no. 4 (2012): 355–371; Mark Blyth, *Austerity: The History of a Dangerous Idea* (Oxford: Oxford University Press, 2013).

[28] Matthias Matthijs and Kathleen McNamara, "The Euro Crisis' Theory Effect: Northern Saints, Southern Sinners, and the Demise of the Eurobond," *Journal of European Integration* 37, no. 2 (2015): 229–245.

[29] Matthias Matthijs, "Powerful Rules Governing the Euro: The Perverse Power and Logic of German Ideas," *Journal of European Public Policy* 23, no. 3 (2016): 375–391.

[30] Craig Parsons and Matthias Matthijs, "European Integration Past, Present and Future: Moving Forward Through Crisis?" in *The Future of the Euro*, eds. Matthias Matthijs and Mark Blyth (New York: Oxford University Press, 2015), 210–232.

[31] Nicolas Véron, *Europe's Radical Banking Union* (Brussels: Bruegel, 2015).

insurance scheme.[32] As Jones, Kelemen, and Meunier have recently pointed out, "Taken together, the series of incremental reforms adopted sequentially in response to the crisis ... has led to one of the most rapid periods of deepening and integration in EU history."[33]

Central to the deepening integration was the fact that political leaders found practical solutions to the Eurozone crisis and, in so doing, effectively reconstituted sovereignty practices. Because sovereignty has remained a cardinal value in the reformed architecture of the Eurozone (and the EU in general), the unfolding of the crisis can be read through the lens of changing sovereignty practices. As I will illustrate in the empirical case of the Eurozone, this path of reconstitution schematically involves four steps – the revelation of the vulnerability of existing practices; a search for remedies at the EU level; the imposition of solutions that incorporate sovereignty concerns; and, coalition-building to institutionalize new sovereignty practices.

First, the Eurozone crisis revealed the vulnerability of existing sovereignty practices. Before the crisis, the practical exercise of sovereignty within the Economic and Monetary Union was divided.[34] Monetary policy was squarely in the hands of the independent European Central Bank. By contrast, economic policy remained a sovereign prerogative primarily in the hands of the Member States. Crucially, "the 'no bail-out rule' was enshrined in treaty form."[35] This rule, in addition to the small size of the EU budget, sharply limited the reciprocal fiscal obligations of the Eurozone Member States. There was a normative basis for this entrenched institutional framework. Throughout the 1990s, German political leaders had peddled the "no bailout" rule of the Economic and Monetary Union as a crucial safeguard against excessive spending by other states. Of course, all Member States had to participate in a "coordination of economic policies" (according to Articles 102 and 103, now Articles 120 and 121 of the Treaty on the Functioning of the European Union) and to abide by fiscal deficit rules (the Stability and Growth Pact, adopted in 1997). Yet these Treaty provisions were extremely vague in comparison to monetary policy provisions, and the Pact was not overly constraining. Attempts at making the Pact very binding on the Member States had repeatedly failed in the late 1990s and the 2000s. Although sanctions against rule violators existed, they were difficult to trigger, as they challenged Member

---

[32] Waltraud Schelkle, *The Political Economy of Monetary Solidarity: Understanding the Euro Experiment* (Oxford: Oxford University Press, 2017).

[33] Jones, Kelemen, and Meunier, "Failing Forward? The Euro Crisis," 3.

[34] For another discussion of this EU law, see Chapter 2, Section II.1.

[35] Kenneth Dyson and Kevin Featherstone, *The Road to Maastricht: Negotiating Economic and Monetary Union* (Oxford: Oxford University Press, 1999), 783.

States' sovereignty. Indeed, a crucial ingredient of the Eurozone crisis was that most national politicians and constituencies – including in Germany and France – were not prepared to easily abandon what they saw as sovereign prerogatives over fiscal matters. Until they were hit by crisis, the Economic and Monetary Union could therefore only remain a halfway house on the path of European integration. In the meantime, the EU pinned its hope in the view that financial markets would impose their "discipline" and prevent excessive indebtedness.

The crisis shattered these normative underpinnings and exposed the fragility of national claims to fiscal sovereignty and self-help. Market actors' sentiment suddenly turned against peripheral Eurozone countries that had accumulated important volumes of public or private debts. In a context of deepening recession, their assessment was that these countries were caught in a debt spiral from which they could not escape, in part because their debt was denominated in euros and they could no longer devalue their currencies or resort to inflation to reduce their debt burden. The increasing fear that Greece, Ireland, and (to a lesser extent) Spain might default on their debts drastically constrained the practice of these Member States' sovereignty over economic policymaking, as they faced soaring debt-financing costs on financial markets. Meanwhile, the Eurozone could not afford to ignore the difficulties of countries that had accumulated unsustainable sovereign debts. After the bankruptcy of Lehman Brothers in 2008, policymakers were especially aware of the risk of contagion of financial crises.[36] If Greece was pushed into default, this heralded trouble for the Eurozone as a whole. The idea that there would be "no bailout" was therefore no longer credible. It also became obvious that scarce EU resources and limited intergovernmental cooperation actually hampered the exercise of sovereign powers. Although German Chancellor Angela Merkel stepped into her predecessors' tracks and took up the mantle of defending Germany's fiscal sovereignty, she also recognized that the EU framework had to change. In the fall of 2010, European Council President Herman Van Rompuy authored a report that recommended "a fundamental shift in European economic governance."[37] That report was drafted in close consultation with the German and French governments, and reflected a widespread view among EU leaders. By then, it was clear to them that the

---

[36] Policymakers interviewed by the author, December 20–22, 2010, Paris.

[37] *Report of the Task Force to the European Council: Strengthening Economic Governance in the EU*, October 21, 2010, 1, www.consilium.europa.eu/uedocs/cms_data/docs/pressdata/en/ec/117236.pdf.

Eurozone could not continue with a strict "no bailout" regime and loosely coordinated Member State budgets.

Second, the revelation of vulnerability in sovereignty practices triggered a search for remedies at the EU level. EU political leaders realized that they could no longer resort to strictly technical fixes and continue with a status quo that had become unsustainable. They became open to change, as habitual practices were no longer effective, and as they reflected on this ineffectiveness. In March 2010, EU heads of government had set for themselves "the objective of an improved crisis resolution framework and better budgetary discipline, exploring all options to reinforce the legal framework."[38] Yet this "exploration" was fraught with political obstacles. EU political leaders could not afford to resolve problems among themselves in a purely technocratic mode, away from the public eye. They were constrained by the limits that their constituents and their partners – and sometimes they themselves – placed on significant redefinitions of sovereignty. The invocation of sovereignty, often by opposition or Euroskeptic politicians, was a call to arms. It threatened to expand what Schattschneider called the "scope of conflict" to the point where political leaders would completely lose control.[39] In the European context of rising right – and left – populism, governments were at risk of electoral defeat – and sometimes were indeed defeated – by challengers who expressed strident sovereignty concerns. They had to deploy new sovereignty practices to cope with adversity, to entrench authority in novel ways, and to adapt the existing order so as to re-legitimate it.

Specifically, EU leaders pursued a two-track approach that involved strengthening both solidarity and discipline within the Eurozone.[40] On the side of solidarity, they established a multilateral fund, the European Stability Mechanism (ESM), which exists by exception to the general "no bailout" rule. For this to be possible, the European Council endorsed in December 2010 a French-German proposal to modify Article 136 of the Lisbon Treaty – barely a year after that major EU treaty reform entered in force.[41] Through an *ad hoc* intergovernmental treaty signed in July 2011, Eurozone member governments then established the ESM. The ESM was created to distribute loans to qualifying Member States, but it was to be activated only as a "last

---

[38] European Council Conclusions, EUCO 7/10 (March 26, 2010), 6.

[39] Elmer Eric Schattschneider, *The Semisovereign People: A Realist's View of Democracy in America* (New York: Holt, Rinehart and Winston, 1960).

[40] For another discussion of this EU law, see Chapter 2, Sections II.1, III.1, and III.2.

[41] The treaty modification was possible under the "simplified revision procedure" (Article 48.6 of the Treaty on European Union), whereby limited treaty modifications can be authorized after a unanimous vote of the member governments.

resort," when the stability of the Eurozone was in jeopardy. Loans were to be extended only to Member States that accepted entry into an agreement with the ESM regarding their future fiscal and economic policies. The ESM did not come into existence right away. It was preceded by the European Financial Stability Facility (EFSF), a private fund established in haste with limited liability (set at €440 billion). Member States were under pressure to come up with an emergency response, yet were initially reluctant to commit the necessary funding to underwrite a public collective guarantee.[42] For these very reasons, many observers and market actors initially doubted European leaders' commitment to extend financial assistance to struggling Member States. In hindsight, however, the Member States did commit massive resources. As Schelkle points out, "the amount of international support given in the course of the Euro Area crisis was unprecedented in the history of multilateral lending."[43] Through the EFSF and later the ESM, the "no bailout" principle was thus successfully circumscribed and solidarity was enhanced.

On the disciplinary side, EU leaders invented a new multilateral authority structure that departed from the principle of self-help and market-driven discipline that was implicit in a strict "no bailout" framework. In effect, this structure expressed a bifurcated understanding of sovereignty with respect to national economic policies. A first understanding applies to Member States that required financial assistance from the EU and the International Monetary Fund and that have been considered "under program" under the newly created European Stability Mechanism (i.e. Greece, Ireland, Portugal, and Cyprus). These states were placed under the close tutelage of a "Troika," i.e. the European Commission, the European Central Bank, and the International Monetary Fund. They had to enter into contractually binding memoranda that specified strict conditions in exchange for economic assistance. In this sense, the new regime is one of conditional bailout, different from the pre-crisis "no bailout" regime. If the conditions set forth by the Troika are not respected, the EU and the IMF can withhold scheduled disbursements of financial assistance, thus exerting considerable pressure on struggling states. As European Commission President Jean-Claude Juncker declared on the eve of the first agreement between Greece and the Troika,

[42] Ledina Gocaj and Sophie Meunier, "Time Will Tell: The EFSF, the ESM, and the Euro Crisis," *European Integration* 35, no. 3 (2013): 239–253.

[43] Schelkle, *The Political Economy of Monetary Solidarity*, 171.

"The sovereignty of Greece will be massively limited."[44] By contrast, the Member States that do not require any financial assistance are left almost completely free to decide on their economic policies. To be sure, they must abide by reinforced EU rules.[45] For states that broadly abide by the rules, however, the EU only issues nonbinding recommendations. For this second group of compliant Member States, the rules therefore do not concretely encroach on sovereign national economic policy prerogatives.

Third, EU political leaders imposed crisis solutions that were transformational yet took on board sovereignty concerns. Struggling to retain the initiative, EU political leaders therefore had little choice but to acknowledge sovereignty concerns while working toward more integrated EU solutions. Both the move toward more solidarity and the reinforcement of discipline were highly problematic from the perspective of sovereignty. There was a danger that Member States in good credit would invoke their sovereignty to refuse an extension of national contributions to the ESM, as well as a danger that indebted Member States would reject the disciplinary measures imposed by the EU as infringements on their sovereignty. The challenge for EU leaders, therefore, was to address domestic concerns with sovereignty while at the same time introducing institutional innovations that would resolve the crisis. EU leaders took advantage of the crises as opportunities to drastically upend existing sovereignty practices and constitutional arrangements. Scholars have sometimes charged that EU crisis management was in fact "extra-legal" and "authoritarian"[46] and based on "domination" rather than "consensus" among Member States.[47] While EU crisis management was in some respects quite questionable from a democratic perspective, it also illustrated the difference between sovereignty as a legal principle and sovereignty as a practice. Legal principles can stand even if they are impractical and routinely disregarded. But when practices become completely impractical, they typically change. This is what happened to sovereignty practices, as opposed to sovereignty as a legal principle.

---

[44] Honor Mahony, "Greece Faces 'Massive' Loss of Sovereignty," *EU Observer*, July 4, 2011, https://euobserver.com/news/32582.

[45] For a discussion of the EU law on economic surveillance and its different impact on Member States depending on their fiscal and economic position, see Chapter 3.

[46] Christian Kreuder-Sonnen, "Beyond Integration Theory: The (Anti-)Constitutional Dimension of European Crisis Governance," *Journal of Common Market Studies* 54, no. 6 (2016): 1350–1366.

[47] Sergio Fabbrini, "From Consensus to Domination: The Intergovernmental Union in a Crisis Situation," *Journal of European Integration* 38, no. 5 (2016): 587–599.

Politicized Integration

On the one hand, leading EU states recognized that the Eurozone institutional framework had to change. At the same time, they naturally had little appetite for revolution and they wanted to preserve the existing order as much as possible. Thus, they became open to unprecedented financing mechanisms such as the European Stability Mechanism so as to prevent disorderly sovereign default, as long as they could keep them well under control. In the name of defending German taxpayers, Merkel consistently opposed a "union of financial transfers" and any form of debt mutualization through a jointly issued public debt instrument, or "Eurobond." She even declared that Eurobonds would not come into existence "as long as I live."[48] EU leaders did not change the EU Treaty – since French presidents did not want to face a new treaty referendum – and they also continued to stress its "no bailout" provisions – as the German chancellor needed to cover herself from adverse rulings by the sovereignty-conscious German constitutional court.[49] Merkel could not afford to ignore the German constitutional court's invocation of Germany's sovereignty and its restrictive definition of the EU as "an association of sovereign states, and, hence, a secondary political entity."[50] She also wanted to reassure other Northern European states that threatened to withdraw their support from the ESM Treaty, especially Finland. In the end, EU leaders agreed to circumvent a strict interpretation of the Treaty, and the ESM Treaty was signed by all Eurozone Member States. In response to concerns expressed by Germany, the Treaty specifies that the new financial assistance mechanism is to be used only in the "last resort" to preserve the integrity of the Eurozone.

On the other hand, states "under program" (i.e. that received financial assistance) resented and wanted to minimize the practical loss of sovereignty due to disciplinary measures being imposed on them. They were obviously less fixated than creditor states on the no bailout rule, but they realized that seeking a bailout meant accepting a greater degree of EU intrusion on their economic policies. For this reason, they were reluctant to request financial assistance from their partners – even when they needed it. Spanish Prime Minister Mariano Rajoy thus bucked market expectations that he would seek an ESM loan until July 2012, despite the escalating costs of financing the

---

[48] "Merkel Vows 'No Eurobonds as Long as I live'," *Spiegel Online*, June 27, 2012, www.spiegel.de/international/europe/chancellor-merkel-vows-no-euro-bonds-as-long-as-she-lives-a-841163.html.

[49] Policymaker interviewed by the author, January 2012, Paris (French President's office).

[50] Frank Schorkoptf, "The European Union as an Association of Sovereign States: Karlsruhe's Ruling on the Treaty of Lisbon," *German Law Journal* 10, no. 8 (2009): 1220. For a discussion of this German jurisprudence, see Chapter 2, Section II.2.

Spanish public debt. Greece's successive governments had no choice but to seek EU loans from the early stage of the crisis, but they constantly pushed back against the austerity measures that were imposed on them by the "Troika." In view of such resentments, the constraints that were placed on Greece and other states "under program" were carefully defined as exceptional and mutually accepted *quid pro quos* for loan financing, rather than permanent infringements on their sovereignty. As it turned out, no Member State was prepared to cling to an absolute notion of national sovereignty if that meant facing the steep economic and political costs of leaving the Eurozone. Not even Greece took that step, despite austerity fatigue and the electoral victory of a left-populist government that put the memorandum of agreement with Greece's creditors to a popular vote by referendum. As Greek Prime Minister Alexis Tsipras tweeted in July 2015: "Honoring the sovereignty of the Greek people to express their will is in no way a decision to rupture w/ Europe."[51] EU elites handled the democratic challenge from Tsipras' government with a characteristic carrot-and-stick approach. Tsipras was bluntly told that political and market pressures would relent only if he accepted continued austerity, which he did shortly after the referendum.

Fourth, a coalition was built to institutionalize the new sovereignty practices. This coalition can be conceived in terms of concentric circles around German and French political leaders, both at the international level and at the domestic level. Coalition building started in October 2010, when German Chancellor Angela Merkel met with French President Nicolas Sarkozy at the seaside resort of Deauville. Although the two leaders were "embattled," they agreed to work together and to propose a deal to their partners that included the establishment of a permanent bailout mechanism as well as debt restructuration ("haircuts") and harsh terms for indebted states.[52] Much of the Deauville agreement subsequently fell apart. Opposition to the bailout mechanism was vehement in Northern Europe, whereas indebted states on the periphery could not accept the French-German idea of depriving them of their voting rights. Meanwhile, market actors voted with their feet against any notion of debt restructuration by dumping peripheral countries' debt securities, thus aggravating the crisis until that part of the plan was set aside. Yet the fact that Germany was prepared to accept the logic of conditional bailouts began to mollify Northern European hardliners, and the fact that France

[51] Alexis Tsipras (@tsipras_eu), "Honoring the sovereignty of the Greek people to express their will is no way a decision to rupture w/Europe." Twitter, June 27, 2015, 16:32. https://twitter.com/tsipras_eu/status/614939404885434368.
[52] Policymaker interviewed by the author, November 3, 2010, Paris (French President's office).

accepted a considerable strengthening of discipline put pressure on states that were concerned about the encroachments of the EU on their sovereignty. The situation was no longer deadlocked, and the French-German proposal to create a permanent bailout institution was effectively ratified by the full European Council of EU leaders in December 2010. From then on, the coalition in favor of reconstituting sovereignty practices was set in motion both at the domestic and international levels.

At the domestic level, national leaders worked to build political momentum behind the change in sovereignty practices. The case of Germany is especially interesting because public opinion was initially so attached to a strict interpretation of the "no bailout" rule, which could have stalled any reform of EU governance. Angela Merkel deftly rallied domestic support in favor of reforms that she could live with. In accepting new institutional mechanisms – the European Stability Mechanism, the Banking Union, and the ECB's increased activism – Merkel increasingly sided against nationalists and ordoliberal fundamentalists in Germany. It was not at all easy for her to choose this course of action in the German context. A new anti-EU party, Alternative for Germany (AfD), began to emerge as a right-wing competitor to her own party, the CDU. There was considerable opposition within the right of her own party.[53] Merkel thus became the de facto spokesperson of a different and increasingly assertive coalition, formed by EU and Member State officials who recognized the need for "governance" and who favored an evolution of sovereignty practices. She declared to the German Parliament: "We need more Europe ... If the euro fails, Europe fails."[54] She capitalized on the credibility that she had acquired in defending Germany's sovereignty concerns and fiscal interests in order to militate for EU governance reforms. If the survival of the Eurozone was at stake and the aid recipients were subjected to strict conditionality, she was prepared to accept a less rigid interpretation of the "no bailout" Treaty clause. The ECB's activist turn under Mario Draghi gave her political cover, and she took the side of Eurozone reform advocates against those who in Germany argued for the defense of narrowly conceived national interests.

At the international level, national leaders increasingly coalesced in favor of "more Europe" as a solution to crisis. As Froud and her coauthors point out, the crisis thus replaced "old familiar liturgies" with "competing stories from

---

[53] Wade Jacoby, "The Politics of the Eurozone Crisis: Two Puzzles behind the German Consensus," *German Politics and Society* 32, no. 2 (2014): 70–85.

[54] Regierungserklärung von Kanzlerin Merkel zum Europäischen Rat und zum Eurogipfel, October 26, 2011, www.bundesregierung.de/ContentArchiv/DE/Archiv17/Regierungserklaerung/2011/2011-10-27-merkel-eu-gipfel.html.

bankers, politicians, and regulators."[55] Within this new context, "more Europe" was a way for leaders to articulate what they were doing to themselves and to their constituencies, as well as of asserting control over crises that threatened to get out of hand. Appeals to "governance" seemed to provide them with the requisite flexibility to adjust to changing circumstances and to avoid chaos. At the same time, the repertoire of "stronger EU governance" contained the debate at the level of pro-EU elites, and was designed both to respond to and to undercut outside interference on the part of Euroskeptic politicians and mass politics. EU officials issued multiple reports on "governance" between the Van Rompuy report[56] and the Five Presidents' Report.[57] The language of governance enabled state actors to experiment with new ways to practice sovereignty. Perhaps the most symbolic change was to give Brussels priority in the discussion of national budgets. First launched in 2011, the "European Semester" mandates that Eurozone member governments draft their yearly budget proposals and get them vetted at the EU level *before* these are submitted to national parliaments. In addition, the EU adopted the "Six Pack," a set of six regulations that strengthens the Stability and Growth Pact by imposing earlier and stiffer sanctions on deviant Member States. It includes an "excessive macroeconomic imbalance" procedure, aimed at monitoring not just fiscal balances but also external balances. Finally, the EU has adopted the "Two Pack," two regulations that authorize "enhanced surveillance" of states that receive EU bailout funds. At the end of the day, the reforms superimposed, on top of the preexisting EMU framework, a more intrusive monitoring regime that effectively changed national practices of sovereignty. Although the reformed regime remained fragile, it enabled the Eurozone to survive the most acute phase of its crisis.

III CONCLUSION

The Eurozone crisis revealed the fragility of the Eurozone but also its plasticity, even in the face of intense politicization. Tensions between the practices of national sovereignty and EU institutions reached a climax, but they ultimately led to new practices of sovereignty. Despite a highly politicized

---

[55] Julie Froud, Adriana Nilsson, Michael Moran, and Karen Williams, "Stories and Interests in Finance: Agendas of Governance before and after the Financial Crisis," *Governance* 25, no. 1 (2012): 35–59.

[56] *Report of the Task Force to the European Council: Strengthening Economic Governance in the EU*.

[57] *The Five Presidents' Report: Completing the Economic and Monetary Union*, June 22, 2015, https://ec.europa.eu/commission/sites/beta-political/files/5-presidents-report_en.pdf.

environment, EU leaders were able to reform existing institutions while carefully attending to Member States' concerns about sovereignty. The reconstitution of sovereignty authorized bailouts of struggling Member States – under strict conditions. To garner support for such a reconstitution, leaders of Member State governments and EU institutions had to engage in political debates touching core questions of what constitutes sovereignty. The fluid coalitional dynamics that we observe are difficult to square with standard political science understandings of the EU, which tend to envision European integration primarily as a process of elite politics and to adopt a dismal view of politicization. The fact that barbarians are at the gates, and in some cases even inside the fortress, does not mean that the EU is necessarily doomed. Remarkably, the victory of a left-populist leader in Greece did not derail the Eurozone reform process. Of course, Greece is a small state at the periphery of the EU, so its capacity to wreak havoc was arguably limited. It remains to be seen whether the formation of a Euroskeptic governing coalition in Italy, a founding Member State of the EU, will fundamentally alter the situation.

There is little doubt that political passions can be paralyzing or even destructive for European integration, but they can also have a creative potential. In a post-Brexit EU, national claims to sovereignty are likely to flare up even more often, and European leaders will need to face up to these claims and incorporate them into future EU reforms. If the EU is to persist (as remains most likely), it will need to keep inventing new ways to reconcile states' sovereignty concerns with the pursuit of its integration. In a world in which international and domestic spheres increasingly overlap, the politicization of sovereignty practices within the EU also exemplifies a broader "politicization of international institutions."[58] In turn, this politicization changes the dynamic of both international and domestic politics. Pierson and Hacker have argued that the world in which we live is increasingly "Schattschneiderian," insofar as voters do not directly impose their preferences and public policies acquire their own momentum.[59] Another facet of this new world is that what Schattschneider called the "scope of conflict" tends to expand and the geometry of coalitions becomes increasingly complex and unpredictable. As politicization accelerates the reconstitution of sovereignty practices, politics makes strange bedfellows who sometimes coalesce in support of remarkably bold institutional reforms.

---

[58] Michael Zürn, Martin Binder, and Matthias Ecker-Ehrhardt, "International Authority and its Politicization," *International Theory* 4, no. 1 (2012): 69–106.

[59] Jacob S. Hacker and Paul Pierson, "After the 'Master Theory': Downs, Schattschneider, and the Re-Birth of Policy-Focused Analysis," *Perspectives on Politics* 12, no. 3 (2014): 643–662.

5

EU Financial Regulation after the Neoliberal Moment

ELLIOT POSNER[*]

I INTRODUCTION

This chapter examines EU financial regulation[1] before and after the financial crisis and in advance of the anticipated break up with the United Kingdom. It provides background and analysis to help readers grasp the current state of affairs and to think clearly about likely future ones. There is no shortage of pressing questions. Will future Brussels policies in this sector contribute to financial markets characterized by a desirable balance of industry risk-taking, systemic stability, and protections for consumers and investors? Will the EU's policies continue to constitute a piece of the international financial architecture or reflect a home-grown approach as in other regulatory areas like data privacy and chemicals? Will Brussels and Washington remain the principal global rulemakers, together setting transnational standards, or can we expect a different configuration of regulatory power, perhaps with London either allied with Washington or becoming the swing player? As these questions suggest, EU financial regulation cannot easily be examined in isolation. More so than the other policy areas covered in this volume, the region's regulation of finance is deeply intertwined with transnational institutions and international politics.[2]

---

[*] The author thanks Anna Gelpern and the other participants of the "EU at a Crossroads: From Technocracy to High Politics?" workshop. He is grateful to Francesca Bignami for her feedback on earlier drafts, to Catalina Milos Sotomayor and Gillian Weiss for editorial assistance, and to IMÉRA Institute for Advanced Study, Aix-Marseille Université, for its generous support.

[1] Financial regulation includes the rules and governance arrangements for banking, securities, investment, and insurance industries and markets.

[2] On this theme, see Daniel Mügge, "Introduction," in *Europe and the Governance of Global Finance*, ed. Daniel Mügge (Oxford: Oxford University Press, 2014), 1–16; Lucia Quaglia, *The European Union and Global Financial Regulation* (Oxford: Oxford University Press, 2014).

At the heart of the chapter's analysis is a late 1990s internal financial regulatory bargain that, unlike Economic and Monetary Union, included the United Kingdom – home to one of the world's leading financial centers as well as to authorities playing pivotal roles in EU and transnational financial policy arenas. The deal tightly tethered EU efforts to integrate financial markets to the emerging standards of transnational rulemaking organizations, at the very moment when neoliberal ideas were taking hold. The list of transnational organizations includes bodies of national authorities such as the Basel Committee on Banking Supervision (BCBS) and the International Organization of Securities Commissions (IOSCO) but also private standard setters such as the International Accounting Standards Board (IASB). Two decades after the EU bargain originated, albeit with few of its original provisions intact, its legacy turns Britain's impending exit from the Union into a portentous moment for EU financial regulation – whose future hinges on the still-undefined terms of the breakup and, in turn, on how the United Kingdom will position itself at the transnational level.

In the years before 2008, the deal made the EU reliant on transnational standards that were moving in a market-friendly direction; propelled Brussels onto the previously US-dominated global rulemaking stage; and guaranteed the polity's status as a dependable financial internationalist. These outcomes – especially the direction of regulatory content – implicate Brussels in the relatively lenient regulation that enabled the 2008 financial crisis[3] and contributed to the Eurozone's troubles, policy responses, and varied political reactions discussed across this volume's chapters.

The turmoil after 2008 triggered across-the-board reforms. The EU ratcheted up regulation, with London often being isolated or part of a losing coalition. Yet the changes (even with some surprises like the remarkable transfer of banking supervisory powers to the European Central Bank) meant that, rather than being at the vanguard of sounder and cutting-edge international regulatory practices, Brussels ended up with mostly incremental reforms. And the divergence between Eurozone and UK priorities and preferences revealed the bargain's fragility and potential pathologies. Combined

---

[3] Abraham L. Newman and Elliot Posner, *Voluntary Disruptions: International Soft Law, Finance, and Power* (Oxford: Oxford University Press, 2018), 63–96; Abraham Newman and Elliot Posner, "Transnational Feedback, Soft Law, and Preferences in Global Financial Regulation," *Review of International Political Economy* 23, no. 1 (January 2016): 123–152; Elliot Posner and Nicolas Véron, "The EU and Financial Regulation: Power without Purpose?" *Journal of European Public Policy* 17, no. 3 (2010): 400–415.

with G20-directed reductions in European representation[4] on transnational standard-setting bodies, the internal divisions widened gaps between transnational standards and EU policy preferences, and contributed to a checkered post-crisis record of financial regulatory internationalism, sometimes casting the EU at odds with new, more robust regulatory practices.[5]

Despite the uncertain terms, this chapter's analysis suggests that some pre-Brexit trends will extend into a post-Brexit period. An EU with diminished international bargaining heft yet concerned about competition from the United Kingdom and the United States would not be well positioned to offer alternatives to one likely eventuality: a London–New York alliance in transnational standard-setting bodies.

The chapter begins with a description of the Union's financial regulatory bargain and a survey of the internal and external effects before the financial crisis. These sections emphasize the adoption of industry-friendly regulation and a pattern of EU internationalism. Turning to the post-crisis period, the chapter covers the declining internationalism and its roots in the bargain's breakdown (especially new fissures between the United Kingdom and the Eurozone) and in the changes in the membership of transnational financial standard setters. Here, the chapter reports on a study that Nicolas Véron and I carried out. The concluding section considers a future of EU financial regulation without the United Kingdom.

II EUROPE'S TURN-OF-THE-MILLENNIUM FINANCIAL REGULATORY BARGAIN

EU financial regulation – both its content and governance arrangements – is part and parcel of the polity's development. The imperative to integrate Member State financial services industries and markets stems directly from the Union's original aspiration to be a region of free-flowing capital. Thus, the impulse to integrate finance, similar to so many aspects of the regional project, guarantees that politics will always be present in technocratic considerations

---

[4] In November 2009, having already added leaders' summits to a forum that had previously been for finance ministers and central bank governors, the Group of 20 (G20) announced that the organization would replace the Group of 7/8 (G7/8) as the primary international forum for coordinating national financial regulatory reform. More or less mirroring the membership of the G20, the transnational financial standard setters (at least the ones that previously had many fewer members reflecting the G7/8) also expanded.

[5] Elliot Posner and Nicolas Véron, "Is the EU a Financial Internationalist? Global Institutional Context and External Regulatory Policy" (Unpublished Paper, 2018).

about how best to manage competing objectives of system stability, allocation efficiency, and international competitiveness.

Recognizing the pervasiveness of politics helps to explain why, despite the achievement in Europe of cross-border capital mobility in the 1980s,[6] national financial systems proved resilient and member governments and EU political institutions struggled to find common market rules.[7] After fits and starts in the late 1980s and early 1990s, a multidimensional political bargain at the turn of the millennium accelerated the integration process. Some aspects of the bargain manifested in EU law; others constituted mutual understandings. Most were deals cut among member governments, with Germany, France, and the United Kingdom exerting the most weight. A few, however, involved the balance of powers among the European Commission, the European Parliament, and the Council of Ministers, the EU's three political institutions with formal legislative roles.[8]

The bargain rested on four pillars.[9] First, unlike in the case of monetary arrangements, *all* Member States – including the United Kingdom, which was the most enthusiastic and leading government[10] – would participate in the EU's proposed single rulebook for financial regulation. Second, two informal tenets would be respected in the creation of EU-wide rules. No legislative initiative would advance without the backing of the region's leading financial center, the United Kingdom, and its most powerful economy, Germany. And transnational soft law,[11] developed in standard-setting bodies, would be the favored solution to the persistent coordination problems that arise from

---

[6] Nicolas Jabko, *Playing the Market: A Political Strategy for Uniting Europe, 1985–2005* (Ithaca, NY: Cornell University Press, 2006), 57–90.

[7] Jonathan Story and Ingo Walter, *Political Economy of Financial Integration in Europe: The Battle of the Systems* (Cambridge, MA: MIT Press, 1997); Richard Deeg and Elliot Posner, "Durability and Change in Financial Systems," in *The Oxford Handbook of Historical Institutionalism*, eds. Orfeo Fioretos, Tulia G. Falleti, and Adam Sheingate (Oxford: Oxford University Press, 2016), 438–452.

[8] Mark A. Pollack, *Engines of European Integration: Delegation, Agency, and Agenda Setting in the EU* (Oxford: Oxford University Press, 2003), 140–144.

[9] The discussion about the EU's financial regulatory bargain is derived from Posner and Véron, "Is the EU a Financial Internationalist?"

[10] David Howarth and Lucia Quaglia, "Brexit and the Single European Financial Market," *Journal of Common Market Studies* 55, no. S1 (2017): 150.

[11] In contrast to international "hard law" (such as treaties and other binding measures agreed by governments), "soft law" is nonbinding, written standards, best practices, and guidance. Created within an array of organizations (private, public and hybrid, and treaty- and non-treaty based), soft law provides advice to market participants and public authorities on issues as wide-ranging as procedures for regulatory cooperation and the amount of capital multinational banks should hold to ensure systemic stability. For a discussion, see Newman and Posner, *Voluntary Disruptions*, 15–19. Most soft law in the area of financial regulation can be found in the

different national regulations and approaches. Borrowing these standards was – to an important extent – a nod to the City of London. Widely seen as technocratic and neutral (as in reflecting no particular national approach), transnational standards largely embodied ideas shared within a transnational network of financiers and authorities and belonging to powerful actors in jurisdictions with the world's biggest financial hubs, the United States and the United Kingdom.[12]

Third, mirroring other areas of EU regulation,[13] financial rulemaking would become more Brussels-centered. In this overhaul of administrative authority, some powers were delegated to new EU-level committees (under what is generally known as the Lamfalussy Process) and, in the case of financial reporting standards, to the IASB (formerly the International Accounting Standards Committee), the private standard-setting body located in London. The Lamfalussy committees, comprising national regulators and tasked with giving advice to the European Commission on the devising of detailed rules and ensuring their consistent application, quickly became key interlocutors with newly congealing Europe-wide industry interests.[14] Nonetheless, despite the elevation of these committees, the bargain limited their binding decision-making powers and maintained the primacy of Member States over implementation and enforcement. In addition, Germany and the United Kingdom were adamant that these powers would not migrate to a

Financial Stability Board's Compendium of Standards (www.fsb.org/what-we-do/about-the-compendium-of-standards/).

[12] Newman and Posner, *Voluntary Disruptions*, 31–62; Eleni Tsingou, "Club Governance and the Making of Global Financial Rules," *Review of International Political Economy* 22, no. 2 (March 2015): 225–256.

[13] Burkard Eberlein and Abraham L. Newman, "Escaping the International Governance Dilemma? Incorporated Transgovernmental Networks in the European Union," *Governance* 21, no. 1 (January 2008): 25–52; Mark Thatcher, "The Creation of European Regulatory Agencies and Its Limits: A Comparative Analysis of European Delegation," *Journal of European Public Policy* 18, no. 6 (September 2011): 790–809; Charles F. Sabel and Jonathan Zeitlin, *Experimentalist Governance in the European Union: Towards a New Architecture* (New York: Oxford University Press, 2012).

[14] Daniel Mügge, "Reordering the Marketplace: Competition Politics in European Finance," *Journal of Common Market Studies* 44, no. 5 (December 2006): 991–1022; Daniel Mügge, *Widen the Market, Narrow the Competition: Banker Interests and the Making of a European Capital Market* (Colchester: ECPR Press, 2010); Elliot Posner, "The Lamfalussy Process: The Polyarchic Origins of Networked Financial Rule-Making in the EU," in *Experimentalist Governance in the European Union: Towards a New Architecture*, eds. Charles F. Sabel and Jonathan Zeitlin (New York: Oxford University Press, 2010), 43–60.

supranational authority, and certainly not to the newly born European Central Bank (ECB).[15]

Lastly, reflecting the same mindset imbuing monetary union, failing banks and other financial entities were the presumed responsibility of national central banks and governments, with no burden-sharing obligations (including bailouts and emergency liquidity provisions) extended to other member governments or the ECB.[16]

III EFFECTS OF EUROPE'S FINANCIAL BARGAIN

What did Europe's financial deal yield in the years before the 2008 financial crisis? The resulting passage of an enormous stream of EU legislation (combined with the new rulemaking procedures and coordination mechanisms of the Lamfalussy Process) contributed much to the purported goal of regional integration of financial markets and the Europeanization of national financial services industries, albeit more so with respect to wholesale markets (in which the participants are banks, other financial service providers, corporations, institutional investors, or the like) than retail ones (such as household banking services).[17]

There were, however, several other consequences. First, it pulled London into a regulatory arrangement with its Continental partners, without making it choose between Europe, on the one hand, and the British approach and competitiveness vis-à-vis New York, on the other.[18] Indeed, Europe's deal consolidated London's position as a leading international financial center as

---

[15] Tom Buerkle, "European Disunion," *Institutional Investor*, July 1, 2002, www.institutional investor.com/article/b151351nvkqjyv/european-disunion.

[16] The determinants of Europe's four-part financial bargain are varied and the subject of scholarly debate that will not be reviewed in this chapter. See Elliot Posner, "Financial Transformation in the European Union," in *Making History: European Integration and Institutional Change at Fifty*, eds. Sophie Meunier and Kathleen R. McNamara (Oxford: Oxford University Press, 2007), 139–155; Shawn Donnelly, *The Regimes of European Integration* (New York: Oxford University Press, 2010); Mügge, *Widen the Market, Narrow the Competition*; Lucia Quaglia, *Governing Financial Services in the European Union: Banking, Securities and Post-Trading* (Oxford: Routledge, 2010).

[17] The European Commission and the ECB publish regular statistics and analysis. For recent examples, see European Central Bank, "Financial Integration in Europe," May 2018, 159, www.ecb.europa.eu/pub/pdf/fie/ecb.financialintegrationineurope201805.en.pdf; European Commission, "European Financial Stability and Integration Review (EFSIR)," https://ec .europa.eu/info/publications/european-financial-stability-and-integration-report-efsir_en.

[18] Posner and Véron, "Is the EU a Financial Internationalist?"

continental banks amplified the trend of moving operations to the United Kingdom.[19]

In addition, while contentious politics surrounded many of the legislative initiatives,[20] European financial regulation as a whole moved in a market-friendly direction[21] that turned the EU into a promoter of global finance and the international financial architecture. The need to accommodate the "light touch" United Kingdom is not the only reason. The timing also mattered. The EU's push to integrate financial regulation coincided with the height of the neoliberal moment in transnational standard-setting bodies.[22] Thus, even with occasional strong national and European Parliament resistance to harmonization measures (such as company law) that directly threatened domestic labor markets and welfare and entitlement programs,[23] the pro-integration faction's use of transnational soft law as a coordination mechanism led to industry-embracing regulation and thus, in hindsight, to a certain shared culpability (with the United States) for enabling the 2008 international financial crisis.[24]

Unlike in the regulation of data privacy, chemicals, the environment, and foods, where the EU adopted distinct European approaches that were widely seen as stringent compared to those of the US,[25] in the domain of financial

[19] Howarth and Quaglia, "Brexit and the Single European Financial Market."

[20] Quaglia, *Governing Financial Services in the European Union.*

[21] In Quaglia's terms, the "market-making" coalitions, with the United Kingdom in the lead, did better than the "market-shaping" ones. Also see Mügge, *Widen the Market, Narrow the Competition.*

[22] Geoffrey R. D. Underhill, Jasper Blom, and Daniel Mügge, *Global Financial Integration Thirty Years On: From Reform to Crisis* (New York: Cambridge University Press, 2010).

[23] John W. Cioffi, "Restructuring 'Germany Inc.': The Politics of Company and Takeover Law Reform in Germany and the European Union," *Law and Policy* 24, no. 4 (October 2002): 355–402; Helen Callaghan and Martin Höpner, "European Integration and the Clash of Capitalisms: Political Cleavages over Takeover Liberalization," *Comparative European Politics* 3, no. 3 (September 2005): 307–332; Neil Fligstein, *Euroclash: The EU, European Identity, and the Future of Europe* (Oxford: Oxford University Press, 2009), 62–122.

[24] Daniel Mügge, "From Pragmatism to Dogmatism: European Union Governance, Policy Paradigms and Financial Meltdown," *New Political Economy* 16, no. 2 (April 2011): 185–206; Posner and Véron, "The EU and Financial Regulation"; Newman and Posner, "Transnational Feedback, Soft Law, and Preferences in Global Financial Regulation"; Newman and Posner, *Voluntary Disruptions*, 63–96.

[25] David Vogel, *The Politics of Precaution: Regulating Health, Safety, and Environmental Risks in Europe and the United States* (Princeton, NJ: Princeton University Press, 2012); Joanne Scott, "Extraterritoriality and Territorial Extension in EU Law," *American Journal of Comparative Law* 62, no. 1 (2014): 87–125; Mark A. Pollack and Gregory C. Shaffer, *When Cooperation Fails: The International Law and Politics of Genetically Modified Foods* (Oxford: Oxford University Press, 2009); Anu Bradford, "The Brussels Effect," *Northwestern University Law Review* 107, no. 1 (2012): 1–67; Abraham Newman, *Protectors of Privacy: Regulating Personal Data in the Global Economy* (Ithaca, NY: Cornell University Press, 2008).

regulation voices normally opposed to US-style capitalism and economic globalization – notably, inside the European Parliament – ended up prioritizing EU integration, which in practice tended to mean the adoption of business-friendly transnational standards.[26] Europe's relatively uncontroversial transposition of the 2004 Basel II accord – arguably the exemplar of neoliberal standards because of a reliance on self-regulation of risk, transparency, and market discipline – is an extreme illustration.[27] The contentious and partial US implementation contrasts with the EU's relatively smooth adoption of the accord, containing minimum bank capital reserve requirements created by a small group of leading central bankers and other banking authorities organized in the Basel Committee on Banking Supervision.[28]

Capital standards for banks were far from the only instance of the EU's market-friendly turn. Even fifteen years after the event, Europe's 2002 requirement that publicly listed companies use international accounting standards (first labeled International Accounting Standards, then International Financial Reporting Standards) stands out as a radical move for continental financial systems with very different accounting traditions.[29] In search of a lingua franca of financial reporting standards, the IASB's circle of accounting experts and professionals were driven by the idea that the main purpose of a company's financial report is transparency, which, they believed, abets market discipline and efficient allocation of capital. Indeed, IFRS are largely based on principles similar to the ones in the United States and the United Kingdom and, in the eyes of many observers, represent an extreme approach to easing cross-border financial integration.[30] By 2008, the EU went further by

[26] Posner and Véron, "The EU and Financial Regulation."

[27] Stijn Claessens, Geoffrey R. D. Underhill, and Xiaoke Zhang, "The Political Economy of Basle II: The Costs for Poor Countries," *The World Economy* 31, no. 3 (March 2008): 313–344; Eleni Tsingou, "Transnational Private Governance and the Basel Process: Banking Regulation and Supervision, Private Interests and Basel II," in *Transnational Private Governance and Its Limits*, eds. Jean-Christophe Graz and Andreas Nölke (London: Routledge, 2008), 62; Andrew Baker, "Restraining Regulatory Capture? Anglo-America, Crisis Politics and Trajectories of Change in Global Financial Governance," *International Affairs* 86, no. 3 (May 2010): 650.

[28] Daniel Mügge, "From Pragmatism to Dogmatism"; Rosemary Foot and Andrew Walter, *China, the United States, and Global Order* (New York: Cambridge University Press, 2010); Kathryn C. Lavelle, *Money and Banks in the American Political System* (New York: Cambridge University Press, 2013).

[29] James Perry and Andreas Nölke, "International Accounting Standard Setting: A Network Approach," *Business and Politics* 7, no. 3 (December 2005): 1–32; Andreas Nölke and James Perry, "The Power of Transnational Private Governance: Financialization and the IASB," *Business and Politics* 9, no. 3 (December 2007): 1–25.

[30] Mügge, "From Pragmatism to Dogmatism," 192–195.

accepting US accounting standards (US GAAP) as equivalent[31] and was the leading global proponent of the IASB's standards and work.[32]

To give a final example, before 2008 the EU also supported market-friendly, internationalist policies for the regulation of over-the-counter (OTC) derivatives.[33] Here, Brussels accepted recommendations by the G-30 and two transnational standard setters (IOSCO and BCBS) advocating self-regulation by industry organizations (such as the International Swaps and Derivatives Association) rather than direct regulation by public authorities.[34] By and large, the EU accommodated the United Kingdom, which, along with the United States, dominated these markets. Similar to the US legal environment (which prohibited direct forms of public regulation), British law upheld the enforceability of speculative derivatives in the UK Financial Services Act of 1986 and offered no mechanism for direct regulation in the UK Financial Services and Market Act 2000.[35]

IV THE EU'S ASCENDANCE AS A GLOBAL FINANCIAL REGULATOR

In addition to market integration, consolidation of London's global position, and Brussels' industry-friendly turn, Europe's bargain had a further consequence. It changed the governance environment of international finance, showcasing the deep entanglement between EU regulation, US policies, and the global financial architecture.

The EU's internal revamp simultaneously turned Brussels into a global rulemaker, ending US financial regulatory hegemony.[36] Before then, the

---

[31] European Commission Press Release IP/08/1962, Accounting: European Commission Grants Equivalence in relation to Third Country GAAPs (December 12, 2008).

[32] Elliot Posner, "Sequence as Explanation: The International Politics of Accounting Standards," *Review of International Political Economy* 17, no. 4 (October 2010): 639–664.

[33] Stefano Pagliari, "Public Salience and International Financial Regulation: Explaining the International Regulation of OTC Derivatives, Rating Agencies, and Hedge Funds," University of Waterloo Thesis, 2013, 128–178, http://stefanopagliari.net/www.stefanopagliari.net/PhD_Thesis.html; Stefano Pagliari, "A Wall around Europe? The European Regulatory Response to the Global Financial Crisis and the Turn in Transatlantic Relations," *Journal of European Integration* 35, no. 4 (2013): 391–408.

[34] Tsingou, "Club Governance and the Making of Global Financial Rules."

[35] Daniel Mügge, "Securities and Derivatives Markets," in *Europe and the Governance of Global Finance*, ed. Daniel Mügge (Oxford: Oxford University Press, 2014), 60–65; Lynn A. Stout, "The Legal Origin of the 2008 Credit Crisis," Law-Econ Research Paper no. 11-05, UCLA School of Law, 2011.

[36] Elliot Posner, "Making Rules for Global Finance: Transatlantic Regulatory Cooperation at the Turn of the Millennium," *International Organization* 63, no. 4 (2009): 665–699. See also Quaglia, *The European Union and Global Financial Regulation* and Mügge, "Introduction."

internationalization of finance had already rendered EU decision-making interdependent – in the sense that Brussels could not easily set policies without consideration of what the United States was doing. Until the early 2000s, however, the United States dominated, with the United Kingdom and sometimes Germany and Japan, having roles, though often limited.[37] The reforms inside Europe improved Brussels' capacities to control access by third-country firms to EU markets, to speak externally with a single voice, and to carry out an international agenda. The improved bargaining leverage was evident in EU–US bilateral relations. In a series of spats over the extraterritorial reach of new legislation on both sides of the Atlantic, Commission officials (speaking on behalf of national member governments under an informal delegation of authority) "discovered" the EU's improved bargaining position. The EU's new external might was at first an unintentional byproduct of an internally focused project. Yet Brussels officials quickly learned how to harness Europe's aggregated markets into strategic bargaining positions. A new "bipolar," largely cooperative relationship quickly took form as multinational US-based banks, concerned that the EU project would disrupt European revenue flows, prodded the US Treasury and regulators (with key members of US Congress in the background) to establish what became known as the Transatlantic Financial Market Regulatory Dialogue.[38]

The EU's strengthened bargaining leverage was also apparent within the global financial architecture, underscoring the importance of the international institutional context. EU policy entrepreneurs, as noted, were using the legitimacy of transnational soft law to advance their internal harmonization agenda. But the effects of another aspect of the international institutional context, the membership composition of standard-setting bodies, are also important, and underappreciated. As highlighted in the discussion of post-2008 developments, my research with Nicolas Véron[39] shows that before the crisis, European national authorities were over-represented in the G7/G8 as well as the many transnational standard-setting bodies. The lopsided numbers were only an EU asset to the extent that European national representatives adopted unified positions – which happened more often after the advent of the EU's turn-of-the-millennium regulatory harmonization program.

One should exercise caution not to take this line of argument too far. Numbers are not everything. In the pre-crisis years, transnational bodies were

---

[37] Beth A. Simmons, "International Politics of Harmonization: The Case of Capital Market Regulation," *International Organization* 55, no. 3 (2001): 589–620.
[38] Posner, "Making Rules for Global Finance."
[39] Posner and Véron, "Is the EU a Financial Internationalist?"

not the only venue for negotiations; the many threads of the EU–US bilateral relationship (where the European Commission usually represented the Union) were often the central forums for hashing out differences, and transatlantic dialogue frequently spanned fluidly across bilateral and transnational venues. Moreover, even with the United Kingdom fully on board in the EU's regulatory project, European national representatives did not always exhibit a united front.[40] These caveats notwithstanding, Europe's over-representation did play to the advantage of the EU before the crisis, which is why it was a factor in 2008 and 2009 in the behind-the-scenes negotiations over the size of the reformed G20, which, as noted, was the new fulcrum of international coordination of financial regulatory reforms.

V WHAT TYPE OF GLOBAL FINANCIAL REGULATOR?[41]

It is one thing to recognize that the internal financial bargain catapulted the EU into a global rulemaker but quite another to understand what kind of a financial regulatory power the EU became. The question belongs to a long-standing public and scholarly debate – with normative overtones – about the EU as an actor in global affairs.

Echoing the literature on the extent to which the polity is sui generis and different from a state,[42] the research on the EU as a global actor asks whether historical evolution, institutional arrangements, and political culture have spawned a particular, if not unique, type of international player. One result has been a long, familiar list of images proposed to characterize the EU's global actorness (including "civilian power,"[43] "normative

---

[40] On the unevenness of European influence, see Daniel Mügge, "The European Presence in Global Financial Governance: A Principal–Agent Perspective," *Journal of European Public Policy* 18, no. 3 (2011): 383–402.

[41] This section and the next two report on the study behind Posner and Véron, "Is the EU a Financial Internationalist."

[42] See for examples: Alberta M. Sbragia, "The United States and the European Union: Comparing Two Sui Generis Systems," in *Comparative Federalism: The European Union and the United States in Comparative Perspective*, eds. Anand Menon and Martin A. Schain (New York: Oxford University Press, 2006), 15–34; Amie Kreppel, "The Normalization of the European Union," *Journal of European Public Policy* 19, no. 5 (June 2012): 635–645; Kathleen R. McNamara, *The Politics of Everyday Europe: Constructing Authority in the European Union* (New York: Oxford University Press, 2017); Abraham L. Newman, "Global European Union Studies: Sometimes Normal Is a Little Weird," *Journal of European Public Policy* 25, no. 7 (July 2018): 959–968.

[43] François Duchêne, "'Europe's Role in World Peace' [in] Europe Tomorrow: Sixteen Europeans Look Ahead," in *Europe Tomorrow: Sixteen Europeans Look Ahead*, ed. Richard

power,"[44] "market power,"[45] and "integrative power"[46]). A few general points are relevant here. On the one hand, scholars find variation by issue area in terms of the EU's support of an open international economy (akin to Wagner's image of a Liberal Power Europe[47]) as opposed to an approach of "managed globalization."[48] On the other hand, scholars tend to depict the Union as a consistent promoter of international cooperation and law and multilateral institutions. Gráinne de Búrca, for example, finds that the EU pursues its international objectives via collective and often multilateral means and that Brussels officials aim to reproduce, at the international level, the EU's internal modes of cooperative governance.[49] The multilateralist presumption runs through otherwise unrelated research such as Kagan's Realist argument that Europe prefers cooperation because of a congenital military weakness (relative to the United States) as well as classic works of Constructivist international relations theory and the literature about "normative" and (to a lesser extent) "civilian" Europe.[50] For many EU experts – though, again, not all – Brussels' internationalist predilection comes with the normative message that, as a pillar of multilateralism and international law, the EU is a force for good in global affairs.

Mayne (London: Fontana/Collins, 1972), 32–47; François Duchêne, "The European Community and the Uncertainties of Interdependence," in *A Nation Writ Large? Foreign-Policy Problems before the European Community*, eds. Max Kohnstamm and Wolfgang Hager (London: Palgrave Macmillan UK, 1973), 1–21.

[44] Ian Manners, "Normative Power Europe: A Contradiction in Terms?" *Journal of Common Market Studies* 40, no. 2 (June 2002): 235–258.

[45] Chad Damro, "Market Power Europe," *Journal of European Public Policy* 19, no. 5 (2012): 682–699.

[46] Joachim Alexander Koops, *The European Union as an Integrative Power: Assessing the EU's "Effective Multilateralism" with NATO and the United Nations* (Brussels: Vubpress Brussels University Press, 2011).

[47] Wolfgang Wagner, "Liberal Power Europe," *Journal of Common Market Studies* 55, no. 6 (November 2017): 1403.

[48] Wade Jacoby and Sophie Meunier, "Europe and the Management of Globalization," *Journal of European Public Policy* 17, no. 3 (2010): 299–317.

[49] Gráinne de Búrca, "EU External Relations: The Governance Mode of Foreign Policy," in *The EU's Role in Global Governance: The Legal Dimension*, eds. Bart Van Vooren, Steven Blockmans, and Jan Wouters (Oxford: Oxford University Press, 2012), 44–45.

[50] Robert Kagan, "Power and Weakness," *Policy Review* 113 (June/July 2002): 30–38; John Gerard Ruggie, "Multilateralism: The Anatomy of an Institution," *International Organization* 46, no. 3 (1992): 561–598; Ian Manners, "Normative Power Europe Reconsidered: Beyond the Crossroads," *Journal of European Public Policy* 13, no. 2 (March 2006): 182–199; Mario Telò, *Europe: A Civilian Power?: European Union, Global Governance, World Order* (Basingstoke: Palgrave Macmillan, 2007); Joakim Kreutz, "Human Rights, Geostrategy, and EU Foreign Policy, 1989–2008," *International Organization* 69, no. 1 (2015): 195–217.

Challenging these views, a new wave of research is resuscitating an earlier effort that conceived of the EU as a "normal" polity. These perspectives do not necessarily expect reliable EU internationalism. Instead, they treat the polity as a global regulator responsive to factors (inside and outside Europe) in ways akin to those of other jurisdictions with large markets and rulemaking capacities.[51] By this way of thinking, even if the EU were consistently internationalist before and after the crisis, it would still be necessary to delve deeper to explore whether the determinants lie in its sui generis characteristics or some other factors – and whether the outcome can be normatively desirable. In the political economy literature, there are several candidate determinants of internationalism. They include internal factors, such as public salience,[52] cohesiveness,[53] and regulatory capacity,[54] and external factors, such as those related to the international institutional context.[55]

Turning specifically to financial regulation, research on the pre-2008 years, as implied at the end of Section III, shows that in harmonizing to largely industry-friendly transnational standards, the EU encouraged financial internationalization and supported soft law and the transnational standard-setting bodies that created it.[56] Apart from some aspects of Member State financial policies not governed by EU legislation, the Union did not exhibit protectionist tendencies in internal policies or with other jurisdictions. By contrast, using equivalence clauses as its main legal tool, it created a largely open,

[51] Alasdair R. Young, "The European Union as a Global Regulator? Context and Comparison," *Journal of European Public Policy* 22, no. 9 (October 2015): 1233–1252; Alasdair R. Young and John Peterson, *Parochial Global Europe: 21st Century Trade Politics* (Oxford: Oxford University Press, 2014); Newman, "Global European Union Studies."

[52] Pagliari, "Public Salience and International Financial Regulation"; Pepper D. Culpepper, *Quiet Politics and Business Power: Corporate Control in Europe and Japan* (New York: Cambridge University Press, 2010).

[53] Eugénia da Conceição-Heldt and Sophie Meunier, "Speaking with a Single Voice: Internal Cohesiveness and External Effectiveness of the EU in Global Governance," *Journal of European Public Policy* 21, no. 7 (2014): 961–979.

[54] Quaglia, *The European Union and Global Financial Regulation*; David Bach and Abraham Newman, "The European Regulatory State and Global Public Policy: Micro-Institutions, Macro-Influence," *Journal of European Public Policy* 14, no. 6 (2007): 827–846.

[55] Tulia G. Falleti and Julia F. Lynch, "Context and Causal Mechanisms in Political Analysis," *Comparative Political Studies* 42, no. 9 (2009): 1143–1166; da Conceição-Heldt and Meunier, "Speaking with a Single Voice," 971–975.

[56] My research with Nicolas Véron, discussed in detail later in this chapter, substantiates these findings. To create a baseline for our study on the years immediately following the crisis, Véron and I examined EU financial regulatory internationalism before the crisis: Across ten regulatory areas, the EU promoted the internationalization of finance with harmonized policies, approaches, and rules broadly compatible with those of the United States; and it supported transnational standard-setting bodies and soft law.

market-friendly approach and rules permitting comparatively easy access for foreign companies from jurisdictions with largely compatible regulation.[57] Similarly, from near seamless transposition of the Basel Committee's capital requirements, to the 2002 adoption of the International Accounting Standards Board's reporting standards and the acceptance of IOSCO and BCBS's recommendations not to impose direct public regulation over OTC derivative markets, the EU proved itself to be intricately part of the international institutional arrangements.[58]

VI EU FINANCIAL REGULATORY INTERNATIONALISM AFTER THE CRISIS

Nicolas Véron and I revisited the issue of EU financial regulatory internationalism for the years immediately following the crisis. We had a range of motivations. In terms of our theoretical interests, financial regulation before and after the 2008 crisis offers a critical set of cases for evaluating the aforementioned propositions about EU internationalism: If the EU is indeed a reliable internationalist, one ought to find supportive evidence at challenging historical moments such as the 2008 crisis when European decision makers face pressure to retreat from internationalist positions. We were aware of some studies that cast doubt on the EU's post-crisis commitment to open access to foreign firms (a variant of the Fortress Europe thesis[59]) and did not always play the leading role in transnational standard setters;[60] and we thought a new one examining a larger number of cases (we looked at ten) was urgently needed. We also wanted to analyze systematically new theoretical ideas about the impact of international institutional context: Specifically, how G20-orchestrated change in the membership composition of standard-setting bodies might have affected external EU behavior.

As for policy, the EU is likely to face critical decisions in the near future – a topic to which I return later in the chapter. After a British exit, financial arrangements between the City of London and EU financial capitals would not only affect Europe and the United Kingdom but also the rest of the world and the global financial architecture. Before and after 2008, Brussels officials

---

[57] Mügge, *Widen the Market, Narrow the Competition*; Posner and Véron, "The EU and Financial Regulation"; Posner, "Financial Transformation in the European Union"; Quaglia, *Governing Financial Services in the European Union.*

[58] Mügge, "Introduction."

[59] Pagliari, "A Wall around Europe?"

[60] Quaglia, *The European Union and Global Financial Regulation.*

made extensive claims about EU financial internationalism.[61] Whether such confidence is merited (and our study is cause for skepticism), there is a need for rigorous analysis that can assist with sound regulatory policymaking.

What did we find? The results are sobering for anyone hoping that the EU might have redeemed itself for not having used its pre-crisis rulemaking influence at the transnational level to check the post-1980s US slide toward overly lax regulation.[62] Yet instead, the EU, in partnership with the United States, spearheaded a G20 regulatory reform lacking the zeal for innovation that Brussels has demonstrated in other sectors and leaving many analysts unconvinced that the program would rid international finance of the unwanted risks.[63] Moreover, the EU's post-crisis record revealed it as a less reliable supporter (than before the crisis) of transnational standard-setting bodies and soft law.

In particular, for the years immediately following the crisis (2010–2014), we find EU internationalism in decline, and increasingly so over time.[64] It is true that some EU unilateralist proposals were never enacted. For instance, European Commission proposals for a financial transaction tax for the EU or a subset of members (an idea contemplated and rejected at the G20) were more bark than bite. And not every area of financial regulation fits the pattern. The EU positions on accounting standards were similar to before-crisis ones.

---

[61] For an example from 2004, see the written testimony (before US Congressional committee) of Alexander Schaub, the then-Director-General of DG Internal Markets (Alexander Schaub, "Testimony of Alexander Schaub, Director–General, DG Internal Market of the European Commission before the Committee on Financial Services, US House of Representatives May 13, 2004," The Committee on Financial Services, US House of Representatives, 2004). For an example from the post-crisis years, see the letter to US Federal Reserve Board Chairman Ben Bernanke by Michel Barnier, then-European Commissioner for the Internal Market and Services (Michel Barnier, "Letter to Ben Bernanke," April 18, 2013, www.federalreserve.gov/ SECRS/2013/April/20130422/R-1438/R-1438_041913_111076_515131431183_1.pdf.).

[62] Elliot Posner, "Is a European Approach to Financial Regulation Emerging from the Crisis?" in *Global Finance in Crisis: The Politics of International Regulatory Change*, eds. Eric Helleiner, Stefano Pagliari, and Hubert Zimmermann (London: Routledge, 2010), 108–120.

[63] For example, see Hans-Jürgen Bieling, "Shattered Expectations: The Defeat of European Ambitions of Global Financial Reform," *Journal of European Public Policy* 21, no. 3 (2014): 346–366.

[64] The study's ten cases were accounting, auditing, bank structure, capital reserves and liquidity, compensation, credit rating agencies, financial transaction tax, hedge funds, OTC derivatives and CCPs, and resolution frameworks. For the EU and the United States (which we included for methodological reasons), we scored each regulatory area before (2007) and after (2014) the crisis for two dimensions of internationalism (support of international finance [integrationism] and of transnational soft law and the standard-setting organizations that create it [transnationalism]).

However, overall, we identify a general pattern of diminishing and lackluster EU financial regulatory internationalism.

There are a number of examples. In the area of banking regulation, the post-crisis internal politics were such that new Brussels rules covering capital and liquidity requirements did not live up to the Basel III accords to which European governments agreed. In fact, BCBS classified parts of the EU rules as "materially non-compliant"[65] and thus contrary to post-crisis efforts to sustain globally integrated banking markets. Similarly, the EU had an uneven record of internationalism for derivatives regulation. The G20 agreed to comprehensive direct regulation of derivatives markets and participants.[66] New EU rules were generally in line with transnational standards,[67] yet the EU was slow to implement and contributed to a botched transatlantic coordination (despite early and earnest efforts to avoid such an outcome)[68] and thus to the fragmentation of markets.[69]

A final illustration comes from the new regime for the resolution of complex, cross-border banks (known as G-SIBs or Global Systemically Important Banks).[70] To avoid a repeat of the disorderly events surrounding the

---

[65] Bank for International Settlements, "Regulatory Consistency Assessment Programme (RCAP): Assessment of Basel III Regulations – European Union," December 2014, 4.

[66] The new regime (overseen by the FSB but involving BCBS, CGFS, CPSS and IOSCO, among other bodies) includes the use of central counterparties for standardized contracts, the trading of standardized derivatives on exchanges or (where appropriate) electronic trading platforms, the reporting of transactions to trade repositories, and the imposition of higher capital and minimum margin requirements for non-centrally cleared contracts. See Eric Helleiner, Stefano Pagliari, and Irene Spagna, "Introduction: Governing the World's Biggest Market," in Governing the World's Biggest Market: The Politics of Derivatives Regulation after the 2008 Crisis, eds. Eric Helleiner, Stefano Pagliari, and Irene Spagna (New York: Oxford University Press, 2018), 2–39.

[67] Lucia Quaglia, "Financial Regulation and Supervision in the European Union after the Crisis," Journal of Economic Policy Reform 16, no. 1 (March 2013): 17–30.

[68] Elliot Posner, "Financial Regulatory Cooperation: Coordination of Derivatives Markets," in Governing the World's Biggest Market: The Politics of Derivatives Regulation After the 2008 Crisis, eds. Eric Helleiner, Stefano Pagliari, and Irene Spagna (New York: Oxford University Press, 2018), 54; Mügge, "Securities and Derivatives Markets," 60–66; Stefano Pagliari and Matthew Gravelle, "Global Markets, National Toolkits: Extraterritorial Derivatives Rulemaking in Response to the Global Financial Crisis," in Governing the World's Biggest Market: The Politics of Derivatives Regulation After the 2008 Crisis, eds. Eric Helleiner, Stefano Pagliari, and Irene Spagna (New York: Oxford University Press, 2018), 119–155.

[69] Peter Knaack, "A Web without a Center: Fragmentation in the OTC Derivatives Trade Reporting System," in Governing the World's Biggest Market: The Politics of Derivatives Regulation After the 2008 Crisis, eds. Eric Helleiner, Stefano Pagliari, and Irene Spagna (New York: Oxford University Press, 2018), 330; Helleiner, Pagliari, and Spagna, "Introduction: Governing the World's Biggest Market."

[70] The FSB makes the designation: www.fsb.org/what-we-do/policy-development/systematically-important-financial-institutions-sifis/global-systemically-important-financial-institutions-g-sifis/.

troubles of Fortis, Dexia, the Icelandic banks, the Royal Bank of Scotland, and Lehman Brothers, financial authorities recognized the need for resolution rules as part of the toolbox of new regulatory tools – beyond capital reserve requirements, which had been their main pre-crisis instrument. Overseen by the Financial Stability Board (the new organization built out of the old Financial Stability Forum and created to coordinate and manage the standard-setting activities of the various transnational organizations), the G20 framework for governing the resolution of distressed banks seeks to limit contagion effects and reduce the need for public bailouts. Like the derivatives measures, the EU's resolution regime[71] dampens the international business of banks by increasing compliance costs. Even for staunch advocates of cross-border finance, slower internationalization might be worth the promised stability. Yet the EU's policies were tarnished by a lagged implementation (compared to Japan and the United States) of the FSB standards.[72]

Based on these and the other cases in our study, we conclude that at least in the domain of financial regulation and for the critical years surrounding the great financial crisis, the EU was not the reliable internationalist that some have portrayed. These findings send us on a search for explanations.

Some of the decline is not surprising, at least if your starting point is the academic research. Public salience, perhaps the most frequently invoked internal factor attributed to shaping regulatory reform, goes a long way to explain why the EU's post-crisis policies and approaches contributed to less financial globalism as well as market fragmentation along jurisdictional frontiers.[73] Public salience is the significance that the public assigns to a given issue. In democratic systems, according to the logic, the degree of public attention affects elections and the relative sway of politicians, regulators, and pressure groups; and in the final analysis, it shapes the type and timing of

---

[71] The EU resolution regime is part of what has become known as Banking Union (discussed later in the chapter) and has two main legal instruments. The first, the Bank Recovery and Resolution Directive (BRRD), harmonizes national resolution rules. See European Parliament and Council Directive 2014/59/EU, 2014 O.J. (L 173) 191. The BBRD has subsequently been amended. See https://ec.europa.eu/info/law/bank-recovery-and-resolution-directive-2014-59-eu_en. The second legal instrument creates the Single Resolution Mechanism (SRM), which establishes a resolution authority and fund for banks supervised by the ECB. See European Parliament and Council Regulation (EU) 806/2014, 2014 O.J. (L 225) 1.

[72] David Howarth and Lucia Quaglia, "Banking Union as Holy Grail: Rebuilding the Single Market in Financial Services, Stabilizing Europe's Banks and 'Completing' Economic and Monetary Union," *Journal of Common Market Studies* 51, no. S1 (2013): 103–123; David Howarth and Lucia Quaglia, "The Steep Road to European Banking Union: Constructing the Single Resolution Mechanism," *Journal of Common Market Studies* 52, no. S1 (2014): 125–140.

[73] Pagliari, "Public Salience and International Financial Regulation"; Culpepper, *Quiet Politics and Business Power.*

adopted regulation. Applying these ideas to financial regulation and specifically to the governance of OTC derivatives, credit rating agencies, and hedge funds, Pagliari argues that when the public is attuned, financial regulatory politics will include a wider range of participants than during periods when only a narrow group of technocrats and industry groups are paying attention and involved.[74] His 2013 investigation finds that elevated levels of public salience account for the post-crisis shift in Europe from industry and market self-regulation to direct public oversight.

Our findings are similar. Echoing themes about crisis-fueled populism in other chapters of this volume,[75] high levels of public salience match up fairly well with the EU's diminished support for global finance. This evidence most likely reflects the general anger in Europe over the reluctance on the part of EU policymakers to deal with the risks to financial system stability. The result, as predicted by the public salience argument, was regulatory reform. Proponents of more stringent regulation were able to influence political processes typically dominated by better organized and concentrated financial lobbies, and the EU put in place regulation that was more rigorous. And despite committing to coordinated "implementation" of G20 principles and transnational standards, the unpredictability, complexity, and idiosyncrasies of the EU's political processes produced financial rules less conducive to cross-border finance and more difficult to coordinate with the United States and other jurisdictions. It is noteworthy that our study finds that the financial reforms in the United States (which also experienced similarly high levels of public salience) followed more or less the same pattern.

With respect to transnational standard-setting bodies and soft law, the EU's dip in support was more pronounced than in the case of the United States. From multiple perspectives, this part of the decline does come as a surprise. As noted, EU specialists typically presume that the EU is strongly multilateralist and an ardent defender of international law. Moreover, the EU's turn-of-the-millennium financial regulatory project was deeply intertwined with transnational standards, and Brussels officials as well as Member State leaders (with Nicolas Sarkozy and Gordon Brown in the lead) were proponents and architects of the G20 reform agenda that came together at the time of the crisis; finance watchers had every early sign to expect strong United States and EU coordination in implementing it.[76] Why then did the EU's relations with transnational standard setters sour from 2010–2014, the years under study? The

---

[74] Pagliari, "Public Salience and International Financial Regulation."

[75] See, in particular, Chapter 1; Chapter 6; Chapter 7; Chapter 8.

[76] Mügge, "Introduction," 1–16.

answers emanate from the two parts of the EU–transnational relationship: internal EU politics and the international institutional context. Both underwent change, to which I turn in the next sections.

VII THE BREAKDOWN OF THE EU FINANCIAL REGULATORY BARGAIN

Starting with internal politics, and specifically the millennial financial bargain, new fissures among Member States contributed to diminished support for transnational processes and standards. The politics of crisis were different inside the United Kingdom than in Eurozone member countries, manifesting in less compatible positions over institutional arrangements and legislative content and putting pressure on the four core pillars of the financial regulatory bargain: a single EU rulebook, informal agreements to adopt rules only when London is on board and to harmonize to UK-influenced soft law, national supervision rather than supranational schemes, and the prohibition against the mutualization of bank bailouts. All of these showed signs of erosion.

Different priorities in London, Berlin, and Paris between 2010 and 2014 undermined the goal of a single EU rulebook and unified governance arrangements. In response to the crisis, three new European Supervisory Authorities (ESAs) began operating in 2011 within the new European System of Financial Supervision (ESFS) – the European Banking Authority (EBA), the European Securities and Markets Authority (ESMA), and the European Insurance and Occupational Pensions Authority (EIOPA).[77] The ESAs replaced the Lamfalussy committees discussed earlier, and they exercised greater, albeit modest and partial, financial decision-making powers. In the process of establishing the ESAs, the United Kingdom successfully watered down their powers, and thus had achieved victory in preserving UK influence over their regulatory output. When, two years later, the EU established a Banking Union,[78] this bargain was revisited and ultimately weakened.

---

[77] The new ESFS also includes the European Systemic Risk Board.

[78] Banking Union – the EU initiative to shore up its banking system – was created in the midst of the Eurozone crisis and has three parts: the Single Supervisory Mechanism or SSM (which transferred supervisory authorities over large banks to the ECB), the Single Resolution Mechanism (SRM), and the Harmonized Deposit Guarantee Scheme (DGS). Nicola Véron, "Europe's Radical Banking Union," Bruegel, May 2015, http://bruegel.org/wp-content/uploads/imported/publications/essay_NV_CMU.pdf.

Among other things, Banking Union gave significant supervisory authority over national banks to the ECB.[79] Although the United Kingdom opted out of Banking Union, it was supportive of the proposals because the United Kingdom had a palpable interest in Eurozone stabilization and was in a position to negotiate and win side deals.[80] However, giving the ECB supervisory powers complicated the deal struck in establishing the ESAs and UK officials again found themselves having to bargain to maintain influence in a future European Banking Authority (EBA) where Eurozone representatives would presumably have unified positions. In the end, British negotiators made a new voting scheme (favoring non-Eurozone Member States) the cost of UK support for the ECB's new powers. London also won an initiative to bolster EU capital markets (that is, Capital Markets Union).[81]

Although these short-term complications were resolved with "side payments," the Banking Union's long-term ramifications remained. Vesting new powers in the ECB contravened the pillar of the EU bargain that prohibited the shifting of supervisory authority to the EU level. The main questions were how much the move would alter power dynamics in EU financial policymaking and to what extent it might prod policy entrepreneurs to exploit the new institutional configuration to alter the rules governing the United Kingdom's financial services industries. Thus, unlike in other domains covered in this volume where the politics of crisis empowered member governments, in finance a supranational institution, the ECB, emerged as the clear winner, a remarkable feat given that governments had been dead-set against such an outcome only a decade earlier.

Lastly, the Eurozone since 2010 has adopted fiscal risk-sharing, even if it does not amount to fiscal federalism.[82] The United Kingdom did not join the European Stability Mechanism (ESM) for country bailouts and the Single Resolution Fund (SRF) for bank bailouts or other related agreements (i.e. Fiscal Compact).[83] And in the one seemingly contrary example, the predecessor to the ESM known as the European Financial Stabilisation Mechanism (later politicized by the pro-Brexit camp as an example of how the sinking EMU would bring Britain down with it), the United Kingdom was only

---

[79] For a discussion of Banking Union, see Antonio Estella, *Legal Foundations of EU Economic Governance* (Cambridge: Cambridge University Press, 2018), 107–133.

[80] Howarth and Quaglia, "Brexit and the Single European Financial Market," 151–153.

[81] Howarth and Quaglia, "Brexit and the Single European Financial Market," 152–153.

[82] For a discussion of the development of EU fiscal policies, see Chapter 2 and Chapter 4.

[83] Ledina Gocaj and Sophie Meunier, "Time Will Tell: The EFSF, the ESM, and the Euro Crisis," *Journal of European Integration* 35, no. 3 (2013): 239–253.

modestly liable for extended funds.[84] Moreover, the ECB's programs, including the 2014 implementation of quantitative easing, did not directly affect the United Kingdom.

Just as the intact bargain encouraged EU support of transnational standards, its demise made it much more challenging. Because of Britain's role as an established leader in the development of transnational standards, they have typically been compatible with UK regulation. Thus, EU financial regulatory agreements that accommodated UK preferences simultaneously yielded close affinities between the EU and international standards, making Brussels a good internationalist. When London and the Continent are divided, by contrast, chances are greater that EU approaches will conflict with transnational standards. The scenario is all the more likely if British participants in standard-setting organizations make use of their leadership roles to win battles there that they lost in Brussels. In this way, the post-crisis unraveling of the internal bargain helps to account for the EU's more difficult relationship with transnational financial law.

VIII THE INTERNATIONAL INSTITUTIONAL CONTEXT

As an explanation, however, the logic of the bargain's breakdown is necessarily incomplete. There are two sides of the complicated relationship between the EU and transnational financial standards, and internal factors represent only one of them. This is why Véron and I also consider the international institutional context, especially change in European representation in global financial bodies.

As part of the post-crisis G20 reforms, European representation, as a proportion, tended to decrease across the array of standard setters. Asia, not Europe, was the G20's main target in enhancing the legitimacy of these organizations by expanding membership. Yet one of the effects was a reduction in the European ratio of representatives. We thus examined the possibility that the post-2008 pattern of declining EU support for transnational law was associated with the decreased proportions of European representation. By this logic, the larger the ratio of European representatives (in terms of GDP and population) in a given rulemaking body, the greater the probability that transnational soft law generated by that body would overlap with EU preferences. Similarly, the larger pre-crisis ratios might have contributed to perceptions of legitimacy (in that European policy stakeholders would consider transnational soft law to be

---

[84] Howarth and Quaglia, "Brexit and the Single European Financial Market," 155–156.

produced via fair procedures and its substance to be sound),[85] which, in turn, might also be expected to bolster EU support of soft law. The post-crisis drop in EU support, by this line of reasoning, would reflect reduced European representation and, by extension, increased preference gaps and reservations about the legitimacy of transnational standards.

At least some evidence points in this direction. The EU presence on the Basel Committee on Banking Supervision, for example, fell from 62 percent in 2007 to 36 percent in 2014,[86] helping to account for the preference gap and subsequent pushback in the EU implementation processes of standards for bank capital reserves and liquidity requirements. A similar correspondence exists between EU representation in the Committee on Payments and Market Infrastructures (responsible for transnational standards for governing central counterparties)[87] and the checkered record of EU implementation of new soft law concerning derivatives and central counterparties. Numbers are obviously not everything. The causal processes are complex and involve multiple factors, and the match between argument and evidence is uneven. As a whole, however, the lower ratio of EU representatives appears likely to have made it more challenging for Brussels to accept transnational standards and to have exacerbated the effects of the new internal EU divisions. The UK–Continental fissures made it harder for the EU to have a single position, further undermining European influence, EU-transnational preference alignment, and perceptions of legitimacy.

Strong evidence also gives credence to a "who represents" variant of this argument. Here, the logic highlights the characteristics of different standard-setting forums[88] and in particular whether EU political institutions, national authorities from Member States, or a combination are the representatives.[89] Again, we emphasize the EU-transnational preference distance, but the key variable is who the representatives are, instead of the ratio. The main proposition is that when EU-level institutions are the representatives, Brussels' backing of transnational soft law is more likely, and the main exception is

---

[85] Fritz Scharpf, *Governing in Europe: Effective and Democratic?* (Oxford: Oxford University Press, 1999).

[86] See figure 7 in Posner and Véron, "Is the EU a Financial Internationalist?"

[87] As part of the G20 reform program, the EU committed itself to requiring that standardized over-the-counter derivatives be cleared through a central body (called a central counterparty or CCP) to reduce exposure to counterparty risk (that is, the possibility that the counterpart in a transaction will not live up to the contractual obligations).

[88] Chris Brummer, *Soft Law and the Global Financial System: Rule Making in the 21st Century* (New York: Cambridge University Press, 2012), chapter 2.

[89] Mügge, "The European Presence in Global Financial Governance"; da Conceição-Heldt and Meunier, "Speaking with a Single Voice," 971–975.

that the argument seems to be contingent on the degree of internal preference alignment among member governments: The "who represents" effect tends not to matter when intra-EU levels of preference overlap are high. Under these circumstances, regardless of who sits at the table, Europeans are able to forge common positions, maximize their influence and minimize gaps between EU policies and transnational soft law.[90] By contrast, when intra-EU preference alignment is lacking, who represents the EU can be more significant, especially so when national authorities sit at the table. The pattern appears to hold even when EU political institutions are represented alongside national authorities (as is the case in the FSB, IOSCO, and the Basel Committee, though only since 2014). In a common scenario, UK authorities seek to win in transnational bodies what they cannot achieve in EU battles. The international stature of London's representatives thus strengthens the "who represents" effect.

The evidence is as follows: After the 2009 introduction of the G20 financial regulatory agenda, national representatives did well when the center of gravity moved from the Transatlantic Financial Market Regulatory Dialogue (which as mentioned featured the European Commission as the main interlocutor with the United States), to the newly created Financial Stability Board (FSB), mostly comprising national authorities. Within the post-crisis international financial architecture, the FSB serves as a central forum for discussing all areas of financial regulation. EU institutions are involved, yet national central bankers, supervisors, and treasury officials are the primary participants. (The main exception to the centrality of national actors is the ECB, which since 2014 has served as the supervisor of the Eurozone's largest banks and is represented on the FSB.) In the years since the FSB's creation, its ascendance sometimes fueled EU conflicts, adding to the difficulty of adopting policies in support of transnational agreements. According to European and US sources, the forum helps the United Kingdom forge alliances with the United States and other countries, which increases the gap between transnational agreements and EU positions. As UK preferences tended to diverge further from the EU mean, the country's sway in transnational organizations arguably strengthened.[91] Similar patterns occurred vis-à-vis the Basel Committee,

---

[90] This scenario is related to what Quaglia and others mean by levels of regulatory capacities and powers in this sector. See Quaglia, *The European Union and Global Financial Regulation*; Bach and Newman, "The European Regulatory State and Global Public Policy"; Posner, "Making Rules for Global Finance"; Abraham L. Newman and Elliot Posner, "International Interdependence and Regulatory Power: Authority, Mobility, and Markets," *European Journal of International Relations* 17, no. 4 (March 2011): 589–610.

[91] In 2013, the Chair of the FSB, Mark Carney, became the Governor of the Bank of England.

whose participants (both European and US) report an absence of European coordination.

IX BREXIT AND THE FUTURE OF EU FINANCIAL REGULATION

To summarize, the Union's turn-of-the-millennium bargain, defined by UK inclusion, is central to understanding the evolution of EU financial regulation and its enmeshment in the global financial architecture. The bargain largely accounts for the pre-crisis rule harmonization toward increasingly industry-friendly standards (rather than representing a home-grown European approach), the EU's ascendance to global rulemaker and its record of internationalism. The post-crisis unraveling of the bargain, rooted largely in UK–Eurozone divisions, moreover, helps explain why the EU became sensitive to G20-led change in the memberships of transnational standard setters and less effective in, and supportive of, such organizations.

These trends are surely a disappointment for those who put faith in the EU's consistent pre-crisis support for international law and technocratically oriented standard-setting bodies, or hoped Brussels might have introduced innovative governance arrangements and a financial system more consistent with societal values as it had attempted to do in other regulatory areas. After the crisis, too, there is cause for discouragement. While new policies that slow the internationalization of finance may be part of a desirable balance between systemic safeguards and industry risk-taking, the EU has shown lackluster support for some of the most robust, stability-inducing transnational soft law, notably banking regulation standards. And again, Brussels failed to offer a viable alternative.

Is there cause for equal pessimism in looking forward to the prospects for financial regulation in an EU without the United Kingdom? Here, I return to the questions posed at the beginning of the chapter about the future content of EU regulation and its relationship to transnational soft law, Brussels' potential stature as a global rulemaker, and the possibility that regulation inside and outside Europe might be better at preventing industry risk-taking from negatively affecting financial systems and economies. Similar to the analysis of the previous sections, answers will likely be contingent on the specifics of the nexus between the United Kingdom and a presumed EU of twenty-seven and must therefore remain provisional: The date for the United Kingdom's departure has come and gone, and yet the terms of EU market access for London-licensed firms have yet to be determined. Even so, some of the contours of plausible scenarios are within view.

Assuming Brexit means Brexit and the United Kingdom will thus no longer have a say in devising EU financial regulation, the extent to which equivalency-in-exchange-for-access requirements by Brussels puts pressure on London to align its rules would matter a great deal. Yet alignment or not, the EU's ability (and willingness) to innovate and lead globally after Brexit is not likely to be much better than it has been since the breakdown of the turn-of-the-millennium bargain. On the one hand, a scenario of close alignment – still a possibility at the time of writing – might seem at first a potential boon for the EU. Close alignment between the United Kingdom and the EU across multiple subsectors might free the EU to devise stiffer, more inventive rules while limiting the United Kingdom's ability to siphon financial activity with laxer regulation. By this scenario, Brexit negotiators would avoid the prospect of a divergent, industry-friendly UK regime that constrains the EU's ability to maintain relatively more stringent regulation and that might even invite a regulatory race to the bottom.

On the other hand, however aligned the UK rules, Brussels would still likely lose global influence relative to Washington's as well as relative autonomy to choose its own path. In other words, any sense of relief by the exit of the leading obstructionist could well be short-lived. Even if the remaining twenty-seven were to see eye-to-eye across more areas of financial regulatory policy (and benefit from Brexit in projected ways, such as the migration of City jobs, operations and markets to Paris, Frankfurt, Dublin, Luxembourg, and Amsterdam), Brussels rules and decisions would affect a smaller portion of US financial firm revenues than before Brexit and thereby diminish its fundamental bargaining leverage vis-à-vis the United States. Moreover, there is a compelling logic for why Brussels' taking an independent regulatory approach (from the United States) could backfire and further diminish EU international bargaining leverage. The more the EU were to veer from the United States (toward more stringent regulation, for instance), the less likely the United Kingdom would be willing to align its regulatory approach with the EU and the more likely London would ally with Washington at the transnational level, further reducing the potential for EU global leadership. From the perspective that the EU might emerge as the new regulatory pace setter, the prospects are thus not good. It is easy to envision Brussels needing to be attentive to Washington but hard to imagine the reverse.

6

The Euro Crisis and the Transformation of the European Political System

RENAUD DEHOUSSE

Ten years after the outbreak of the euro crisis, i.e. the economic and financial turmoil that followed the bankruptcy of Lehman Brothers, it appears clear that this series of events has had a lasting impact on European policy-making, and possibly on European politics. According to a long-held view of EU policy-making, the latter is characterised by the absence of politicisation. European policies are generally seen as shaped primarily by the interaction of national and European bureaucracies with stakeholders of various kinds.[1]

European elections are described as 'second-order elections' that unfold according to the template established by the first direct election of members of the European Parliament in 1979: candidates are selected by national parties and national issues dominate both the campaign and the vote.[2] The lack of a strong European party system and the almost complete absence of 'parties at the European level' – to use the language of the Treaty on the Functioning of the European Union – have also been emphasised.[3] The vast literature on the catchall concept of Europeanisation has focused on Europe's influence over domestic policies, rather than over national political systems. In his 2000 study of the impact of European integration on national party systems, Peter Mair identified a gap between the actual responsibilities of the European Union and its Member States, and the themes that are at the heart of electoral

---

[1] Claudio Radaelli, *Technocracy in the European Union* (London: Longman, 1999).

[2] Karlheinz Reif and Hermann Schmitt, "Nine Second-Order National Elections: A Conceptual Framework for the Analysis of European Election Results," *European Journal of Political Research* 8, no. 1 (1980): 3–44.

[3] Luciano Bardi et al., "How to Create a Transnational Party System," European Parliament, 2010, http://cadmus.eui.eu/bitstream/handle/1814/14744/StudyTransnationalPartySystem.pdf?sequence=1&isAllowed=y; Thomas Poguntke et al., "The Europeanisation of National Party Organisations: A Conceptual Analysis," *European Journal of Political Research* 46, no. 6 (2007): 747–771.

competition at each of these levels. Major decisions on the direction and scope of the integration process, he argued, continued to be central in European elections even though the European Parliament, despite its repeated requests, had little influence over these issues. Conversely, national elections continued to be dominated by confrontations on 'national' policy issues even though these were increasingly shaped by choices made at the European level. As a result, wrote Mair, voter choices only had a limited impact on important decisions made at both levels.

Since this diagnosis was made, however, a number of works have suggested that domestic politics are increasingly influenced by developments at the European level. This evolution is said to affect both the behaviour of parties and that of voters. As regards the former, expert surveys and manifesto data have shown that European issues have become more salient for political parties across the Union.[4] In some instances, dissent was so strong that it led to the emergence of new political parties, such as *Front de gauche* in France or ANEL in Greece.[5] With regard to electoral behaviour, a number of scholars suggest we might be shifting to a new era, as contestation over European issues has appeared at the national level. Van der Eijk and Franklin have evoked the image of the 'sleeping giant': whereas voters increasingly have clearer attitudes towards the EU, political parties tend to downplay European issues since the latter are fairly divisive for their traditional base.[6] However, they argue, the issue is now 'ripe for politicisation': 'it is only a matter of time before policy entrepreneurs in some countries seize the opportunity ... to differentiate themselves from other parties in EU terms.'[7] Writing a few years later, Hooghe and Marks stress that European integration is increasingly becoming the focus of high-profile political debate at the domestic level.[8] The elites have had to make room for European integration as a 'field of strategic interaction among

---

[4] Marco R. Steenbergen and David J. Scott, "Contesting Europe? The Salience of European Integration as a Party Issue," in *European Integration and Political Conflict*, eds. Gary Marks and Marco R. Steenbergen (Cambridge: Cambridge University Press, 2004), 165–192.

[5] *Front de gauche* in France was created following the 2005 referendum on the Constitutional Treaty and the Independent Greeks (ANEL) was formed in reaction to the first set of austerity measures contained in the bailout memorandum imposed by the EU in 2010–2011.

[6] Cees Van Der Eijk and Mark N. Franklin, "Potential for Contestation on European Matters at National Elections in Europe," in *European Integration and Political Conflict*, eds. Gary Marks and Marco R. Steenbergen (Cambridge: Cambridge University Press, 2004), 32–50.

[7] Van Der Eijk and Franklin, "Potential for Contestation on European Matters at National Elections in Europe," 47.

[8] Liesbet Hooghe and Gary Marks, "A Postfunctionalist Theory of European Integration: From Permissive Consensus to Constraining Dissensus," *British Journal of Political Science* 39, no. 1 (2009): 1–23.

party elites in their contest for political power."[9] As a result, they argue, the future of Europe is more likely to be shaped by political conflict than by the functionalist, efficiency-driven pressures that played a crucial role in the first decades of the integration process. A number of studies have documented the development of contestation over European issues in some countries at the time of national elections, stressing *inter alia* that the salience of EU-related issues played a key role in cross-national variations.[10]

Although these analyses predate the economic and financial crisis triggered by the bankruptcy of Lehman Brothers in 2008, there are good reasons to believe that this crisis has acted as a catalyst for further politicization. It has led to a massive transfer of authority to the European level in an area, macroeconomic policy, which has enormous re-distributive implications and has a radiating influence over a large range of public policies. This, in turn, has dramatically enhanced the domestic salience of EU membership because of the central role that European decisions have played in successive rescue packages and in the development of fiscal austerity. The purpose of this chapter is to review the manifold influences of the euro crisis over EU policy-making. I will argue that the crisis has, in several respects, aggravated the well-known legitimacy problem of the European Union by triggering an attempt at further depoliticising major EU policies, despite the overt opposition of European leaders to further transfers of authority to the EU (Section I). This has fed hostility to European integration, notably in domestic elections (Section II). In parallel, however, one has witnessed an attempt at reinforcing the accountability of European institutions with the so-called *Spitzenkandidaten* system, discussed in Section III. While the result of these contrasting forces remains to be seen, it has to date aggravated the European democracy conundrum: the Union and its policies are, yes, more present in domestic political debates, but the normative principles underlying their legitimacy remain both unclear and disputed.

---

[9] Hooghe and Marks, "A Postfunctionalist Theory of European Integration," 9.

[10] Matthew J. Gabel, "European Integration, Voters, and National Politics," *West European Politics* 23, no. 4 (2000): 52–72; Erik R. Tillman, "The European Union at the Ballot Box? European Integration and Voting Behavior in the New Member States," *Comparative Political Studies* 37, no. 5 (2004): 590–610; Catherine E. De Vries, "Sleeping Giant: Fact or Fairytale? How European Integration Affects Vote Choice in National Elections," *European Union Politics* 8, no. 3 (2007): 363–385; Catherine E. De Vries, "EU Issue Voting: Asset or Liability? How European Integration Affects Parties' Electoral Fortunes," *European Union Politics* 11, no. 1 (2010): 89–117.

I THE ATTEMPT AT DEPOLITICISING MACROECONOMIC POLICY

The European response to the euro crisis, slow and piecemeal as it may have been,[11] has nonetheless led to a substantial consolidation of European economic governance.[12] A first part of the reform was to set up backstop devices aiming to assist countries threatened by default, culminating in the creation of the European Stability Mechanism in 2012. From the very beginning, however, in exchange for their solidarity 'creditor countries' demanded a significant tightening of the surveillance system to prevent the resurgence of similar problems in the future. In slightly over a year, this led to the adoption of two important legislative packages (the 'Six Pack' and the 'Two Pack'), and a new treaty – the 'Fiscal Compact' imposed by Chancellor Merkel. While this is not the place for a systematic analysis of these reforms,[13] it is important to note that they significantly strengthened the Commission's hand in the surveillance of Member States' fiscal policy.

First, the scope of the Commission's control powers was expanded far beyond public finances through the establishment of the macroeconomic surveillance procedure (the excessive macroeconomic imbalance procedure [MIP]) based on a scoreboard of indicators covering the whole of macroeconomic policy. In the same vein, the newly created 'European Semester' increased the interactions between the national authorities and the Commission before draft budgets are submitted.[14] Finally, to ensure the effectiveness of the new regulatory system, there was a general shift 'from soft law measures without binding consequences toward a binding framework.'[15] The authority of the Commission was considerably enhanced to avoid a repetition of the 2004 episode, in which its recommendation of sanctions against France and Germany for excessive deficits was reversed by the Economic and Financial Affairs (ECOFIN) Council. Under the new framework, if the Commission

---

[11] Peter A. Hall, "The Economics and Politics of the Euro Crisis," *German Politics* 21, no. 4 (2012): 355–371.

[12] For a legal and constitutional analysis of these developments, see Chapter 2; for a political science analysis from the perspective of integration theory, see Chapter 4.

[13] Michael Bauer and Stefan Becker, "The Unexpected Winner of the Crisis: The European Commission's Strengthened Role in Economic Governance," *Journal of European Integration* 36, no. 3 (2014): 213–229; Renaud Dehousse, "Le 'pacte budgétaire': incertitudes juridiques et ambiguïté politique," *Les brefs de Notre Europe*, no. 33 (2012): 1–4; Jean-Paul Keppenne, "Institutional Report," in *The Economic and Monetary Union: Constitutional and Institutional Aspects of the Economic Governance within the EU*, eds. Ulla Neegaard, Catherine Jacqueson, and Jens Hartig Danielsen (Copenhagen: DJØF Publishing, 2014), 179–257.

[14] For a critique of the European Semester, see Chapter 3.

[15] Keppenne, "Institutional Report," 211.

deems the rules of the Stability and Growth Pact (SGP) to be violated, its 'recommendations' become binding unless the Council rejects them through a qualified majority decision within ten days. This 'reverse qualified majority' system, introduced by the Six Pack and consolidated by the Fiscal Compact,[16] heavily tilts the balance of power in favour of the Commission, whose choices are now very difficult to reverse.[17]

In discussions over SGP reform, the introduction of the 'reverse qualified majority' was presented as a shift towards 'quasi-automatic' sanctions.[18] However, this description obscures the fact that the enforcement mechanism involves a fair degree of discretion. This is because budget deficit targets are defined no longer in nominal, but in structural terms, i.e. they are to take into consideration business cycle swings and filter out the effects of one-off and temporary measures.[19] Similarly, in the MIP, a negative result does not lead to the automatic conclusion that there is an imbalance, since from an economic standpoint it is difficult to determine the exact threshold at which a macroeconomic imbalance might become harmful. In other words, the attempt to refine the rules and render them less mechanical has enhanced the discretion enjoyed by the Commission.

The breadth of the Commission's margin for manoeuvre is by its very nature indeterminate.[20] Remarkably, the Commission has departed from the previous practice, in which codes of conduct on the implementation of the SGP were endorsed by the ECOFIN Council: in January 2015, the Commission issued, without Council involvement, a communication detailing how it would apply the flexibility provisions of the SGP to encourage growth-friendly

---

[16] See European Parliament and Council Regulation (EU) 1173/2011, On the Effective Enforcement of Budgetary Surveillance in the Euro Area, 2011 O.J. (L 306) 1, arts. 4(2), 5(2) and 6(2), and European Parliament and Council Regulation (EU) 1174/2011, On Enforcement Measures to Correct Excessive Macroeconomic Imbalances in the Euro Area, 2011 O.J. (L 306) 8, art. 3(3) [Six Pack]; see also European Parliament and Council Regulation (EU) 1303/2013, Laying Down Common Provisions on the European Regional Development Fund, the European Social Fund, the Cohesion Fund, 2013 O.J. (L 347) 320, art. 23(10).

[17] Wim van Aken and Lionel Artige, "A Comparative Analysis of Reverse Majority Voting: The WTO's Dispute Settlement Mechanism, the EU Anti-dumping Policy and the Reinforced SGP and Fiscal Compact," EUSA Thirteenth Biennial Conference, Baltimore, 2013.

[18] This view was expressed by the German government, the Commission and the ECB. See, e.g., Olli Rehn, Why EU Policy Co-ordination has Failed, and How to Fix It, The Ludwig Ehrard Lecture, 26 October 2010, http://europa.eu/rapid/press-release_SPEECH-10-590_en.htm?locale=en.

[19] Treaty on Stability, Coordination and Governance (TSCG), Article 3(3) [Fiscal Compact].

[20] Interview with Mario Buti, Director General, DG ECOFIN, May 2015.

fiscal consolidation.[21] Some of the decisions taken by the Juncker Commission in this area clearly flew in the face of Northern European 'creditor' countries' preferences. In early 2015, for instance, it proposed that France, which had failed to meet its deficit target, be granted a two-year extension of the deadline to correct its excessive deficit and merely insisted that France carry out comprehensive and ambitious structural reforms.[22] This soft policy line earned the Commission a scathing rebuke from Bundesbank President Jens Weidmann:

> As a lesson of the crisis the rules were stiffened somewhat. But at the same time, the Commission was granted more leeway in interpreting the rules. So far, the Commission has made ample use of this additional leeway, thereby thwarting the original intention of the rule overhaul.[23]

Developments in the field of banking regulation have followed a similar path.[24] At the time of the Maastricht Treaty, Germany and France had systematically opposed any role for the new central bank in supervising banks, which remained in the hands of national authorities, because the right to control their own market was deemed to be of central importance.[25] The following two decades, however, saw the cross-border integration of the banking sector and the emergence of a number of large banking groups operating in several countries. As is known, the European banking sector was subsequently hit by a series of crises beginning in 2008: the credit crunch following the bankruptcy of Lehman Brothers; the turmoil deriving from banks' exposure to the sovereign debt of countries like Greece; the real estate bubbles in Ireland and Spain – all of which contributed to undermining public confidence in European banks. Thus it was recognized that a nationally based supervisory model was inadequate to oversee an integrated financial market in which capital could move freely and the idea of centralized bank supervision gained traction. In a first step, new regulatory authorities were established following recommendations from a high-level group of financial

---

[21] Communication from the Commission, *Making the Best Use of the Flexibility within the Existing Rules of the Stability and Growth Pact*, COM (2015) 12 final (13 January 2015).

[22] *Commission Recommendation for a Council Recommendation with a View to Bringing an End to the Excessive Government Deficit in France*, COM (2015) 115 final (27 February 2015).

[23] At the Crossroad: The Euro-Area between Sovereignty and Solidarity, Speech delivered at Sciences Po, Paris, 12 November 2015, www.bundesbank.de/Redaktion/EN/Reden/2015/2015_11_12_weidmann.html.

[24] For a discussion of EU banking regulation highlighting the United Kingdom's role and the international dimension, see Chapter 5.

[25] Mourlon-Druol, "Don't Blame the Euro: Historical Reflections on the Roots of the Eurozone Crisis," *West European Politics* 37, no. 6 (2014): 1282–1296.

experts chaired by a former *Banque de France* governor.[26] However, due to opposition from countries with large financial centres, the new structures were granted only limited competences, and their decisions were subject to the control of national authorities through voting and appeals procedures.[27] When in the spring of 2012, Spain and Italy pushed heavily for a rescue package to rescue their ailing banks, 'creditor' countries insisted that the supervision of European banks be removed from the hands of national authorities and entrusted to a strong European regulator, and that EU regulation be tightened. Given the urgent character of the crisis, the European Central Bank (ECB) appeared as a more reliable alternative than the newly created authorities.[28]

Once the decision was made, it took only a few months to agree on the blueprint for a Single Supervisory Mechanism (SSM). The ECB has now become the sole decision-maker for granting or revoking banking licenses in the Eurozone; it has had to recruit around 1,000 officials for its supervisory arm and now employs a fifth of all banking supervisory staff in the Eurozone.[29] Moreover, the move towards a banking union had broader political ramifications: not only did it entail a degree of fiscal union (through the prospect of cross-border liabilities for failing banks and transfers of public funds) but it was also perceived by many actors as 'a vote of confidence ... from the euro area's political leaders,'[30] which enabled Mario Draghi to announce a few weeks later that the ECB would do 'whatever it takes' to save the euro.

This episode, together with the bolstering of the Commission's surveillance powers over macroeconomic policy, illustrates the remarkable character of the developments that have unfolded over the course of the euro crisis. In both cases, despite Member States' traditional sovereignty concerns, supranational institutions have seen their powers significantly increased in areas of strategic importance. Equally remarkably, the final result appears to owe much to the agency of the most directly concerned institutions, namely the Commission and the European Central Bank, which played a major role in the design of

---

[26] De Larosière Group, "The High Level Group on Financial Supervision in the EU," 25 February 2009, http://ec.europa.eu/economy_finance/publications/pages/publication14527_en.pdf.

[27] Alexandre Hennessy, "Redesigning Financial Supervision in the European Union (2009–13)," *Journal of European Public Policy* 21, no. 2 (2014): 151–168; Lucia Quaglia, "Financial Regulation and Supervision in the European Union after the Crisis," *Journal of Economic Policy Reform* 16, no. 1 (2013): 17–30.

[28] Renaud Dehousse, "Why Has EU Macroeconomic Governance Become More Supranational?," *Journal of European Integration* 38, no. 5 (2016): 617-31.

[29] Nicolas Véron, *Europe's Radical Banking Union* (Brussels: Bruegel, 2015).

[30] Véron, *Europe's Radical Banking Union*, 18.

key innovations of the period and advocated for reform. Both the process and the output are difficult to reconcile with the 'new intergovernmentalism' literature that has developed in the wake of the crisis, for which the crisis confirmed the pre-eminence acquired by the European Council in the post-Maastricht era.[31]

Be that as it may, in both cases transfers of authority to the European level were a response to the perceived weakness of earlier enforcement mechanisms in which national authorities were supposed to apply the rules to themselves, and therefore had incentives for collusion and horse-trading.[32] North-South mistrust had reached such high levels that creditor countries insisted on the 'depoliticisation' of enforcement mechanisms. And, as stressed by former President of the European Council Herman van Rompuy, 'in the EU, there is only one way to depoliticise a process: it is to "communitarise" it.'[33] By so doing, however, the democratic deficit has been aggravated. Innovations such as the European Semester and the creation of fiscal policy councils in the constitutional system of the Member States, imposed by the Fiscal Compact, were deliberately conceived to curtail the autonomy enjoyed by national authorities in the handling of their fiscal policy. The hope of creditor countries was clearly that the more detailed character of the revised and extended SGP would likewise constrain EU institutions. Elections could no longer reverse the stream: as illustrated by Greece's failed attempt to reject austerity in 2015, the alternative was between staying within the Eurozone and complying with its rules or leaving it altogether.

To make things worse, these fundamental changes were adopted against a background of fading support for European integration in the general public. Tellingly, national leaders' reactions at the beginning of the crisis downplayed the part to be played by EU institutions. French President Nicolas Sarkozy was quite blunt:

> The crisis has prompted the heads of state and government to assume greater responsibilities because at the end of the day, they alone have the democratic legitimacy to make decisions. European integration will be intergovernmental because Europe will have to make strategic, political choices.[34]

---

[31] Christopher Bickerton, Dermot Hodson, and Uwe Puetter, *The New Intergovernmentalism* (Oxford: Oxford University Press, 2015).

[32] Marco Buti, Sylvester Eijffinger, and Daniele Franco, "Revisiting the Stability and Growth Pact: Grand Design or Internal Adjustment," ECPR Discussion Paper, No. 180, 2003.

[33] Interview with Herman Van Rompuy, April 2015.

[34] Nicolas Sarkozy, Speech delivered in Toulon on 1 November 2011 [Author's translation].

In softer language, Chancellor Merkel heralded the emergence of a new 'Union Method,' in which intergovernmental actors were to play a larger role than before. However, the dramatic character of the crisis, which called into question the very existence of the common currency, forced national leaders to accept as necessary decisions which did not respond to their deep preferences,[35] through a process which some of them subsequently denounced as a plot orchestrated by European technocrats.[36]

II THE EUROPEANISATION OF DOMESTIC POLITICS

As the European Union underwent arguably the most severe crisis of its history, with potentially radical consequences for its member countries, EU membership came to feature more prominently in domestic political debates. This was in line with earlier studies, which had highlighted similar phenomena in previous years. Looking at votes in Austria, Sweden, and Finland at the time of their accession to the EU, for instance, Tillman had already found that the membership issue garnered much attention on these occasions, and that voters' assessment of political parties' stance on this issue had an impact on their voting choice.[37] Similarly, in a comparison of elections in the 1992–2002 period, De Vries determined that European integration matters had a strong impact in several countries.[38]

Returning to the euro crisis, as is known, the financial market turmoil that followed the discovery of a huge deficit in Greece in 2009 led to the adoption of financial aid packages for several countries that could no longer finance themselves on the market. In addition, the countries that benefitted from such programmes were forced to accept strict austerity programmes in order to restore their public finances. In such a context, it is hardly surprising that partisan conflict developed over European issues.

The Europeanisation of domestic politics has been most acute in the country most affected by the crisis, i.e. Greece. Following a massive assistance package put together by the IMF and the EU in April 2010 – the largest in the history of all international bailouts – the government led by George Papandreou had to commit to a programme of stringent austerity measures coupled with a number of controversial reforms, thereby triggering a wave of

---

[35] Frank Schimmelfennig, "European Integration in the Euro Crisis: The Limits of Postfunctionalism," *Journal of European Integration* 36, no. 3 (2014): 321–337.
[36] Matteo Renzi, *Avanti: Perché l'Italia non si ferma* (Milan: Feltrinelli, 2017).
[37] Tillman, "The European Union at the Ballot Box?"
[38] De Vries, "Sleeping Giant: Fact or Fairytale?"

protests. The ensuing elections shook the pillars of the Greek political system. In May 2012, the two parties that had dominated post-dictatorship politics, consistently securing over three quarters of the vote, PASOK (centre-left) and New Democracy (centre-right), only gained 32 per cent of the vote, while anti-bailout, anti-establishment and populist forces made substantial gains, with left-wing party Syriza emerging as one of the main winners.[39] Subsequently, the fiscal adjustment programme, with its corollary of privatisation, welfare cuts, and dismissals of public officials, exacted high social costs, particularly for vulnerable categories such as young persons and elderly pensioners; Greece witnessed a brutal GDP collapse and a dramatic increase in unemployment (close to 28 per cent in 2013). No wonder then that elections were largely orchestrated as a debate on austerity and the country's continued membership in the Eurozone. This 'Europeanisation' of Greek politics culminated in a dramatic sequence in 2015, with the victory of Syriza in the January parliamentary elections, the rejection of the adjustment programme proposed by the EU in a referendum organised in June, and ultimately the confirmation of Syriza's leader, Alexis Tsipras, as prime minister in the parliamentary elections held in September.

In an analysis of the January 2015 parliamentary vote, Katsanidou and Otjes argue that it is no longer possible to think of economic issues without considering the relationship between Greece and the Union.[40] They therefore develop a two-dimensional model of the Greek party system: one dimension for cultural issues such as immigration and security, and another for European issues, including both economic policy and matters related to European integration. This structuring makes it easier to understand Syriza's decision to seek an alliance with the right-wing ANEL party, with which they agreed on the most burning issue of the time, i.e. the necessity to renegotiate the terms of the bailout, even though the two parties were opposed on many socio-cultural issues.

In many respects, the Greek elections represent an extreme form of Europeanisation, since membership in the EU was at stake, with potentially dramatic repercussions. Yet such situations remain rare outside of crisis periods. Most analyses of the Europeanisation of parties or political systems,

---

[39] Sofia Vasilopoulou and Daphne Halikiopoulou, "In the Shadow of Grexit: The Greek Election of 17 June 2012," *South European Society and Politics* 18, no. 4 (2013): 523–542.

[40] Alexia Katsanidou and Simon Otjes, "Mapping the Greek Party System after the 2015 Elections: How the Economy and Europe Have Merged into a Single Issue," *LSE European Politics and Policy (EUROPP) Blog*, February 25, 2015, http://blogs.lse.ac.uk/europpblog/2015/02/25/mapping-the-greek-party-system-after-the-2015-elections-how-the-economy-and-europe-have-merged-into-a-single-issue/.

however, continue to reduce the debate over Europe to a single overarching issue: support for European integration or for membership in the EU.[41] One might however wonder whether this approach is appropriate in view of the multifaceted nature of the integration process. EU public policy now covers a wide range of areas that extends well beyond the original core of internal market policies. The Europeanisation literature has shown that the impact of Europe can be strong even in the absence of any legislative action, for instance as a result of the macroeconomic surveillance procedure.[42] As a result, even when a policy debate does not explicitly revolve around the need for more or less integration, EU membership may matter a lot. When asked about the subjects that influence their vote, respondents routinely mention issues such as immigration, unemployment, education or the future of the welfare system.[43] Although all these fields fall under national jurisdiction more so than under EU jurisdiction, the interdependence of European countries and the control exercised by the Union over domestic public finances makes it difficult to discuss such matters without taking into account the existence of European constraints.

The relation to Europe can therefore no longer be reduced to a single issue of support for integration. In their attempt to differentiate themselves from their rivals, parties and candidates will increasingly mobilise 'Europeanised' issues, i.e. issues which can be directly or indirectly influenced by EU membership, even if they are not primarily interested in integration matters. This will in turn affect the way the issues in question are perceived by the general public. Surveys and other efforts to assess the importance of European issues in domestic elections should therefore take account of the full range of EU-related issues. The 'European discourse' is being transformed. It is no longer merely limited to offering a broad view on the best way to organise the continent, but rather indicates how Member State parties and politicians intend to manage their relationship with Brussels and other Member States in key areas.[44] Considering the range of issues addressed at the EU level, there

---

[41] De Vries, "Sleeping Giant: Fact or Fairytale?"; Hanspeter Kriesi, "The Role of European Integration in National Election Campaigns," *European Union Politics* 8, no. 1 (2007): 83–108.

[42] Maarten P. Vink and Paolo Graziano, *Europeanization: New Research Agendas* (Basingstoke: Palgrave Macmillan, 2007); Bruno Palier and Yves Surel, eds., *L'Europe en action: L'européanisation dans une perspective comparée* (Paris: L'Harmattan, 2007).

[43] TNS Sofres, "Le second tour de l'élection présidentielle, sondage jour du vote," 6 May 2012, https://docs.google.com/viewer?a=v&pid=sites&srcid=aWVwZy5mcnxocmllb GVjfGd4OjdkNTdkMzIyNTkoNzQ5Yw.

[44] Thus, a lexicometric analysis of the importance given to a variety of subjects in the main candidates' campaign materials in the 2012 elections in France has shown that while "the EU issue" was a topic of relatively minor importance in the discourse of most candidates,

are reasons to believe that this is not a temporary development, but rather a structural shift in domestic politics.

Another remarkable feature of crisis-time elections is their negative character. When European issues are addressed in election campaigns, it is generally to underscore the parties' and candidates' opposition to developments in Brussels. Contestation over issues regarding Europe can, however, take different forms.[45] The first is radical and complete opposition: the very idea of integration is rejected, along with its attendant sovereignty losses. This is traditionally the position of many anti-establishment political entrepreneurs from both the far left and the far right, who have regularly mobilised the EU issue to reap electoral gains.[46] A second, less direct, line of opposition focuses on the policies pursued by the European Union or on the position of other Member States, but stops short of calling into question the very existence of the Union – a tack taken by many centre-left parties across Europe. The novelty of the crisis period, however, has been that many representatives of 'mainstream' parties, traditionally well disposed towards the EU, have come to adopt a similar stance. Political leaders such as Nicolas Sarkozy in France and Matteo Renzi in Italy deliberately surfed on the loss of support for European integration to engage in systematic 'Brussels bashing' or in a critique of other European countries. Even former European Commissioner Mario Monti found it necessary to warn of the dangers of 'creditocrazia,' a system in which all decisions would be dictated by countries with sound public finances, irrespective of their partners' situation.[47] As a rule, this discursive shift has contributed to fanning the flames of Euro-scepticism.[48]

"Europeanised issues," i.e. issues directly or indirectly related to Europe, featured prominently on all candidates' agendas. Dominique Labbé and Denis Monière, *La campagne présidentielle de 2012: Votez pour moi!* (Paris: L'Harmattan, 2013).

[45] Peter Mair, "Political Opposition and the European Union," *Government and Opposition* 42, no. 1 (2007): 1–17.

[46] Paul Taggart, "A Touchstone of Dissent: Euroscepticism in Contemporary Western European Party Systems," *European Journal of Political Research* 33, no. 3 (1998): 363–388; Van Der Eijk and Franklin, "Potential for Contestation on European Matters at National Elections in Europe"; De Vries, "Sleeping Giant: Fact or Fairytale?"; Kriesi, "The Role of European Integration in National Election Campaigns."

[47] Sylvie Goulard and Mario Monti, *La democrazia in Europa: Guardare lontano* (Milan: Rizzoli, 2012).

[48] See, e.g., Renaud Dehousse and Angela Tacea, "The French 2012 Presidential Election: A Europeanised Contest," *Cahiers Européens de Sciences Po*, no. 2 (2012): 2–16, for the French 2012 presidential elections, or Aldo Di Virgilio et al., "Party Competition in the 2013 Italian Elections: Evidence from an Expert Survey," *Government and Opposition* 50, no. 1 (2015): 65–89, for the 2013 parliamentary elections in Italy.

III TOWARDS POLITICISATION OF EU POLICY-MAKING?

Politicisation has also gained ground at the European level. With the innovation known as the system of *Spitzenkandidaten*, introduced in the 2014 European Parliament elections, the European Parliament has gained influence over the appointment of the Commission president. The *Spitzenkandidaten* system drew on a practice dating back to the beginning of the 1980s: the 'confirmation vote' – an investiture of sorts, later codified by the Treaty of Maastricht, which also aligned the term of commissioners with that of the Parliament. Although these reforms were introduced without any real debate, they clearly indicated a desire to strengthen the links between the Parliament and the body that most resembles an 'executive' at the European level, i.e. the Commission. Subsequently, Members of the European Parliament requested the establishment of a system of hearings to confirm Commission candidates, based on the US Congress' oversight of certain presidential nominations. After some hesitation, Commission president Jacques Santer accepted the principle, which was then enshrined in the Parliament's rules of procedure.[49] The hearings have proven to be a formidable challenge for certain candidates whose skills and opinions failed to impress the members of parliamentary committees. In each confirmation process, the Parliament has managed to impose changes in the distribution of portfolios, or even reject outright certain candidates. The forced resignation of the Santer Commission in 1999, triggered by the threat of a parliamentary vote of censure, reinforced the idea of a strong link between the Parliament and the executive.

Given this momentum, it did not take very much imagination to see that political parties at the European level – another creation of the Maastricht Treaty – might one day be tempted to use elections as a lever to impose their choice of Commission president on governments.[50] By 1998, Jacques Delors and a number of EU figures called for European political parties to list their candidate for the presidency before the European elections.[51] The idea was to give voters an opportunity to influence the choice of president, and even the Commission's programme. The European socialist party in particular embraced this idea, following a number of electoral setbacks; many saw it as

---

[49] European Parliament, Rules of Procedure (8th Parliamentary Term, September 2015), rule 118.3 and annex XVI, www.europarl.europa.eu/sides/getDoc.do?pubRef=-//EP//NONSGML +RULES-EP+20140701+0+DOC+PDF+Vo//en&language=en.

[50] Renaud Dehousse, "Constitutional Reform in the European Community: Are There Alternatives to the Majoritarian Avenue?" *West European Politics* 18, no. 1 (1995): 118–136.

[51] Jacques Delors et al., "Politiser le débat européen," https://institutdelors.eu/wp-content/ uploads/2018/01/ceo1999.pdf.

a possible remedy to citizens' disenchantment with Europe. During the seventh legislature (2009–2014), European Parliament President Martin Schulz followed this playbook, leading to his selection as candidate of the European Socialist Party (PES). Despite the many reservations, especially within the European People's Party (EPP), where heads of government frowned upon an initiative that could only reduce their leeway, once several parties put forward their candidates in the autumn of 2013, it began to appear inevitable. At a time when personalisation is an important element of political life, it was inconceivable to leave the media spotlight entirely to candidates from other parties.[52] Thus Jean-Claude Juncker was chosen as the EPP's candidate, and when the EPP won the plurality of the votes, he was named Commission president. His success, despite the opposition from prominent figures from within his own party such as Angela Merkel and Herman Van Rompuy, powerfully backed by British Prime Minister David Cameron after the elections, gives credence to the idea that a change did occur. Its magnitude remains to be assessed.

A first observation is that the 2014 election results only very partially met the expectations of the new system's proponents. The victory of the European People's Party was only relative: while it remained the largest group in the European Parliament, it lost close to 20 per cent of its parliamentary representation (a total of fifty-three seats). The striking element of these elections was the decline of the four main European parties: in most countries, both left- and right-wing populist movements made the largest gains. Moreover, personalisation does not seem to have played a decisive role in voter choice. According to a post-election survey conducted in seven EU countries, on average only 36 per cent of respondents (a mere 21 per cent in Greece) believed that the choice of Commission president was important or very important, while 44 per cent, (with a maximum of 48 per cent in Germany), held the opposite view.[53]

The only consolation for the supporters of the *Spitzenkandidaten* system was that the idea appeared to be more popular with voters from the two largest parties (EPP and PES), whose candidates received the most media coverage because they were considered the only truly electable candidates. Furthermore, the countries where the *Spitzenkandidaten* campaigned experienced

---

[52] Nereo Penalver Garcia and Julian Priestley, *The Making of a European President* (Basingstoke: Palgrave Macmillan, 2015).

[53] Nicolas Sauger, Renaud Dehousse, and Florent Gougou, "Comparative Electoral Dynamics in the European Union in 2014 (CED- EU14)," *Cahiers Européens de Sciences Po*, no. 2 (2015): 1–36.

The Euro Crisis and the Transformation of the European Political System 149

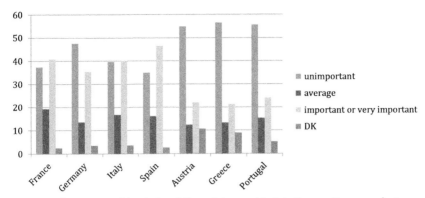

FIGURE 1. Importance of the choice of Commission presidents in the 2014 European elections
Source: Sauger, Dehousse, and Gougou, "Comparative Electoral Dynamics in the European Union in 2014"

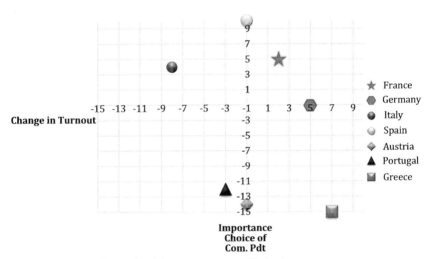

FIGURE 2. Impact of Spitzenkandidaten on turnout at EU election
Source: Sauger, Dehousse, and Gougou, "Comparative Electoral Dynamics in the European Union in 2014"

greater participation.[54] This, however, did not suffice to reverse the well-established trend which has seen turnout at the polls decline at each successive election: in 2014, an all-time low of 42.6 per cent was registered.

Figure 2 compares variations in the turnout at the 2009 and 2014 elections with the intensity of support for the indirect election of the Commission

---
[54] Hermann Schmitt, Sara Hobolt, and Sebastian Adrian Popa, "Does Personalization Increase Turnout? Spitzenkandidaten in the 2014 European Parliament Elections," *European Union Politics* 16, no. 3 (2014): 347–368.

president (operationalised as the number of points beyond the average in all countries polled in the survey). Evidently, there is little relation between the two. The country in which support was highest, i.e. Spain, even saw a decline in turnout. Conversely, in Greece, where the upsurge of interest for EU elections was strongest, support for the indirect election was the lowest. This result obtained despite the fact that the clear winner of the European elections in Greece, Alexis Tsipras, was the radical left's candidate for the Commission presidency. In other words, there is no apparent correlation between strong public support for the idea of electing the Commission president and the turnout registered in 2014.

This anointing of sorts through universal suffrage nonetheless sufficed to propel Jean-Claude Juncker to the head of the Commission. No alternative proposal emerged from European Council negotiations, and the virulence of the British and Hungarian opposition ended up rallying less enthusiastic Member States to his candidacy. In the Parliament, Juncker was subsequently confirmed by a 'grand coalition' of the EPP, socialist, and liberal members. While some raised the prospect of a true coalition agreement, similar to those that exist in some parliamentary systems, the achievements were more modest in the European context. Leadership positions in the Parliament were distributed to the detriment of euro-sceptic groups, which did not secure the committee chairs that the principle of proportional representation suggested they might aspire to. And the relatively weak majority obtained by the Commission in the confirmation vote of 22 October 2014 (423 for, 209 against and 67 abstaining), with many abstentions among socialist representatives from Southern Europe, shows that no solid majority existed in the Parliament. As in the past, each piece of legislation that has gone forward has been based on ad hoc parliamentary coalitions.

The new structure of the EU executive has mostly attracted attention because it includes a tier of vice-presidents, tasked with the implementation of key aspects of Juncker's programme. At the same time, it confirms the necessarily multi-partisan nature of the Commission's operations: the economic and financial affairs portfolio, which was awarded to the French socialist Pierre Moscovici after much wrangling, places him in two working groups, respectively headed by the Finnish liberal Jyrky Kattainen and by the EPP-affiliated Latvian conservative Valdis Dombrovskis. That being said, the executive's priorities are directly drawn from Juncker's campaign platform.[55] The official discourse thus tends to emphasise the existence of a chain of

---

[55] European Commission Press Release IP/14/984, The Juncker Commission: A Strong and Experienced Team Standing for Change (10 September 2014).

command that connects the executive's choices to the preferences that emerged from the vote. All in all, even though the idea of a leadership contest at the European level, in which voters have a decisive role, has had relatively little success in the polls, it seems to have been important for many actors in the nascent European political system.[56]

That the European Parliament strongly supported this initiative is not a surprise, since the process is viewed (perhaps too hastily) as reinforcing its influence. What is most surprising, however, is the way Member State governments accepted an institutional path that inevitably led to a reduction of their own room for manoeuvre. This choice, which does not seem to be driven by self-interest, can probably be explained by ideational factors: with regard to democracy, the parliamentary system remains the reference political system in most European countries. As a result, when the issue of democracy arises it is difficult to oppose simple ideas that resonate with national political cultures.[57] UK Prime Minister David Cameron, who made every effort to oppose the choice of Jean-Claude Juncker after the 2014 European elections, learned this lesson through bitter experience. The process that led to the latter's appointment was presented as self-evident. Parliamentary group leaders argued that since his party had won the elections, Juncker should naturally be chosen as Commission president, even though some of them had been his rivals in the presidential race, a principled discourse which proved to be difficult to rebuke.

As this book goes to press, the election process for the 2019–2024 cycle has come to a close, and the outcome for the *Spitzenkandidaten* system has been disappointing. The major parties did indeed select leading candidates, who ran for the Commission presidency in spring 2019. However, the result of the vote was even more splintered than in the previous election cycle, continuing the trend of electoral fragmentation. The EPP and the PES both experienced losses, while the Liberals and Greens, as well as right-wing populist parties, advanced in the polls. When both the EPP's leading candidate (Manfred Weber) and the PES's leading candidate (Frans Timmermans) proved contentious among European leaders, the European Council selected a *Spitzenkandidaten* outsider as their nominee, the German CDU politician Ursula von

---

[56] This idea has been championed *inter alia* in the works of Simon Hix. Simon Hix, *What's Wrong with the European Union and How to Fix It* (Cambridge: Polity Press, 2008).

[57] Olivier Costa and Paul Magnette, "Idéologie et changement institutionnel dans l'Union européenne: Pourquoi les gouvernements ont-ils constamment renforcé le Parlement européen?" *Politique européenne* 9 (2003): 49–75; Stefan Goetze and Berthold Rittberger, "A Matter of Habit? The Sociological Foundations of Empowering the European Parliament," *Comparative European Politics* 8, no. 1 (2010): 37–54.

der Leyen. The European Parliament, of course, remained constitutionally entitled to reject von der Leyen's nomination as Commission president, but the inability of any single party or coalition of parties to secure a majority of the seats put it in a weak position. And indeed, in July 2019, von der Leyen was elected by a narrow majority of the European Parliament to the office of Commission president. It remains to be seen whether Juncker's pronouncement that he was the "first and last Spitzenkandidat" is correct. However, it is evident that the transformation of the election process of the Commission president is far from complete.

IV THE EUROPEAN DEMOCRACY CONUNDRUM

The euro crisis has had important consequences for the political system of the European Union. In several respects, it appears to have aggravated the well-known 'democratic deficit' of the European Union.[58] Under the pressure of events, national governments have accepted transfers of powers to supranational institutions in areas of strategic importance. As a result, the discretion they enjoyed in the conduct of macroeconomic policy has been further eroded, particularly in debtor countries, submitted to a strict surveillance programme. This change, taking place in a period of weakened support for European integration, has had a strong impact on domestic politics, particularly in Eurozone countries. The influence of the EU is now felt more clearly in a large number of fields, which has fed opposition to Europe and/or its policies. In parallel, one has witnessed an attempt to enhance the importance of European elections and possibly the responsiveness of the EU political system with the development of the so-called *Spitzenkandidaten* system. The increased prominence of European elections will make it difficult for future Commission presidents, even those not selected from the *Spitzenkandidaten*, to ignore the party coalitions that emerge in the Parliament.

To sum up, reactions to the crisis have exposed the contradictions between two models of European governance: delegation of powers to independent supranational bodies, which is the hallmark of the 'Community method', and a form of parliamentary government. EU politics seem to oscillate between these two poles, at times anxious to keep partisan politics at bay; at other times

---

[58] On which see, e.g., Giandomenico Majone, "Europe's 'Democratic Deficit': The Question of Standards," *European Law Journal* 4, no. 1 (1998): 5–8; Andrew Moravcsik, "In Defence of the 'Democratic Deficit': Reassessing Legitimacy in the European Union," *Journal of Common Market Studies* 40, no. 4 (2002): 603–624; Andreas Follesdal and Simon Hix, "Why There is a Democratic Deficit in the European Union: A Response to Majone and Moravcsik," *Journal of Common Market Studies* 44, no. 3 (2006): 533–562.

eager to see political parties mobilise themselves around European issues. The contradiction between a 'trusteeship' model and a form of parliamentary government is by no means new. It was already present at earlier stages of the construction of the EU institutional architecture.[59] However, with the euro crisis and the accelerated institutional development that has resulted, some blatant incompatibilities have emerged.

Consider for instance the way in which the Juncker Commission used its enhanced control powers over domestic fiscal policies. In recent years, countries like France and Italy, whose fiscal policies did not fully respect European recommendations, were granted a considerable degree of flexibility.[60] In so doing, the Juncker Commission followed a line that was clearly less drastic than that of the Barroso Commission. To its critics in 'creditor countries,' the Commission responded that it was now (read: after Juncker's election) a political body, which had to take into consideration the domestic situation in the Member States. It is highly likely that the large swing towards Eurosceptic parties registered in the 2014 European elections played a role in its evaluations.

Although the introduction of politics through the *Spitzenkandidaten* system has been used by some to legitimize the Commission, others have drawn precisely the opposite conclusion. For supporters of rules-based governance, the idea that the European executive claims for itself the right to decide, on the basis of a variety of factors, including political ones, how best to implement the rules appears to be nonsense. In this view, the Commission enjoys the powers it does precisely because of the neutral, *super partes* status it enjoys in the EU. In other words, the logic of delegation of powers to neutral agents that characterised the first decades of European integration[61] is at odds with a logic of politicisation of EU policy-making.[62] Unsurprisingly, in the last few years there have been signals indicating a willingness in some quarters to re-examine the role devoted to the European Commission. In 2015, for instance, Germany's powerful finance minister Wolfgang Schäuble resurrected an old plan to strip the Commission of certain regulatory and oversight functions, beginning with competition policy, and to give them to

---

[59] See, e.g., Renaud Dehousse, "European Institutional Architecture after Amsterdam: Parliamentary System or Regulatory Structure?" *Common Market Law Review* 35, no. 3 (1998): 595–627.

[60] Dehousse, "Why Has EU Macroeconomic Governance Become More Supranational?"

[61] For an extended discussion of the principal-agent model of European integration, see Chapter 18.

[62] Giandomenico Majone, "The Two Logics of Delegation: Agency and Fiduciary Relations in EU Governance," *European Union Politics* 2, no. 1 (2001): 103–122.

independent authorities in order to maintain 'depoliticised' supervision of state activities.[63] A few months later, the German government wrote to German members of the European Parliament to stress that the Commission could not claim both the status of political representative and the role of impartial guardian of the Treaties.[64]

To make things worse, today's Europe is characterised by widespread opposition to 'Brussels' and by growing polarisation. To the well-known North–South cleavage on economic issues, one must add an East–West split over the free movement of persons. Even populist movements, which share a common aversion to the establishment, appear to pursue different objectives: the South, with movements like Syriza in Greece and Podemos in Spain, has predominantly left-wing populism, whereas, in the North, right-wing populism with strong identity components is pervasive. Given these divisions, steering a course that rallies majority support is anything but easy, irrespective of the governance model – parliamentary or trusteeship – that one has in mind.

In the long run, the fundamental contradictions between these two governance models will have to be addressed. One possibility is to draw a line between areas in which a more politicised logic is accepted and those in which neutral third parties acting in the general interest is preferred. In the turbulent environment in which Europe finds itself, it is hard to say how the tension between the two governance models will play out over time. Moreover, the growth of populism and opposition to Europe registered in a number of countries is likely to lead Member State governments to insist on retaining a central role in EU governance. The logic of incremental change experienced by the EU throughout the course of its history may no longer suffice to define a new balance.

---

[63] Stephan Brown, "Schäuble: Commission Must Give Up Power," *Politico*, 30 July 2015, www.politico.eu/article/schauble-european-commission-power-eurogroup-juncker-dijsselbloem-grexit/.

[64] Florian Eder, "5 Reasons Germany's Influence Is Fading," *Politico*, 15 January 2016, www.politico.eu/article/5-reasons-germanys-influence-is-fading-angela-merkel-epp-meeting/.

II

Human Migration

7

On Equal Treatment, Social Justice and the Introduction of Parliamentarism in the European Union

ULF ÖBERG AND NATHALIE LEYNS

I INTRODUCTION

From the beginning of European integration, the principles of equality and non-discrimination have played a central role in shaping European labour markets. On the one hand, they guarantee nationals of one Member State equal access to employment and the right to provide services in other Member States. On the other hand, they protect nationals in the host Member State from the unfavourable consequences that could result from the existence of lower pay or employment standards for foreign workers as compared to those enjoyed by domestic workers. These principles of equal pay for equal work at the same workplace are far-reaching and impact both labour law and social security law.[1]

This part of the European Social Contract has been challenged over the past twenty years, due to a combination of ideological, economic, legal, technical and social factors. Following the 2004 enlargement of the European Union to Central and Eastern European countries, which were mostly low-wage economies, the European Union witnessed a shift in the treatment of labour competition within the internal market. From legitimate social

---

[1] Labour law defines the rights and obligations of workers and employers. Social security law establishes the various programmes designed to insure against the ordinary hazards of labour market participation and to guarantee a minimum level of social welfare. The EU's numerous social directives aim at protecting workers and give them rights in areas such as health and safety, non-discrimination at work and working conditions (e.g. rights for posted workers). These social directives also give the right to information and consultation on collective redundancies, transfers of companies and other work-related issues. As for social security law, each Member State has its own social security schemes. However, EU law coordinates national systems to ensure that people who move from one Member State to another maintain their social security coverage (such as pension rights and healthcare).

158 Ulf Öberg and Nathalie Leyns

demands, calls for equal pay for equal work came to be viewed as xenophobic, protectionist and contrary to free movement principles.

The tide, however, has slowly started to turn. The tendency by some companies to resort to social dumping[2] within the European Union has provoked populist and nationalist backlash, which has placed the social dimension of the European construction at the forefront of contemporary debates. As a result, there appears to be a swing of the pendulum occurring in the positive law and the case law of the EU, in favour of equal pay and working conditions. This social and political shift has also contributed to contemporary EU constitutional debates and has prompted calls for more political accountability and the introduction of a measure of parliamentarism.

Against the backdrop of growing public distrust in the European construction, this chapter places the free movement of persons and services in a legal and judicial context. It analyses the evolving case law of the European Court of Justice and traces a number of important historical periods: from the initial recognition of the equal treatment and non-discrimination principles, to the acceptance of labour and social regulation at the national level, to the promotion of a regulatory competition model that contained little room for higher standards of worker protection at the national level, to the recent turn in the tide in favour of labour and social rights. The chapter concludes by turning briefly from the Court of Justice to the EU's political institutions and argues that the challenge and renewal of the European Social Contract has had a positive effect on democratic debate and political accountability.

II AT THE BEGINNING: THE ECONOMIC RATIONALE

1 *Establishing a European Union*

In the aftermath of the Second World War, the founding members of the then-European Economic Community wished to create stability and the conditions for peace. Beginning with the *Brussels Report on the General Common Market* (the Spaak Report), which set the groundwork for the Treaty of Rome, it was clear that the foundation stone of the European project's

---

[2] The European Court of Justice has found that social dumping is a set of practices aimed at gaining an advantage over competitors in the host Member State, such as the use of migrant (and/or undeclared) workers as a cheaper labour force, which has negative consequences on worker rights and economic processes. Case C-244/04, *Commission v. Germany*, ECLI:EU: C:2006:49, paras. 54–61.

Equal Treatment, Social Justice & Introduction of Parliamentarism   159

social dimension was the exclusion of structural competition on wages.[3] The Spaak Report stated that it would not be permissible for national legislation or trade unions, through industrial action, to use the arrival of immigrant workers to lower pay and working conditions.[4] Neither did the drafters believe that employers would use immigrant labour to exert downward pressure on labour conditions. The Spaak Report highlighted that the principle of free movement was necessary for the creation of a common market and did not only involve products and services, but was also to apply progressively to capital and persons. Faith was placed in an untapped workforce that would be transformed into a resource for Europe, and an integration process where structural competition on wages would be excluded.

In line with the Spaak Report, the view reflected in the contemporaneous *Ohlin Report on Social Aspects of European Economic Co-operation* (the Ohlin Report)[5] was that 'objective, scientific analysis' revealed that even significant differences in labour costs between Member States would not, in the ordinary course of events, distort competition.[6] The Ohlin Report stated that it was consistent with the goal of market integration to use national

---

[3]   The Spaak Report was drafted by an Intergovernmental Committee headed by Paul-Henri Spaak in 1956. It pursued horizontal integration of the economy through the gradual elimination of trade barriers, with the aim of achieving a customs union.

[4]   *Report of the Heads of Delegation to the Ministers of Foreign Affairs, The Brussels Report on the General Common Market (Spaak Report)*, April 21, 1956, 89. Available in French at http://aei .pitt.edu/996/1/Spaak_report_french.pdf. The relevant text is as follows: 'the third condition is related to the wages: if, on one hand, all discrimination is effectively forbidden between national workers and immigrants workers, and if, on the other hand – by state law or the action of unions – any decrease in wages is prohibited, employers will not have any incentive to resort to more immigrant workers than the ones they effectively require to fill the vacancies available. Hence, all downward pressure on wages levels is avoided and the labour market will tend toward a natural equilibrium.' [Own translation]

[5]   The Ohlin Report was drafted by a group of experts of the International Labour Organisation led by the Swedish economist and liberal politician Bertil Ohlin in 1956. Ohlin and the British economist James Meade were awarded the Nobel Memorial Prize in Economic Sciences in 1977 'for their path-breaking contribution to the theory of international trade and international capital movements.'

[6]   The "distortion of competition" concept has two somewhat distinct consequences in EU law and can refer to Member State regulation that is considered too 'high' or too 'low' relative to that of other Member States: (1) as a trigger for internal market treaty rights, to challenge state measures and practices that are said to distort competition; (2) as a justification for EU legislation and administrative action, to harmonize regulation or enforce competition law in areas in which national laws and practices are said to distort competition. Integration of the EU market seeks to guarantee that market actors in one Member State are not placed at a competitive disadvantage because of the distorting laws and unfair competitive practices of other Member States. These operate as an illegitimate barrier to the free movement principle.

regulation and collective bargaining to end unjustified differences in labour costs for the benefit of low wage groups. At that time, it was also common ground in Europe that wages and labour conditions were largely the product of collective bargaining by the social partners.[7] In the words of the Ohlin Report, there was 'widespread agreement that government interference with the freedom of collective bargaining, if it becomes necessary at all, should be kept to a minimum'.

Together, the Spaak and Ohlin Reports presented an underlying economic rationale for non-discrimination and the principle of equal pay for equal work at the same workplace.[8] In their view, non-discrimination and equal treatment would induce workers to move from regions with high unemployment to Member States offering better employment prospects. The Reports led to the signing of the Treaty of Rome on 25 March 1957 establishing the European Economic Community, and laying down the plan that would create a common market to cover the whole European Economic Community.

Although this chapter focuses on the social dimension of the internal market, and the free movement of natural and legal persons, it is helpful to briefly place this law in the broader context of free movement law. The stated aim of the Treaty of Rome was to abolish obstacles to the free circulation of goods, persons, services and capital.[9] For persons, defined as both natural and legal persons, i.e. firms, these freedoms comprised: (1) the right to move freely and establish themselves within the European Economic Community as workers or self-employed persons, (2) the right to set up a company, a branch or a subsidiary, and (3) the right to provide services in another Member State. All of these free movement rights were bound to the principle of non-discrimination based on nationality.[10] The principle of non-discrimination

---

[7] As defined in one leading source, "[c]ollective bargaining is the process of negotiation between unions and employers regarding the terms and conditions of employment of employees, and about the rights and responsibilities of trade unions. It is a process of rule-making, leading to joint regulation." "Collective Bargaining," European Foundation for the Improvement of Living and Working Conditions website, 4 September 2017, www.eurofound.europa.eu/sr/node/52052.

[8] In the European Union, the principle of "equal pay for equal work" stems from the idea that workers doing the same work in the same place have a right to the same pay.

[9] Article 3(c) Treaty Establishing the European Economic Community [hereinafter EEC Treaty].

[10] While the definition of worker, self-employed persons and setting up a company do not require much elaboration, the definition of services as applied to natural and legal persons is not self-evident. Article 60 of the EEC Treaty states: "Services within the meaning of this Treaty shall be deemed to be services normally supplied for remuneration, to the extend they are not governed by the provisions relating to the free movement of goods, capital and persons. Services

Equal Treatment, Social Justice & Introduction of Parliamentarism 161

also included employment, remuneration and working conditions.[11] Based on a political philosophy and an economic theory that relied mainly on the liberation of market forces – not government regulation – to stimulate economic growth, the Treaty of Rome left social and labour policies largely in the hands of the Member States.

In 1986, the Single European Act revised the Treaty of Rome and set the objective of establishing a single market by 31 December 1992. The concept of the free movement of persons was originally used in connection with economically active persons only – i.e. workers, the self-employed and legal entities that moved from one Member State to another. However, in the late 1980s, the objective of a single market had still not been attained. Despite the liberalisation of intra-Community trade, the rapid elimination of quotas and the gradual lowering of customs barriers, many obstacles to the free movement of persons and services remained.

The concept of EU citizenship for Member State nationals, introduced in the 1992 Treaty on European Union (Treaty of Maastricht), extended the freedom of movement to all EU citizens, including non-economically active persons such as students, retirees and family members. This European citizenship strengthened the rights of all persons to move and reside freely within the territory of the Member States. Those rights were later confirmed by the Treaty of Lisbon[12] and included in the general provisions of the Area of Freedom, Security and Justice.[13]

In sum, the currently applicable Treaty on the Functioning of the European Union (TFEU) restates the original Treaty of Rome's commitment to the common market and defines the internal market as 'an area without internal frontiers in which the free movement of goods, persons, services

---

shall include in particular: (a) activities of an industrial character, (b) activities of a commercial character, (c) artisan activities, (d) activities of the liberal professions." Thus, services is a residual category of economic activity, and applies when persons move to perform what would ordinarily be considered work or self-employment but on a temporary basis. This is important for understanding the social dumping debate of recent years, because when free movement of services is used as the legal basis for working in another Member State, the individual is generally not subject to the standard regulatory requirements of that Member State since the movement, by definition, is considered temporary.

[11] Article 48 EEC Treaty.

[12] The Treaty of Lisbon Amending the Treaty on European Union and the Treaty Establishing the European Community, December 13, 2007 O.J. (C 306) 1 [hereinafter Treaty of Lisbon].

[13] The European Union's area of freedom, security and justice (AFSJ) was created to ensure the free movement of persons, irrespective of their economic function, and to provide a high level of security, as well as rights, for European citizens. For an overview of the development of the AFSJ over the past decade, see Chapter 14.

and capital is ensured'.[14] These four fundamental freedoms are the cornerstone of the EU internal market. Being one of the aspects of the free movement of persons and services within the EU, the labour market is framed within the broader concept of the internal market.

2 The Principles of Equality and Non-discrimination among Workers before the European Court of Justice

In this economic and legal environment, non-discrimination and the right to equal pay emerged early on as a core element of the case law of the European Court of Justice ('the Court'). In the absence of harmonisation of the labour legislation, social conditions and welfare systems of the Member States, the legal conditions of establishment for companies and workers varied significantly depending on their country of origin. On the one hand, imposing high national standards on foreign workers would have had the effect of protecting national workers from foreign competition to the detriment of the free movement principle. On the other hand, failing to impose any standards on foreign workers from one Member State employed in another Member State would have placed national workers at a structural disadvantage in those cases in which national standards were higher than those of the foreign workers' country of origin. The early case law of the Court operated to mediate between these two extremes.

In 1974, the Court recognised that the principle of non-discrimination in Article 48 of the Treaty of Rome (current Article 45 TFEU) was a legal norm directly applicable in national proceedings. In that case, involving a challenge to a national seaman quota in the French Merchant Seaman Code, the Court held that Article 48 had direct effect. The Court also elaborated on the non-discrimination principle in Article 48 and found that it served to protect both foreign and domestic workers. On the one hand, it guaranteed Member State nationals the right of equal access to employment and the provision of services in other Member States. On the other hand, it guaranteed nationals of the host Member State that their wages and working conditions would not be undercut by workers from Member States with less favourable employment conditions.[15] In other words, the Court balanced worker access to the labour markets in Europe where jobs were available with the protection of national workers in high-employment Member States from unfair external wage competition.

---

[14] Article 26 TFEU.

[15] Case C-167/73, *Commission v. France (French Merchant Seamen)*, ECLI:EU:C:1974:35.

In subsequent cases, the Court highlighted the dual economic and social purpose of the non-discrimination principle – between not only nationals and non-nationals but also men and women.[16] In *Defrenne* v. *Sabena*, the first in this important line of the cases, the Court stated that the aim of Article 119 of the Treaty of Rome (current Article 157 TFEU), which sets down the principle of equal pay for men and women, was to avoid the distortion of competition between undertakings established in different Member States, as some Member States had already implemented the principle, while others had not yet eliminated pay discrimination between men and women. In that case, the Court continued by indicating that the guarantees of Article 119 were central to European integration. It reasoned that the EU was not merely an economic union but was also created to promote, through common action, social progress and the constant improvement of living and working conditions.

In more recent cases, the Court has expanded on the interrelationship between the social and economic goals of the principle of equal pay for equal work set out in Article 157 TFEU.[17] In its case law, the right not to be discriminated against on grounds of sex has emerged as a fundamental human right guaranteed by the Court. As such, the economic aim pursued by Article 157 TFEU, namely the elimination of distortions of competition between undertakings established in different Member States, is secondary to the social aim pursued by the same provision, which constitutes the expression of a fundamental human right.[18]

III THE POSTING OF WORKERS IN THE EUROPEAN UNION

1 *A Core Set of Mandatory Rules in EU Law*

The intensification of labour mobility has prompted employers to provide cross-borders services and to temporarily send or post workers to other Member States within the European Union. Article 56 TFEU provides for the elimination of discrimination on grounds of nationality against service providers established in another Member State, as well as the abolition of any restriction that would prohibit, impede or render less advantageous the activities of a service provider established in another Member State where s/he

---

[16] Case C-43/75, *Defrenne* v. *Sabena*, ECLI:EU:C:1976:56.
[17] Cases C-270/97 and C-271/97, *Deutsche Port AG* v. *Sievers and Schrage*, ECLI:EU:C:2000:76; Case C-50/96, *Deutsche Telekom AG* v. *Schröder*, ECLI:EU:C:2000:72.
[18] *Deutsche Telekom AG*, para. 57; *Sievers and Schrage*, para. 57.

lawfully provides similar economic activities.[19] Exercising this freedom to provide services, companies have been increasingly posting workers in various sectors, including construction, financial and business services, transport, media and communications, and agriculture.

The principal legislation in this domain is Directive 96/71/EC of the European Parliament and of the Council of 16 December 1996 concerning the posting of workers in the framework of the provision of services (Posting of Workers Directive).[20] The Directive defines a posted worker as 'a worker who, for a limited period of time, carries out his [or her] work in the territory of an EU Member State other than the state in which he [or she] normally works'. By contrast, the definition of 'worker' is 'that which applies in the law of the Member State to whose territory the worker is posted'.[21]

Aimed at ensuring that posted workers benefit from a certain minimum level of social protection, the Posting of Workers Directive imposes a series of obligations on host Member States. These include the duty to ensure that service providers respect a core set of mandatory terms and conditions of employment when workers are posted to the host Member State. This minimum set of labour standards, whose mandatory nature stems from Article 3(1) of the Posting of Workers Directive,[22] follows three main objectives: (i) the avoidance of any distortion of competition that could result from applying different national rules on labour protection to undertakings providing services within the same Member State; (ii) the guarantee of a minimum standard of social protection for workers posted within the EU; and (iii) the elimination of

---

[19] Article 56 first paragraph TFEU: 'Within the framework of the provisions set out below, restrictions on freedom to provide services within the Union shall be prohibited in respect of nationals of Member States who are established in a Member State other than that of the person for whom the services are intended'; *inter alia*, Cases C-49/98, C-50/98, C-52/98 to C-54/98 and C-68/98 to C-71/98, *Finalarte and others*, ECLI:EU:C:2001:564, para. 28 (and the case law cited therein).

[20] European Parliament and Council Directive 96/71/EC, Concerning the Posting of Workers in the Framework of the Provision of Services, 1997 O.J. (L 18) 1.

[21] European Parliament and Council Directive 96/71/EC, art. 2.

[22] Article 3 of the Posting of Workers Directive requires Member States to ensure that posted workers are subject to the host country's laws, regulations or administrative provisions concerning: "maximum work periods and minimum rest periods; minimum paid annual holidays; minimum rates of pay, including overtime rates; conditions of hiring out workers, in particular the supply of workers by temporary employment undertakings; health, safety and hygiene at work; protective measures in the terms and conditions of employment of pregnant women or those who have recently given birth, of children and of young people; equality of treatment between men and women and other provisions on non-discrimination."

obstacles to the free movement of services and of uncertainty for service providers.[23]

The Directive does not harmonise the content of the mandatory rules guaranteeing a minimum level of labour protection. Rather, Member States are given the freedom to set those standards in accordance with their own labour legislation and social policy. However, the standards adopted by a host Member State, which are imposed upon service providers that post workers to that host Member State, are viewed as restrictions to the free movement of services. In the case law of the Court, for such restrictive measures to satisfy the free movement guarantees of Article 56 TFEU, they must be proportionate, namely they must be appropriate for securing their labour-protection objectives and they must not go beyond what is necessary to attain it.[24]

Inevitably, the transposition of the Posting of Workers Directive at the national level has given rise to differences in the choice of applicable labour standards and social protection norms. In many cases, the Member States have used the latitude conferred by the Directive to go beyond the minimal provisions of the Directive, with the aim of guaranteeing the principle of equal pay for equal work and reconciling the provisions of the Posting of Workers Directive with their industrial relations systems. This has led to conflicts between, on the one hand, the rights of posted and domestic workers, and, on the other hand, the rights of service providers. From the perspective of service providers, satisfying two sets of labour and social standards – that of their country of origin and that of the host Member State – can be cumbersome and can deter the cross-border provision of services. At the same time, domestic firms and workers have a legitimate interest in preserving the national conditions in their labour markets.

2 *The Delicate Balance between the Rights of Posted Workers and the Freedom to Provide Services in the Court's Case Law*

The Court has had several opportunities to rule on the compliance of national measures with Article 56 TFEU and to give guidance on how to strike the balance between the freedom of services and the protection of workers' rights. In a first generation of case law, the need for equality between posted and local workers prevailed in the Court's reasoning. In *Rush Portuguesa*, the Court

---

[23] See Opinion of Advocate General Trstenjak, Case C-319/06, *Commission of the European Communities v. Grand Duchy of Luxembourg*, ECLI:EU:C:2007:516, para. 33.

[24] Cases C-369/96 and C-376/96, *Arblade and Others*, ECLI:EU:C:1999:575, para. 35; Case C-165/98, *Mazzoleni and ISA*, ECLI:EU:C:2001:162, para. 26; *Finalarte*, para. 32.

ruled that the freedom to provide services included the right to temporarily move one's workforce from one Member State to another.[25] At the same time, however, the Court clarified that EU law does not prohibit Member States from extending their legislation, or collective labour agreements, to any person who is employed, even temporarily, within their territory, irrespective of the country in which the employer is established.[26] National measures of restrictions on free movement could be justified when they met overriding requirements relating to the public interest, which included the protection of workers,[27] provided that employers were not already liable for similar contributions under the legislation of their home Member State, and that such measures were appropriate for securing the attainment of their objective and did not go beyond what was necessary in order to attain it.[28]

In *Finalarte*, the Court expanded on this reasoning.[29] It made clear that EU law did not preclude host Member States from imposing national rules on companies established in another Member State, such as those guaranteeing an entitlement to paid leave for posted workers. However, the Court set two conditions: (i) the workers do not enjoy an essentially similar level of protection under the law of the (home) Member State where their employer is established, so that the application of the national rules of the host Member State confers a genuine benefit on the workers concerned, which significantly adds to their social protection and (ii) the application of those rules by the host Member State is proportionate to the public interest objective pursued.[30] The Court also indicated that whereas such a restriction may be legitimately justified if it is necessary to safeguard, effectively and by appropriate means,

---

[25] Case C-113/89, *Rush Portuguesa* v. *Office National d'immigration*, ECLI:EU:C:1990:142.

[26] Cases C-62/81 and 63/81, *Seco* v. *EVI*, ECLI:EU:C:1982:34, para. 14; *Rush Portuguesa*, paras. 11 and 18; Case C-164/99, *Portugaia Construções*, ECLI:EU:C:2002:40; Alexandre Defossez, "Le détachement des travailleurs: concurrence loyale ou dumping social?" in *La concurrence réglementaire, sociale et fiscale dans l'Union européenne*, eds. Eric Carpano, Manuel Chastagnaret, and Emmanuelle Mazuyer (Brussels: Larcier, 2016), 219–236; Louis-Marie Le Rouzic, "Le dumping social et la crise de confiance dans l'Union européenne," *Revue de droit public* 4 (2017): 977–996; Sjoerd Feenstra, "How Can Viking/Laval Conundrum be Resolved? Balancing the Economics and the Social: One Bed for Two Dreams?" in *A European Social Union after the Crisis*, eds. Frank Vandenbroucke, Catherine Barnard, and Geert De Baere (Cambridge: Cambridge University Press, 2017), 315–319.

[27] *Arblade and Others*, para. 36; *Mazzoleni and ISA*, para. 27.

[28] *Portugaia Construções*, para. 19.

[29] *Finalarte*. In *Finlarte*, the European Court of Justice considered the compatibility of German law, which required temporary construction workers to make contributions to a social security scheme providing holidays for construction workers, with Article 56 TFEU.

[30] *Finalarte*, para. 53.

the overriding public interest of the social protection of workers,[31] it is not the case when the measures at hand pursue economic aims, such as the protection of national businesses.[32]

According to this line of reasoning, when national courts consider restrictive measures, they must balance the administrative and economic burdens imposed on employers against the increased social protection for workers (by comparison with the social protection afforded under the law of the workers' home Member State). Any rules purporting to offer a benefit for workers must thus provide a genuine benefit and significantly add to their social protection.

The Court also held that this reasoning applied to collective labour agreements. In *Arblade and Others*, the Court said that Article 56 TFEU does not preclude a host Member State from imposing on an undertaking established in another Member State, and temporarily carrying out work in the host Member State, a minimum wage requirement as fixed in a collective labour agreement.[33] As with state-based rules, the Court set conditions: the provisions of the collective labour agreement had to be sufficiently precise and accessible and could not render it impossible or excessively difficult in practice for an employer to determine the obligations with which s/he was required to comply.[34] Additionally, the Court confirmed that one of the justifications that Member States were permitted to advance, in defending national restrictions on the free movement of services, was the prevention of social dumping. In *Commission* v. *Germany*, the Court held that Member States could rely on the objective of preventing social dumping to extend their legislation or collective agreements relating to minimum wages to any person who was employed, even temporarily, within their territory.[35]

The equality principle developed in this case law carved out an important role for regulatory autonomy at the national level. The idea emerged that Member States enjoyed considerable authority both in defining the core of mandatory rules for the minimum protection of workers in their territory and in legitimately imposing national regulations on posted workers in seeking to

---

[31] *Finalarte*, para. 37 and 72; *Portugaia Construções*, para. 20 (and case law cited); Case C-60/03, *Wolf & Müller* v. *Pereira*, ECLI:EU:C:2004:610, para. 35.

[32] *Finalarte*, para. 39.

[33] *Arblade and Others*, para. 43.

[34] *Arblade and Others*, para. 43.

[35] *Arblade and Others*, para. 41; *Commission* v. *Germany*, paras. 54–61. "Social dumping" is a set of practices used by firms engaged in transborder market activities that seek to gain advantage over competitors in the host Member State through the use of a cheaper migrant (and/or undeclared) labour force, and in doing so harm worker rights and collective bargaining processes.

protect worker rights and prevent fraud and social dumping.[36] However, as explored in the next section, the Court subsequently turned away from the equality principle and instead moved towards a more economic rationale for the principle of non-discrimination. In a new line of cases, the Court considerably reduced Member State authority to impose measures on service providers and undertakings posting workers in their territory. The reason advanced for this shift in free movement law was that national regulatory measures involved additional expense, administrative and economic burdens and as such were liable to prohibit, impede or render less attractive the activities of said service providers or undertakings, even when such measures were intended to protect workers or fight against social dumping.

IV A NEW MILLENNIUM: A CHANGE OF PERSPECTIVE

1 *The Enlargement of the EU and Its Impact on EU Law*

On 1 May 2004, ten countries were simultaneously admitted to membership of the EU: Cyprus, the Czech Republic, Estonia, Hungary, Latvia, Lithuania, Malta, Poland, the Slovak Republic and Slovenia. This historical accession of mainly Central and Eastern European countries prompted a heated debate, motivated by the fear of a levelling downwards of services quality and unfair competition from service providers originating in countries with less stringent labour legislation, social protection and welfare rights. The debate came to a head in the national referenda on the Constitutional Treaty, held in the course of 2005. There emerged a real fear of a 'race to the bottom' for social protection, not only through the posted workers mechanism reviewed in the previous section but also through the outsourcing of jobs and companies to Central and Eastern European countries, manufacturing-based economies likely to be less sensitive to calls for labour-market regulation and social protection. The rhetoric of a 'race to the bottom' fuelled a political campaign targeting the concept of European integration.[37]

---

[36] Miguel Rodriguez-Piñero Bravo-Ferrer and Miguel Rodriguez-Piñero Royo, "The Rüffert Case: Posted Workers, Social Dumping and the European Court of Justice," in *Individuelle und kollektive Freiheit im Arbeitsrecht: Gedächtnisschrift für Ulrich Zachert*, eds. Thomas Dieterich et al. (Baden: Nomos, 2011), 95.

[37] Marie-Ange Moreau, "Le dumping social: une donnée construite par le droit de l'Union européenne," in *La concurrence réglementaire, sociale et fiscale dans l'Union européenne*, eds. Eric Carpano, Manuel Chastagnaret, and Emmanuelle Mazuyer (Brussels: Lacier, 2016), 187–201.

The current discrepancy between the living and social standards of the different Member States is unquestionable. The enlargement of the EU, coupled with the fundamental principles of freedom of movement of persons, workers and services, made it possible for nationals from Central and Eastern European countries to move and work in other Member States, performing similar economic activities as those offered by local workers at a more competitive price. Since labour costs vary significantly between the Member States, the free movement of services allows firms in Member States with high labour costs to take advantage of the favourable economic conditions offered by the national labour markets of Member States with lower labour costs. Economically, the practice of posting workers presents a clear competitive advantage for undertakings which employ or even outsource cheaper workers in the home Member State and post them to a host Member State for employment purposes.

This very real risk that Member States with stricter social regulations would become less competitive prompted various reactions among market actors and the general public. At least in Sweden the trade union movement resisted this temptation, welcomed accession of the new Member States as well as their workforce and opposed transitional rules for workers from new Member States, trusting that industrial action would remain a viable and legal strategy for safeguarding the principle of equal pay for equal work. By contrast, the fear of social dumping gave wind to nationalist and protectionist forces in a number of Member States, and contributed to the failure to ratify the Constitutional Treaty.

The heated popular debate on social dumping also animated the discussions on the Directive on Services in the Internal Market (the Services Directive), adopted in December 2006,[38] which led to it being stripped of its most politically controversial content. The original intention was to reduce obstacles to cross-border trade and to facilitate the freedom of establishment and the freedom to provide services, thereby promoting competitiveness within the EU. To achieve this objective, the European Commission initially proposed the introduction of a 'country-of-origin' principle, which would have allowed service providers and individuals to sell their services in other Member States, merely subject to the legislation of their country of origin and not to any of the requirements of the host Member State.

---

[38] European Parliament and Council Directive 2006/123/EC, On Services in the Internal Market, 2006 O.J. (L 376) 36; see Emiliano Grossman and Cornelia Woll, "The French Debate Over the Bolkestein Directive," *Comparative European Politics* 9, no. 3 (2011): 334–366.

However, some Member States and trade unions were concerned that the application of the country-of-origin principle to services would prompt most companies to establish themselves in, or create subsidiaries in, Member States with the lowest levels of social protection, from which they could provide services in all Member States. Additionally, it was argued that the workers posted by such companies would be subject to less stringent health and safety standards, which would lead to a further decline in consumer protection and social welfare. Last, the opponents of the country-of-origin principle in the Services Directive pointed to the danger that it would undermine the social protections in existing EU legislation on posted and temporary workers.

Rejection of the country-of-origin principle was driven by the deeply rooted *lex loci laboris* principle in labour law.[39] Opponents of the proposed Services Directive were motivated by the desire to protect national sovereignty, promote equal treatment of workers on the territory in which they are employed, and avoid competition on the basis of wages and working conditions.[40] Concerns about foreign competition for low-skill jobs and the consequences of such competition for the social protection systems of certain Member States dominated the debate and crystallised in the 'Polish plumber' controversy.[41] The symbol of the Polish plumber was used to exacerbate the protectionist tendencies of public opinion and enflamed the debate against social dumping.

The contentious country-of-origin principle was eventually removed from the Services Directive. The final text simply reaffirmed the general principles of free movement of services and mutual recognition.[42] According to the

[39] According to the *lex loci laboris* principle, an economically active person is subject to the legislation of the Member State in which territory s/he is employed, even if s/he resides in the territory of another Member State. Franzen describes this principle in the following terms: "The employee – according to the basic idea behind this view – is economically too weak to the resist the choice of law imposed by the employer. Thus, this choice would typically deprive the employee of the protection afforded by the law which would normally be applicable. 'Normally applicable' means the law of the place of work." Martin Franzen, "Conflicts of Laws in Employment Contracts and Industrial Relations," in *Comparative Labour Law and Industrial Relations in Industrialized Market Economies*, ed. Roger Blanpain (Alphen aan den Rijn: Wolters Kluwer, 2007), 224.

[40] Frank Hendrickx, "The Services Directive and Social Dumping: National Labour Law under Strain?" in *The Services Directive: Consequences for the Welfare State and the European Social Model*, eds. Ulla Neergaard, Ruth Nielsen, and Lynn Roseberry (Copenhagen: Djøf Publishing, 2008), 250.

[41] The Polish plumber (*le plombier polonais*) was a phrase first used in France by the French writer Philippe Val in the political satirical magazine *Charlie Hebdo*. It was used as a symbol of cheap labour coming from Central Europe as a result of the Services Directive during the 2005 French referendum on the EU Constitutional Treaty.

[42] Hendrickx, "The Services Directive and Social Dumping," 244.

principle of mutual recognition, as restated in Article 16 of the Services Directive, Member States may impose national laws on posted workers where such laws are not discriminatory with regard to nationality, are justified for reasons of public policy, public security, public health or environmental protection, are appropriate, and do not go beyond what is necessary to attain that objective.[43]

2 Return of the Country-of-Origin Principle through the Court

With no harmonisation of national laws on the establishment of companies and individuals, social conditions and welfare provision, it was inevitable that the Court would be called upon to clarify the application of the free movement principles. Amongst others, the posting of workers from their home Member State to a host Member State, as regulated by the Posting of Workers Directive, has led to many judgments, some of which have been highly controversial.[44]

---

[43] Alexandre Saydé, "Freedom as a Source of Constraint: Expanding Market Discipline through Free Movement," in *Research Handbook on the Law of the EU's Internal Market*, eds. Panos Koutrakos and Jukka Snell (Cheltenham: Elgar, 2017), 37.

[44] This case law has spawned a considerable scholarly literature. See, e.g., Ciaran O'Mara, "European Developments," *Irish Employment Law Journal* 5, no. 1 (2008): 39–43; Catherine Barnard, "The European Court of Justice as a Common Law Court? Viking and Laval in the United Kingdom," *Neue Zeitschrift für Arbeitsrecht*, (2011):122–125; Patrick Chaumette, "Les actions collectives syndicales dans le maillage des libertés communautaires des entreprises: CJCE 11 décembre 2007, ITF & The Finish Seamen's Union, aff. C-483/05, CJCE 18 décembre 2007, Laval & Partnery Ltd, aff. C-341/05," *Droit social* 2 (2008): 210–220; Bernard Teyssié, "Esquisse du droit communautaire des conflits collectif," *Étude doctrine, JCP/La Semaine juridique – Édition sociale*, no. 6 (2008): 15–18; Joël Cavallini, "Une action collective licite en droit interne peut être contraire à la libre prestation de services consacrée par le Traité de Rome," *JCP/La Semaine juridique – Édition sociale*, no. 6, (2008): 38–40; Christophe Vigneau, "Encadrement par la Cour de l'action collective au regard du Traité de Rome," *JCP/La Semaine juridique – Édition générale*, no. 13 (2008): 31–36; Charles-Eric Clesse, "Le plombier polonaise est-il de retour? Incidence de l'arrêt Laval sur le système belges et le respect des rémunérations y contenues," *Journal des tribunaux du travail* (2008): 219–223; Stefano Guadagno, "The Right to Strike in Europe in the Aftermath of Viking and Laval," *European Journal of Social Law* 4 (2012): 241–277; Le Rouzic, "Le dumping social et la crise de confiance dans l'Union européenne," 977–996; Simon Tans, "Case Report on *Laval*, 18 December 2007 (Case C-341/05) and *Viking*, 11 December 2007 (Case C-438/05)," *European Journal of Migration and Law* 10 (2008): 249–275; Barend Van Leeuwen, "An Illusion of Protection and an Assumption of Responsibility: The Possibility of Swedish State Liability after Laval," *Cambridge Yearbook of European Legal Studies* 14 (2012): 453–473; Catherine Barnard, "Social Dumping or Dumping Socialism?," *The Cambridge Law Journal* 67, no. 2 (2008): 262–264; Stefano Giubboni, "European Citizenship and Social Rights in Times of Crisis," *German Law Journal* 15, no. 5 (2015): 945–952.

The freedom to provide services and the concomitant posting of workers have always been closely linked to the question of wages and conditions of employment of posted workers, which ultimately depends on the law applicable to their employment contracts and the scope of industrial action to prevent the undercutting of wages. In some circumstances, the full application of the law of the country of origin generates a risk of social dumping, especially in the case of laws that are less protective than those of the host Member State. Thus, the Court has often been called upon to rule on the application of the Posting of Workers Directive in the context of host Member States with high social protection standards that exceed the minimum protection rules set down in the Posting of Workers Directive.

As explained earlier, the first generation of case law recognised that the protection of workers and the fight against social dumping could operate as an overriding reason of public interest that could legitimate the restriction of the freedom to provide services. The Court endorsed Member States' right to impose restrictions beyond the minimum standards set in the Posting of Workers Directive, provided those measures were justified by public interest objectives. As will be explained in this section, the Court changed its approach after the 2004 accession and circumscribed Member States' prerogatives, in favour of economic competition and to the detriment of worker rights and protection.

2.1 The Political and Economic Reasons for Jurisprudential Inconsistency

The inconsistencies in the free movement case law and the changes that occurred after accession can be put down to the co-existence of two paradigms on which European economic integration is based – regulatory neutrality versus regulatory competition. As Alexandre Saydé has argued, these two paradigms pervade free movement law and are strongly opposed.[45] On the one hand, the regulatory neutrality paradigm 'seeks to ensure that the competition among private businesses is not distorted by national regulations.'[46] From this angle, the principle of equal pay for equal work operates as a legitimate tool to ensure the neutrality of costs and labour law for businesses competing in the host Member State. Social dumping is considered an obstacle to economic integration, prosperity and innovation, and a distortion of competition among competing companies. By contrast, the regulatory

---

[45] Alexandre Saydé, "One Law, Two Competitions: An Enquiry into the Contradiction of Free Movement Law," *Cambridge Yearbook of European Legal Studies* 13 (2011): 365–415.

[46] Saydé, "One Law, Two Competitions," 366.

competition paradigm 'seeks to ensure the proper functioning of the competition among Member States'.[47] In that context, the country-of-origin principle, according to which service providers are entitled to sell their services in host Member States while only abiding by the legislation of their country of origin, is conceptualised as the natural functioning of economic integration.[48]

Thus, at the root of free movement principles is a foundational normative dilemma – between the contradictory missions of guaranteeing competition between Member States, on the one hand, and between private companies, on the other hand. This implies different prescriptions for the regulation of the internal market and has led to inconsistencies within the free movement case law of the Court. The first generation of cases followed the regulatory neutrality paradigm. The Court recognised Member States' rights and sovereignty to restrict the free movement principle under certain conditions. By contrast, the second generation of cases, which began after the 2004 enlargement, favoured the regulatory competition view. In this case law, analysed in the remainder of this section, differences in national labour standards were held to operate as unlawful restrictions on the free movement principle.

2.2 Interpreting the Core Set of Mandatory Rules as a Ceiling

The *Laval*,[49] *Rüffert*[50] and *Viking*[51] line of cases called into question the idea that Member States could impose restrictive measures on service providers and justify such measures based on the protection of social values and the fight against social dumping. In essence, the Court ruled that host Member States were confined to the mandatory rules of minimum protection provided under the Posting of Workers Directive and were barred from imposing higher labour standards on service providers, such as average levels of pay.

In *Laval*, a Latvian construction company won a public tender to renovate a school in Vaxholm, a small and affluent town in the outer suburbs of Stockholm.[52] None of their employees were members of a Swedish trade union. The Swedish Construction Workers Union (*Byggnads*) started

---

[47] Saydé, "One Law, Two Competitions," 366.
[48] Saydé, "One Law, Two Competitions," 410.
[49] Case C-341/05, *Laval un Partneri v. Svenska Byggnadsarbetareförbundet*, ECLI:EU:C:2007:809 [hereinafter *Laval*].
[50] Case C-346/06, *Rüffert v. Land Niedersachsen*, ECLI:EU:C:2008:189 [hereinafter *Rüffert*].
[51] Case C-438/05, *International Transport Workers' Federation and Finnish Seamen's Union v. Viking Line ABP and OÜ Viking Line Eesti*, ECLI:EU:C:2007:772 [hereinafter *Viking*].
[52] For the sake of transparency, it should be noted that Ulf Öberg represented the Swedish trade unions before the European Court of Justice in the *Laval* case.

negotiations with Laval to sign collective agreements which were to include, *inter alia*, pay rates. Since the company refused to sign a collective agreement and provide average rates of pay to its workers, the Swedish trade unions took collective action, including picketing at the work site. Although the Swedish Labour Court (*Arbetsdomstolen*) found that the Swedish trade unions had acted in accordance with Swedish law, it made a reference to the Court for a preliminary ruling on the question of whether such industrial action and Swedish law were in breach of EU law.

Advocate General Mengozzi, in his opinion, concluded that the Posting of Workers Directive and Article 49 of the Treaty of Rome (current Article 56 TFEU) should not be interpreted as preventing trade unions from taking collective action to compel a foreign service provider to subscribe to pay rates determined in accordance with a domestic collective agreement, as long as the collective action was motivated by public interest objectives and was not disproportionate. The Advocate General stated that when examining the proportionality of the collective action, the national court would have to consider whether the conditions laid down by the rules of the host Member State conferred a real advantage, such as significantly contributing to the social protection of posted workers, and did not duplicate any identical or essentially comparable protection available in the home state.[53] He added that EU law should refrain from intruding on national approaches to regulating industrial relations.[54] As a consequence, the Advocate General found that even though the Swedish system of collective bargaining gave trade unions more latitude to undertake collective action against foreign undertakings operating in Sweden, to set wages and working conditions in line with those applied in the rest of the country, it should be considered a functional equivalent of the Posting of Workers Directive's framework.[55]

The Court did not follow this line of reasoning. Instead, its judgment highlighted the supposed intrinsic uncertainty and lack of transparency of the Swedish system of industrial relations,[56] which relies on case-by-case negotiation between employers and trade unions. The Court found that the possibility that undertakings established in another Member State could be

---

[53] Opinion of Advocate General Mengozzi, Case C-341/05, *Laval un Partneri Ltd* v. *Svenska Byggnadsarbetareförbundet*, ECLI:EU:C:2007:291, para. 282.

[54] Opinion of Advocate General Mengozzi, para. 260.

[55] Opinion of Advocate General Mengozzi, para. 185.

[56] For an analysis of the Nordic model and its economies, see Jonas Pontusson, "Whither Social Europe?" *Challenge* 49, no. 6 (2006): 35–54; Jonas Pontusson, "The Comparative Politics of Labor-Initiated Reforms: Swedish Cases of Success and Failure," *Comparative Political Studies* 25, no. 4 (1993): 548–578.

forced by means of trade union action to sign a collective agreement constituted a restriction to the freedom to provide services within the meaning of Article 56 TFEU.[57] In the view of the Court, the restriction was especially problematic because of the lack of sufficiently precise and accessible provisions that would allow the undertaking to anticipate in advance the labour standards it would have to comply with.[58] In ruling as it did, the Court dismissed an interpretation of the Posting of Workers Directive that would have allowed Member States like Sweden to make the provision of services in its territory conditional on the observance of terms and conditions of employment going beyond the mandatory rules for minimum protection.

Article 3(7) of the Posting of Workers Directive provides that the mandatory rules in Articles 3(1) to 3(6) 'shall not prevent the application of terms and conditions of employment which are more favourable to workers'. In addition, Recital 13 of this Directive states that it provides for a '... nucleus of mandatory rules for minimum protection'. Read together, the two provisions strongly suggested that the intent of the Directive was to give Member States the latitude to impose higher labour standards on service providers. Furthermore, as indicated by Advocate General Mengozzi, the Posting of Workers Directive allows Member States to apply terms and conditions of employment which are more extensive than those established by virtue of Article 3(1), provided that such favourable terms and conditions do not infringe on the freedom to provide services.[59]

The Court, however, rejected these arguments, and ruled that the Directive could not be interpreted as allowing host Member States to make the provision of services in its territory conditional on the observance of terms and conditions of employment going beyond the mandatory rules for minimum protection. The floor of mandatory rules for minimum protection became a ceiling that significantly curtailed the employment regulation of Member States and the possibility for trade unions to undertake industrial action to ensure the respect of the principle of equal pay for equal work at the workplace.

The issue concerning the level of national social protection afforded to posted workers was raised again in *Rüffert*, a case involving a German building site and the wages paid to construction workers from Poland.[60] Once more, the Advocate General and the Court disagreed on the interpretation of the

---

[57] *Laval*, paras. 99 and 100.
[58] *Laval*, para. 110.
[59] Opinion of Advocate General Mengozzi, Case C-341/05, paras. 33 and 34.
[60] *Rüffert*.

Posting of Workers Directive in combination with Article 56 TFEU. According to the Advocate General, the minimum rate of pay required by the collective agreements under national law constituted the implementation of an enhanced level of social protection for workers as provided for under Article 3(7) of the Posting of Workers Directive.[61] By contrast, the Court found that Article 3(7) could not be interpreted as allowing the host Member State to make the provision of services on its national territory conditional on the observance of terms and conditions of employment going beyond the mandatory rules of minimum protection as provided for under the Directive.[62] The national legislation forcing undertakings to pay higher wages than those of their home Member State was seen as imposing an economic burden that might prohibit, impede or render less attractive the provision of services by employers in those Member States, and therefore the legislation was held to be an unjustified restriction on the free movement of services.[63]

In this second generation of free movement cases, the Court rejected the regulatory neutrality model of the *Rush Portuguesa* line of cases, in which the principles of equal pay for equal work and non-discrimination had figured so prominently to protect workers, prevent social dumping and endorse the social aspects of European integration. Instead, the Court endorsed the regulatory competition model of free movement law and upheld economic freedoms and the mutual recognition principle to the detriment of social rights.

With the *Laval* and *Rüffert* judgments, the Court held, contrary to the until-then predominant view, that the minimum standard of protection in the Posting of Workers Directive – a floor with room for improvement – was indeed the maximum ceiling above which there was no room for national regulation or industrial action. The competitive advantage provided by cheaper labour in another Member State was thus clearly permitted and constitutionally protected within the European Union under the free movement principle. In other words, the freedom to provide services trumped the principle of equal pay for equal work enshrined in the Treaty rules on the free movement of workers and services.

This interpretation had a number of possible unintended consequences. The *Laval* and *Rüffert* judgments effectively barred Member States and their trade unions from using the traditional tools of labour and employment law to

---

[61] Opinion of Advocate General Bot, Case C-346/06, *Dirk Rüffert* v. *Land Niedersachsen*, ECLI: EU:C:2007:541, paras. 94 and 95.

[62] *Rüffert*, para. 33.

[63] *Rüffert*, paras. 40–41; Case C-549/13, *Bundesdruckerei GmbH* v. *Stadt Dortmund*, ECLI:EU: C:2014:2235, para. 30.

require higher levels of worker protection from foreign companies, most notably the requirement that foreign undertakings operating within their territory use their average rates of pay, if such wages were higher than those of the home Member State. Thus, foreign service providers were exempted from industrial action and public procurement regulation in the host Member State, while local companies were subject to the unconditional application of these national measures. This form of reverse discrimination obviously placed local companies and their workforce at a significant competitive disadvantage.[64] Article 56 TFEU was essentially transformed into an instrument for undermining national labour law legislation designed to protect workers by restricting, among other things, unfair wage competition.[65]

Another important judgment in this second generation of case law was *Viking*. Decided in 2007, *Viking* involved a Finnish shipping company that operated a ferry sailing under the Finnish flag, with a Finnish crew, between Helsinki and Tallinn. After the company gave notice of its intention to reflag the ferry by registering it in Estonia and to replace the crew with Estonian workers, the International Transport Workers' Federation and its affiliate announced that they would take industrial action to prevent the company from using what they considered to be a "flag of convenience" (i.e. registering a ship in a country with lower labour standards). The Court ruled that a trade union's threat to strike, with the aim of pressuring an employer to sign a collective agreement, may constitute a restriction on the freedom of establishment if the terms of the collective agreement are likely to deter the company from exercising its freedom of establishment. The Court went on to say that such a restriction on freedom of establishment may be legitimate if it aims at protecting jobs or working conditions, and if all other ways of resolving the conflict are exhausted.[66] The Court also recognised the right to take collective action and the right to strike for the protection of workers are fundamental rights, which can legitimately justify a restriction to the free movement principles. However, in the specific facts of the case, the Court decided that the threat to strike amounted to an unlawful restriction of the freedom of establishment.

---

[64] For a more detailed analysis of the competitive pressures issue, see Saydé, "Freedom as a Source of Constraint," 45–46.

[65] Cathal Flynn, "The Protection of Workers' Rights and the Freedom of Movement: Compatible Objectives in the EU Legal Order? A Critical Analysis of the Laval and Rüffert Judgments of the ECJ," *Irish Journal of European Law* 16, no. 1 & 2 (2009): 191–192; but see Damjan Kukovec, "Law and the Periphery," *European Law Journal* 21, no. 3 (2015): 406–428.

[66] *Viking*, paras. 75–90.

Different from *Laval* and *Rüffert*, *Viking* involved a direct conflict between the freedom of establishment for companies and the right of workers to take collective action to block business decisions affecting their rights. This ruling thus illustrates another aspect of the free movement and mutual recognition principles: companies can strategically choose to establish themselves in Member States with low labour and social regulations and engage in strategic litigation and forum shopping in other Member States to relocate industrial disputes to jurisdictions more favourable to business interests.

V A POSSIBLE TURN OF THE TIDE? HOST EQUALITY AND THE PRINCIPLE OF EQUAL PAY FOR EQUAL WORK

1 *Growing Distrust in the European Construction*

1.1 Legislative Changes

The *Laval*, *Rüffert* and *Viking* cases revived the heated debate on social dumping and abuse of the mutual recognition and country-of-origin principles.[67] The European trade union movement mobilised against the Court's case law and argued that companies should not be allowed to freely elect the national law of low-regulation Member States and then rely on the free movement principle to provide services in high-regulation Member States. They pointed to the distortion of competition and structural disadvantage for domestic workers caused by permitting cheaper labour forces to 'export' their home employment law and work conditions to the host country. Instead, they advocated for equality of companies under the law of the host Member State, which would eliminate social dumping and would allow for merit-based competition between domestic and posted workers.[68]

---

[67] Simon Deakin, "Brexit, Labour Rights and Migration: Why Wisbech Matters to Brussels," Brexit Special Supplement, *German Law Journal* 17 (2016): 15–18. (Amongst others, the United Kingdom saw a rise in nationalism, and it can be argued that the presence of cheap posted workers from Central and East European countries was one of the factors leading to the Brexit vote.) See also Le Rouzic, "Le Dumping Social et la Crise de Confiance Dans l'Union Européenne," 977–996; Dorte Sindbjerg Martinsen, "The European Social Union and EU Legislative Politics," in A *European Social Union after the Crisis*, eds. Frank Vandenbroucke, Catherine Barnard, and Geert De Baere (Cambridge: Cambridge University Press, 2017): 467–474.

[68] Saydé, "Freedom as a Source of Constraint," 48–49.

In response to these concerns and distrust towards the Court's interpretation of the free movement principles, a new law was adopted in 2014.[69] The Enforcement Directive complements the Posting of Workers Directive and seeks to prevent companies from avoiding host Member State regulatory requirements by claiming that they operate primarily in another (home) Member State.

Generally speaking, under EU law, a company's place of business is important for determining which country's labour, tax, social security and other regulatory requirements are applicable. Drawing on the Court's place-of-business case law,[70] Article 4 of the Enforcement Directive states that '[i]n order to determine whether an undertaking genuinely performs substantial activities, other than purely internal management and/or administrative activities, the competent authorities shall make an overall assessment of all factual elements characterising those activities, taking account of a wider timeframe, carried out by an undertaking in the Member State of establishment, and where necessary, in the host Member State.' This inquiry is designed, among other things, to uncover letter-box entities that have no real connection to the jurisdiction claimed to be the primary jurisdiction. To conduct the assessment, and prevent abuses of the free movement principle, the Enforcement Directive requires a high degree of cooperation and mutual assistance among the public authorities of the Member States.

1.2 Labour and Social Rights in the Court's Case Law

Progressively, the Court has also started to back-track from its *Laval*, *Rüffert* and *Viking* reasoning. Although it is perhaps too early to speak of a third generation of case law, the Court appears to be retreating from the country-of-origin principle and the regulatory competition paradigm.

In the 2015 *RegioPost* case, the Court was asked to give a preliminary ruling on the Posting of Workers Directive. At issue was a German regional public procurement law which required that tender offers contain a commitment to pay either the rate established in the applicable collective agreement, or, in

---

[69] European Parliament and Council Directive 2014/67/EU, On the Enforcement of Directive 96/71/EC Concerning the Posting of Workers in the Framework of the Provision of Services and Amending Regulation (EU) N° 1024/2012 on Administrative Cooperation through the Internal Market Information System, 2014 O.J. (L 159) 11 [hereinafter "Enforcement Directive"].

[70] See, e.g., Case C-73/06, *Planzer Luxembourg v. Bundeszentralamt für Steuern*, ECLI:EU:C:2007:397, paras. 60-61; Case C-421/10, *Finanzamt v. Markus Stoppelkamp*, ECLI:EU:C:2011:640, para. 31.

the absence of such an agreement, the minimum rate set down in the regional law.[71] This condition applied to all workers, domestic and posted. In the facts of the case, the minimum rate established by law applied since there was no collective agreement at the time of the public tender. The Court found that the minimum pay requirement was permissible, notwithstanding the clear parallels with the *Rüffert* judgment. It added that the fact that the minimum pay set down in the regional law only applied to public contracts, not to private contracts, and therefore was somewhat in tension with the universality and transparency conditions of the Posting of Workers Directive, did not change the outcome.[72]

In *Sähköalojen*,[73] decided at roughly the same time, a group of Polish electricians that had been posted to Finland to build a nuclear power plant challenged their employment contract with their Polish employer. They claimed that the contract failed to respect the pay rates guaranteed under Finnish law for electricians (which incorporated the Finnish collective agreements in the sector), in violation of the minimum wage guarantee in the Posting of Workers Directive. While the Advocate General's opinion relied heavily on the earlier, free movement reasoning in *Laval*, the Court signalled a clear departure from that approach, in favour of equal pay for equal work, and held for the Polish electricians.

To elaborate: The Finnish collective agreements in question calculated pay based on a number of criteria, which included assigning individuals to specific pay groups, time-based hourly pay and piecework pay. They also included a number of different forms of remuneration, including holiday pay and compensation for travel time. Following *Laval*, the Advocate General underscored the burden on the Polish employer's free movement rights and the protectionist effect of these pay provisions for the domestic labour market. As a result, the Advocate General found that the Finnish pay rates could not be considered the 'minimum wage' guaranteed by the Posting of Workers Directive.

---

[71] Case C-115/14, *RegioPost v. Stadt Landau in der Pfalz*, ECLI:EU:C:2015:760 [hereinafter *RegioPost*].

[72] *RegioPost*, para. 64; Adrian Brown, "The Lawfulness of a Regional Law Requiring Tenderers for a Public Contract to Undertake to Pay Workers Performing that Contract the Minimum Wage Laid Down in that Law: Case C-115/14, RegioPost," *Public Procurement Law Review* 2 (2016): 49–55; Marco Rocca, "Arrêt 'RegioPost': Marché Public et Salaire Minimal," *Journal de Droit Européen* 2 (2016): 57–58; Safia Cazet, "Obligation de Versement d'un Salaire Minimal et Libre Prestation de Services," *Europe* 1 (2016): comm. 12.

[73] Case C-396/13, *Sähköalojen ammattiliitto v. Elektrobudowa Spółka Akcyjna*, ECLI:EU:C:2015:86 [hereinafter *Sähköalojen*].

The Court, however, did not follow the Advocate General's opinion. Rather than dwelling on the freedom to provide services, the Court emphasised the Directive's objective of ensuring fair competition between enterprises operating on the same territory and affording social protection for posted workers.[74] It also pointed to the extensive authority given to the host Member State to define the mandatory rules of worker protection, in particular the constituent elements of the minimum wage. The Court also limited that discretion so as to protect the interests of foreign undertakings in legal certainty: it stated that national rules must be binding and must meet the requirements of transparency, which means, in particular, that they must be accessible and clear.[75] Overall, however, the Court recognised that systems for calculating pay like the one in the Finnish collective agreements could be legitimately used to determine the mandatory wages to be paid to posted workers – equal pay for equal work.[76] The end result was that the Polish electricians, under the Posting of Workers Directive, had to be afforded the same treatment as workers employed by Finnish firms.

This last case, although encouraging for the protection of workers' rights, does not end the debate on social dumping. Another way in which enterprises can take advantage of national differences in social regulation is by posting workers from Member States with low social security contributions (and less generous social benefits) to Member States that require high social security contributions of their employers and employees. When an individual is employed across national borders, there is a long-standing EU scheme that applies (the 'Social Security Regulation').[77] The Social Security Regulation assigns individuals to a single national social security system and entrusts the social security body in that Member State with issuing a certificate that serves as proof that the individual is registered with the system and is paying contributions. For posted workers, who by definition are in the host Member State on a short-term basis, their social security system is that of their home Member State.

---

[74] *Sähköalojen*, para. 30.
[75] This transparency requirement echoes Article 5, para. 2, of the Enforcement Directive, which aims at improving access to information for Member States.
[76] *Sähköalojen*, para. 39.
[77] This scheme was initially set down in Council Regulation (EEC) 1408/71, On the Application of Social Security Schemes to Employed Persons, to Self-Employed Persons and to Members of their Families Moving within the Community, 1971 O.J. (L 149) 2. Since 1 May 2010, Regulation (EEC) 1408/71 has been replaced by European Parliament and Council Regulation (EC) 883/2004, On the Coordination of Social Security Systems, 2004 O.J. (L 166) 1 [hereinafter "Social Security Regulation"].

Over the past decade or so, there has been growing evidence of undertakings improperly obtaining certificates from (home) national authorities for their workers posted in other Member States. Before the Court, this issue has been raised by social security institutions in host Member States that have questioned the *bona fides* of the certificates issued by the social security institutions of home Member States. The traditional position under EU law is that social security bodies are bound by the principle of sincere cooperation and have a duty to trust one another.[78] As a result, the certificate issued by a Member State's social security institution establishes a presumption that the worker concerned is properly affiliated with the social security system of that Member State.

This is the view that prevailed in the case of *A-Rosa Flussschiff*. The Court stated that as long as a social security certificate is not withdrawn or declared invalid by the (home) Member State in which it was issued, it is binding on the competent institution of the (host) Member State in which that person actually works.[79] In *A-Rosa Flussschiff*, the regulatory imperative of affiliating individuals with a single social security system, and of entrusting the network of national social security institutions with administering this regulatory imperative, led the Court to conclude that the presumption applies even when the national body issued the certificate to workers falling outside the material scope of the Social Security Regulation, e.g. the work was performed on a permanent basis in the host Member State.[80] The Court dismissed arguments made by the national authorities regarding the need to prevent social dumping and to combat avoidance schemes that allow service providers to officially enrol in a Member State with low social contributions and pretend to 'temporarily' post workers in other Member States where such contributions are higher.

Recently, however, in the *Altun* judgment, the Court has given more credence to such claims.[81] In the facts of that case, a Belgian construction company sub-contracted all of the work on its Belgian construction sites to a firm established in Bulgaria that posted workers to the Belgian sites. Those workers had social security certificates issued by the responsible Bulgarian

---

[78] Article 4(3) TFEU.

[79] Case C-620/15, *A-Rosa Flussschiff* v. *Urssaf*, ECLI:EU:C:2017:309, paras. 40–41 [hereinafter *A-Rosa Flussschiff*]. See also Opinion of Advocate General Saugmandsgaard Øe, Case C-527/16, *Soziales und Konsumentenschutz* v. *Alpenrind GmbH*, ECLI:EU:C:2018:52, para. 43; Laetitia Driguez, "Portée des formulaires A1, sécurité sociale des travailleurs migrants," *Europe* 6 (2017): comm. 227.

[80] *A-Rosa Flussschiff*.

[81] Case C-359/16, *Altun and Others*, ECLI:EU:C:2018:63, paras. 49 and 61 [hereinafter *Altun*].

authority, but when the Belgian authorities investigated the matter, they found that the Bulgarian firm carried out no significant activity in Bulgaria and therefore the certificates, which were based on their status as temporary, posted workers based in Bulgaria, had been improperly granted. When the Belgian construction company was criminally prosecuted, the Belgian court referred the issue of status of the certificate to the Court. The Court reiterated that such certificates establish the presumption that the worker concerned is covered by (and employer and employee are paying into) the social security system of the home Member State in which the undertaking employing him/her is established and that they have binding effect. However, the Court went on to carve out an exception for certificates obtained through fraud or fraudulently relied upon by undertakings in the host state. It ruled that the application of EU law cannot be extended to cover transactions carried out for the purpose of fraudulently or wrongfully obtaining advantages provided for by EU law. As a result, the Court held that a national court may disregard the certificate if, on the basis of evidence and with due regard to the safeguard inherent in the right to a fair trial, it finds the existence of fraud.

The *Alpenrind* case decided in 2018 clarified the extent of the presumption of good faith attached to social security documents.[82] In that set of facts, an Austrian meat packing and processing firm used posted workers employed by a series of Hungarian undertakings. At issue was not a certificate, but a so-called portable document issued by the Hungarian social security institution and attesting to the coverage of the posted workers under the Hungarian social security scheme. In his opinion, Advocate General Øe drew a parallel between a portable document and the social security certificates at issue in the *A-Rosa Flussschiff* and *Altun* judgments, and concluded that such documents are binding on the competent institution of the host Member State, i.e. Austria, with the exception of cases involving fraud.

Although the Advocate General's opinion attached binding effect to portable documents, it did indicate that there are circumstances in which it is appropriate for host Member States to second guess the official determinations of home Member States, with the aim of uncovering the fraudulent use of posted workers to avoid the social contributions required by host Member States. Under the Social Security Regulation, for an individual to be considered a posted worker for social security purposes, that individual cannot be sent to replace another posted worker.[83] In interpreting this provision, the

---

[82] Case C-527/16, *Salzburger Gebietskrankenkasse v. Alpenrind GmbH*, ECLI:EU:C:2018:669 [hereinafter *Alpenrind*].

[83] Social Security Regulation, art. 12(1).

Advocate General departed from the restrictive position taken by Austria (and the other typically host Member States that appeared in the litigation). He found that the non-replacement provision was intended to prevent situations in which the same employer rotates its staff in order to circumvent the condition relating to the maximum term, i.e. twenty-four months, during which a worker will be considered a posted worker.[84] Therefore, successive postings by different employers are not in principle affected by the non-replacement condition. However, the result is different if there are personnel and/or organisational links between such employers. In that case, the Advocate General warned that there was a risk of fraud or abuse of rights and the host Member State would be entitled to examine whether the employers were attempting to circumvent the non-replacement condition. In the event of an affirmative conclusion of the investigation, the host Member State would be entitled to disregard the portable document or certificate.[85]

The Court followed the Advocate General in confirming the binding nature of portable documents but gave a broad interpretation of the 'non-replacement' condition. According to the Court, 'if a worker who is posted by his employer to carry out work in another Member State is replaced by another worker posted by another employer, the latter employee must be regarded as being "sent to replace another person"' in the sense of the Social Security Regulation.[86] According to this interpretation, one has to consider whether there is a recurrent use of posted workers to fill the same position or activity at the premises of the (same) host Member State undertaking. This is *regardless* of the location of the registered office of the employers concerned, and *irrespective of* whether there are personnel or organisational links between them.[87] Such posted workers are subject to the social security legislation of the host Member State.

2 The European Pillar of Social Rights and Beyond

On 17 November 2017, the European Parliament, the Council and the Commission endorsed the European Pillar of Social Rights in a proclamation signed at a summit for fair jobs and growth.[88] The Social Pillar sets out twenty key principles and rights. These concern equal opportunities and access to the

---

[84] Opinion of Advocate General Saugmandgaard Øe, Case C-527/16, para. 89.

[85] Opinion of Advocate General Saugmandgaard Øe, paras. 109–113.

[86] *Alpenrind*, para. 100.

[87] *Alpenrind*, paras. 96–100.

[88] Martinsen, "The European Social Union and EU Legislative Politics," 473; European Parliament, European Commission, and Council of the European Union, European Pillar of

labour market, fair working conditions, and social protection and inclusion, all of which are considered to be essential elements of fair and well-functioning labour markets and welfare systems in the twenty-first century. The right to fair and equal treatment regarding working conditions clearly provides for the need to foster the transition towards open-ended, flexible forms of employment while combating employment relationships based on precarious working conditions and the abuse of atypical contracts.

Additionally, in 2016, the European Commission introduced two proposals that forecast significant changes in the field of free movement: amendments to the Posting of Workers Directive and to the Social Security Regulation, the EU legislation at the centre of the litigation and the changing case law canvassed earlier in this chapter. These proposals aimed at enhancing the protection of workers, eliminating wage differences between posted and local workers, and improving fairness within the European internal market. Although the legislative debate on the amendments to the Social Security Regulation is still ongoing, the amended version of the Posting of Workers Directive was approved in June 2018.[89]

Turning to the specifics of the amendments to the Posting of Workers Directive, the Commission's proposal represented a departure from the country-of-origin and mutual recognition principles and a return to the principle of equal treatment of workers. Under a reinforced commitment to equal pay for equal work, posted workers would receive the same remuneration as local workers in the same position in the host Member State. Thus, the Commission proposed replacing the original guarantee of a minimum wage for posted workers with the 'same remuneration' for posted and local workers. In addition, the proposal introduced a limit on the application of the home Member State's labour law to the employment contract: if the anticipated or actual length of the posting exceeded twenty-four months, the law of the home Member State would no longer apply, but rather that of the host Member State.

These proposals proved to be extremely contentious in the Council, pitting Member States that routinely send out workers against Member States that generally receive them. National parliaments in several Central and Eastern European countries indicated their opposition to the harmonisation of remuneration and the establishment of a principle of equality of treatment between

---

Social Rights (2017), https://ec.europa.eu/commission/sites/beta-political/files/social-summit-european-pillar-social-rights-booklet_en.pdf.

[89] European Parliament and Council Directive (EU) 2018/957, Amending Directive 96/71/EC Concerning the Posting of Workers in the Framework of the Provision of Services, 2018 OJ (L 173) 16.

posted and local workers.[90] They took the position that wage differentials are an economic factor and do not result in unfair competition and argued that the Commission's proposal was in breach of the subsidiarity principle. In October 2017, however, an agreement was worked out in the Council, and after intensive negotiations involving the European Parliament, Commission and Council, the amendments were adopted in June 2018.[91] The new legislation provides for, among other things, the remuneration of posted workers in accordance with host Member State law and practices; the application of universally applicable collective agreements to posted workers across all sectors; and the equal treatment of temporary agency workers and local workers. All rules on remuneration which apply to local workers will also have to apply to posted workers, and remuneration will not only include the minimum rates of pay but also other elements such as bonuses and allowances. The maximum period contained in the Commission proposal (twenty-four months) for the application of foreign labour law has been shortened to twelve months, with the possibility of a sixth-month extension. The problem of avoidance by undertakings of host state law through the repeated replacement of posted workers with other posted workers is dealt with by making the calculation of the duration of the posting cumulative.

In its Annual Growth Survey 2018, the European Commission underscored the need to put in place labour and social protection legislation that responds to the new realities of employment, as well as the importance of Member State measures designed to help people build the skills necessary to navigate today's flexible and quickly evolving labour market.[92] The Commission called for an adaptation of social protection and labour market policies to evolving forms of employment and increased labour mobility. As one indication of the lag between social protection schemes and the current realities of the labour market, the Commission noted that more than half of independent workers in Europe are not covered by unemployment benefits. Overall, the Annual Growth Survey stressed that social protection systems should adapt to new ways of working: entitlements should be portable from one job to the next, cumulating contributions from multiple jobs should be facilitated and transitions between jobs should be secured.

All of these legislative and policy initiatives strongly suggest a departure from the regulatory competition paradigm, in favour of regulatory neutrality

---

[90] Bulgaria, the Czech Republic, Estonia, Hungary, Lithuania, Poland, Slovakia and Romania.

[91] See "Posting of workers," Council of the European Union website, last visited 23 October 2018, www.consilium.europa.eu/en/policies/labour-mobility/posting-workers/.

[92] Communication from the Commission, *Annual Growth Survey 2018*, COM (2017) 690 final.

and the principle of equal pay for equal work.[93] The current historical moment may in fact be a tipping point, in favour of a new general political direction and new priorities on employment. The changes do not only draw from the non-discrimination principles of the early decades of European integration. They also draw attention to the problem of adapting labour and social security regulations to the new realities and social abuses of contemporary labour markets, so that their guarantees can be equally effective in an economic panorama of short-term, 'atypical', 'non-standard forms of employment' and precarious work.

VI CONCLUDING REMARKS

The fine line between economic competition and social dumping is difficult to draw. Until recently, legitimate social claims of equality of treatment and equal pay for equal work were branded as xenophobic and protectionist. The recent rise of populism and nationalism challenges some of the core values of the European Union, but there is no doubt that a new political era has placed the social dimension of the European construction at the forefront.

It cannot be denied that the neoliberal stamp of EU legislation and the *Laval* line of cases contributed to the growing distrust of EU institutions and the revival of protectionism among national publics. Rising fear and anxiety can be traced to a number of sources, but one of the most prominent has been a perception of an increasing number of nationals immigrating from other Member States and third countries. This has led many European citizens to question the idea of the internal market and to favour a return to national isolation.[94] The current attempt in various Member States to restrict free movement of persons is not just a passing phenomenon but an expression of general distrust in the European foundational principle of free movement and its negative implications for national sovereignty.

Among the many examples of the relationship between EU free movement policies and national populist politics, Brexit is probably the most salient.[95]

---

[93] Some share the view that the European Union is currently economically driven, which exalts the principle of competition over that of cooperation and cannot be the basis for true equality. See Charlotte O'Brien, *Unity in Adversity, EU Citizenship, Social Justice and the Cautionary Tale of the UK* (Oxford: Hart Publishing, 2017).

[94] Éva Lukács Gellerne, "Brexit: A Point of Departure for the Future in the Field of the Free Movement of Persons," *Elte Law Journal* 1 (2016): 141–162; Deakin, "Brexit, Labour Rights and Migration," 15–18.

[95] Catherine Barnard, "Remains of the Day: Brexit and EU Social Policy," in *A European Social Union after the Crisis*, eds. Frank Vandenbroucke, Catherine Barnard, and Geert De Baere (Cambridge: Cambridge University Press, 2017), 477–501.

During and after the referendum, Brexiteers have promised that the free movement of persons and services will be restricted in order to protect national jobs and national workers from European migrants. The common economic view, repeated often in the public debate, that migration has a net positive effect on Member State economies, has not stemmed the political backlash.

However, the most profound – and promising – legacy of the ongoing political and legal debate may not be nationalism, but EU constitutional transformation. As correctly predicted by European trade unions, the undermining of the principles of non-discrimination and equal pay for equal work has indeed caused nationalistic and xenophobic reactions. In many cases, however, the political reaction of adversely affected social and economic groups was not a retreat to national politics but vigorous activation of democratic procedures at the EU and national levels to attempt to reverse the course taken by the EU's legislature and judiciary. This process contributed to the post-*Laval* legislative developments analysed in this chapter, including the Enforcement Directive and the amendments to the Posting of Workers Directive.

More generally speaking, disappointment with the EU's political direction in the 2000s has led to a call for political accountability through the introduction of a degree of parliamentarism within the European Union.[96] The process for electing the president of the European Commission offers a good example of the first germs of such parliamentarism, especially since the 2014 European Parliament elections and the adoption of the so-called *Spitzenkandidaten* process. According to the Treaty on European Union, the president of the European Commission is elected by the European Parliament, based on a proposal by the European Council, which must act by qualified majority and takes into account the results of the European Parliament's elections.[97] The innovation of the European Parliament elections of 2014 was that the major European political parties agreed to each put forward a 'lead candidate' (*Spitzenkandidat*) who, depending on which party won the most seats in the elections, would become the Commission's president. The rationale for this innovation was that it would improve legitimacy and

---

[96] "The Commission Bears a Political Responsibility for the Lindsey Strikes," European Federation of Building and Woodworkers website, last visited 23 October 2018, www.efbww .org/default.asp?Index=732&Language=en; see also Frank Vandenbroucke, Catherine Barnard, and Geert De Baere, eds., *A European Social Union after the Crisis* (Cambridge: Cambridge University Press, 2017); Teija Tiilikainen, "Concepts of Parliamentarism in the EU's Political System." The Finnish Institute of International Affairs, ECPR General Conference, Panel: Concepts in the EU Multilevel System, Montreal, 26–29 August 2015.

[97] Article 17.1 TEU.

democratise the selection of the head of the EU executive branch, namely, the Commission president.[98] The use of the *Spitzenkandidaten* process in 2014 led to the appointment of Jean-Claude Juncker (lead candidate of the European People's Party) as president of the European Commission.[99]

The fate of the *Spitzenkandidaten* process going forward is uncertain. After the 2014 elections, the European Parliament took a number of steps to transform the practice into an institutional fixture. In November 2015, the Parliament sought to constitutionally anchor the *Spitzenkandidaten* process to secure its repetition in future elections.[100] In 2017, the Parliament also adopted two resolutions that would enhance parliamentarism in the EU, including through the *Spitzenkandidaten* process. Critics argued that the process undermined the duty of the European Council and the European Parliament to select the best candidate, and forced them to accept the candidate that can win elections in the various Member States. They pointed to the lack of transparency of the process and the increased politicisation of the Commission, which was intended by the European founders to be a neutral body independent of national interests.

In the run up to the elections for the 2019–2024 legislature, France, the Czech Republic, Hungary, Lithuania, the Netherlands, Poland, Portugal, and Slovakia voiced their opposition to the process. Lurking behind some of the criticism was the fear that the elections could well be won by Eurosceptic groups, which would then be entitled to appoint their lead candidate as Commission president. The European Parliament, however, warned that it was ready to use its power to elect the Commission president to reject any candidate that was not appointed according to the *Spitzenkandidaten* process, reiterating the view that this process supports European democracy and solidarity.[101] Indeed, in the May 2019 elections, the main European political

---

[98] "Spitzenkandidaten: The Underlying Story," European Parliament website, last visited 23 October 2018, www.europarltv.europa.eu/programme/others/spitzenkandidaten-the-underlying-story; Johannes Müller Gómez, "The European Council and the Future of European Democracy, Prospects of an Enhanced Multi-level Parliamentarism." EUSA Conference, Miami, 2017; Johannes Müller Gómez and Wolfgang Wessls, "The EP Elections 2014 and Their Consequences: A Further Step towards EU Parliamentarism?" *Cuadernos Europeos de Deusto* 52 (2015): 39–66.

[99] For further analysis of the process, see Chapter 6; and Gert-Jan Put, Steven Van Hecke, Corey Cunningham, and Wouter Wolfs, "The Choice of *Spitzenkandidaten*: A Comparative Analysis of the Europarties' Selection Procedures," *Politics and Governance* 4, no. 1 (2016): 9–22.

[100] Resolution of 11 November 2015 on the reform of the electoral law of the EU (2015/2035(INL)).

[101] European Parliament Press Release, "Spitzenkandidaten" Process Cannot Be Overturned, Say MEPs (7 February 2018), www.europarl.europa.eu/news/en/press-room/20180202IPR97026/spitzenkandidaten-process-cannot-be-overturned-say-meps. However, even though the European Parliament and its constituent political parties are supporters of the process, it has

parties announced *Spitzenkandidaten* and ran political campaigns on that basis. However, the election results were even more fragmented than in the previous election cycle, and no party or coalition of parties was able to command a clear majority to back one of the *Spitzenkandidaten*. The Member States governments in the European Council proceeded to select a *Spitzenkandidaten* outsider as their nominee, the German CDU politician Ursula von der Leyen. Although her nomination gained the support of all European leaders minus Germany, which abstained from the vote, it de facto departed from the *Spitzenkandidaten* process. The European Parliament, of course, remained constitutionally entitled to reject von der Leyen's nomination as Commission president, but the inability of any single party or coalition of parties to secure a majority of the seats placed it in a weak position to do so. Despite the strong criticism surrounding the process and the nomination of a candidate who did not participate in the European elections and had not originally been supported by any of the major European political parties, Ursula von der Leyen was elected by a narrow majority on 16 July 2019 to be president of the European Commission.

In conclusion, the rise of nationalism and populism in the European Union is a predicted and predictable reaction to a polity – including courts and their policymaking – that failed to put the economic and political interests of a majority of workers and EU citizens at the core of the political, economic and social priorities of the past years. Although the future is uncertain, the solution is not to retreat to the nation state or to the old system of EU governance, but rather to affirm the ideal of an ever closer political union that is accountable before the European electorate.

---

been noted that national parties (which form the European political parties) are themselves often reluctant to centre their campaign efforts on their respective *Spitzenkandidaten*; in the 2014 elections, *Spitzenkandidaten* figured prominently only in those Member States where there were strong links between the lead candidate and the national party. See Daniela Braun and Tobias Schwarzbözl, "Put in the Spotlight or Largely Ignored? Emphasis on the *Spitzenkandidaten* by Political Parties in Their Online Campaigns for European Elections," *Journal of European Public Policy* (online) (2018), https://doi.org/10.1080/13501763.2018 .1454493.

8

The Emerging Architecture of EU Asylum Policy

Insights into the Administrative Governance of the Common European Asylum System

EVANGELIA (LILIAN) TSOURDI

I INTRODUCTION

Crisis vocabulary has consistently dominated public discourse on asylum in both the EU and its Member States since 2015. The spike in arrivals of individuals seeking asylum in the EU highlighted the limitations inherent in the legal design and implementation modes of EU asylum policy, most notably the existence of a structural solidarity deficit.[1] These developments came shortly after the completion of the second phase of legislative harmonisation in the EU asylum policy in June 2013 and the establishment of a Common European Asylum System (CEAS), which was heralded as a historic achievement. At that point, EU institutions and Member States believed that asylum policy had been fully hammered out and they heralded the dawn of the 'age of implementation'.[2]

Nevertheless, a mere two years later, increased arrivals in the summer and early autumn of 2015 overwhelmed the EU and triggered several political and

---

[1] See Daniel Thym, "The 'Refugee Crisis' as a Challenge of Legal Design and Institutional Legitimacy," *Common Market Law Review* 53, no. 6 (2016): 1545–1574; Evangelia (Lilian) Tsourdi, "Solidarity at Work? The Prevalence of Emergency-Driven Solidarity in the Administrative Governance of the Common European Asylum System," *Maastricht Journal of European and Comparative Law* 24, no.5 (2017): 667–686; Maarten Den Heijer, Jorrit Rijpma, and Thomas Spijkerboer, "Coercion, Prohibition, and Great Expectations: The Continuing Failure of the Common European Asylum System," *Common Market Law Review* 53, no. 3 (2016): 607–642; and, Augustín José Menéndez, "The Refugee Crisis: Between Human Tragedy and Symptom of the Structural Crisis of European Integration," *European Law Journal* 22, no. 4 (2016): 388–416.

[2] See European Council Conclusions, EUCO 79/14 (27 June 2014), and for a commentary, Philippe De Bruycker, "The Missed Opportunity of the 'Ypres Guidelines' of the European Council Regarding Immigration and Asylum," *Migration Policy Centre Blog*, 29 July 2014, https://blogs.eui.eu/migrationpolicycentre/the-missed-opportunity-of-the-ypres-guidelines-of-the-european-council-regarding-immigration-and-asylum/.

legal reactions at the national level. Notably, Member States detected 1.82 million illegal border crossings in 2015, with the largest number reported on the so-called Eastern Mediterranean route between Turkey and the Greek islands in the Eastern Aegean Sea (885,386 crossings).[3] Further illegal border crossings occurred through the so-called Central Mediterranean route to Italy (154,000 crossings).[4] However, few applied for asylum in Greece and instead crossed the border to the Former Yugoslav Republic of Macedonia and continued onwards, towards the Hungarian border with Serbia, and then to their final destinations in the EU (so-called secondary movements). Those arriving in Italy also conducted secondary movements. While it is not possible to give exact numbers, the EU's external borders management agency, Frontex, estimated that there were close to one million secondary movements.[5] Great numbers of those arriving were fleeing the Syrian civil war. Of the approximately 1.4 million applications for international protection that were lodged in the EU28 in 2015, 383,710 were filed by Syrian applicants.[6]

Asylum seekers faced harsh material conditions at entry points, reaching the level of a humanitarian emergency. Certain Member States at the external borders raised physical barriers with their non-EU neighbours in the hope of stopping refugee movements; for example, Hungary constructed a temporary technical obstacle on its border with Serbia which led to a shift of the route towards the Croatian border with Serbia. Others refused to welcome refugees in the name of their national cultural and religious identity.[7] One after the other, states participating in the Schengen area reinstated border controls at internal EU frontiers, invoking a serious threat to their internal security and public policy related to secondary movements of irregular migrants. (Between September 2015 and March 2016, the countries concerned were Belgium, Denmark, Germany, Hungary, Austria, Slovenia, Sweden and Norway.)[8] These unilateral decisions, while found to be in compliance with the

---

[3] Frontex, *Risk Analysis for 2016*, 2016, 6.
[4] Frontex, *Risk Analysis for 2016*, 6.
[5] Frontex, *Risk Analysis for 2016*, 6.
[6] European Asylum Support Office, *Annual Report on the Situation of Asylum in the European Union*, 2016, 8, 10.
[7] See, e.g., Matthew Karnitschnig, "Orban Says Migrants Threaten 'Christian' Europe," *Politico Europe*, 3 September 2015, www.politico.eu/article/orban-migrants-threaten-christian-europe-identity-refugees-asylum-crisis/. Referring to the Hungarian PM's op-ed for the German newspaper *Frankfurter Allgemeine Zeitung*.
[8] Communication from the Commission, *Back to Schengen: A Roadmap*, COM (2016) 120 (4 March 2016), 9.

The Emerging Architecture of EU Asylum Policy

Schengen Borders Code,[9] eroded the Schengen *acquis* guaranteeing border-free travel within the Schengen area. Faced with these events, the EU institutions adopted an array of additional policy, legal and operational measures to prevent a collapse of the CEAS and the unravelling of the EU's area of free movement. Although, objectively, the number of those arriving at the EU's external borders has significantly dropped since then, the issue of asylum still dominates the EU policy agenda, revealing a deep rift between Member States. The rift is political. At its heart lies contestation over a number of central issues: the nature of the obligation to provide asylum and whether it is a common obligation at EU level or one that binds each Member State individually; the scope for central EU action to enhance solidarity in the field of asylum; and the appropriateness of 'people-sharing' as a tool for achieving a fair sharing of responsibilities between Member States.

What explains the CEAS's poor performance? One important factor is path dependence, which has led to the entrenchment of a responsibility-allocation scheme that was conceived almost a decade before the EU came to exercise powers in the policy area. The Dublin system, initially established in a 1990 convention outside of EU law, was largely blind to fair sharing, let alone to the preferences of asylum seekers; it created asymmetrical burdens by assigning the primary duty to examine an asylum claim and to provide materially for asylum seekers to the state 'responsible' for the asylum seeker's presence in the EU.[10] Another important reason for the CEAS's current troubles is the over-reliance on legislative harmonisation as the main avenue for achieving the goals of a common policy, at the expense of attention to implementation. By failing to attend to the administrative dimension of asylum policy, the EU has sought to provide what is effectively a regional public good[11] by allocating the

---

[9]   See European Parliament and Council Regulation (EU) 2016/399, On the Rules Governing the Movement of Persons Across Borders (Schengen Borders Code), 2016 O.J. (L 77) 1 [hereinafter Schengen Borders Code]. The decisions were initially based on Article 25 of the Schengen Borders Code, which allows for reintroduced controls at internal borders for a period of up to two months. The controls have been subsequently prolonged based on Articles 23 and 24 of the Schengen Borders Code, which allows for reintroduced controls at internal borders for a period of up to six months.

[10]   Reference is mainly made to the Convention Determining the State Responsible for Examining Applications for Asylum Lodged in One of the Member States of the European Communities, 15 June 1990, 1997 O.J. (C 254) 1 (entered into force 1 September 1997) [hereinafter Dublin Convention].

[11]   Suhrke conceptualises refugee protection as a global public good, a good whose benefits once provided: (i) cannot be excluded from other members of the international community (non-excludability) and (ii) do not diminish or become scarce when enjoyed (non-rivalry). See Astri Suhrke, "Burden-Sharing During Refugee Emergencies: The Logic of Collective versus National Action," *Journal of Refugee Studies* 11, no. 4 (1998): 396. Betts argues that in refugee

vast majority of governance obligations – including financial ones – to Member States with different levels of economic development and different conceptualisations of welfare. One important goal of this chapter is to shine light on the administrative and implementation dimension of asylum policy, as a first step to improving the EU's record in the asylum field.

Scratching beneath the superficial layer of the ongoing political and media debate, this contribution holistically analyses the content of the EU's Common European Asylum System, a notion that despite its centrality to the EU's asylum policy lacks a precise definition. Beyond legislative harmonisation, I point to the central role of implementation, which should be viewed as an integral part of the system design, and critically assess the impact of the principle of solidarity and fair-sharing of responsibility. Thereafter, the chapter examines the CEAS's changing implementation modes, critically assessing to what extent they signal a passage towards an emerging integrated European administration. It also traces the relationship between the events of the 2015–2016 refugee crisis and developments in the administrative architecture of the CEAS. The chapter concludes by highlighting how Member State unilateralism and externalisation, i.e. the transfer of obligations to third countries, are increasingly taking centre stage and are operating as a parallel – or indeed even alternative – track to harmonisation and intra-EU cooperation on asylum matters.

II EMERGENCE OF THE COMMON EUROPEAN ASYLUM SYSTEM

1 *Beginnings*

Until 1999, coordination of Member State asylum policy (directly linked to their international law obligations under the 1951 Refugee Convention and other international instruments) was done largely outside the EU framework. The 1990 Dublin Convention, a public international law instrument, allocated responsibility among EU countries for examining asylum applications. Although the Maastricht Treaty made asylum an EU competence, it was placed in the Treaty on European Union and very little was decided because of the limitations of the intergovernmental method that applied.

---

protection it is unlikely these non-excludable benefits will accrue equally to all members of the international community. States with greater proximity to a given refugee outflow benefit more from a neighbouring state's contribution, thus making refugee protection a regional public good. See Alexander Betts, *Protection by Persuasion: International Cooperation in the Refugee Regime* (Ithaca, NY: Cornell University Press, 2009), 29.

The entry into force of the Treaty of Amsterdam[12] in 1999 and of the Tampere European Council conclusions[13] later that year marked a turn in both the level of ambition and the *telos* of a European asylum policy. The Tampere conclusions called for the development of a common EU policy on asylum and migration[14] and introduced the goal of developing a Common European Asylum System.[15] Although the Amsterdam Treaty avoided reference to the notions of a common policy or a CEAS, it provided for the adoption of three types of measures: on asylum,[16] refugees and displaced persons,[17] and immigration policy.[18] The inclusion of asylum policy in the Amsterdam Treaty was somewhat ambivalent. Certain elements were conceived of as a corollary to the establishment of an internal market and the need to guarantee freedom of movement of persons. In particular, measures related to responsibility allocation for the examination of asylum claims, as well as those related to the establishment of minimum standards for giving temporary protection to displaced persons, were explicitly formulated as 'directly related flanking measures' that would support the aim of a common external border – and the abolition of internal borders – within the Schengen area.[19] However, the remainder of the contemplated asylum measures were broadly categorised as 'other measures in the fields of asylum, immigration and safeguarding the rights of nationals of third countries'.[20] The fact that this latter set of measures was distinguished indicated that they were not to be understood *per se* as corollary measures but rather as contributing to a European asylum policy in its own right.

2 Lisbon Treaty: Aim of a Common Policy and Output of a Common Asylum System

With the entry into force of the Lisbon Treaty in 2009, the ambition to create a CEAS that had been expressed throughout the years as a political commitment was reflected for the first time in law.

---

[12] See Treaty of Amsterdam Amending the Treaty on European Union, the Treaties Establishing the European Communities and Certain Related Acts, 2 October 1997, 1997, O.J. (C 340) 1.

[13] European Council, Tampere Presidency Conclusions (15–16 October 1999).

[14] European Council, Tampere Presidency Conclusions, para. 10.

[15] European Council, Tampere Presidency Conclusions, para. 13.

[16] See Article 63(1) Treaty Establishing the European Community [hereinafter TEC].

[17] See Article 63(2) TEC.

[18] See Article 63(3) TEC. The latter were relevant in what concerns the issuance of residence permits for recognised beneficiaries.

[19] See Article 61(a) TEC, read in conjunction with Articles 63(1)(a) and 63(2)(a). Article 14(2) TEC stated the following: 'the internal market shall comprise an area without internal frontiers in which the free movement of goods, persons, services and capital is ensured'.

[20] See Article 63(1)(a) TEC.

To begin with, a general legal basis frames the creation of the entire Area of Freedom, Security and Justice (AFSJ). Article 67 TFEU stipulates:

> [t]he Union shall constitute an area of freedom, security and justice with respect for fundamental rights and the different legal systems and traditions of the Member States.[21] It shall ensure the absence of internal border controls for persons and shall frame a common policy on asylum, immigration and external border control, based on solidarity between Member States, which is fair towards third-country nationals.[22]

Thus, common policies on asylum, immigration and external border control became an integral part of the AFSJ.[23] Although the text of Article 67 TFEU refers to the three constituent parts as 'a' common policy, further legal bases clarify that each of these, i.e. asylum, immigration and external border controls, constitutes a separate policy with distinct aims.[24] These articles, i.e. Articles 77, 78 and 79 TFEU, can be considered as *lex specialis* compared to Article 67 TFEU. All aspects of this policy are qualified in the following manner: they should be based on 'solidarity between Member States' and they should be 'fair for third country nationals'. Therefore, inter-state solidarity and fairness towards third country nationals emerge as overarching principles in the entire AFSJ area.[25]

Turning now to Article 78 TFEU establishing the EU's competence specifically in the asylum field, there are two important concepts that serve as the legal foundation for significant EU powers in the field: (i) in Article 78(1) TFEU, there is an overarching aim of developing 'a common policy on asylum, subsidiary protection and temporary protection';[26] and (ii) in Article 78(2) TFEU, the output of this policy should be 'a common European asylum system'.[27] Although the term 'asylum' figures in both provisions, it takes on different meanings, and it is important to explore both to understand fully the concept of the CEAS.

The first meaning, asylum *in the strict sense*, is included in Article 78(1) TFEU, which proclaims the development of a 'common policy on asylum, subsidiary protection and temporary protection'. 'Asylum' here refers to the

---

[21] See Article 67(1) TFEU.
[22] See Article 67(2) TFEU.
[23] For an overview of AFSJ, see Chapter 14.
[24] See Article 77 TFEU, for the external border controls policy, Article 78 TFEU for the asylum policy and Article 79 TFEU for the immigration policy.
[25] See also Article 80 TFEU, and Subsection II.3 of this chapter.
[26] See Article 78(1) TFEU.
[27] See Article 78(2) TFEU.

protection status that is linked with the 1951 Refugee Convention, same as in the Amsterdam Treaty. More specifically, in the Amsterdam Treaty, the provisions on asylum made direct reference to 'refugees'[28] and 'refugee status',[29] bearing links with the 1951 Refugee Convention. That Convention defines a 'refugee' as an individual who is outside her country of nationality or, if stateless, former habitual residence, and is unable or unwilling to avail herself of the protection of that country owing to a well-founded fear of being persecuted for reasons of race, religion, nationality, membership of a particular social group or political opinion.[30] In addition, the Convention stipulates a number of civil and political, as well as economic and social, rights for refugees, such as the rights to religion, wage-earning employment and public education.[31] It also lays down the rule of *non-refoulement* in binding terms.[32]

In light of the intended continuity in this field, 'asylum' in Article 78(1) TFEU should be interpreted in the same sense. This conclusion is also supported by the fact that 'asylum' is juxtaposed with 'subsidiary protection' and 'temporary protection' as additional elements of the same 'common policy'. In view of their importance to the overall scheme, it bears dwelling for a moment on these two other forms of protection. *Subsidiary protection* is a new protection status introduced by EU law. As suggested by the name, it is *subsidiary* to refugee status, meaning additional to refugee protection, and concerns individuals who would not qualify as refugees but are still considered to have protection needs. These needs are linked to Member States' obligations under international and European human rights law, including the prohibition of *refoulement*, i.e. the prohibition of return to a location where the individual faces a real risk of being subjected to torture or inhuman or degrading treatment.[33] Nevertheless, the introduction of subsidiary protection

---

[28] See Article 63(1)(c) TEC.

[29] See Article 63(1)(d) TEC.

[30] See United Nations Convention Relating to the Status of Refugees, July 25, 1951, 189 U.N.T.S. 150, Article 1(A)2 [hereinafter 1951 Refugee Convention].

[31] For a detailed commentary of the Convention see Andreas Zimmermann, ed., *The 1951 Convention Relating to the Status of Refugees and Its 1967 Protocol* (New York: Oxford University Press, 2011), as well as Guy Goodwin-Gill and Jane McAdam, *The Refugee in International Law* (New York: Oxford University Press, 2007), and James Hathaway and Michelle Foster, *The Law of Refugee Status* (Cambridge: Cambridge University Press, 2014).

[32] See 1951 Refugee Convention, Article 33(1), which reads as follows: '[n]o Contracting State shall expel or return ("refouler") a refugee in any manner whatsoever to the frontiers of territories where his life or freedom would be threatened on account of his race, religion, nationality, membership of a particular social group or political opinion.'

[33] For the precise content of subsidiary protection see European Parliament and Council Directive 2011/95/EU, On Standards for the Qualification of Third-Country Nationals or Stateless Persons as Beneficiaries of International Protection, for a Uniform Status for Refugees

has not resulted in a comprehensive and systematic consolidation of all protection possibilities within international law.[34] Indeed, Member States continue to operate various types of non-harmonised complementary statuses.[35] Beneficiaries of subsidiary protection in the EU enjoy a number of civil and political, as well as economic and social, rights, the majority of which are the same as for recognised refugees.[36] With respect to *temporary protection* under EU law, it applies when there is a mass influx of migrants. In these situations, the normal rules of CEAS can be 'frozen' and exceptional procedures resulting in a special protection status can be temporarily activated by a unanimous decision of the Council of the European Union.[37] Temporary protection includes special rules for asylum procedures (they are temporarily frozen); reception conditions (they are more elementary than those normally foreseen); and responsibility-allocation (through voluntary burden-sharing arrangements). To date there is no commonly agreed definition of temporary protection at the international level. However, the temporary protection schemes that have been operationalised contain a number of common elements: it is a grant of protection of a temporary nature from the receiving state to specific groups or individuals; there is an expectation that it is an interim solution until either return or transfer to another third country is possible; and

---

or for Persons Eligible for Subsidiary Protection, and for the Content of the Protection Granted, 2011 O.J. (L 337) 9, art. 15 [hereinafter 2011 Qualification Directive] and Evangelia (Lilian) Tsourdi, "What Protection for Persons Fleeing Indiscriminate Violence? The Impact of the European Courts on the EU Subsidiary Protection Regime," in *Refuge from Inhumanity: War Refugees and International Humanitarian Law*, eds. David James Cantor and Jean-Francois Durieux (Leiden: Brill/Martinus Nijhoff, 2014), 270.

[34] See Jane McAdam, *Complementary Protection in International Refugee Law* (New York: Oxford University Press, 2007), 56.

[35] For an overview of national statuses of complementary protection in nine Member States after the adoption of the predecessor Qualification Directive from 2004, see European Council on Refugees and Exiles, "Complementary Protection in Europe," July 2009. The 2010 Odysseus Academic Network study on the future of the CEAS identified this as an element which undermined harmonisation, as currently there is no common minimum level of protection for all individuals in need (understood as encompassing all international obligations of Member States that prevent expulsion). See Philippe De Bruycker et al., *Setting up a Common European Asylum System: Report on the Application of Existing Instruments and Proposals for the New System* (European Parliament, 2010), 191, 196.

[36] See 2011 Qualification Directive, recital 39. See also Articles 20–35 for analysis.

[37] See Council Directive 2001/55/EC, On Minimum Standards for Giving Temporary Protection in the Event of a Mass Influx of Displaced Persons and on Measures Promoting a Balance of Efforts Between Member States in Receiving Such Persons and Bearing the Consequences Thereof, 2001 O.J. (L 212) 12 [hereinafter Temporary Protection Directive or TPD].

The Emerging Architecture of EU Asylum Policy

it usually affords fewer rights to the individual than those prescribed by the 1951 Refugee Convention.[38]

Beyond the definition in international refugee law, the term 'asylum' can also be used *in the broad sense*, i.e. a shorthand for the entire common policy. This second meaning is employed both in Article 67 TFEU, which, as explained previously, frames the entire AFSJ, and in Article 78(2), which directs the EU institutions to establish 'a common European asylum system'.[39] The Union can adopt legally binding acts in the material field of asylum (referred to here in the broader sense) with the aim of developing a common policy, but, as a shared competence and not an area of exclusive competence,[40] Union action is framed by the principles of subsidiarity and proportionality.[41] This general obligation, enhanced under the Treaty of Lisbon,[42] is stressed explicitly in the Area of Freedom, Security and Justice,[43] presumably due to the political sensitivity of its subject matter. The principle of proportionality is defined as not exceeding what is necessary to achieve the objectives of the Treaties.[44] Despite the limitations of subsidiarity and proportionality, the objective of setting up a 'common' policy can be understood as entailing a high harmonisation imperative. The next section examines how this imperative is further refined by the principle of solidarity and fair-sharing of responsibility, which might arguably entail an additional imperative for action at EU level. It also is important to point out that Article 78(1) TFEU specifically requires that the common policy be compatible with the 1951 Refugee Convention and other treaties.

More broadly speaking, the language in the Lisbon Treaty largely frees asylum policy of its 'sidekick status' status – so apparent in the Amsterdam Treaty – with respect to the Schengen area and the establishment of an internal market. Although this development had taken place much earlier at

---

[38] See Susan M. Akram and Terry Rempel, "Temporary Protection as an Instrument for Implementing the Right of Return for Palestinian Refugees," *Boston University International Law Journal* 22, no.1 (2004): 11–12 and Meltem Ineli-Ciger, *Temporary Protection in Law and Practice* (Leiden: Brill, 2018).

[39] This interpretation of 'asylum' is supported by the use of the term in policy documents, including various European Council conclusions, as well as by the list of the specific measures and legal bases that are included within the broader CEAS – a status of asylum, a status of subsidiary protection and a system of temporary protection. See Article 78(2)(a), (b), (c) TFEU.

[40] See Article 4(2)(j) TFEU.

[41] See Article 5(1) TEU.

[42] See for details, Article 5 TEU, and Protocol No. 2 to the TFEU, On the Application of the Principles of Subsidiarity and Proportionality. In a nutshell, this Protocol introduces an 'early warning system' providing a watchdog status for national parliaments.

[43] See Article 69 TFEU.

[44] See Article 5(4) TEU.

the political level, the Lisbon Treaty affirms the change in the law. Indeed, certain authors even more ambitiously argue that the creation of an AFSJ is the ultimate *telos* of the entire EU integration project: 'the constitutional structure of the Union has also undergone a gradual change from an Internal Market, to an Area of Freedom, Security and Justice which complements and overcomes the stage of economic integration'.[45]

After setting down the objective of a 'common European asylum system', Article 78(2) TFEU details the different 'measures on asylum' that comprise such a system, nuancing the notion of asylum under EU law as compared to international law.[46] These legislative harmonisation measures concern: the definition of who qualifies as a refugee or a beneficiary of subsidiary protection; common procedures for the examination of asylum claims; reception conditions that should be afforded to asylum seekers during the examination of their claims including a number of socio-economic rights; and the standards of treatment of recognised refugees and subsidiary protection beneficiaries including their right to a residence permit on the basis of protection grounds.[47] An additional clause refers to the external dimension of the system, namely 'partnership and cooperation with third countries for the purpose of managing inflows of people applying for asylum or subsidiary or temporary protection'.[48]

Although legislative harmonisation is an important element of a CEAS, it is not the only one. As research in the social sciences and public policy studies have demonstrated, systems designed to achieve certain ends comprise a variety of public and private actors, and require attention to all phases of the policymaking cycle and the feedback loops that exist among the various components.[49] What, then, are the parts of the asylum system? I argue that

---

[45] See Sara Inglesias-Sanchez, "Free Movement of Third Country Nationals in the European Union? Main Features, Deficiencies and Challenges of the New Mobility Rights in the Area of Freedom, Security and Justice," *European Law Journal* 15, no. 6 (2009): 795, referring to the writings of Oliver Suhr, "Besondere Bestimmungen über den Raum der Freiheit, der Sicherheit und des Rechts," in *Verfassung der Europäischen Union. Kommentar der Grundlagenbestimmungen*, eds. Christian Callies and Matthias Ruffert (Munich: CH Beck, 2006), 506.

[46] Article 78(2) (a)–(g) TFEU.

[47] Article 78(2) (a)–(f) TFEU.

[48] Article 78(2) (g) TFEU.

[49] See, e.g., Robert E. Goodin, Martin Rein, and Michael Moran, "The Public and its Policies," in *The Oxford Handbook of Public Policy*, eds. Robert E. Goodin, Martin Rein, and Michael Moran (Oxford: Oxford University Press, 2008), 3–35; Edward C. Page, *Policy Without Politicians Bureaucratic Influence in Comparative Perspective* (Oxford: Oxford University Press, 2012); Michael Hill and Peter Hupe, *Implementing Public Policy: Governance in Theory and Practice* (London: Sage Publications, 2002); Morten Egeberg, ed., *Multilevel Union*

they are not merely the legislative rules that form the system but also the actors that are meant to implement these rules. Therefore, the implementation phase, rather than being distinct, is part and parcel of the system. The CEAS *is* the rules and it *also is* their implementation. In view of this understanding, I contend that the goal in Article 78(2) TFEU to establish a 'common system' enhances the integration imperative, because it entails not only the enactment of highly harmonised norms but also putting into place significant, high-quality cooperation between the concerned actors.

In sum, the Common European Asylum System should be understood as an output that encompasses both the legislative harmonisation component, and its operationalisation. The legally harmonised norms are an essential part of this system, but not the sole one. Modes of implementation, including the interaction between the EU and national levels, equally form part of the system. Alongside the harmonised norms is therefore an administrative system that connects relevant EU and international institutions, national authorities, including but not necessarily limited to public administration, as well as private actors such as civil society on asylum matters. Hence, the study of EU asylum policy from an EU administrative law perspective is crucial if one is to understand its shortcomings, and conceptualise effective ways to overcome them.

3 The Impact of the Principle of Solidarity and Fair-Sharing of Responsibility

The principle of solidarity is central to the development of the Common European Asylum System. In the analysis of EU law generally speaking, solidarity is often said to be a foundational principle, but there is controversy over whether it should be viewed as a binding legal principle or as a political norm.[50] Although it is recognised as foundational in the Treaty on European Union, those provisions are largely aspirational; furthermore, the status of solidarity as a binding general principle of law is highly controversial.

    Administration: The Transformation of Executive Politics in Europe (Basingstoke: Palgrave Macmillan, 2006).

[50] Daniel Thym and Evangelia (Lilian) Tsourdi, "Searching for Solidarity in the EU Asylum and Border Policies," *Maastricht Journal of European and Comparative Law* 24, no. 5 (2017): 607. See also Armin von Bogdandy, "Founding Principles," in *Principles of European Constitutional Law*, eds. Armin von Bogdandy and Jürgen Bast (Oxford: Hart Publishing, 2009), 53–54; and Malcolm Ross, "Solidarity: A New Constitutional Paradigm for the EU?," in *Promoting Solidarity in the European Union*, eds. Malcolm Ross and Yuri Borgmann-Prebil (New York: Oxford University Press, 2010), 41–44.

However, more specific expressions of solidarity appear in different provisions of the EU Treaties.[51] These solidarities are both state-centred and individual-centred, and they often operate as the source of legally binding duties.[52]

In EU asylum policy, there are different solidarities at play. First, as already mentioned, state-centred solidarity and fairness towards third country nationals underpins the entire AFSJ area.[53] The Treaty also introduces in Article 80 TFEU a far-reaching statement of the principle of solidarity and fair-sharing of responsibility that underpins (or should underpin) the EU's asylum policy; this can be called *structural solidarity*. Finally, through Article 78(3) the Treaty provides for the adoption of provisional measures 'in the event of one or more Member States being confronted by an emergency situation characterised by a sudden inflow of nationals of third countries'; this can be called *emergency solidarity*.[54] All of these are state-centred,[55] intra-EU, forms of solidarity.

As I have analysed elsewhere,[56] the principle of solidarity and fair sharing of responsibility under Article 80 TFEU profoundly impacts the goal of asylum policy, dictates a certain 'quality' in the cooperation among the different actors and arguably unsettles its implementation modes. Article 80 TFEU says:

> The policies of the Union set out in this Chapter and their implementation shall be governed by the principle of solidarity and fair sharing of responsibility, including its financial implications, between the Member States. Whenever necessary, the Union acts adopted pursuant to this Chapter shall contain appropriate measures to give effect to this principle.

---

[51] See Peter Hilpold, "Understanding Solidarity within EU law: An Analysis of the 'Islands of Solidarity' with Particular Regard to Monetary Union," *Yearbook of European Law* 34, no. 1 (2015): 257–285; Esin Küçük, "Solidarity in EU Law: An Elusive Political Statement or a Legal Principle with Substance?" *Maastricht Journal of European and Comparative Law* 23, no. 6 (2016): 965–983; Michele Knodt and Anne Tews, *Solidarität in der EU* (Baden-Baden: Nomos, 2014).

[52] An example of state-centred solidarity is the so-called solidarity clause in EU disaster law established in Article 222 TFEU; see analysis in Theodore Konstadinides, "Civil Protection Cooperation in EU Law: Is there Room for Solidarity to Wriggle Past?" *European Law Journal* 19, no. 2 (2013): 267–282. An example of individual-centred solidarity is communitarian solidarity between EU citizens; see conceptualisation in Floris De Witte, *Justice in the EU: The Emergence of Transnational Solidarity* (Oxford: Oxford University Press, 2015), 123–168.

[53] Article 67(2) TFEU.

[54] Article 78(3) TFEU.

[55] See Valsamis Mitsilegas, "Humanizing Solidarity in European Refugee Law: The Promise of Mutual Recognition," *Maastricht Journal of European and Comparative Law* 24, no. 5 (2017): 722–724.

[56] See Tsourdi, "Solidarity at Work?" 672–675.

This provision creates binding legal obligations and should impact both the legislative and implementation phases. The Article's wording not only permits, but in fact *requires* the adoption of concrete measures, whenever necessary. Special importance should be attached to the Article's reference to 'solidarity *and* fair sharing of responsibility', which ratchets up the duty – 'solidarity plus'.[57] The aim is to provide support up to the point where each Member State is contributing its fair share. More ambitiously, the objective should be to structure the policy and its implementation in such a way that asymmetrical burdens do not occur in the first place.

Inter-state solidarity is therefore a vital legal principle in the context of the CEAS. It is structural to this policy area and should be vested with far-reaching effects. Merely limiting its scope to adopting partial palliative measures is not enough. It arguably requires new measures to offset those effects of the CEAS that existing solidarity measures do not compensate for. It can even require a redesign of the CEAS' legislative instruments and, possibly, its implementation modes.

Notwithstanding the importance of inter-state solidarity and fair sharing, the CEAS currently lacks a genuine system for allocating responsibility among the Member States based on objective indicators.[58] Member States often assert that they are 'overburdened', but such claims cannot be objectively substantiated and they raise the suspicion, among other Member States, that the failure to comply with EU law obligations derives not from 'inability' but from 'unwillingness'. Generally speaking, the claim of migratory 'pressure' is not based on pre-defined objective criteria but is merely ascertained on a common-sense basis. Even when objective criteria are evoked to support common-sense assessments, e.g. number of migrants arriving, there is no clarity as to whether migratory pressure should be evaluated on an absolute or a relative basis. Instinctively, almost any observer would agree that the arrival of, say, 20,000 asylum seekers (an objective metric) will have a different impact in Germany than in Malta. Thus, a more complete understanding of fair sharing would seek to relativise pressure by taking into account characteristics of the receiving state, such as population, GDP, unemployment rates and so on. Remarkably though, as will be analysed later, even the measures that have most recently been adopted or proposed for the CEAS are not keyed to the relative migratory pressures faced by Member States.

---

[57] Tsourdi, "Solidarity at Work?" 673–674.
[58] See Philippe De Bruycker and Evangelia (Lilian) Tsourdi, "In Search of Fairness in Responsibility-Sharing," *Forced Migration Review* 51 (2015): 64.

III IMPLEMENTATION MODES IN THE CEAS: FROM EXECUTIVE FEDERALISM TOWARDS AN INTEGRATED ADMINISTRATION?

Academic commentary on EU asylum policy has largely focused on the legislative component and the content of the harmonised legal norms that have been set down for the Member States.[59] The administrative component, however, is equally important, and indeed, the visible failures of EU asylum policy of the past years can be attributed in no small part to shortcomings in the CEAS' administrative architecture. To fill the important gap in the academic literature and to engage critically with the transformations that are taking place, this chapter adopts the analytical perspective of administrative governance. In this vein, this section provides an overview of implementation in the CEAS and examines how it has shifted in recent years, drawing on the more general literature on EU administrative law and paying special attention to the role of the solidarity principle. It also explores the relationship between the events of the 2015–2016 refugee crisis and changes in EU asylum policy.

The initial implementation design of the CEAS was broadly underpinned by the theory of executive federalism.[60] This theory can be summed up as follows: apart from exceptional cases where the EU level directly implements policies (direct implementation), national executives assume responsibility in the main for the application of European law (indirect implementation).[61] Strictly applied, this leads to a neat division of labour for most policies, where legislation is adopted at EU level, and the implementation of EU law is a matter of predominantly national concern. The realisation of a common policy is thus secured primarily through legal harmonisation, aided by the European Court of Justice as the authoritative interpreter of EU law.

---

[59] See, e.g., Steve Peers, Violeta Moreno-Lax, Madeline Garlick, and Elspeth Guild, eds., *EU Immigration and Asylum Law (Text and Commentary): Second Revised Edition* (Leiden: Martinus Nijhoff, 2015); Kay Hailbronner and Daniel Thym, *EU Immigration and Asylum Law Commentary* (Munich: Beck/Hart Publishing, 2016); Helen O'Nions, *Asylum-A Right Denied: A Critical Analysis of European Asylum Policy* (Farnham: Ashgate, 2014); Marcelle Reneman, *EU Asylum Procedures and the Right to an Effective Remedy* (Oxford: Hart Publishing, 2014).

[60] Lenaerts describes 'executive federalism' in the following sense: ' . . . the division of powers between the central government and the component entities is not just one defined in terms of areas in which each government holds substantive competence, but relates also to the split between the central government holding the legislative power and the component entities holding the executive power in a given areas'; see Koen Lenaerts, "Regulating the Regulatory Process: 'Delegation of Powers' in the European Community," *European Law Review* 18, no. 1 (1993): 28.

[61] See, e.g., Jürgen Schwarze, *European Administrative Law: Revised 1st Edition* (London: Sweet and Maxwell, 2006), 6–8.

The Emerging Architecture of EU Asylum Policy · 205

Exceptionally, the Commission is involved in its role of guardian of the treaties, to pursue infringements of EU law.

The theory of executive federalism, however, increasingly fails to capture the reality of implementation of EU law, and the intricate links that increasingly exist between the EU and the national levels. Examples of this more complex reality include comitology committees,[62] networks[63] and agencies.[64] Thus a significant body of research on EU administrative law points to the rise of 'integrated administration', which defies the old categories of direct and indirect implementation. As poignantly observed by Hofmann and Türk, 'integrated administration in Europe is therefore not so much a multi-level system in the sense of a hierarchy superimposed on Member States' administrations. It is a system of integrated levels.'[65]

As traced later, contemporary developments in asylum policy implementation broadly follow the more general pattern. The common European asylum system as set down in the Lisbon Treaty was conceptualised as a 'common system of national variants'. What is common is the set of legal rules Member States are called on to implement, rather than the implementation stage itself. Neither the Treaties nor secondary legislation initially foresaw intense administrative interaction at the implementation stage. On the contrary, each Member State holds primary responsibility for implementation at national level of the harmonised legal rules set at EU level. This can be clearly inferred from Article 78 TFEU, which foresees that 'a Member State' is ultimately responsible for the examination of an asylum application.[66] Secondary EU legislation on asylum is also explicit on this point: the norms contained in

---

[62] See, for example, Christian Joerges and Jürgen Neyer, "From Intergovernmental Bargaining to Deliberative Political Processes: The Constitutionalisation of Commitology," *European Law Journal* 3, no. 3 (1997): 253.

[63] See Paul Craig and Gráinne De Búrca, *EU Law: Texts, Cases and Materials*, 6th ed. (New York: Oxford University Press, 2015), 162–183, for an analysis of decision-making and new forms of governance.

[64] One of the first works to formulate the necessity to give a proper account to the legal reality going beyond a dichotomy of implementation by either the European or national level was Edoardo Chiti, "The Emergence of a Community Administration: The Case of European Agencies," *Common Market Law Review* 37, no. 2 (2000): 309. More recently, Chamon understands agencies to contribute to an atypical form of administrative integration since the typical form would be further reliance on direct administration (by the Council or the Commission); see Merijn Chamon, *EU Agencies: Legal and Political Limits to the Transformation of the EU Administration* (New York: Oxford University Press, 2016).

[65] See Herwig C. H. Hoffmann and Alexander H. Türk, "Conclusions: Europe's Integrated Administration," in *EU Administrative Governance*, eds. Herwig C.H. Hofmann and Alexander H. Türk (Cheltenham: Edward Elgar, 2006), 583.

[66] See Article 78(2)(e) TFEU.

these instruments impose specific duties on Member States with a view to establishing functioning and well-resourced national asylum systems.[67] Nonetheless, three key elements in the design of asylum implementation link Member States with each other, as well as with the EU institutions. These are: responsibility assignation; practical cooperation; and EU funding. The links were initially modest, but they have all been reinforced in recent times, both through the adoption of additional legal instruments and through administrative practice, leading to the emergence of an incipient integrated administration.

1 The 'Dublin System': From Responsibility Assignation towards People Sharing?

Even if the EU's common asylum system essentially consists of twenty-eight national systems, one element had to be coordinated from the outset: responsibility assignation. This term refers to the identification of the responsible Member State for examining a specific asylum claim. On the one hand, responsibility assignation sought to counter 'forum shopping',[68] meaning the filing by the same individual of multiple asylum claims in different Member States, which had been facilitated by the abolition of internal border controls. On the other hand, it sought to avoid the situation of 'refugees in orbit',[69] meaning the abdication of responsibility by each Member State, with the attendant risk of leaving asylum seekers in limbo.

Currently, it is the Dublin III Regulation that assigns responsibility within the CEAS.[70] This instrument contains criteria and mechanisms for

---

[67] See European Parliament and Council Directive 2013/33/EU, Laying Down Standards for the Reception of Applicants for International Protection, 2013 O.J. (L 180) 96, art. 29(2) stating Member States should: 'allocate the necessary resources in connection with the national law implementing this Directive' and European Parliament and Council Directive 2013/32/EU, On Common Procedures for Granting and Withdrawing International Protection, 2013 O.J. (L 180) 60, art. 2(f) [hereinafter 2013 Procedures Directive] clarifying that a 'determining authority' should be understood as 'any quasi-judicial or administrative body *in a Member State* responsible for examining applications for international protection competent to take decisions at first instance in such cases' [emphasis added].

[68] See for elaboration of this point in Joined Cases C-411/10 and 493/10, N.S. and M.E., ECLI: EU:C:2011:865, para. 79.

[69] For an early account of this phenomenon see Göran Melander, *Refugees in Orbit* (Geneva: International University Exchange Fund, 1978).

[70] To be precise, Ireland and the United Kingdom, which benefit from opt-out/opt-in possibilities for some of the measures pertaining to the Area of Freedom, Security and Justice, have exercised their right to opt into this legal instrument. Denmark, which cannot be bound by non-'Schengen-relevant' Area of Freedom, Security and Justice measures based on EU law, has

determining 'the Member State responsible for examining an application for international protection lodged in one of the Member States'.[71] The basic premise of Dublin III is that a single Member State is responsible for each application.[72] The Regulation provides a hierarchy of criteria for identifying the responsible state.[73] Apart from limited cases related to unaccompanied minors and safeguarding family unity, this is in principle the State primarily responsible for the person's presence in the EU.[74] In practice, this usually means the State of first irregular entry, i.e. entry to the EU territory that has not been conducted through an authorised border crossing point. Where asylum seekers are present in the territory of a Member State other than the 'responsible Member State' as understood under the Regulation, they are to be transferred to the responsible Member State. However, Member States *must* abstain from such a transfer when 'there are substantial grounds for believing that there are systemic flaws in the asylum procedure and in the reception conditions for applicants in that Member State, resulting in a risk of inhuman or degrading treatment within the meaning of Article 4 of the Charter of Fundamental Rights of the European Union'.[75] In addition, they *may* abstain from a transfer for any other reasons, including on humanitarian and compassionate grounds.[76] Finally, they retain the right to return the applicant to a safe third country outside the EU territory, provided the rules

signed an agreement under international law with the EU, associating itself with the contents of the Dublin Regulation. Moreover, the four EFTA States participate in EU responsibility assignation, based on international treaties which require them to apply the Dublin rules. The Regulation currently in force is European Parliament and Council Regulation (EU) 604/2013, Establishing the Criteria and Mechanisms for Determining the Member State Responsible for Examining an Application for International Protection Lodged in One of the Member States by a Third-Country National or a Stateless Person, 2013 O.J. (L 180) 31 [hereinafter Dublin III Regulation]. As mentioned previously, the EU's responsibility-allocation system was first developed during the phase of intergovernmental cooperation based on the Dublin Convention, signed under international law (see Note 10). When asylum became a shared competence, a new Regulation was adopted, namely Council Regulation (EC) 343/2003, Establishing the Criteria and Mechanisms for Determining the Member State Responsible for Examining an Asylum Application Lodged in one of the Member States by a Third-Country National, 2003 O.J. (L 50) 1 [hereinafter Dublin II Regulation], which remained in force until 2013 when that instrument was replaced as part of the adoption of a new generation of asylum legislative instruments.

[71] See Dublin III Regulation, art. 1.

[72] See Dublin III Regulation, art. 3(1).

[73] See Dublin III Regulation, chap. III.

[74] E.g. the Member State which issued a residence document or a visa. See Dublin III Regulation, art. 12.

[75] See Dublin III Regulation, art. 3(2).

[76] See Dublin III Regulation, chap. IV.

and safeguards contained in the Directive establishing common asylum procedures are ensured.[77]

This system does not lead to fair sharing of responsibility between the Member States, since that responsibility will largely depend on the geographical location of each State. The problems created by the application of the Dublin system long predated the surge of asylum seeker arrivals in 2015–2016. They have been critically assessed by a wealth of academic commentators,[78] and have formed the basis of a rich body of pre-crisis litigation before the Court of Justice of the European Union and the European Court of Human Rights.[79]

In terms of administration, the Dublin system incorporates elements of intense horizontal transnational cooperation between national administrations, e.g. information exchange, to finalise the determination of responsibility and to conduct eventual transfers of asylum seekers to the responsible Member State.[80] Nevertheless, the system is not underpinned by an understanding of asylum provision as a common EU responsibility and a regional public good. Instead, once responsibility is assigned, it is for the individual Member State alone to provide for the refugee; any further EU measures, such as EU funding, are of a limited scale. No people-sharing measures, i.e. further redistribution of asylum seekers or recognised beneficiaries of international protection, are currently incorporated in the CEAS. As soon as possible after international protection is granted, the Member State that granted status must issue the beneficiary with a residence permit on protection grounds;[81] under EU law, the beneficiary does not enjoy the right of free movement to other Member States.

Despite the unfair distributive effect of Dublin, the responsibility-assignation aspect of the policy design had shifted very little prior to the refugee crisis. The only concrete initiatives had been the extremely small-scale relocation projects in Malta, based on voluntariness, which had yielded

---

[77] See Dublin III Regulation, art. 3(3) and 2013 Procedures Directive.

[78] See, e.g., Paul McDonough and Evangelia (Lilian) Tsourdi, "The 'Other' Greek Crisis: Asylum and EU Solidarity," *Refugee Survey Quarterly* 31, no. 4 (2012): 67–100 and Francesco Maiani, "The Dublin III Regulation: A New Legal Framework for a More Humane System?" in *Reforming the Common European Asylum System: The New European Refugee Law*, eds. Vincent Chetail, Philippe De Bruycker, and Francesco Maiani (Leiden: Brill, 2016), 104–114.

[79] See, in particular: *MSS v. Belgium and Greece*, App. No. 30696, ECLI:CE:ECHR:2011:0121, Judgment 2011 and N.S. and M.E.

[80] See Dublin III Regulation, arts. 34–35.

[81] See 2011 Qualification Directive, art. 24.

The Emerging Architecture of EU Asylum Policy

extremely modest results.[82] The refugee crisis brought about a remarkable shift in the administration modes of CEAS through the establishment of emergency relocation, meaning intra-EU transfer of asylum seekers between Member States as a short-term exception to the normal responsibility-assignation rules.[83] Emergency relocation was established for the benefit of Greece and Italy, which under the normal application of the Dublin system rules would have been responsible for the asylum seekers. After the transfer from Italy and Greece, the 'Member State of relocation' acquired responsibility for examining the asylum applications and, if the assessment was positive, for providing international protection, including a residence permit on that basis. These relocation schemes were more numerically robust than in the past;[84] moreover, the established quotas were obligatory, thus representing a first attempt to frame solidarity *and* fair-sharing as an obligation, rather than as a discretionary act.

The effectiveness of emergency relocation was, however, undercut by several factors. First, some Member States in Eastern Europe refused to implement their obligations under the schemes and did not cooperate in effectively relocating asylum seekers to their territories, leading the Commission to open infringement proceedings against them.[85] Two of the Member States in question, notably Hungary and Slovakia, mounted a legal challenge of their own against the Council decision establishing mandatory emergency relocation before the Court of Justice. They constructed a series of imaginative arguments regarding procedural failings that had occurred during the adoption process of the legal instrument, and they also argued substantive violations of EU law, notably the principle of proportionality. The Court rejected

---

[82] See European Asylum Support Office, "Fact Finding Report on Intra-EU Relocation Activities from Malta," July 2012.

[83] Council Decision (EU) 2015/1523, Establishing Provisional Measures in the Area of International Protection for the Benefit of Italy and of Greece, 2015 O.J. (L 239) 146 [hereinafter 1st Emergency Relocation Decision] and Council Decision (EU) 2015/1601, Establishing Provisional Measures in the Area of International Protection for the Benefit of Italy and Greece, 2015 O.J. (L 248) 80 [hereinafter 2nd Emergency Relocation Decision]. For analysis see Salvatore Fabio Nicolosi, "Emerging Challenges of the Temporary Relocation Measures under European Union Asylum Law," *European Law Review* 41, no. 3 (2016): 338–361.

[84] A total of 160,000 persons were to be relocated. See 1st Emergency Relocation Decision, art. 4, and 2nd Emergency Relocation Decision, art. 4.

[85] Case C-715/17, *Commission v. Poland*, 2018 O.J. (C 112) 18; Case C-718/17, *Commission v. Hungary*, 2018 O.J. (C 112) 19; Case C-719/17, *Commission v. Czech Republic*, 2018 O.J. (C 112) 18.

all of Hungary and Slovakia's arguments,[86] and found them to be in violation of EU law, but they continued to resist implementation.

Another factor that hindered the effectiveness of the relocation schemes was their nature as emergency-driven responses.[87] Both Emergency Decisions numerically capped the beneficiaries concerned,[88] restrictively defined the eligible applicants for relocation, and expired after two years.[89] As a result, Member States at the external border were given very little assurance that there would be the requisite level of solidarity and that it would be sustainable over the long run. Finally, in the same way as the general Dublin III Regulation, both Decisions failed to take into account the preferences of asylum seekers. They thus failed to ensure the full collaboration of asylum seekers.

In terms of the administrative set up of the emergency relocation schemes, the process exhibited elements of transnational administrative cooperation familiar from the Dublin III Regulation, but which were further enhanced. In addition, the EU level was more operationally involved, for example deploying experts under the aegis of the EU's asylum agency, the European Asylum Support Office (EASO). These experts were involved in information provision, registration and matching procedures for eligible applicants.[90] Nonetheless, the process also uncovered the current limits of transnational administrative cooperation. The lack of mutual trust among the Member State authorities pushed them to instruct their liaison officers deployed in Greece and Italy to conduct additional checks and personal interviews,[91] making the process lengthy and administratively burdensome.

The Commission's proposal to amend the Dublin system ('Dublin IV proposal') builds on this experience and would include, in a more permanent

---

[86] See Joined Cases C-643/15 and C-647/15, *Slovak Republic and Hungary v. Council of the European Union*, ECLI:EU:C:2017:631, and for analysis Bruno De Witte and Evangelia (Lilian) Tsourdi, "Confrontation on relocation – The Court of Justice endorses the emergency scheme for compulsory relocation of asylum seekers within the European Union: Slovak Republic and Hungary v. Council," *Common Market Law Review* 55, no. 5 (2018): 1457–1491.

[87] See Tsourdi, "Solidarity at Work?" 679–681.

[88] The first relocation decision applied until 17 September 2017 and the second until 26 September 2017. See respectively 1st Emergency Relocation Decision, art. 13(2) and 2nd Emergency Relocation Decision, art. 4.

[89] See 1st Emergency Relocation Decision, art. 3(2) and 2nd Emergency Relocation Decision, art. 3(2) establishing the notion of applicants 'in clear need of international protection'.

[90] See for an example of EASO's involvement in registering applicants eligible for relocation in Communication from the Commission, *First Report on Relocation and Resettlement*, COM (2016) 165 (16 March 2016), 12.

[91] Communication from the Commission, 10.

manner, obligatory people-sharing in situations of disproportionate pressure.[92] This would be underpinned by a new automated system, operated jointly by eu-LISA (the European Agency for the operational management of large-scale IT systems in the Area of Freedom, Security and Justice) and the Member States.[93] All applications would be registered there, and the system would calculate disproportionate pressure on the basis of objective indicators in real time.[94] This system would thus render an application lodged with one Member State, an 'EU-lodged application', even though the processing itself would not be conducted at the EU level.

There are a number of flaws, however, in this proposed mechanism. The Dublin IV proposal introduces a new *obligatory* admissibility procedure.[95] The system as it currently operates gives the Member States the discretion to operate admissibility procedures, but does not require them.[96] The new required procedure would weed out applications as inadmissible where, for example, the applicant could be returned to a third, non-EU country that complies with the criteria of 'safety' under EU law. It would also channel certain applications, such as those of persons holding the nationality of a country of origin that is considered 'safe' under EU law, into an accelerated processing procedure. All such applicants for asylum protection would be excluded from relocation to another Member State, a fact which undermines the mechanism's effect on fair-sharing.[97] Moreover, the relocation process included in Dublin IV openly antagonises applicants by disregarding completely their reasons for seeking asylum and their preferences,[98] and by seeking instead to achieve compliance through coercion.[99]

---

[92] *Proposal for a Regulation Establishing the Criteria and Mechanisms for Determining the Member State Responsible for Examining an Application for International Protection Lodged in One of the Member States by a Third-Country National or a Stateless Person*, COM (2016) 270 final (4 May 2016) [hereinafter Dublin IV proposal].

[93] Dublin IV proposal, recitals 29, 30 and art. 44.

[94] Dublin IV proposal, art. 22.

[95] Dublin IV proposal, art. 3(3).

[96] For instance, currently, under the admissibility procedure in Greek law, certain applicants are returned from Greece to Turkey based on the assessment that Turkey is a safe third country (based on criteria established by EU law). Of course, there needs to be the agreement of the third country involved. Thus, returns are operationalised through EU-wide or bilateral readmission agreements, and the entire cooperation framework often involves political bargaining and financial commitments by the EU. A case in point is the EU-Turkey statement, a non-legally binding document, which mentions explicitly commitments of the EU and its Member States towards Turkey as part of the cooperation 'bargain'. European Council Press Release 144/16, EU-Turkey Statement (18 March 2016).

[97] See Dublin IV proposal, art. 36(3).

[98] Dublin IV proposal, art. 38(2)–(3).

[99] Dublin IV proposal, art. 5.

Currently, the emergency relocation mechanisms have come to an end, while the Dublin IV proposal faces resistance from several Member States, on various grounds. Insofar as administrative integration is concerned, both the operationalisation of the emergency relocation schemes and the Commission's Dublin IV proposals attest to a shift, albeit modest, in that direction. These developments also manifest a modicum of intra-EU solidarity. Obligatory people sharing, even on a time-limited scale, contributes to the notion of a common obligation to provide protection. When the national level is unable to live up to the implementation of its obligations, asylum applicants are to be shared by the Member States. It remains to be seen whether this shift will be sustainable or whether it will be abandoned in the future development of the CEAS.

2 Practical Cooperation: From Support towards Joint Implementation?

In the initial policy design, practical cooperation between Member States was to support Member States in the implementation stage. It basically consisted of information exchange through administrative networks and *ad hoc* projects.[100] These collaborative efforts soon met their limits in boosting Member States' implementation capacity; their inadequacy led to an institutionalisation push. Institutionalisation came to fruition in 2010, with the establishment of the European Asylum Support Office.[101]

Articles 74 and 78 (1) and (2) TFEU constitute the legal basis for the creation of EASO. Therefore, the agency was conceptualised as a 'measure to ensure administrative co-operation', in view of attaining the goal of establishing a CEAS. It does not hold decision-making powers[102] or powers to adopt general rules.[103] The agency undertakes several activities, mainly revolving around training and quality, information and analysis, as well as operational support. The latter makes EASO particularly akin to an instrument of solidarity, as its mandate is to support Member States subject to particular

---

[100] See, e.g., Communication from the Commission, *On Strengthened Practical Cooperation-New Structures, New Approaches: Improving the Quality of Decision Making in the Common European Asylum System*, COM (2006) 67 (17 February 2016).

[101] European Parliament and Council Regulation (EU) 439/2010, Establishing a European Asylum Support Office, 2010 O.J. (L 132) 11 [hereinafter EASO Regulation].

[102] See EASO Regulation, recital 14: '[t]he Support Office should have no direct or indirect powers in relation to the taking of decisions by Member States' asylum authorities on individual applications for international protection'. See also EASO Regulation, art. 2(6).

[103] EASO Regulation, art. 12(2). More broadly, for the argument that agencies could not formally possess the power to adopt normative acts, see Paul Craig, *EU Administrative Law* (New York: Oxford University Press, 2012), 151; Chamon, *EU Agencies*, 40.

The Emerging Architecture of EU Asylum Policy

pressures that place exceptionally heavy and urgent demands on their reception facilities and asylum systems.[104]

Regarding operational support, apart from data collection and exchange, the legislator foresaw that EASO, at the request of the Member State concerned, would coordinate actions on the ground.[105] Three main types of action were outlined: actions to facilitate an initial analysis of asylum applications under examination by the competent national authorities; actions designed to ensure that appropriate reception facilities, including emergency reception, are made available; and the deployment of Asylum Support Teams (ASTs).[106] ASTs are made up of seconded national experts, including interpreters, participating in the Asylum Intervention Pool.[107] Member States contribute to this Pool by proposing experts that correspond to the required profiles.[108] The Member States that contribute retain autonomy regarding the selection of the number and profiles of deployed experts, as well as the duration of their deployment.[109]

The first such operations were launched shortly after the EASO's establishment and they gradually grew in number and scope. EASO provided operational assistance to six Member States between 2011 and the summer of 2016: Bulgaria, Cyprus, Greece, Italy, Luxembourg and Sweden. It adopted a flexible definition of what constitutes pressure and the determination was a relative one, not based on a fixed calculation.[110] Assessed on an absolute scale, the number of experts sent to these smaller Member States was not impressive. This, however, does not detract from the value of the operation, since the lion's share of responsibility remains with the Member States, through their own financial and human resources, and what may appear to be a rather modest contribution on an EU-wide scale greatly enhances the capacity of a smaller Member State. The AST deployments were not operational like the border guard teams deployed by Frontex (the European Border and Coast Guard Agency), which interacted with individual migrants at external borders.[111] Rather, their work consisted of expert advice in ministry

---

[104] EASO Regulation, art. 8.
[105] EASO Regulation, arts. 10 and 13.
[106] EASO Regulation, art. 10(a)–(c).
[107] EASO Regulation, art. 15.
[108] EASO Regulation, art. 15(2).
[109] EASO Regulation, art.16(1).
[110] See European Asylum Support Office, "Operating Plan for the Deployment of Asylum Support Teams to Luxembourg," 26 January 2012 and European Asylum Support Office, "EASO Special Support Plan to Cyprus," 5 June 2014, 3.
[111] For the current regulation of Frontex-led deployments see European Parliament and Council Regulation (EU) 2016/1624, On the European Border and Coast Guard, 2016 O.J. (L 251) 1, arts.

departments, or involved training and study visits of members of national administrations.[112]

Gradually, the EASO separated deployments from increases in refugee influxes, testing joint-processing pilots. The content of the term 'joint processing' is yet to be clarified and can theoretically encompass different options ranging from assistance in emergency scenarios through agency deployments, to a completely harmonised approach, meaning centralised processing.[113] Cognisant of the legal limitation included in the EASO Regulation, it is useful to distinguish between three possible scenarios: assisted processing, common processing and EU-level processing. Assisted processing refers to the examination of asylum applications by officials of the competent Member State with the support of officials of one or other Member States, possibly coordinated through EASO. This would mean in practice either that national officials are active at every procedural stage and are merely assisted by the EU (coordinated) level, or that deployed experts conduct independently only preparatory acts and do not undertake actions or adopt decisions that involve administrative discretion.

Common processing essentially refers to 'mixed' or 'composite' administrative proceedings.[114] Broadly speaking:

15–26. Political agreement on a new Frontex regulation was reached in April 2019, and it is expected that the new Regulation will be formally adopted in autumn 2019. See also commentary in Philippe De Bruycker, "The European Border and Coast Guard: A New Model Built on an Old Logic," *European Papers* 1, no. 2 (2016): 559. Frontex-led deployments of seconded national border guards were introduced in 2007 as part of an emergency response mechanism. In the 2011 amendments to Frontex's founding regulation, deployments were decoupled from emergencies, and border guards could also be deployed in normal, i.e. unrelated to emergency joint operations. Such deployments have always been significant, both with respect to the number of personnel involved, as well as the breadth of operational activities entailed. For commentary on one of the first such deployments see Sergio Carrera and Elspeth Guild, "Joint Operation RABIT 2010': FRONTEX Assistance to Greece's Border with Turkey: Revealing the Deficiencies of Europe's Dublin Asylum System," CEPS, 22 November 2010; for a global appraisal see Jorrit J. Rijpma, "Frontex and the European System of Border Guards: The Future of European Border Management," in *The European Union as an Area of Freedom, Security and Justice*, eds. Maria Fletcher, Ester Herlin-Karnell, and Claudio Matera (Oxford: Routledge, 2017), 217.

[112] See McDonough and Tsourdi, "The 'Other' Greek Crisis," 80–96.

[113] Ramboll and Eurasylum, "Study on the Feasibility and Legal and Practical Implications of Establishing a Mechanism for the Joint Processing of Asylum Applications on the Territory of the EU," 13 February 2013, 2–4, http://ec.europa.eu/dgs/home-affairs/e-library/documents/policies/asylum/common-procedures/docs/jp_final_report_final_en.pdf.

[114] On mixed or composite administrative proceedings in EU law more broadly see characteristically: Giacinto della Cananea, "The European Union's Mixed Administrative Proceedings," *Law and Contemporary Problems* 68 (Winter 2004): 197–218; Mario P. Chiti, "Forms of European Administrative Action," *Law and Contemporary Problems* 68 (Winter 2004): 37–60; Herwig C. H.

they ensure that input into single administrative procedures can be given from authorities from various jurisdictions. Irrespective of whether a final decision will be taken by a Member State or an EU authority, both levels can thus be directly involved in a single administrative procedure.[115]

Their 'mixed' or 'composite' character refers to the variety of jurisdictions involved in a single administrative procedure. In our context, they concern asylum-related decision-making. They occur if the EU (coordinated) level is exclusively responsible for one or more parts of the decision-making procedure involving administrative discretion (such as responsibility determinations under Dublin III, or proposing asylum decisions on the basis of interviews). The final scenario is EU-level processing, where the joint elements disappear, and the decision is taken entirely by an EU authority instead of the Member States.

Of these three scenarios, only the first (assisted processing) is within EASO's current mandate. The second scenario (common processing) is beyond the limits of the current mandate of EASO, which is expressly prohibited from exercising power with respect to decisions (of the Member States' asylum authorities) on individual applications for international protection.[116] The third, EU-level processing, is legally impossible under the TFEU, which envisages that 'a Member State' is ultimately responsible for the examination of an application.[117]

Several pilot joint-processing exercises took place between June 2014 and June 2015. In 2014, twenty-two experts took part in the joint-processing pilot projects conducted by EASO in nine Member States, and in 2015, eighteen experts from fifteen Member States were involved in three EASO pilot projects.[118] These activities were not clearly anchored in the EASO Regulation. At the beginning, the joint-processing activities involved tasks that did not entail administrative discretion, such as initial registration, or data archiving.[119] They evolved beyond that, including, for example in the Netherlands, the assessment of the merits of individual cases by deployed experts that had conducted the asylum interview.[120] However, these joint-processing exercises were small scale and short term.

Hofman, "Composite Decision-Making Procedures in EU Administrative Law," in *Legal Challenges in EU Administrative Law: Towards an Integrated Administration*, eds. Herwig C. H. Hofman, and Alexander Türk (Cheltenham: Edward Elgar, 2009), 136.

[115] Diana-Urania Galetta et al., *The Context and Legal Elements of a Proposal for a Regulation on the Administrative Procedure of the European Union's Institutions, Bodies, Offices and Agencies*, European Parliament, 2015, 17.

[116] EASO Regulation, recital 14 and art. 2(6).

[117] See Article 78(2)(e) TFEU.

[118] European Asylum Support Office, "Five Years of EASO: Results and Perspectives," 2015, 14.

[119] European Asylum Support Office, "Newsletter-March 2015," 2 April 2015, 6.

[120] European Asylum Support Office, 10.

The next push came during the 2015–2016 refugee crisis and the operationalisation of the hotspot approach to migration management.[121] There are a variety of administrative tasks that must be completed at hotspots, including registration and identification of migrants, and channelling of migrants into further procedures, e.g. return or assessment of an international protection claim.[122] Previous deployments, although beneficial, could not address the structural weaknesses of Member State asylum systems, undermined by insufficient human and financial resources. During this subsequent period, EASO deployees moved away from expert consulting and began to undertake more hands-on tasks, such as providing information to arriving third-country nationals, and assisting with the emergency relocation process. As pressures increased, forms of common rather than assisted processing emerged in Greece, with deployed experts undertaking admissibility interviews[123] and submitting opinions that, despite being advisory and non-binding on national authorities, entailed the exercise of administrative discretion.[124]

The Commission proposal on a European Union Agency on Asylum, which is still under negotiation, confirms these integrative trends, enhancing the Agency's mandate and resources.[125] If adopted,[126] the Agency's functions would evolve to include monitoring-like functions and processes that have the

---

[121] The hotspot *approach* involves inter-agency collaboration, in which deployed national experts, under the coordination of a specific agency, operationally assist national administrations. See also Communication from the Commission, *Managing the Refugees Crisis: Immediate Operational, Budgetary and Legal Measures under the European Agenda on Migration*, COM (2015) 490 (29 September 2015), annex II. A *hotspot* is in essence an EU external border section facing high numbers of arrivals of third-country nationals. In practice, these arrivals most often present a mixture of individuals, some of whom qualify for international protection since they are fleeing persecution or generalised violence, and others who do not.

[122] For a detailed list of the tasks to be performed at hotspots by different agencies see: Darren Neville, Sarah Sy, and Amalia Rigon, *On the Frontline: The Hotspot Approach to Managing Migration* (European Parliament, 2016), 27–29.

[123] As elaborated previously, admissibility represents a preliminary stage in the asylum procedure, where a determination is made as to whether the asylum application should be examined on the merits, or whether the application should be discontinued as inadmissible, for instance, because the individual can safely be returned to a third country.

[124] Evangelia (Lilian) Tsourdi, "Bottom-up Salvation? From Practical Cooperation towards Joint Implementation through the European Asylum Support Office," *European Papers* 1, no. 3 (2016): 1021–1026.

[125] See *Proposal for a Regulation of the European Parliament and of the Council on the European Union Agency for Asylum and Repealing Regulation (EU) No 439/2010*, COM (2016) 271 (4 May 2016) [hereinafter EUAA proposal].

[126] A political agreement was reached between the two co-legislators for several chapters of the EUAA proposal in late 2017 but, at the time of this writing, negotiations on a number of contentious issues remain pending.

potential to steer implementation.[127] In addition, elements of not only assisted but also common processing would be ingrained in the Agency's mandate. The envisaged measures, as part of operational support, are variegated. They include preparatory acts of the asylum procedure that do not entail administrative discretion, such as assistance with the identification and registration of third country nationals, and assistance with the provision of information on the international protection procedure.[128] The proposed regulation also includes a form of common processing: migration management teams deployed in areas under pressure could potentially be tasked with the 'examination of claims',[129] even though the final decision on protected refugee status would remain the competence of Member States.[130] These trends are further enhanced in the Commission's amended proposal, released in September 2018, which in many respects complements, rather than repeals, the earlier proposal.[131] Overall, the workings of the EU asylum agency, both *de facto* currently, and *de jure* prospectively, point towards the emergence of an increasingly integrated European administration.

3 EU Funding: From Symbolic Politics towards a Structural Response?

Member States are expected to fund the operationalisation of the common asylum policy mainly through their own national budgets. While EU funding in this area has existed since 2000 and the adoption of a European Refugee Fund (ERF),[132] it was always meant to complement predominantly national spending rather than to compensate Member States through the EU budget. EU funding was initially extremely limited, namely €216 million, over a four-year period,[133] leading academic commentators to label it 'symbolic politics'.[134]

---

[127] See for analysis of these elements, Evangelia (Lilian) Tsourdi, "Monitoring and Steering through FRONTEX and EASO 2.0: The Rise of a New Model of AFSJ Agencies?" *EU Immigration and Asylum Law and Policy* (blog), 29 January 2018, http://eumigrationlawblog.eu/monitoring-and-steering-through-frontex-and-easo-2-0-the-rise-of-a-new-model-of-afsj-agencies/.

[128] EUAA proposal, art. 16(3)(a), (3), (h).

[129] EUAA proposal, art. 21(2)(b).

[130] EUAA proposal, recital 46.

[131] *Amended Proposal for a Regulation of the European Parliament and of the Council on the European Union Agency for Asylum and Repealing Regulation (EU) No 439/2010*, COM (2018) 633 final (12 September 2018).

[132] Council Decision 2000/596/EC, Establishing a European Refugee Fund, 2000 O.J. (L 252) 12 [hereinafter 2000 ERF Decision].

[133] 2000 ERF Decision, art. 2(1).

[134] See Eiko Thielemann, "Symbolic Politics or Effective Burden-Sharing? Redistribution, Side Payments and the European Refugee Fund," *Journal of Common Market Studies* 43, no. 4 (2005): 807.

A specific financial envelope was foreseen for the case of emergency, but emergency was linked exclusively with the activation of the EU Temporary Protection Directive.[135] As that instrument was never activated, Member States could not access that dedicated amount.

The ERF was renewed for the 2005 to 2010 period, containing a slightly enhanced financial envelope,[136] and largely following the initial design. In the 2007–2013 financial framework, the EU undertook a substantial overhaul of Home Affairs funding, which led to the establishment, alongside a revamped ERF,[137] of the following: the European Integration Fund,[138] the European Return Fund[139] and the External Borders Fund.[140] The new ERF Decision expanded the scope of the financial reserve for emergency measures so that it covered, not only as before temporary protection but also 'situations of particular pressure'.[141] Emergency funding came with strict requirements. Member States had to implement actions 'immediately', and their duration could not exceed six months.[142] Moreover, its activation was heavily tied to administrative requirements, burdening the administration of the Member State invoking it, and the maximum amount of EU co-financing was 80 per cent, meaning that the rest of the amount had to come from the national budget.

The setup of the Home Affairs financial framework for 2014–2020 marked a departure from previous funding periods with asylum, return and integration funding streamlined into a single fund.[143] The global resources (that is, the funding available for the entire period from 2014–2020) initially available for

[135] 2000 ERF Decision, art. 6.
[136] Council Decision 2004/904/EC, Establishing the European Refugee Fund for the Period 2005 to 2010, 2004 O.J. (L 381) 52 [hereinafter 2004 ERF Decision].
[137] European Parliament and Council Decision 573/2007/EC, Establishing the European Refugee Fund for the Period 2008 to 2013 as Part of the General Programme Solidarity and Management of Migration Flows and Repealing Council Decision 2004/904/EC, 2007 O.J. (L 141) 1 [hereinafter 2007 ERF Decision].
[138] Council Decision 2007/435/EC, Establishing the European Fund for the Integration of Third-Country Nationals for the Period 2007 to 2013 as Part of the General Programme 'Solidarity and Management of Migration Flows', 2007 O.J. (L 168) 18 [hereinafter 2007 EIF Decision].
[139] European Parliament and Council Decision 575/2007/EC, Establishing the European Return Fund for the Period 2008 to 2013 as Part of the General Programme 'Solidarity and Management of Migration Flows', 2007 O.J. (L 144) 45 [hereinafter 2007 RF].
[140] European Parliament and Council Decision 574/2007/EC, Establishing the External Borders Fund for the Period 2007 to 2013 as Part of the General Programme 'Solidarity and Management of Migration Flows', 2007 O.J. (L 144) 22 [hereinafter 2007 EBF].
[141] 2007 ERF Decision, recitals 21 and 22, and art. 5(1)–(2).
[142] 2007 ERF Decision, art. 5(3).
[143] European Parliament and Council Regulation (EU) 516/2014, Establishing the Asylum, Migration and Integration Fund, Amending Council Decision 2008/381/EC and Repealing

The Asylum, Migration and Integration Fund (AMIF) amounted to €3,137 billion.[144] This is more than the combined amount of the funds that were merged during the previous multi-annual financial framework (2007–2013), which was €2,200 billion.[145] Still, at the time of its adoption the Fund accounted for a mere 0.29 per cent[146] of the EU's entire Multi-Annual Financial Framework (MFF).[147] The overall result is that EU funding still covers only a limited portion of national spending in this area, and it does not compensate for the asymmetric pressures created by the EU's responsibility allocation rules.

The new AMIF also provides for greater flexibility in the emergency funding component. It adopts a broad definition of what constitutes an emergency,[148] encompassing a situation of heavy migratory pressure that affects only one Member State, and taking into account relative pressures. In addition, the broad scope of the new fund, which includes not only refugees but also irregular economic migration, is better suited to the reality of arrivals of mixed migration flows that demand a cross-policy approach. The process for the activation of emergency funding has been simplified, and the six-month limit for spending has been lifted. The Horizontal Regulation, which sets down the rules for the administration of the funding, clarifies that emergency assistance may amount to 100 per cent of the eligible expenditure.[149]

    Decisions No. 573/2003/EC and No. 575/2007/EC of the European Parliament and of the Council Decision 2007/435/EC, 2014 O.J. (L 150) 168 [hereinafter AMIF Regulation].

[144] AMIF Regulation, art. 14(1).

[145] See European Council of Refugees and Exiles, "Information Note on the Regulation (EU) No 2014/516 of the European Parliament and the Council of 16 April 2014 Establishing the Asylum, Migration and Integration Fund," 29 May 2015, 9, www.ecre.org/ecre-publish-note-on-the-asylum-migration-and-integration-fund/?option=com_downloads&id=1022.

[146] Calculation included in Alessandro D'Alfonso, "How the EU Budget is Spent: Asylum, Migration and Integration Fund (AMIF)," EU Parliamentary Research Service Briefing 2015, 1, www.europarl.europa.eu/RegData/etudes/BRIE/2015/551316/EPRS_BRI(2015)551316_EN.pdf.

[147] Council Regulation (EU, Euratom) 1311/2013, Laying Down the Multiannual Financial Framework for the Years 2014–2020, 2013 O.J. (L 347) 884.

[148] According to Article 2(k) of the AMIF Regulation, there is an emergency situation in the following scenarios: (i) heavy migratory pressure in one or more Member States characterised by a large and disproportionate inflow of third-country nationals, which places significant and urgent demands on their reception and detention facilities, asylum systems and procedures or (ii) the implementation of temporary protection mechanisms within the meaning of Directive 2001/55/EC or (iii) heavy migratory pressure in third countries where refugees are stranded due to events such as political developments or conflicts.

[149] European Parliament and Council Regulation (EU) 514/2014, Laying Down General Provisions on the Asylum, Migration and Integration Fund and on the Instrument for Financial Support for Police Cooperation, Preventing and Combating Crime, and Crisis

Under the AMIF, there are two types of funded actions. The first consist of Union actions, emergency assistance, funding for the European Migration Network (EMN) and funding for technical assistance, to be implemented under the centralised management model.[150] The second are actions to be included in national programmes and implemented under the shared management model.[151] The latter constitute the bulk of the EU funding. In broad strokes, centralised administration captures the idea that the Commission is either tasked with making the relevant decisions,[152] or implements programmes without formal, systematic cooperation with national bureaucracies.[153] In shared administration, the enabling legislation formally gives the Commission and Member States distinct administrative tasks, which are interdependent, and both must discharge their respective roles for the Union policy to be implemented successfully.[154]

Overall, the AMIF contains moderate design improvements that have led to a relative simplification of management processes and that carry enhanced potential to influence policy implementation, i.e. steering capacity. An example of the first point is the merging of three different budget lines for asylum, migration and integration into a single one. With respect to funding of national programmes, the obligation for Member States to draw up annual programmes has been eliminated, and instead funding operates on a multi-annual planning cycle, thus avoiding some of the repetitive paperwork for Member State authorities.[155] Although multi-annual programming existed prior to the 2014–2020 period, the multi-annual component contained the general priorities, while the European Refugee Fund was implemented on the basis of annual programmes. The synergies between the different actors in

---

Management, 2014 O.J. (L 150) 112, preamble, art. 20(2), and recital 15 [hereinafter HA Funds Horizontal Regulation].

[150] AMIF Regulation, art. 14(3)(b)–(e).

[151] AMIF Regulation, art. 14(3)(a).

[152] See, for example, the area of state aid.

[153] This does not necessarily mean that the Commission carries out the entirety of the activity itself, 'in house'. See Craig, *EU Administrative Law*, 31.

[154] Committee of Independent Experts, *Second Report on Reform of the Commission, Analysis of Current Practice and Proposals for Tackling Mismanagement, Irregularities and Fraud*, 10 September 1999, vol. I, para. 3.2.2.

[155] There are five main stages in the multi-annual programming cycle: a newly introduced stage of policy dialogue; preparation of draft programmes by Member States to be approved by the Commission; thereafter, annual implementation reporting. Halfway through the implementation period is a mid-term review that includes enhanced reporting and evaluation, and could lead to the review of national programmes. The final stage consists of implementation reporting and ex-post evaluations that feed into the next multi-annual programming cycle. See HA Funds Horizontal Regulation, arts. 13–15.

the various stages of the process were also not as clearly articulated. The multi-annual programmes are now the sole source of concrete implementation planning, and the legislative instruments have clarified the interactions between the different actors. As for the second point – the Fund's enhanced steering capacity – one example is the newly introduced policy dialogue phase in the multi-annual planning cycle that allows the Commission to enter into structured consultations with Member States at an early stage.[156]

Nonetheless, there are factors which limit EU funding's steering and solidarity potential in the national programmes component of the AMIF. As mentioned earlier, the overall available amount remains extremely modest, and hence can only cover a limited part of national spending in this field. The pre-determined share available to Member States is largely based on absolute indicators, indirectly taken up from the previous period, that fail to account for relative pressures.[157] The management and control systems that Member States are called to set up are intricate and demand human and financial resources for their effective operation. It is for this reason that taking EU funding 'costs'.

The centralised emergency funding component of the AMIF has emerged as somewhat more successful than shared management of national programmes. Emergency funding better serves the purpose of fair-sharing because it foresees no co-financing from the side of the Member State, and is released on the basis of migratory pressure. It can now be activated swiftly and its implementation is more flexible since the six-month operationalisation window has been suppressed. It should therefore come as no surprise Member States heavily relied on emergency funding during the 2015–2016 refugee crisis.[158] The new element is that next to the 'usual suspects', such as Greece and Italy, a host of Member States with stronger national economies, such as France, Germany and the Netherlands, have also had recourse to emergency funding under AMIF to implement their obligations.[159] This points to an increasing demand for structural, meaning both permanent and substantial, forms of European funding in the asylum area.

---

[156] HA Funds Horizontal Regulation, art. 13.

[157] See AMIF Regulation, recital 37 and annex I.

[158] By August 2018, a total of €734,474,723 in emergency funding under AMIF had been awarded. See Communication from the Commission, *Managing the Refugee Crisis: State of Play of the Implementation of the Priority Actions under the European Agenda on Migration*, COM (2015) 510 (14 October 2015), updated annex 8 (25 June 2018).

[159] Communication from the Commission, COM (2015) 510.

There have been two further developments in the resources arena. First, several Member States demanded for the first time the activation of the Civil Protection Mechanism for migration-related purposes.[160] This process allows for the pooling and transfer of non-financial resources and depends on the voluntary contribution of Member States. In the case of the 2015–2016 refugee crisis, the non-financial resources consisted of items such as tents, blankets, etc. that were vital for emergency humanitarian assistance for those arriving. Items were undersupplied compared to demand.[161] The second development was the birth of an intra-EU humanitarian aid budget line.[162] This budget line, which draws from the general EU budget, is not specific to migration. However, its first activation related to the refugee crisis: several tranches of money were released for projects in Greece, mainly supporting reception capacity.[163]

Commission proposals for the next multi-annual framework (covering the period 2021–2027) are currently under negotiation. Overall, the proposals foresee a significant augmentation for the combined migration and border management financial envelope which would reach the amount of €34.2 billion, compared to €12.4 billion for the period 2014–2020.[164] This overall figure includes the amount foreseen for the new Asylum and Migration Fund, which is €10.2 billion,[165] and is almost three times the existing allocation. The omission of 'integration' from the name of the new Asylum and Migration Fund indicates the fact that although it covers immediate integration measures, it excludes long-term integration measures, such as integration into the labour market and social inclusion support. These are to be covered instead by

---

[160] See Council Decision 1313/2013/EU, On a Union Civil Protection Mechanism, 2013 O.J. (L 347) 924 [hereinafter Union Civil Protection Mechanism Decision].

[161] See Communication from the Commission, *On the State of Play of Implementation of the Priority Actions under the European Agenda on Migration*, COM (2016) 85 (10 February 2016), annex 9 Accepted Member States' Support to Civil Protection Mechanism for Serbia, Slovenia, Croatia and Greece, 4.

[162] See Council Regulation (EU) 2016/369, On the Provision of Emergency Support within the Union, O.J. (L 70) 1 [hereinafter Humanitarian Assistance Regulation].

[163] By April 2018 Greece had received a total of €605.3 million under that instrument. See "The EU Announces €180 Million in Emergency Support to Support Refugees in Greece," European Commission website, 2 April 2018, https://ec.europa.eu/echo/news/eu-announces-180-million-emergency-support-support-refugees-greece_en.

[164] See Communication from the Commission, *A Modern Budget for a Union That Protects, Empowers and Defends: The Multiannual Financial Framework for 2021–2027*, COM (2018) 321 (2 May 2018), 14–15.

[165] See *Proposal for a Regulation of the European Parliament and of the Council Establishing the Asylum and Migration Fund*, COM (2018) 471 final (12 June 2018), art. 8(1) [hereinafter AMF proposal].

other budget lines, for instance EU structural funds.[166] Overall, notwithstanding the increased funding, it still is not sufficient to approximate a compensatory and solidaristic logic for the investment Member States undertake in this policy area.

The Commission proposals include some elements that might ease the administrative burden for implementing national authorities, such as streamlining the implementation modes for the EU structural and migration funds through the adoption of a single cross-cutting Horizontal Regulation.[167] In addition, linking the mid-term review of funding implementation, to be conducted by the Commission, with a financial adjustment to the initial national allocations could increase the Fund's steering potential.[168] Nevertheless, the proposed Fund's still modest overall allocation, combined with the fact that once again solely absolute indicators are to be used in order to allocate the funding among Member States,[169] limits both its steering and its fair-sharing potential. The instruments of the next funding period, if adopted as they now stand, would bring about targeted improvements but would not revolutionise the function of EU migration funding.

IV EPILOGUE: EU ASYLUM POLICY BETWEEN INTEGRATION, EXTERNALISATION AND UNILATERALISM

Initially based on executive federalism, the implementation design of EU asylum policy has started to shift. An integrated European administration is gradually emerging, and is becoming visible throughout the CEAS. The refugee crisis fuelled this trend, while the Commission's 2016 proposals embed integration among Member State and EU asylum authorities in the CEAS' institutional design. The working methods of the European Asylum Support Office exemplify integrated administration, most notably through EASO deployments that are made up predominantly of seconded national experts.

At first, EASO Asylum Support Teams mainly acted as advisors to relevant national ministries and asylum services, assisting, for example, through the creation of refined tools and processes, or conducting training sessions for

---

[166] AMF proposal, Legislative Financial Statement, point 1.4.4.

[167] See *Proposal for a Regulation of the European Parliament and of the Council Laying Down Common Provisions on the European Regional Development Fund, the European Social Fund Plus, the Cohesion Fund, and the European Maritime and Fisheries Fund and Financial Rules for Those and for the Asylum and Migration Fund, the Internal Security Fund and the Border Management and Visa Instrument*, COM (2018) 375 final (29 May 2018).

[168] See AMF proposal, arts. 11(1) and 14(1).

[169] See AMF proposal, annex I.

decision-makers. The first move towards a more operational function was the rolling out of a series of ad hoc, joint-processing pilots. The pilot programmes originally involved tasks that did not entail administrative discretion, such as initial registration and archiving data, but then evolved to include more discretionary tasks, including, for example, the assessment of the merits of individual cases. The next push came during the 2015–2016 refugee crisis. EASO deployees in Greece and Italy began to move away from expert consulting and to undertake more hands-on tasks, such as providing information to arriving third-country nationals, and assisting with responsibility assignation. Moreover, a mix of Greek and Italian administration, Member State 'liaison officers' and EASO deployees were in direct contact on Greek and Italian soil, and were actively involved in the emergency relocation of migrants. As the months passed, and pressures increased, forms of common rather than assisted processing emerged in Greece. Today, deployed experts are involved in the admissibility procedure required under Greek law, including conducting admissibility interviews and issuing opinions on protected status; although these opinions are advisory and non-binding on national authorities, they require the exercise of administrative discretion. The Commission proposal to improve the powers of the EASO and transform it into an EU Asylum Agency confirms these trends. It enlarges the scope of deployments beyond emergencies, while retaining their short-term character. Finally, it tasks potentially deployed experts with the 'examination of claims', while repeating that the final decision remains in the competence of Member States.

Apart from admissibility decision-making in hotspots, Dublin IV as proposed would entail the establishment of a new automated system, operated jointly by eu-LISA and the Member States, where all applications would be registered, and which would calculate disproportionate pressure on the basis of objective indicators in real time. This system would thus render an application lodged with one Member State an EU-lodged application, even though processing would still occur at the Member State level, not the EU level. In the funding area, the Asylum, Migration and Integration Fund's operationalisation of the shared management component interlinks more closely the Commission and Member State administrations and sets up a 'national partnership' for designing, implementing and controlling EU funding.

If administrative integration is the prevailing trend, externalisation and unilateralism are also apparent. Initially subterranean, externalisation is gradually taking centre stage, and is becoming increasingly embedded in the design of EU asylum policy. A modest apparition of this trend was the

The Emerging Architecture of EU Asylum Policy

inclusion of external dimension activities under the AMIF. The EU–Turkey agreement accelerated developments.[170] It spurred amendments in the Dublin IV proposal, such as the introduction of an obligatory admissibility phase, geared at weeding out applicants that could be returned to safe third countries, and the exclusion of those inadmissible from relocation. It has led to the emergence of several new funding lines that pool together EU and Member State funds and target third countries. Externalisation is increasingly gaining ground as the new optimum, a sweep-under-the-rug operation that will render a radical redesign of CEAS implementation modes unnecessary.[171]

Another parallel development is the emergence of unilateralism. One manifestation of this tendency was the unilateral closure of internal borders by Member States along the Western Balkans route during 2015. More recently, Hungary, the Czech Republic and Poland undertook unilateral (and illegal) action with their outright rejection of emergency relocation. Their total refusal to implement their obligations under the relocation decisions – linked exclusively with unwillingness rather than inability – led the Commission to launch infringement actions against them, which are currently pending before the Court of Justice. Unilateralism is also exhibited in the impossibility for Member States to come to a compromise on a viable redesign of the Dublin system,[172] which has driven Germany, Greece and Spain to enter into an agreement among themselves to ensure the implementation of obligations under the Dublin III Regulation currently in force.[173] Finally, threats by the German Minister of Interior that he would order border guards to unilaterally summarily reject asylum seekers at the border prompted a June 2018 mini-summit between a coalition of sixteen Member State leaders willing to address asylum issues,[174] foreshadowing the potential for enhanced cooperation in this area.

The future of CEAS is uncertain. On the one hand, slipping towards unilateral responses might mean the end of EU's CEAS, while simultaneously

---

[170] European Council Press Release 144/16. According to that statement of 18 March 2016, those newly arrived are to be returned to Turkey, including asylum seekers. For every Syrian being returned to Turkey from the EU, another Syrian will be resettled from Turkey to the EU.

[171] See European Council Conclusions, EUCO 9/18 (28 June 2018), point 5.

[172] European Council, point 12.

[173] Fiona Maxwell and Ryan Heath, "Spain, Greece and Germany Seal Migrant Swap Deal," Politico Europe, 30 June 2018, www.politico.eu/article/spain-greece-and-germany-seal-migrant-swap-deal/.

[174] See commentary in Catherine Woolard, "The Story of the Summit: European Solutions Not EU Solutions," ECRE, 29 June 2018, www.ecre.org/editorial-the-story-of-the-summit-european-solutions-not-eu-solutions/.

jeopardising the entire free movement area. The alternative path involves the slow but steady emergence of an increasingly integrated European administration. The advantages of such an implementation mode are a greater steering potential, in favour of improved harmonisation, and a slight enhancement of fair-sharing, to the extent that deployments would become lengthier and more numerically robust. This is not to say that enhanced administrative integration should be celebrated as something which is inherently positive. Administrative integration brings its own challenges, of both a constitutional and practical nature, and requires a rethink of accountability processes so that it does not lead to a *de facto* watering down of procedural guarantees.[175]

At the same time, externalisation of protection obligations seems to have become the primary goal. Yet it is not the panacea that several policy-makers think that it is cut out to be. Externalisation ultimately rests on the viability of political agreements struck with third-country partners. This also renders the EU hostage to the whims of foreign political leaders, shaky ground for any redesign of the EU's implementation architecture. Presented as the principal way to achieve some relief from unfairly shared obligations, it incentivises governments to become zealous participants in operations with dubious fundamental rights implications. In this sense, externalisation and administrative integration are not necessarily antithetical terms. An integrated European administration might be channelled entirely towards operationalising externalisation, instead of providing asylum protection, despite the stated goal in the Treaties. It is hoped that future developments will be more constructive, and will not simply focus on finding quick, and unstable, fixes that circumvent the imperative of creating a full-fledged Common European Asylum System.

---

[175] Among the broad literature on public accountability see Mark Bovens, Thomas Schillemans, and Robert E. Goodin, "Public Accountability," in *The Oxford Handbook of Public Accountability*, eds. Mark Bovens, Robert E. Goodin, and Thomas Schillemans (New York: Oxford University Press, 2014), 1–20; E. Madalina Busuioc, *European Agencies: Law and Practices of Accountability* (Oxford: Oxford University Press, 2013); Richard Mulgan, "'Accountability': An Ever-Expanding Concept?" *Public Administration* 78, no. 3 (2000): 555–573.

9

Databases for Non-EU Nationals and the Right to Private Life

Towards a System of Generalised Surveillance of Movement?

NIOVI VAVOULA

I INTRODUCTION

The creation of pan-European centralised databases that process the personal data of non-EU citizens is inextricably linked with the emergence of 'a Europe without internal frontiers'. The story begins in the mid-1980s with the evolution of European integration and the addition of borders to the list of responsibilities shared by the Member States and the EU (then European Community). In parallel, a more limited number of Member States decided to abolish their internal border controls within the framework of the so-called Schengen Agreement and Convention:[1] a person allowed to enter the territory of one of the participating countries was automatically permitted to circulate within the Schengen area, without being subjected again to checks at the border. As irregular migrants and criminals were not excluded from free circulation, the dismantlement of internal checks was accompanied by so-called compensatory or flanking measures providing for, among other things, a common set of rules on external borders, short-stay visas and asylum applications.[2] With the Treaty of Amsterdam, the law developed under the Schengen

---

[1] Agreement between the Governments of the States of the Benelux Economic Union, the Federal Republic of Germany and the French Republic on the Gradual Abolition of Checks at their Common Borders, 14 June 1985, 2000 O.J. (L 239) 13 [hereinafter Schengen Agreement]; Convention Implementing the Schengen Agreement of 14 June 1985 between the Governments of the States of the Benelux Economic Union, the Federal Republic of Germany and the French Republic on the Gradual Abolition of Checks at their Common Borders, 19 June 1990, 2000 O.J. (L 239) 19 (signed 1990, entered into force 1993, applied 1995) [hereinafter CISA]. For parallel developments at EC level that led to the Schengen cooperation see Elspeth Guild, *European Community Law from a Migrant's Perspective* (The Hague: Kluwer, 2001), chapters 7–8.

[2] For the development of the Schengen *acquis* see Monica den Boer, ed., *Schengen, Judicial Cooperation and Policy Coordination* (Maastricht: European Institute of Public Administration, 1997).

227

Convention, the so-called Schengen *acquis*, was integrated within EU law.[3] At the same time, the EU competence in Justice and Home Affairs (JHA) that had been introduced with the Maastricht Treaty was modified to include the overarching objective of establishing an Area of Freedom, Security and Justice (AFSJ).[4] Since then, a substantial corpus of legislation regulating access to, stay in and removal from the Schengen area has been progressively constructed.[5] Efforts to control the movement of non-EU nationals within the Schengen area have been coupled with efforts to prevent them from reaching the EU external border,[6] thus necessitating action outside the physical border.[7] In all of these developments, the growing tendency to associate non-EU nationals with irregular migration and criminality has been critical.

---

[3] Council Decision 1999/435/ EC, Concerning the Definition of the Schengen *Acquis*, 1999 O.J. (L 176) 1; Council Decision 1999/436/EC, Determining the Legal Basis for Each of the Provisions or Decisions which Constitute the Schengen *Acquis*, 1999 O.J. (L 176) 17. For an analysis see, among others, Eckart Wagner, "The Integration of Schengen into the Framework of the European Union," *Legal Issues of European Integration* 25, no. 2 (1998): 1–60; Pieter Jan Kuijper, "Some Legal Problems Associated with the Communitarization of Policy on Visas, Asylum and Immigration under the Amsterdam Treaty and Incorporation of the Schengen Acquis," *Common Market Law Review* 37, no. 2 (2000): 345–366.

[4] Article 61 Treaty Establishing the European Community and Article 2 Treaty on European Union [hereinafter TEU]. The Member States participating in the Schengen area and the AFSJ must be distinguished. The United Kingdom, Ireland and Denmark are non-Schengen States, but have the possibility to opt in to measures that develop those parts of the Schengen *acquis* that they subscribed to previously under their respective arrangements. Switzerland, Iceland, Norway and Liechtenstein are Schengen Associated States, without being EU Member States.

[5] A series of Schengen instruments have been recast as EU legislation, including the conditions under which a non-EU national may enter and reside on national territory. See European Parliament and Council Regulation (EU) 2016/399, On a Union Code on the Rules Governing the Movement of Persons across Borders (Schengen Borders Code), 2016 O.J. (L 77) 1. Furthermore, a Common European Asylum System (CEAS) setting common standards in administering applicants for international protection has been set up; this system includes rules on the Member State responsible for an asylum application, reception conditions, qualification and procedures. See Section II.1.2.

[6] Didier Bigo and Elspeth Guild, eds., *Controlling Frontiers: Free Movement into and within Europe* (Aldershot: Ashgate, 2005); Valsamis Mitsilegas, "Human Rights, Terrorism and the Quest for 'Border Security'," in *Individual Guarantees in the European Judicial Area in Criminal Matters*, eds. Marco Pedrazzi, Ilaria Viarengo, and Alessandra Lang (Brussels: Bruylant, 2011), 85–112; Valsamis Mitsilegas, "Immigration Control in an Era of Globalisation: Deflecting Foreigners, Weakening Citizens, Strengthening the State," *Indiana Journal of Global Legal Studies* 19, no. 1 (2012): 3–60; Valsamis Mitsilegas, "The Law of the Border and the Borders of Law: Rethinking Border Control from the Perspective of the Individual," in *Rethinking Border Control for a Globalizing World*, ed. Leanne Weber (Oxford: Routledge, 2015), 15–32.

[7] For an analysis see Bernard Ryan and Valsamis Mitsilegas, eds., *Extraterritorial Immigration Control* (Leiden: Martinus Nijhoff, 2010).

Asylum and visa applications, as well as entry and exit procedures, have been instrumentalised for the purpose of the prevention and investigation of crimes, particularly of terrorism.[8] More broadly speaking, security considerations have had a major impact in determining the objectives and rules of immigration control instruments.[9]

The evolution of digital technologies has been an indispensable component of these efforts, enabling the *en masse* storage and further processing of personal data collected on different groups of non-EU citizens. As Bonditti points out, technology has been the 'servant mistress of politics'[10] resulting in 'the digitalisation of the European migration policy'.[11] In this framework, technological advances, particularly the most controversial ones, such as fingerprinting, 'terrorist profiling' and travel surveillance, 'have been (and are still being) "tested" on migrants and refugees or otherwise legitimised at the border'.[12] Biometry in particular has been championed as a tool to reliably determine whether a third-country national is whom he claims to be.[13] The move to identify individuals based on their biological characteristics is attributed to a number of advantages of biometric over alphanumeric identifiers, including their universality, distinctiveness and permanence.[14]

Technological evolution has enabled the EU legislator to set up a 'mille-feuille' of information-processing schemes, currently comprising three

---

[8] For instance, the Hague Programme states: 'the management of migration flows, including the fight against illegal immigration, should be strengthened by establishing a continuum of security measures that effectively links visa application procedures and entry and exit procedures at external border crossings. Such measures are also of importance for the prevention and control of crime, in particular terrorism.' The Hague Programme: Strengthening Freedom, Security and Justice in the European Union, 2004 O.J. (C 53) 1, 7.

[9] For instance, see Communication from the Commission, *The European Agenda on Security*, COM (2015) 185 final (28 April 2015).

[10] Philippe Bonditti, "From Territorial Spaces to Networks: A Foucaultian Approach to the Implementation of Biometry," *Alternatives: Global, Local, Political* 29, no. 4 (2004): 465–482.

[11] Michiel Besters and Frans Brom, "'Greedy' Information Technology: The Digitalization of the European Migration Policy," *European Journal of Migration and Law* 12, no. 4 (2010): 455–470.

[12] Ben Hayes, "NeoConOpticon: The EU Security-Industrial Complex," Transnational Institute/ Statewatch, 2009, 35; see Katja Lindskov Jacobsen, "Making Design Safe for Citizens: A Hidden History of Humanitarian Experimentation," *Citizenship Studies* 14, no. 1 (2010): 89–103.

[13] For a thorough analysis on biometrics see Els Kindt, *Privacy and Data Protection Issues of Biometric Identifiers* (Dordrecht: Springer, 2013).

[14] Anil Jain, Ruud Bolle, and Sharath Pankanti, *Biometrics. Personal Identification in Networked Society* (New York: Springer, 2006). For an analysis of implementing biometrics at the borders see European Commission, "Biometrics at the Frontiers: Assessing the Impact on Society," 2005, www.statewatch.org/news/2005/mar/Report-IPTS-Biometrics-for-LIBE.pdf. Their reliability has been criticised. See Elspeth Guild, Sergio Carrera and Alejandro Eggenschwiler, "Informing the Borders Debate," CEPS, 2009, 3, www.ceps.eu/system/files/book/1843.pdf.

large-scale information systems: the Schengen Information System (SIS II, formerly named SIS), which includes alerts on unwelcome third-country nationals, criminals and irregular migrants; Eurodac, where fingerprints are stored, primarily of asylum seekers; and the Visa Information System (VIS), which contains personal data collected from short-stay visa applicants. At present, the momentum for EU immigration databases is greater than ever. In addition to consecutive enhancements to the three existing databases, centralised systems are bound to proliferate via the establishment of an Entry/Exit System (EES), the European Travel Information and Authorisation System (ETIAS) and the European Criminal Record Information System for third-country nationals (ECRIS-TCN). Each system is set up as a network of databases, consisting of a central database, located in Strasbourg, and national databases in each participating Member State. Moreover, the different systems are established as separate entities. In view of this compartmentalisation, interoperability – different ways of linking information from the different data pots – is also in the pipeline.

This elaborate framework of databases exemplifies the gradual transformation of traditional immigration control to a system of mass surveillance of movement:[15] different groups of third-country nationals are classified according to the dangers they pose to society and surveillance techniques become the vehicle for managing these dangers. As Gammeltoft-Hansen has eloquently observed, EU immigration databases operate as a series of concentric 'risk filters' serving to categorise and identify migrants.[16] In this context, Broeders has framed immigration databases as forming part of 'panopticon Europe', an ever-growing strategy designed to exclude third-country nationals through delegitimatisation and criminalisation.[17] Bigo has instead coined the

---

[15] Annaliese Baldaccini, "Counter-Terrorism and the EU Strategy for Border Security: Framing Suspects with Biometric Documents and Databases," *European Journal of Migration and Law* 10, no. 1 (2008): 31–49; Valsamis Mitsilegas, "Border Security in the European Union: Towards Centralised Controls and Maximum Surveillance," in *Whose Freedom, Security and Justice? EU Immigration and Asylum Law and Policy*, eds. Elspeth Guild, Helen Toner, and Annaliese Baldaccini (Portland: Hart, 2007), 359–394; Valsamis Mitsilegas, "The Border Paradox: The Surveillance of Movement in a Union without Internal Frontiers," in *A Right to Inclusion and Exclusion? Normative Fault Lines of the EU's Area of Freedom, Security and Justice*, ed. Hans Lindahl (Oxford: Hart, 2009), 33–64. Clarke has coined the term 'dataveillance' to denote this type of surveillance through the collection of personal data. See Roger Clarke, "Introduction to Dataveillance and Information Privacy, and Definitions of Terms," *Roger Clarke's Website*, 15 August 1997.

[16] Thomas Gammeltoft-Hansen, "Filtering Out the Risk Migrant: Migration Control, Risk Theory and the EU," Working Paper 52/2006, AMID Working Paper Series 2006, 8.

[17] Dennis Broeders, "The New Digital Borders of Europe: EU Databases and the Surveillance of Irregular Migrants," *International Sociology* 22, no. 1 (2007): 71–92.

term 'banopticon', designed to highlight the fact that these systems are not intended to monitor everybody, but only the designated risk groups, constituting an exclusionary form of control that seeks to banish and prevent or deny entry.[18]

The aim of the present chapter is to map the landscape of pan-European centralised databases involving non-EU nationals by tracing three historical periods in the surveillance of movement: the initial, hesitant steps to employ technological means for purposes of immigration control; the systematisation of immigration databases and the gradual expansion of their capacities; and the current stage of generalised and normalised surveillance of movement through the processing of personal data on practically the entire non-EU population. Furthermore, as these many databases come into direct conflict with the rights to private life and personal data protection, this chapter offers an anthology of the issues of concern. The privacy guarantees and compliance standards are drawn from the jurisprudence of the Court of Justice of the EU (CJEU) and the European Court of Human Rights (ECtHR), both of which have placed limits on mass surveillance, albeit in different factual contexts. Due to space constraints, the assessment focuses on the necessity of setting up or maintaining information systems, their personal scope, the categories of personal data processed (including biometric identifiers), access to stored data for law enforcement purposes and interoperability among the systems.

II THE THREE WAVES OF SURVEILLANCE OF MOVEMENT OF NON-EU NATIONALS

1 The First Wave: Establishing Centralised Databases for the Purpose of Modernising Immigration Control

In the early 1990s, the first EU immigration databases were created: the emblematic Schengen Information System (SIS) and Eurodac, designed to facilitate the allocation of responsibility for examining asylum applications among the Member States. At the time, the technology was still fairly rudimentary, and therefore these two databases necessarily followed a compartmentalised approach. In addition, compartmentalisation was framed as a means of safeguarding the limited purposes and personal scope of each

---

[18] Didier Bigo, "Globalized (In)Security: The Field and the Ban-Opticon," in *Terror, Insecurity and Liberty: Illiberal Practices of Liberal Regimes after 9/11*, eds. Didier Bigo and Anastassia Tsoukala (Oxford: Routledge, 2008), 10–48.

232 Niovi Vavoula

database, thus conforming with one of the key principles of EU data protection law, the purpose limitation principle.[19]

1.1 Keeping Away the Unwanted: The SIS

Perhaps the best-known centralised database in the AFSJ is the SIS, which, as discussed later, has since been replaced by SIS II. At the heart of the compensatory measures for the abolition of internal border controls,[20] the SIS was conceived in 1987 and became operational in 1995.[21] The system held data categorised in the form of alerts on various categories of persons and objects, in particular on people (EU and non-EU nationals alike) wanted for arrest and extradition,[22] missing persons,[23] witnesses or persons summoned to appear before the judicial authorities or to serve a penalty,[24] persons or objects subject to discreet surveillance (where the individual is not made aware of the surveillance) or specific checks[25] and objects sought for the purpose of seizure or their use as evidence in criminal proceedings.[26] In addition, the SIS held alerts on non-EU nationals to be refused entry or stay in the Schengen area.[27] The variety of possible alerts reflected the system's overall purpose of ensuring a high level of security in the Schengen area by facilitating both border control and police investigations.[28] On the one hand, the SIS was meant to be used by national police, customs and border control authorities when performing checks on persons at their external borders or on national territory. On the other hand, it was designed to assist immigration officers when processing third-country nationals, particularly in relation to issuing visas

---

[19] According to the principle, personal data must be collected for specified, explicit and legitimate purposes and not further processed in a way incompatible to those purposes. See European Parliament and Council Regulation (EU) 2016/679, On the Protection of Natural Persons with Regard to the Processing of Personal Data and on the Free Movement of Such Data, and Repealing Directive 95/46/EC, 2016 O.J. (L 119) 1, art. 5(1)(b) [hereinafter General Data Protection Regulation].

[20] Bernd Schattenberg, "SIS: Privacy and Legal Protection," in *Free Movement of Persons in Europe: Legal Problems and Experience*, eds. Henry Schermers et al. (Dordrecht: Martinus Nijhoff, 1993), 43.

[21] For a detailed overview of the setting of the SIS see Evelien Brouwer, *Digital Borders and Real Rights: Effective Remedies for Third-Country Nationals in the Schengen Information System* (Leiden: Martinus Nijhoff, 2008), 47–57.

[22] Article 95 CISA.

[23] Article 97 CISA.

[24] Article 98 CISA.

[25] Article 99 CISA.

[26] Article 100 CISA.

[27] Article 96 CISA.

[28] Article 93 CISA.

Databases for Non-EU Nationals and the Right to Private Life   233

and residence permits.[29] By its very (mixed) nature, the SIS thus served as both an immigration and a criminal law instrument.

In practice, alerts on third-country nationals dominated the system.[30] Data could be inserted on two main grounds.[31] First, alerts could be registered on the basis of public policy, public security or national security grounds.[32] This could be the case when third-country nationals had been convicted of an offence carrying a penalty involving deprivation of liberty for at least one year,[33] or there were serious grounds for believing that they had committed serious criminal offences, or there was clear evidence that they planned to commit such offences in the territory of a signatory state.[34] Second, alerts could be inserted with respect to third-country nationals who had not complied with national immigration law, on the basis of a deportation order or refusal of entry, including or accompanied by a prohibition on entry or a prohibition on residence.[35]In connection with each alert, the SIS stored basic alphanumeric information – name, nationality, the type of alert, any specific objective physical characteristics and so on – and operated on a hit/no hit basis. In the event of a hit, national authorities would perform searches for supplementary information in another system named Supplementary Information Request at the National Entries (SIRENE).[36]

---

[29] Article 92 CISA.
[30] Elspeth Guild, "Moving the Borders of Europe," Inaugural lecture, University of Nijmegen 2000, 24, http://cmr.jur.ru.nl/cmr/docs/oratie.eg.pdf; Brouwer, *Digital Borders and Real Rights*, 66–68; Schengen Joint Supervisory Authority, *Final Report of the Schengen Joint Supervisory Authority on the Follow-Up of the Recommendations Concerning the Use of Article 96 Alerts in the Schengen Information System* (26 November 2010).
[31] In the early days of the SIS, under Article 96 CISA all alerts were inserted at the discretion of national authorities, on the basis of a national decision either by an administrative or judicial authority.
[32] National security is understood as encompassing surveillance by the intelligence services of the Member States, particularly with regard to the fight against terrorism. Public security is not defined under EU law. Drawing from the case law on free movement law, public security covers both internal and external security (Case C-367/89, *Aimé Richardt and Les Accessoires Scientifiques SNC*, ECLI:EU:C:1991:376) and can involve a risk of serious disturbances to foreign relations or to the peaceful coexistence of nations (Case C-83/94, *Peter Leifer, Reinhold Otto Krauskopf and Otto Holzer*, ECLI:EU:C:1995:329). Furthermore, in *P.I.*, the term 'imperative grounds of public security' was interpreted as meaning 'a particularly serious threat to one of the fundamental interests of society, which might pose a direct threat to the calm and physical security of the population'. See Case C-348/09, *P. I. v. Oberbürgermeisterin der Stadt Remscheid*, ECLI:EU:C:2012:300.
[33] Article 96(2)(a) CISA.
[34] Article 96(2)(b) CISA.
[35] Article 96(3) CISA.
[36] Each Member State operates a SIRENE Bureau, available 24/7, responsible for any supplementary information exchange and coordination of activities connected to SIS alerts.

1.2 Monitoring the Territorial Belonging of Asylum Seekers and Irregular Migrants: Eurodac

Parallel to the establishment of the SIS and also in response to the abolition of border controls within the Schengen area, national governments set out common rules on how to determine which Member State would be responsible for examining individual asylum applications.[37] The Dublin Convention, which was signed in 1990 and entered into force in 1997,[38] allocated asylum applications to a single Member State based on prescribed hierarchical criteria. A necessary corollary was a central registration system that would process the fingerprints of asylum seekers and assist in the implementation of the Dublin system. Eurodac (standing for European Dactyloscopy), the first pan-European *biometric* database, was created by Regulations 2725/2000[39] and 407/2002[40] and became operational in 2003.[41] According to its basic rules, every asylum seeker over the age of fourteen must enter their fingerprints when they apply for international protection. The collected fingerprints are stored in its Central System and are compared with fingerprints that have already been transmitted by other participating countries.[42] As with the SIS, Eurodac functions on a hit/no hit basis; if a Eurodac check reveals that the

---

The SIS should thus be understood as an index, which enables national authorities, after a hit, to exchange further information stored in SIRENE.

[37] For a comprehensive analysis of EU asylum law and policy, see Chapter 8.

[38] Convention Determining the State Responsible for Examining Applications for Asylum Lodged in One of the Member States of the European Communities, 15 June 1990, 1997 O.J. (C 254) 1 [hereinafter Dublin Convention]. The Convention superseded the refugee section in CISA. It was later replaced by Council Regulation 343/2003, 2003 O.J. (L 50) 1 [hereinafter Dublin II Regulation] and European Parliament and Council Regulation (EU) 604/2013, 2013 O.J. (L 180) 31 [hereinafter Dublin III Regulation]. The Dublin IV Regulation is currently being negotiated. See *Proposal for a Regulation Establishing the Criteria and Mechanisms for Determining the Member State Responsible for Examining an Application for International Protection Lodged in One of the Member States by a Third-Country National or a Stateless Person*, COM (2016) 270 final (4 May 2016).

[39] Council Regulation (EC) 2725/2000, Concerning the Establishment of 'Eurodac' for the Comparison of Fingerprints for the Effective Application of the Dublin Convention, 2000 O.J. (L 316) 1 [hereinafter Eurodac Regulation].

[40] Council Regulation (EC) 407/2002, Laying Down Certain Rules to Implement Regulation (EC) No 2725/2000 Concerning the Establishment of 'Eurodac' for the Comparison of Fingerprints for the Effective Application of the Dublin Convention, 2002 O.J. (L 62) 1.

[41] For a detailed overview of the story behind Eurodac see Jonathan Aus, "Eurodac: A Solution Looking for a Problem?" *European Integration Online Papers* 10 (2006): 1–26; Steve Peers and Nicole Rogers, eds., *EU Immigration and Asylum Law* (Leiden: Martinus Nijhoff, 2006), 263–268; Niovi Vavoula, *Immigration and Privacy in the Law of the European Union: The Case of Databases* (Leiden: Brill, 2019), chapter 4.

[42] Eurodac Regulation, arts. 4–7.

fingerprints have already been recorded in another Member State, the asylum seeker may be sent to that Member State. In addition, the system processes the data of all migrants that are apprehended in connection with irregular border crossings by land, sea or air or that are found to be irregularly staying on the territory of a Member State.[43] This category of data is also connected with the operation of the Dublin system, as a key criterion for assigning responsibility among the Member States is the asylum seeker's country of first entry into the EU.[44] Storing the fingerprints of irregular migrants at the EU's external border enables national authorities to track the (possible) movement of asylum seekers prior to their lodging of an application.

As for the type of data stored in Eurodac, apart from a full set of fingerprints, it only contains limited biographical information. The person's name and nationality are not included and, thus, individuals are identified by no more than their fingerprints.[45] The fingerprints of asylum seekers are retained for a period of ten years, while those of individuals found irregularly entering for two years only (now eighteen months).[46] The fingerprints of migrants found irregularly staying are not centrally stored, but only compared on the spot with the existing Eurodac data for the sole purpose of determining whether the irregular migrant has formerly applied for international protection in another Member State.

2 The Second Wave: Immigration Databases and the 'War on Terror'

The events of 9/11 signalled a new era for pan-European immigration databases. In response to the terrorist attacks, policies on immigration control, public security and criminality have become extensively intertwined. The migration-risk nexus fuelled by the events in the United States, and then the attacks in Madrid (2004) and London (2005), coincided with technological advances, and the combination resulted in the creation of a new database and the expansion of old ones. As detailed in the following section, the VIS was

---

[43] Eurodac Regulation, arts. 8–10.

[44] Dublin III Regulation, art. 13.

[45] Elspeth Guild, "Unreadable Papers? The EU's First Experiences with Biometrics: Examining Eurodac and the EU's Borders," in *Are You Who You Say You Are? The EU and Biometric Borders*, ed. Juliet Lodge (Nijmegen: Wolf Legal Publishers, 2007), 32.

[46] See European Parliament and Council Regulation (EU) 603/2013, 2013 O.J. (L 180) 1 [hereinafter Recast Eurodac Regulation]. The Regulation is discussed later in this chapter, but it bears mentioning here that the retention period was only partially justified. According to Article 13(1) of the Dublin III Regulation, a Member State remains responsible as the first country of entry for a period of one year; there is no reason why the retention period is eighteen months rather than one year.

created for the administration of the common EU visa policy and the data of short-stay visa applicants. SIS (SIS II) was significantly expanded through the insertion of additional features and the collection and storage of biometrics. Eurodac was reformed to encompass not only the primary purpose of administering the asylum allocation system but also the ancillary purpose of assisting in the fight against terrorism and serious crime.

2.1 Targeting Visa Applicants: The VIS

Visas are an emblematic symbol of the state's right to control entry of aliens. They first became a matter of collective interest in the Schengen framework, which contained extensive rules on short-stay (Schengen) visas,[47] supplemented by provisions on freedom to travel.[48] With the entry into force of the Amsterdam Treaty, EU competences in the field of short-stay visas were significantly reinforced.[49] However, progress on establishing a common visa policy was rather slow until the events of 9/11. Immediately afterwards, the EU Member States decided to reform the EU common visa policy by establishing a network for information exchange among their national authorities responsible for issuing short-stay visas.[50] The underlying rationale was to reinforce extraterritorial immigration control by storing the personal data collected from visa applicants and, at the same time, to exploit this pool of information for law enforcement purposes. The premise was that visa applicants constitute a risky population not only for immigration-control purposes but also for crime prevention, justifying measures that would potentially pre-empt and deter their movement.[51] As was explicitly stated '(t)he events of 11 September 2001 ... radically altered the situation, showing that visas are not just about

[47] Articles 9–17 CISA. The duration of a short-stay is no more than three months in any six-month period from the date of first entry in the territory of the Member State.
[48] Articles 19–24 CISA.
[49] Articles 62(2)(b), 62(3), 67 Treaty Establishing the European Community. For an overview see Annalisa Meloni, "The Development of a Common Visa Policy under the Treaty of Amsterdam," Common Market Law Review 42, no. 5 (2005): 1357–1381.
[50] For an overview of the discussions see Council Document 12019/01 (20 September 2001); Council Document 14523/01 (26 November 2001); Council Document 15577/01 (21 December 2001); Council Document SN 300/1/01 (15 December 2001). On the emphasis on 'border security' see Valsamis Mitsilegas, "Borders, Security and the Transatlantic Cooperation in the Twenty-First Century: Identity and Privacy in an Era of Globalized Surveillance," in Immigration Policy and Security, eds. Terri Givens, Gary Freeman, and David Leal (New York: Routledge, 2009), 148–166.
[51] Louise Amoore and Marieke de Goede, eds., Risk and the War on Terror (Oxford: Routledge, 2008).

controlling immigration but are above all an issue of EU member states' internal security.'[52]

The VIS database was established by a series of instruments: Decision 2004/512/EC,[53] which formed the legal basis for the VIS; Regulation 767/2008[54] governing the use of the system for border control purposes; and Council Decision 2008/633/JHA[55] prescribing the modalities by which visa data was to be consulted by law enforcement authorities and Europol.[56] After numerous years of complications, the gradual rollout of the VIS concluded in February 2016.[57] The database operates in tandem with the EU rules on short-stay visas. The current legal framework comprises a 'black list' of countries whose nationals must be in possession of a visa prior to their entry in the Schengen area, the Visa Code prescribing procedures and standards for national authorities, and rules on the uniform format of visas. Long-stay visas remain regulated at the national level only.

The VIS database currently constitutes the largest information exchange scheme in the EU. As of 30 September 2017, the VIS contained over 49 million visa applications and almost 42 million fingerprint sets.[58] Reflecting the post-9/11 migration-risk nexus, the VIS is designed for multiple purposes. Article 2 of the VIS Regulation stipulates that the overarching purpose of the database is to improve the implementation of the common visa policy by facilitating the

---

[52] Council Document 14523/01 (26 January 2002).

[53] Council Decision 2004/512/EC, Establishing the Visa Information System (VIS), 2004 O.J. (L 213) 5.

[54] European Parliament and Council Regulation (EC) 767/2008, 2008 O.J. (L 218) 60 as amended by the European Parliament and Council Regulation (EC) 810/2009, Visa Code, 2009 O.J. (L 243) 1 [hereinafter VIS Regulation].

[55] Council Decision 2008/633/JHA, 2008 O.J. (L 218) 129 [hereinafter VIS Decision]. The need for different legal instruments reflects the (former) pillar structure under which rules on immigration and asylum matters were (in the vast majority of cases) adopted under co-decision between the European Parliament and the Council, whereas rules on judicial and police cooperation in criminal matters were subject to unanimity in the Council and mere consultation of the European Parliament.

[56] Europol is the EU Agency for Law Enforcement Cooperation aimed at supporting cooperation between domestic law enforcement authorities through the collection, storage, further processing, analysis and exchange of personal data, whether provided by Member States or produced by the agency itself. In operation since 1999, Europol is currently governed by the European Parliament and Council Regulation (EU) 2016/ 794, On the European Union Agency for Law Enforcement Cooperation (Europol) and Replacing and Repealing Council Decisions 2009/ 371/ JHA, 2009/ 935/ JHA, 2009/ 936/ JHA, and 2009/ 968/ JHA, 2016 O.J. (L 135) 53.

[57] Commission Implementing Decision (EU) 2016/281, Determining the Date from which the Visa Information System (VIS) Is to Start Its Operations at External Border Crossing Points, 2016 O.J. (L 52) 64.

[58] eu-LISA, Technical Reports on the Functioning of VIS (May 2018), 4.

exchange of short-stay visa data; however, it further sets out no fewer than seven sub-purposes.[59] In practice, the VIS is meant to be used in a variety of fora: when processing an application for a Schengen visa in a consulate; when verifying the identity of the visa holder at the border against the data stored in the system; when performing checks on national territory to verify the identity and status (visa holder, asylum seekers, irregular migrant) of a third-country national; and in the context of the prevention, detection or investigation of serious crimes.

The system stores a wide array of personal data of visa applicants, irrespective of whether their application has been granted, refused, revoked, renewed or discontinued. These data include bibliographic information, biometrics (a full set of fingerprints and a photograph), information on persons who have issued an invitation and/or are liable to pay for the applicant's subsistence costs, purpose of the travel, residence and occupation.[60] By including such extensive information on visa applicants, the VIS implies an element of suspicion of visa applicants – they need to be monitored even though they have an a priori legitimate reason for travel to the EU. Crucially, this shadow of suspicion accompanies not only the travellers as such but also the family members, organisations or companies that have issued invitations or sponsored a stay within the Schengen area. Everyday activities are transformed into risks to be managed and prevented by gathering an extensive array of private information and putting it in the hands of a wide range of domestic authorities.

Turning to data access, outside of immigration authorities, access to VIS data is not routinely granted. Law enforcement authorities are allowed access only when necessary in a specific case, and only when there are reasonable grounds to believe that consultation of the system will substantially contribute to the prevention, detection or investigation of terrorist offences and other

---

[59] These include: (a) Facilitating the visa application procedure; (b) Preventing 'visa shopping'; (c) Facilitating the fight against fraud; (d) Facilitating checks at external border crossing points and within national territory; (e) Assisting in the identification of persons that do not meet the requirements for entering, staying or residing in a Member State; (f) Facilitating the implementation of the Dublin mechanism for determining the Member State responsible for the examination of an asylum application and for examining such applications, which is meant to assist in cases when a visa applicant has applied for international protection, as according to the Dublin criteria the Member State that has granted a Schengen visa will be responsible and (g) Contributing to the prevention of threats to Member States' internal security. For a critical examination of the VIS purposes see Vavoula, *Immigration and Privacy in the Law of the European Union*, chapter 3. The ranking of the purposes has been subject to litigation before the EU Court of Justice. See Case C-482/08, *UK* v. *Council*, ECLI:EU:C:2010:631.

[60] VIS Regulation, art. 9.

Databases for Non-EU Nationals and the Right to Private Life 239

serious crimes.[61] These conditions must be verified by the Member State's Central Access Point following a reasoned electronic request by the designated authority.[62] More ambiguously, access to VIS data by Europol is allowed 'within the limits of its mandate and when necessary for the performance of its tasks'.[63]

2.2 From the SIS to the SIS II: The Transformation of the System from a Reporting to an Investigation Tool

A second strand of action as regards the operation of immigration databases in the wake of the 9/11 events has been the reinforcement of the functions of the SIS. At a Spanish initiative, Regulation 871/2004[64] and Council Decision 2005/211/JHA[65] were adopted stipulating wider access to certain types of data by visa, judicial and law enforcement authorities, among which Europol and Eurojust were included.[66] In the case of Europol, however, access was not granted to immigration data. At the same time, it became obvious that there was a pressing need to develop a second generation SIS – the SIS II – to accommodate the expanded EU family after the 2004 enlargement. The migration from the SIS to the SIS II was also regarded as a first-class opportunity to insert new functionalities into the system by taking advantage of the latest developments in the field of information technology.[67] Two Regulations and a Decision were formally adopted in 2006;[68] due to numerous technical complications the SIS II only commenced its operation in April 2013.

---

[61] VIS Decision, art. 5(1).

[62] VIS Decision, art. 4.

[63] VIS Decision, art. 7.

[64] Council Regulation (EC) 871/2004, Concerning the Introduction of Some New Functions for the Schengen Information System, Including in the Fight against Terrorism, 2002 O.J. (L 162) 29.

[65] Council Decision 2005/211/JHA, Concerning the Introduction of Some New Functions for the Schengen Information System, Including in the Fight against Terrorism, 2005 O.J. (L 68) 44.

[66] Eurojust is the counterpart of Europol in relation to judicial cooperation. See Council Decision 2009/426/JHA, On the Strengthening of Eurojust and Amending Decision 2002/187 JHA Setting Up Eurojust with a View to Reinforcing the Fight against Serious Crime, 2009 O.J. (L 138) 14.

[67] For an overview see Joanna Parkin, "The Difficult Road to the Schengen Information System II - The Legacy of Laboratories and the Cost for Fundamental Rights and the Rule of Law," CEPS, 2011.

[68] European Parliament and Council Regulation (EC) 1987/2006, On the Establishment, Operation and Use of the Second Generation Schengen Information System (SIS II), 2006 O.J. (L 381) 4 [hereinafter SIS II Regulation]; Council Decision 2007/533/JHA, On the Establishment, Operation and Use of the Second Generation Schengen Information System (SIS II), 2007 O.J. (L 205) 63 [hereinafter SIS II Decision]; European Parliament and Council

The reforms made to the SIS II signal its gradual transformation from a mere reporting mechanism to a general investigation tool.[69] In this respect, one major shift has been the possibility of interlinking alerts involving different individuals or events that are inserted under different legal bases.[70] Such interlinking is allowed only if there is a clear operational need. Whether or not the option is used is subject to the national law of the public authority's Member State, which raises the prospect of the creation of significantly different systems across the EU. The potential for profiling through the interlinking of alerts is significant: 'the person is no longer "assessed" on the basis of data relating only to him/her, but on the basis of his/her possible association with other persons',[71] which may lead to their being treated with greater suspicion if they are deemed to be associated with criminals or wanted persons. Even though authorities with no right of access to certain categories of alert will not be able to see the link to an alert to which they do not have access, for instance motor vehicle authorities with respect to immigration alerts, such authorities will not necessarily be unaware of the existence of a link.[72]

Another major change involves the possibility of including biometric identifiers (photographs and fingerprints) within the system.[73] This change is part of a more general trend to introduce biometrics in all EU databases and documents: as described previously, both VIS and Eurodac are based on the collection and storage of biometrics; EU rules on the format for residence

---

Regulation (EC) 1986/2006, Regarding Access to the Second Generation Schengen Information System (SIS II) by the Services in the Member States Responsible for Issuing Vehicle Registration Certificates, 2006 O.J. (L 381) 1. On the need for separate instruments see Note 55.

[69] For the sake of a holistic approach it must be noted that under the revised SIS II rules, the registration of alerts on public policy, public security and national security grounds became mandatory. See SIS II Regulation, art. 24.

[70] Examples of interlinking include: (a) an EU national wanted for arrest based on a European Arrest Warrant related to a convicted companion who should be refused entry; (b) family members in respect of whom SIS II alerts have been registered; (c) a third-country national parent who should be refused entry related to a missing child (third-country national); (d) a third-country national to be refused entry and the possibility of them being a witness in an illegal immigration case; (e) a husband convicted criminal to be refused entry whose wife is a suspected terrorist; (f) a third-country national to be refused entry who is also a suspect in an illegal immigration case; (g) a third-country national to be refused entry using his or her own car, boat or aircraft; and (h) a third-country national to be refused entry using a stolen identity document. Council Document 12573/3/04 (30 November 2004), 3.

[71] Opinion of the European Data Protection Supervisor, 2006 O.J. (opinion on proposed SIS II regulations and decision).

[72] Valsamis Mitsilegas, *EU Criminal Law* (Oxford: Hart, 2009), 241.

[73] SIS II Regulation, art. 22.

Databases for Non-EU Nationals and the Right to Private Life 241

permits and EU passports also require the use of biometrics.[74] According to Article 22 of the SIS II Regulation, biometrics will be introduced in two phases: (i) in the first stage, they will be used only for identity verification by comparing the biometric identifiers of the person of interest with those – and only with those – existing in the SIS II under that person's name (one-to-one searches); (ii) the second stage would allow the use of the biometrics to identify other individuals of interest (one-to-many searches). This development has significant implications: it transforms the database into a general intelligence weapon, as biometrics can be used in the course of investigations to conduct speculative searches in the database's pool of suspected population – so-called fishing expeditions.[75] In this respect, biometrics will operate as a vital search key for revealing links to other alerts. A Commission report on the readiness and availability of fingerprints for identification purposes confirms these concerns, as it is stated that a comparison of fingerprints with those already stored 'might identify links with other alerts'.[76] In sum, biometrics are not merely collected and stored to sort out the 'welcome' from the 'unwanted' but also to enhance the investigative powers of national law enforcement authorities.

2.3 The Use of Eurodac Data for Law Enforcement Purposes

A paradigmatic example of how the boundaries between immigration and police databases have been blurred and how the specified purpose of personal data collection no longer serves as a limit on data processing activities is the reconfiguration of Eurodac from a tool serving the Dublin system to a weapon in the fight against terrorism and serious crime. A year after the database had begun its operation, the Hague Programme called for the maximisation of effectiveness and interoperability of EU information systems and 'an innovative approach to the cross-border exchange of law enforcement information'.[77] Shortly afterwards, the Commission published a Communication on

---

[74] Evelien Brouwer, "The Use of Biometrics in EU Databases and Identity Documents: Keeping Track of Foreigners' Movements and Rights," in *Are You Who You Say You Are? The EU and Biometric Borders*, ed. Juliet Lodge (Nijmegen: Wolf Legal Publishers, 2007), 45–66; Baldaccini, "Counter-Terrorism and the EU Strategy for Border Security."

[75] Ben Hayes, "From the Schengen Information System to the SIS II and the Visa Information System (VIS): The Proposals Explained," Statewatch, February 2004, 4; Baldaccini, "Counter-Terrorism and the EU Strategy for Border Security," 38.

[76] Report from the Commission, *The Availability and Readiness of Technology to Identify a Person on the Basis of Fingerprints Held in the Second Generation Schengen Information System (SIS II)*, COM (2016) 93 final (29 February 2016), 7.

[77] See The Hague Programme: Strengthening Freedom, Security and Justice in the European Union, 7.

improved effectiveness, enhanced interoperability and synergies of EU information systems stating that 'authorities responsible for internal security could … have access to Eurodac in well-defined cases, when there is a substantiated suspicion that the perpetrator of a serious crime had applied for asylum'.[78] After four proposals and largely under the pressure of finalising the second phase of the Common European Asylum System (CEAS),[79] the recast Eurodac Regulation was adopted in June 2013,[80] allowing consultation of asylum seekers' fingerprints for the purposes of prevention, detection and investigation of terrorist offences and other serious crimes.

As with the VIS, law enforcement access is listed as an ancillary purpose; the principal purpose remains that of supporting the implementation of the Dublin asylum rules. Following the VIS model, consultation of Eurodac data does not take place on a routine basis and involves only the prevention, detection and investigation of terrorist offences and other serious crimes.[81] The conditions for access are somewhat stricter than the ones prescribed in the VIS Decision.[82] There is an additional step for accessing the Eurodac data: the national authority must have already consulted national fingerprint databases, as well as the automated fingerprinting identification systems (AFIS) of other Member States[83] and the VIS, and such consultation must have proven futile.[84] This step is meant to ensure that consultation of Eurodac is reserved only for cases in which other pools of information have been exhausted. Furthermore, compared to VIS, the necessity of consulting the database is defined more carefully: according to Article 20(1)(b), 'there must be an overriding public security concern which makes the searching of the database

---

[78] Communication from the Commission, *Improved Effectiveness, Enhanced Interoperability and Synergies among European Databases in the Area of Justice and Home Affairs*, COM (2005) 597 final (11 November 2005).

[79] See Brigitta Juster and Vassilis Tsianos, "Erase Them! Eurodac and Digital Deportability," *Transversal/EIPCP Multilingual Webjournal*, February 2013, http://eipcp.net/transversal/0313/kuster-tsianos/en.

[80] See Recast Eurodac Regulation.

[81] Recast Eurodac Regulation, recital 31. See Opinion of the European Data Protection Supervisor, 2013 O.J. (C 28) 3, para. 54 (opinion on proposal for recast Eurodac, executive summary); Standing Committee of Experts on International Immigration, Refugee and Criminal Law (Meijers Committee), Note on the Proposal for a Regulation on the Establishment of Eurodac (COM(2012)254), CM1216 (2012).

[82] These conditions apply also in the case of Europol access to Eurodac data.

[83] Such consultation is conducted on the basis of Council Decision 2008/615/JHA, On the Stepping up of Cross-Border Cooperation, Particularly in Combating Terrorism and Cross-Border Crime, 2008 O.J. (L 210) 1 [hereinafter Prüm Decision].

[84] Recast Eurodac Regulation, art. 20(1). There is a caveat: Article 20(1) prescribes that prior consultation is not necessary if there are reasonable grounds to believe that a comparison with such systems would not lead to the establishment of the identity of the data subject.

Databases for Non-EU Nationals and the Right to Private Life   243

proportionate'. Verification that these data access conditions have been met is entrusted to a verifying authority assigned at the national level.

3 The Third Wave: The Generalisation of Surveillance of Movement of Non-EU Citizens

The most recent burst of database activity has been prompted by the terrorism events in France in November 2015 and Belgium in March 2016. A number of proposals that had remained in the EU legislative drawer for years, successfully opposed by those against normalising surveillance of movement,[85] re-emerged as part of a comprehensive, multi-faceted response at EU level, encapsulated in the concept of establishing a 'genuine Security Union'.[86] Dossiers that were particularly contentious in the past (Entry/Exit System and European Travel Information and Authorisation System [ETIAS]) have been prioritised and speedily adopted. At the same time, existing databases have been re-jigged to explicitly encompass security considerations.[87] Overall, the development of pan-European immigration databases has accelerated tremendously: new systems have been established to fill perceived 'informational gaps' created by the compartmentalised approach of the 1990s and 2000s; the existing systems have been reformed to enhance and magnify their use and effectiveness; and interoperability has been heavily promoted, to enable the connection of the 'data pots' in a variety of ways.

3.1 Visa-Free Travellers as a Risk: The Establishment of the EES and the ETIAS

Although the databases discussed previously in the chapter create a rather comprehensive network of information exchange schemes concerning third-country nationals, they do not cover those originating from countries not subject to the visa regime. Influenced by similar initiatives in the United States, particularly the US-VISIT programme (now IDENT), the European Council hinted at this 'informational gap' in the Hague Programme[88] and so

---

[85] Valsamis Mitsilegas and Niovi Vavoula, "The Normalisation of Surveillance in an Era of Global Mobility," in *Handbook of Migration and Security*, ed. Philippe Bourbeau (Cheltenham: Edward Elgar, 2017), 232–251.

[86] See Communication from the Commission, COM (2015) 185 final.

[87] Communication from the Commission, *Stronger and Smarter Information Systems for Borders and Security*, COM (2016) 205 final (6 April 2016).

[88] See The Hague Programme: Strengthening Freedom, Security and Justice in the European Union, 7.

too did the Commission in its Communication on improved effectiveness, enhanced interoperability and synergies among information systems.[89] After years of discussions,[90] in 2013 the Commission presented three legislative proposals commonly referred to as the 'Smart Borders Package'. This Package was composed of a proposal to establish the EES at the EU external borders,[91] a proposal for a 'Registered Travellers Programme' (RTP) to facilitate the border crossing of pre-screened *bona fide* travellers,[92] and one on amendments to the Schengen Borders Code to reflect the changes.[93] Due to proportionality concerns,[94] the Commission originally left the registration of biometrics and law enforcement access outside the scope of that proposal, and later entirely withdrew the package and committed to submitting revised proposals in early 2016. However, in the aftermath of the 2015 terrorist events, the EES rose high on the EU agenda, including a far-reaching proposal to further extend the reach of the EES to cover EU nationals.[95] The EES was ultimately adopted in November 2017 and certain rules were slightly modified, but the basic policy choices remained the same.[96] The idea of the RTP was abandoned.

The system is designed to register border crossing both at entry and exit for all non-EU nationals admitted for a short stay, irrespective of whether they are required to obtain a Schengen visa or not.[97] It will also apply to non-EU nationals whose entry for a short stay has been refused at the border, which

---

[89] See Communication from the Commission, COM (2005) 597 final, 9.

[90] Vavoula, *Immigration and Privacy in the Law of the European Union*, chapter 5.

[91] *Commission Proposal for a Regulation of the European Parliament and of the Council Establishing an Entry/Exit System (EES) to Register Entry and Exit Data of Third Country Nationals Crossing the External Borders of the Member States of the European Union*, COM (2013) 95 final (28 February 2013).

[92] *Commission Proposal for a Regulation of the European Parliament and of the Council Establishing a Registered Traveller Programme*, COM (2013) 97 final (28 February 2013).

[93] *Commission Proposal for a Regulation of the European Parliament and of the Council Amending Regulation (EC) No 562/2006 as Regards the Use of the Entry/Exit System (EES) and the Registered Traveller Programme (RTP)*, COM (2013) 96 final (28 February 2013).

[94] For criticism, see among others Opinion of the European Data Protection Supervisor, 2014 O.J. (C 32) 25 (executive summary); Article 29 Data Protection Working Party, Opinion 05/2013 on Smart Borders, WP206 (6 June 2013); Standing Committee of Experts on International Immigration, Refugee and Criminal Law (Meijers Committee), Note on the Smart Borders proposals (COM(2013) 95 final, COM(2013) 96 final and COM(2013) 97 final), CM1307 (3 May 2013).

[95] Council Document 12272/15 (25 September 2015).

[96] European Parliament and Council Regulation (EU) 2017/2226, 2017 O.J. (L 327) 20 [hereinafter EES Regulation].

[97] According to Article 2(3) of the EES Regulation, there are a few exceptions for non-EU nationals: those who have residence permits; are family members of an EU national and hold a residence card; or are family members of another non-EU national who enjoys free movement rights or has a residence card.

means that even though these persons will be physically kept outside of the EU, their data will be stored in the EES for future use. Following the VIS model, the EES is a multi-purpose tool: it will enhance the efficiency and automation of border checks; assist in the identification of irregular migrants; allow the identification and detection of overstayers; allow refusals of entry to be checked electronically; enable visa authorities to check the use of previous visas; inform non-EU nationals of the duration of their authorised stay; gather statistics; combat identity fraud and misuse of travel documents; and strengthen internal security and the fight against terrorism by allowing law enforcement authorities access to travel history records.[98] To these ends, once the system becomes operational, it will record the identities of third-country nationals, by storing alphanumeric data, four fingerprints and a facial image, along with details of their travel documents, which will be linked to electronic entry and exit records.[99] The retention periods foreseen vary depending on whether an exit record exists or not; if so, it is three years, but in case of *potential* overstayers, the records will be kept for five years.[100] The current practice of stamping travel documents will be abolished. Instead, the system will automatically calculate the maximum term of authorised stay in accordance with the Schengen Borders Code.[101] An information mechanism will be included to identify cases where there are no records of exit.[102] Access to EES data for the purposes of the prevention, detection and investigation of terrorist offences and other serious crimes is envisaged under a mixture of rules combining the Eurodac and the VIS models.[103] For example, verification that the conditions of access have been met is the responsibility of each Member State's Central Access Point; intelligence services are not excluded from accessing the EES data.[104] Furthermore, the EES Regulation allows national authorities to search the database to identify 'an unknown suspect perpetrator or suspected victim of a terrorist offence or other serious criminal offence' if they meet the listed conditions and have already (unsuccessfully) consulted their national databases or, in the case of fingerprints, their national AFIS.[105]

---

[98] EES Regulation, art. 6(1).

[99] EES Regulation, arts. 14–20.

[100] EES Regulation, art. 34.

[101] See Note 5.

[102] EES Regulation, art. 12.

[103] EES Regulation, arts. 29–33.

[104] EES Regulation, art. 29. Compare with Article 3 of the VIS Decision.

[105] EES Regulation, art. 32(2). Compare with Article 20(1) of the Eurodac Regulation.

The movement of visa-free travellers will also be monitored through the European Travel Information and Authorisation System (ETIAS), enacted in September 2018.[106] The ETIAS was initially conceptualised alongside the EES, with the Commission briefly mentioning that it would examine the possibility of introducing an Electronic System of Travel Authorisation (ESTA) to pre-screen non-EU nationals. The system, which was a transplantation of the US standards in the EU context, foresaw the pre-screening of non-EU nationals who were not subject to a visa requirement in order to verify that they fulfilled the entry conditions before travelling to the EU.[107] In 2011, the project was shelved 'as the potential contribution to enhancing the security of the Member States would neither justify the collection of personal data at such a scale nor the financial cost and the impact on international relations'.[108] Nonetheless, following the removal of numerous countries from the 'black' list of countries whose nationals require a visa to enter the Schengen territory and under the influence of the 2015/2016 terrorist events, the idea re-emerged.[109] Reminiscent of the SIS II, the ETIAS Regulation solidifies the link between immigration control and security, as one of its main objectives is to contribute to a high level of security by thoroughly assessing whether travellers pose a 'security risk'.[110] There are many other purposes of the database: preventing illegal migration, protecting public health, enhancing the effectiveness of border checks, supporting the SIS II, and contributing to the prevention, detection and investigation of terrorist offences or of other serious criminal offences.[111]

To achieve these aims, all visa-exempt travellers shall be obliged to obtain authorisation prior to their departure through an online application in which they must disclose a series of personal data including biographical data, travel arrangements, home and email address, phone number, level of education and current occupation.[112] The pre-screening and provision of authorisation

---

[106] European Parliament and Council Regulation (EU) 2018/1240, 2018 O.J. (L 61) 1.

[107] Communication from the Commission, *Preparing the Next Steps in Border Management*, COM (2008) 69 final (13 February 2008); see also Commission, "Policy Study on an EU Electronic System for Travel Authorisation," Price Waterhouse Coopers, February 2011.

[108] Communication from the Commission, *Smart Borders – Options and the Way Ahead*, COM (2011) 680 final (25 October 2011), 7.

[109] Communication from the Commission, COM (2016) 205 final, 13.

[110] See European Parliament and Council Regulation (EU) 2018/1240, Establishing a European Travel Information and Authorisation System (ETIAS), 2018 O.J. (L 236) 1, art. 4(a) [hereinafter ETIAS Regulation]. According to Article 3(6), security risk is defined as the risk of a threat to public policy, internal security or international relations for any of the Member States.

[111] See ETIAS Regulation, art. 4(b)–(f).

[112] ETIAS Regulation, art. 17.

Databases for Non-EU Nationals and the Right to Private Life   247

shall take place on the basis of automated processing[113] (comparison) of the applicant's personal data with three elements: (a) data held in existing immigration and law enforcement databases;[114] (b) screening rules *enabling profiling* on the basis of risk indicators, consisting of a combination of data including age range, sex, nationality, residence, level of education and occupation;[115] and (c) a special ETIAS watch list of individuals suspected of having participated in terrorism or other serious crimes or in respect of whom there are factual indications or reasonable grounds to believe that they will commit such offences.[116] In practice, the ETIAS will be used both at the borders by carriers and border authorities and by immigration authorities to verify travel documentation.[117] If authorisation is granted, data will be held for three years; otherwise, it will be held for five years.[118] Law enforcement authorities and Europol will be granted access under rules largely mirroring those in the VIS Decision.[119]

The EES and the ETIAS introduce mobility surveillance for almost all travellers. They are grounded on automaticity and almost blind reliance on technology.[120] As with the earlier databases, they are based on the collection and further processing of biometrics and they reinforce the link between immigration control and law enforcement. In many respects, the value and significance of short-stay (Schengen) visas are diminished: on the one hand, individuals who have obtained a visa are surveilled not only in the VIS but also in the EES; on the other hand, nationals from visa-exempt countries are nonetheless placed under suspicion, because they will soon be monitored in the EES and the ETIAS. This complex framework of consecutive surveillance of movement strongly supports the idea that all non-EU nationals are suspicious and form part of the risky population. In other words, in the eyes of the EU legislator, every non-EU national potentially constitutes a 'security risk'.

---

[113] The automated processing will be handled by the Central Unit, but in cases of a hit, manual processing will follow by the National Unit of the Member State responsible. See ETIAS Regulation, art. 26.

[114] These are: SIS II, VIS, Eurodac, EES, Europol database, the Interpol Stolen and Lost Travel Document Database, the Interpol Travel Documents Associated with Notices Database and the ETIAS.

[115] ETIAS Regulation, art. 33.

[116] ETIAS Regulation, art. 34.

[117] ETIAS Regulation, arts. 45–49.

[118] ETIAS Regulation, art. 54.

[119] ETIAS Regulation, arts. 50–53.

[120] See Article 20 of the EES Regulation about the rebuttable presumption of irregularity in lack of an exit record.

To conclude this discussion, it bears highlighting that the ETIAS will constitute as large a database as the EES and will contain as much personal information as the VIS, thus combining the worst of both worlds. Based on the ETIAS data, the authorities will be able to construct complete profiles of visa-exempt travellers who are previously unsuspected of any offence. Even though no biometrics will be stored, the categories of data collected and stored are quite extensive. Coupled with the EES, the ETIAS will constitute both a massive catalogue of third-country nationals and a powerful surveillance tool driven by the logic of risk prevention transplanted once again into immigration control.[121] Importantly, the ETIAS is understood as a platform for mining and profiling personal data, not simply issuing automated or manual travel authorisation decisions. The ETIAS screening rules are meant to identify persons who are otherwise unknown to national competent authorities but are *assumed* to be of interest for immigration control or security purposes and therefore are *likely* to commit criminal offences in the future. These persons will be flagged not because of any specific actions they have engaged in but because they display particular category traits in a probabilistic logic devoid of concrete evidence.[122]

3.2 The SIS II, Eurodac and VIS under Refurbishment

Efforts to fill in 'informational gaps' have been accompanied by radical reforms to all three operational databases. The Eurodac proposal was tabled in May 2016 and political agreement has been reached, even though formal adoption is still pending due to complications in other asylum-related files.[123] The proposal signals a landmark change in Eurodac's purpose – from a system aimed at the effective implementation of the Dublin mechanism into an instrument for *wider immigration purposes*, including the return of irregular migrants. The anticipated Eurodac reform is both quantitative and qualitative. Quantitavely, the scope *ratione personae* has been expanded and additional categories of data, including sensitive ones, are to be entered into the system. In particular, on top of a full set of fingerprints, Member States shall be obliged to take and transmit a facial image.[124] The age threshold for

---

[121] Vavoula, *Immigration and Privacy in the Law of the European Union*, chapter 6.

[122] Susie Alegre, Julien Jeandesboz, and Niovi Vavoula, *European Travel Information and Authorisation System (ETIAS): Border Management, Fundamental Rights and Data Protection*, Study for the European Parliament, PE 583.148, 2017, 23–26.

[123] *Commission Proposal for a Regulation of the European Parliament and of the Council*, COM (2016) 272 final (4 May 2016).

[124] *Commission Proposal*, COM (2016) 272 final, art. 2(1).

Databases for Non-EU Nationals and the Right to Private Life 249

fingerprinting children is significantly reduced to the age of six.[125] The categories of data held in the database are also considerably expanded, in order to 'allow immigration and asylum authorities to easily identify an individual'.[126] Furthermore, for the first time since the establishment of the database, information on persons who are found irregularly present on the national territory will be centrally stored.[127] As these new categories of persons and information suggest, the transformation is also qualitative: Eurodac has been detached from its original Dublin context and re-conceptualized as a multi-purpose immigration tool.

The SIS II also underwent a refurbishment.[128] The Commission proposal of December 2016 followed an evaluation of the system, which found that a major flaw was the lack of harmonised national criteria for entering alerts.[129] Regulations 2018/1860 and 2018/1861 rectify this issue, albeit taking the lowest-common-denominator approach and making the registration of entry bans and return decisions mandatory.[130]

As for the contemplated VIS reform, it is of perhaps greatest interest for the purposes of the present chapter. This is because it seeks to fill the one outstanding gap in the coverage of third-country nationals in EU databases[131] – holders of residence permits, residence cards and long-stay visa holders.[132] The

---

[125] *Commission Proposal*, COM (2016) 272 final, art. 2(2).

[126] *Commission Proposal*, COM (2016) 272 final, art. 13.

[127] See *supra*, section II.1.2.

[128] *Proposal for a Regulation of the European Parliament and of the Council on the Establishment, Operation and Use of the Schengen Information System (SIS) in the Field of Border Checks*, COM (2016) 882 final (12 December 2016); *Proposal for a Regulation of the European Parliament and of the Council on the Establishment, Operation and Use of the Schengen Information System (SIS) in the Field of Police Cooperation and Judicial Cooperation in Criminal Matters*, COM (2016) 883 final (21 December 2016); *Proposal for a Regulation of the European Parliament and of the Council on the Use of the Schengen Information System for the Return of Illegally Staying Third Country Nationals*, COM (2016) 881 final (21 December 2016) [hereinafter collectively SIS II Proposal].

[129] *Commission Proposal for a Regulation of the European Parliament and of the Council*, COM (2018) 882 final (12 December 2016); *Commission Proposal for a Regulation of the European Parliament and of the Council*, COM (2018) 883 final (12 December 2016); *Commission Proposal for a Regulation of the European Parliament and of the Council*, COM (2018) 881 final (12 December 2016).

[130] European Parliament and Council Regulation (EU) 2018/1860, On the Use of the Schengen Information System for the Return of Illegally Staying Third-Country Nationals, 2018 O.J. (L 312) 1, art. 3; European Parliament and Council Regulation (EU) 2018/1861, On the Establishment, Operation and Use of the Schengen Information System (SIS) in the Field of Border Checks, 2018 O.J. (L 312) 14, art. 24.

[131] Communication from the Commission, COM (2016) 205 final, 3.

[132] For the discussion on the merits of registering residence permit holders see Council Document 12527/15 (8 October 2015).

VIS proposal[133] would extend the system to these groups of non-EU nationals as well as lower the threshold age for fingerprinting (six years). With this reform, *almost all* third-country nationals will be monitored. The only exception will be family members of EU nationals who hold residence cards and thus benefit from free movement rights. The underlying logic for including legal residents and long-stay holders is the need to manage a decentralised system of residence permits issued at the national level, but this decentralised structure has been deemed to have a collateral effect on immigration control *and security*.[134] In particular, the inability to verify biometrically the identities of residence card and long-stay visa holders is considered a security risk.

3.3 The ECRIS-TCN: Bridging Law Enforcement with Immigration Control and Non-EU with EU Nationals?

The European Criminal Records Information System for Third-Country Nationals (ECRIS-TCN) was proposed in June 2017.[135] This system emerged as a necessity purely in the law enforcement context, as in order to obtain complete information on previous convictions of non-EU nationals, requesting Member States were obliged to send 'blanket requests' to all Member States, thus creating a heavy administrative burden.[136] The ECRIS-TCN will be a centralised system for the exchange of criminal records on convicted third-country nationals and stateless persons and is meant to complement the already existing, decentralised ECRIS system through which information on the criminal records of EU nationals is exchanged among Member States.[137]

---

[133] *Commission Proposal for a Regulation of the European Parliament and of the Council*, COM (2018) 302 final (16 May 2018).

[134] See *Commission Proposal*, COM (2018) 302 final, art. 1(2).

[135] *Commission Proposal for a Regulation of the European Parliament and of the Council*, COM (2017) 344 final (29 June 2017); *Commission Proposal for a Directive of the European Parliament and of the Council*, COM (2016) 7 final (19 January 2016).

[136] Until now exchange of criminal records on non-EU nationals has been taking place under Council Decision 2009/316/JHA, On the Establishment of the European Criminal Records Information System (ECRIS) in application of Article 11 of Framework Decision 2009/315/JHA, 2009 O.J. (L 93) 33; Council Framework Decision 2009/315/JHA, On the Organisation and Content of the Exchange of Information Extracted from the Criminal Record between Member States, 2009 O.J. (L 93) 22.

[137] European Parliament and Council Regulation (EU) 2019/816, Establishing a Centralised System for the Identification of Member States Holding Conviction Information on Third-Country Nationals and Stateless Persons (ECRIS-TCN) to Supplement the European Criminal Records Information System and Amending Regulation (EU) 2018/1726, 2019 O.J. (L 135) 1 [hereinafter ECRIS-TCN Regulation]; European Parliament and Council Directive 2019/884, Amending Council Framework Decision 2009/315/JHA, as Regards the Exchange of Information on Third-Country Nationals and as Regards the European Criminal Records

Databases for Non-EU Nationals and the Right to Private Life   251

In cases where a record exists, data will be transferred by the convicting Member State to the requesting Member State on a bilateral basis, as per the rules in the ECRIS. All queries will be submitted through the central ECRIS-TCN system, which will contain biographical and biometric data; the retention period is not universal and will depend upon the retention period for the criminal records in the national databases. A particularly thorny issue in the negotiations involved the inclusion of dual nationals, that is, EU citizens who also hold the nationality of a third State, which creates potential discrimination compared to other EU citizens.[138] The final text formally adopted in April 2019 indeed prescribes that the personal scope of the system includes 'citizens of the Union who also hold the nationality of a third country'.[139] Like the possibility raised in some quarters of expanding the EES to EU nationals, the ECRIS-TCN illustrates how data on EU nationals can make their way into databases for non-EU nationals.

3.4 Compartmentalisation Is Dead! Long Live Interoperability

With all non-EU nationals effectively captured by at least one database, the final step towards an EU 'Big Brother' is the interconnection of the different 'data pots' under the umbrella term of interoperability.[140] The interoperability debates first started in the aftermath of 9/11.[141] In its 2005 Communication, the Commission defined interoperability as the 'ability of IT systems and of the business processes they support to exchange data and to enable the sharing of information and knowledge'.[142] However, details on the legal aspect of interoperability were spared, as the concept was reduced to a technical rather than a legal or political matter.[143] Since the Paris attacks of 13 November 2015, the

---

Information System (ECRIS), and Replacing Council Decision 2009/316/JHA, 2019 O.J. (L 151) 143.

[138] See Council Document 10828/18 (10 July 2018), where it is mentioned that the proposed solution would involve the registration of both dual nationals and non-EU nationals.

[139] ECRIS-TCN Regulation, art. 2.

[140] For an analysis of interoperability from the perspective of improving internal security, see Chapter 10.

[141] Council Document 13176/01 (24 October 2001).

[142] Communication from the Commission, COM (2005) 597 final.

[143] For a critique see Paul De Hert and Serge Gutwirth, "Interoperability of Police Databases within the EU: An Accountable Political Choice?" *International Review of Law Computers & Technology* 20, no. 1–2 (2006): 21–22; European Data Protection Supervisor, Comments on the Communication of the Commission on interoperability of European databases (10 March 2006).

connection of the 'data jars' has gained fresh impetus,[144] leading to the introduction of two proposals[145] which have recently been adopted.[146]

Interoperability is conceived as information systems 'speaking to each other' and as an evolutionary tool that will enable further uses through the aggregation of data from different sources. Its four main components are a European Search Portal (ESP), a shared Biometric Matching Service (BMS), a Common Identity Repository (CIR) and a Multiple Identity Detector (MID). The ESP will enable competent authorities to simultaneous query the underlying systems and the combined results will be displayed on one single screen. Even though the screen will indicate in which databases the information is held, access rights will remain unaltered and will proceed following the rules of each database.[147] The BMS will generate and store templates from all biometric data recorded in the underlying systems,[148] thus effectively becoming a new database that compiles biometrics from the SIS II, VIS, Eurodac, EES and ECRIS-TCN and that will replace separate searches in the other databases. At the core of interoperability lies the CIR, which will store an individual file for each person registered in the systems, containing both biometric and biographical data as well as a reference indicating the system from which the data were retrieved.[149] CIR's main objectives are to facilitate identity checks of third-country nationals,[150] assist in the detection of individuals with multiple identities and streamline law enforcement access. With respect to law enforcement, the rules explained earlier are substituted by a two-step process in which law enforcement authorities can first consult all databases to check whether records on an individual exist in any of the

---

[144] European Council, Conclusions, EUCO 28/15 (18 December 2015), 3; Council Document 7371/16 (24 March 2016), pt. 55. A High Level Expert Group on Information Systems and Interoperability was appointed and it delivered its final report in May 2017. The report gave the green light to implementing a number of aspects of interoperability, but interconnectivity was dismissed. See High Level Expert Group on Information Systems and Interoperability, Final Report (May 2017), http://ec.europa.eu/transparency/regexpert/index.cfm?do=groupDetail .groupDetailDoc&id=32600&no=1.

[145] One part of the legislative package deals with the databases that build on the Schengen Acquis, namely the EES, the VIS, ETIAS and those parts of SIS II that deal with border control cooperation. The other part covers Eurodac, the law enforcement aspects of the SIS II and the ECRIS-TCN.

[146] European Parliament and Commission, Regulation (EU) 2019/817, 2109 O.J. (L 135) 27 (EES, VIS, ETIAS, border control) [hereinafter Interoperability Regulation I]; European Parliament and Commission, Regulation (EU) 2019/818, 2109 O.J. (L135) 85 (Eurodac, law enforcement, ECRIS-TCN) [hereinafter Interoperability Regulation II].

[147] Interoperability Regulations I and II, arts. 6–11.

[148] Interoperability Regulations I and II, arts. 12–16.

[149] Interoperability Regulations I and II, arts. 17–24.

[150] Interoperability Regulations I and II, art. 20.

databases without obtaining prior authorisation by a verifying authority. In the event of a 'hit', the second step is to obtain access to each individual system that contains the matching data through the procedure prescribed for each database.[151] Finally, the MID will use the alphanumeric data stored in the CIR and the SIS II to detect multiple identities; it will create links between identical data to indicate whether the individual is lawfully registered in more than one system or whether identity fraud is suspected.[152]

III SURVEILLANCE OF MOVEMENT AND PRIVACY: A BALANCE RIGHTLY STRUCK?

1 A Concise Typology of Standards of Privacy Protection

The collection, storage and further processing of personal data through databases inevitably raises questions regarding the protection of the right of third-country nationals to private life, as enshrined in Article 8 European Convention on Human Rights (ECHR) and Article 7 EU Charter of Fundamental Rights (EUCFR), and personal data protection as encompassed in Article 8 EUCFR.[153] Both rights are not absolute and may be limited pursuant to Article 52(1) EUCFR, provided that the limitations to the right are provided for by law, genuinely meet an objective of general interest to the EU, safeguard the essence of the rights and respect the principle of proportionality, which entails considerations of appropriateness and strict necessity. Perhaps unsurprisingly, the proliferation of databases has not been accompanied by a substantial privacy assessment by the Court of Justice of the European Union (CJEU), presumably due to lack of awareness of or interest in the privacy issue, given the other more pressing rights at stake, such as non-refoulement.

Be that as it may, there is significant Strasbourg and Luxembourg jurisprudence on surveillance practices at the national and EU levels that contains important standards. In both Courts, the systematic collection and storage of personal data has been repeatedly found to constitute an interference with the

---

[151] Interoperability Regulations I and II, art. 22.

[152] Interoperability Regulations I and II, arts. 25–36.

[153] See also Article 16 TFEU. The relationship between the two rights has been the subject of extensive debate. The view taken here is that the right to personal data protection safeguards and reinforces the right to private life, rather than replaces it. As such, emphasis is placed on the standards set down in the case law of the European Courts, rather than the data protection principles that are implicitly embedded in and inform the judicial analysis. For an analysis of this thesis and a detailed typology of privacy standards see Vavoula, *Immigration and Privacy in the Law of the European Union*, chapter 1.

right to private life – or in EU terms as a limitation to the right to private life – irrespective of whether the data will be further used or the collection took place in an intrusive manner.[154] A central consideration has been whether the personal data processing 'taken as whole' allows for precise conclusions to be drawn on the private lives of the individuals affected.[155] Retention of biometric identifiers has been singled out as 'not inconsequential, irrelevant or neutral'.[156] Furthermore, the transmission of data to, and subsequent use by, other public authorities is considered a separate interference with the right to privacy since it expands the group of individuals with knowledge of the personal data.[157]

The principles of necessity and proportionality are a key requirement in the area of mass surveillance, featuring prominently in the case law of both European Courts.[158] In *Digital Rights Ireland* and *Tele2*, the Grand Chamber of the CJEU condemned generalised surveillance through the collection, retention and storage of everyday personal data – a practice which 'is likely to generate in the minds of the persons concerned the feeling that their private lives are the subject of constant surveillance'.[159] Therefore, the CJEU found the indiscriminate collection of personal data without any differentiation, limitation or exception to be unlawful.[160] Rather, the Court held that data collection must be confined to situations that pose a threat to public security – restricted to a time period, a geographical zone, groups of persons likely to be involved in a serious crime, or more broadly persons whose communications may contribute to law enforcement.[161] In Opinion 1/15, the transfer of Passenger Name Records (PNR) data by air carriers and their subsequent use by

---

[154] *Amann v. Switzerland*, ECLI:CE:ECHR:2000:0216; *Rotaru v. Romania*, ECLI:CE: ECHR:2000:0504.

[155] Joined Cases C-293/12 and C-594/12, *Digital Rights Ireland Ltd v. Ireland*, ECLI:EU: C:2014:238, para. 27; Joined Cases C-203/15 and C-698/15, *Tele2 Sverige AB v. Post-och Telestyrelsen*, and *Secretary of State for the Home Department v. Tom Watson, Peter Brice, Geoffrey Lewis*, ECLI:EU:C:2016:970, para. 99; Opinion 1/15 of the Court (Grand Chamber) (26 July 2017), ECLI:EU:C:2017:592, para. 150 ('very specific information').

[156] *S and Marper v. UK*, ECLI:CE:ECHR:2008:1204, para. 84. Also see Case C-291/12, *Schwarz v. Stadt Bochum*, ECLI:EU:C:2013:670.

[157] *Weber and Saravia v. Germany*, 46 EHRR SE5 (2008).

[158] As I explain elsewhere, in the jurisprudence of the ECtHR, a series of privacy standards have been pronounced under the doctrinal label of legality rather than proportionality. See Vavoula, *Immigration and Privacy in the Law of the European Union*, chapter 1.

[159] *Digital Rights Ireland*, para. 37.

[160] *Digital Rights Ireland*, para. 57; *Tele2 Sverige AB*, paras. 105–108; Case C-362/14, *Maximillian Schrems v. Data Protection Commissioner*, ECLI:EU:C:2015:650, para. 93.

[161] *Maximillian Schrems*, para. 93.

Canadian authorities was accepted as an appropriate instrument for the purpose of fighting terrorism and other serious crimes.[162]

As regards biometrics, in *S and Marper* v. *UK*, the ECtHR held that the retention of biometrics in connection with persons who are not suspected of a criminal offence may lead to discrimination and stigmatisation and may undermine the presumption of innocence.[163] Furthermore, in the *Schwarz* case, which concerned the storage of two fingerprints in EU biometric passports, the CJEU stressed the impact on the individual both in terms of the possibility of a false match (between the fingerprints of the passport holder and the fingerprints in the passport) and as regards the registration of fingerprint data *per se*. The Court found that storage of these fingerprints in a medium, such as the passport, is proportionate, as it remains with their owner[164] and the fingerprints are used for verification purposes.[165] A possible mismatch would not entail the automatic refusal of entry to the EU, but would merely draw the attention of authorities to that person, resulting in a more detailed check in order to establish their identity.[166]

Ex post access, further processing and retention periods are subject to further requirements: they must be restricted to what is strictly necessary, respect procedural and substantive conditions, and be limited to the purposes of preventing, detecting and prosecuting well-defined serious offences.[167] In *Zakharov* v. *Russia*, the ECtHR took the view that surveillance was lawful and proportionate only if based on reasonable suspicion, understood as 'factual indications for suspecting that person of planning, committing or having committed criminal acts or other acts that may give rise to secret surveillance measures.'[168] In addition, the ECtHR found that surveillance and access to data should be subject to prior review by a court or independent administrative body entrusted with ensuring compliance with constitutional and legislative limits on data processing.[169]

Moreover, retention periods should be limited on the basis of the data's potential usefulness and should remain as short as possible.[170] In Opinion 1/15

---

[162] Opinion 1/15 of the Court (Grand Chamber), paras. 186–189.

[163] *S and Marper*, para. 122.

[164] *Schwarz*, para. 48.

[165] *Schwarz*, para. 56.

[166] *Schwarz*, para. 43.

[167] *Digital Rights Ireland*, paras. 60–62; *Tele2 Sverige AB*, para. 115.

[168] *Zakharov* v. *Russia*, ECLI:CE:ECHR:2015:1204, para. 260.

[169] *Digital Rights Ireland*, para. 62; *Tele2 Sverige AB*, para. 120; in Opinion 1/15 of the Court (Grand Chamber) the CJEU even stated that such review is 'essential' (para. 202).

[170] *S and Marper*, para. 119; *Digital Rights Ireland*, paras. 63–64.

on the EU-Canada PNR Agreement the Grand Chamber of the CJEU distinguished between different situations: the transfer and storage of PNR data prior to (and for the purpose of) the entry into Canada; further use and storage during the passenger's stay; and the retention of PNR data after his or her departure. Whereas *storage* before entry was found to be proportionate,[171] the *use* of data during the stay had to be based on new circumstances and objective evidence.[172] Importantly, after departure, passengers subject to entry and exit checks should be regarded as 'not presenting, in principle, a risk' for terrorism and serious crime. Once a passenger leaves Canada, therefore, there is no prima facie connection – not even indirect – between their PNR data and the objective of the agreement (fighting terrorism and serious crime) that would justify retaining the data.[173] Consequently, *continued storage* of all air passengers' data after departure is not justified and only in specific cases, on the basis of objective evidence, is storage of certain passengers' data.[174]

2 *The Case of Databases for Non-EU Nationals*

The standards analysed in the previous section are applicable to the collection of personal data for immigration and border control purposes and, even more specifically, to the use of that data by law enforcement authorities. The personal data contained in the EU's immigration databases reveal very specific information about the privates lives of individuals – regarding their travel habits, their personal status, possible personal associations, in the case of the VIS, and even their educational and occupational background, in the case of the ETIAS. The following section unpacks the key privacy concerns by providing paradigmatic examples from the various databases on the issues of the necessity of specific information systems, the personal scope of such systems, the categories of personal data collected, the retention periods foreseen and the law enforcement access granted.[175]

2.1 Appropriateness Revisited: 'Mind the (Informational) Gap'

A key issue underpinning the operation of databases is whether their initial establishment and operation are appropriate for the purposes pursued.

---

[171] Opinion 1/15 of the Court (Grand Chamber), paras. 197–198.

[172] Opinion 1/15, paras. 199–202.

[173] Opinion 1/15, paras. 204–208.

[174] Opinion 1/15, paras. 204–208.

[175] For an in depth analysis see Vavoula, *Immigration Control and Privacy in the Law of the European Union*.

Databases for Non-EU Nationals and the Right to Private Life 257

A primary example of the appropriateness issue is the operation of Eurodac as a support mechanism for an arguably ill-functioning Dublin system.[176] Although Eurodac's initial establishment was not necessarily problematic,[177] it is broadly accepted that the Dublin system is not currently 'working' for either asylum seekers or Member States. On the one hand, asylum seekers are not deterred from defying the Dublin rules and moving on to Member States in the EU core, to seek decent reception conditions and to lodge their asylum applications.[178] On the other hand, both the CJEU[179] and the ECtHR[180] have released landmark rulings condemning appalling reception conditions, leading to the halt of transfers to Greece since 2011 in view of its systemic deficiencies. The case of Greece is not the sole example. Available statistics demonstrate that during the period 2008–2012, only around 25 per cent of outgoing requests resulted in transfers, meaning that Dublin transfers take place in only around 3 per cent of all European asylum cases.[181] A Commission evaluation of the Dublin III Regulation confirms the very low number of transfers in comparison to the number of Dublin requests.[182] In light of this, the failings of Dublin have a domino effect on the operation of Eurodac, stripping away its necessity and appropriateness. Since the allocation mechanism is problematic and, therefore, must be fundamentally reformed, the need for maintaining the instrument assisting in this allocation, namely Eurodac, must also be questioned. In the light of this, the refurbishment and reconceptualisation of Eurodac as a tool for 'wider migration purposes' is questioned and it could be argued that this tweak has been promoted in order to disentangle the system from its asylum origins and thus legitimise its existence in view of the challenges surrounding the operation of the Dublin

---

[176] Elspeth Guild et al., *New Approaches, Alternative Avenues and Means of Access to Asylum Procedures for Persons Seeking International Protection*, Doc. PE509.989, 2014.

[177] This pronouncement is with a caveat about the fingerprinting of irregular border crossers. See Vavoula, *Immigration Control and Privacy in the Law of the European Union*, chapter 4.

[178] On this issue, see among others, Jesuit Refugee Service, "Protection Interrupted: The Dublin Regulation's Impact on Asylum Seekers' Protection The DIASP Project," 2013, www.refworld.org/docid/51d152174.html; Susan Fratzke, "Not Adding Up: The Fading Promise of Europe's Dublin System," Migration Policy Institute, 2015.

[179] Joined Cases C-411/10 and C-493/10, *NS v. Secretary of State for the Home Department* and *ME and Others v. Refugee Applications Commissioner and Minister for Justice, Equality and Law Reform*, ECLI:EU:C:2011:865.

[180] *MSS v. Belgium and Greece*, ECLI:CE:ECHR:2011:0121; *Tarakhel v. Switzerland*, ECLI:CE:ECHR:2014:1104.

[181] Guild, "Moving the Borders of Europe," 9.

[182] European Commission, *Evaluation of the Implementation of Dublin III Regulation – Final Report*, DG-Home (2016), 56–57.

system. Eurodac's expansion also seems to disregard the fact that the SIS II already stores alerts on persons who must be refused entry or stay.

Furthermore, the added value of establishing the EES and the ETIAS as new databases monitoring the movement of almost all foreign travellers is not evident, particularly in light of the operation of the VIS, which was only fully rolled out worldwide in 2016.[183] Whether the EES will tackle the issue of overstayers is highly uncertain: the information mechanism envisaged does not signify that the person is necessarily an overstayer, as there may be other reasons why a person has not exited properly, e.g. human error, illness, application for asylum, death.[184] Importantly, national authorities will not have further information as regards the whereabouts of the person in question.[185] Moreover, the necessity of the ETIAS has been based on the perceived risk posed by visa-exempt travellers, without, however, substantiating the existence of that risk. The lack of an impact assessment prior to the adoption of the proposal and the pre-2015 decision to discard the project are testaments of the logic underpinning this field:[186] fill any and all 'information gaps', rather than address clear evidence-based operational needs. In this logic, necessity and appropriateness are based on data greediness, technological availability and an evolving understanding of travel as an a priori suspicious activity that legitimises the intervention of the EU as a norm creator. The new generation of databases is being created with a view to completing, through systematic personal data processing, the 'puzzle' of non-EU nationals interacting with the EU in any way, be it administrative or law enforcement.

2.2 Non-EU Nationals Concerned

The puzzle approach to databases is also evident in the personal scope of immigration databases. A key example of the EU's sweeping monitoring of the movement of third-country nationals, irrespective of proportionality considerations, is the grounds for entering alerts in the SIS II. In the first years of operation of the system, it was estimated that 77 per cent of alerts were entered

---

[183] Valsamis Mitsilegas, *The Criminalisation of Irregular Migration in Europe: Challenges for Human Rights and the Rule of Law* (London: Springer, 2015), 34.

[184] Ben Hayes and Mathias Vermeulen, *Borderline – The EU's New Border Surveillance Initiatives* (Berlin: Heinrich Böll Stiftung, 2012), 41.

[185] Meijers Committee, Note on the Smart Borders Proposals, CM1307, 2.

[186] See Alegre, Jeandesboz, and Vavoula, "European Travel Information and Authorisation System (ETIAS)," 27.

Databases for Non-EU Nationals and the Right to Private Life   259

for the wrong reasons, raising questions of procedural fairness in SIS decision-making.[187] In a similar vein, the decision to register irregular migrants in the SIS rested entirely within the discretion of national authorities, resulting in significant discrepancies in the implementation.[188] Certain Member States, Germany and Italy in particular, were more rigorous in inserting alerts[189] and, therefore, third-country nationals faced differential treatment depending on the State in which they were found to be irregularly entering or staying. Over time, efforts to harmonise the recording of alerts stepped up, but divergences still persist.[190] In certain Member States the threshold for entering alerts is significantly higher than in others. For instance, in Lithuania, the refusal or annulment of a visa and the refusal or withdrawal of a residence permit triggers a SIS II alert, whereas in other Member States the categories set out in the Regulation are followed.[191] In numerous States an expulsion decision (return) is automatically accompanied by an alert.[192] The mandatory registration of entry bans and return decisions in the refurbished SIS II will signify a further watering down of the SIS II standards and will lead to automatic storage of personal data of essentially all irregular migrants irrespective of how serious the violation of immigration law. By inclusion of this data, registration in the SIS II becomes unavoidable, even in cases when the individual has voluntarily left the national territory, which is disproportionate in view of the personal conduct of the person concerned. The proportionality criterion for the registration of alerts is thus nullified, substituted by race-to-the-bottom harmonisation.

The expansive approach to personal scope, this time explicitly linked to security concerns, is also illustrated by the proposal to expand the VIS to include holders of residence permits, residence cards and long-stay visas. In the VIS reform, the inability to verify the identity and documentation of these categories of persons against a centralised system is framed as a potential

---

[187] Stephen Kabera Karanja, *Transparency and Proportionality in the Schengen Information System and Border Control Cooperation* (Leiden: Martinus Nijhoff, 2008), 216.

[188] Brouwer, *Digital Borders and Real Rights*, 61–62.

[189] Schengen Joint Supervisory Authority, Article 96 Inspection – *Report of the Schengen Supervisory Authority on the Inspection of the Use of Article 96 Alerts in the Schengen Information System* (20 June 2005).

[190] For an analysis see Vavoula, *Immigration and Privacy in the Law of the European Union*, chapter 2.

[191] European Migration Network, "Ad Hoc Query on Procedures for Entering Foreigner's Data into the Schengen Information System," 2014, http://ec.europa.eu/dgs/home-affairs/what-we-do/networks/european_migration_network/reports/docs/ad-hoc-queries/border/505_emn_ahq_procedures_entering_foreigners_data_into_the_sis__7jan2014_%wider_dissemination%29.pdf.

[192] European Migration Network, "Ad Hoc Query on Procedures for Entering Foreigner's Data."

'threat to the security of one of the Member States'.[193] In other words, in an era of 'Security Union', security and migration are fully intertwined and a permanent cloud of suspicion surrounds not only individuals who may have undergone a series of checks for obtaining legal documentation but also the Member States who granted the residence status, who can only trust each other if an EU technological fix intervenes. In addition, from the perspective of the allocation of competences, it is questionable whether the VIS, as a Schengen *acquis* instrument, may be expanded to include categories of nationals whose documentation is not regulated by EU rules, but remains a competence of the Member States.

2.3 Categories of Collected Information

The categories of personal data collected, stored and further processed within databases merits some attention, as the high volume of personal data collected in certain cases goes beyond necessity and proportionality. For example, in the VIS, a category of personal data that raises proportionality concerns is that of persons issuing an invitation or sponsoring the stay of a visa applicant, persons who may be EU citizens or third-country long-term residents. In the course of routine implementation of the EU visa policy, the processing of these data is excessive and disproportionate and may lead to the creation of a mini-register on the side. Furthermore, in light of law enforcement access to the VIS data, their registration and consultation raises further concerns, as their data may be used in police investigations. Another example of disproportionate collection comes from the ETIAS and the processing of data on the applicant's level of education; the US ESTA does not collect this category of information and it is not clear why the ETIAS needs to do so.

Furthermore, the routine storage of biometrics – a special category of personal data – in all databases but the ETIAS is questionable. In contrast with the storage of fingerprints in biometric passports, at issue in the *Schwarz* case, in databases biometrics are stored centrally and therefore the individuals concerned lose control of their personal data. Furthermore, when biometrics are centrally stored, the error rates are impacted by the number of persons contained in the system.[194] Therefore, the larger the system, the greater the probability of a 'hit' based on an error. In cases of large-scale databases holding millions of records, the possibility of a false match is enhanced,

---

[193] *Commission Proposal*, COM (2018) 302 final.
[194] Kindt, *Privacy and Data Protection Issues of Biometric Identifiers*, 59.

Databases for Non-EU Nationals and the Right to Private Life   261

particularly if there are data quality issues.[195] Such an error can have severe consequences: the wrongful return of the individual to another Member State on the basis of a Eurodac hit; refusal of entry into the Schengen area; or even implication of the person in criminal proceedings in the framework of law enforcement. In addition, a full set of fingerprints is arguably disproportionate for immigration control purposes and can only reasonably be justified if their use is limited to criminal law purposes. Indeed, given that the VIS – and the revised Eurodac, if agreed – includes a digital photo, the collection of fewer fingerprints would have sufficed for identification purposes, even though that would frustrate the ancillary purpose of the systems to assist in crime prevention or investigation.

2.4 Retention Periods

The period during which personal data must be retained is vital, as continued storage and use of data perpetuates the effects of the interference with the right to private life. In the case of Eurodac, the ten-year retention period for asylum seekers was never properly justified; even though the Parliament had suggested reducing it to five years, the amendment was ignored by the Council.[196] As for the current eighteen-month retention period for the fingerprints of irregular border crossers, it does not correspond to the one-year responsibility of Member States for asylum seekers under Dublin rules. Furthermore, in the case of the SIS II, broad leeway has been granted to Member States: the three-year rule for deletion of the data subject to review without any maximum retention period being imposed on the Member States. The current trend points to an emerging default retention period of five years (SIS II,[197] VIS,[198] Eurodac,[199] EES,[200] ETIAS[201]). Among other things, this default for all EU databases appears to be useful for the purposes of interoperability.

Importantly, in light of the CJEU Opinion 1/15 on the EU-Canada PNR agreement, the EU's existing and proposed databases make no distinction between the different phases of a non-EU national's journey. For example,

---

[195] For data quality issues of the VIS in particular, see Vavoula, *Immigration and Privacy in the Law of the European Union*, chapter 3.

[196] Aus, "Eurodac: A Solution Looking for a Problem?"

[197] SIS II Proposal, art. 34.

[198] Excluding visa holders whose data are kept for ten years. See VIS Regulation, art. 23.

[199] See *Commission Proposal*, COM (2016) 272 final, art. 17(2) and (3).

[200] In the case of potential overstayers, see EES Regulation, art. 34(3).

[201] In cases of refusal, annulment, revocation of the travel document. See ETIAS Regulation, art. 54.

both the EES and the ETIAS – the latter as a result of Member State pressure – will continue to store personal data even after the departure of the individual concerned in order to serve immigration-control purposes. However, according to the CJEU case law, after the departure of travellers, storage is justified only in relation to certain individuals on the basis of objective evidence. Therefore, the premise of databases as systems which may encompass an array of purposes creates a paradox, whereby the continued storage of personal data of all individuals captured by the database may be justified for administrative purposes, but has a significant spillover effect because of law enforcement access to their data, and perpetuates the risk for the individuals concerned.

2.5 Law Enforcement Access

There are also a number of issues related to law enforcement access to databases for non-EU nationals. As explained earlier, in the case of the SIS II, the interrelation between immigration control and law enforcement was pre-embedded in the structure of the system, which had no unitary and limited purpose. Even though its main preoccupation was and continues to be immigration control, a *de facto* mission creep into law enforcement has thus been evident. Furthermore, the ECRIS-TCN is a law enforcement tool aimed at enabling Member States to exchange criminal records on non-EU nationals. With regard to the remaining databases, law enforcement access is an ancillary purpose – an add-on to the overarching functions of the system and as such, for the time being, such consultation may take place under specific circumstances only. Nevertheless, it must be stressed that law enforcement access is not obvious[202] and compelling evidence justifying the addition of this purpose must be adduced. As with the necessity of setting up the databases in the first place, justification of the need for law enforcement access has often been fragile.[203] Furthermore, the Eurodac example clearly illustrates the inherent danger of mission creep when personal data is centrally stored: once information is stored for a specific purpose, there is a real possibility of the system being re-purposed for objectives that were not initially contemplated.

[202] As is demonstrated by the fact that in designing the EES, the Commission initially left out law enforcement, and a proposal for recasting the Eurodac Regulation, including law enforcement access to asylum seekers' data, was blocked by the European Parliament in 2009.

[203] For the case of Eurodac see Niovi Vavoula, "The Recast Eurodac Regulation: Are Asylum Seekers Treated as Suspected Criminals?" in *Seeking Asylum in the European Union: Selected Protection Issues Raised by the Second Phase of the Common European Asylum System*, eds. Céline Bauloz et al. (Leiden: Brill, 2015), 260.

Databases for Non-EU Nationals and the Right to Private Life   263

As for the modalities of law enforcement access, these substantially fall short of the standards set out by the European Courts. Whereas the conditions are indeed set out and no routine access is foreseen in the individual legal instruments, a series of loopholes remain. The national authorities allowed to consult the data are those responsible for the prevention, detection and investigation of terrorist offences or of other serious criminal offences as designated at the national level.[204] As is evident from this expansive definition, national governments have considerable leeway to designate a wide array of agencies.[205] There is no other guidance, requirement or limit contained in the EU legal instruments. Indeed, national intelligence agencies may also be given access if the Member State so chooses; only in the case of Eurodac have intelligence services been explicitly excluded.[206] The inclusion of intelligence services is worrisome; although it is to be welcomed that they are bound by the same rules as the rest of national authorities,[207] their operation is obscure when compared to police agencies. Once a Member State determines which authorities are to be given law enforcement access, the list of designated authorities is communicated to the Commission and published in the Official Journal, but there is no EU-level control and oversight. Finally, with regard to the procedure for consulting the data, in all cases, the designated authorities must submit a reasoned electronic request to an authority (Central Access Point or in the case of Eurodac to a Verifying Authority) that ascertains that the conditions for obtaining access have been met. Nevertheless, this procedure is not in line with the criteria set out in *Digital Rights Ireland, Tele2,* and Opinion 1/15, where the CJEU explicitly required that law enforcement access to the data be made dependent on prior review carried out by a court or by an independent administrative body. Considering that requesting and verifying authorities may be part of the same law enforcement agency, the independence and objective judgment of the necessity of access may be jeopardised.

2.6 (Not so Innocent) Interoperability

With the adoption of the new Regulations on interoperability, the landscape of information processing through centralised databases will be forever

---

[204] The list of competent authorities is published in the Official Journal, but may differ significantly both across the different databases and among Member States.

[205] Mitsilegas, "Human Rights, Terrorism and the Quest for 'Border Security'," 109.

[206] Eurodac Regulation, art. 5(1).

[207] Opinion of the European Data Protection Supervisor on the Proposal for a Regulation of the European Parliament and of the Council Concerning the Visa Information System (VIS) and the Exchange of Data between Member States on Short-Stay Visas (COM(2004)835 final), 2005 O.J. (C 181) 13.

changed. Whereas it has been correctly pointed out that interoperability will not frustrate existing limits on *access* rights of national authorities, it must be highlighted that the *use* of personal data will be attached to new purposes, which are not to be found in the respective legal instruments. For instance, in the interoperability legislation, Eurodac data will be used to detect persons with multiple identities even though Eurodac's mandate does not specify this use. Another worrisome change involves the possibility for a Member State *police* authority to query the CIR with the biometric data of a person taken during an identity check, solely for the purpose of identifying that person.[208] This function of the CIR is not supported by the existing legal framework and current EU law, aside from the Interoperability Regulations, does not spell out the circumstances and conditions under which their identity checks shall take place.[209] Overall, interoperability further downplays the importance of the purpose limitation principle and 'disrespects the importance of separated domains and cuts through their protective walls'.[210]

Importantly, the operationalisation of interoperability involves the masked setting up of new databases based on combining data from different sources – the BMS, the CIR and the MID.[211] The fancy wording that is used ('component' and 'repository') should not distract from the dangerous reality of massive catalogues of third-country nationals at EU level.[212] The aggregation of data through databases signifies a new information-processing paradigm of mass and indiscriminate surveillance. By combining information from different systems, brand new systems emerge, authorities are empowered to draw more precise conclusions on the private lives of individuals, and data subjects are unable to foresee how their collected information will be used. It is not far-fetched to characterise interoperability as a decisive step away from a compartmentalised system of independent databases and towards a single EU information system in the service of an EU Big Brother.

Another key change brought about by interoperability involves law enforcement access to non-EU nationals' data. Although, as mentioned previously, access is currently reserved for specific cases based on the necessity of consulting the data, interoperability marks a significant step towards routine access.

---

[208] Interoperability Regulations I and II, art. 20.

[209] Tony Bunyan, "The Point of No Return – Interoperability Morphs into the Creation of a Big Brother Centralised EU State Database Including All Existing and Future Justice and Home Affairs Databases," Statewatch, May 2018, 10.

[210] De Hert and Gutwirth, "Interoperability of Police Databases within the EU," 27.

[211] Presumably the MID will not store personal data *per se*, but confirmation files that contain the links between alphanumeric data related to identity stored in the CIR and the SIS.

[212] Opinion 4/2018 of the European Data Protection Supervisor (16 April 2018), 11.

The regulations stipulate a two-step approach, in which designated authorities shall first check all systems through the CIR on a hit/no hit basis and then, if they get a hit, satisfy the conditions applicable to each of the underlying databases to obtain access to the individual data pots.[213] Yet even just a hit is significant since it reveals elements of an individual's personal life, for instance that they are visa free travellers, and therefore the first step of checking whether there is personal data should be covered by the conditions of access. Importantly, it is hard to believe that upon finding that a database holds information on a person, the verifying authority ensuring the conditions for access have been met will not allow such access. In other words, not only the independence and objectivity but also the very existence of a verifying authority may be biased by the two-step approach.

IV CONCLUSION

The aim of this chapter has been twofold: to map the evolution of pan-European databases for non-EU nationals and to highlight a series of privacy concerns that have been triggered by their establishment, operation and reconfiguration over time. Through the systematic categorisation of EU information systems in three distinct eras, it has been demonstrated that their operation entails the collection and storage of a wide range of personal data, including biometrics, and their further processing for multiple and often diverging purposes, which are anything but fixed. In the future, driven by the logic of closing information gaps, lack of EU citizenship will entitle State authorities to require individuals to provide extensive personal data, including sensitive data. The big picture is that of systematic expansion of the personal scope of EU databases: once the aforementioned systems are fully operational, no non-EU citizen will be left un-surveyed through at least one database. Apart from expanding the groups of individuals concerned and the purposes and the categories of data to be collected, the initial compartmentalised approach has been abandoned in favour of interoperability, enabling the data pots to interact. The aggregation of data will not only generate new databases and new data (MID) but will also transform existing databases – particularly those originally created for administrative, immigration control purposes – into powerful intelligence tools.

---

[213] See Teresa Quintel, "Connecting Personal Data of Third Country Nationals: Interoperability of EU Databases in the Light of the CJEU's Case Law on Data Retention," University of Luxembourg Law Working Papers, March 2018, 16.

These trends have utterly blurred the boundaries between immigration and criminal law.[214] They had been driven by, and will in turn feed, the perception of non-EU nationals as potential risks for EU internal security, and have significant repercussions for their privacy. This chapter had provided concrete examples of disproportionate data processing by scrutinising the operating rules of the many databases, as well as their interoperability, against the jurisprudential benchmark of the European Courts. The necessity and appropriateness of information systems has been taken for granted rather than robustly justified; the existence of the old generation of databases has generated a domino effect, in which their operational flaws are used to unreflexively justify the new and revised systems. Furthermore, specific categories of information should not be available to certain authorities. With the routine registration of biometrics, the provision of extensive retention periods and the use of data for law enforcement purposes, the administration of non-EU nationals through electronic databases has progressively been transformed into a system of mass surveillance of movement. Particularly in the VIS, the EES and the ETIAS, everyday legitimate activities are monitored.[215] Travel has emerged as an inherently dangerous activity and mobility operates as a trigger for state surveillance.

With surveillance of movement becoming the norm, a key question remains: will it expand to cover EU nationals, undermining not only their privacy but also EU citizenship rights? This is more than a rhetorical question. As explained earlier, with respect to both the EES and the ECRIS-TCN, it was suggested that EU nationals also be included. These examples seem to tentatively confirm the dystopian predictions, raised in the introduction, that the new technologies are being tested on foreigners so that they can then be extended to EU nationals. In light of the comprehensive coverage of non-EU nationals, it appears that the trial period has come to an end. Indeed, in an era when every non-EU national is potentially a risk justifying security surveillance, the divide between the privacy safeguards for EU and non-EU nationals will become acute. Might, in the future, the standards of privacy protection for EU nationals be lowered to close this gap? It remains to be seen what the future will bring to the ongoing battle between security and privacy. It is only hoped that the outcome has not already been decided.

---

[214] For further exploration of this theme, see Chapter 11.
[215] See David Lyon, *Surveillance Society: Monitoring Everyday Life* (Buckingham: Open University Press, 2001).

III

Internal Security

10

The EU and International Terrorism

Promoting Free Movement of Persons, the Right to Privacy and Security

GILLES DE KERCHOVE AND CHRISTIANE HÖHN[*]

I INTRODUCTION

Since 2015, there has been a sea change in the scope and depth of cooperation in the EU on counter-terrorism (CT). Although the issue has been on the EU's policy agenda since 9/11, the string of terrorist attacks that have occurred since early 2015 have prompted a series of political initiatives that have transformed the EU's presence in the field.[1] The politics have been mirrored by public opinion: Eurobarometer polls show that 82% of EU citizens want the EU to do more on security and counter-terrorism.

Following the Charlie Hebdo Paris attacks in January 2015, there have been a number of political initiatives at the EU level. First, in February 2015, leaders of the twenty-eight Member States announced an ambitious agenda for EU

---

[*] EU Counter-Terrorism Coordinator Gilles de Kerchove holds an LL.M. from Yale Law School and teaches European law at several Belgian universities. Dr Christiane Höhn, Principal Adviser to the EU Counter-Terrorism Coordinator, holds an LL.M. from Harvard Law School. The opinions expressed in this chapter are those of the authors alone and do not necessarily reflect the positions of the Council of the European Union or the European Council.

[1] Attacks with high numbers of victims and on symbolic targets in the EU include: January 2015 attacks in Paris on Charlie Hebdo (12 people killed, terrorist attack on a satirical magazine killing a number of the cartoonists) and kosher supermarket (killing several Jewish customers); November 2015 attacks in Paris in multiple locations, including the Bataclan theatre and the Stade de France (137 victims killed, 413 injured); March 2016 attacks on Brussels airport and Maelbeek metro station in Brussels (32 victims dead, 340 injured); July 2017 attack in Nice during national day celebrations using a car (86 victims killed, 434 injured); December 2017, Christmas market attack in Berlin, using a car (12 victims dead, 56 injured); May 2017 attack in Manchester (at least 23 dead and 250 injured) at a pop concert attended by youth; Barcelona, Las Ramblas, truck attack in July 2017 (14 people killed and at least 130 injured). The figures of victims quoted are approximate. A detailed overview of terrorist attacks in the EU can be found in Europol's annual TE-SAT reports, www.europol.europa.eu/activities-services/main-reports/eu-terrorism-situation-and-trend-report.

counter-terrorism efforts.[2] They directed the EU to focus on three broad areas: (i) security, including information sharing, border security, firearms, judicial cooperation and updating the definition of terrorist crimes; (ii) prevention of radicalisation and safeguarding of values, including working with Internet companies, supporting the development of rehabilitation programmes inside and outside prisons and of communication strategies to promote tolerance, non-discrimination, fundamental freedoms and solidarity throughout the EU, stepping up inter-faith and other community dialogue, narratives to counter terrorist ideologies, creating economic, educational and cultural opportunities; and (iii) partnerships with priority third countries, in particular in the EU's direct neighbourhood in North Africa, the Middle East, Turkey and the Western Balkans.

Second, in April 2016, Commission President Juncker announced an EU Security Union,[3] and appointed a responsible Commissioner,[4] underlining the growing importance of the issue for the Commission. Indeed, during the Juncker Commission (2014–2019), Justice and Home Affairs (the policy competences most directly related to counter-terrorism) have generated the highest number of legislative proposals out of all the Commission's services. Third, in September 2016, in response to Brexit, the President of the European Council Tusk and the twenty-seven Heads of State or Government set down a positive agenda that includes, importantly, increased cooperation in internal security, border security and counter-terrorism.[5]

Although the terrorist threat that provoked this wave of policy action is evolving, there are a number of continuing and novel challenges. The terrorist threat in Europe remains high. Of the around 5,000 European foreign terrorist fighters who travelled to Syria and Iraq, about 1,500 have already returned, around 1,000 have been killed and 2,500 are still in the conflict zone (some may have been killed in the battle of Mosul/Raqqa but their death has not been ascertained or they may have travelled to other

---

[2] European Council Press Release 56/15, Informal Meeting of the Heads of State or Government, Brussels, 12 February 2015 – Statement by the Members of the European Council (2 February 2015).

[3] Communication from the Commission, *Delivering on the European Agenda on Security to Fight Against Terrorism and Pave the Way Towards an Effective and Genuine Security Union*, COM (2016) 230 final (20 April 2016).

[4] The first Commissioner for the Security Union, Sir Julian King, was appointed in September 2016. His mission letter can be found here: https://ec.europa.eu/commission/commissioners/sites/cwt/files/commissioner_mission_letters/mission-letter-julian-king_en.pdf.

[5] Bratislava Declaration and Roadmap, European Council website, last visited 6 July 2018, www.consilium.europa.eu/en/policies/eu-future-reflection/bratislava-declaration-and-roadmap/.

conflict zones). Hence, EU Member States have to cope with these foreign terrorist fighter returnees, as well as high numbers of accompanying women and children. In addition, Daesh[6] has changed its strategy and is now promoting home-grown terrorism – attacks by persons who stayed at home and were radicalised there. Many of the latest terrorist attacks in Europe were committed by such 'home-growns'. Daesh also has affiliates in many regions of the world, such as North Africa, including Libya, the Sinai (Egypt), the Sahel and the Philippines. Further, it would be a mistake to underestimate Al Qaeda and its affiliates. In the future, use of new technologies such as miniaturisation, synthetic biology, drones and cyber capabilities could also increase the threat.

The United States is the EU's closest partner in the fight against terrorism. Strong EU–US cooperation is indispensable to fight terrorism effectively. The EU Member States strongly rely on the United States for the fight against terrorism. Since 9/11, many EU–US tools have been adopted for the fight against terrorism, such as EU–US Mutual Legal Assistance and Extradition Agreements, cooperation agreements between the United States and the EU agencies Europol and Eurojust, and the EU–US Passenger Name Record (PNR) and Terrorist Financing Tracking Program (TFTP) agreements. Information sharing is strong. Cooperation also includes transport and aviation security, prevention of radicalisation, e-evidence, battlefield information, terrorist financing and foreign terrorist fighters. Best practices are also shared. The EU and the United States cooperate on counter-terrorism capacity building in third countries, including in the UN and Global Counter-Terrorism Forum (GCTF) contexts.

This chapter provides an overview of the law and policy of EU counter-terrorism. The next section lays out the legal framework and institutional actors that govern in this policy area. The chapter then turns to one very important component of the EU's counter-terrorism strategy – establishing an information sharing environment by collecting, sharing and analysing information related to terrorism investigations. After explaining the recent developments in the field, the chapter points to future directions and challenges for information sharing, including the use of artificial intelligence, the determination of when 'home-growns' should be placed on terrorist watch lists or other databases, and privacy concerns.

---

[6] Daesh is a synonym for the terrorist group Islamic State in Iraq and the Levant (ISIL), which is different from Al Qaeda.

II THE LEGAL AND INSTITUTIONAL CONTEXT OF EU CT COOPERATION

1 *Historical Trajectory of EU CT Cooperation*

Although EU Member States experienced terrorism in the early days of European integration, in the 1970s and 1980s, it was mainly nationalist/separatist or left-wing terrorism specific to one or two Member States. There was the *Euskadi Ta Askatasuna* (ETA) in Spain and France, the Red Army Faction (RAF) in Germany, the Irish Republican Army (IRA) in Northern Ireland, as well as other groups, but since the terrorist organisations were limited territorially, they were generally not perceived as a Europe-wide problem. Only after 9/11 and the attacks in Madrid (2004) and London (2005), with the emergence of the common threat of jihadi terrorism, did EU cooperation in the fight against terrorism really take off. Efforts accelerated and intensified considerably in 2013, with the increasing number of foreign terrorist fighters leaving for Syria and Iraq from the EU,[7] and again in early 2015, with the beginning of what turned out to be a string of major terrorist attacks in Europe.

The growth of EU powers in the CT domain has followed a typically European path. It has been spurred not only by developments in the terrorist threat but also by policy spillover from the Schengen area of free movement without internal border controls. The Schengen commitment to facilitating free movement of persons, through borderless travel within the EU, did not eliminate the traditional state function of monitoring citizen movements for purposes of immigration control and law enforcement. The elimination of passport and other types of checks at Member State borders was therefore compensated by a number of new EU tools (so-called flanking measures) designed to assist Member State officials in their border security, law enforcement and, most recently, counter-terrorism functions. Over time, this EU law and policy has gradually become less intergovernmental, based on direct

---

[7] Individuals referred to as 'foreign terrorist fighters' travel abroad for the purpose of terrorism. The definition is contained in the European Parliament and Council Directive 2017/541/EU, On Combating Terrorism and Replacing Council Framework Decision 2002/475/JHA and Amending Council Decision 2005/671/JHA, 2017 O.J. (L 88) 6, para. 4. For an overview of the EU's policy related to foreign terrorist fighters see Gilles de Kerchove and Christiane Höhn, "The Regional Answers and Governance Structure for Dealing with Foreign Fighters: The Case of the EU," in *Foreign Fighters under International Law and Beyond*, eds. Andrea de Guttry, Francesca Capone, and Christophe Paulussen (The Hague: T.M.C. Asser Press, 2016), 299–331.

cooperation between the Member States, and more supranational, governed by common EU institutions.

There are several types of international and European cooperation in the fight against terrorism, and in justice and home affairs, i.e. police, borders and judicial cooperation, more broadly. The United Nations is fully intergovernmental, based on treaties and the classical concepts of extradition and mutual legal assistance (MLA). The Council of Europe is more integrated, with more specific instruments (still based on extradition and MLA) and stronger human rights protection through the European Convention on Human Rights and the jurisprudence of the European Court of Human Rights. Schengen, the European area of free travel without internal border controls, was initially developed by a subset of Member States, under an international treaty, and only later on was it incorporated into EU law.[8] Schengen, like the UN and Council of Europe systems, was based on MLA and extradition, but it also included flanking measures to compensate for the lack of internal border controls.[9] Since the Treaty of Maastricht, which entered into force in 1993, the EU went a step further than the Council of Europe: in the context of MLA and extradition the procedural requirements of the requesting State would apply.[10] The Treaty of Amsterdam (entry into force 1999) introduced the common area of freedom, security and justice (AFSJ), which includes not only justice and home affairs (JHA) but also fundamental rights, and the Lisbon Treaty (entry into force 2009) further developed the concept.

Today, the EU is the worldwide most integrated region with regard to cooperation in justice and home affairs. JHA includes two key innovative principles: 'availability of information', according to which information is available to the relevant authorities of all Member States through common databases such as the Schengen Information System; and 'mutual recognition of judicial decisions', under which the judicial decision of one Member State is recognised and carried out by the law enforcement and judicial authorities of the other Member States. Examples of mutual recognition are the European Arrest Warrant[11] and the European Investigation Order.[12] To

---

[8] Amsterdam Treaty, Protocol 2 (signed 1997, entered into force1999).

[9] Schengen Convention of 1990, which implemented the Schengen Agreement of 1985.

[10] Convention on Mutual Legal Assistance in Criminal Matters between the Member States of the European Union, 29 May 2000, 2000 O.J. (C 197) 1.

[11] For information and legal texts on the European Arrest Warrant: https://ec.europa.eu/info/law/cross-border-cases/judicial-cooperation/types-judicial-cooperation/european-arrest-warrant_en.

[12] Press release and link to legal text in European Commission Press Release IP/17/1388, As of Today the "European Investigation Order" Will Help Authorities to Fight Crime and Terrorism (22 May 2017).

compensate for this intensive collaboration among justice and home affairs officials, safeguards for fundamental rights have been put into place: jurisdiction to review EU measures was given to the European Court of Justice (ECJ); data protection and procedural safeguards have been written into the relevant EU law; and there are specifically applicable provisions in the EU Charter of Fundamental Rights. Furthermore, all Member States are signatories to the European Convention on Human Rights and subject to the jurisprudence of the European Court of Human Rights. Democratic oversight has also been enhanced: today, the regular legislative co-decision procedure applies to JHA measures, which are therefore decided no longer through purely intergovernmental cooperation, but through the equal say of the Council and the European Parliament. Member States have the primary responsibility for counter-terrorism, but they are not the only ones.

Turning specifically to counter-terrorism law and powers, the situation is somewhat different. There is significant overlap between the objectives of fighting serious crime and fighting terrorism and many of the JHA legal instruments that have been introduced to facilitate law enforcement and judicial cooperation can be used for counter-terrorism. Moreover, since 9/11, many developments in the JHA field have been launched because of the terrorism threat, even though the instruments are broader and cover also other (serious) crime (for example, the EU–US Mutual Legal Assistance and Extradition Agreement[13] and the EU Passenger Name Record Directive).[14] At the same time, in response to terrorist attacks, the EU has introduced several measures targeted specifically at counter-terrorism. In 2004, the position of the EU Counter-Terrorism Coordinator was created by the European Council.[15] In 2005, the EU adopted its Counter-Terrorism Strategy based on the four pillars of 'prevent, protect, pursue, respond'.[16]

To roughly summarise the EU's role in the CT domain: the EU provides a common legal framework for CT and related areas such as countering

---

[13] Press release with link to the agreements in Council of the European Union Press Release 14826/09, EU/US Agreements on Extradition and on Mutual Legal Assistance (23 October 2009).

[14] European Parliament and Council Directive 2016/681/EU, On the Use of Passenger Name Record (PNR) Data for the Prevention, Detection, Investigation and Prosecution of Terrorist Offences and Serious Crime, 2016 O.J. (L 119) 132.

[15] European Council, Declaration on Combatting Terrorism, 25 March 2004, www.consilium.europa.eu/uedocs/cms_data/docs/pressdata/en/ec/79637.pdf.

[16] The European Union Counter-Terrorism Strategy, 30 November 2005, http://register.consilium.europa.eu/doc/srv?l=EN&f=ST%2014469%202005%20REV%204.

terrorist financing, external border controls and firearms.[17] The EU provides funding to support Member States and increase capacities, including common capacities such as the cyber-related centres of excellence at Europol.[18] It provides a forum for the sharing of best practices and lessons learned, including for practitioners via the Radicalization Awareness Network[19] and through the European Strategic Communications Network. It also allows for the development of common policy responses and approaches on issues such as foreign terrorist fighters. It provides major funding for security research and platforms and tools for operational cooperation of law enforcement, judicial and border authorities. It also provides funding to support capacity building in priority third countries. The projects are often implemented with Member States' expertise and increasingly participation of EU JHA agencies (detailed in this chapter).

The events of the past couple of years related to jihadi terrorism have led some to question the continued viability of the Schengen area. Yet re-introducing internal border controls would eliminate one of the EU's main achievements for its citizens and would concede victory to the terrorists by giving up a core element of EU citizenship. Furthermore, re-introducing border controls would be ineffective against the growing home-grown terrorist threat, since home-grown terrorist fighters do not travel. Rather, the Schengen area of free movement without internal border controls requires strong external border controls, information sharing and operational law enforcement and judicial cooperation. More checks in the territory of the Member States, including in border areas, are also possible. Temporary reinstatement of border controls in some areas has also been authorised. When discussing privacy and data protection in the context of information collection, sharing and analysis, the importance of these security tools as flanking measures for safeguarding the freedom of movement must be kept in mind. Citizens will only continue to support core fundamental rights such as free movement in the Schengen area and admission of refugees if security checks are as effective as possible.

---

[17] For progress on EU action related to CT, see the monthly progress reports on the implementation of the Security Union by the Commission https://ec.europa.eu/home-affairs/what-we-do/policies/european-agenda-security.

[18] On the European Cybercrime Centre EC3, see "Europol Cybercrime Center EC3," Europol website, last visited 21 August 2018, www.europol.europa.eu/about-europol/european-cybercrime-centre-ec3. About the Internet Referral Unit (IRU), see "EU Internet Referral Unit-EU IRU," Europol website, last visited 21 August 2018.

[19] "Radicalisation Awareness Network (RAN)," European Commission website, last visited 19 October 2018, https://ec.europa.eu/home-affairs/what-we-do/networks/radicalisation_awareness_network_en.

2 EU Legal Framework for CT

In the EU, the focus is on cooperation between law enforcement and judicial actors; among border guards and customs officers; and with the private sector (such as Internet companies). Civil society organisations can also play an important role in the prevention of radicalisation.

Under the Lisbon Treaty, internal security, which is interpreted as cooperation between law enforcement authorities, for instance the *Bundeskriminalamt* in Germany, is a shared competence between the EU and the Member States. EU criminal law has been adapted over recent years to respond effectively to the evolving terrorist threat. The Council Framework Decision on combatting terrorism as updated in 2008 includes crimes such as membership in a terrorist organisation and providing terrorist training as well as inciting terrorist acts.[20] Especially in the context of foreign terrorist fighters, with the UN Security Council Resolution 2178,[21] the Council of Europe Additional Protocol to the Convention on Prevention of Terrorism[22] and the new EU Directive on combatting terrorism,[23] criminalisation has been further expanded and includes many preparatory acts, such as preparation of terrorist travel or receiving terrorist training. Therefore, criminal law and law enforcement cover actions long before attacks are committed. The traditional distinction between forward-looking prevention of terrorist attacks, entrusted to security services, and backwards-looking investigation and prosecution of attacks, handled by the police and prosecutors, is no longer valid, and therefore law enforcement cooperation has a significant role to play in the CT domain.[24] Law enforcement and judicial authorities also play an important role in the prevention of terrorist attacks by investigating and prosecuting the preventive terrorist offenses that apply to certain behaviour long before an attack has happened.

---

[20] Council Framework Decision 2008/919/JHA, Amending Framework Decision 2002/475/JHA on Combating Terrorism, 2008 O.J. (L 330) 21.

[21] Security Council Resolution 2178 (24 September 2014).

[22] Council of Europe, Additional Protocol to the Council of Europe Convention on the Prevention of Terrorism, 22 October 2015, https://rm.coe.int/CoERMPublicCommon SearchServices/DisplayDCTMContent?documentId=09000016804/c5ea.

[23] The European Parliament (EP) and the Council reached political agreement on 17 November 2016. The Directive was adopted by the Council on 7 March 2017 after the vote of the EP Plenary on 15 February 2017. It was signed on 15 March 2017. The text can be found here: European Parliament and the Council Directive 2015/0281(COD), On Combating Terrorism and Replacing Council Framework Decision 2002/275/JHA and Amending Council Decision 2005/671/JHA (23 February 2017).

[24] But see Chapter 11.

As for border controls, as will be discussed later, there are many databases that have been developed over the previous decades that are gradually being made available for internal security purposes. The legacy of the pillar structure (law enforcement was in a separate treaty from border control), which was finally abolished in the Lisbon Treaty, remains a challenge, since many of the instruments created for migration and border control officials did not include a law enforcement objective. Recently, however, a number of EU laws have adopted an integrated approach that is better adapted to today's threat environment.

In contrast to internal security (to repeat, law enforcement cooperation), which under the Lisbon Treaty is a shared competence between the EU and the Member States, national security remains the sole responsibility of the Member States (Article 4(2) TEU).[25] National security is interpreted as covering the cooperation of security services and intelligence agencies. Security services are domestic intelligence services of EU Member States, such as MI5 in the United Kingdom, the *Bundesamt für Verfassungsschutz* (BfV) in Germany and the *Direction Générale de la Sécurité Intérieure* (DGSI) in France. The division of labour between these security services and law enforcement/police varies among the Member States, and in some, the security service is double hatted as a police service. Intelligence agencies are foreign intelligence services of EU Member States, such as MI6 in the United Kingdom, the *Bundesnachrichtendienst* (BND) in Germany and the *Direction Générale de la Sécurité Extérieure* (DGSE) in France. Cooperation among the security and intelligence services of the Member States ('intelligence cooperation') is taking place outside of the EU context. The security services are cooperating in the Counter-Terrorism Group (CTG). The difference between the terms 'national security' and 'internal security', in particular with regard to the fight against terrorism, may not be entirely clear. Potentially, the concept of European security would also need to be added to the debate, as terrorist groups operate transnationally, preparing attacks in one EU Member State and carrying them out in another. The national security provision has not yet been interpreted by the European Court of Justice, but this could change as the Court may pronounce itself on this in the context of a currently pending case.[26]

---

[25] For a more detailed analysis of the EU and intelligence in the CT context, see Gilles de Kerchove and Christiane Höhn "The Role of European Intelligence Cooperation," in *Intelligence Law and Policies in Europe*, eds. Jan-Hendrik Dietrich and Satish Sule (Baden-Baden: Nomos, 2019).

[26] In 2017, the United Kingdom's Investigatory Powers Tribunal made a preliminary reference to the ECJ to clarify whether the powers of the security and intelligence agencies to collect and access bulk communications data fall within the scope of EU law. *Privacy International*

Before concluding this overview of the EU's legal powers in the CT domain, it bears mentioning common foreign and security policy. The EU has taken a law enforcement and judicial approach to the fight against terrorism.[27] Terrorism is a crime to be investigated and prosecuted. However, when terrorist groups are present in conflict zones such as Syria and Iraq, military action is important and also has an impact on the terrorist threat internally. A number of EU Member States contribute, for example, militarily in the context of the Global Coalition against Daesh.[28] The internal–external link is much stronger today: What happens in regions such as North Africa, the Middle East and the Western Balkans has a direct impact on the EU's security. Information found on the battlefield in Syria and Iraq is relevant for investigations, prosecutions and border control in Europe. Foreign terrorist fighters are on the battlefield in Syria and Iraq, but when they return, they become subjects of interest to law enforcement and judicial authorities. Under the Lisbon Treaty, the EU has improved powers in the foreign and security policy domain, although they continue to be exercised largely through the intergovernmental method.

3 EU Institutional Actors

Mirroring this legal framework, there are numerous EU institutional actors involved in the fight against terrorism. The following section presents an inventory of the most important institutional players, proceeding in order from those with broader to more specific policy tasks.

The role of the **EU Counter Terrorism Coordinator** is to ensure implementation and evaluation of counter-terrorist strategy, coordinate counter-terrorist work within the Union and foster better communication between the Union and third countries.[29]

Different parts of the **European Commission** are involved in the fight against terrorism. They come together in the Security Union Task Force chaired by the Commissioner for the Security Union.

---

v. *Secretary of State for Foreign et al.*, Final Judgment of 23 July 2018, IPT/15/110/CH. This could lead to an interpretation of the term 'national security' by the ECJ.

[27] For a description of the EU's approach, also in light of the US approach adopted after 9/11, see Gilles de Kerchove and Christiane Höhn, "Counter-Terrorism and International Law since 9/11, Including in the EU-US Context," in *Yearbook of International Humanitarian Law*, eds. Terry D. Gill et al. (The Hague: T.M.C. Asser, 2013), 267–295.

[28] "The Global Coalition," last visited 24 July 2018, http://theglobalcoalition.org/en/home/.

[29] European Council, Stockholm Programme, 10/11 December 2010.

The **European External Action Service (EEAS)**, created to assist with EU foreign and security policy, has also stepped up its engagement on CT: counter-terrorism partnerships with priority third countries, in particular in North Africa, the Middle East (MENA) and the Western Balkans, are developed together by the EEAS, the Commission and the EU Counter-Terrorism Coordinator. The EEAS has deployed CT experts (seconded from Member States) in the EU's delegations in the MENA region, the Western Balkans and other priority regions for CT cooperation.

The **EU Intelligence and Situation Centre (INTCEN)** is located in the EEAS.[30] It deals with strategic intelligence analysis, not operational intelligence. It relies on contributions from the security and intelligence services of EU Member States. Together with the EU Military Staff Intelligence Directorate it creates joint civil/military situational analysis and strategic foresight (Single Intelligence Analysis Capacity). A counter-terrorism team within the INTCEN staffed by experts from Member State security and intelligence services is providing strategic analysis on the various aspects of the terrorist threat to Europe. The EU and the United States have an agreement on the exchange of classified information.

A number of **EU JHA agencies** also contribute to the fight against terrorism:[31]

On 1 January 2016, Europol launched the **European Counter-Terrorism Centre (ECTC)**.[32] This is a platform through which Member States can increase information sharing and operational cooperation with regard to the monitoring and investigation of foreign terrorist fighters; the trafficking of illegal firearms; and terrorist financing and the identification of additional lines of investigation. Member States can make use of Europol's full range of capabilities in the area of organised and cyber-crime, such as cross-checking the relevant data. The ECTC serves as an information hub for counter-terrorism for law enforcement and other relevant authorities in EU Member States and beyond. It provides operational support, coordination and expertise

---

[30] See "Fact Sheet EU INTCEN," European Union website, last visited 24 July 2018, https://eeas .europa.eu/factsheets/docs/20150206_factsheet_eu_intcen_en.pdf. See also Björn Fägersten, "Intelligence and Decision-Making within the Common Foreign and Security Policy," *European Policy Analysis* 22 (October 2015): 1–12.

[31] For a recent overview of the activities of EU JHA agencies relevant to CT, see EU Counter-Terrorism Coordinator, JHA Agencies' Role in Counter-Terrorism, Docs. 6146/18, 6146/18 ADD 1/EXT 1, and 6146/18 ADD 2, 2018.

[32] Conclusions of the Council of the EU and of the Member States Meeting within the Council on Counter-Terrorism, 14406/15 (20 November 2015). For an overview of the ECTC and its activities, see www.europol.europa.eu/about-europol/european-counter-terrorism-centre-ectc.

for Member State investigations, as well as a strategic support capability, including tackling the use of social media for radicalisation purposes.[33] Europol is developing an interesting capacity for supporting Internet-based investigations of the Member States in the context of the Internet Referral Unit and the European Cybercrime Centre EC3. For this, it will be necessary to attract top talent, such as PhDs in IT and mathematics. Increasingly, Member States are asking Europol to provide support on major counter-terrorism investigations, such as after the Paris and Brussels attacks in 2015 and 2016. The ECTC has strongly increased operational support for Member States: between 2016 and 2017, the number of supported operations more than tripled from 127 to 439. Around a third of this support is provided by the Internet Referral Unit (IRU). The relevant US authorities are closely cooperating with Europol, including information sharing and cooperation on investigations.

Eurojust has a distinctive operational and strategic role in the fight against terrorism by facilitating multilateral judicial cooperation, coordination and exchange of information in cross-border terrorism cases.[34] Member States are making increased use of Eurojust in counter-terrorism cases with an international dimension. A majority of EU Member States have already relied on Eurojust in cross-border terrorism cases, for instance using Eurojust to agree upon common and coordinated approaches, speed up the execution of European Arrest Warrants, European Investigation Orders and Mutual Legal Assistance requests, exchange information and evidence in ongoing investigations, set up Joint Investigation Teams (JITs), deal with extradition requests, etc. There are different reasons for using Eurojust, including the time-sensitivity of judicial cooperation and coordination in ongoing investigations. The United States has a liaison prosecutor at Eurojust and has started to participate in Joint Investigation Teams.

The **European Police College (CEPOL)** has considerably stepped up its training offerings in the area of counter-terrorism with the support of its

---

[33] See the report by the EU Counter-Terrorism Coordinator, *State of Play on the Implementation of the Statement of the Members of the European Council of 12 February 2015, the JHA Council Conclusions of 20 November 2015 and the Conclusions of the European Council of 18 December 2015*, 6785/16 (4 March 2016). On the ECTC, see also Europol Press Release, Europol's European Counter-Terrorism Centre Strengthens the EU's Response to Terror (25 January 2016), www.europol.europa.eu/content/ectc (see also the infographic). Finally, see the analysis by Chertoff et al., "Globsec Intelligence Reform Initiative, Reforming Transatlantic Counter-Terrorism," 2016, 16*ff*, www.globsec.org.

[34] "Eurojust website," last visited 24 July 2018, www.eurojust.europa.eu/Pages/home.aspx.

network, which includes national police training institutes in the Member States.[35] CEPOL's activities include residential training courses at its Budapest headquarters, opportunities under the CEPOL Exchange Programme to build up contacts with peers, and online modules and webinars. Its activities are addressed to both counter-terrorism specialists and law enforcement officials who might need to deal with terrorism in the context of their more general policing duties. A structured strategic and operational training-needs assessment at EU level is the basis for the development of training offerings, which allows CEPOL to turn policy-level priorities into concrete instruction. CEPOL has also developed CT training partnerships with neighbouring countries, in particular, around the Mediterranean.

The **European Border and Coast Guard Agency (Frontex)**[36] also contributes to CT in the context of border control.[37] Frontex cooperates with Europol and Eurojust and provides support to Member States in circumstances requiring increased technical and operational assistance at the external border in the fight against organised cross-border crime and terrorism. Frontex has included the detection of suspected foreign terrorist fighters (FTFs) as an operational objective in most of its operations. Activities are carried out in the context of Frontex-coordinated operations at the external EU borders, where a large number of undocumented migrants are apprehended.

The **Fundamental Rights Agency (FRA)** is collecting and analysing information and data to provide Member States and EU institutions with independent, evidence-based advice on fundamental rights.[38] FRA research could be relevant in particular in the context of prevention of radicalisation, including underlying factors such as integration.

eu-LISA manages the EU's large-scale information systems (databases), which are relevant in CT.[39]

---

[35] "Cepol website," last visited 24 July 2018, www.cepol.europa.eu/.

[36] "European Border and Coast Guard Agency," European Union website, last visited 24 July 2018, https://europa.eu/european-union/about-eu/agencies/frontex_en; "Frontex website," last visited 24 July 2018, https://frontex.europa.eu/.

[37] CT was included in the Frontex regulation that entered into force in 2016. See European Parliament and Council Regulation (EU) 2016/1624, On the European Border and Coast Guard, 2016 O.J. (L 251) 1, art. 8.

[38] "European Union Agency for Fundamental Rights," European Union website, last visited 24 July 2018, https://europa.eu/european-union/about-eu/agencies/fra_en; "FRA website," last visited 24 July 2018, http://fra.europa.eu/en.

[39] "eu-LISA Website," last visited 24 July 2018, www.eulisa.europa.eu/.

III THE INFORMATION SHARING ENVIRONMENT

As explained earlier, the EU's counter-terrorism strategy is multi-faceted. One of the most important dimensions is the use of information and pan-European databases to detect planned terrorist attacks and apprehend suspected terrorists.[40] Creating such an information-sharing environment requires attention to three phases, all of which are equally important: information collection, information sharing and information analysis.

1 Information Collection

A pre-condition for information exchange is the collection of information and access to the information in the first place.

1.1 New EU Tools

The EU has a number of longstanding databases that are relevant to counter-terrorism investigations, including the **Schengen Information System** and the **Europol Information System**. Recently, several new tools have been created to assist national authorities, as listed here:

The **EU–US Terrorist Financing Tracking Programme** provides access to information on cross-border payments.[41] It has provided a large number of leads in terrorism-related investigations. The Programme, however, only covers the SWIFT system for bank transfers, and not the euro payment area. The EU is contemplating a complementary Terrorist Financing Tracking System to close this gap.

In May 2018, the **EU Passenger Name Record (PNR) System** entered into force, which will oblige airlines to transmit passenger-related data to the competent authorities in the Member States.[42] This is a de-centralised system, meaning that each Member State is required to implement it. Connections need to be established between the Passenger Information Units (PIUs) of

---

[40] For another account of these developments, see Chapter 9.

[41] For more information on the EU–US TFTF and the legal text, see "Terrorist Finance Tracking Program," European Commission website, last visited 24 July 2018, https://ec.europa .eu/home-affairs/what-we-do/policies/crisis-and-terrorism/tftp_en. See also Mara Wesseling, "An EU Terrorist Finance Tracking System," Royal United Services Institute for Defence and Security Studies, Occasional Paper (September 2016).

[42] For more information, see the press release with the relevant links: European Commission Statement, Security Union: New Rules on EU Passenger Name Record Data, STATEMENT/ 18/3910 (25 May 2018).

Member States for information exchange. Running algorithms on PNR data will allow Member States to identify unknown terrorist suspects before departure, who can then undergo more in-depth checks upon arrival. While the 2015 and 2016 terrorist attacks were the major drivers of the EU PNR directive, it will also be useful for other forms of serious and organised crime.

Prüm has existed for many years and is also a de-centralised system.[43] Through the Prüm system, Member States can run fingerprints, DNA and vehicle registrations on the police databases of other Member States to check for hits. Information based on these hits is then exchanged bilaterally.

A new database recently adopted will enable the sharing of conviction records of third-country nationals (**ECRIS-TCN**).[44] It will contain an index which will allow for the identification of whether, and in which Member State, a third-country national has a previous criminal record, which can then be requested. The **European Criminal Records Information System (ECRIS)** already exists for EU nationals. It is a de-centralised system, which allows Member States to check whether a person has already been convicted of a crime in another EU Member State.

The new databases that are being created for EU borders (**Entry-Exit System [EES]**[45] and **European Travel Information and Authorization System [ETIAS]**)[46] will contain additional sources of information. The entry and exit of third-country nationals into the EU will be recorded in the EES, including their fingerprints, so that visa-overstayers can be identified. The information may also be relevant for security purposes. Hence, it will now be possible to know the dates of entry and exit of third-country nationals and to identify those third-country nationals who overstay the three months allowed on a Schengen visa. ETIAS is modelled on the US ESTA and allows national authorities to assess the risk of travellers (third-country nationals that are visa exempt) prior to arrival in the EU. ETIAS also facilitates secure, visa-free travel to the EU. To request a visa, information must be provided and security

---

[43] For more information, see "Stepping up Cross-Border Cooperation (Prüm Decision)," last visited 24 July 2018, https://eur-lex.europa.eu/legal-content/EN/TXT/HTML/?uri= LEGISSUM:jl0005&from=EN.

[44] For more information, see European Commission Press Release IP/16/87, Commission Proposes to Strengthen the Exchange of Criminal Records on Non-citizens (19 January 2016).

[45] See European Council Press Release 671/17, Entry-Exit System: Final Adoption by the Council (20 November 2017) and, European Commission, "Fact Sheet: Stronger and Smarter Borders for the European Union. The Entry-Exit System," https://ec.europa.eu/home-affairs/sites/homeaffairs/files/what-we-do/policies/securing-eu-borders/fact-sheets/docs/factsheet_-_entryexit_system_en.pdf.

[46] For more information, see "ETIAS Europe website," last visited 24 July 2018, www.etiaseurope.eu/.

checks are carried out before arrival, through the Visa Information System (VIS), and it is only logical that there also be a system for visa-free travellers. ETIAS is a centralised system which combines security, border and migration objectives and has in-built interoperability, hence serving as a possible example for a new generation of EU information systems. ETIAS allows Member States to identify terrorist suspects prior to travel into the EU; in those cases, travel authorisation will be denied.

1.2 Cross-Cutting Issues Related to Information Collection

Although information is fed into a plethora of EU databases and information systems, there are a number of common issues and challenges for information collection. These are related to data protection law, to the opportunities and challenges presented by the evolution of digital technologies, and to the interconnected nature of counter-terrorism policy, which requires cooperation across a variety of policy domains.

First, developments in data protection jurisprudence have made it difficult to collect certain types of data that are vital to counter-terrorism investigations. Access to traffic and location metadata is key, both for prevention of terrorist attacks and for investigations and prosecutions after attacks. For instance, traffic metadata, e.g. not the content of the communications but whom a person emailed, messaged or called, can be used after a terrorist attack to identify the perpetrators' accomplices, to quickly discover whether further attacks are planned and to investigate and prosecute the perpetrators. Among other things, location metadata enables the authorities to prove the presence of an FTF in Daesh-controlled territory in Syria or Iraq. In some Member States, this evidence can secure a conviction for FTF-related offenses.

The retention of such metadata has been called into question by the European Court of Justice's *Tele2* ruling of December 2016.[47] That judgment found that imposing an obligation of generalised data retention on private telecommunications companies was not proportionate. According to the ECJ, generalised data retention contradicts the structure of the e-privacy directive, the secondary law upon which Member States' data retention legislation is based, as well as the proportionality principle with regard to the rights of privacy and data protection in the EU Charter of Fundamental Rights. As a result of the *Tele2* ruling, in some Member States there is no longer a legal framework that requires telecommunications companies and Internet Service

---

[47] Joined Cases C-203/15 and C-698/15, *Tele2 Sverige AB v. Post-och Telestyrelsen* and *Secretary of State for the Home Department v. Tom Watson, Peter Brice, Geoffrey Lewis*, ECLI:EU:C:2016:970.

Providers to retain certain categories of metadata for a certain time period. Since not all the necessary information is retained by communications providers for business purposes, this can have a negative impact on terrorist prevention, investigations and prosecutions. The EU and the Member States are working on a solution that would satisfy both security needs and fundamental rights law, but it has not proven easy. Since it is not possible to determine in advance who is likely to commit an offence, the targeted retention mentioned by the Court may not be feasible. Moreover, one of the possibilities alluded to in the *Tele2* judgment – retention of data for those neighbourhoods where there is a high risk that attacks are being prepared – may be considered discriminatory. One possible way forward which is being discussed is the concept of 'restricted data retention' – retaining only the absolutely necessary data categories. This could be combined with strict rules for access to the data as well as protection of the retained data. It will be important either for Member States to adopt a coordinated approach in their national data retention regimes or for the EU to consider data retention legislation in the future.

Second, the challenges and opportunities of evolving digital technologies: in response to the Snowden leaks, more and more Internet-based communications are encrypted. Encryption poses challenges for the authorities with regard to access to content. In the past, this risk was mitigated by access to the metadata, through which it could be known with whom a terrorist suspect communicated and how often. As explained earlier, however, retention of this metadata has been put into question, and, combined with encryption, there is the risk of services going dark. The Commission has committed to strengthening the capacities of Europol to support Member States in Internet-based investigations, including upgrading their technical, decryption capabilities and developing alternative investigation methods.[48] Europol could become the hub of a knowledge community and could serve as a good example of pooling resources in an expensive and challenging field. Europol's European Cybercrime Center (EC3) and its Internet Referral Unit (IRU) are already supporting Member States in this field.

The migration of more and more crime-related electronic data to private servers in the cloud presents another challenge for information collection.[49] Most of the private service providers are not based in the EU and do not store

---

[48] For the recommendation of the Commission, see Communication from the Commission, *Eleventh Progress Report towards an Effective and Genuine Security Union*, COM (2017) 608 final (18 October 2017).

[49] For a discussion of these issues, see Chapter 12.

their data in the EU. If a terrorist attack takes place in a Member State and the perpetrators communicate in that Member State, it is illogical to force police and prosecutors to resort to the cumbersome process for Mutual Legal Assistance from the third country where the data or the company is located, most often the United States. Under US legislation, US-based companies can cooperate voluntarily with EU Member States to respond to requests for subscriber information and transaction information (communications meta-data), albeit not the content of communications. Europol has created the SIRIUS platform, a tool that helps investigators and prosecutors to contact the relevant companies in the most efficient way.[50] The EU is cooperating with Internet Service Providers (ISPs) to streamline voluntary cooperation. There have also been legislative developments in the United States and the EU on this issue: in spring 2018, the US CLOUD Act was adopted and the Commission proposed EU legislation on e-evidence.[51] Negotiations on the draft e-evidence legislation are progressing, which would impose legal obligations to cooperate on ISPs that offer services in the EU.

To turn to the opportunities, the widespread availability and accuracy of biometric technologies such as fingerprint matching and facial recognition offers the possibility of substantially improving the efficiency and utility of information systems. The EU is further developing biometric capabilities. Biometrics are particularly important at external borders, where they can be used to identify, for example, Daesh infiltration of undocumented migrants or cases of document fraud. For example, in one Member State, a picture allowed authorities to detect an FTF from Syria at the external border via facial recognition. It would be key for this information and technology to be present everywhere at the EU external border.

Soon, biometric (fingerprint) searches will be possible in the Schengen Information System (SIS). The SIS is a centralised EU database which is systematically checked when individuals cross the EU's external borders. By entering data into SIS, Member States can flag terrorist suspects and indicate arrest warrants, and therefore the system enables the detection and tracking of known terrorist suspects. The full roll-out of SIS fingerprint searches is expected to happen next year. Facial recognition, a much-needed development, will be added in the future. Europol is also developing a biometric

---

[50] Europol Press Release, Europol Launches the Sirius Platform to Facilitate Online Investigations (31 October 2017), www.europol.europa.eu/newsroom/news/europol-launches-sirius-platform-to-facilitate-online-investigations.

[51] For more information see "E-evidence," European Commission website, last visited 24 July 2018, https://ec.europa.eu/home-affairs/what-we-do/policies/organized-crime-and-human-trafficking/e-evidence_en.

capability. But these efforts to strengthen the biometric capabilities of EU databases are not enough – the Member States must also cooperate, by feeding the biometric-enabled databases with biometric data.

A third challenge of information collection is related to the multivalent nature of CT policy. One important source of biometric and other data on FTFs is information found on the battlefield, for example in Syria and Iraq. A wealth of information is available on the cell phones of FTFs and the Daesh documents and computers that were found when territory such as Raqqa was liberated by the anti-Daesh coalition. This battlefield information is not only relevant for future military efforts and for protecting forces on the ground but is also needed to protect the homeland. Vice versa, in a context of FTF movement between the EU and Syria/Iraq, Daesh influence on attacks, and radicalisation in the West, police efforts at home to degrade the terrorist groups can also have a direct impact on the battlefield, dismantling facilitation networks and so on.

It is critical to share this battlefield information not only with intelligence services but also with border control systems and with law enforcement. If it is entered – quickly – into the SIS, such information can help prevent infiltration of FTFs and other terrorist fighters into the EU. It can also support investigations and prosecutions of returning FTFs, for which obtaining evidence about what happened in Syria and Iraq is a challenge.[52] (The more evidence there is of participation in specific crimes in Syria and Iraq, the longer the prison sentence that can be imposed.) It is also relevant for security services, which can use the Daesh information to prevent terrorist attacks.

Although the importance of battlefield information for civilian authorities at home has been recognised, challenges to communicating the information remain. Information found by the military is often overclassified and it takes a long time to de-classify and share. The US special operations command has now taken the decision to no longer classify information it finds on the battlefield. Only when the information has been enriched by analysis will the products be classified. Procedures are being streamlined for sharing this

---

[52] See also Security Council Resolution 2396 (21 December 2017), para. 20. 'Calls upon Member States, including through relevant Central Authorities, as well as UNODC and other relevant UN entities that support capacity building, to share best practices and technical expertise, informally and formally, with a view to improving the collection, handling, preservation and sharing of relevant information and evidence, in accordance with domestic law and the obligations Member States have undertaken under international law, *including information obtained* from the internet, or *in conflict zones*, in order to ensure foreign terrorist fighters who have committed crimes, including those returning and relocating to and from the conflict zone, may be prosecuted.'

unclassified information with international partners. The United States is reviving project Vennlig, successfully used in the earlier Iraq war, to declassify and share battlefield information via Interpol.[53] The EU is supporting Iraq to strengthen its capacities to collect and share battlefield information. Overall, the topic of good practices on battlefield information requires further reflection and action, as demonstrated by the recent initiatives in the UN, the Global Counter-Terrorism Forum and the Council of Europe.

A last topic that bears mentioning is the quality of the data that is fed into the EU systems and enriching the data with contextual information. Take the example of an FTF returnee back in the EU: in addition to the name, it is also important to have information on the assessed risk, his location and whether he is under investigation.

2 Information Sharing

Information needs not only to be collected but also shared. This is especially important in the Schengen zone of free movement, where flanking measures are needed to compensate for the lack of internal border controls. Terrorist groups such as Daesh and Al Qaeda operate across borders; hence the authorities of the Member States need to share information, both within the Member State and among Member States. For instance, if an FTF of one Member State returns to the EU but enters via another Member State, it is crucial that his information be included in the SIS, so that his entry to the EU will be detected, in particular as onward travel is possible without border controls. Other examples are attacks that are prepared in one Member State and carried out in another (the Paris attacks of November 2015 were in part planned from Brussels); and cells and facilitators within terrorist organisations that consist of several nationalities and are linked to several countries.

Feeding information into and consulting EU databases to the maximum extent possible is key to the fight against terrorism in an increasingly complex and transnational world. The following section canvasses the main avenues for doing so in each of the relevant policy areas – border controls, criminal justice, and security and law enforcement cooperation. It then considers information sharing implications of interoperability and cybersecurity.

---

[53] For more information see the Interpol Press Release, G7 Ministers Call for Sharing of Battlefield Data on Terrorists via INTERPOL (20 October 2017), www.interpol.int/News-and-media/News/2017/N2017-144.

2.1 External Border Controls

Over the past few years, external border controls have been considerably strengthened. The Schengen Borders Code, which establishes the procedure and criteria to be used by national border guards, mandates systematic database checks for both third-country nationals and EU citizens and residents.[54] In 2016, Frontex, the EU's border agency, was transformed into the European Borders and Coast Guard Agency (but is still known as Frontex) and counter-terrorism is among its legal bases.[55] Frontex is increasingly providing technical and operational assistance to frontline Member States to protect external borders, including with respect to organised cross-border crime and terrorism. Alongside Frontex, Europol has deployed to hotspots to assist Italy and Greece with the processing of irregular migrants, and is carrying out second-line security checks in its databases.[56] In 2017, 9,896 persons, 1,242 documents and 10,388 communication means (mobile devices, email accounts, etc.) were referred to Europol for such secondary security checks.[57]

The EU is also modernising the SIS database and is making improvements to the counter-terrorism related functions.[58] The SIS is key to identifying terrorist suspects entering the EU; it can also be used to monitor their movements after entry, since the system can be accessed during police checks in-country. Both police authorities and security services share information via the SIS. For security services, there is a special function (Article 36 (3)) that allows for discreet checks and hence protects the information of the service entering the information. (In the case of discreet checks, the person being

---

[54] See the press release with link to the legislation, European Council Press Release 113/17, Schengen Borders Code: Council Adopts Regulation to Reinforce Checks and External Borders" (7 March 2017).

[55] See European Parliament and Council Regulation (EU) 2016/1624, On the European Border and Coast Guard, 2016 O.J. (L 251) 1.

[56] Europol Press Release, Europol Setting Up Team of 200 Investigators to Deploy to Migration Hotspots (12 May 2016), www.europol.europa.eu/newsroom/news/europol-setting-team-of-200-investigators-to-deploy-to-migration-hotspots.

[57] EU Counter-Terrorism Coordinator, JHA Agencies' Role in Counter-Terrorism, 6146/18 ADD 1/EXT 1.

[58] On the SIS, see the European Commission, "Fact Sheet: The Schengen Information System," June 2018, https://ec.europa.eu/home-affairs/sites/homeaffairs/files/what-we-do/policies/european-agenda-security/20180612_agenda-on-security-factsheet-sis_en.pdf; and generally, "Schengen Information System," European Commission website, last visited 24 July 2018, https://ec.europa.eu/home-affairs/what-we-do/policies/borders-and-visas/schengen-information-system_en. See also the press release about the update with relevant links in European Commission Statement, Security Union: Commission Welcomes Agreement on a Reinforced Schengen Information System, STATEMENT/18/4133 (12 June 2018).

checked is not informed of a hit, questioned or arrested, but the hit is communicated to the Member State which entered the alert, so that the service which entered the information can follow the whereabouts of the person without the person being aware.) Information sharing via the SIS on terrorist suspects, in particular FTFs, has strongly increased over the past years. This is important since FTFs often re-enter the EU through Member States with which they do not have a connection, and the SIS enables their detection at the EU external borders. Based on the recent change to the Schengen Borders Code, EU nationals are now also being checked against the SIS when they re-enter the Schengen area, which permits the identification of FTFs that are European nationals. Progress has also been made on including contextual information on terrorist suspects and enabling this information to be communicated rapidly, so that in the case of a 'hit', border authorities can take the appropriate action. A possible future development under discussion is the broader dissemination of terrorism-related hits: today, in the event of a hit, only the Member State having entered the information (in the context of a border control or an in-country check) is informed. However, in the Schengen area of free movement, this information is also relevant for the other Member States and Schengen partners.

It is also key to check Interpol databases at EU external borders.[59] Interpol databases contain information about terrorist suspects from third countries and stolen and lost passports.[60] Member States are increasing these checks.

2.2 Europol

Member States have also enormously strengthened information sharing via Europol. The creation of the European Counter-Terrorism Center within Europol in January 2016 has enabled the pooling of the various Europol resources related to terrorism. Member States are sharing information via the Europol Information System (EIS) and analytical work files, for example, on FTFs. At the end of 2017, the EIS contained 46,166 persons linked to terrorism, compared to around 350 at the end of 2014.[61] Europol is also cross-checking terrorism-related data against organised crime databases and has

---

[59] On Interpol and CT, see "Terrorism," Interpol website, last visited 24 July 2018, www.interpol .int/Crime-areas/Terrorism/Terrorism.

[60] "Border Management," Interpol website, last visited 24 July 2018, www.interpol.int/ INTERPOL-expertise/Border-management/SLTD-Database.

[61] EU Counter-Terrorism Coordinator, JHA Agencies' Role in Counter-Terrorism, 6146/18 ADD 1/EXT 1.

found a high number of hits. Upon request, Europol is also supporting Member States in their investigations after terrorist attacks, such as after the Paris and Brussels attacks. In addition to Europol's support for investigations after terrorist attacks have been committed, investigators from the most concerned Member States and partner countries are working together in Joint Liaison Teams to identify leads and facilitate cross-border investigations.[62] Europol has very strict handling codes, so that the Member States retain control over the information they share with Europol.

Joint Investigation Teams with the support of Europol and Eurojust provide a framework for in-depth information and evidence sharing in multi-national investigations.[63] JITs have been put in place, for example, after the Paris and Brussels attacks and are a highly effective form of judicial cooperation and replace the more cumbersome procedure for judicial assistance. The evidence obtained through JITs can be used in court, Europol and Eurojust are often members of JITs, and even the United States has begun participating in JITs together with Member States.

It is also important for Europol to strengthen information exchange with third countries in the fight against terrorism. There is already considerable information sharing with the United States, Canada, Norway and Switzerland. It is now necessary to move beyond these traditional partners. Therefore, recently, the Council authorised the Commission to open negotiations for agreements between the EU and eight countries in the MENA region on the exchange of personal data between Europol and these countries' competent authorities for fighting serious crime and terrorism.[64] This is challenging given the strict data protection requirements that partner countries must satisfy. In addition, in December 2017, Europol's Management Board adopted a list of priority partners for the conclusion of working arrangements for strategic-level cooperation.[65] The Management Board has adopted a model for the working arrangements to be concluded with third-country partners.

---

[62] In a statement issued following the terrorist attacks in Brussels on 22 March 2016, Ministers for Justice and Home Affairs and representatives of the EU institutions called for the setting-up of a joint liaison team of national counter-terrorism experts at Europol's European Counter Terrorism Centre. This team would support Member States in investigating the wider European and international dimensions of the current terrorist threat.

[63] On JITs, see "Joint Investigation Teams-JITS," Europol website, last visited 25 July 2018, www.europol.europa.eu/activities-services/joint-investigation-teams.

[64] Algeria, Egypt, Israel, Jordan, Lebanon, Morocco, Tunisia and Turkey.

[65] First-tier priorities are: Algeria, Egypt, Israel, Jordan, Lebanon, Morocco, Tunisia and Japan.

2.3 Eurojust

Member States are also sharing information about prosecutions and convictions via Eurojust, which allows national authorities to identify links to prosecutions in other Member States, to exchange information and to share their approaches to similar judicial questions. Since the Charlie Hebdo attacks in early 2015, there has been an increase in the use of Eurojust for CT cases, including in the prosecutions of the attacks in Paris, Brussels, Berlin, Barcelona and Cambrils. The number of operational terrorism cases Eurojust has supported over recent years has increased sixfold – from fourteen in 2014 to eighty-seven in 2017. The number of CT coordination meetings at Eurojust has remained stable over recent years, at around fifteen per year. (Case coordination allows parties to align approaches, exchange information and facilitate judicial cooperation in a multilateral framework.) Over the last three years, information sharing about ongoing prosecutions on terrorist offenses more than tripled: from 110 in 2015 to 375 in 2017. Information on 218 convictions was shared with Eurojust in 2015, and on 345 in 2017.[66] Overall, upon request, Eurojust facilitates the cooperation with other Member States and third countries with regard to prosecutions, providing a modern framework for judicial cooperation.

Eurojust is committed to further step up information sharing on prosecutions and convictions.[67] It is important to collectively re-think how to apply Council Decision 2005/671/JHA, which obliges Member States to share information about prosecutions and convictions with Eurojust if the cases affect two or more Member States.[68] In the case of Daesh or Al Qaeda-inspired terrorism, information about all related judicial investigations, prosecutions and convictions is relevant for all other EU Member States. Therefore, it may affect two or more EU Member States and should be shared with Eurojust. This interpretation would considerably increase information sharing. This

---

[66] EU Counter-Terrorism Coordinator, JHA Agencies' Role in Counter-Terrorism, 6146/18 ADD 1/EXT 1.

[67] See Eurojust Press Release, France, Germany, Belgium and Spain Call for the Creation of a European Judicial Counter-Terrorist Register (21 June 2018), www.eurojust.europa.eu/press/ PressReleases/Pages/2018/2018-06-21.aspx. The Ministers of Justice of Germany, France, Belgium and Spain have called for the creation of a European Judicial Counter-Terrorism Register, which will make it possible to proactively establish possible links between cases and to identify coordination needs for the investigations. The legal basis for working together is already in place (Council Decision 2005/671/JHA), which should be systematically applied in all Member States.

[68] Council Decision, 2005/671/JHA, On the Exchange of Information and Cooperation Concerning Terrorist Offences, 2005 O.J. (L 253) 22, para. 3.

information includes the names of the suspects, a short summary of the case and requests for judicial cooperation. The Member State keeps control over the information. All information Eurojust registers into the case management system is kept private by default. Eurojust cross-checks the information against its database. In case of a hit, Eurojust asks the authorities which provided the information whether it can be shared with the country of the hit, therefore leaving full control with the Member State as data owner. Such cross-checks can identify links between ongoing investigations and prosecutions, links with other countries or links with organised crime cases. This may trigger national authorities to launch new investigations or extend ongoing ones. For this system to work well, there must be timely and systematic sharing by all Member States whenever a judicial proceeding related to FTFs starts. The information about the cases should be updated, for example, when additional suspects are added. There is no overlap with what Europol is already doing, because the information shared with Eurojust is of a judicial nature. It is important that Eurojust also provide feedback to the national authorities. Europol and Eurojust should work closely together, as police and judicial work complement one another. It is good practice to invite Europol to Eurojust coordination meetings, as Europol can contribute important information.

2.4 Multilateral Information Sharing among Security and Intelligence Services

Strategic information about the terrorist threat picture is shared via the EU INTCEN, which produces strategic analysis of various aspects of the terrorist threat based on input from Member State services. Security and intelligence services cooperate outside of the EU framework. The cooperation of the security services is mostly conducted under the umbrella of the Counter-Terrorism Group. In 2016, the CTG set up a common platform under the Dutch Presidency, which will allow for the electronic exchange of information and closer cooperation through posting of members of the services of the Member States to the platform.[69] This is an important development which has already produced operational results. Since it is important for law

---

[69] Netherlands Presidency of the EU Press Release, New Platform for Deepening Cooperation between European Intelligence and Security Services (January 2016); see also European Council Press Release 158/16, Joint Statement of EU Ministers for Justice and Home Affairs and Representatives of EU Institutions on the Terrorist Attacks in Brussels on 22 March 2016 (24 March 2016), para. 8

enforcement and security services to exchange information, not only within the Member States but also at the European level, Europol and the CTG are exploring avenues for cooperation.

Traditionally, security services have been careful to exchange information out of a concern for protecting sources and methods and other issues. But counter-terrorism is different from counter-espionage, where information needs to be kept very restricted and there is the risk of infiltration.[70] Today's terrorist groups consist of criminals, and, unless very sensitive sources need to be protected, it is important to share as much as possible not only bilaterally but also multilaterally, as is happening in the CTG context. In advance, it is not always possible to know what information is relevant for other countries. Therefore, it seems necessary in counter-terrorism to expand the information sharing approach and to couple the need-to-know transfer of information with a dare-to-share culture, not removing the need to know but significantly broadening it.

2.5 Interoperability of Information Systems

Interoperability is a critical issue on which the EU can achieve major progress. It is a priority at the highest political level: as the European Council has stated in its Conclusions of 18 December 2015: 'The recent terrorist attacks demonstrate in particular the urgency of enhancing relevant information sharing, notably as regards ... ensuring the interoperability of the relevant databases with regard to security checks.'[71]

Even though the EU has developed multiple information systems over recent decades, they have been underutilised for lack of interoperability. One culprit is the legacy of the previous EU legal framework, described previously, under which migration and border control was artificially separated from internal security. As a result, databases that are very relevant for internal security, such as the fingerprint registration database of asylum seekers (Eurodac), could be accessed by law enforcement only under restricted conditions, for limited purposes. Another reason for the interoperability problem is the historical legacy of a patchwork of EU databases, both alphanumerical and biometric, created for various purposes, without a framework designed to link them. As a result, identity fraud can go undetected – for

---

[70] On this, see Alain Bauer, "L'avenir du terrorisme," *Les Carnets des Dialogues du Matin* (Hiver 2015–2016): 9–32.

[71] European Council Meeting (17 and 18 December 2015) – Conclusions, EUCO 28/15 (18 December 2015), para. 5.

instance, the perpetrator of the terrorist attacks in Berlin, an asylum seeker, had multiple identities that had gone undetected. Moreover, available information is not cross-checked or not always properly used.

The Commission tabled an interoperability legislative proposal in late 2017 and it was adopted in spring 2019.[72] It will allow authorities to 'connect the dots' and to carry out identity checks, cross-checking information from the relevant EU centralised databases. The legislation creates a European Single Search Portal, which will show the results of all searched (alpha-numeric) databases on the same screen, hence avoiding the need for the lengthy, separate checking of databases. It also creates a Shared Biometric Matching System, which will provide results across the biometric databases. Most importantly, it establishes a common identity repository, which cross-checks identity data from all relevant databases, both alpha-numeric and biometric, and flags irregularities. This will facilitate the detection of identity fraud. A new type of 'identity check' is also introduced, which facilitates the access of relevant authorities to the system.

In developing this legislative proposal, data protection concerns were extensively taken into account. The High Level Expert Group that was involved in developing the various concepts underpinning the legislation included representation of EU data protection institutions and experts – the European Data Protection Supervisor, the Fundamental Rights Agency, DG Just and the Commission Legal Service – as well as the Civil Liberties, Justice and Home Affairs (LIBE) secretariat from the European Parliament.[73] This led to very data protection conscious choices: The flagging of irregularities and the availability of information from all databases avoids fishing expeditions and prevents officials from requesting access to databases which do not contain relevant information. It also affords security officials a quick overview of potentially relevant data, but for access to the data itself, a (streamlined) request remains necessary.

For now, the first phase of interoperability only covers the EU's centralised databases and will take several years to implement. Europol and Frontex are fully involved. However, in the future, interoperability could be expanded to de-centralised systems such as PNR data or a (modernised) Prüm: the exchange of the police fingerprint data of Member States is currently based

---

[72] A comprehensive overview, background documents and the legislative texts can be found here: http://europa.eu/rapid/press-release_IP-17-5202_en.htm.

[73] High Level Expert Group on Information Systems and Interoperability, *Final Report* (May 2017), http://ec.europa.eu/transparency/regexpert/index.cfm?do=groupDetail.groupDetail Doc&id=32600&no=1 (see Annex 5 by the EU Counter-Terrorism Coordinator).

on a multitude of bilateral IT connections, but could be replaced by a hub-and-spoke system and could be designed in light of interoperability. It is interesting that ETIAS, the newest database to be established, incorporates interoperability with other databases and EU agencies from the beginning and has both border/migration and security purposes. This would be a good model for the future.

2.6 Cybersecurity

Information sharing is also key in cybersecurity, where many silos exist. At the national level, defence, intelligence services, law enforcement, Computer Emergency Response Teams (CERTs), private companies and other actors need to exchange critical information. At the EU level, there exists a similar compartamentalisation – between Europol, EU-CERT[74] and the EU Agency for Network and Information Security (ENISA),[75] which needs to be addressed.

3 Information Analysis

The information needs not only to be collected and shared but also analysed. This is increasingly the challenge today, given the huge amount of information which is being generated and the diversity of the terrorist threat. The transformation of the threat to more home-grown radicalisation and terrorism makes information analysis even more important. Europol has taken initiatives on this score. For instance, with regard to FTFs, it supports the common analysis of information through the Focal Point Travellers initiative;[76] relevant US authorities are participating in the initiative.[77] Likewise, it is critical to

---

[74] "CERT-E," Enisa website, last visited 24 July 2018, www.enisa.europa.eu/topics/csirts-in-europe/capacity-building/european-initiatives/cert-eu.

[75] "Enisa website," last visited 24 July 2018, www.enisa.europa.eu/.

[76] "Europol Analysis Projects," Europol website, last visited July 24, 2018, www.europol.europa .eu/crime-areas-trends/europol-analysis-projects: 'Analysis Project Travellers coordinates investigations into, and data analysis on, foreign terrorist fighters, and supports law enforcement efforts to counter foreign fighters when they return to Europe or the US from i.e. Syria or Iraq. In response to the concerted efforts of EU Member States, with Europol's help, the amount of data on foreign terrorist fighters within AP Travellers has increased substantially since early 2015.'

[77] See, e.g., Europol Press Release, FBI and Europol Strengthen Joint Fight against Foreign Terrorist Fighters (7 April 2016), www.europol.europa.eu/newsroom/news/fbi-and-europol-strengthen-joint-fight-against-foreign-terrorist-fighters.

train analysts. For law enforcement, the European Police College (CEPOL) is increasingly providing counter-terrorism related training, in cooperation with the training academies of the EU Member States.[78] Notwithstanding these efforts, a number of challenges remain, which are discussed in the next section.

4 Challenges with Regard to the Information Sharing Environment and Possible Future Developments

4.1 Information Analysis

The more diverse terrorist threat that exists in Europe today, combined with the availability of huge amounts of information, create challenges for the analysis of information. The current state of 'infobesity' has generated a need for more and better analysts and analytical tools. With respect to training, in September 2017, French President Macron proposed a European Intelligence Academy for the joint training of intelligence analysts in the context of counter-terrorism to bring intelligence capacities in Europe closer together and contribute to creating a common culture.[79] This Academy will likely be set up outside of the EU legal framework.

It is also necessary to make far more use of big data analytics and artificial intelligence to detect early signs of radicalisation. Internet companies use data on customer activities and preferences to place advertisements and to propose content or items for consumers to buy. This same technology should also be able to help spot individuals on the path to radicalisation. However, even in the case of increased use of technology, the need for a sufficient number of trained analysts will remain.

Even once individuals are identified as possible terrorists, it is imperative to prioritise the potential threat. The public statements of the heads of the security services of France, Germany and the United Kingdom collectively indicate that some 50,000 individuals have come to their attention in the context of now-closed investigations. This points to the difficulty of identifying those previously investigated individuals – likely only a very small subset of the

---

[78] EU Counter-Terrorism Coordinator, JHA agencies' role in counter-terrorism, 6146/18 ADD 1/ EXT 1.

[79] Initiative pour l'Europe- Discours d'Emmanuel Macron Pour une Europe souveraine, unie, democratique, 26 September 2017, www.elysee.fr/declarations/article/initiative-pour-l-europe-discours-d-emmanuel-macron-pour-une-europe-souveraine-unie-democratique/. English translation available here: www.elysee.fr/assets/Initiative-for-Europe-a-sovereign-united-democratic-Europe-Emmanuel-Macron.pdf.

50,000 – who may now or at some point in the future reach a tipping point, and go from extremism to violence. The challenge is particularly acute for home-grown radicalised persons who, unlike FTFs, do not travel to conflict zones. It is difficult to prioritise among such individuals, both with respect to monitoring (given the number of officers required for 24/7 monitoring, even the largest Member States have very limited capacities) and the decision of which names to enter into EU databases such as the SIS or the Europol Information System. On this score, there may be lessons to be learned from the United States, where since 9/11 there have been long and difficult inter-agency discussions on the threshold for placing individuals in counter-terrorism databases. The United States has also found a way to share the whole list with border guards and even Europol without compromising sources and methods.

4.2 Digitalisation of Security

Digitalisation of security is a reality. Public authorities need to keep up with the technology and use it to a maximum. Information is no longer the monopoly of state authorities, but is available through a variety of private sources: for example, an NGO is using Facebook to collect and crowd source information about war criminals, including Daesh, from refugees. Private companies that operate globally have an enormous amount of information. A lot of open source information is available on the Internet.

We need to adapt and transform our way of operating to make the most of the opportunities that digitalisation of security provides. This requires much stronger public–private partnerships, staying on top of technological developments such as artificial intelligence and using them in the most efficient way for security purposes.

At the same time, it is important to understand how the terrorist threat will evolve thanks to technology. In the future, there is the risk that terrorist groups will use technologies such as drones, synthetic biology, miniaturisation and artificial intelligence and will use techniques and technologies such as crowd-funding, bitcoin and the dark web to finance their operations and procure weapons.

4.3 Data Protection and Privacy

There have been a number of developments in the privacy and data protection spheres that have proved challenging for counter-terrorism efforts. Since the Snowden revelations, there appears to have been a 'privacy spring' in the

The EU and International Terrorism

European Court of Justice.[80] The General Data Protection Regulation (GDPR), which entered into force in May 2018, may have an impact on security since certain services based on data may no longer be possible or difficult to carry out in Europe.[81] Of even greater concern may be the draft e-privacy regulation, which also includes a restrictive regime.[82] Beyond security, this data protection law may hinder the development of artificial intelligence in Europe, which is an important future industry and requires huge amount of data to 'learn'.

The European Parliament and its LIBE committee responsible for terrorism-related legislation also have a very strong focus on privacy and data protection. It is important to re-balance the debate in Europe, and develop a stronger voice on security. To this end, it is useful to hold briefings of security policymakers and heads of security services, law enforcement agencies and judicial actors for the European Parliament, to share the challenges and needs of security. This has already happened in the work of the European Parliament's temporary Terrorism (TERR) committee, which is finalising a report on how the EU could strengthen the fight against terrorism.[83]

In the United States, there are yearly seminars bringing together justices of the US Supreme Court with key stakeholders from the US security community for an exchange of views and to learn from each other. It may be time to replicate such a format in Europe with the judges from the European Court of Justice and the European Court of Human Rights in Strasbourg.

It will also be key to take a more modern approach, using fully privacy by design.[84] This principle is enshrined in the GDPR, but has not yet fully come

---

[80] See, e.g., Case C-362/14, *Maximillian Schrems* v. *Data Protection Commissioner*, ECLI:EU: C:2015:650 (concerning data transfers to the United States in the context of the Safe Harbour Agreement); Joined Cases C-293/12 and C-594/12, *Digital Rights Ireland Ltd.* v. *Minister for Communications, Marine and Natural Resources et al.*, ECLI:EU:C:2014:238 (concerning the EU's data retention directive); *Tele2 Sverige* (concerning national data retention legislation); Case C-131/12, *Google Spain* v. *AEPD and Mario Costeja González*, ECLI:EU:C:2014:317 (concerning the 'right to be forgotten'); Opinion 1/15 of the Court (Grand Chamber), ECLI: EU:C:2017:592 (on the EU–Canada PNR agreement).

[81] For more information see "GDPR Portal: Site Overview," Eugdpr website, last visited 24 July 2018, www.eugdpr.org/.

[82] "Proposal for an ePrivacy Regulation," European Commission website, last visited 24 July 2018, https://ec.europa.eu/digital-single-market/en/proposal-eprivacy-regulation.

[83] "European Parliament Committees: Terrorism," European Parliament website, last visited 24 July 2018, www.europarl.europa.eu/committees/en/terr/home.html.

[84] Pioneering work has been carried out by Dr Ann Cavoukian, former Privacy Commissioner of Ontario. For the foundational principles, see Ann Cavoukian, "Privacy by Design: The 7 Foundational Principles," August 2009, www.ipc.on.ca/wp-content/uploads/Resources/7foundationalprinciples.pdf.

to life. New technologies can be used to protect privacy, while still allowing big data to be used for security purposes. Big data and new technologies also provide opportunities for creative privacy-by-design solutions that protect privacy while responding to security needs.[85] More creative solutions should be considered in order to reconcile data protection principles and access to the data, such as, for example, homomorphic encryption.

IV CONCLUSION

Terrorism has become a priority area for EU policymaking and has been a driver for further EU integration. The information sharing environment has been one of the key areas of work for the EU over the past three years. Considerable progress has been made,[86] but challenges remain which need to be addressed as a matter of urgency and priority. New technologies provide opportunities and risks for the CT field. In this context, close EU–US exchanges and sharing of experience will be important moving forward. The EU and the United States have built a close CT partnership, which is leading to practical cooperation on investigations and prosecutions of terrorists. A number of EU developments have been inspired by similar debates in the United States, such as the interoperability of databases. Information exchange with the United States is increasing, underpinned by strong privacy protections on both sides.[87]

---

[85] On privacy by design and big data, see, for example, Ann Cavoukian and Michelle Chibba, "Start with Privacy by Design in All Big Data Applications," in *Guide to Big Data Applications*, ed. S. Srinivasan (n.p.: Springer, 2018), 29–48.

[86] For details on the progress related to CT and the Security Union, Commissioner King's monthly Security Union progress reports are instructive.

[87] This includes the EU–US umbrella agreement on data protection in criminal investigations. See European Commission "Fact Sheet: Questions and Answers on the EU–US Data Protection 'Umbrella Agreement'," 1 December 2016, http://europa.eu/rapid/press-release_MEMO-16-4183_en.htm; "Conclusion of the EU–US Data Protection Umbrella Agreement," Europarl website, last visited 24 July 2018, www.europarl.europa.eu/legislative-train/theme-area-of-justice-and-fundamental-rights/file-conclusion-of-the-eu-us-data-protection-umbrella-agreement.

11

The Preventive Turn in European Security Policy
Towards a Rule of Law Crisis?

VALSAMIS MITSILEGAS[*]

I INTRODUCTION

Security has been at the heart of European integration, in one way or another, since the entry into force of the Maastricht Treaty. A series of terrorist attacks in the 2000s, including 9/11, 7/7 and the Madrid bombings, has been followed by a plethora of responses by the EU legislator, with EU intervention being justified as emergency law and pushing boundaries in criminal law and the constitutional systems of the Union and its Member States. This pattern of EU response has been replicated after successive terrorist incidents, resulting in a patchwork of measures adopted swiftly, without detailed justification or impact assessment and resembling at times kneejerk reactions or quick fixes to complex issues, while presenting significant challenges to fundamental rights and the rule of law in Europe. In recent years, the development of a European security strategy and the publication of regular reports on the Security Union might be said to represent a more strategic response. The Security Union reports, however, betray a tendency to pursue relentlessly and uncritically a security agenda without due consideration for the protection of fundamental rights and the rule of law.

The aim of this contribution is to distil the main features of the EU security agenda that has emerged in recent years, and to outline the challenges for citizenship, fundamental rights and the rule of law, by viewing developments within the EU in the light of parallel developments across the Atlantic. A central element of the argument is that the European Union has embraced a paradigm change from repression to prevention, marked by a shift from criminal to 'security' law, leading towards a paradigm of preventive justice. In

---

[*] I would like to thank Francesca Bignami for her insightful comments on an earlier draft. The usual disclaimer applies.

this process, a number of boundaries have been blurred: the boundaries between migration and security; the boundaries between security and foreign policy and militarisation; the boundaries between internal and external security; the boundaries between public and private prevention, and the increasing role of the private sector in the EU security model; the boundaries between the technical and the legal; and, ultimately, the boundaries between reactive criminal law based on investigations of specific acts and generalised surveillance, embracing surveillance of everyday, perfectly legitimate activities by all of us. By highlighting these parameters of the EU preventive justice paradigm, the chapter concludes by flagging up the profound challenges this paradigm poses for fundamental rights and the rule of law. The contribution urges a rethink of the Security Union to place fundamental values of the Union at the heart of the European security strategy.

II THE EUROPEAN UNION AND PREVENTIVE JUSTICE

Preventive justice is understood here as the exercise of state power in order to prevent future acts that are deemed to constitute security threats. There are three main shifts in the preventive justice paradigm when compared to classic criminal justice: a shift from an investigation of acts which have taken place to an emphasis on suspicion; a shift from targeted action to generalised surveillance; and, underpinning both, a temporal shift from the past to the future. Preventive justice is thus forward rather than backward looking; it aims to prevent potential threats rather than punishing past acts; and in this manner it introduces a system of justice based on the creation of suspect individuals, identified by virtue of ongoing risk assessment.[1] This model of preventive justice has been a key post-9/11 response by the United States, linked with the evolution of a highly securitised, emergency agenda[2] and has been largely transposed to EU law since.

Preventive justice has materialised in a number of areas of state regulation, including criminal law and immigration and border control law. In the field of criminal law, the link between criminalisation and prosecution of concrete

---

[1] Valsamis Mitsilegas, "The European Union and Preventive Justice: The Case of Terrorist Sanctions," in *EU Criminal Law after Lisbon* (Oxford: Hart, 2016), 236–262.

[2] See *inter alia* David Cole, "The Difference Prevention Makes: Regulating Preventive Justice," in *Criminal Law and Philosophy* 9, no. 3 (2015): 501–519; Bruce Ackerman, *Before the Next Attack* (New Haven, CT: Yale University Press, 2006); and Jeremy Waldron, *Torture, Terror and Trade-Offs* (Oxford: Oxford University Press, 2010).

The Preventive Turn in European Security Policy   303

acts is gradually removed;[3] criminal justice is placed within the framework of the 'preventive state',[4] transforming criminal law into 'security law'.[5] The scope of the criminalisation of terrorism is a key example – as evidenced clearly in the recent amendment of the EU substantive criminal law on terrorism to address the phenomenon of 'foreign fighters'.[6] Preventive justice can also be implemented through immigration and border control law, using immigration control to extensively monitor human mobility for security purposes[7] and establish a form of generalised, pre-emptive surveillance.

Key to the development of preventive justice is the collection, processing and exchange of a wide range of personal data. Legal scholar Jacqueline Ross calls this the new surveillance paradigm, which:

> emphasises the aggregation of vast quantities of data about people who are not themselves suspected terrorists, for the purpose of making threat assessments, that is to say, predictive judgments about what kinds of patterns of activity may characterize incipient terrorist plots; what individuals may be particularly susceptible to recruitment as future terrorists; and what patterns of spending and communication tend to be associated with ongoing terrorist conspiracies.[8]

In the EU context, the preventive justice trend is apparent in the development of new databases, the broad access given to security authorities to consult these databases (including on immigration) and the introduction of systems of generalised surveillance through data retention (requiring telecommunication

---

[3] Andrew Ashworth and Lucia Zedner, *Preventive Justice* (New York: Oxford University Press, 2014).

[4] See *inter alia* Peter-Alexis Albrecht, "La Politique Criminelle dans L'État de Prévention," *Déviance et Société* 21, no. 2 (1997): 123–136.

[5] Ulrich Sieber, "Der Paradigmenwechsel vom Strafrecht zum Sicherheitrecht," in *Die Verfassung moderner Strafrechtpflege. Erinnerung an Joachim Vogel*, eds. Klaus Tiedemann et al. (Baden-Baden: Nomos, 2016), 351–372.

[6] See Mitsilegas, "The European Union and Preventive Justice: The Case of Terrorist Sanctions."

[7] Didier Bigo and Elspeth Guild, eds., *Controlling Frontiers: Free Movement into and within Europe* (Aldershot: Ashgate, 2005); Valsamis Mitsilegas, "Human Rights, Terrorism and the Quest for 'Border Security'," in *Individual Guarantees in the European Judicial Area in Criminal Matters*, eds. Marco Pedrazzi, Ilaria Viarengo, and Alessandra Lang (Brussels: Bruylant, 2011), 85–112; Valsamis Mitsilegas, "Immigration Control in an Era of Globalisation: Deflecting Foreigners, Weakening Citizens, Strengthening the State," *Indiana Journal of Global Legal Studies* 19, no. 1 (2012): 3–60.

[8] Jacqueline Ross "The Emergence of Foreign Intelligence Investigations as Alternatives to the Criminal Process: A View of American Counterterrorism Surveillance through German lenses," in *Comparative Criminal Procedure*, eds. Jacqueline Ross and Stephen Thaman (Cheltenham: Edward Elgar, 2016), 494.

304 Valsamis Mitsilegas

companies to retain and transfer customer data to state authorities) and passenger name records (PNR systems requiring airlines to collect and transfer passenger data to state authorities).[9]

The preventive justice paradigm is particularly prominent in the Union's security strategy building the Security Union.[10] As explored later, the consequence has been an all-encompassing agenda that has broken down a number of traditional dividing lines and categories in the law, and in doing so has put pressure on fundamental rights and the rule of law.

III BLURRING THE BOUNDARIES BETWEEN MIGRATION, MOBILITY AND SECURITY

For almost two decades, a key component of EU security policy has been the blurring of the boundaries between immigration control and the fight against crime and terrorism. As the French philosopher and legal scholar Didier Bigo argues, an (in)security continuum has developed, transferring the security considerations of crime control to the field of migration.[11] The insecurity continuum was accentuated after 9/11: the policy and legal response in both Europe and America expressly linked – under the term *'border security'* – border controls with counter-terrorism.[12] In the United States, a key recommendation of the 9/11 Commission Report was to target what was termed 'terrorist travel',[13] resulting in the development of systems of generalised surveillance of mobility such as the establishment of PNR systems aimed to intervene pre-departure and prevent movement if necessary. On the European side, the nexus between migration and security was eloquently captured in the 2004 Hague Programme for EU action in Justice and Home Affairs:

[9] David Lyon, *Surveillance Society: Monitoring Everyday Life* (Buckingham: Open University Press, 2001); Kevin Haggerty and Richard Ericson, "The Surveillant Assemblage," *British Journal of Sociology* 51, no. 4 (2000): 605–622; Louise Amoore and Marieke de Goede, eds., *Risk and the War on Terror* (Oxford: Routledge, 2008); Valsamis Mitsilegas, "The Transformation of Privacy in an Era of Pre-Emptive Surveillance," *Tilburg Law Review* 20, no. 1 (2015): 35–57.

[10] On the foundations of this strategy, see the Communication from the Commission, *The European Agenda on Security*, COM (2015) 185 final (28 April 2015).

[11] Didier Bigo, "Frontier Controls in the European Union: Who Is in Control?" in *Controlling Frontiers: Free Movement into and within Europe*, eds. Didier Bigo and Elspeth Guild (Aldershot: Ashgate, 2005): 49–99.

[12] Valsamis Mitsilegas, "Human Rights, Terrorism and the Quest for 'Border Security'," 85–112.

[13] National Commission on Terrorist Attacks, *The 9/11 Commission Report*, 2004, 385, http://govinfo.library.unt.edu/911/report/911Report.pdf.

the management of migration flows, including the fight against illegal immigration should be strengthened by establishing a continuum of security measures that effectively links visa application procedures and entry and exit procedures at external border crossings. Such measures are also of importance for the prevention and control of crime, in particular terrorism.[14]

Border control measures have thus been adopted and developed as security measures and data obtained in the context of immigration and border control (e.g. data on visa applications, passenger information, etc.) are also viewed as security data which must be available not only to immigration authorities for immigration purposes but also to intelligence and law enforcement authorities for security purposes.[15] In this manner, the law of the border becomes security law, and border controls become avenues of surveillance for counter-terrorism purposes.

The Commission's Communication on the European Agenda for Security, adopted in 2015, emphasised once again the need for a joined-up inter-agency and cross-sectoral approach.[16] This approach reflects a blurring of the boundaries between different areas of EU law and policy, ranging from immigration to criminal justice, foreign policy and defence. The post-9/11 developments chronicled earlier have served as an important laboratory for this security agenda.[17] The 2015 Communication, however, carries the preventive paradigm even further, and announces the intention to monitor the movement not only of third country nationals but also of citizens. For EU law, such a move represents considerable challenges for free movement within an area without internal frontiers and ultimately EU citizenship and the rights which it entails.[18]

This cross-policy and inter-agency approach is based on maximum collection and exchange of personal data and access to EU databases irrespective of

---

[14] European Council, The Hague Programme: Strengthening Freedom, Security and Justice in the European Union, 2004 O.J. (C 53) 1.

[15] For a comprehensive description of these immigration and border control databases, see Chapter 9.

[16] Communication from the Commission, COM (2015) 185 final. For an overview of the EU's internal security strategy, see Chapter 10.

[17] Valsamis Mitsilegas, "Border Security in the European Union: Towards Centralised Controls and Maximum Surveillance," in Whose Freedom, Security and Justice? EU Immigration and Asylum Law and Policy, eds. Elspeth Guild, Helen Toner, and Anneliese Baldaccini (Portland, OR: Hart Publishing, 2007), 359–394.

[18] Valsamis Mitsilegas, "The Borders Paradox: The Surveillance of Movement in a Union without Internal Frontiers," in A Right to Inclusion and Exclusion? Normative Faultlines of the EU's Area of Freedom, Security and Justice, ed. Hans Lindahl (Oxford: Hart, 2009), 33–64. See also part IV infra.

their main purpose or rationale. A constant theme in the seventh and eighth Commission progress report towards the Security Union has been the prioritisation of the interoperability of databases,[19] which has now resulted in EU legislation on interoperability.[20] This blurring of boundaries between the use of various databases has significant consequences for fundamental rights and citizenship. Enabling access to immigration databases such as the Visa Information System (known as VIS, a database containing data of individuals who apply for a Schengen visa and their sponsors) and Eurodac (a database containing data of asylum applicants in the EU) by law enforcement and security authorities overlooks the purpose of immigration law and poses significant challenges to privacy, data protection and non-discrimination.[21] The shift from border control to the generalised surveillance of mobility further serves to extend control and surveillance to *all* travellers, including EU citizens – undermining fundamental principles of free movement and citizenship within the European Union.[22] Blurring boundaries in this manner results in an all-encompassing, yet at the same time amorphous, concept of security, which is constantly prioritised but may serve to undermine key distinctions and limits to the reach of the state in the lives of individuals.

Recent developments on the use of UN Security Council Resolutions to boost EU Common Foreign and Security Policy (CFSP) action on border security under the banner of operation EUNAVFOR MED confirm the blurring of boundaries between immigration, security and defence and result in the militarisation of the border.[23] EUNAVFOR MED is a military crisis management operation that was initially established by Council Decision (CFSP) 2015/778.[24] Its mission is to contribute to the disruption of the business model of human smuggling and trafficking networks in the Southern Central Mediterranean; this is to be achieved by undertaking systematic efforts to identify, capture and dispose of vessels and assets used or suspected of being

---

[19] Communication from the Commission, *Seventh Progress Report towards an Effective and Genuine Security Union*, COM (2017) 261 final (16 May 2017); Communication from the Commission, *Eighth Progress Report towards an Effective and Genuine Security Union*, COM (2017) 354 final (29 June 2017).

[20] See Section VI.

[21] Niovi Vavoula, *Immigration and Privacy in the Law of the European Union: The Case of Databases*, (Leiden: Brill, 2019).

[22] Mitsilegas, "The Borders Paradox," 33–64.

[23] Didier Bigo, "The (In)securitization Practices of the Three Universes of EU Border Control: Military/Navy- Border Guards/Police- Database Analysts," *Security Dialogue* 45, no. 3 (2014): 209–225.

[24] Council Decision (CFSP) 2015/778, On a European Union Military Operation in the Southern Central Mediterranean (EUNAVFOR MED), 2015 O.J. (L 122) 31.

The Preventive Turn in European Security Policy

used by smugglers or traffickers.[25] In June 2015, EUNAVFOR MED officially launched its first phase.[26] The evolution of the EU's legislative framework has been inextricably linked with action by the UN Security Council. On 9 October 2015, the UN Security Council adopted Resolution 2240(2015),[27] which reinforced the authority to take measures against the smuggling of migrants and human trafficking from the territory of Libya and off its coast. Resolution 2240/2015 would be implemented in the framework of Operation Sophia, as agreed by the Council (of the EU) on 18 January 2016. As a result, the operation was authorised to conduct boarding, search, seizure and diversion on the high seas of any suspicious vessels.[28]

This approach continued in the next year with parallel developments at UN and EU level. In June 2016, Resolution 2292(2016) was adopted by the UN Security Council concerning an arms embargo to Libya. The Council (of the EU) extended until 27 July 2017 the mandate of EUNAVFOR MED Operation Sophia, adding two supporting tasks: capacity building and training the Libyan coastguards and navy, particularly in law enforcement tasks at sea; and contributing to the implementation of the UN arms embargo as agreed upon in Resolution 2292(2016) and to information sharing.[29] On 19 December 2016, the Council adopted Decision (CFSP) 2016/2314, increasing the authorisations granted to EUNAVFOR MED Operation Sophia to exchange information with relevant actors.[30] Then, in June 2017, the UN Security Council renewed the authorisations prescribed in Resolution 2292(2016)[31] and the European Council stressed the key role of training and equipping the Libyan Coast Guard as a means of dismantling the business model of smugglers and traffickers.[32] With the deadline of the operation's mandate approaching, on 25 July 2017 the Council (of the EU) extended the mandate of Operation Sophia until 31 December 2018 and further increased the information

---

[25] Council Decision (CFSP) 2015/778, art. 1.
[26] Council Decision (CFSP) 2015/972, Launching the European Union Military Operation in the Southern Central Mediterranean (EUNAVFOR MED), 2015 O.J. (L 157) 51.
[27] Security Council Resolution 2240 (9 October 2015).
[28] Political and Security Committee Decision (CFSP) 2016/118, Concerning the Implementation by EUNAVFOR MED operation SOPHIA of United Nations Security Council Resolution 2240 (2015) (EUNAVFOR MED operation SOPHIA/1/2016), 2016 O.J. (L 23) 63.
[29] Council Decision (CFSP) 2016/993, Amending Decision (CFSP) 2015/778 on a European Union Military Operation in the Southern Central Mediterranean (EUNAVFOR MED operation SOPHIA), 2016 O.J. (L 162) 18, arts. 1 and 3.
[30] Council Decision (CFSP) 2016/2314, Amending Decision (CFSP) 2015/778 on a European Union Military Operation in the Southern Central Mediterranean (EUNAVFOR MED operation SOPHIA), 2016 O.J. (L 345) 62.
[31] Security Council Resolution 2357 (12 June 2017).
[32] European Council Meeting (22 and 23 June 2015) – Conclusions, EUCO 8/17 (23 June 2017).

308 Valsamis Mitsilegas

exchange possibilities, by enabling the transmission not only of data on vessels and their equipment, but also of the relevant information acquired during the performance of core operation tasks.[33]

IV BLURRING THE BOUNDARIES BETWEEN INTERNAL AND EXTERNAL SECURITY

Another key element of the emergence of the preventive justice paradigm, linked inextricably with calls for a multi-purpose and cross-cutting approach, is the merging of internal and external security. This trend is acknowledged by the Commission's 2015 European Agenda on Security. In addition to the blurring of boundaries between internal security and immigration and borders, analysed earlier in the chapter, the Commission focuses on the need to overcome the internal/external security distinction:

> we need to bring together all internal and external dimensions of security. Security threats are not confined by the borders of the EU. EU internal security and global security are mutually dependent and interlinked. The EU response must therefore be comprehensive and based on a coherent set of actions combining the internal and external dimensions, to further reinforce links between Justice and Home Affairs and Common Security and Defence Policy. Its success is highly dependent on cooperation with international partners. Preventive engagement with third countries is needed to address the root causes of security issues.[34]

The emergence of the European Union as a global security actor is not a novel phenomenon. The European Union has played a leading role in negotiating major international and regional conventions on transnational crime and security. Its institutions and certain Member States participate in non-traditional, global security, norm-setting bodies such as the G20 Financial Action Task Force (FATF) and the UN Security Council, both key actors in developing a paradigm of preventive justice in the field of terrorist sanctions.[35] In the normal chain of events, the EU revises its internal *acquis* to comply with the international standards it has contributed to making, claiming that it

---

[33] Council Decision (CFSP) 2017/1385, Amending Decision (CFSP) 2015/778 on a European Union Military Operation in the Southern Central Mediterranean (EUNAVFOR MED operation SOPHIA), 2017 O.J. (L 194) 61, art. 1.

[34] Communication from the Commission, COM (2015) 185 final.

[35] Valsamis Mitsilegas, "The European Union and the Globalisation of Criminal Law," *Cambridge Yearbook of European Legal Studies* 12 (2010): 337–407.

The Preventive Turn in European Security Policy

is essential for the EU legal order to align with global norms.[36] There is thus a process of synergy, which can result in the introduction of far-reaching norms in the EU legal order that may challenge fundamental legal principles.

The evolution of criminal law on 'foreign fighters' is characteristic of this international–EU dynamic.[37] Norms first developed by the UN Security Council have been transplanted into the legal orders of EU Member States first via the revision of the Council of Europe Counter-terrorism Convention and subsequently via the revision of EU substantive criminal law on terrorism.[38] Initially, UN Security Council Resolution 2178 called upon states to ensure that their domestic laws and regulations establish serious criminal offenses for prosecuting foreign terrorist fighters and those involved in their financing and recruitment. The Resolution was transposed in the Additional Protocol to the Council of Europe Convention on the Prevention of Terrorism adopted by the Council of Europe.[39] In addition to widening the categories of preparatory offences,[40] the Protocol introduces a series of provisions expressly criminalising mobility and travel. States are called to adopt such measures as may be necessary to establish 'travelling abroad for the purpose of terrorism' *from its territory or by its nationals*, when committed unlawfully and intentionally, as a criminal offence under its domestic law.[41] Attempt is also criminalised.[42] Travelling abroad for the purpose of terrorism is defined as travelling to a State, which is not that of the traveller's nationality or residence, for the purpose of the commission of, contribution to or participation in a terrorist offence, or the providing or receiving of training for terrorism.[43] The

[36] Valsamis Mitsilegas, "The EU and the Implementation of International Norms in Criminal Matters," in *The External Dimension of the Area of Freedom, Security and Justice*, eds. Marise Cremona, Jörg Monar, and Sara Poli (Brussels: P.I.E. Peter Lang, 2011), 239–272.

[37] For a detailed discussion of foreign terrorist fighters, see Gilles de Kerchove and Christiane Höhn, Chapter 10, this volume.

[38] Valsamis Mitsilegas, "The European Union and the Global Governance of Crime," in *Globalisation, Criminal Law and Criminal Justice: Theoretical, Comparative and Transnational Perspectives*, eds. Valsamis Mitsilegas, Peter Alldridge, and Leonidas Cheliotis (Oxford: Hart, 2015), 153–198.

[39] For a background to the Protocol see Nicola Piacente, "The Contribution of the Council of Europe to the Fight against Foreign Terrorist Fighters," *Eucrim* 1 (2015): 12–15.

[40] Additional Protocol to the Council of Europe Convention on the Prevention of Terrorism (22 October 2015). See the provisions on criminalising the participation in an association or group for the purpose of terrorism (Article 2) and receiving training for terrorism (Article 3).

[41] Additional Protocol to the Council of Europe Convention on the Prevention of Terrorism, art. 4(2).

[42] Additional Protocol to the Council of Europe Convention on the Prevention of Terrorism, art. 4(3).

[43] Additional Protocol to the Council of Europe Convention on the Prevention of Terrorism, art. 4(1).

Protocol also criminalises funding travelling abroad for the purpose of terrorism[44] and organising or otherwise facilitating travelling abroad for the purpose of terrorism.[45] The Additional Protocol has now been ratified by the European Union,[46] which has also revised its internal legislation on the criminalisation of terrorism by adopting a new Directive to align EU law with UN Security Council and Council of Europe standards.[47] As with the regular revisions of EU internal anti-money laundering and terrorist finance law (justified as essential to align the EU acquis with the new standards by the FATF),[48] the extension of EU substantive criminal law on terrorism has followed a paradigm developed initially by the Security Council.

This internalisation of external norms has also occurred in the context of transatlantic security co-operation. A key example in this context is the emergence of preventive legislation on PNR data. The conclusion of a series of EU–US international agreements enabling the transfer of PNR data to US authorities has been the outcome of the need for the EU to comply with unilateral US legal requirements and has been controversial in challenging fundamental rights in the EU legal order.[49] However, and notwithstanding these concerns, recent terrorist incidents in Europe have provided political justification for the internalisation of this model of preventive surveillance in the EU, via the adoption of an 'internal' PNR Directive.[50] The adoption of this Directive poses a significant challenge to EU free movement law, by extending the targets of surveillance from third-country nationals to EU citizens and giving rise to what I have termed 'the Borders Paradox';[51] as far

[44] Additional Protocol to the Council of Europe Convention on the Prevention of Terrorism, art. 5.

[45] Additional Protocol to the Council of Europe Convention on the Prevention of Terrorism, art. 6.

[46] Council Decision (EU) 2018/890, On the Conclusion, on Behalf of the European Union, of the Additional Protocol to the Council of Europe Convention on the Prevention of Terrorism, 2018 O.J. (L 159) 15.

[47] European Parliament and Council Directive (EU) 2017/541, On Combating Terrorism and Replacing Council Framework Decision 2002/475/JHA and Amending Council Decision 2005/671/JHA, 2017 (L 88) 6. See Preamble, recitals 5 and 6.

[48] For the latest EU Directive, see Valsamis Mitsilegas and Niovi Vavoula, "The Evolving EU Anti-Money Laundering Regime: Challenges for Fundamental Rights and the Rule of Law," *Maastricht Journal of European and Comparative Law* 23, no. 2 (2016): 261–293.

[49] Valsamis Mitsilegas, "Transatlantic Counter-terrorism Cooperation and European Values: The Elusive Quest for Coherence," in *A Transatlantic Community of Law*, eds. Deirdre Curtin and Elaine Fahey (Cambridge: Cambridge University Press, 2014), 289–315.

[50] European Parliament and Council Directive (EU) 2016/681, On the Use of PNR Data for the Prevention, Detection, Investigation and Prosecution of Terrorist Offences and Serious Crime, 2016 O.J. (L 119) 132.

[51] Mitsilegas, "The Borders Paradox," 33–64.

The Preventive Turn in European Security Policy 311

as certain Member States are concerned, the PNR Directive applies not only to flights into the EU but also to intra-EU flights.[52] The challenges to EU values that this internalisation of external standards in the field of security can pose should not be underestimated. The recent Opinion of the Court of Justice of the European Union (CJEU) on the EU–Canada PNR Agreement[53] confirms that PNR systems as currently devised fall foul of fundamental rights in the EU.

V BLURRING THE BOUNDARIES BETWEEN THE PUBLIC AND THE PRIVATE: EVERYDAY DATA AND DANGEROUSNESS

The model of preventive justice focuses increasingly on the collection by the state of personal data and the co-option of the private sector in the fight against crime. The collection of personal data involves data generated by ordinary, everyday life activities. This includes records of financial transactions,[54] airline travel (PNR) reservations,[55] mobile phone telecommunications[56] and digital evidence.[57] The focus on monitoring everyday life may thus result in mass surveillance, marked by the collection and storage of personal data in bulk. Inextricably linked with the focus on the monitoring of everyday life for preventive purposes is the privatisation of surveillance under a model of what has been named a 'responsibilisation strategy' aiming to co-opt the private sector in the fight against crime:[58] banks and other financial and non-financial

---

[52] At the time of writing, twenty-three Member States have notified the Commission of their decision to apply the PNR Directive to intra-EU flights. "PNR: List of Member States Who Have Decided to Apply the Directive (EU) 2016/681 to Intra-EU Flights," European Commission website, last visited 10 July 2019, https://ec.europa.eu/home-affairs/news/list-member-states-applying-pnr-directive-intra-eu-flights_en.

[53] Opinion 1/15 of the Court on the EU-Canada PNR Agreement, 26 July 2017, ECLI:EU: C:2017:592.

[54] Valsamis Mitsilegas, *Money Laundering Counter-Measures in the European Union: A New Paradigm of Security Governance versus Fundamental Legal Principles* (The Hague: Kluwer Law International, 2003); Marieke de Goede, *Speculative Security: The Politics of Pursuing Terrorist Monies* (Minneapolis: University of Minnesota Press, 2012).

[55] Valsamis Mitsilegas, "Contrôle des Étrangers, des Passagers, des Citoyens: Surveillance et Anti-Terrorisme," *Cultures et Conflits* 58 (2005): 155–182.

[56] Valsamis Mitsilegas, *EU Criminal Law* (Oxford: Hart, 2009); Arianna Vedaschi and Valerio Lubello, "Data Retention and Its Implications for the Fundamental Right to Privacy: A European Perspective," *Tilburg Law Review* 20, no. 1 (2015): 14–34.

[57] Sergio Carrera, Gloria Gonzalez-Fuster, Elspeth Guild, and Valsamis Mitsilegas, *Access to Electronic Data by Third-Country Law Enforcement Authorities: Challenges to EU Rule of Law and Fundamental Rights* (Brussels: CEPS, 2015).

[58] David Garland, "The Limits of the Sovereign State," *British Journal of Criminology* 36, no. 4 (1996): 445–471.

institutions (including lawyers), airlines, mobile phone and internet providers among others are legally obliged to collect, store and reactively or proactively transfer personal data to state authorities. The privatisation of preventive justice in this manner expands considerably the reach of the state and poses grave challenges to fundamental rights. Everyday and sensitive personal data is now being collected *en masse* and legislation imposes growing demands for bulk data transfers from the private sector to state authorities. This has led to what has been called the 'disappearance of disappearance' – a process whereby it is increasingly difficult for individuals to maintain their anonymity, or to escape the monitoring of social institutions.[59] The use of personal data in these terms leads to a process whereby individuals embarking on perfectly legitimate everyday activities are constantly being assessed and viewed as potentially dangerous without having concrete opportunities to know and contest such assessments. Indeed, even if such opportunities do exist, as privacy law scholar Daniel Solove has noted, predictive determinations about one's future behaviour are much more difficult to contest than investigative determinations about one's past behaviour.[60]

The European Court of Justice has issued a number of judgments condemning this omnipresent surveillance. As the Court of Justice noted in *Tele2* regarding retention metadata:

> That data, taken as a whole, is liable to allow very precise conclusions to be drawn concerning the private lives of the persons whose data has been retained, such as everyday habits, permanent or temporary places of residence, daily or other movements, the activities carried out, the social relationships of those persons and the social environments frequented by them . . . In particular, that data provides the means . . . of establishing a profile of the individuals concerned, information that is no less sensitive, having regard to the right to privacy, than the actual content of communications.[61]

The impact of state intervention on the individual is intensified when one considers the potential of combining personal data from different databases collected for different purposes in a landscape of blurring of boundaries and interoperability, described earlier, in order to create a profile of risk or dangerousness. Mass surveillance is linked closely with ongoing risk

---

[59] Haggerty and Ericson, "The Surveillant Assemblage."

[60] Daniel J. Solove, "Data Mining and the Security-Liberty Debate," *The University of Chicago Law Review* 75, no. 1 (2008): 359.

[61] Joined Cases C-203/15 and C-698/15, *Tele2 Sverige AB v. Post-och Telestyrelsen*, and *Secretary of State for the Home Department v. Tom Watson, Peter Brice, Geoffrey Lewis*, ECLI:EU: C:2016:970, para. 99.

assessment in the preventive justice model. As was noted by a number of Governments intervening in the CJEU EU–Canada litigation, the use of PNR data

> is intended to identify persons hitherto unknown to the competent services who present a potential risk to security, while persons already known to present such a risk can be identified on the basis of advance passenger information data. If solely the transfer of PNR data concerning persons already reported as presenting a risk to security were authorised, *the objective of prevention could consequently not be attained.*[62]

VI BLURRING THE BOUNDARIES BETWEEN THE LEGAL AND THE TECHNICAL

Another dimension of challenges to the rule of law concerns the blurring of boundaries between the legal and the technical, or legislation and technocracy. Since 2007, I have raised these challenges in the emerging EU landscape of border security, noting the dangers of de-politicisation that a growing emphasis on the technical as a basis of EU action may entail.[63] I noted the growing emphasis on the technical in relation to both the creation and development of EU agencies such as the European Border and Coast Guard Agency (Frontex), and to the establishment and interlinking of EU databases. With respect to EU databases, I drew attention to the first iteration of the principle of interoperability in a European Commission Communication from 2005, according to which interoperability is a technical rather than a legal/political concept.[64] These rule of law challenges are particularly acute in the database field as the move to the technical – which will signify enabling surveillance without and outside democratic scrutiny and controls – may have profound implications for civil liberties and the relationship between the individual and the state.

The same rule of law concerns apply even more acutely today, where interoperability appears to be central to the development of an EU system where EU databases containing large quantities of sensitive personal data can be interconnected and accessed by a number of different agencies. Blurred boundaries between the legal and the technical are here superimposed upon

---

[62] Opinion 1/15 of the Court on the EU–Canada PNR Agreement, para. 58 [emphasis added].
[63] Mitsilegas, "Border Security in the European Union."
[64] Communication from the Commission, *On Improved Effectiveness, Enhanced Interoperability and Synergies among European Databases in the Area of Justice and Home Affairs*, COM (2005) 597 final (24 November 2005), 3 in Mitsilegas, "Border Security in the European Union," 391.

blurred boundaries as to the purpose of these databases – as analysed in previous sections, blurred boundaries between migration, mobility and security. Interoperability is deemed to apply notwithstanding the fact that the various EU databases were constructed to serve very diverse purposes, ranging from the facilitation of the assessment of visa and asylum applications (VIS and Eurodac respectively) to police co-operation and counter-terrorism (aspects of the Schengen Information System, established to compensate for the abolition of EU internal borders and the earliest of EU databases), and the databases of Europol (the European Police Office, whose main task is to provide intelligence analysis to EU Member States). Reflecting their different purposes, these databases contain quite diverse categories of data. Interoperability – especially if it is justified under the blanket need for a 'war on terror' – renders meaningless data protection safeguards based on purpose limitations on access and use of these databases. By envisaging maximum linkage of databases, and the extension of the categories of databases included within the interoperability system,[65] the EU is moving into a paradigm where the uncritical application of the technical has the potential to lead to maximum surveillance without strong built-in legal safeguards to protect human rights.[66] This paradigm of maximum information access is reminiscent of a similar approach in the United States[67] to establish a 'Total Information Awareness' programme.[68] The continuous emphasis on the technical and on the possibilities of technology at the expense of the legal and without fully ascertaining the legal consequences of interoperability poses serious challenges to fundamental rights and the rule of law.

The move to the technical is reflected, at the organisational level, by the creation of further layers of technocracy to confuse and undermine democratic oversight. Specialised agencies have been tasked with regulating EU databases and interoperability. The key example is eu-Lisa: an EU agency

---

[65] See the recently passed Regulations on interoperability of databases, European Parliament and Commission, Regulation (EU) 2019/817, 2109 O.J. (L 135) 27 and European Parliament and Commission, Regulation (EU) 2019/818, 2109 O.J. (L135) 85.

[66] The Explanatory Memorandum to the proposal for Regulation 2019/818 refers to 'the urgent need to join up and strengthen in a comprehensive manner the EU's information tools for border management, migration and security.' *Proposal for a Regulation of the European Parliament and of the Council*, COM (2017) 794 final (12 December 2017) 1.

[67] For an early EU–US comparison see Valsamis Mitsilegas, "Borders, Security and Transatlantic Co-operation in the 21st Century: Identity and Privacy in an Era of Globalised Surveillance," in *Immigration Policy and Security: US, European and Commonwealth Perspectives*, eds. Terri Givens, Gary Freeman, and David Leal (New York: Routledge, 2009), 148–166.

[68] For a recent critique, see Bernard E. Harcourt, *The Counterrevolution: How Our Government Went to War against Its Own Citizens* (New York: Basic Books, 2018), 58–59.

established to 'run' the proliferating EU databases, and whose mandate is currently being extended to the regulation of interoperability.[69] It is questionable whether this technical, single-agenda institution is best placed to address the serious legality challenges posed by technical developments at EU level.

VII FROM 'SECURITY LAW' TO PREVENTIVE JUSTICE: CHALLENGES TO HUMAN RIGHTS, CITIZENSHIP AND THE RULE OF LAW

The evolution of Europe's Security Union within a paradigm of preventive justice poses significant challenges for the rule of law, the protection of fundamental rights and citizenship in the European Union. For the rule of law, preventive justice poses serious challenges *ex ante*, since the more nebulous the state action authorised, the more difficult it is to monitor the existence and exercise of EU competence to legislate, to justify the EU action and to guarantee transparency and democratic control. Preventive justice also presents challenges to the rule of law *ex post*:[70] the limits to the arbitrariness of state action and ensuring full and effective judicial scrutiny and control are highly unsatisfactory, as illustrated by the extensive *Kadi* litigation in the CJEU.[71] In these cases, the CJEU ultimately upheld the model of preventive terrorist sanctions and avoided ruling on whether long-term preventive terrorist sanctions amounted, in effect, to criminal sanctions triggering the safeguards of criminal law.[72] The move towards preventive justice further undermines *ex ante* rule of law because it generally is coupled with efforts to bypass standard democratic scrutiny processes by framing matters as responses to emergency security threats. A key example is the recent criminalisation of conduct related to 'foreign fighters', discussed earlier. The EU

---

[69] See European Council Press Release 285/18, eu-LISA: Agreement between the Council Presidency and the European Parliament (24 May 2018), according to which new legislation has been agreed to entrust the agency with developing and operating new EU systems and for eu-LISA to contribute *to the development of technical solutions to achieve interoperability* [emphasis added]. The repeated emphasis on the technical is noteworthy.

[70] On the distinction between rule of law *ex ante* and *ex post* see Valsamis Mitsilegas, "Rule of Law: Theorising EU Internal Security Cooperation from a Legal Perspective," in *Theorising European Internal Security*, eds. Raphael Bossong and Mark Rhinard (Oxford: Oxford University Press, 2016), 113–114.

[71] Joined Cases C-402/05 and C-415/05, *Kadi and Al Barakaat International Foundation* v. *Council and Commission*, ECLI:EU:C:2008:461 [hereinafter *Kadi I*]; Joined Cases C-584/10, C-593/10, and C-595/10, *Commission and Others* v. *Kadi*, ECLI:EU:C:2013:518 [hereinafter *Kadi II*].

[72] Mitsilegas, "The European Union and Preventive Justice. The Case of Terrorist Sanctions."

legislation was framed as 9/11-style emergency law, with no impact assessment and without full scrutiny of the constitutional implications of these proposals.

A paradigm of security based upon preventive justice challenges a number of fundamental rights, including the principle of legality in criminal offences and sanctions and the presumption of innocence (via the preventive criminalisation of terrorism and organised crime). The paradigm also compromises the right to an effective remedy and effective judicial protection. Moreover, with respect to the data surveillance measures discussed earlier in this chapter, the rights to non-discrimination, privacy and data protection are undermined. In a series of landmark rulings, the CJEU has upheld the importance of the rights to data protection and privacy and found generalised pre-emptive surveillance contrary to EU law.[73] The Court has further confirmed that the EU fundamental rights benchmark is also applicable in the Union's external action, both in the field of judicial co-operation in criminal matters[74] and in the field of data exchange.[75]

A string of constitutional cases on preventive data retention measures has highlighted the close link between protecting the right to privacy and upholding citizenship ties by safeguarding trust in the relationship between the individual and the state.[76] This trust is being eroded under a system of maximum surveillance under interoperability, where every citizen is seen as a potential threat.[77] It also breaks the fundamental link between privacy, democracy and citizenship which underpins the social contract in liberal societies today. According to the German Constitutional Court:

> a preventive general retention of all telecommunications traffic data . . . is, among other reasons, also to be considered as such heavy infringement because it can evoke a sense of being watched permanently . . . The individual does not know which state official knows what about him or her, but the individual does know that it is very possible that the official does know a lot, possibly also highly intimate matters about him or her.[78]

---

[73] Joined Cases C-293/12 and 594/12, *Digital Rights Ireland and Seitlinger*, ECLI:EU:C:2014:238; *Tele2 Sverige AB*; Opinion 1/15 of the Court on the EU–Canada PNR Agreement.

[74] Case C-182/15, *Petruhhin v. Latvijas Republikas*, ECLI:EU:C:2016:630.

[75] Case C-362/14, *Schrems v. Data Protection Commissioner*, ECLI:EU:C:2015:650.

[76] Valsamis Mitsilegas, "The Value of Privacy in an Era of Security," *International Political Sociology* 8, no. 1 (2014): 104–108.

[77] For instance, in one of the Commission's proposals on interoperability, the aim is laid out as *the correct identification of bona fide persons* and combating identity fraud. *Proposal for a Regulation of the European Parliament and of the Council*, COM (2017) 794 final, 7 [emphasis added].

[78] Bundesverfassungsgericht, Judgment 1 BvR 256/08, 1 BvR 263/08, 1BvR 586/08 of 2 March 2010, para. 214.

The Romanian Constitutional Court has noted that data retention addresses all law subjects, regardless of whether they have committed criminal offences or they are the subject of a criminal investigation, which is likely to overturn the presumption of innocence and to transform *a priori* all users of electronic communication services or public communication networks into people susceptible of committing terrorism crimes or other serious crimes. According to the Romanian Court, continuous data retention is sufficient to generate in the mind of the persons legitimate suspicions regarding the respect of their privacy and the perpetration of abuses [by the state].[79] These concerns have been reflected in the case-law of the CJEU, where the adverse impact of generalised preventive surveillance without an explicit link to a specific suspicion has been highlighted.[80] In its recent ruling in *Tele2*, which built upon the Court's ruling in *Digital Rights Ireland*, the CJEU noted that the interference of systematic and continuous data retention with the rights to privacy and data protection is very far-reaching and must be considered to be particularly serious, as the fact that the data is retained without the subscriber or registered user being informed is likely to cause the persons concerned to feel that their private lives are the subject of constant surveillance.[81] The Court noted that the national legislation in question, which was found to be contrary to EU law, affects all persons using electronic communication services, even though those persons are not, even indirectly, in a situation that is liable to give rise to criminal proceedings.[82] In the context of surveillance and data technologies, protecting the right to privacy is essential for upholding citizenship ties in a democratic society.

VIII THE WAY FORWARD: FROM A 'SECURITY CRISIS' MENTALITY TO THE RESTORATION OF THE RULE OF LAW

Behind the preventive justice paradigm and the many blurrings and rule-of-law challenges covered in this chapter has been the emergence of a 'security

---

[79] Romanian Constitutional Court, Decision No. 1258 of 8 October 2009.

[80] For an overview and on the specific link between surveillance and suspicion see Valsamis Mitsilegas, "Surveillance and Digital Privacy in the Transatlantic 'War on Terror': The Case for a Global Privacy Regime," *Columbia Human Rights Law Review* 47, no. 3 (2016): 1–77.

[81] *Tele2 Sverige AB*, para. 100.

[82] *Tele2 Sverige AB*, para. 105. See also Opinion 1/15 of the Court on the EU–Canada PNR Agreement, where the Court noted that 'as regards air passengers in respect of whom no such risk has been identified on their arrival in Canada and up to their departure from that non-member country, there would not appear to be, once they have left, a connection – even a merely indirect connection – between their PNR data and the objective pursued by the envisaged agreement which would justify that data being retained' (para. 205).

crisis' mentality. A key factor behind this transformation has been the emergence of perceived 'global threats', the prime one being, of course, terrorism, with the 9/11 attacks and the subsequent attacks in London and Madrid in the 'oos. These justified the blurring of boundaries of legality at many levels, not only in the EU but also in the United States, and have resulted in a transatlantic paradigm of preventive justice.

At least initially, the transatlantic convergence was not total. EU law provided resilient defences to a number of attempts to blur boundaries in the name of security, in particular as regards attempts to blur boundaries between immigration control and security. In recent years, however, it seems that such resistance has become increasingly futile. There is now a new 'security crisis' mentality, a political reflex to new terrorist attacks in Europe (including in Paris, Berlin and Nice), as well as by the influx of refugees into Europe during the war in Syria. This crisis mentality has been stoked by a deliberate confluence – if not confusion – between responses to terrorist attacks and responses to refugee flows. The new political environment has resulted in a further blurring of the boundaries of legality and a re-invigorated focus on the maximum collection, processing, exchange and transfer of personal data as a simple solution to the perceived crises.

This chapter has attempted to cast light on the significant perils of the preventive justice paradigm to human rights and the rule of law, as well as to fundamental structures of liberal societies today. Political institutions involved in law-making in the EU are demonstrating less and less appetite for departing from the securitised paradigm of mass surveillance. Resistance has emerged largely from the judiciary: it has taken the judiciary on both sides of the Atlantic to push back on security excesses stemming from the post 9/11 crisis mentality. The CJEU is still holding strong in defending privacy in view of concerted efforts at mass surveillance, but it has many other battles to fight and courts are inevitably reactive in this context. This chapter calls for growing vigilance and for an attempt to reframe the debate. It is necessary to leave behind the 'security crisis' mentality and the associated knee-jerk emergency responses and to adopt a more reflective approach, aimed at managing security within a solid framework of human rights and the rule of law.

12

The Opening Salvo

The CLOUD Act, e-Evidence Proposals, and EU–US Discussions Regarding Law Enforcement Access to Data across Borders

JENNIFER DASKAL[*]

On March 23, 2018, the Clarifying Lawful Overseas Use of Data (CLOUD) Act went into effect, mooting a pending US Supreme Court case and establishing a new mechanism for bilateral cooperation on law enforcement access to data.[1] Specifically, the Act updates the Stored Communications Act (SCA)[2] and specifies that US warrants for stored communications data require service providers to disclose all responsive data in their custody, or control, regardless of where the underlying data is stored.

The Act also authorizes the United States to enter into executive agreements with partner governments, pursuant to which the partner governments can, in specified situations and in accordance with a number of statutorily required safeguards, directly request both stored and real-time communications content from US-based companies.

Less than a month later, on April 17, 2018, the European Commission put forth its legislative proposals related to law enforcement access to electronic evidence: a draft Regulation on European Production and Preservation Orders[3] and a draft Directive on the appointment of legal representatives.[4] Akin to provisions in the CLOUD Act, the Regulation would, if adopted,

---

[*] Special thanks to Francesca Bignami for putting together such a terrific volume, inviting me to contribute, and editing my work.

[1] Clarifying Lawful Overseas Use of Data (CLOUD) Act, Pub. L. No. 115-141, div. V (2018) (enacted) (to be codified in scattered sections of 18 U.S.C.) [hereinafter CLOUD Act].

[2] Stored Communications Act (SCA)18 U.S.C. §§ 2701–2713 (2018).

[3] *Commission Proposal for a Regulation of the European Parliament and of the Council on European Production and Preservation Orders for Electronic Evidence in Criminal Matters,* COM (2018) 225 final (April 17, 2018) [hereinafter Draft e-Evidence Regulation].

[4] *Commission Proposal for a Directive of the European Parliament and of the Council Laying Down Harmonised Rules on the Appointment of Legal Representatives for the Purpose of Gathering Evidence in Criminal Proceedings,* COM (2018) 226 final (April 17, 2018) [hereinafter Draft e-Evidence Directive].

319

authorize law enforcement officials from one EU Member State to directly request electronic data from a service provider located in another Member State. The Directive, if adopted, would require service providers that operate in the EU to designate at least one legal representative in the EU, thereby ensuring that there is a place to serve process and compel production of sought-after data, even if the service provider is located outside the territorial boundaries of the EU.

This chapter addresses and analyzes these parallel and independent, yet remarkably similar, developments. It begins by identifying the key, underlying issues that motivated these initiatives. It then delves into details about both the CLOUD Act and e-evidence proposals – highlighting their many similarities and uncovering their differences. And it concludes with some thoughts about the implications for international law making and norm-setting in this space.

I THE BACKGROUND

1 *The Changing Dynamic*

Until relatively recently, most evidence sought in the prosecution of criminal activity was based in the investigating and prosecuting jurisdictions' territory. To be sure, there have long been cartels and other criminal actors that operate across multiple states. And globalization and other shifts in technology (i.e. think of the shifts spurred by airplanes) have facilitated the movement of people and goods across borders. But, historically, most investigations have been local. And the relevant evidence local as well. As a result, criminal investigations that required access to evidence or witnesses across territorial borders remained the exception rather than the rule.

The development of a globally interconnected Internet and cloud storage has changed that. Increasingly, users in State A contract with and use email services or social media companies that are based in State B. Meanwhile, service providers may store a user's data across an international border, perhaps even across an ocean.[5] The user may have never stepped foot in, or have any other connection to, the jurisdiction where either the service provider is located or the data is stored.

---

[5] I use the term "service provider" broadly to refer to email service providers, social media companies, and the range of other entities that manage or hold digital information of their users that is or may be of interest to law enforcement entities.

The Opening Salvo

321

These technological shifts have created a range of challenges for law enforcement. This is so for three key reasons. First, digital evidence is increasingly critical to many, if not most, criminal investigations. Second, the digitalization of communications and other information brings an additional, but critically important, and often quite powerful, player into the mix. Rather than tracking or searching a target and his or her possessions directly, law enforcement increasingly seeks – and arguably needs – information that is held in the hand of third-party service providers. As a result, these service providers significantly control, via a combination of technological, business, and policy decisions, how much evidence is available to law enforcement. Third, data sought by law enforcement is often either held outside the investigating nation's territorial border or controlled by service providers located across international borders – or perhaps both. A recent European Commission report found that over half of all criminal investigations involve a cross-border request for digital evidence.[6]

This third factor in particular – the fact that digital evidence is often held or controlled by providers across territorial borders – creates a number of both legal uncertainties and practical difficulties. As a matter of law, a combination of international law norms and longstanding state practice generally prohibit law enforcement in State A from unilaterally searching and seizing property located in State B, absent State B's consent. This makes good sense. After all, most of us would feel pretty uneasy about, say, a law enforcement agent from Moscow showing up on the doorstep of a target in, say, Chicago or London, and asserting the right to search his or her home based on an authorization issued by the Kremlin. Instead, states are generally required to employ what is known as the mutual legal assistance (MLA) process – making a diplomatic request for the evidence and waiting for the jurisdiction with control over the data to respond.

The MLA process, however, is slow and cumbersome. It depends on the recipient (what I call "assisting") government agreeing with and assisting the requesting government in its investigation. More often than not, this is low on the priority list for the assisting government. Even when seeking to facilitate access, it often takes assisting governments months or longer to respond, due

---

[6] Commission Staff Working Document, Impact Assessment Accompanying Proposal for a Regulation of the European Parliament and of the Council on European Production and Preservation Orders for Electronic Evidence in Criminal Matters and Proposal for a Directive of the European Parliament and of the Council Laying Down Harmonised Rules on the Appointment of Legal Representatives for the Purpose of Gathering Evidence in Criminal Proceedings, SWD (2018) 118 final (April 17, 2018), 14 [hereinafter EC Impact Assessment].

in part to the number of steps that each response requires. If, for example, a foreign government seeks emails held by a US-based provider, the request is first evaluated by the Department of Justice. If approved, the request is sent to a US attorney's office, which must seek a warrant for the data based on a probable cause standard from a US judge. (Needless to say, requesting data on behalf of foreign governments is not always a top priority for prosecutors that have their own cases to investigate and pursue.) Once obtained, the warrant is served on the service provider. The service provider transmits the data back to the prosecutor, and the Department of Justice then does another review before transmitting the data to the requesting government. According to a 2013 study, the US government took an average of ten months to respond to incoming MLA requests.[7] Since then, there have been some efforts to streamline the process. But the volume of requests continues to increase, which likely increases wait times as well.

Perhaps more importantly, effective use of the MLA system requires clarity as to which territorial state has jurisdiction over the data of interest. Put another way, it requires background agreement as to when a state can unilaterally compel production and when it must make a diplomatic request for data of interest. But these are issues that are the subject of ongoing discussion and dispute. Should sovereign control be based on where the underlying data is located.[8] The place where the provider that manages the data is headquartered? Any place that the provider or his or her legal representative is located? Or perhaps it should turn on factors totally separate from the location of either the provider or underlying data – such as the location or nationality of the target of the search? Equally importantly, who decides – particularly when sovereign interests collide?

Governments have, via domestic legislation, sometimes taken steps to dictate the answers to these questions. US law, for example, has long prohibited the disclosure of US-held communications content to foreign governments, thereby requiring that foreign governments employ the MLA system if they are seeking US-held content from a US-based provider.[9] The

---

[7] Richard Clarke et al., "Liberty and Security in a Changing World," December 12, 2013, 227, https://obamawhitehouse.archives.gov/sites/default/files/docs/2013-12-12_rg_final_report.pdf.

[8] This was the position of Microsoft and several amici in briefing to the United States Supreme Court. See generally Jan Philipp et al., *Brief of Amici Curiae in United States v. Microsoft*, No. 17-2, 138 S.Ct. 1186 (2018).

[9] See Stored Communications Act (SCA), 18 U.S.C. §§ 2702, 2703, 2711(4) (together establishing that disclosures can, pursuant to specified procedures and rules, be made to US governmental officials, but not to foreign officials).

EU's General Data Protection Regulation similarly prohibits the transfer of EU-held data regarding EU citizens and residents outside the EU, unless certain conditions are met; this has the effect of, among other things, shifting law enforcement requests for EU-held data regarding EU citizens and residents into the MLA system or other government-to-government agreements on cooperation in law enforcement matters.[10] The EU's telecommunications framework also currently prohibits national telecommunications providers from responding directly to requests from foreign authorities.[11] These kinds of transfer restrictions are known as blocking statutes.

But absent consensus as to the jurisdictional rules that apply, such kinds of blocking statutes create potent conflicts of laws. Imagine State A asserting the authority to directly compel the production of data that State B says cannot be shared. Companies are caught in the middle – forced to choose which law to violate and which to comply with, and sometimes with dramatic consequences. This is more than a hypothetical concern. A Microsoft executive in Brazil, for example, was arrested and detained for failing to disclose data that US law prohibited him from sharing.[12] Others have been arrested or threatened with arrest for failure to disclose.

Both the CLOUD Act and the draft e-evidence proposals are a direct response to these challenges. They seek to facilitate law enforcement access to data across borders and to set baseline norms both as to the jurisdictional rules and as to the minimal substantive and procedural protections required. Both initiatives move away from location of data as key to determining access and control. Both acknowledge and address the risk and reality of legal conflict. And both identify baseline protections that all requesting governments must comply with.

But they also differ in key ways. Most obviously, the CLOUD Act is now law, whereas the EU e-evidence proposals remain just that – proposals. But they also differ in scope and effect. The following details these two efforts, highlighting the many similarities as well as the key differences.

---

[10] See European Parliament and Council Regulation (EU) 2016/679, On the Protection of Natural Persons with Regard to the Processing of Personal Data and on the Free Movement of Such Data, and Repealing Directive 95/46/EC, 2016 O.J. (L 119) 1, arts. 48 and 49 [hereinafter General Data Protection Regulation]; see also Jennifer Daskal, "Microsoft Ireland, CLOUD Act, International Lawmaking 2.0," *Stanford Law Review Online* 71 (May 2018): 9.

[11] EC Impact Statement, 2.2.2

[12] Brad Smith, "In the Cloud We Trust," *Microsoft News*, January 21, 2015, https://news.microsoft.com/stories/inthecloudwetrust/.

II THE LEGISLATIVE SOLUTIONS: ENACTED AND PROPOSED

1 *The CLOUD Act*

1.1 CLOUD Act Part I: The Reach of US Warrants

The CLOUD Act contains two parts. The first part (what I call "CLOUD Act Part I") clarifies the reach of the warrant authority under the SCA – the issue that was at the heart of the then-pending *Microsoft Ireland* case in the US Supreme Court.[13] The case dates to December 2013, when the US government sought emails that were held by Microsoft but stored in Dublin, Ireland. Microsoft refused to turn over the emails; it argued that the United States' warrant authority was territorially limited and that the Department of Justice could not use its warrant authority to access them. According to Microsoft, it needed to make an MLA request to Ireland to obtain the sought-after emails.

The US government countered that Microsoft controlled and could access the data from its headquarters in Washington; what mattered was the location of Microsoft, not the underlying os and 1s. This was, according to the government, a territorial exercise of its warrant authority that did not require resort to a mutual legal assistance request directed at Ireland.

The magistrate and district court judges sided with the government.[14] But the Second Circuit reversed, ruling in favor of Microsoft.[15] The result, according to the Second Circuit: the US warrant under the SCA authority only reaches US-held data, even if the target, crime, and victims are all US-based. Any time the data is held outside the United States, US law enforcement must seek the data from the country where the data is located.

But while this rule worked relatively well for Microsoft, which holds its data in relatively stable locations, it created a range of problems when applied to other companies. Data held by Google, for example, is constantly being moved around; Google operates what Professor Paul Schwarz has labeled

---

[13] See *United States* v. *Microsoft*, No. 17-2, 138 S.Ct. 1186 (2018).

[14] *In re* Warrant to Search a Certain E-mail Account Controlled and Maintained by Microsoft Corp., 15 F.Supp.3d 466, 477 (S.D.N.Y. 2014).

[15] *Microsoft Corp.* v. *United States* (*In re* Warrant to Search a Certain E–Mail Account Controlled and Maintained by Microsoft Corp.) (*Microsoft Ireland*), 829 F.3d 197 (2d Cir. 2016), *reh'g denied, Microsoft Corp.* v. *United States* (*In re* Warrant to Search Certain E-Mail Account Controlled and Maintained by Microsoft Corp.), 855 F.3d 53 (2d Cir. 2017) (en banc).

the Data Shard model.[16] Sometimes single accounts are split up into different parts (or shards), with, say, the text of emails in one location and attachments including photos in another. This creates numerous problems for law enforcement: First, even a single target's emails and attachments could be held in multiple different jurisdictions, meaning that law enforcement may have to make multiple different requests to multiple different locations. Second, the locations themselves are constantly shifting meaning there is no stable location for requests. Third, there is often no way for law enforcement to learn the relevant location absent disclosure by the company. Fourth, some companies, such as Google, assert that only its US law enforcement team can access the data, regardless of where the underlying os and 1s are located. Thus, even if law enforcement could identify the location where extraterritorially located data is held, the relevant foreign government would not have jurisdiction over the people that could produce it.[17]

A rule that limits access based solely on location of data is also often hard to justify on a normative level. Data location is, after all, generally the result of private sector business decisions based on things like tax rates, energy costs, and efficiency. Thus, whereas the data may be in the same territorial location as the crime or user being investigated, it might not be. In fact, there might not be any connection whatsoever between where the data happens to be located and the criminal activity at issue or the individual whose data is sought. In such situations, there is no good justification in applying the access rules of the place where the data is located. The host government likely has no interest in the case. And the user will have no say in the rules governing access and no mechanism – via mechanisms of democratic accountability or otherwise – in expressing a preference about those rules.[18]

The CLOUD Act responds to these concerns. It effectively overturns the Second Circuit's ruling in the Microsoft case and makes clear that US warrant authority reaches all data within the relevant company's custody or control, without regard to the location of the underlying os and 1s. But as the Act also explicitly recognizes, the reach of US warrant authority to any and all data within US-based tech companies' custody and control risks conflict with

---

[16] Paul M. Schwartz, "Legal Access to the Global Cloud," *Columbia Law Review* 118 (2018): 1681–1762.

[17] *In re* Search Warrant No. 16-960-M-01 to Google, 232 F. Supp.3d 708, 712–713 (E.D. Pa. 2017).

[18] See Jennifer Daskal, "Borders and Bits," *Vanderbilt Law Review* 71, no. 1 (2018): 188–191; Jennifer Daskal, "The Un-Territoriality of Data," *Yale Law Journal* 125, no. 2 (2015): 390–391; Schwartz, "Legal Access to the Global Cloud," 1695 (noting that data held in what he labels a data shard cloud is "constantly in motion"; "national boundaries are largely irrelevant").

foreign law. It thus includes two provisions addressing the issue of "comity" – the legal test that a court uses when deciding how to deal with conflicting legal regimes.

First, it creates a new statutory basis for providers to move to quash based on comity grounds.[19] When a covered conflict arises, a reviewing court must consider the "totality of the circumstances" in deciding whether to enforce the warrant. In so doing, the court is directed to take into account factors such as the relevant interests of both the United States and foreign government, the location and nationality of the person whose communications are being sought, the likelihood that the provider would be subject to penalties for disclosing the data to the United States, the importance of the data to the investigation, and the likelihood that it could be obtained in an alternative timely and effective matter.[20] The statute thus provides guidance as to the relevant factors to consider, although leaves unspecified how to resolve that conflict in any given case.

That said, this new statutory provision applies in very limited situations – when the United States seeks the data of a foreigner located outside the United States and the request generates a conflict with the law of a "qualifying" foreign government. Qualifying foreign governments are those with an executive agreement with the United States. At the time of writing, this was a null set. Moreover, the whole point of becoming a qualifying government is to minimize legal conflict, meaning that the set of cases in which the statutory comity provisions can and will be invoked are likely to be few and far between.

Second, the CLOUD Act explicitly preserves the availability of so-called common-law comity claims in those situations where the request generates a legal conflict and the new statutory-based comity claims are not available – because, for example, the conflict is not with a qualifying foreign government.[21] The statute does not, however, specify the factors that apply to the evaluation of the common-law comity claim, leaving it up to the courts to determine how to evaluate such claims, if and when they arise. The factors identified in connection with the new statutory-based comity claims will presumably provide guidance, but they are not binding. And even if they were binding, they do not specify the resolution of any specific case or fact pattern.

---

[19] CLOUD Act §103(b).
[20] CLOUD Act §103(b).
[21] CLOUD Act §103(c).

1.2 CLOUD Act Part II: Foreign Government Access

The second part of the Act (what I call "CLOUD Act Part II") responds to foreign government concerns resulting from the blocking provisions that prohibit the sharing of US-held content with foreign governments.[22] It allows for these blocking provisions to be lifted, but only pursuant to executive agreements between the United States and partner foreign nations and subject to a number of conditions that limit which foreign governments would be eligible for such agreements, whose data they can obtain, and how the data is both requested and used. Importantly, the agreements do not compel providers to comply with foreign government requests or place any other affirmative obligations on the providers. They simply lift blocking provisions that would otherwise prohibit such sharing.

The scope and details of these agreements are subject to numerous conditions. First, foreign governments are only eligible if the Attorney General, in conjunction with the Secretary of State, certifies in writing, and with an accompanying explanation, that the foreign government "affords robust substantive and procedural protections for privacy and civil liberties" with respect to relevant data collection activities.[23]

Second, the agreements only cover the data of foreigners located outside the United States. Foreign governments seeking data of persons located in the United States or US citizens or legal permanent residents, regardless of where they are located, must still employ the mutual legal assistance process and make a diplomatic request for the data. In other words, if a foreign government seeks the communications content of a US citizen or resident, it must ultimately obtain a US-issued warrant based on a standard of probable cause. If, however, it seeks the data of a foreigner outside the United States, it can seek to directly compel production, pursuant to its own domestic laws. This reflects a normative view that US law and procedure should govern access to US citizen and resident data, even when the data is being sought by a foreign government. Conversely, however, the United States has no equivalent justification in insisting on the application of US-specific rules and procedures when the foreign government seeks access to foreigners' data, so long as baseline conditions are met.

Third, the Act specifies a number of baseline requirements that foreign government requests must satisfy. The requests must be particularized, meaning they must target a *specific* person, account, address, personal device, or other

---

[22] CLOUD Act §105.
[23] CLOUD Act §105.

identifier. The requests must be based on "articulable and credible facts" – a standard that is more readily understandable to non-US law enforcement than the US-specific standard of probable cause. The requests must be subject to review or oversight by a court, judge, or magistrate or other independent authority. And the data may not be used to infringe the freedom of speech.

Fourth, the agreements also include a number of requirements as to use of collected data. The data must be stored on a "secure system" accessible only to those "trained in applicable procedures."[24] The foreign government is required to segregate, seal, or delete non-relevant information.[25] Notably, these use-based requirements are *added* protections compared to the status quo. Under the current mutual legal assistance process, the US government has little say as to how data is handled or used once it has been disclosed.

Fifth, the agreements are subject to accountability provisions. The partner government must agree to compliance reviews by the United States to ensure that these requirements are in fact met.[26] And the executive agreements must be renewed every five years or they expire.

Sixth, the partner government must agree to analogous and reciprocal rights of access for US law enforcement seeking data that is held in and controlled by service providers located in their country. Thus, the foreign government must agree to lift and otherwise avoid any blocking provisions that would preclude a provider located within that foreign government's jurisdiction from disclosing data directly to the United States, pursuant to lawful process and baseline standards.

No such agreement can go into effect until it has been sent up to Congress and 180 days have passed without objection. As of this writing, no such agreement has been finalized and sent to Congress, let alone implemented. But the United Kingdom and United States have reportedly been in discussions about a potential agreement along these lines for several years; it is expected that a US–UK agreement will be ultimately completed and sent to Congress. The EU is possibly next. In June 2019, the Council of the EU authorized the Commission to open negotiations with the United States on an agreement on access to e-evidence, although there are a range of issues to be resolved, including basic issues as to whether an agreement can and should be made with the EU as a whole or state-by-state.[27]

---

[24] CLOUD Act §105.

[25] CLOUD Act §105.

[26] CLOUD Act §105.

[27] Council of the EU Press Release 421/19, Council Gives Mandate to Commission to Negotiate International Agreements on e-Evidence in Criminal Matters (June 6, 2019); see also Jennifer Daskal and Peter Swire, "A Possible EU-US Agreement on Law Enforcement Access to Data?"

2 *The e-Evidence Regulation*

Akin to the data sharing provisions included in the CLOUD Act Part II, the draft e-Evidence Regulation sets up a mechanism for authorities in one EU Member State to compel the production of stored data held by a service provider established or represented in another Member State. The draft Regulation is coupled with a draft e-Evidence Directive that requires service providers offering services in the EU to locate a representative in at least one Member State so as to ensure the possibility to compel production.

If enacted, the e-Evidence Regulation would mark a significant shift in how intra-EU data sharing takes place. Since the 1990s, several EU laws have been adopted to facilitate judicial and police cooperation in criminal investigations. But all such provisions provide for varying degrees of government-to-government cooperation. Even the newly implemented European Investigation Order, which went into effect in May 2017 and was widely hailed as speeding up cross-border investigations, relies on principles of mutual recognition and requires the investigating prosecutor to work through the prosecutor in the state with jurisdiction over sought-after data in order to preserve or access the sought-after evidence.[28] The draft e-Evidence Regulation, by contrast, allows the investigating prosecutor to go directly to the provider to make the request.

In so doing, it contains many similarities to the CLOUD Act. It shifts the focus away from the location of data as the key determinant of jurisdiction. And it sets up an expedited mechanism for an EU Member State to obtain data held by providers in another Member State.

But there are also key differences. It is significantly more ambitious in scope. Whereas the CLOUD Act Part II serves simply to lift blocking provisions that prohibit providers from sharing data across borders, the draft e-Evidence Regulation goes much farther. It sets out a comprehensive scheme that both eliminates blocking provisions and other barriers that prevent cross-border sharing *and* sets out affirmative compliance obligations on the part of service providers to respond within specified (and short) time frames.

But it is also narrower in scope in some key regards as well. Notably, the bilateral agreements authorized by the CLOUD Act cover requests for both

---

Lawfare (blog), May 21, 2018, www.lawfareblog.com/possible-eu-us-agreement-law-enforcement-access-data/.

[28] See, e.g., European Commission Press Release IP/17/1388, As of Today the 'European Investigation Order' Will Help Authorities to Fight Crime and Terrorism (May 22, 2017); European Parliament and Council Directive 2014/41/EU, Regarding the European Investigation Order in Criminal Matters, 2014 O.J. (L 130) 1.

stored data and real-time intercepts. The draft e-Regulation, by contrast, explicitly excludes real-time intercepts from its scope.

The following describes how the e-Evidence Regulation operates, highlighting the similarities and differences between its operation and that of the CLOUD Act. In so doing, it focuses primarily on the draft regulation as initially proposed by the European Commission in April 2018. But it is also worth noting that these provisions are the subject to ongoing revision. The Council of the EU has subsequently adopted its own modified draft, which will ultimately need to be reconciled with a separate, and yet to be agreed upon, Parliament draft in order to become law.[29]

2.1 Location of Data

Like the CLOUD Act, the draft e-Evidence Regulation rejects location of data as a basis for delimiting access. As described in the European Commission's explanatory text:

> [The draft Regulation] moves away from data location as a determining connecting factor [for determining jurisdiction], as data storage normally does not result in any control by the state on whose territory data is stored. Such storage is determined in most cases by the provider alone, on the basis of business considerations.[30]

The European Commission thus makes clear that service providers' obligation to produce data in response to a lawful order applies "regardless of the location of data."[31] And it includes an exclusive list of grounds for the service provider to object to either a Production or Preservation Order. Location is not included on the list. Moreover, while the draft Regulation recognizes the possibility of legal conflict, it explicitly states that location of data is not, in and of itself, a valid basis for asserting conflict with foreign law.

There is thus consistency across the Atlantic on this question, at least for purposes of the draft Regulation and CLOUD Act: location of data should not determine or delimit access. (That said, other parts of EU law make location of data key.[32]) As I have written extensively elsewhere, this is a result that

---

[29] Council of the EU, Note, 2018/0108(COD) (November 30, 2018), www.data.consilium.europe .eu/doc/document/ST-15020-2018-INT/en/pdf.

[30] Draft e-Evidence Regulation, 13.

[31] Draft e-Evidence Regulation, art. 1(1).

[32] See, e.g., General Data Protection Regulation, art. 48 (seeking to control transfers of data outside the EU, thereby implicitly imposing something akin to a data localization mandate, albeit with numerous exceptions).

The Opening Salvo

makes sense; location of data should not be determinative of law enforcement jurisdiction.[33]

2.2 Breadth and Specificity

The draft e-Evidence Regulation is broader in scope than the CLOUD Act Part II in that it defines and covers a full range of stored digital evidence – not just communications content. It defines four categories of data – ranging from the name of a subscriber (labeled "subscriber data") to the time and duration of logins ("access data") to location data and routing information ("transactional data") to communications content ("content data").[34] But it is also narrower in one critical way as well: it covers stored data only; it does not authorize real-time intercepts or prospective collection.

The draft Regulation also sets out different requirements for accessing the different kinds of data, depending on the sensitivity of the data. Thus, orders for subscriber and access data can be issued or otherwise validated by prosecutors, whereas orders for transactional and content data can only be issued or validated by a judge or court.[35] Orders can be issued for subscriber or access data in connection with any criminal investigation; orders for content and transactional data can only be issued in connection with specified offenses.[36]

2.3 Baseline Requirements/Rights Protections

As with the CLOUD Act Part II, the draft e-Evidence Regulation seeks to set a range of baseline requirements that must apply. Requests for data must, in all cases, be necessary and proportionate.[37] This is akin to, albeit not identical to, the requirements of particularity and a finding of specific and articulable facts supporting cross-border requests under the bilateral agreements anticipated by the CLOUD Act Part II.[38] Orders for content and transactional data must, as stated previously, be signed off by a judge or

---

[33] See Daskal, "Borders and Bits"; Daskal, "The Un-Territoriality of Data."

[34] Draft e-Evidence Regulation, art. 2 (7)–(10) (defining the separate categories of data covered).

[35] Draft e-Evidence Regulation, art. 4(1)–(2).

[36] Draft e-Evidence Regulation, art. 5(3)–(4).

[37] Draft e-Evidence Regulation, art. 5(2).

[38] See Jennifer Daskal and Peter Swire, "Why the CLOUD Act Is Good for Privacy and Human Rights," *Lawfare* (blog), March 14, 2018, www.lawfareblog.com/why-cloud-act-good-privacy-and-human-rights/. But see Neema Singh Guilani and Naureen Shah, "The Cloud Act Doesn't Help Privacy and Human Rights: It Hurts Them," *Lawfare* (blog), March 16, 2018, www.lawfareblog.com/cloud-act-doesnt-help-privacy-and-human-rights-it-hurts-them; Jennifer Daskal and Peter Swire, "Privacy and Civil Liberties under the CLOUD Act: A Response,"

court. These also are analogous to requirements in the CLOUD Act, also requiring judicial or independent review.

But there are also important differences in the requirements between the CLOUD Act and Commission e-Evidence proposals. The draft Commission e-Evidence Regulation, for example, explicitly addresses the question of notice to the target of the investigation. Pursuant to the draft Regulation, the issuing government can preclude the provider from notifying the target that his or her data is being sought. But the issuing government is required to provide notice at some point – once there is no longer a necessary and proportionate basis for the delay. The Council's draft differs in that it incorporates a default gag order on the provider informing the target. But it too requires governmental notice, albeit with an exception if necessary and proportionate to protect the fundamental rights and legitimate interests of another person.

By contract, neither Part I nor Part II of CLOUD Act requires governmental notice. Under the first part – dealing with the scope of US compulsion orders – and coupled with other provisions of the SCA, the US government is not required to notify the target of an investigation that his or her data has been collected if the data is obtained via warrant. In such situations, there is no requirement of governmental notice, unless and until the data is being used in a criminal prosecution. The United States also can seek, consistent with the Commission draft, a court order to preclude the provider from disclosing this information to the target "for such period as the court deems appropriate."[39] Once the delayed notification order expires, however, the provider is permitted to inform the target.

In addition, the long list of requirements that foreign governments must meet in order to be eligible to enter into executive agreements with the United States, as laid out in the CLOUD Act Part II, do not include any requirements with respect to target notice. That said, the CLOUD Act only specifies the minimum requirements that each agreement must include. Nothing precludes the executive from adding additional requirements – including on notice – as it negotiates specific agreements.

2.4 Comity

As with the CLOUD Act Part I, the draft e-Evidence Regulation explicitly recognizes the risk that data requests conflict with the laws of third countries

---

Lawfare (blog), March 21, 2018, www.lawfareblog.com/privacy-and-civil-liberties-under-cloud-act-response/.

[39] Stored Communications Act (SCA), 18 U.S.C. § 2705(b).

The draft Commission e-Evidence Regulation is much more specific than the CLOUD Act in this regard, laying out certain redlines and clear procedure for how these claims are raised.[40] If the conflict is based on protections for either fundamental rights of individuals or the fundamental interest of the third country in national security or defense, the third country's laws trump. In such situations, the order will not be enforced.

The draft Commission e-Evidence Regulation also sets out clear procedures for considering the interests of third party countries in determining whether such a conflict exists. If a reviewing court agrees that there is in fact a conflict and that the conflict is based on fundamental rights or interest of a third country, it must notify that third-country government. The government then has a specified amount of time to raise an objection. Absent objection, the issuing authority can proceed. But if there is an objection and if the court agrees that it is based on fundamental rights or interests, then the order is quashed.

If, however, the conflict is based on something other than fundamental rights or interests, then the court engages in a multi-factored test without directly engaging the third-country government. The court is told to consider, among other considerations, the relevant interests of the countries, the location, nationality and residence of the person whose data is being sought, the location, nationality and residence of any victims, the place where the criminal offense occurred, and the degree of connection between the service provider and the third country.

The draft e-Evidence Regulation thus differs from the CLOUD Act in two important respects. First, the CLOUD Act's provisions on comity are found in Part I only and thus only address challenges to the reach of US warrant authority. The CLOUD Act Part II is silent as to this issue. It does not address the possibility that a foreign government request for US data might impinge on third countries' laws and interests. And it does not give any guidance as to how such conflicts should be handled.

Second, the CLOUD Act applies a balancing test to all conflicts that arise; unlike the Commission e-Evidence Regulation, it does not recognize any redlines designed to protect fundamental rights or interests of third countries. Notably, the draft Council regulation is much more akin to the CLOUD Act in this regard. Among other changes, it eliminates the obligation to notify third party states and to dismiss in certain circumstances – thus applying a

---

[40] Draft e-Evidence Regulation, arts. 15 and 16.

334 Jennifer Daskal

balancing test in all cases, as is done in the CLOUD Act, and without clear redlines or any clear mechanism for obtaining third-party input.[41]

2.5 Obligations on Service Providers

The CLOUD Act Part II and its anticipated bilateral agreements serve merely to lift US blocking provisions, thereby protecting against US rules that prohibit service providers from disclosing data to a foreign government. It does not place any affirmative obligations on service providers to comply, although the law of the foreign government could in theory impose such obligations.

Reflecting the quasi-federalist, as opposed to international, character of the EU, the draft e-Evidence Regulation goes much further, placing specific obligations on service providers and setting out the possibility of penalties for non-compliance. It sets out very specific obligations of the service providers – to respond within ten days to production orders and within six days in cases of emergency. It requires that providers provide a reason for rejection and imposes a preservation obligation during the pendency of a dispute. And it specifies the specific instances in which a provider may refuse compliance. Under the Commission proposal, this can be due to an impossibility (e.g. lack of relevant data), a belief that the request "manifestly" violates the EU's Charter of Fundamental Rights, or a belief that is "manifestly" abusive.[42] The draft Council Regulation, however, eliminates the possibility of objection based on a concern of manifest abuse or violation of fundamental rights, thereby eliminating a key basis by which individual rights might be protected. It also provides the option of large fines being imposed on providers for noncompliance.[43]

2.6 Enforcement Procedure

Because the CLOUD Act does not place any affirmative obligation on service providers to comply, it is silent as to the question of enforcement if and when a service provider fails to respond to a foreign government demand for data. The draft e-Evidence Regulation, by contrast, sets out clear enforcement proced-ures. The so-called competent authority – meaning the relevant authority in

---

[41] Theodore Christakis, *E-Evidence in a Nutshell*, Cross Border Data Forum (January 14, 2019), www.crossborderdataforum.org/e-evidence-in-a-nutshell-developments-in-2018-relations-with-the-cloud-act-and-the-bumpy-road-ahead/?cn-reloaded=1.

[42] See Draft e-Evidence Regulation, art. 9.

[43] Draft e-Evidence Regulation, art. 9(5).

The Opening Salvo

the state in which the provider is based – is required to enforce the order, absent a legitimate and specified basis for objection. Legitimate grounds for not transferring the information include a finding that the data is protected by a privilege or immunity under the competent authority's national law or that the disclosure will impact governmental interests such as national security and defense.[44]

III BROADER IMPLICATIONS AND GOING FORWARD

The CLOUD Act and draft e-Evidence proposals resulted from independent, yet parallel, initiatives on both sides of the Atlantic. They were motivated by similar concerns about the need for evidence across state borders and the difficulties in accessing this evidence in a timely and efficient manner. Notably, both deal exclusively with law enforcement access – saying nothing about separate security services or intelligence agencies. And both recognize the need for baseline protections governing access to data – although they do so in different ways.

Importantly, the CLOUD Act is now law, whereas the e-Evidence Regulation and Directive remain drafts. This has led some Europeans – and others – to complain that the United States is imperialistically setting the standards. It is, after, all, an example of what I have called international lawmaking 2.0 – with key international norms regarding privacy and access to data being set unilaterally and then imposed extraterritorially, as opposed to the more traditional process of nation states coming together and negotiating norms and rules.[45]

But this is a phenomenon that is not just limited to data access, and not just limited to the United States. Consumer safety, environmental regulations, and an array of intellectual property rules have long been imposed unilaterally by states with significant market power and then exported elsewhere.[46] And with respect to consumer privacy, the EU has largely taken the lead, with the

---

[44] Draft e-Evidence Regulation, art. 14.

[45] See Daskal, "Microsoft Ireland, CLOUD Act, International Lawmaking 2.0," 15–16. I am hardly the only one to have noted this phenomenon. See also Anu Bradford, "The Brussels Effect," *Northwestern University Law Review* 107, no. 1 (2012): 1–68; Gregory Shaffer, "Globalization and Social Protection: The Impact of EU and International Rules in the Ratcheting Up of US Privacy Standards," *Yale Journal of International Law* 25, no. 1 (2000): 1–88; Austin L. Parrish, "Reclaiming International Law from Extraterritoriality," *Minnesota Law Review* 93 (2009): 815–874.

[46] See, e.g., Bradford, "The Brussels Effect"; Joanne Scott, "From Brussels with Love: The Transatlantic Travels of European Law and the Chemistry of Regulatory Attraction," *American Journal of Comparative Law* 57, no. 4 (2009): 897–942.

United States on the receiving end of extraterritorially imposed obligations – and complaining about EU unilateralism.[47] The EU's General Data Protection Regulation and data transfer restrictions are key examples.[48] In these situations, it is the EU that is imposing its vision of data privacy and protection on those that want to do business in Europe or transfer data out of Europe.

Whatever one thinks of the merits, this kind of lawmaking is the reality. It is simply not a workable solution for states, at least in the short-term, to come together and achieve global consensus as to access and disclosure rules, although that does seem like a laudable long-term goal.[49] Moreover, there is a risk that any attempt at international consensus building will lead to a watering down of protections, with things like standard of proof, role (or not) of independent review, and obligations (or not) of particularity devolving to the lowest common denominator.

The following addresses some of the benefits, costs, and opportunities provided by this approach. In so doing, I largely focus on Part II of the CLOUD Act, both because it is current law and because it has broader, geographic implications than the e-Evidence proposals, which have primary effect exclusively within the EU.

1 *The Benefits*

Whatever one thinks of the CLOUD Act, Part II of the Act includes a long list of requirements that each and every foreign government must meet in order to be eligible for an executive agreement. And despite the shortcomings, this list is more privacy protective than the domestic rules applicable in many, if not most, countries around the world and likely more privacy protective than any set of requirements that would have emerged from a broad, multilateral process. Among other key elements, the requirements incorporate key restrictions on use, requirements of particularity, and mandated independent oversight or review.

These requirements need to be understood in comparison not just to the status quo, but in comparison as to future, anticipated developments. Some have complained that the executive agreements envisioned permit foreign governments to access US-held communications content based on standards

---

[47] See, e.g., Mark Scott and Laurens Cerulus, "Europe's New Data Protection Rules Export Privacy Standards Worldwide," *Politico*, February 6, 2018, www.politico.eu/article/europe-data-protection-privacy-standards-gdpr-general-protection-data-regulation//.

[48] See General Data Protection Regulation, art. 48.

[49] See, e.g., Brad Smith, "The Need for a Digital Switzerland," *Microsoft Blog*, February 14, 2017, https://blogs.microsoft.com/on-the-issues/2017/02/14/need-digital-geneva-convention/.

The Opening Salvo 337

that are less protective than the otherwise applicable warrant based on probable cause.[50] But such critiques of the CLOUD Act assume a stable status quo pursuant to which the United States holds much of the world's content data and the requests for such data are channeled through the MLA process – a likelihood that seems unrealistic given the growing interest and need for cross-border data. Absent some mechanism to better facilitate law enforcement access across borders, states are developing – and in key respects, already have developed – unilateral means to obtain data of interest, whether via data localization mandates or unilateral extraterritorial assertions of jurisdiction.

Thus, the key comparison is not US standards versus CLOUD Act standards, but foreign government standards versus CLOUD Act standards. And in *this* regard, the CLOUD Act provides protections that are often greater than, and incentivizes foreign governments to adopt protections that are more privacy-protective than, the status quo. In fact, some have expressed concerns that the Act is so demanding that few countries will be able to meet the standards laid out. If that is ultimately the case, then the greatest promise of the CLOUD Act will be lost.

Importantly, the agreements envisioned by the CLOUD Act must also include a number of requirements that provide *added* protections, even above the status quo. Under the MLA system, the United States has relatively little say in how foreign governments use data once it has been disclosed. The Act, by contrast, requires foreign governments to put in place numerous protections focused on use. Among other requirements, the data must be stored on a "secure system" accessible only to those "trained in applicable procedures."[51] The foreign government is required to segregate, seal, or delete non-relevant information.[52] In addition, the foreign government must agree to periodic reviews by the United States government to ensure that the provisions of the executive agreement are being followed.[53] These use-based requirements are additional protections over the current regime.

---

[50] See, e.g., Neema Singh Guilani and Naureen Shah, "The CLOUD Act Doesn't Help Human Rights: It Hurts Them," *Lawfare* (blog), March 16, 2018, www.lawfareblog.com/cloud-act-doesnt-help-privacy-and-human-rights-it-hurts-them.

[51] CLOUD Act (to be codified at 18 U.S.C. § 2523 (b)(4)(F)).

[52] CLOUD Act (to be codified at 18 U.S.C. § 2523 (b)(4)(G)).

[53] CLOUD Act (to be codified at 18 U.S.C. § 2523 (b)(4)(J)). There are other precedents in the data protection field for such audits. Both the US–EU Passenger Name Records (PNR) Agreement and the US–EU Terrorist Finance Tracking Program (TFTP) Agreement provide for periodic joint reviews of how the transferred data is being handled. For the latest EU reports, see *Report from the Commission to the European Parliament and the Council on the Joint Review of the Implementation of the Agreement between the European Union and the United States of America on the Processing and Transfer of Passenger Name Records to the*

2 Limits and Costs

This kind of unilateral standard-setting also has both limitations and costs. First, and most obviously, the absence of multilateral consensus building means, in many cases, the absence of multi-state buy-in and support. Second, if the standards imposed are too high, too contested, or too contrary to foreign government rules and approaches, the entire exercise may be rejected. States can and will simply continue to find alternative means of acting on their own, and thus the promise of unilateral standard-raising, at least of the kind envisioned by part II of the CLOUD Act, is lost. Third, and relatedly, the sense of exclusion of those governments that are not currently, and may never be, eligible for CLOUD Act-like agreements, may incentivize those governments to actually accelerate efforts to identify other means of access, whether via data localization or by extraterritorial means of either compelling production or accessing directly (i.e. direct, remote hacking).

On a more substantive level, the elimination of assisting state review – pursuant to both part II of the CLOUD Act and the draft e-Evidence Regulation – eliminates a key protection for targets of investigation. Under the MLA system, there are two governmental checks, one by the requesting government and the other by the assisting government, before evidence is disclosed. Both the executive agreements envisioned by the CLOUD Act and e-Evidence proposals eliminate that second-layer review.

In one respect, this is no different than what would happen if the data were held locally, within the requesting state's territorial borders. In such situations, there is only one layer of review: that of the requesting state where the data is located. But in such situations, the provider is local, meaning that the provider is or at least should be expected to be familiar with the requesting government's laws, policies, and practices – and hence can effectively assess the legitimacy of the request. By contrast, the nature of cross-border requests means that the requesting government is asking a provider located in *another* jurisdiction to review the request and respond. This requires providers to be familiar with and responsive to laws and practices of multiple different, requesting jurisdictions, including jurisdictions in which the provider lacks

---

United States Department of Homeland Security, COM (2017) 29 final (January 19, 2017); *Report from the Commission to the European Parliament and the Council on the Joint Review of the Implementation of the Agreement between the European Union and the United States of America on the Processing and Transfer of Financial Messaging Data from the European Union to the United States for the Purposes of the Terrorist Finance Tracking Program*, COM (2017) 31 final (January 19, 2017).

any physical presence. This puts a burden and responsibility on providers to understand and assess the legitimacy of multiple different governmental requests, something that can be difficult for providers to do.

At a minimum, this shift highlights the need for robust standards and procedural protections on the front end, in terms of what kind of requests can be made, as well as increased accountability and transparency on the back end to protect against abuse. It also highlights the need for, and benefit of, default third-party notification, if and when the target of the data request is located in a state other than that of the issuing government. Such notification ensures that the state where the target resides can, if it so chooses, launch a complaint and thereby take steps to protect its own residents. Unhelpfully, the draft Council e-Evidence Regulation includes such a third-party notification requirement, if and when the issuing state is seeking the data of someone located outside its territory, but directs the notice to the state where the service provider is located. The location of the service provider may be totally separate from the location of the target, however. In those situations, the state where the service provider is located likely will not, as a result, have any incentive to protect the interests of the individual whose data is being sought. A preferable approach would be to notify the state where the target of the request is located.

3 Ongoing Opportunities

Both the CLOUD Act and the e-Evidence initiative can and should be considered the opening salvo in a set of ongoing conversations and developments that will shape future developments on access to data and the baseline protections that apply. The specifics of e-Evidence are, as of this writing, subject to ongoing debate and there are thus ongoing opportunities to set the baseline rules.

Moreover, the CLOUD Act lays out the baseline requirements only. It thus creates a *floor* that each and every agreement must meet as a matter of US law, without setting or identifying the ceiling. Additional provisions can be added to any agreement that is reached to deal with a range of potential issues, such as target notice, protections of fundamental rights, enforcement mechanisms, and standards for resolving legal conflict, if and when such conflicts occur. At a minimum, executive agreements entered into under the CLOUD Act can and should lay out steps to be taken if foreign government requests do not satisfy the range of baseline requirements included in either the Act or specific agreements. In such situations, the provider should be required to preserve the data in question but also given the opportunity to seek review from the US government. And it should be protected from foreign government action during the pendency of review. This will allow for greater accountability and help ensure enforcement of the baseline norms.

The agreements also can and should crib from the Commission e-Evidence proposal and specify that requests for data cannot infringe on the fundamental rights of third parties (meaning non-residents and non-citizens of either the United States or partner government) or fundamental interests of third-party governments. If and when a provider concludes that a request conflicts with such fundamental rights or interests, it can and should elevate that request to either the government or court where it operates. If there in fact appears to be a legal conflict affecting fundamental rights or interests, the third-party government should be given a reasonable opportunity to weigh in.

Meanwhile, some of the innovative features of the CLOUD Act can and should migrate into other parts of US law. The CLOUD Act Part II requires a number of use-based protections on collected information. As stated previously, any unreviewed information must be on a secure server accessible only by authorized individuals. Partner governments also must segregate, seal, or delete, and not disseminate, irrelevant information.[54]

These kinds of use limitations should be applied more broadly. A combination of case law and statutory law already sets stringent limits on law enforcement access to communications content – requiring a US warrant approved by a judge and subject to the relatively robust standard of probable cause.[55] But most of the statutory provisions focus on collection, rather than use. In fact, an increased focus on use is something that the EU may require as a condition of accessing and transferring EU-resident data. European Court of Justice cases such as the 2017 judgment striking down the EU–Canada agreement on the collection and use of passenger name records suggest that absent adequate protections in how data is used and disseminated, data sharing agreements may be found to violate the EU Charter of Fundamental Rights.[56] Meanwhile, Privacy Shield is already in

---

[54] CLOUD Act §105.

[55] See Stored Communications Act (SCA), 18 U.S.C. §2703; United States v. Warshak, 631 F.3d 266, 288 (6th Cir. 2010) (holding individual retains reasonable expectation of privacy in contents of emails stored with, or sent or received through a commercial provider); United States v. Carpenter, 819 F.3d 880 (6th Cir. 2016) (holding individual retains reasonable expectation of privacy in record of movements obtained through cell-site location information), rev'd, 138 S.Ct. 2206, 2217 (2018).

[56] See European Court of Justice (Grand Chamber) Opinion 1/15, 2017 O.J. (C 309) 3, 4.

trouble because of analogous concerns about how US-held data is collected and used.[57]

IV CONCLUSION

The CLOUD Act and draft e-Evidence Regulation and Directive are important developments, both designed to better facilitate law enforcement access to data and also to set baseline standards. They are opening salvos in what is likely to be an ongoing discussion about law enforcement access to data across borders and the baseline rules that apply. And, in fact, the parties to the Council of Europe's Budapest Convention on Cybercrime are currently at work on a draft protocol designed to also facilitate cross-border access to data.[58] There is, undoubtedly, much more work to be done to harmonize approaches, ensure adequate protection of collected data, and safeguard the legitimate interests of affected individuals and states. But both the EU and United States have made important – and largely progressive – starts. These efforts should be supported, built on, and monitored – and thereby improved and strengthened in their implementation and development over time.

---

[57] See European Parliament Press Release, Suspend EU–US Data Exchange Deal, Unless US Complies by 1 September, Say MEPs (July 5, 2018), www.europarl.europa.eu/news/en/press-room/20180628IPR06836/suspend-eu-us-data-exchange-deal-unless-us-complies-by-1-september-say-meps.

[58] Specifically, in June 2017, Member States gave themselves eighteen months to draft an additional protocol to the Convention that would, among other things, allow for direct cooperation between law enforcement and service providers located across borders for a range of non-content data. Cybercrime Convention Committee, "Preparation of a Draft 2nd Additional Protocol to the Budapest Convention on Cybercrime," June 1, 2017, 3, https://rm .coe.int/-draft-terms-of-reference-for-the-preparation-of-a-draft-2nd-additiona/168071b794.

13

Preserving Article 8 in Times of Crisis

Constraining Derogations from the European Convention on Human Rights

MARC ROTENBERG AND ELENI KYRIAKIDES

The European Convention on Human Rights (ECHR) has been enormously influential among international instruments in defining and defending individual rights around the world. Article 8, in particular, is the most widely recognized source of legal authority for privacy as a claim of fundamental rights.[1] However, even under ideal conditions these values are maintained only with "eternal vigilance," as the truism states. Especially in times of emergency, states are under pressure to constrict rights enshrined in international instruments and domestic law. One attempt to sustain rights through times of crisis is Article 15 of the ECHR, which permits some derogation of human rights as an extraordinary measure. The Convention provides for derogation only where the very "life of the nation" is under threat, the response strictly limited, and as consistent with other obligations under international law. In this way, the European Convention allows for limited state deviation from established international norms; by providing for the conditional and supervised derogation from their obligations under the Convention,[2] Article 15 recognizes state needs while incentivizing states not to abandon the commitment to defend rights. In total, nine states have relied on Article 15 since the Convention was

[1] See, e.g., Gianclaudio Malgieri and Paul De Hert, "European Human Rights, Criminal Surveillance, and Intelligence Surveillance: Towards 'Good Enough' Oversight, Preferably but not Necessarily by Judges." Working Paper vol. 3, no. 9, Brussels Privacy Hub, 2017, 1. For more on the importance of international instruments for privacy protection, see Marc Rotenberg, "From European to International Standards on Data Protection," Remarks before Council of Europe and European Commission in Brussels, Belgium for Data Protection Day, January 28, 2011. https://epic.org/privacy/intl/coeconvention/ROTENBERG_COE_Jan28.pdf.

[2] Research and Library Division, European Court of Human Rights, Guide on Article 15 of the European Convention on Human Rights (2018), 5, www.echr.coe.int/Documents/Guide_Art_15_ENG.pdf.

established – Ukraine, Albania, Armenia, France, Georgia, Greece, Ireland, Turkey, and the United Kingdom.[3] France and Turkey most recently called states of emergency.[4]

However, citing the threat of international terrorism, today national "states of emergency" are arising more frequently among parties to the Convention, and at a significant cost to human rights. In particular, encroachment on the Article 8 right to respect for private and family life, the home, and correspondence is endemic. A state of emergency initiated by France in 2015 granted the government sweeping authority to track individuals electronically and conduct digital searches. The state of emergency terminated in 2017, only to be replaced by anti-terrorism legislation that made certain powers permanent. Meanwhile, under a state of emergency declared in 2016, Turkey has broadly surveilled social media activities and banned the use of privacy protective technologies like Virtual Private Networks (VPNs); there too, the termination of the state of emergency in July 2018 did not bring significant improvements in the rule of law. France's arguably more moderate emergency contrasts with Turkey's derogation, marked by largely untethered discretion. These expansions of derogation authority demand new solutions to ensure members of the Council of Europe do not abandon their longstanding human rights obligations. This derogation from Article 8, important in its own right, is a case study in a larger Western crossroads; it is representative of a modern tension between the national and international. In the face of today's new challenges, will international institutions rise to the task of reinforcing human rights, or will they falter in favor of national action?

Section I of this chapter reviews the procedures for derogation under Article 15 of the Convention, as developed by the European Court of Human Rights (ECtHR). Next, Section II describes recent case studies in derogation from Convention obligations in France and Turkey, with a focus on Article 8 privacy rights. Section III assesses the validity of the derogations based on the Article 15 standards described in Section I. Finally, Section IV sets out recommendations to ensure state compliance with human rights obligations, proposing collaborative response between NGOs and the Council of Europe to cabin derogation from the Convention.

---

[3] Press Unit, European Court of Human Rights, Derogation in Time of Emergency (2018), 2, www.echr.coe.int/Documents/FS_Derogation_ENG.pdf.

[4] Press Unit, European Court of Human Rights, 2.

I DEROGATION UNDER THE ECHR

Article 15 "Derogation in Time of Emergency" of the ECHR governs any official derogation, such as the recent decisions of France and Turkey to declare a "state of emergency" described in Section II. In the Council of Europe's history, only eight nations out of the forty-seven parties to the convention have claimed the benefits of Article 15 (Albania, Armenia, France, Georgia, Greece, Ireland, Turkey, and the United Kingdom) and four (Greece, Ireland, the United Kingdom, and Turkey) have had cases brought against them before Council of Europe (CoE) institutions.[5] Other human rights instruments like the International Convention on Civil and Political Rights (ICCPR) also contain similar derogation articles.[6]

Article 15 sets out the basic conditions for parties to the Convention to validly derogate from the Convention obligations during a time of national emergency. Article 15 reads:

1. In time of war or other public emergency threatening the life of the nation any High Contracting Party may take measures derogating from its obligations under this Convention to the extent strictly required by the exigencies of the situation, provided that such measures are not inconsistent with its other obligations under international law.

2. No derogation from Article 2, except in respect of deaths resulting from lawful acts of war, or from Articles 3, 4 (paragraph 1) and 7 shall be made under this provision.

3. Any High Contracting Party availing itself of this right of derogation shall keep the Secretary General of the Council of Europe fully informed of the measures which it has taken and the reasons therefor. It shall also inform the Secretary General of the Council of Europe when such measures have ceased to operate and the provisions of the Convention are again being fully executed.[7]

In sum, Article 15's three sections: first, set the conditions for valid derogation, second, prohibit derogation from certain rights, and, third, require official notification of derogation measures.

---

[5] Press Unit, European Court of Human Rights, 1.

[6] International Covenant on Civil and Political Rights art. 4, December 16, 1966, 999 U.N.T.S. 171 (entered into force March 23, 1976).

[7] Convention for the Protection of Human Rights and Fundamental Freedoms art. 15, November 4, 1950, 213 U.N.T.S. 222 [hereinafter ECHR].

Supervising Convention parties' reliance on the article, ECtHR case law spanning half a century[8] has developed each of these Article 15 requirements.[9] And while the ECtHR indicated any review of Article 15 derogations is limited, this same precedent makes equally clear that Article 15 is available to parties only as an extraordinary measure and subject to certain basic strictures.[10] Each of the requirements of sections of Article 15, as detailed in ECtHR precedent, is described in turn in the subsections that follow.

1 Article 15(1): Criteria for Valid Derogation

Section 1 of Article 15 sets out the criteria for valid derogation under the ECHR. A party may derogate only if the three criteria of 15(1) are satisfied: (i) there is a "time of war or other public emergency threatening the life of the nation," (ii) any measures are limited to what is "strictly required by the exigencies of the situation," and (iii) the measures do not conflict with the nation's other international law obligations.[11]

1.1 "Time of War or Other Public Emergency Threatening the Life of the Nation"

First, for a valid derogation from the ECHR the party must be facing a "time of war or other public emergency threatening the life of the nation."[12] In *Lawless* v. *Ireland*, the ECtHR further defined the second clause ("other public emergency") as "an exceptional situation of crisis or emergency which affects the whole population and constitutes a threat to the organised life of the community of which the State is composed."[13] Nations receive deference in determining whether a "time of war or other public emergency threatening

---

[8] Key ECtHR Article 15 jurisprudence has also occasionally been supplemented by the now defunct European Commission of Human Rights, including the influential Commission opinion in the "Greek Case." *Denmark* v. *Greece*, App. No. 3321/67, 1969 Y.B. Eur. Conv. on H.R. 12 (European Commission on Human Rights) [hereinafter the *Greek Case*].

[9] Edward Crysler, "Brannigan and McBride v. UK: A New Direction on Article 15 Derogations under the European Convention on Human Rights?" *Nordic Journal of International Law* 65, no. 1 (1996): 92–121.

[10] See, e.g., Frederick Cowell, "Sovereignty and the Question of Derogation: An Analysis of Article 15 of the ECHR and the Absence of a Derogation Clause in the ACHPR," *Birkbeck Law Review* 1, no. 1 (2013): 143–144.

[11] ECHR art. 15, §1.

[12] ECHR art. 15, §1.

[13] *Lawless* v. *Ireland* (no. 3), 3 Eur. Ct. H.R. (ser. A) (1961), para. 28.

the life of the nation" exists.[14] This "wide margin of appreciation" is warranted because of national authorities' "direct and continuous contact with the pressing needs of the moment, the national authorities are in principle better placed than the international judge."[15] However, this deference is not absolute,[16] and the Court will still review state compliance with this requirement of Article 15 section 1.

To qualify for Article 15 derogation the ECtHR has also stated that the national emergency:

> should be actual or imminent; that it should affect the whole nation to the extent that the continuance of the organised life of the community was threatened; and that the crisis or danger should be exceptional, in that the normal measures or restrictions, permitted by the Convention for the maintenance of public safety, health and order, were plainly inadequate.[17]

A flexible analysis, the Court will accommodate a "broad[] range of factors" in its assessment.[18] For instance, the sheer extent and difficulty of effectively combatting Kurdish separatist violence in south-east Turkey rose to the level of a "public emergency threatening the life of the nation."[19] Following the 9/11 terrorist attacks in the United States, the Court found a "threat to the life of the nation," where the Secretary of State of the United Kingdom had issued credible evidence to show a threat of serious terrorist attacks against the United Kingdom, even though no attack had taken place.[20] The Court has not expressly held that an emergency measure must be temporary. Case law has demonstrated that a valid "public emergency" within the meaning of Article 15 may be years long.[21] However, the Court has, albeit inconsistently, considered temporality in assessing the second prong of Article 15(1), namely the proportionality of the measures.[22]

---

[14] *Ireland* v. *United Kingdom*, 25 Eur. Ct. H.R. (ser. A) (1978), para. 207.
[15] *Aksoy* v. *Turkey*, 1996-VI Eur. Ct. H.R., para. 68.
[16] See, e.g., *Greek Case* (rejecting the nation's assessment that there were grounds for derogation under Article 15).
[17] *Greek Case*, para. 153.
[18] *Greek Case*, para. 179.
[19] *Aksoy*, paras. 69–70.
[20] A. v. *United Kingdom*, 2009-II Eur. Ct. H.R., para. 177.
[21] See, e.g., *Ireland* v. *United Kingdom*, paras. 11–12 (citing the "tragic and lasting crisis in Northern Ireland" continuing for a period of four years).
[22] For further discussion of ECtHR assessments of temporality of emergency measures under Article 15(1), see Jan-Peter Loof, "Crisis Situations, Counter Terrorism and Derogation from the European Convention of Human Rights: A Threat Analysis," in *Margins of Conflict: The ECHR and Transitions to and from Armed Conflict*, ed. Antoine Buyse (Antwerp: Intersentia, 2010), 35–56.

1.2 "To the Extent Strictly Required by the Exigencies of the Situation"

Second, for a valid derogation from the ECHR, any measures undertaken to address the emergency must be limited to that which is "strictly required by the exigencies of the situation."[23] Again, parties to the ECHR are entitled to "a wide margin of appreciation" to determine what type and scope of the measures are required.[24] However, as with the analysis of any alleged "emergency" the Court will still review the party's emergency measures to determine whether they were "strictly required."[25] Likewise, the ECtHR will evaluate all relevant factors bearing on whether the measures were "strictly required" in a particular emergency.[26] Among many other considerations,[27] the Court has looked to whether the measures were used for a "purpose other than that for which they were granted,"[28] "whether ordinary laws would have been sufficient to meet the danger,"[29] whether "it was a genuine response to the emergency situation,"[30] "whether adequate safeguards were provided against abuse,"[31] "whether the need for the derogation was kept under review,"[32] "whether a derogating measure encroaches on a fundamental convention right,"[33] and whether the measure was unjustifiably discriminatory.[34]

1.3 "Not Inconsistent with Its Other Obligations under International Law"

Third, and straightforwardly, the derogation from the ECHR may not be inconsistent with the party's other obligations under international law.[35] Where the party's other international commitments are violated – e.g. obligations under the International Convention of Civil and Political Rights, the Universal Declaration of Human Rights, or another key international instrument – that party's derogation from the ECHR cannot be valid. For instance,

---

[23] ECHR art. 15, § 1.

[24] *Aksoy*, para. 68.

[25] A. v. *United Kingdom*, paras. 186, 184. See also *Brannigan* v. *United Kingdom*, 258-B Eur. Ct. H.R. (ser. A) (1993), para. 43.

[26] A. v. *United Kingdom*, para. 84.

[27] See Research and Library Division, European Court of Human Rights, Guide on Article 15 of the European Convention.

[28] *Lawless*, para. 38.

[29] *Ireland* v. *United Kingdom*, para. 212.

[30] *Brannigan*, para. 51.

[31] *Aksoy*, paras. 79–84.

[32] *Brannigan*, para. 54.

[33] A. v. *United Kingdom*, para. 184.

[34] A. v. *United Kingdom*, para. 190.

[35] ECHR art. 15, § 1.

in *Brannigan* v. *United Kingdom* the complainant argued that the United Kingdom's derogation from the ECHR was invalid because the United Kingdom had violated the derogation notification requirements under the ICCPR.[36] The Court determined it would be outside its role to try to define the ICCPR's requirements.[37] Nonetheless, the Court lightly reviewed the character of the United Kingdom's notice of derogation from the ICCPR, concluding it was sufficient to avoid invalidating the United Kingdom's derogation from the ECHR.[38]

2 Article 15(2): Non-Derogable Rights

In addition to the requirements for valid derogation under section 1, section 2 of Article 15 mandates that parties not derogate from certain Convention rights.[39] These non-derogable rights are the Article 2 "Right to Life," the Article 3 "Prohibition on Torture," the Article 4 paragraph 1 "Prohibition on Slavery or Servitude," and the Article 7 "Prohibition on Punishment without Law."[40] Three protocols to the Convention also prohibit derogation from certain other rights: Protocol No. 6 (the abolition of the death penalty in time of peace and limiting the death penalty in time of war), Protocol No. 7 (the *ne bis in idem* principle only, as contained in Article 4 of that protocol), and Protocol No. 13 (the complete abolition of the death penalty).[41] Some of these rights are, however, by their own text subject to inherent limitations.[42] For instance, infringement of the right to life is permissible when the use of force is strictly necessary in defense of unlawful violence against a person.[43] These textual limitations continue to operate notwithstanding Article 15(2).

3 Article 15(3): Notification Procedures

Finally, Article 15 section 3 sets out procedures for a party to provide notice of any derogation in reliance on Article 15. The section requires that the derogating nation notify the Secretary General of the Council of Europe of the

---

[36] *Brannigan*, para. 73.

[37] *Brannigan*, paras. 72–73.

[38] *Brannigan*, paras. 72–73.

[39] ECHR art. 15, § 2.

[40] ECHR arts. 2, 3, 4, and 7.

[41] Research and Library Division, European Court of Human Rights, Guide on Article 15 of the European Convention, 8.

[42] Research and Library Division, European Court of Human Rights, 8.

[43] ECHR art. 15, § 2(a).

measures undertaken, its reasons for such measures, and when the measures have been ceased.[44] This notice publicizes the derogation to facilitate oversight and collective enforcement of the ECHR. Parties frequently submit the full text of the relevant derogating legislation, as well as full information regarding any administrative measures taken.[45] Incomplete or partial notice of the pertinent details will restrict the Article's application. For instance, in *Sakis* v. *Turkey*, "when assessing the territorial scope of the derogation" the ECtHR refused to "extend its effects to . . . territory not explicitly named in the notice of derogation."[46] *Prompt* notice is an implicit requirement of Article 15 (3), the ECtHR has also concluded.[47] For instance, a four-month delay by the Greeks in submitting the reasons for derogation after its initial notice was deemed an "undue delay."[48] Finally, Article 15 section 3 is not a static notice requirement. The spirit of the notification procedures calls for a "process of continued reflection"; the party must continuously "re-evaluate whether a there is ongoing need for derogation and whether greater conformity with the Convention can be achieved" and update the Council of Europe about its activities accordingly.[49]

II CASE STUDIES ON DEROGATION AND THE IMPACT ON ARTICLE 8 RIGHTS: FRANCE AND TURKEY

While many nations face an evolving range of national security threats in the twenty-first century, national authorities have often overreached. Some states have used the threat to impose strong-arm measures – to the detriment of fundamental rights, such as Article 8 of the Convention. Article 8 states:

1. Everyone has the right to respect for his private and family life, his home and his correspondence.
2. There shall be no interference by a public authority with the exercise of this right except such as is in accordance with the law and is necessary in a democratic society in the interests of national security, public safety or the economic well-being of the country, for the prevention of

---

[44] ECHR art. 15, § 3; *Lawless*.
[45] See, e.g., *Greek Case*, para. 39 (noting the failure of the Greek government to "furnish complete texts of its emergency legislation" and "full information with regard to the administrative measures taken").
[46] *Sakık* v. *Turkey*, 1997-VII Eur. Ct. H.R., para. 39.
[47] *Lawless*, para. 47.
[48] See, e.g., *Greek Case*, para. 45.
[49] *Brannigan*, para. 54.

disorder or crime, for the protection of health or morals, or for the protection of the rights and freedoms of others.[50]

France and Turkey have avoided expressly acknowledging the ECHR obligations from which they may have derogated, including whether digital searches authorized by national laws compromised Article 8. The ECtHR has not reviewed any complaints alleging derogation from Article 8 by Turkey and, indeed, has not reviewed France's Article 15 claim at all. Nonetheless the legal provisions and factual information reported on the states of emergency in France and, in a more extreme iteration, Turkey illustrate the dramatic effects of these derogations for the Article 8 right to privacy.

Following civilian terrorist attacks in 2015, France became the only European country to issue a state of emergency. Turkey, after a brief but deadly military coup, called a state of emergency in 2016, which has since transformed into an authoritarian crackdown in the name of combatting terrorism. Both examples feature prolonged, expansive derogation from Convention obligations, raising real questions about compliance with the ECHR's Article 15 standards for derogation.

1 France

A state of emergency initiated by France in 2015 ushered in sweeping legal authorizations for the French government to track individuals electronically and conduct digital searches. This state of emergency carried on for nearly two years until finally terminated in November 2017. However, the French coordinated the end of the state of emergency with a legislative expansion of ordinary surveillance powers, making permanent powers previously only available during a time of emergency.[51]

In addition to the rules under ECHR Article 15 and other international instruments, emergency procedures are also typically regulated under national law. In France, emergency procedures are located in two provisions of the French constitution and in statutory law. The French constitution allows an emergency to be called in two circumstances: under Article 16, where the "proper functioning of public constitutional powers is interrupted," and under Article 36, where there is a "state of siege."[52] A 1955 state-of-emergency statute never enshrined in the constitution also provides for a state of emergency

---

[50] ECHR art. 8.
[51] Loi 2017-1510 du 30 october 2017, J.O., October 31, 2017, p. 130.
[52] 1958 Constitution, arts. 16, 36.

Preserving Article 8 in Times of Crisis

where there is "imminent danger resulting from serious breaches of public order."[53] The French president in consultation with the Council of Ministers may invoke a state of emergency for twelve days.[54] In order to extend the emergency, parliament must then pass a law incorporating a date of sunset.[55]

On November 13, 2015, terrorist attacks by the Islamic State in Paris killed over one hundred people and injured hundreds more. Suicide bombs were detonated at a sports stadium in a Paris suburb, followed by shootings at busy restaurants, bars, and a concert venue in the city center.[56] That day, French President François Hollande ordered a state of emergency throughout France and closed French borders.[57] The French government acknowledged Articles 16 or 36 of the constitution were inapplicable, and instead President Hollande relied on the 1955 emergency statute as the legal basis for an initial executive-ordered twelve-day state of emergency.[58] On November 20, an act of the French parliament extended the emergency for three months.[59] France formally notified the Secretariat General of its intent to claim the benefits of Article 15 on November 24, 2015,[60] enclosing the emergency French legislation[61] and official decrees initiating the state of emergency.[62] The state of emergency would be extended six times until ultimately terminated on November 1, 2017, nearly two years later.[63]

---

[53] Loi 55-385 du 3 avril 1955, J.O. April 7, 1955, p. 3479.

[54] Loi 55-385.

[55] Loi 55-385, art. 2.

[56] "Paris attacks: What Happened on the Night," *BBC News*, December 9, 2015, www.bbc.com/news/world-europe-34818994.

[57] CCTV+, "Hollande Orders State of Emergency, Borders Closed." YouTube, November 13, 2015. www.youtube.com/watch?v=Mg1TmjVOK4I.

[58] See, e.g., Filip G. Bozinovic, "Finding the Limits of France's State of Emergency." Claremont-UC Undergraduate Res. Conference on the E.U., 2017, 21–22 (explaining the national debate over the constitutional status and use of the 1955 emergency statute in 2015).

[59] Loi 2015-1501 du 20 novembre 2015, J.O., November 21, 2015, p. 21665, art. 1.

[60] Council of Europe, Declaration Contained in a Note Verbale from the Permanent Representation of France, dated 24 November 2015, registered at the Secretariat General on November 24, 2015, Or. Fr. (2016), https://wcd.coe.int/com.instranet.InstraServlet?command=com.instranet.CmdBlobGet&InstranetImage=2847547&SecMode=1&DocId=2333388&Usage=2 [hereinafter Council of Europe, French Declaration November 25, 2015].

[61] Loi 55-385.

[62] See, e.g., Décret 2015-1475 du 14 novembre 2015, J.O., November 14, 2015, p. 21297.

[63] Council of Europe, Declaration Contained in a Letter from the Permanent Representative of France to the Council of Europe, dated 2 November 2017, registered at the Secretariat General on November 7, 2017, Or. Fr. (2017), www.coe.int/en/web/conventions/full-list/-/conventions/treaty/005/declarations?p_auth=IRgBNXH.

The government's powers under the state-of-emergency law are found in the same 1955 statute,[64] and these powers were subsequently expanded by the French parliament during the first vote to extend the emergency.[65] Many of the law's problematic powers, like the authority to close places of worship, are unrelated to Article 8 privacy rights. For the purposes of this chapter, we focus on those provisions with a privacy nexus.

The law gives a range of broad powers to the Minister of the Interior and prefects, which are the national authorities that govern in a department or region of France.[66] These powers tend not to require prior judicial approval and may be used broadly to preserve "security" and "order."[67] The provisions for electronic monitoring and searches under the French emergency law are expansive. Article 6 of the French emergency law permits the Minister of Interior to order, without judicial authorization, the house arrest of persons in decreed zones for whom "there are serious reasons to think that his behavior constitutes a threat to public security and public order" in those territories.[68] Importantly, a house arrest order for certain crimes can include an alternative of mobile electronic tracking.[69] Under Article 11, electronic searches may also be conducted "anywhere, including a home, day and night ... when there are serious reasons to believe that this place is frequented by a person whose behavior constitutes a threat to public safety and order."[70] This includes access to and copying of *any* data that can be reached from any "initial system" discovered on the premises, like data stored on the cloud.[71] Judicial approval is required only for law enforcement to subsequently access and review the data collected during the search, not to initially collect the data.[72] Individuals have the right to file a request with an advisory commission to withdraw emergency house arrest orders and other travel restrictions; they can also challenge such orders as excessive in court. However, when the law was extended, the ability to contest emergency measures was eliminated.[73]

---

[64] Loi 55-385 du 3 avril 1955, J.O., April 7, 1955, p. 3479.

[65] Loi 2015-1501.

[66] Loi 55-385.

[67] Loi 55-385.

[68] Loi 55-385, art. 6.

[69] Loi 55-385, art. 6.

[70] Loi 55-385, art. 11.

[71] Loi 55-385, art. 11.

[72] Loi 55-385, art. 11.

[73] Loi 2015-1501 (in part, repealing Article 7 of the 1955 law); see also Daniel Severson, "France's Extended State of Emergency: What New Powers Did the Government Get?" *Lawfare* (blog), November 22, 2015, www.lawfareblog.com/frances-extended-state-emergency-what-new-powers-did-government-get.

On October 30, 2017, France promulgated new legislation – Law 2017-1510 on Strengthening Internal Security and the Fight Against Terrorism – and officially terminated the state of emergency on November 1, 2017.[74] The new law extends powers once only available during an emergency, including some that bear on Article 8 rights.[75] Article 3 permits – in this iteration, solely for purpose of preventing terrorist acts – restrictions on persons for "whom there are substantial reasons to believe that his or her conduct constitutes a particularly serious threat" and who regularly makes contact with "persons or organizations inciting, facilitating or participating in acts of terrorism."[76] After this determination is made these persons may be placed under mobile electronic surveillance, requiring the individual to wear a tracking device, subject to appeal to a judge.[77] Directly inspired by the 2015 state-of-emergency law,[78] Article 4 permits, *to prevent acts of terrorism*, searches and seizures of any document, object, or data that is found on the premises of the person determined to constitute a particularly serious threat.[79] However, now the search is subject to prior judicial approval in addition to the judicial approval to subsequently review data copied during that search.[80] Finally, the law extends new authority to intelligence services and the armed forces to monitor wireless communications.[81] The law creates a French system of passenger transport records, separate from the EU system.[82]

2 *Turkey*

Turkey initiated a state of emergency in 2016 following an attempted coup. This state of emergency was in place for two years until it was terminated in July 2018. However, expansive counterterrorism legislation adopted in August

---

[74] Loi 2017-1510, p. 130.

[75] Olivier Le Bot, "Un 'etat d'urgence permanent? (Loi n° 2017-1510 du 30 Octobre 2017 renforçant la sécurité intérieure et la lutte contre le terrorisme)," *Revue française de droit administratif* 6 (November–December 2017): 1118 ("The law of 30 October 2017 considerably extends the administrative police powers available to public authorities, by including in the ordinary legislation four powers totally ... or partially ... of the state of emergency law").

[76] Loi 2017-1510, art. 3(1).

[77] Loi 2017-1510, art. 3.

[78] Le Bot, "Un 'etat d'urgence permanent?," 1118.

[79] Loi 2017-1510, art. 4.

[80] Loi 2017-1510, art. 4.

[81] Loi 2017-1510, art. 15. For further discussion, see Jean-Charles Jobart, "La loi renforçant la sécurité intérieure et la lutte contre le terrorisme: À propos de la loi n° 2017-1510 du 30 octobre 2017," *La Semaine Juridique Administrations et Collectivités territoriales* 45 (2017): 11.

[82] Loi 2017-1510, art. 14.

2018, combined with the aggrandizement of presidential powers through a set of constitutional amendments, allowed for the practices that began during the state of emergency to continue, in effect, indefinitely. The state of emergency brought several interferences with privacy rights, including broad-based authority for communications interception.

The Turkish emergency procedures reside in several constitutional provisions: Article 15 (establishing that rights may be suspended during emergency), Article 119 (providing for emergencies during natural disaster or economic crisis), Article 120 (providing for emergencies during widespread acts of violence or serious deterioration of public order), and Article 121 (the procedures for calling a state of emergency). Under Articles 119 and 120, the Council of Ministers, meeting under the oversight of the President, may call a state of emergency for a maximum of six months.[83] Under Article 121, the Grand National Assembly must then immediately review the decision and decide whether to alter or lift the emergency.[84] The Assembly can continually extend the emergency for a maximum of four months at a time at the request of the Council of Ministers.[85] The article also permits the Council of Ministers under the oversight of the President to issue decrees with the force of law, subject to same-day approval by the Assembly.[86] Ordinary statute also contains procedures analogous to these constitutional provisions.[87]

Turkish authorities declared a state of emergency on July 15, 2016, after a failed coup, resulting in the deaths of over 200 people.[88] As its legal basis, the Turkish government cited each of the constitutional and statutory authorities set out in the previous paragraph. On July 21, Turkish authorities notified the Council of Europe of its reliance on Article 15 to temporarily suspend the ECHR,[89] attaching the text of the emergency constitutional articles and statutory sections, and a July 20 decision of the Council of Ministers extending

---

[83] 1982 Constitution, arts. 119–120.

[84] 1982 Constitution, art. 121.

[85] 1982 Constitution, art. 121.

[86] 1982 Constitution, art. 121.

[87] Law No. 2935 of October 25, 1983, on State of Emergency (Turkey).

[88] Henri Barkey, "One Year Later, the Turkish Coup Attempt Remains Shrouded in Mystery," *Washington Post*, July 14, 2017, www.washingtonpost.com/news/democracy-post/wp/2017/07/14/one-year-later-the-turkish-coup-attempt-remains-shrouded-in-mystery/?utm_term=.3a86c31c04f2.

[89] Council of Europe Press Release, Secretary General Receives Notification from Turkey of Its Intention to Temporarily Suspend the European Convention on Human Rights (July 21, 2016), https://wcd.coe.int/ViewDoc.jsp?p=&Ref=DC-PR132(2016)&Language=lanEnglish&Ver=original&Site=DC&BackColorInternet=F5CA75&BackColorIntranet=F5CA75&BackColorLogged=A9BACE&direct=true.

the state of emergency for ninety days.[90] On July 25, Turkey delivered a declaration, as well as a description of the attack and the measures taken under the state of emergency to the Council of Europe.[91] Subsequently, Turkey provided brief notifications each time measures were extended and the decrees issued under the state of emergency.[92] Turkey extended the state of emergency seven times before it ended in July 2018.[93]

While the first notice contained a description of the legal authority for the declaration of a state of emergency, not the actual powers triggered by the state of emergency,[94] the second communication of July 25 was slightly more attuned to the procedural demands of Article 15(3). The Turkish declaration was a joint statement by the Turkish Grand National Assembly, nodding to the threat of the coup and to the need for unity. It stated the Turkish Assembly had defended the nation and "again demonstrated that it is an Assembly worthy of its people."[95] Two descriptions followed the declaration, explaining the current danger calling for a state of emergency, as well as some of the measures taken in response.[96] The informational states that the Fethullah Gülen Terrorist Organization (FETÖ) "is carrying out its activities as cell-type structures in various public institutions, particularly within the judicial institutions, the Turkish Armed Forces and Police," and that public officials are using their "positions and authorities, equipment and the personnel of the institution they work in line with the aims of the organization."[97] These facts serve as the reasons for the measures taken by Turkish authorities, including "10,000 members of FETÖ ... taken into custody" in the days after the coup and the detention of "1352 judges and prosecutors."[98] The Turkish government

---

[90] Directorate of Legal Advice and Public International Law, Note Verbale, Ref: JJ8187C Tr./005-191 (2016), https://wcd.coe.int/com.instranet.InstraServlet?command=com.instranet .CmdBlobGet&InstranetImage=2929966&SecMode=1&DocId=2380676&Usage=2.

[91] Council of Europe, Treaty Office, Notification of Communication, Communication Transmitted by the Permanent Representative of Turkey and Registered by the Secretariat General on 24 July 2016 Or. Engl. (2016), https://wcd.coe.int/com.instranet.InstraServlet? command=com.instranet.CmdBlobGet&InstranetImage=2930086&SecMode=1&DocId= 2380804&Usage=2 [hereinafter Council of Europe, Turkish Notification July 24, 2016].

[92] See, e.g., Council of Europe, Treaty Office, Notification of Declaration dated 18 October 2016 (2016), https://wcd.coe.int/ViewDoc.jsp?p=&Ref=NotificationJJ8239C&Language= lanEnglish&Ver=original&Site=COE&BackColorInternet=F7F8FB&BackColorIntranet= F7F8FB&BackColorLogged=F7F8FB&direct=true.

[93] Human Rights Watch, *World Report 2019* (2019) 588.

[94] Directorate of Legal Advice and Public International Law, Note Verbale, Ref: JJ8187C Tr./005-191.

[95] Directorate of Legal Advice and Public International Law.

[96] Directorate of Legal Advice and Public International Law, 5.

[97] Directorate of Legal Advice and Public International Law, 9.

[98] Directorate of Legal Advice and Public International Law, 9.

noted the possibility of a new coup attempt, supporting the need for the Article 15 derogation.[99]

In particular, Turkish decrees (an executive emergency measure that needs no ordinary legislative approval) 670 and 671 submitted to the Council of Europe better illuminate the state of emergency's specific effect on Article 8 privacy rights.[100] The French emergency measures, while overbroad, included some restraints on the discretion of public authorities such as judicial approval to exploit collected data. In contrast, the Turkish decrees authorize almost wholly unbounded authority,[101] set out in terms open to flexible interpretation.[102]

For instance, Article 3 of Decree 670 required public and private entities to transfer any information authorities deem necessary concerning those investigated during the state of emergency investigation, as well as on their spouses and children. This information also includes digital communications.[103] No independent review, oversight, or appeal is included.

More broadly speaking, in order to maintain "national security, public order, prevention of crime, protection of public health and public morals, or protection of the rights and freedoms,"[104] Decree Law no. 671 permits the government's Information and Communications Technologies Authority to take any measures ordered by the Prime Minister concerning electronic communications services.[105] "[O]perators, access providers, data centres and the relevant content and hosting providers" are required to implement an order within two hours, while the decision is submitted to a judge within twenty-four hours for review.[106] The Authority may also take "all kinds of measures or have them taken in order to protect public institutions and

---

[99] Directorate of Legal Advice and Public International Law, 9.

[100] Bilge Yesil and Efe Kerem Sozeri, "Online Surveillance in Turkey: Legislation, Technology and Citizen Involvement," *Surveillance and Society* 15, no. 3/4 (2017): 546.

[101] Platform for Peace and Justice, "Construction of a New Regime by Decree Laws," 2018, 27, www.platformpj.org/wp-content/uploads/Construction-of-a-New-Regime-By-Decree-Laws-1.pdf ("[The Information and Communications Technologies Authority] has been furnished with unlimited authority to gather information and documents from public entities and private individuals and institutions").

[102] Bilge Yesil, Efe Kerem Sozeri, and Emad Khazraee, "Turkey's Internet Policy after the Coup Attempt: The Emergence of a Distributed Network of Online Suppression and Surveillance," 2017, 12–27, http://globalnetpolicy.org/wp-content/uploads/2017/02/Turkey1_v6-1.pdf.

[103] Decree with Force of Law No. 670, August 17, 2016, art. 3, https://rm.coe.int/CoERM PublicCommonSearchServices/DisplayDCTMContent?documentId=090000168069f40e.

[104] 1982 Constitution, art. 22.

[105] Decree with Force of Law No. 671, August 17, 2016, art. 25, https://rm.coe.int/CoERM PublicCommonSearchServices/DisplayDCTMContent?documentId=090000168069f410.

[106] Decree with Force of Law No. 671, art. 25.

organizations" and persons against cyberattack and deter attacks.[107] Finally, the Authority may "receive information, documentation, data, and records," "benefit from archives, electronic data processing centres and the communication infrastructure," and "may take other necessary measures."[108]

III ASSESSING FRENCH AND TURKISH COMPLIANCE WITH ARTICLE 15 RULES FOR DEROGATION

France and Turkey expressly claimed the benefits of Article 15, and, accordingly, their compliance with the Convention's requirements is reviewable. The ECtHR has yet to assess France's and Turkey's treatment of Article 8 privacy rights.[109] Anticipating the Court's response, this paper conducts precisely that review: insofar as France and Turkey derogated Article 8 privacy rights, did they comply with Article 15 standards?

Notably, neither country indicated the specific Convention rights derogated under the state of emergency. We assume for our analysis that Article 8 rights were in fact derogated by both France and Turkey. Additionally, because of this work's focus on ECHR Article 8 privacy rights, we set aside aspects of the Article 15 analysis that fall outside of that assessment – Article 15 (1)'s requirement not to violate other obligations under international law and Article 15(2)'s requirement not to derogate from certain Convention rights, both considerations being outside the scope of this work.

The following subsections assess, in turn, France's and Turkey's derogation of Article 8 rights for compliance with Article 15. First, we assess whether any derogation from Article 8 rights was valid under Article 15(1)'s requirements for both a "time of war or a public emergency threatening the life of the nation" and limiting measures to what is "strictly required by the exigencies of the situation." Second, we assess whether the Article 15(3) notification procedures were followed by the two countries. We conclude that neither France's nor Turkey's derogation was likely valid under Article 15(1). Though a closer call, there are also compelling reasons to conclude each also fell short of Article 15(3) notification procedures.

---

[107] Decree with Force of Law No. 671, art. 25.
[108] Decree with Force of Law No. 671, art. 25.
[109] While the ECtHR issued two opinions involving Turkey's state of emergency, neither case has involved Article 8 rights. See *Alpay* v. *Turkey*, App. No. 16538/17, ECLI:CE: ECHR:2018:0320JUD001653817, Judgment 2018, paras. 66-71 (concerning challenge to pre-trial detention); *Altan* v. *Turkey*, App. No. 13237/17, ECLI:CE:ECHR:2018:0320JUD001323717, Judgment 2018, paras. 82–87 (also concerning challenge to pre-trial detention).

1 France

France's derogation of Article 8 privacy rights during the 2015–2017 state of emergency likely did not comply with Article 15 standards. The prolonged state of emergency does not clearly meet the 15(1) threshold requirement for a "time of war or public emergency threatening the life of the nation." The electronic searches and tracking permitted by law were also unlikely to be "strictly required" given the exigencies as required by Article 15(1). Whether France's perfunctory notification would satisfy ECtHR review for Article 15(3) compliance is a closer call. Nonetheless, there are good reasons to find France's notification also falls short of Article 15 requirements.

1.1 Article 15(1): Did France Validly Derogate?

France's prolonged state of emergency may fall short of the threshold requirement of Article 15(1) for a valid derogation – the existence of a "time of war or public emergency threatening the life of the nation." However, the sweeping legal authorization for electronic searches and tracking, with little oversight or connection to the emergency's originating threat, probably went beyond what is "strictly required by the exigencies of the situation" as mandated by 15(1).

First, it is unclear whether the two-year French state of emergency met the Article 15(1) requirement that there be a "public emergency threatening the life of the nation." There can be little doubt that France initially met this requirement when the state of emergency was called. For instance, in *Aksoy* v. *Turkey* the "extent and impact of PKK [Kurdistan Workers' Party] terrorist activity in South-East Turkey," which claimed thousands of lives over a decade, had "undoubtedly" created an emergency.[110] Here, hundreds were killed and countless more injured in France's capital *in one single night* and the coordinated nature of the attacks indicated a credible risk of further attacks. There is little question these events constituted a state of emergency. However, six extensions of the state of emergency later, no similar threat persisted to clearly justify a valid claim to Article 15. While attacks continued, there was only one attack of comparable scale on July 14, 2016, when a truck was driven into a crowd in Nice, France.[111] This attack was carried out by a single "lone wolf" actor who was promptly shot and killed by police,

---

[110] *Aksoy*, paras. 8, 70.
[111] "Timeline: Attacks in France," *BBC News*, July 26, 2016, www.bbc.com/news/world-europe-33288542.

eliminating the immediate danger.[112] While this tragic attack must be condemned, it is not clearly based on ECtHR precedent that this could give rise to a threat to the very life of the nation, particularly without producing further credible evidence of serious terrorist attacks planned against France. For instance, as was a consideration weighing against finding a "state of emergency" in the *Greek Case*, the terrorist threat in France "[did] not differ markedly from that in many other countries in Europe over a similar period," yet France was the only European nation to initiate a state of emergency.[113] On the other hand, in surprisingly perfunctory analyses, in two recent cases the ECtHR did not scrutinize Turkey's claimed state of emergency where the applicants did not challenge this element of the Article 15 claim, and where the Turkish Constitutional Court had ruled below that a state of emergency was present.[114] As a result, whether the French state of emergency met Article 15(1) may turn on the findings of the national court below and whether an applicant challenged this element of a state's emergency claim.

Second, the measures taken by the French government in derogation of Article 8 privacy rights were also likely not limited to what is "strictly required by the exigencies of the situation" as mandated by Article 15(1). As explained earlier, Article 15(1) requires a close nexus between any measures taken and the specific demands of the state of emergency.[115] The French measures were not closely tailored to the particulars of the French emergency, instead permitting a sweeping invasion of Article 8 rights.[116]

The emergency measures went beyond addressing the terrorist threat underlying the state of emergency to target larger public safety concerns. For instance, under the emergency law, Article 11 electronic searches could be authorized "anywhere" under a low standard which *did not require any relationship to terrorism* – "when there are serious reasons to believe that this place is frequented by a person whose behavior constitutes a threat to public safety and order."[117] To the credit of the French Assembly, Article 6 emergency

---

[112] "Timeline: Attacks in France."

[113] *Greek Case*, para. 161; see also, Christopher Michaelsen, "Derogating from International Human Rights Obligations in the 'War against Terrorism'? A British-Australian Perspective," *Terrorism and Political Violence* 17, no. 1/2 (2005): 142. But see A. v. *United Kingdom*, para. 180 (acknowledging that "each Government . . . make[s] their own assessment on the basis of the facts known to them").

[114] *Alpay*, paras. 76–77, and *Altan*, paras. 92–93.

[115] A. v. *United Kingdom*, para. 190.

[116] See *supra* Section II.1.

[117] Loi 55-385, art. 11.

provisions for individualized electronic tracking of individuals on house arrest were at least restricted to the monitoring of those convicted of certain crimes.[118] However, even these provisions were still not restricted solely to those convicted of a crime of terrorism but also swept in crimes with a sentence of "ten years' imprisonment" where that person had served less than eight years.[119] French authorities' limited success at addressing the terrorist threat under the state of emergency likewise raises concerns about the necessity of the emergency measures. The expanded powers "led to only 20 terror-related prosecutions,"[120] and "[l]ess than 1 percent of raids have resulted in new terrorism investigation."[121]

Moreover, the invasion of Article 8 rights permitted under the French measures was also sweeping, rather than tailored to the specific exigencies. For instance, as explained previously, the emergency legislation provided indiscriminate copying of any data, including data stored in the cloud, which was accessible from an "initial system" discovered during a search of the premises.[122] Authorities could access "any type of information on any type of electronic device of any French resident and especially any information available via usernames, passwords collected during a police search, [and] any content stored online."[123] Also, in contrast with cases such as *Lawless* v. *Ireland*, where the Court approved emergency detention because of the system of safeguards in place, there were few safeguards available in the French state of emergency.[124] Electronic searches did not require prior judicial approval. Only subsequent access to the data was subject to judicial review, after the fact of searching and copying,[125] and individuals' ability to contest emergency measures was eliminated under the first of six extensions of the French law, only a week into the French state of emergency.[126]

---

[118] Loi 55-385, art. 6.

[119] Loi 55-385, art. 6.

[120] Anne-Sylvaine Chassany, "France: The Permanent State of Emergency," *Financial Times*, October 2, 2017, www.ft.com/content/f5309ff8-a521-11e7-9e4f-7f5e6a7c98a2.

[121] Alissa J. Rubin, "Muslims in France Say Emergency Powers Go Too Far," *New York Times*, February 17, 2016, www.nytimes.com/2016/02/18/world/europe/frances-emergency-powers-spur-charges-of-overreach-from-muslims.html.

[122] Loi 55-385, art. 11.

[123] "A Police State to Avoid Any Critical Evaluation?," *La QuaDrature Du Net*, November 19, 2015, www.laquadrature.net/en/police-state-in-france.

[124] *Lawless*, para. 37.

[125] Loi 55-385, art. 11.

[126] Loi 2015-1501, p. 21665; see also Severson, "France's Extended State of Emergency."

1.2 Article 15(3): Did France Provide Proper Notice of Derogation?

Whether France's notice of derogation in reliance on Article 15 would satisfy Article 15(3)'s requirements is unclear based on ECtHR precedent. However, there are compelling reasons to believe the French notification would fall short. France almost certainly met the requirement for *prompt* notice of derogation as held in *Lawless v. Ireland*,[127] having notified the Secretary General of its intent to derogate twelve days after claiming a state of emergency domestically.[128] France also issued subsequent notices upon extension of the state of emergency,[129] according with the requirement for continued assessment of the need for reliance on Article 15.[130] French authorities also appropriately attached the texts of the emergency legislation and decrees in its communications to the Council of Europe.[131] However, France's notices still lacked meaningful detail. For instance, France did not provide a justification for the necessity of the emergency measures undertaken beyond that they were "necessary to prevent the commission of further terrorist attacks."[132] Likewise, the notice provided only "that some of the emergency measures 'may involve a derogation from the obligations' under the ECHR, without explaining which measures exactly do, in fact, require a derogation and to what extent, let alone why precisely were those specific measures strictly required by the exigencies of the situation."[133] France also did not identify the specific Convention rights to be derogated.

ECtHR case law has yet to rule on how robust a notice of derogation must be. The ECtHR has accepted similarly vague justifications for specific measures from parties to the Convention, where the text of the legal measures was provided. For instance, in *Lawless v. Ireland* the Court accepted Ireland's explanation that "the measures had been taken in order 'to prevent the commission of offences against public peace and order and to prevent the

---

[127] *Lawless*, para. 45.

[128] Council of Europe, French Declaration November 25, 2015.

[129] "Reservations and Declarations for Treaty No.005 – Convention for the Protection of Human Rights and Fundamental Freedoms: Declarations in Force as of Today," Council of Europe website, last visited August 15, 2018, www.coe.int/en/web/conventions/full-list/-/conventions/treaty/005/declarations?p_auth=N5hF4XrW.

[130] *Brannigan*, para. 54.

[131] *Brannigan*, para. 54.

[132] Council of Europe, French Declaration November 25, 2015.

[133] Marko Milanovic, "France Derogates from ECHR in the Wake of the Paris Attacks," *EJIL: Talk!* (blog), December 13, 2015, www.ejiltalk.org/france-derogates-from-echr-in-the-wake-of-the-paris-attacks/.

maintaining of military or armed forces other than those authorised by the Constitution.'"[134] On the other hand, more recently in *A. v. United Kingdom*, the Court accepted an Article 15 notice from the United Kingdom that specified that Article 5(1)(f) on detention and deportation may be derogated, explained why this specific right was being derogated based on the specific terrorist risks present, *and* provided the applicable emergency law.[135] The failure to justify why the specific measures taken are necessary and from which rights the French were derogating does little to facilitate Article 15(3)'s goal of collective oversight of the Convention. Vague attestations of compliance with Article 15's standards suggest less than meaningful adherence, and, without further detail about the grounds for compliance, the Council can only engage in superficial review. At a minimum, there are significant questions about the adequacy of the French Article 15(3) notice of derogation.

2 Turkey

Turkey's derogation from Article 8 privacy rights during its two-year state of emergency almost certainly did not comply with Article 15 standards. As with France's derogation, it is not clear whether the prolonged state of emergency meets the threshold requirement of a "time of war or public emergency threatening the life of the nation." The significant interference with privacy rights under the Turkish state of emergency – from banning privacy technologies to sweeping social media surveillance – all conducted for the generalized purpose of combatting terrorism – in all likelihood go beyond what is "strictly required" under 15(1). The validity of Turkey's perfunctory notification, like France's, is a closer call. However, there are similar reasons to believe Turkey's notification falls short of Article 15 requirements.

2.1 Article 15(1): Did Turkey Validly Derogate?

It is unclear whether Turkey's extended state of emergency meets the threshold of the Article 15(1) requirement for a "time of war or public emergency threatening the life of the nation." However, the sweeping surveillance authorized under the state of emergency – particularly combined with the accelerated social media monitoring and bans on privacy protective technologies also conducted *in practice* during the state of emergency – very likely goes

---

[134] *Lawless*, para. 47.
[135] *A. v. United Kingdom*, para. 11.

beyond what is "strictly required by the exigencies of the situation" under Article 15(1).

First, as with France, it is unclear whether the two-year Turkish state of emergency satisfies the Article 15(1) requirement for a "time of war or public emergency threatening the life of the nation." As with France, Turkey clearly experienced a "time of war or other public emergency threatening the life of the nation" when the state of emergency was first initiated. However, in contrast to the French derogation the Turkish was far more widely applicable, its original limits expanding significantly over time, rendering it far more questionable. An attempted coup amounting to hundreds dead and thousands injured is unquestionably such an emergency. However, after this immediate threat was quelled, the credibility of the Turkish claim of to a "public emergency" diminished.[136] As observed by the CoE advisory body, the Venice Commission:

> Turkish authorities insist that even though the "active phase" of the coup lasted only for a few hours, a risk of a repeated coup attempt still remains, because many supporters of Mr Gülen are still present in the State apparatus. This claim seems highly speculative, especially after over a hundred thousand public servants had been dismissed and tens of thousands arrested.[137]

Perhaps in part out of recognition of these optics, Turkey subsequently claimed that the continuation of the state of emergency was necessary simply to combat terrorism, deviating from the original purpose for the determination.[138] A party's claim to Article 15 need not be entirely static.[139] However, to preserve Article 15's status as an extraordinary measure, a state of emergency that initially only targeted individuals who specifically "belong to, connect to, or have contact with the Fetullahist Terrorist Organization," but was expanded to broadly target "persons who have 'membership, affiliation, link or connection with'" any terrorist groups must be viewed with skepticism.[140]

---

[136] See, e.g., Ignatius Yordan Nugraha, "Human Rights Derogation during Coup Situations," *International Journal of Human Rights* 22, no. 2 (2018): 200 (evaluating when a coup warrants Article 15 derogation, and noting that in the *Greek Case* the unlikely prospect of an actual "communist takeover" precluded finding an "emergency").

[137] Council of Europe, Venice Commission, Opinion No. 865/2016, On Emergency Decree Laws Nos. 667–676 Following the Failed Coup of 15 July 2016 (2016), 10, www.venice.coe.int/webforms/documents/default.aspx?pdffile=CDL-AD (2016)037-e

[138] Venice Commission, 11.

[139] Venice Commission, 11.

[140] Venice Commission, 11; see also, David Kaye (Special Rapporteur on the Promotion and Protection of the Right to Freedom of Opinion and Expression), *Report on Mission to Turkey*, U.N. Doc. A/HRC/35/22/Add.3 (June 21, 2017), para. 46.

Where the threat is this "nonspecific, the government's burden of justification in respect of the existence of a 'public emergency' is particularly high" – here, a burden as of yet unmet.[141] As noted previously, in two recent decisions the ECtHR accepted without closely scrutinizing Turkey's prolonged state of emergency where the Turkish Constitutional Court had ruled below that a state of emergency was present.[142] However, this interpretation should not necessarily prevail in subsequent cases before the Court. The applicants in *Alpay* v. *Turkey* and *Altan* v. *Turkey* did not contest this element of Turkey's Article 15 claim.[143] The cases also involved pre-trial detentions initiated only a few weeks and several months after the original state of emergency was called, respectively, while years later the state of emergency continues under dramatically different circumstances.[144]

Second, the measures taken by the Turkish government in derogation of Article 8 privacy rights have also almost certainly not been limited to what is "strictly required by the exigencies of the situation," as mandated by Article 15(1). Like France, the Turkish measures cannot pass muster under Article 15 because they are not directed at addressing the source of the emergency and permit an overbroad invasion of Article 8 rights. However, Turkey's measures went far further than France's.

The Turkish emergency measures are not tailored toward addressing the national emergency. The expanding official basis for the state of emergency just described shows that the measures have been used for "purpose other than that for which they were granted" rather than restricted to what was "strictly required."[145] Still further, as described in Section II.2, the Turkish authorities have used procedures reserved for a state of emergency (the "decree" mechanism) to introduce permanent measures that implicate Article 8 rights.[146] Under the Turkish constitution, during a state of emergency the Council of Ministers under the oversight of the President may issue decrees with the force of law to meet the specific needs of the necessity.[147] These decrees do not go through ordinary legislative processes, and have limited, expedited legislative review.[148] Permanent measures by their very nature are aberrant to Article 15,

---

[141] Michaelsen, "Derogating from International Human Rights Obligations," 142.

[142] *Alpay*, paras. 76–77; *Altan*, paras. 92–93.

[143] *Alpay*, para. 76; *Altan*, para. 93.

[144] *Alpay*, paras. 19–28; *Altan*, paras. 19–33.

[145] *Lawless*, para. 38.

[146] See Section II.2.

[147] 1982 Constitution, art. 121.

[148] 1982 Constitution, art. 121.

an *exceptional* Convention mechanism, says the Venice Commission.[149] This is particularly true where those permanent measures are introduced via emergency legal channels outside ordinary legislative processes.[150] The French expanded ordinary legal authorities at the close of the state of emergency; however, France did so using standard legislative procedures and pared back certain authorities available under the emergency – for instance with requirements that investigative authority be tied to "acts of terrorism" and that privacy-intrusive measures undergo prior judicial review.[151] In contrast, Turkey instituted extreme emergency measures as part of permanent law *and* circumvented the ordinary legislative process.

The Article 8 effects of the Turkish decrees are also sweeping, rather than tailored to the specific exigencies of the situation. As delineated in Section II, Decree 670 permits indiscriminate access to digital communications to further the coup investigations,[152] and Decree 671 permits generalized and swift control of communications companies to further ordinary aims like crime prevention, rather than genuine emergency need.[153] Indiscriminate application of surveillance to communications without clear, precise safeguards for access has been roundly condemned by the ECtHR in *Zakharov* v. *Russia*.[154] Against this backdrop, without a close nexus to the needs of the emergency, which these Turkish decrees lack, the Court would have little basis to greenlight that indiscriminate access in an emergency.[155]

Finally, it is noteworthy that, because the broad discretion granted to authorities under the emergency was layered over a preexisting legal regime of aggressive surveillance and internet restrictions, Turkish treatment of Article 8 rights during the state of emergency was, in practice, more aggressive than the emergency legal texts might suggest.[156] The state of emergency also

---

[149] Council of Europe, Venice Commission, Opinion No. 865 / 2016, 19–21.

[150] Venice Commission, 19 ("Permanent changes to legislation should not be introduced through such decree laws, but must be left to ordinary legislation.").

[151] See Section II.1.

[152] Decree No. 670, art. 3.

[153] Decree No. 671, art. 25.

[154] See, e.g., *Zakharov* v. *Russia*, App. No.47143/06, ECLI:CE:ECHR:2015:1204 JUD004714306, paras. 302–305 (invalidating the Russian communications surveillance regime).

[155] Başak Bağlayan, "The Turkish State of Emergency under Turkish Constitutional Law and International Human Rights Law," *ASIL Insights* 21, no. 1 (2017) (explaining Turkish emergency laws are applied with an "alarming level of arbitrariness").

[156] See generally Office of the U.N. High Commissioner for Human Rights, *Report on the Impact of the State of Emergency on Human Rights in Turkey, Including an Update on the South-East, January–December 2017* (March 2018), www.ohchr.org/Documents/Countries/TR/2018-03-19_ Second_OHCHR_Turkey_Report.pdf; Freedom House, *Freedom on the Net 2017: Turkey*,

ushered in a general ratcheting up of authoritarian tactics,[157] raising questions about whether the measures were a "genuine response" to the demands of the emergency situation – a consideration which kept the Court from disapproving of detention without judicial review in *Brannigan* v. *United Kingdom*.[158] For instance, in November and December 2016, respectively, Turkish authorities banned privacy-protective technologies VPN and TOR.[159] The ban is expected to become permanent.[160] Tens of thousands of individuals have been detained for "alleged use of the encrypted communications app ByLock," based on a disputed claim that "the app was primarily used by members of the Gülen movement."[161] Social media monitoring has also increased since the date of the attempted coup, and at the start of 2017 "almost 70,000 social media accounts have been put under surveillance."[162] Journalists and newspaper staff have been tried in court based on evidence garnered from "surveillance of their journalistic work."[163]

2.2 Article 15(3): Did Turkey Provide Proper Notice of Derogation?

With shortcomings analogous to the French notice, it is unclear whether Turkey's notice of derogation would satisfy Article 15(3)'s requirements based on ECtHR precedent if challenged. Notably, while the ECtHR issued two decisions concerning Turkey's state of emergency neither involved a challenge to Turkey's notice of derogation and, as a result, the Court accepted the notice without review.[164] Nonetheless, there are again good reasons to believe the Turkish notification would fall short of Article 15 standards upon review.[165]

2017, https://freedomhouse.org/report/freedom-net/2017/turkey; Kaye, *Report on Mission to Turkey.*

[157] See Fevzi Doruk Ergun, "National Security vs. Online Rights and Freedoms in Turkey: Moving Beyond the Dichotomy," March 4, 2018, http://edam.org.tr/en/national-security-vs-online-rights-and-freedoms-in-turkey-moving-beyond-the-dichotomy/ (describing the Turkish state of emergency's "significant ramifications for the surveillance and censorship debate").

[158] *Brannigan*, para. 51 (finding the needs of detention without judicial control to be clearly linked to the needs of combatting terrorism, such that there was "no indication derogation was other than a genuine response").

[159] Yesil, Kerem Sozeri, and Khazraee, "Turkey's Internet Policy after the Coup Attempt," 14–15.

[160] Yesil, Kerem Sozeri, and Khazraee, "Turkey's Internet Policy after the Coup Attempt," 14–15.

[161] Yesil, Kerem Sozeri, and Khazraee, "Turkey's Internet Policy after the Coup Attempt," 14–15.

[162] Freedom House, "Freedom on the Net 2017: Turkey."

[163] Office of the U.N. High Commissioner for Human Rights, Report on the Impact of the State of Emergency on Human Rights in Turkey, para. 91.

[164] *Alpay*, paras. 66–71; *Altan*, paras. 82–87.

[165] See, e.g., Martin Scheinin, "Turkey's Derogation from the ECHR: What to Expect?" *EJILL Talk!* (blog), July 27, 2016, www.ejiltalk.org/turkeys-derogation-from-the-echr-what-to-expect/.

As explained earlier, Turkey's initial notification to the Council of Europe came promptly as required under ECtHR precedent. It was delivered to the Secretary General within days of the declared national emergency.[166] Turkey also provided subsequent notices when the state of emergency was extended.[167] However, using nearly identical language to the French Declaration, the Turkish notice only stated generally that the "measures taken may involve derogation from the obligations under" the ECHR and failed to mention the specific Articles which would be derogated.[168] Turkey did attach the texts of the relevant constitutional and statutory sections relied on to initiate the emergency, and appears to have forwarded the relevant emergency decrees, though full data are not available.[169] As described at length in reference to France in Section III.1.2, the ECtHR case law has not clearly ruled on just how robust a notice of derogation must be, and has accepted party notices with varied levels of detail. Nonetheless, because the failure to justify why specific measures are necessary and to specify which rights are derogated does little to advance the oversight goal of Article 15(3), at a minimum there are significant questions about the adequacy of the Turkish notice.

2.3 Conclusion

Neither the recent French nor the more egregious Turkish states of emergency likely comply with Article 15 standards for derogation under the ECHR. Both parties continually extended the state of emergency beyond the initial immediate and extraordinary needs that precipitated the emergency, and therefore fall short of the requirement that there be a "public emergency threatening the life of the nation" under Article 15(1). Sweeping effects on Article 8 rights during the state of emergency without a clear relationship to the threat justifying the emergency cannot meet the Article 15(1) requirement to limit measures to those "strictly required by the exigencies of the situation." Finally, both countries provided prompt notice to the Council of Europe on their claims to Article 15, but with no real explanation of the necessity of the measures taken and the Articles affected. There are, therefore, significant questions about French and Turkish compliance with the Article 15(3) notice provision.

---

[166] Council of Europe Press Release, Secretary General Receives Notification from Turkey.
[167] "Reservations and Declarations for Treaty No.005," Council of Europe website.
[168] See, e.g., Directorate of Legal Advice and Public International Law, Note Verbale, Ref: JJ8187C Tr./005-191.
[169] See, e.g., Council of Europe, Turkish Notification July 24, 2016.

IV STRATEGIES FOR CURTAILING EXCESSIVE DEROGATION OF ARTICLE 8

This expansion of derogation authority by France and Turkey calls for new solutions to ensure members of the Council of Europe do not abandon their longstanding human rights obligations. As discussed in previous sections, the success of the Council of Europe relies on willing compliance of its members, collective enforcement, and monitoring. As such, up until forced withdrawal of a party to the Convention, arguably the strongest available mechanisms are "naming and shaming." Accordingly, the Council of Europe should step up efforts to identify and publicize excessive derogation of Article 8 rights, relying on NGOs and academic experts with regional ties and privacy expertise.

Cultivating an NGO response to the issue of excessive derogations has a number of advantages over other avenues for action.[170] Civil society can fill in critical information gaps about state activity under a state of emergency: NGOs frequently have ties with groups poorly understood by institutions, can "be less inclined to distort the information in the interest of some broader political agenda, or skew it to fit some official government version," understand a particular society on a more granular level, and can help evaluate claims made by their government.[171] These unique civil society functions are especially relevant to curbing derogations from the ECHR, in which vulnerable or disfavored groups may be most affected and heightened state power is prone to excess.[172] While increased institutional participation of NGOs is politically sensitive for certain Member States, this resistance should be outweighed by the unique role of civil society in ensuring that European institutions protect ECHR rights.[173]

---

[170] See, e.g., Els ten Hulscher, "Investigating NGO Influence on the Council of Europe and on Domestic Policies," 2015, http://theses.ubn.ru.nl/bitstream/handle/123456789/996/Hulscher%2C_Els_ten_1.pdf?sequence=1.

[171] Douglas Chalmers, "How Do Civil Society Associations Promote Deliberative Democracy?" Paper presented at the 23rd Latin American Studies Association International Conference, Washington DC, September 6–8 (2001). www.columbia.edu/~chalmers/Chalmers_LASA.htm#_ftn1.

[172] Sections II and III.

[173] See, e.g., Rachel A. Cichowski, "Civil Society and the European Court of Human Rights," in *The European Court of Human Rights between Law and Politic*, eds. Jonas Christoffersen and Mikael Rask Madsen (New York: Oxford University Press, 2011), 77–97. For more detailed information on the role that NGOs play in the CoE, see Catharina Harby, "The Experience of the AIRE Centre in Litigating before the European Court of Human Rights," in *Civil Society, International Courts and Compliance Bodies*, eds. Tullio Treves et al. (The Hague: TMC Asser Press, 2005), 41–46.

Preserving Article 8 in Times of Crisis 369

First, the jurisdiction of the Venice Commission should be expanded, empowering it to issue advisory opinions upon the request of NGOs and academic experts who may be able to identify flawed measures taken by parties to the Convention. Second, the Conference of INGOs to the Council of Europe should undertake country visits and opinions concerning extended states of emergency and their Article 8 effects. Finally, an expert network dedicated to monitoring derogations should be established. We do not address all traditional mechanisms for civil society engagement.[174] Instead, we seek to supplement the debate with new calls to action.

1 *Venice Commission: Expand Jurisdiction and Solicit NGO and Expert Input*

First, the jurisdiction of the Venice Commission should be expanded to empower it to issue advisory opinions upon the request of NGOs who may be able to identify flawed measures taken by parties to the Convention. The Commission should also fully capitalize on the mechanism for NGO consultations already available to it.

The Venice Commission has the power to issue influential advisory legal opinions, but its jurisdiction is strictly limited.[175] The European Commission for Democracy through Law, more commonly called the "Venice Commission," is a powerful advisory body to the Council of Europe, composed of independent experts.[176] The Venice Commission guides the Council of Europe on legal and constitutional issues:

> The role of the Venice Commission is to *provide legal advice* to its member states and, in particular, to help states wishing to bring their legal and institutional structures into line with European standards and international experience in the fields of democracy, human rights and the rule of law. It

[174] "The Collective Complaints Procedure," Council of Europe website, last visited July 6, 2018, www.coe.int/en/web/turin-european-social-charter/collective-complaints-procedure1. For a discussion of shortcomings and successes of the complaint procedure, see Holly Cullen, "The Collective Complaints System of the European Social Charter: Interpretative Methods of the European Committee of Social Rights," *Human Rights Law Review* 9, no. 1 (2009): 61–93.

[175] For a discussion of the influence of the Venice Commission, see generally Wolfgang Hoffmann-Riem, "The Venice Commission of the Council of Europe: Standards and Impact," *European Journal of International Law* 25, no. 2 (2014): 579–597. For instance, the European Court of Human Rights frequently refers to Venice Commission documents in judgments and decisions. See, e.g., *Partisi* v. *Turkey*, App. No. 48818/17, Eur. Ct. H.R. (2017), para. 21; *Işikirik* v. *Turkey*, App. No. 41226/09, Eur. Ct. H.R. (2017), para. 34.

[176] "For Democracy through Law: The Venice Commission of the Council of Europe," Council of Europe website, last visited July 6, 2018, www.venice.coe.int/WebForms/pages/?p=01_Presentation.

also helps to ensure *the dissemination and consolidation of a common constitutional heritage,* playing a unique role in conflict management, and provides "emergency constitutional aid" to states in transition.[177]

The Commission's assessments of Turkey's state of emergency have been among the most rigorous guidance available from the CoE on Article 15's scope of application (as well as arguably the strongest official condemnation of excessive derogation).[178]

Few other avenues for such thorough guidance on Article 15 and credible "naming and shaming" exist. However, under the statute that defines the Venice Commission's work, these influential opinions may currently only be made under strictly limited conditions: "upon request submitted by the Committee of Ministers, the Parliamentary Assembly, the Congress of Local and Regional Authorities of Europe, the Secretary General, or by a state or international organisation or body participating in the work of the Commission."[179] This jurisdiction should be expanded to enhance the ability of the Council of Europe to highlight deviations from Convention obligations. This Venice Commission should be given *permissive* jurisdiction to issue opinions upon the request of NGOs and academic experts. NGOs and independent experts are often closer to the ground and have an intimate understanding of any privacy infringements that parties to the Convention may be affecting. By allowing the NGOs and independent experts to solicit advisory opinions, the Venice Commission has an opportunity to shed light on developments that may not be identified by official Council of Europe bodies.

Even if, at this historical juncture, it is not politically feasible to extend the Venice Commission's power to issue advisory opinions, at a minimum and toward the same end, the Venice Commission should increase consultation with NGOs and academic experts. Under its mandate, the Commission may:

> hold hearings or invite to participate in its work, on a case-by-case basis, any qualified person or non-governmental organisation active in the fields of competence of the Commission and capable of helping the Commission in the fulfilment of its objectives.[180]

---

[177] Ibid.

[178] Council Opinion (Venice Commission) No. 875 / 2017, On the Amendments to the Constitution Adopted by the Grand National Assembly on 21 January 2017 and to be Submitted to a National Referendum on 16 April 2017 (March 13, 2017).

[179] European Commission for Democracy through Law Resolution Res(2002)3, Adopting the Revised Statute of the European Commission for Democracy through Law (2002), 4, www.venice.coe.int/WebForms/documents/?pdf=CDL(2002)027-e&lang=EN.

[180] European Commission for Democracy through Law Resolution Res (2002)3, 5.

Preserving Article 8 in Times of Crisis

There is little evidence the Venice Commission has taken full advantage of this mechanism. For instance, the most recent annual report of Venice Commission activities lists only one collaboration with NGOs and experts:[181] NGOs were included in a working group to prepare a new Ukrainian law on parliamentary elections.[182] To be fully apprised of all relevant details of any legal or constitutional question that comes before it, the Venice Commission should increase its collaboration with NGOs in Council of Europe countries.

Both expanding the jurisdiction of the powerful Venice Commission to permissively issue opinions at the request of NGOs and increasing NGO consultations would enhance the reach and effect of the Venice Commission's rigorous advice. These shifts could be a productive step toward combatting excessive derogation from Convention obligations.

2 Conference of INGOs of the Council of Europe: Undertake Country Visits and Issue Opinions on Limits to Convention Derogations

As a second means of "naming and shaming," the Conference of INGOs to the Council of Europe, the NGO wing of the CoE, should undertake country visits to France and Turkey and report on their compliance with Convention obligations. The Conference should also issue reports documenting state parties' reliance on Article 15 and the effect of states of emergency on Article 8 rights.

NGOs acquired consultative status with the CoE in 1952, just a few years after the CoE itself was founded in 1949.[183] Recognizing increased need for NGO participation, in 2003 the CoE granted participatory status to International NGOs ("INGOs")[184] and formally established the "Conference of INGOs" as a body in 2005.[185] INGOs are non-governmental organizations that obtain participatory status after having satisfied the requirements set by the

---

[181] European Commission for Democracy through Law, *Annual Report of Activities 2016* (2017), 42, www.venice.coe.int/webforms/documents/default.aspx?pdffile=CDL-RA(2016)001-e.

[182] Ibid., 42.

[183] "Conference of INGOs: Participatory Status," Council of Europe website, last visited May 14, 2018, www.coe.int/en/web/ingo/participatory-status.

[184] Committee of Ministers Resolution Res(2003)8, On Participatory Status for International Non-Governmental Organisations with the Council of Europe (November 19, 2003), https://search .coe.int/cm/Pages/result_details.aspx?ObjectID=09000016805de70b.

[185] Committee of Ministers Resolution Res(2005)47, On Committees and Subordinate Bodies, Their Terms of Reference and Working Methods (December 14, 2005), https://search.coe.int/ cm/Pages/result_details.aspx?ObjectID=09000016805d91ee.

CoE, among which are having a non–profit-making aim (political parties are excluded) and signing a declaration accepting the principles set out in basic statutes and documents of the CoE.[186] The Conference of INGOs is an institution of the CoE and participates in decision making in the "CoE 'quadrilogue' alongside the Committee of Ministers, the Parliamentary Assembly and the Congress of Local and Regional Authorities."[187]

The Conference of INGOs acts by adopting texts, conducting country visits, and publishing a range of other documents on key CoE developments.[188] Through its participatory status, the Conference of INGOS helps supervise parties' adherence to Convention obligations.[189] For instance, among the Conference of INGO duties, as defined by a Committee of Ministers resolution, are:

a. promote the respect of the Council of Europe's conventions and legal instruments in the member States;
b. contribute to the implementation of Council of Europe standards and policies in collaboration with local, regional and national NGOs; [and to] . . .
e. furnish, either spontaneously or at the request of the Council of Europe's different bodies, information, documents or opinions relating to their own field(s) of competence on matters which are under consideration or which could be addressed by the Council of Europe.[190]

Despite these responsibilities, the Conference of INGOs has been remarkably quiet concerning France's and Turkey's states of emergency. The Conference has conducted no country visits to Turkey or France since 2015,[191] though the Conference can be credited for recently "commit[ting] itself" to a fact-finding mission in certain parts of Turkey.[192] While the Conference did adopt a

---

[186] Committee of Ministers Resolution Res(2016)3, On Participatory Status for International Non-Governmental Organisations with the Council of Europe (July 6, 2016), https://search.coe.int/cm/Pages/result_details.aspx?ObjectId=090000168068824c; Heike Krieger, "The Conference of International Non-Governmental Organisations of the Council of Europe," in *The Council of Europe: Its Law and Policies*, eds. Stefanie Schmahl and Marten Breuer (Oxford: Oxford University Press, 2017), 318.

[187] "Conference of INGOs: Participatory Status," Council of Europe website.

[188] See, e.g., "Conference of INGOs, Publications," Council of Europe website, last visited February 20, 2018, www.coe.int/en/web/ingo/publications.

[189] Committee of Ministers Resolution Res(2016)3.

[190] Committee of Ministers Resolution Res(2016)3.

[191] Conference of INGOs Resolution, Protecting the Freedoms of Association and Expression in Turkey under the State of Emergency, CONF/PLE(2017)RES1 (January 27, 2017), 3.

[192] Conference of INGOs Resolution, CONF/PLE(2017)RES1, 3.

resolution in January 2017 on "Protecting the freedoms of association and expression in Turkey under the State of Emergency," which condemned the "disproportionate measures" during the state of emergency, this resolution focused almost exclusively on the emergency's effect on the functioning of civil society.[193]

The Conference of INGOs should focus new attention on the challenge facing the Council of Europe of excessive derogation from the Convention. The Conference should conduct visits to Turkey and France and issue reports on their compliance with Convention obligations. The Conference should also *sua sponte* issue reports dedicated to party reliance on state of emergency derogations under Article 15 and the effect of such derogations on privacy rights under Article 8. Through these activities, the Conference has an opportunity to define appropriate boundaries for states of emergency in an era of international terrorism.

3 *Establishment of an Expert Network to Focus on the Problem of ECHR Derogations*

An additional suggestion is for civil society to undertake the formation of a network explicitly dedicated to the monitoring of derogations under the Council of Europe Human Rights Convention. Such an observatory could be incorporated into other ongoing reporting on human rights.[194] Alternatively, it could exist as a free-standing entity with an independent secretariat and it could have the specific mission of responding to any state action under Article 15. An independent entity could provide a repository of relevant case law and international instruments, as well as a roster of experts and international NGOs.

Both approaches have advantages and disadvantages. A civil society network that draws on existing efforts to report on human rights violations would take advantage of the current structure and support for human rights work, but it may lack the ability or the resources to respond quickly and effectively when emergency circumstances trigger state derogations. For example, several NGOs deserve recognition for publicizing problems with the French and

---

[193] Conference of INGOs Resolution, CONF/PLE(2017)RES1, 3.

[194] Current human rights reporting mechanisms in which NGOs can participate are described in Philip Alston and Ryan Goodman, *International Human Rights* (Oxford: Oxford University Press, 2013) (UN system) and Gauthier de Beco, ed., *Human Rights Monitoring Mechanisms of the Council of Europe* (Oxford: Routledge, 2012) (CoE).

Turkish derogations in blogs, the media, and letters to the Council of Europe.[195] However, there is still an opportunity for consistent, coordinated NGO efforts against the derogations. The second approach, a free-standing entity, would require a new commitment of resources. However, it may have a more lasting impact, since it would be tasked with the specific responsibility of engaging the Council of Europe when member states seek to derogate. Most critically, an independent NGO network could provide the basis for ongoing reporting on states and their track record on fundamental rights when they invoke derogations over long periods of time.

V CONCLUSION

The need to combat a shifting terrorist threat – in some instances an authentic national security concern and in others a cover for authoritarian encroachment – has ushered in a new phenomenon of excessive derogation from human rights obligations. In the digital era, it is no surprise that these derogations from Convention obligations have been to the detriment of Article 8 privacy rights. The examples of France and Turkey and their extended derogations under Article 15 underscore the urgent need for new solutions to human rights encroachments.

The Council of Europe should increase collaboration with NGOs and academic experts to address the new threat to international human rights, with a bent toward accurately identifying and widely publicizing evidence of excessive derogation from Article 8 rights. As first steps, we propose a number of measures. The CoE should expand the jurisdiction of the Venice Commission to empower it to issue advisory opinions upon the request of NGOs. The Conference of INGOs to the Council of Europe should increase its activity and analysis concerning Article 15 states of emergency and their Article 8 effects. Last, we urge the creation of an NGO network dedicated to monitoring ECHR derogations.

---

[195] See, e.g., Amnesty International, Article 19, Human Rights Watch, and PEN International, "Letter to the Members of the Parliamentary Assembly of Council of Europe: Deterioration of Human Rights in Turkey Requires Parliamentary Assembly's Immediate Attention," January 20, 2017, www.hrw.org/news/2017/01/23/letter-members-parliamentary-assembly-council-europe (calling attention to the state of emergency in Turkey); Human Rights Watch, "France: New Emergency Powers Threaten Rights," November 24, 2015, www.hrw.org/news/2015/11/24/france-new-emergency-powers-threaten-rights.

14

Progress and Failure in the Area of Freedom, Security, and Justice

EMILIO DE CAPITANI

I INTRODUCTION

Almost one decade ago, the Lisbon Treaty came into force. It promised great advances for European governance, particularly in the policy areas that collectively come under the Area of Freedom, Security, and Justice (AFSJ).[1] Fundamental rights, law and order, civil justice, and migration are policy areas that citizens typically care a great deal about, but they surfaced relatively late in EU law and politics. Only in the Maastricht Treaty (1993) were these matters placed on the EU agenda, and until the Amsterdam Treaty (1999) they were decided exclusively through the intergovernmental method. Then, in the Amsterdam Treaty, a first block of competences dealing with borders, migration, asylum, and judicial cooperation in civil matters was transferred to the ordinary Community, i.e. supranational, method of EU policymaking.[2] In the Lisbon Treaty (2009) the process was completed: police and judicial cooperation on criminal matters also became subject to the Community

---

[1] According to the European Commission: "The three notions of freedom, security and justice are closely interlinked. Freedom loses much of its meaning if it cannot be enjoyed in a secure environment and with the full backing of a system of justice in which all Union citizens and residents can have confidence. These three inseparable concepts have one common denominator – people – and one cannot be achieved in full without the other two. Maintaining the right balance between them must be the guiding thread for Union action." Communication from the Commission, *Towards an Area of Freedom, Security and Justice*, COM (1998) 459 (July 14, 1998).

[2] Although the Lisbon Treaty changed the name of the European Community to European Union, the term "Community method" is still useful. It has been employed since the 1960s and refers to the decision-making method that gives more weight to supranational institutions (as compared to the Member States), and hence tends to expedite European integration. The Community method generally entails the power of proposal for the European Commission, qualified majority voting (as opposed to unanimity voting) in the Council, and a vote in the European Parliament.

method, and the EU Charter of Fundamental Rights (CFR) was given binding effect, thus boosting legislative efforts in the fundamental rights area.

By mainstreaming the AFSJ and placing it on the same footing as classic common market powers, the Lisbon Treaty promised to spur more effective, fair, and democratic AFSJ policies. Yet even in normal times, EU intervention in these areas of core state power never promised to be easy and, as is widely known, the past decade has been anything but normal for European politics and society. This chapter examines how the AFSJ has evolved in the turbulent years since the Lisbon Treaty entered into force. My perspective is shaped by over thirteen years (1998–2011) in the European Parliament's secretariat responsible for AFSJ matters.[3] The approach taken in this chapter is a detailed, hands on, policy analysis of the improvements that have been made in AFSJ governance and the deep flaws that persist.

The chapter proceeds as follows: It first explores the main innovations made by the Lisbon Treaty to the AFSJ. Section III then surveys the legislative output in the AFSJ over the past decade. Section IV analyzes the problematic aspects of the democratic governance of the AFSJ, including the withholding by the Member States of information essential for the policymaking process; poorly defined institutional roles; the use of the Common Foreign and Security Policy as a legal basis, circumventing the Community method; and the empowerment of EU agencies to undertake policymaking functions. The chapter concludes with a number of recommendations for improving AFSJ governance.

II LEGAL INNOVATIONS OF THE LISBON TREATY

In the AFSJ domain, the major innovation of the Lisbon Treaty was the creation of an integrated policy sphere that is governed according to the same general principles and through the same supranational institutional method.[4]

---

[3] Before that I was in the European Parliament Secretary General for Interinstitutional Relations (1985–1998) where I worked on the so-called Legislative Backbone, which coordinates the European Parliament services working on legislative files (Parliamentary Committees and Plenary Services).

[4] Maria Fletcher, Ester Herlin-Karnell, and Claudio Matera, *The European Union as an Area of Freedom, Security and Justice* (London: Routledge, 2016); Steve Peers, *EU Immigration and Asylum Law*, vol. I of *EU Justice and Home Affairs Law*, 4th ed. (Oxford: Oxford University Press, 2016); Steve Peers, *EU Criminal Law, Policing, and Civil Law*, vol. II of *EU Justice and Home Affairs Law*, 4th ed. (Oxford: Oxford University Press, 2016); Steve Peers, Violeta Moreno-Lax, Madeline Garlick, and Elspeth Guild, *EU Asylum Law*, vol. III of *EU Immigration and Asylum Law (Text and Commentary)*, 2nd ed. (Leiden: Brill/Nijhoff, 2015); Christian Kaunert, "The Area of Freedom, Security and Justice in the Lisbon Treaty: Commission Policy Entrepreneurship?" *Journal European Security* 19, no. 2 (2010): 169–189;

As is well known, the Maastricht Treaty had set into place a so-called pillar structure, in which the First Pillar covered the European Community common market and its four freedoms as defined in the founding Rome Treaty (1958), the Second Pillar, external security, and the Third Pillar, cooperation on Justice and Home Affairs. The internal market policies that fell in the First Pillar were generally governed by the Community method, while the external and internal security policies that fell in the Second and Third Pillars were governed by the intergovernmental method. In the Amsterdam Treaty, cooperation on Justice and Home Affairs was reframed as part of the general objective of developing the EU as an Area of Freedom, Security, and Justice (AFSJ) and the border, immigration, asylum, and civil justice elements of the AFSJ were transferred into the First Pillar. In the Lisbon Treaty, that process was completed: the pillar structure was abolished, police and judicial cooperation in criminal matters was consolidated with the rest of the AFSJ, and the entire domain is now governed through the Community method.[5] The following section reviews the most important legal and institutional ramifications of the decision to apply the principles and procedures of the Community method to AFSJ.

1 Jurisdiction of the European Court of Justice

Before the Lisbon Treaty, the Court's jurisdiction over AFSJ matters was circumscribed and governed by a special set of rules. Since Lisbon, the general rule is that the AFSJ is subject to the full jurisdiction of the Court of Justice.[6] The one persisting exception is for judicial cooperation in criminal matters and police cooperation, according to which the Court has "no

---

Jörg Monar, "A New 'Area of Freedom, Security and Justice' for the Enlarged EU? The Results of the European Convention," in *The Area of Freedom, Security and Justice in the Enlarged Europe*, ed. Karen Henderson (Basingstoke: Palgrave Macmillan, 2005), 110–134; Valentina Bazzocchi, "The European Charter of Fundamental Rights and the Area of Freedom, Security and Justice," in *The EU Charter of Fundamental Rights*, ed. Giacomo Di Federico (Heidelberg: Springer, 2011): 177–197; Emilio De Capitani, "The Evolving Role of the European Parliament in the AFSJ," in *The Institutional Dimension of the European Union's Area of Freedom, Security and Justice*, ed. Jörg Monar (Brussels: P.I.E Peter Lang, 2010), 113–144.

[5] It should be noted, however, that even though the pillar structure was eliminated, the former "second pillar" covering common foreign and security policy still survives as a domain of intergovernmental cooperation with specific rules and procedures (albeit excluding the possibility of adopting EU legislation).

[6] See Koen Lenaerts, "The Contribution of the European Court of Justice to the Area of Freedom, Security and Justice," *International and Comparative Law Quarterly* 59, no. 2 (2010): 255–301. It is worth recalling that there was a five-year transitional period that has since expired

jurisdiction to review the validity or proportionality of operations carried out by the police and other law-enforcement services of a Member State or the exercise of the responsibilities incumbent upon Member States with regard to the maintenance of law and order and the safeguarding of internal security."[7] In view of the entry into force of the Charter of Fundamental Rights and its impact for criminal justice, migration, and border control policies, the expanded role for the Court is highly significant and has already produced extensive litigation.

It is also important to note that the Court now also has full jurisdiction over international agreements on subjects related to the AFSJ. Thus, under Article 218(11) of the Treaty on the Functioning of the European Union (TFEU), a Member State, the Council, the Commission, or the European Parliament "may obtain the opinion of the Court of Justice as to whether an agreement envisaged is compatible with the treaties. Where the opinion of the Court is adverse, the agreement envisaged may not enter into force unless it is amended, or the Treaties are revised." This extension of the Court's jurisdiction has so far resulted in several Judgments and Opinions,[8] which have given the Court the opportunity to flesh out the new post-Lisbon constitutional framework, including the *Opinion on the European Union's Accession to the European Convention on Human Rights*[9] and the *Opinion on the EU–Canada Agreement on Passenger Name Records*.[10]

2 *Direct Effect and Primacy in Criminal Law*

The decision to consolidate criminal law with the rest of AFSJ policies has led to the application of the constitutional principles of direct effect and primacy, a development which is quite remarkable in light of how central criminal law is to state sovereignty. Since Lisbon, criminal law measures are generally adopted as directives,[11] which, unlike pre-Lisbon Framework Decisions, can have direct effect in the Member States. Moreover, now that the European

---

for EU measures in judicial and police cooperation in criminal matters adopted before the entry into force of the Lisbon Treaty. See Protocol 36 TEU and TFEU.

[7] Article 276 TFEU. However, it is quite likely this exception cannot be invoked when the intervention has a cross-border dimension.

[8] See Henri Labayle, "Architecte ou spectatrice?, La Cour de justice de l'Union dans l'Espace de liberté, de securité et de justice," *Revue trimestrielle de droit européen* 42, no. 1 (2006): 1–46.

[9] Opinion 2/13 of the Court (Full Court), December 18, 2014, ECLI:EU:C:2014:2454.

[10] Opinion 1/15 of the Court (Grand Chamber), July 26, 2017, ECLI:EU:C:2017:592.

[11] Recently, however, the European Parliament and the Council adopted a regulation on the mutual recognition of confiscation and freezing orders. Regulation (EU) 2018/1805, 2018 O.J. (L 303) 1.

Court of Justice (CJEU) has jurisdiction over the entire AFSJ, primacy, i.e. supremacy, also extends to EU measures on police and judicial cooperation in criminal law. This was confirmed by the Court in the *Melloni* judgment.[12] In *Melloni*, the Spanish Constitutional Court referred the question of whether its execution of a European Arrest Warrant, issued by the Italian authorities under the EU Framework Decision, could be conditioned on the Italian *in absentia* conviction being opened up for review, in accordance with the rights of the defense under Spanish constitutional law. The Spanish Constitutional Court raised the question based on Article 53 of the Charter of Fundamental Rights, which says that the rights guaranteed therein shall not be interpreted as restricting rights guaranteed under Member State constitutions. The Spanish Constitutional Court reasoned that this provision gave it license to apply the standard of protection of fundamental rights guaranteed by its constitution when that standard was higher than that deriving from the Charter and, where necessary, to give it priority over the application of provisions of EU law. The CJEU answered in the negative. The CJEU stated that the proposed interpretation of Article 53 of the Charter would undermine the principle of primacy of EU law "which is an essential feature of the EU legal order" so that "rules of national law, even of a constitutional order, cannot be allowed to undermine the effectiveness of EU law on the territory of that State."[13] It should be noted that, recently, the CJEU has followed a less drastic approach in a pair of cases referred by the Italian Constitutional Court. In *Taricco I* and *Taricco II*, the Court of Justice recognized that on matters of fundamental rights, Member State constitutional courts possess a wider margin of appreciation.[14]

3 Principle of Conferral

Under the constitutional principle of conferral, the EU is competent only for the missions foreseen by the Treaties and only to the extent provided for by the Treaties (exclusive, shared or support competence).[15] The principle of

---

[12] Case C-399/11, *Stefano Melloni v. Ministerio Fiscal*, ECLI:EU:C:2013:107.

[13] *Stefano Melloni*, paras. 58–59.

[14] Case C-105/14, *Criminal Proceedings against Ivo Taricco and Others*, ECLI:EU:C:2015:555; Case C-42/17, *Criminal Proceedings against M.A.S. and M.B.*, ECLI:EU:C:2017:936; see Chiara Amalfitano and Oreste Pollicino, "Two Courts, Two Languages? The Taricco Saga Ends on a Worrying Note," *VerfBlog*, June 5, 2018, https://verfassungsblog.de/two-courts-two-languages-the-taricco-saga-ends-on-a-worrying-note/.

[15] Article 5 TEU; Stephen C. Sieberson, "How the New European Union Constitution Will Allocate Power between the EU and Its Member States: A Textual Analysis," *Vanderbilt*

conferral also applies to the AFSJ. The latter is considered a "shared competence" (Article 4(2) TFEU). The Member States shall exercise their powers in the field to the extent that the Union has not yet exercised its competence but once the EU adopts an act, the issues covered become the EU's exclusive competence (so called pre-emption principle under Article 2(2) TFEU).

The EU's powers in AFSJ are subject to a general and a specific limitation. The general limitation is contained in Protocol 25 Treaty on European Union (TEU) and TFEU, which makes clear that when the EU exercises power in areas of shared competence, it preempts Member State action only on those elements governed by the Union act in question and not in the related policy field. The AFSJ's specific limitation is stated in Article 4(2) TEU, according to which the EU shall respect the "essential State functions, including ensuring the territorial integrity of the State, maintaining law and order and safeguarding national security."[16] In particular, national security remains the sole responsibility of each Member State. (As mentioned earlier, this bar on EU competence over national security is paralleled by the exclusion of CJEU jurisdiction in the national security domain.) The specific AFSJ limitation is also confirmed by Article 67(1) TFEU, according to which the AFSJ has to be developed by respecting "the different legal systems and traditions of the Member States."

These limitations on the AFSJ competence present significant challenges, especially with respect to the national security limitation. Internal security at EU level is one of the overarching policy missions of AFSJ, and the Lisbon Treaty envisions policymaking through a Council committee called the Committee for Internal Security (Article 71 TFEU) and implementation and administration by the specialized agencies of Europol (Article 88 TFEU) and Eurojust (Article 85 TFEU). It is difficult to see how the policy scheme can operate with a carve-out for "national security." Following a pragmatic approach, the EU Counter-Terrorism Coordinator considers that the notion of "national security" in Article 4(2) TEU covers principally the activities of those national intelligence and security services that are tasked with protecting the essential structure of the State, as opposed to the generic law and order domain.[17] Since this Member State "exclusive" competence operates as an exception to the general rule of "shared" responsibility in

---

Journal of Transnational Law 37 (2004): 993–1042; Bazzocchi, "The European Charter of Fundamental Rights and the Area of Freedom, Security and Justice."

[16] Sieberson, "How the New European Union Constitution Will Allocate Power between the EU and Its Member States," 1036.

[17] See Chapter 10.

Progress and Failure in the Area of Freedom, Security, and Justice 381

AFSJ, it should be interpreted restrictively and the last word will be for the Court of Justice.[18]

4 *Subsidiarity, Proportionality, and Information*

The principle of subsidiarity, and the related proportionality inquiry, is particularly relevant in a domain of shared responsibility between the EU and the Member States, as is the case for AFSJ policies.[19] The principle of subsidiarity requires that the "Union shall act only if and in so far as the objectives of the proposed action cannot be sufficiently achieved by the Member States, either at central level or at regional and local level, but can rather, by reason of the scale or effects of the proposed action, be better achieved at Union level." (Article 5(3) TEU). In the AFSJ domain, making this subsidiarity assessment is particularly difficult because of the importance of information on the situation in the Member States and the relative dearth of such information.[20] Member States still jealously safeguard their powers over criminal and immigration law, and information on their policies is hard to come by, or when available, not easily comparable. As a result, the EU has been obliged to begin virtually from scratch and to establish general and specific obligations for the Member States to transmit to the EU the information necessary for the new EU policies.

A clear example of the general obligation to transmit information is afforded by Regulation 862/2007 on European statistics on migration and international protection.[21] According to a recent Commission Report, this Regulation

[18] The CJEU has already circumscribed the national security exception in the context of freedom of movement of EU citizens. See Cases C-331/16 and C-366/16, *K. v. Staatssecretaris van Veiligheid en Justice* and *H.F. v. Belgische Staat*, ECLI:EU:C:2018:296.

[19] Stephen David Coutts, "The Lisbon Treaty and the Area of Freedom, Security and Justice as an Area of Legal Integration," *Croatian Yearbook of European Law and Policy* 7, no. 7 (2011): 87–107; Gerard Conway, "Conflicts of Competence Norms in EU Law and the Legal Reasoning of the ECJ," *German Law Journal* 11, no. 9 (2010): 966–1005.

[20] As the Commission observed in Communication from the Commission, *Towards an EU Criminal Policy: Ensuring the Effective Implementation of EU Policies through Criminal Law*, COM (2011) 573 final (September 20, 2011): "To establish the necessity for minimum rules on criminal law, the EU institutions need to be able to rely on clear factual evidence about the nature or effects of the crime in question and about a diverging legal situation in all Member States which could jeopardise the effective enforcement of an EU policy subject to harmonisation. This is why the EU needs to have at its disposal statistical data from the national authorities that allow it to assess the factual situation."

[21] European Parliament and Council Regulation (EC) 862/2007, On Community Statistics on Migration and International Protection, 2007 O.J. (L 199) 23. An amendment to this Regulation has recently been approved by the European Parliament, but it is still awaiting the Council

together with Regulation 1260/2013 and related implementing measures have resulted in clear improvements in data availability, completeness, quality, and timeliness.[22] It has also triggered the need for further information and the Commission has proposed legislation that would expand the information to include better statistics on returns (more frequent, and disaggregated, figures to be reported), resettlement, intra-EU mobility, newly granted permanent/ long-term residence permits, family reunification for those given international protection, child immigration, and more. This information is essential not only for the legislator but also, when made available to the public, for raising the awareness of EU citizens and for improving public debate – a point highlighted by the popularity of Eurostat's webpage with migration data.[23]

5 Principle of Sincere Cooperation and Loyalty

The principle of sincere cooperation and loyalty is established between the EU and the Member States (Article 4(3) TEU) and between the EU institutions (13(2) TEU). According to Article 4(3) TEU: "The Member States shall take any appropriate measure, general or particular, to ensure fulfilment of the obligations arising out of the Treaties or resulting from the Union's tasks and refrain from any measure which could jeopardise the attainment of the Union's objectives."

In the AFSJ domain, these principles are especially important because national authorities are critical for both transposing EU law and for promoting human mobility, security, and dignity in the day-to-day operation of the area. Without sincere cooperation and the related principle of mutual trust, mutual recognition by Member States of criminal justice and migration measures issued by other Member State administrations and courts is at risk, with grave implications for the AFSJ. Sincere cooperation is important for virtually every dimension of the AFSJ, not only administration but also, as noted in the previous section, the exchange of information necessary for the legislative process.[24]

---

vote. European Parliament legislative resolution of 16 April 2019 (COM(2018)0307 – COM0182/2018 – 2018/0154(COD)).

[22] See the latest *Report from the Commission on the Implementation of Regulation (EC) No 862/ 2007 on Community Statistics on Migration and International Protection*, COM (2018) 594 final (August 16, 2018).

[23] "Migration and Migrant Population Statistics," Eurostat website, last visited October 31, 2018, https://ec.europa.eu/eurostat/statistics-explained/index.php/Migration_and_migrant_ population_statistics.

[24] See Chapter 15 for a discussion of mutual trust and the mutual recognition of European Arrest Warrant decisions.

Progress and Failure in the Area of Freedom, Security, and Justice 383

6 *Principle of Solidarity and Fair Sharing of Responsibility*

Related to sincere cooperation is the principle of solidarity and fair sharing of responsibility including the financial consequences of fair sharing (Article 80 TFEU). This principle applies to the border (Article 77 TFEU), asylum (Article 78 TFEU), and migration (Article 79 TFEU) aspects of AFSJ.[25] There is also a specific commitment to solidarity in the event of terrorist attacks or natural disasters (Article 222 TFEU). Increasingly, EU legislation in the borders, asylum, and migration domain establishes detailed procedures in order to detect potential risks and to intervene in case of emergencies. These alert and intervention systems are triggered by reports drafted by specialized EU agencies: the European Border and Coast Guard Agency (Frontex) for the external borders, the European Asylum Support Office (EASO) for refugee influxes, Europol for emerging threats to be dealt with through police cooperation, and European Civil Protection and Humanitarian Aid Operations (ECHO, a specialized Commission Service, which has recently been replaced by a full-fledged Civil Protection Mechanism) for natural disasters and humanitarian aid.[26]

7 *Indirect Administration*

The Lisbon Treaty affirms the principle of indirect administration, whereby the responsibility for implementing and applying EU law belongs primarily to the Member States (Article 4(3), 2nd subparagraph TEU, and Article 291(1) TFEU). This principle extends to the AFSJ but with some important specificities. As has been demonstrated by the experience with the Schengen Area, a common legal framework is not enough to effectively guarantee an area of free travel and security.[27] Rather, to overcome the difficulties arising from the coexistence of twenty-eight different administrative cultures, tools, and regulations, it has been necessary to create institutional mechanisms to promote administrative, organizational, and financial integration.

---

[25] See Chapter 8 for a detailed discussion on the principle of solidarity and fair sharing of responsibility, with particular focus on EU asylum law.

[26] See European Parliament and Council, Decision (EU) 2019/420, 2019 O.J. (L 771) 1 on the Civil Protection Mechanism; Chapters 8 for a discussion of Frontex and EASO; and 10 for a discussion on Europol. See also Lena Karamanidou and Bernd Kasparek, "Border Management and Migration Control in the European Union," Working Paper 2018/14, Global Migration: Consequences and Responses, Respond, July 2018, http://uu.diva-portal.org/smash/get/diva2:1248445/FULLTEXT01.pdf.

[27] For a description of the Schengen Area, see the next section.

There are many examples of this trend toward what is often called "integrated administration." One of the primary functions of EU agencies is to foster integration of national administrations through information exchange and the coordination of joint proceedings and operations.[28] The Treaty contains the legal basis for two security-related agencies, Europol (Article 88 TFEU) and Eurojust (Article 85 TFEU), and a European Public Prosecutor (Article 86 TFEU). Moreover, even in the absence of a legal basis in the Treaties, a number of new EU agencies have been established by EU legislation since 1999. These include Frontex, EASO, the EU cyber-security agency ENISA, the EU human rights agency FRA, the European Observatory of Drugs, and eu-LISA (which is in charge of the management of AFSJ databases).

Even outside the agency framework, there has been a significant effort to monitor and evaluate Member State participation in AFSJ policies. This kind of monitoring is essential for mutual trust, mutual recognition, and the smooth operation of the area of borderless travel and security. The Lisbon Treaty anticipates a "mutual evaluation" mechanism for potentially all AFSJ policies (Article 70 TFEU). So far, the only one to have been adopted is for border control and the application of the Schengen *acquis*.[29] With the informal agreement of the European Parliament, the Council unanimously agreed that this evaluation mechanism should remain a "peer evaluation" exercise, with Commission involvement. Evaluations cover all aspects of the Schengen *acquis*, including the absence of border controls at internal borders, and can entail both announced and unannounced on-site visits. Frontex is also involved, through annual risk analyses, and related recommendations. In case of deficiencies, the Member State concerned is required to submit an action plan to remedy it.

8 Flexibility Clause

Article 352 TFEU authorizes the EU to adopt measures that are not foreseen by the Treaty but that are needed to obtain one of its objectives (known as the

---

[28] Madalina Busuioc, *EU Justice and Home Affairs Agencies: Securing Good Governance*, Study for European Parliament, PE 596.812, 2017; Ester Herlin-Karnell, "Constructing Europe's Area of Freedom, Security, and Justice through the Framework of 'Regulation': A Cascade of Market-Based Challenges in the EU's Fight against Financial Crime," *German Law Journal* 16, no. 1 (2015): 49–73; Estella Baker and Christopher Harding, "From Past Imperfect to Future Perfect? A Longitudinal Study of the Third Pillar," *European Law Review* 34, no. 1 (2009): 47.

[29] See Council Regulation (EU) 1053/2013, Establishing an Evaluation and Monitoring Mechanism to Verify the Application of the Schengen Acquis, 2013 O. J. (L 295) 27.

"flexibility clause" or "implicit powers"). The flexibility clause covers the AFSJ but there are a couple of more specific clauses applicable to criminal justice measures. Under Article 83 (1) TFEU, the Council after consent of the European Parliament may identify new types of serious crime subject to harmonization measures, in addition to those crimes already listed in the Treaty. Moreover, the European Public Prosecutor's Office is currently empowered to prosecute only crimes involving "the financial interests of the Union," but the European Council acting unanimously and with consent of the European Parliament may extend its powers to include serious crime having a cross-border dimension (Article 86 TFEU).

9 *Principle of Democracy*

Last but not least, the principle of democracy has been strengthened in the Lisbon Treaty. All AFSJ legislation, including the police and judicial cooperation measures previously in the Third Pillar, must now be adopted by co-decision with the European Parliament and by qualified majority in the Council (including those domains where the European Parliament (EP) before Lisbon was only consulted or simply informed).[30] Abandoning the unanimity voting rule in the Council was not easy and was only made possible by preserving Member State influence at both the front end and back end of the legislative process: On the front end, Member States (one quarter or more) may initiate legislative proposals without the filter of the Commission (Article 76 TFEU) and, on the back end, specifically with respect to criminal law, a Member State may block a legislative measure if it considers that the text would affect fundamental aspects of its criminal justice system (Article 83 TFEU).

The Lisbon Treaty has also improved the powers of national parliaments in the AFSJ.[31] They now have a role to play in assessing the observance of the

---

[30] See Emilio De Capitani, "The Democratic Accountability of the EU's Area of Freedom, Security and Justice Ten Years On," in *Area of Freedom, Security and Justice Ten Years on Successes and Future Challenges under the Stockholm Programme*, eds. Elspeth Guild, Sergio Carrera, and Alejandro Eggenschwiler (Brussels: Centre for European Policy Studies, 2010), 23–30; Michael Dougan, "The Treaty of Lisbon 2007: Winning Minds, Not Hearts," *Common Market Law Review* 45, no. 3 (2008): 683. For an example, see Ester Herlin-Karnell, "What Principles Drive (or Should Drive) European Criminal Law?" *German Law Journal* 11, no. 10 (2010): 1115–1130.

[31] Angela Tacea, "The Role of National Parliaments in the Area of Freedom, Security and Justice: High Normative Expectations, Low Empirical Results," in *The Routledge Handbook of Justice and Home Affairs*, eds. Ariadna Ripoll Servent and Florian Trauner (Abingdon: Routledge, 2018): 434–444; Katrin Auel and Christine Neuhold, "Multi-Arena Players in the Making? Conceptualizing the Role of National Parliaments since the Lisbon Treaty," *Journal of*

subsidiarity principle in the areas of judicial cooperation in criminal matters and police co-operation (Article 69 TFEU), in evaluating the implementation of the Union's policies (Article 70 TFEU), in being periodically informed by the Council's Committee for the Internal Security strategy (Article 71 TFEU), in evaluating Eurojust's activities (Articles 85(1) TFEU), and in scrutinizing Europol's activities (Article 88(2) TFEU). These provisions complement and strengthen the role for national parliaments set down in Article 12 TEU and Protocol 2 on the application of the principles of subsidiarity and proportionality (TEU and TFEU).

10 Horizontal Differentiation: Opt-Out Countries and Enhanced Cooperation

Even though the EU's ordinary constitutional regime has been extended to all AFSJ policies, important exceptions have been made for Denmark, Ireland, and the United Kingdom. Known as "horizontal differentiation" in European integration, these countries continue to benefit from a special opt-out regime for the AFSJ under Protocols to the Treaties.[32] To allow for opt-outs, a number of issues that previously were found in other parts of the Treaties were consolidated in the AFSJ in the Lisbon Treaty: the regulation of passports, identity cards, residence permits, or any other such document, which before the Lisbon Treaty were included under citizenship title, are now in the AFSJ (Article 78 TFEU); and the legal basis enabling the Council to adopt measures on the freezing of assets to fight terrorism and related activities has been inserted into the AFSJ (Article 75 TFEU) instead of the Chapter on capital and payment (although on this last issue, the opt-out possibility does not apply to Ireland). Needless to say, this special status for Denmark, Ireland, and the United Kingdom is more due to political reasons than objective reasons linked with the situation of these countries. As a result, the nationals of Denmark, Ireland, and the United Kingdom are not subject to the same obligations nor do they enjoy the same protection as EU citizens of the other Member States.[33]

European Policy 24, no. 10 (2016): 1547–1561; Christine Neuhold and Julie Smith, "Conclusion: From 'Latecomers' to 'Policy Shapers'? The Role of National Parliaments in the 'Post-Lisbon' Union," in The Palgrave Handbook of National Parliaments and the European Union, eds. Claudia Hefftler, Christine Neuhold, Olivier Rozenberg, and Julie Smith (London: Palgrave Macmillan, 2015), 668–686.

[32] Dirk Leuffen, Berthold Rittberger, and Frank Schimmelfennig, Differentiated Integration: Explaining Variation in the European Union (Basingstoke: Palgrave Macmillan, 2013), 1.

[33] On paper, the three countries can at any moment draw to an end their special status, but the opposite is true. At the time of this writing, the United Kingdom is headed for Brexit; Ireland is

At the same time, the opt-out countries have accepted that other Member States can advance in certain domains under "enhanced cooperation." The first and still more important case is cooperation on the Schengen Area, which covers external borders policy, and certain aspects of irregular migration, as well as police cooperation.[34] As was explained earlier, cooperation on the Schengen Area has been strengthened since the Lisbon Treaty came into effect. The Schengen Area gradually expanded from the original five to include Italy (November 1990), Spain and Portugal (June 1991), Greece (November 1992), Austria (April 1995) and Denmark, Finland and Sweden, as well as Iceland and Norway (December 1996). The Czech Republic, Estonia, Latvia, Lithuania, Hungary, Malta, Poland, Slovenia, and Slovakia joined in December 2007; so too, in 2008, the associated country Switzerland and thereafter Liechtenstein. Romania and Bulgaria await unanimous approval from the other Schengen members before they can join, while Cyprus has not completed preparations to join because of the island's division. Overall, the Schengen Area comprises the territory of twenty-two EU and four non-EU Member States, in which more than 400 million citizens are able to travel without being subject to internal border controls. It covers a total area of 4.3 million km², has 42,673 km of external maritime borders, 7,721 km of external land borders, and 1,792 external frontier checkpoints, including international airports.

III THE LEGISLATIVE TRACK RECORD POST-LISBON

Almost ten years after the entry into force of the Treaty of Lisbon and its undeniable constitutional advances, the Freedom, Security, and Justice Area is still far from achieving its promise. To be sure, in quantitative terms, AFSJ remains one of the most active domains of EU policymaking and represents 25–30 percent of all EU legislative activity. Overall, however, the policy results have been rather limited and unbalanced compared to the ambitions targets set out in the Lisbon Treaty. In addition, only a few of the legislative instruments from before Lisbon have been upgraded (the so-called

---

maintaining its exceptional status, which was justified because of the passport union with the United Kingdom; and Denmark decided in a 2015 referendum to even opt out of Europol.

[34] Emilio De Capitani, "The Schengen System after Lisbon: From Cooperation to Integration," *ERA Forum* 15, no. 1 (2014): 101–118; William Walters, "Mapping Schengenland: Denaturalizing the Border," *Environment and Planning D: Society and Space* 20, no. 5 (2002): 561–580; Ruben Zaiotti, *Cultures of Border Control: Schengen and the Evolution of European Frontiers* (Chicago: University of Chicago Press, 2011).

388 *Emilio De Capitani*

Lisbonisation process) to reflect the constitutional developments discussed in the first part of this chapter.

1 *Protecting and Promoting Fundamental Values and Rights*

At legislative level the biggest achievement since the entry into force of the Lisbon Treaty has been the adoption of the new EU legal framework for the protection of personal data as foreseen by Article 16 TFEU and Article 8 of the Charter of Fundamental Rights. The two main texts already in force are Regulation 2016/679, known as the General Data Protection Regulation,[35] and Directive 2016/680 with regard to the processing of personal data for public security purposes.[36] These measures will soon be followed by a Regulation on protection of personal data for EU institutions[37] and by a specific Directive dealing with protection of personal data in the electronic services (E-Privacy).[38] By protecting individuals from all kinds of data protection abuses, by both private actors and public authorities at national and supranational level, this body of regulation is an important achievement. Not only has it set the standard for Europe but it has also shaped data protection guarantees in the third countries to which EU personal data is transferred.[39]

The Lisbon Treaty also strengthened the legal basis for the right of access to documents of EU institutions (Article 15 TFEU and Article 42 of the Charter of Fundamental Rights). Unfortunately, the revision of the pre-Lisbon rules in

[35] European Parliament and Council Regulation (EU) 2016/679, On the Protection of Natural Persons with Regard to the Processing of Personal Data and on the Free Movement of Such Data, 2016 O.J. (L 119) 1.

[36] European Parliament and Council Directive (EU) 2016/680, On the Protection of Natural Persons with Regard to the Processing of Personal Data, 2016 O.J. (L 119) 89.

[37] See the text of the *Proposal for a Regulation of the European Parliament and of the Council on the Protection of Individuals with Regard to the Processing of Personal Data*, COM (2017) 8 final (January 10, 2017) as confirmed by the EP in the European Parliament Resolution, On the Proposal for a Regulation of the European Parliament and of the Council on the Protection of Individuals with Regard to the Processing of Personal Data by the Union Institutions, Bodies, Offices and Agencies and on the Free Movement of Such Data, and Repealing Regulation (EC) No 45/2001 and Decision No 1247/2002/EC, P8_TA-PROV(2018)0348 (September 13, 2018).

[38] See the latest version of the *Proposal for a Regulation of the European Parliament and of the Council Concerning the Respect for Private Life and the Protection of Personal Data in Electronic Communications and Repealing Directive 2002/58/EC*, COM (2017) 10 final (January 10, 2017).

[39] Jan Philipp Albrecht, "How the GDPR Will Change the World," *European Data Protection Law Review* 2, no. 3 (2016): 287–289; see also Lukas Feiler, Nikolaus Forgó, and Michaela Weigl, *The EU General Data Protection Regulation (GDPR): A Commentary* (Woking: German Law Publishers, 2018).

this domain[40] is still blocked in the Council because of the strong resistance of the Council and the Commission to implementing the EU principles. There are a number of weak points that require a thorough rewriting of the current legislation. For instance, the legal standards for classifying information as confidential, secret, and top-secret documents are very poorly defined in Article 9 of Regulation 1049/01, a flaw that affects not only citizens but also the European Parliament's work on freedom, security, and justice matters. The real standards applicable to the access and exchange of this information are those adopted on the basis of the Council's Rules of Procedure with a specific implementing decision,[41] which transpose the EU–NATO agreement in this domain.[42]

The only real progress on transparency has been made thanks to the jurisprudence of the Court of Justice. It has enforced different components of the post-Lisbon framework: the requirement that not only votes but also legislative debates in the European Parliament and Council be public (Article 15(3)TFEU), permitting the public to learn of the position of the different national delegations;[43] and the duty to disclose information related to the foreseeable impact of a legislative procedure.[44] The General Court has recently issued an important ruling holding in favor of disclosure of the documents exchanged during "legislative trilogues" designed to expedite the legislative process, notwithstanding the "informal" character of these interinstitutional meetings.[45] Unfortunately, similar progress on transparency has not been made with respect to documents connected with the implementing phase of EU legislation.[46]

---

[40] European Parliament and Council Regulation (EC) 1049/2001, Regarding Public Access to European Parliament, Council and Commission Documents, 2001 O.J. (L 145) 43.

[41] See Council Decision 2013/488/EU, On the Security Rules for Protecting EU Classified Information, 2013 O.J. (L 274) 1.

[42] Agreement between the European Union and the North Atlantic Treaty Organisation on the Security of Information, March 14, 2003, 2003 O.J. (L 80) 36; see also Council Decision (EU) 2019/292, On the Authorisation To Release EU Classified Information to Third States and International Organisations, 2019 O.J. (L 48) 20.

[43] See Joined Cases C-39/05 P and C-52/05 P, *Sweden and Turco v. Council*, ECLI:EU: C:2008:374; Case C-280/11 P, *Council v. Access Info Europe*, ECLI:EU:C:2013:671, para. 63; Case T-540/15, *De Capitani v. Parliament*, ECLI:EU:T:2018:167; Case C-57/16 P, *ClientEarth v. European Commission*, ECLI:EU:C:2018:660; and Case T-128/14, *Daimler v. Commission*, ECLI:EU:T:2018:643.

[44] See *ClientEarth*.

[45] *De Capitani v. Parliament*.

[46] See, e.g., Case C-562/14, *Sweden v. Commission*, ECLI:EU:C:2017:356, dealing with the so-called EU Pilot Procedure.

390   *Emilio De Capitani*

Another legislative procedure designed to give positive expression to a fundamental right, albeit not technically in the AFSJ, is a proposal for a new directive on the principle of equal treatment between persons irrespective of religion or belief, disability, age, or sexual orientation.[47] Since 2008, the text has been blocked in the Council, mainly because of a strong reservation of the German delegation. To partially compensate, the Commission has issued a number of nonbinding recommendations on the powers, structure, and functions of the equality bodies that have been created in each Member State.[48]

2 *Human Mobility and Protection of EU Borders*

In the years after the Amsterdam Treaty, when border control policy was first transferred to the Community method, a number of important legislative measures had already been passed. The generic term "measures" in the relevant Treaty article paved the way to strengthen the rules governing border guards contained in the Schengen Borders Code,[49] to establish the EU borders agency (Frontex),[50] and to develop administrative networks and EU-wide information systems.[51]

Since Lisbon, the most important legislative accomplishment on borders, indeed perhaps in the entire AFSJ, has been EU Regulation 2016/1624 on the European Border and Coast Guard.[52] Adopted over thirty years after the

---

[47] The latest consolidated provisional text of the *Proposal for a Council Directive on Implementing the Principle of Equal Treatment between Persons Irrespective of Religion or Belief, Disability, Age or Sexual Orientation*, COM (2008) 426 final (July 2, 2018), is the result of ten years negotiation by the Council.

[48] See *Commission Recommendation on Standards for Equality Bodies*, C (2018) 3850 final (June 22, 2018).

[49] Recently codified: European Parliament and Council Regulation (EU) 2016/399, On a Union Code on the Rules Governing the Movement of Persons across Borders (Schengen Borders Code), 2016 O.J. (L 77) 1.

[50] See Council Regulation (EC) 2007/2004, Establishing a European Agency for the Management of Operational Cooperation at the External Borders of the Member States of the European Union, 2004 O.J. (L 349) 1. The regulation has already been modified in 2007, 2011, 2013, and 2014.

[51] European Parliament and Council Regulation (EU) 1077/2011, Establishing a European Agency for the Operational Management of Large-Scale IT Systems in the Area of Freedom, Security and Justice, 2011 O.J. (L 286) 1. Since Lisbon, another system has been created specifically for external border crossing. See European Parliament and Council Regulation (EU) 1052/2013, Establishing the European Border Surveillance System (Eurosur), 2013 O.J. (L 295) 11.

[52] European Parliament and Council Regulation (EU) 2016/1624, 2016 O.J. (L 251) 1. Political agreement on a new Frontex regulation was reached in April 2019, and it is expected that the new Regulation will be formally adopted in autumn 2019.

first Schengen agreement, this Regulation outlines at the legislative level for the first time the main "measures necessary for the gradual establishment of an integrated management system for external borders."[53] The Regulation advances the objective of stronger integration among national border police and control systems and between the national and European levels in several ways. It announces a full-fledged integrated border policy, develops Frontex into a multilevel national-European border agency, and amends the Schengen Borders Code. The Regulation also enhances Frontex's role in migration hotspots, enabling it to coordinate national responses and to participate in search and rescue operations and in the return of illegal migrants.[54] The Regulation has made clear that solidarity is not tied to the simple goodwill of the Member States but is the consequence of a shared "in solido" responsibility for the Schengen Area. This new legislative framework will undoubtedly drive future developments not only on borders but also on complementary policies dealing with asylum, migration, and even internal security.

3 A Common EU Asylum Policy

Article 78 TFEU is the legal basis for the common asylum policy.[55] Before the Lisbon Treaty, certain minimum rules were adopted; after Lisbon, between 2009 and 2013, the central components of the system were put into place. Five of these texts are again under revision: (i) The "Dublin Regulation," which defines which Member State has a duty to examine requests for asylum (generally the Member State of first entry into the EU). Since the current system puts extreme pressure on the Member States whose borders are also the external borders of the EU there have been several unsuccessful proposals put forward by the Commission and the European Parliament for sharing this burden by relocating the asylum seekers, notably in cases of mass influxes of refugees.[56] (ii) The "Reception Conditions" Directive, which defines the conditions (such as housing) to be granted to asylum seekers and protects their fundamental rights by ensuring that detention is only applied as a

---

[53] Article 77 TFEU.
[54] For more discussion of hotspots, see Chapter 8.
[55] For a detailed discussion of the common asylum policy, see Chapter 8.
[56] *Proposal for a Regulation of the European Parliament and of the Council Establishing the Criteria and Mechanisms for Determining the Member State Responsible for Examining an Application for International Protection Lodged in One of the Member States by a Third-Country National or a Stateless Person*, COM (2016) 270 final/2 (May 4, 2016).

measure of last resort.[57] (iii) The "Qualification Regulation," which clarifies the grounds for granting international protection. It will also improve access to rights and integration measures for beneficiaries of international protection.[58] (iv) The "Asylum Procedure" Regulation, which aims at fairer, quicker, and better-quality asylum decisions, notably for the most vulnerable people such as unaccompanied minors and victims of torture.[59] (v) The Eurodac Regulation, which requires the fingerprints of asylum seekers to be stored in a European database (to avoid multiple requests for asylum by the same refugee). In the current proposed text, law enforcement authorities would have access to the EU database in order to prevent, detect, or investigate the most serious crimes, such as murder, and terrorism.[60] The Common European Asylum System (CEAS) will be completed by an EU measure defining which countries should be considered safe, thereby simplifying the asylum procedure and expediting the return of individuals who do not qualify for international protection.

At the time of writing, negotiations on what is collectively known as the "Asylum Package" have reached a stalemate. After numerous trilogue meetings, a partial agreement between the Council and the European Parliament was reached in June 2018 on three measures: the Qualifications Regulation, the Reception Directive, and the Resettlement Regulation.[61] In the Council, however, each of the measures has been held up because of the opposition of a minority of delegations, who have come out against the position of the Council in the trilogue talks.[62] The diminished number of asylum requests in

---

[57] *Proposal for a Directive of the European Parliament and of the Council Laying Down Standards for the Reception of Applicants for International Protection*, COM (2016) 465 final (July 13, 2016).

[58] *Proposal for a Regulation of the European Parliament and of the Council on Standards for the Qualification of Third-Country Nationals or Stateless Persons as Beneficiaries of International Protection*, COM (2016) 466 final (July 13, 2016).

[59] *Proposal for a Regulation of the European Parliament and of the Council Establishing a Common Procedure for International Protection in the Union and Repealing Directive 2013/32/EU*, COM (2016) 467 final (July 13, 2016).

[60] *Proposal for a Regulation of the European Parliament and of the Council on the Establishment of 'Eurodac' for the Comparison of Fingerprints*, COM (2016) 272 final (May 4, 2016).

[61] *Proposal for a Directive of the European Parliament and of the Council Establishing a Union Resettlement Framework*, COM (2016) 468 final (July 13, 2016).

[62] See "Reform of the Common European Asylum System (CEAS) is in a Mess," Statewatch website, last visited November 1, 2018, www.statewatch.org/news/2018/oct/eu-council-ceas-in-a-mess.htm; Council of the European Union, Reform of the Common European Asylum System and Resettlement, Doc. No. 12420-18 (October 2, 2018).

Progress and Failure in the Area of Freedom, Security, and Justice   393

2017 and 2018[63] has slowed down matters further, since reform of the CEAS appears less urgent. Interinstitutional negotiations in this politically sensitive domain will have to be resumed after the 2019 European elections, in the 2019–2024 legislature.

4 An EU Migration Policy Still in the Making

Article 79 TFEU is the new ambitious legal basis for migration policy. Notwithstanding the potential for a common migration policy, it is under-developed at present. The measures that currently exist deal with visas and irregular migration.

On the subject of irregular migration, the most important text is the "Return Directive,"[63] which was adopted in 2008, and contains obligations to return irregular migrants and sets down minimum standards for their treatment.[64] Recently, the European Parliament and the Council have decided to use the Schengen Information System for the registration of Member State return decisions and entry bans of illegal third-country nationals.[65] Other measures target the traffickers[66] and smugglers[67] of human beings and the employers of illegal third-country nationals.[68]

On visas, the EU has a common list of countries whose citizens are required to have a visa to travel to the Schengen Area.[69] Generally speaking, citizens

---

[63] See the EASO latest statistics here, "Asylum Applications Remain Stable in the EU throughout Summer Months," EASO website, last visited November 1, 2018, www.easo.europa.eu/news-events/asylum-applications-remain-stable-eu-throughout-summer-months.

[63] European Parliament and Council Directive 2008/115/EC, On Common Standards and Procedures in Member States for Returning Illegally Staying Third-Country Nationals, 2008 O.J. (L 348) 98.

[64] The procedures contained in the Return Directive are currently being revised. See *Proposal for a Regulation of the European Parliament and of the Council on a European Travel Document for the Return of Illegally Staying Third-Country Nationals*, COM (2015) 668 final (December 15, 2015); *Proposal for a Regulation of the European Parliament and of the Council on the European Border and Coast Guard*, COM (2018) 631 final (September 12, 2018).

[65] European Parliament and Council, Regulation (EU) 2018/1860, 2018 O.J. (L 312) 1.

[66] See "Together against Trafficking in Human Beings," European Commission website, last visited November 1, 2018, https://ec.europa.eu/anti-trafficking/.

[67] Council Framework Decision 2002/946/JHA, On the Strengthening of the Penal Framework to Prevent the Facilitation of Unauthorised Entry, Transit and Residence, 2002 O.J. (L 328) 1.

[68] European Parliament and Council Directive 2009/52/EC, Providing for Minimum Standards on Sanctions and Measures against Employers of Illegally Staying Third-Country Nationals, 2009 O.J. (L 168) 24.

[69] See the Regulation recently codified, European Parliament Resolution, On the Proposal for a Regulation of the European Parliament and of the Council Listing the Third Countries Whose Nationals Must Be in Possession of Visas When Crossing the External Borders and

who have a Schengen visa can travel within the Schengen Area for up to 90 days in any 180-day period. In addition, the EU is currently adopting, based on the example of countries like the United States, Australia, and Canada, a European Travel Information and Authorisation System (ETIAS) for all third-country nationals entering the Schengen Area.[70] This will be paired with an ambitious system for monitoring the presence on Schengen territory of visa overstayers (the so-called Entry-Exit system).[71]

The policy field of regular, economic migration is the least developed of all. Similar to other advanced economies, Europe seeks to attract highly skilled workers. It has adopted several measures to standardize long-term residence applications and rights for long-term residents, including the Single Permit Directive,[72] the Researchers Directive,[73] and the Blue Card Directive.[74] These Directives also facilitate movement between Member States, but the issue of how many economic migrants to admit remains within the prerogative of the single Member States.

5 A Criminal Justice Area under Construction

Since the entry into force of the Lisbon Treaty, most of the legislation in the criminal justice area has been focused on sanctions and has been adopted on the basis of Articles 82, 83, 85, and 86 TFEU.[75] Much of this legislation is based on the mutual recognition of national measures, including on the freezing and confiscation of the proceeds of crime,[76] search warrants,[77] and criminal discovery of electronic communications.[78] EU criminal law seeks to

---

Those Whose Nationals are Exempt from That Requirement, P8_TA-PROV(2018)0359 (October 2, 2018).

[70] European Parliament and Council Regulation (EU) 2018/1240, 2018 O.J. (L 61) 1.

[71] European Parliament and Council Regulation (EU) 2017/2226, 2017 O.J. (L 327) 20.

[72] European Parliament and Council Directive 2011/98/EU, 2011 O.J. (L 343) 1.

[73] Council Directive 2005/71/EC, 2005 O.J. (L 289) 15.

[74] Council Directive 2009/50/EC, 2009 O.J. (L 155) 17. Revisions to the Blue Card Directive are currently pending. *Proposal for a Directive of the European Parliament and of the Council*, COM (2016) 378 final (7 June 2016).

[75] For an extensive discussion of EU criminal and counter-terrorism policies, see Chapter 10.

[76] European Parliament and Council Directive 2014/42/EU, On the Freezing and Confiscation of Instrumentalities and Proceeds of Crime in the European Union, 2014 O.J. (L 127) 39.

[77] European Parliament and Council Directive 2014/41/EU, Regarding the European Investigation Order in Criminal Matters, 2014 O.J. (L 130) 1.

[78] *Proposal for a Regulation of the European Parliament and of the Council on European Production and Preservation Orders for Electronic Evidence in Criminal Matters*, COM (2018) 225 final (April 17, 2018). At the time of writing this proposal is still under negotiation.

Progress and Failure in the Area of Freedom, Security, and Justice   395

develop tools for preventing crime[79] and for detecting and sanctioning crime.[80] Criminal sanctions have also been imposed by resorting to the specific legal basis of the single market activities being regulated,[81] and therefore, unfortunately, in the absence of a general criminal law strategy. In parallel with these internal measures, the EU has also concluded or is currently negotiating international agreements with third countries.[82] It is also

[79] The texts currently in force are: European Parliament and Council Directive (EU) 2016/681, On the Use of Passenger Name Record (PNR) Data for the Prevention, Detection, Investigation and Prosecution of Terrorist Offences and Serious Crime, 2016 O.J. (L 119) 132; European Parliament and Council Regulation (EU) 2019/816, Establishing a Centralised System for the Identification of Member States Holding Conviction Information on Third-Country Nationals and Stateless Persons (ECRIS-TCN); European Parliament and Council Directive 2019/884 Amending Council Framework Decision 2009/315/JHA, as Regards the Exchange of Information on Third-Country Nationals and as Regards the European Criminal Records Information System (ECRIS), 2019 O.J. (L 151) 143.

[80] The main texts adopted are the following: European Parliament and Council Directive 2011/36/EU, On Preventing and Combating Trafficking in Human Beings and Protecting Its Victims, 2011 O.J. (L 101) 1; European Parliament and Council Directive 2011/92/EU, On Combating the Sexual Abuse and Sexual Exploitation of Children and Child Pornography, and Replacing Council Framework Decision 2004/68/JHA, 2011 O.J. (L 335) 1; European Parliament and Council Directive (EU) 2017/541, On Combating Terrorism and Replacing Council Framework Decision 2002/475/JHA and Amending Council Decision 2005/671/JHA, 2017 O.J. (L 88) 6; Council Framework 2001/413/JHA, Combating Fraud and Counterfeiting of Non-Cash Means of Payment, 2001 O.J. (L 149) 1; European Parliament and Council Directive 2013/40/EU, On Attacks against Information Systems and Replacing Council Framework Decision 2005/222/JHA, 2013 O.J. (L 218) 8; European Parliament and Council, Directive (EU) 2017/2103, Amending Council Framework Decision 2004/757/JHA, 2017 O.J. (L 305) 12; European Parliament and Council, Directive (EU) 2018/1673, On Combating Money Laundering by Criminal Law, 2018 O.J. (L 284) 22.

[81] According to Article 83(2) TFEU, criminal sanctions could be foreseen not only for the so-called Eurocrimes such as terrorism and trafficking of human beings but also when harmonization of criminal law shall prove "essential to ensure the effective implementation of a Union policy," for instance, linked with the internal market, environment, consumers policy, etc. Early examples of this legislation include the European Parliament and Council Directive 2003/6/EC, On Insider Dealing and Market Manipulation (Market Abuse), 2003 O.J. (L 96) 16; European Parliament and Council Regulation (EU) 596/2014, On Market Abuse, 2014 O.J. (L 173) 1; European Parliament and Council Directive (EU) 2017/1371, On the Fight against Fraud to the Union's Financial Interests by Means of Criminal Law, 2017 O.J. (L 198) 29 (providing common definitions of offences against the EU budget as fraud or the misuse of public procurement procedures).

[82] See Agreement between the EU and the United States on the Processing and Transfer of Financial Messaging Data from the EU to the USA for the Purposes of the Terrorist Finance Tracking Program, 2010 O.J. (L 195) 5, the first version of which was rejected by the EP; Agreement between the United States of America and the European Union on the Use and Transfer of Passenger Name Record to the United States Department of Homeland Security, 2012 O.J. (L 215) 5; Agreement between the EU and Japan on Mutual Legal Assistance in Criminal Matters, 2010 O.J. (L 39) 20. It is worth recalling that the EP withheld its consent on the Anti-Counterfeiting Trade Agreement, in particular because the inclusion of criminal

396   *Emilio De Capitani*

in the process of acceding to certain Council of Europe Conventions in this domain, such as the Convention on Terrorism[83] and its protocol on foreign fighters.[84] It is worthwhile noting that only a relatively small proportion of the EU's legislation in the criminal justice field is focused on improving the rights of the defense and victims' rights.[85]

On the institutional front, since the entry into force of the Lisbon Treaty, the EU has strengthened the role of EU agencies such as Europol[86] and Eurojust,[87] and has adopted the Regulation on the European Public Prosecutor (EPPO).[88] The intention is for Europol to become an information

---

    sanctions for violation of intellectual property rights was considered neither clearly defined nor proportionate.

[83] See "Details of Treaty No.196. Council of Europe Convention on the Prevention of Terrorism," Council of Europe website, last visited November 1, 2018, www.coe.int/en/web/conventions/full-list/-/conventions/treaty/196.

[84] Additional Protocol to the Council of Europe Convention on the Prevention of Terrorism (October 22, 2015), https://rm.coe.int/168047c5ea.

[85] Establishing procedural rights in criminal proceedings at the EU level was already proposed in the 2003 European Commission Green Paper on "Procedural Safeguards for Suspects and Defendants in Criminal Proceedings throughout the EU." It became a reality only after the Stockholm Programme was adopted by the European Council, ten days after the entry into force of the Lisbon Treaty, which has lifted the unanimity rule in this domain. The main texts are the following: European Parliament and Council Directive 2012/13/EU, On the Right to Information in Criminal Proceedings, 2012 O.J. (L 142) 1; European Parliament and Council Directive 2010/64/EU, On Right to Interpretation and Translation in Criminal Proceedings, 2010 O.J. (L 280) 1; European Parliament and Council Directive 2013/48/EU, On the Right of Access to a Lawyer in Criminal Proceedings and in European Arrest Warrant Proceedings, and on the Right to Have a Third Party Informed upon Deprivation of Liberty and to Communicate with Third Persons and with Consular Authorities While Deprived of Liberty, 2013 O.J. (L 294) 1; European Parliament and Council Directive 2016/343, On Strengthening of Certain Aspects of the Presumption of Innocence and of the Right to be Present at Trial in Criminal Proceedings, 2016 O.J. (L 65) 1; European Parliament and Council Directive 2016/800, On Procedural Safeguards for Children Who Are Suspects or Accused Persons in Criminal Proceedings, 2016 O.J. (L 132) 1; European Parliament and Council Directive 2016/1919, On Legal Aid for Suspects and Accused Persons in Criminal Proceedings for Requested Persons in European Arrest Warrant Proceedings, 2016 O.J. (L 297) 1; European Parliament and Council Directive 2011/99/EU, On the European Protection Order, 2011 O.J. (L 338) 2.

[86] European Parliament and Council Regulation (EU) 2016/794, On the European Union Agency for Law Enforcement Cooperation (Europol) and Replacing and Repealing Council Decisions 2009/371/JHA, 2009/934/JHA, 2009/935/JHA, 2009/936/JHA and 2009/968/JHA, 2016 O.J. (L 135) 53.

[87] European Parliament and Council Regulation (EU) 2018/1727, On the European Union Agency for Criminal Justice Cooperation (Eurojust), 2018 O.J. (L 295) 138. Eurojust will need to cooperate closely with the EPPO. Moreover, Eurojust will continue to be responsible for judicial cooperation in relation to crimes against EU financial interests in respect of those Member States that do not yet participate in the EPPO.

[88] Council Regulation (EU) 2017/1939, Implementing Enhanced Cooperation on the Establishment of the European Public Prosecutor's Office ('the EPPO'), 2017 O.J. (L 283) 1.

hub for law enforcement so that Member States can work more closely and effectively. Complex investigations require sound analysis. The other major improvement foreseen by Article 88 TFEU is the democratic scrutiny by the European Parliament together with national parliaments. Europol's legal basis has been aligned with the Treaty of Lisbon, and there are ongoing efforts to make Europol more accountable, effective, and efficient. Europol's data protection has been improved, even though it still must be coordinated with the Data Protection Directive applicable in the security domain,[89] as well as new data protection rules that have been introduced for EU institutions and agencies.

As far as Eurojust is concerned, it is increasingly active. In 2017, Eurojust supported Member States in more than 2,500 criminal cases and organized 200 joint investigative teams. The European Parliament and national parliaments have acquired a greater role in assessing Eurojust activities. There is institutional agreement on applying the Regulation on Access to Documents to all Eurojust documents, including those related to operational matters. This will ensure more transparency for citizens and greater oversight by the European Parliament. In addition, the harmonized data protection laws for EU institutions and bodies will also apply to Eurojust.

The Regulation establishing the European Public Prosecutor Office (EPPO),[90] foreseen by Article 86 TFEU, was passed only after long and extremely complex negotiations within the Council and was made possible only because of the decision to go forward with enhanced cooperation among twenty Member States. The EPPO, which will be in operation by the end of 2020, will become the centerpiece of a new system, joining together national law enforcement, judicial authorities, and EU actors such as the European Anti-Fraud Office (OLAF), Eurojust, and Europol. In its first phase, EPPO will be a specialized body with investigatory powers dedicated to the fight against crimes related to the EU budget such as fraud, corruption, money laundering, and Value Added Tax (VAT) fraud. The Regulation also provides for a specific and robust set of procedural rights for suspects and accused persons. The EPPO will carry out this task on the basis of a truly European investigation and prosecution policy. The existing administrative body OLAF will closely cooperate with the EPPO to ensure complementarity of their respective mandates. In the future, the

---

[89] European Parliament and Council Directive (EU) 2016/680.
[90] Council Regulation (EU) 2017/1939.

EPPO may also acquire the power to investigate and prosecute cross-border terrorist offences.[91]

6 A Still-Virtual Internal Security Strategy

Beyond specific criminal justice measures, the EU has sought to develop an internal security strategy (ISS) that covers all stages of security, from the strategic to the legislative and operational levels. The first post-Lisbon ISS, adopted by the European Council, covered the period 2010–2014.[92] It was followed by a new ISS covering the period 2015–2020.[93] These documents aim to establish a shared agenda for the Member States, EU institutions, civil society, local authorities, and, interestingly enough, the EU security industry.[94] As foreseen by Article 83 TFEU, the ISS is aimed at the most serious crimes of "terrorism, trafficking in human beings and sexual exploitation of women and children, illicit drug trafficking, illicit arms trafficking, money laundering, corruption, counterfeiting of means of payment, computer crime and organised crime." The ISS calls for information exchange between the Member States and the EU following the "availability principle," according to which national law enforcement authorities should share among themselves the information needed, in particular in the context of joint operations. These strategic documents have since been followed by a Commission "European Agenda on Security,"[95] adopted in 2015, which is constantly updated[96] by

---

[91] See Communication from the Commission, *A Europe That Protects: An Initiative to Extend the Competences of the European Public Prosecutor's Office to Cross-Border Terrorist Crimes*, COM (2018) 641 final (September 12, 2018).

[92] European Council, "The Internal Security Strategy for the European Union: Towards an European Security Model," March 2010, www.consilium.europa.eu/media/30753/qc3010313enc.pdf.

[93] Draft Council Conclusions on the Renewed European Union Internal Security Strategy 2015–2020, Doc. No. 9798/15 (June 10, 2015).

[94] Sergio Carrera and Elspeth Guild, "The EU Internal Security Strategy and the Stockholm Programme: A Challenge to Rule of Law and Liberty in Europe," CEPS Paper, institutdelors.eu/wp-content/uploads/2018/01/tgae20114ccarreraguild-.pdf.

[95] See Communication from the Commission, *The European Agenda on Security*, COM (2015) 185 final (April 28, 2015), as well as the relevant Factsheet, European Commission, "A European Agenda on Security State of Play: September 2017," https://ec.europa.eu/home-affairs/sites/homeaffairs/files/what-we-do/policies/european-agenda-security/20170907_a_european_agenda_on_security_-_state_of_play_en.pdf.

[96] Communication from the Commission, *Delivering on the European Agenda on Security to Fight against Terrorism and Pave the Way towards an Effective and Genuine Security Union*, COM (2016) 230 final (April 20, 2016).

Progress and Failure in the Area of Freedom, Security, and Justice 399

periodic reports[97] adopted under the responsibility of the Commissioner for internal security, in close cooperation with the Commissioner in charge of migration and home affairs. There is also an EU Global Strategy for Foreign and Security Policy (EUGS), adopted in 2016, which makes clear the interaction between internal and external EU security.[98]

There are several weaknesses with these initiatives. As suggested by their titles, the various strategies are not binding. They are adopted without the involvement of the European Parliament, and, quite likely, without that of national parliaments. Moreover, these internal security efforts cover only activities at EU level and make practically no reference to the situation on the ground in the Member States because of the lack of data, which in most cases are inaccessible or unverifiable. Last, and most troubling, each Member State operates with a different system of democratic accountability for internal security. In theory, Member State governments are subject to oversight by their national parliaments, but it is unclear how effective this has been; moreover, accountability to national parliaments has been used as a reason for avoiding accountability at the EU level, notably with respect to EU external security operations.

Unlike cooperation among border control authorities, which has been built bottom-up since 1995, when the Convention Implementing the Schengen Agreement entered into force, police cooperation is still fragmented. This is true not only of cooperation among the Member States, but even inside the Member States themselves, most notably in federalist systems.

To establish an effective area of internal security, it will be necessary to take stock of how much progress has been made on national implementation of existing EU security measures. Most of these security measures, for instance the EU Policy Cycle for organized and serious international crime, for 2013–2017 and 2018–2021,[99] have been developed on a voluntary basis and without associating the European Parliament.

---

[97] The latest (16th) periodic report is Communication from the Commission, *Sixteenth Progress Report towards an Effective and Genuine Security Union*, COM (2018) 690 final (October 10, 2018).

[98] See "EU Global Strategy," European Union website, last visited November 1, 2018, https://europa.eu/globalstrategy/en/global-strategy-foreign-and-security-policy-european-union.

[99] See Council of the European Union, "EU Policy Cycle to Tackle Organised and Serious International Crime," 2014, www.consilium.europa.eu/media/30232/qc0114638enn.pdf; "The EU Policy Cycle to Tackle Organized Crime," European Council website, last visited November 1, 2018, www.consilium.europa.eu/en/documents-publications/publications/eu-policy-cycle-tackle-organized-crime/; "EU Policy Cycle – Empact," Europol website, last visited November 1, 2018, www.europol.europa.eu/crime-areas-and-trends/eu-policy-cycle-empact; "The EU Fight against Organised Crime 2018–2021," European Council website, last

IV THE GOVERNANCE TRACK RECORD POST-LISBON

Even though the expectation was that, after Lisbon, the AFSJ would be governed through the Community method and the ordinary principles of constitutional law, the experience has been quite different. As will be argued in this section, the Member States, either alone or through the intergovernmental method in the Council and the European Council, have continued to control the AFSJ. As a result, there is little coherent policy at the EU level, and to the extent that it does exist, it lacks transparency, European Parliament participation, and European Parliament oversight.

The main devices that have been used by the Member States, through the European Council and the Council, to preserve the pre-Lisbon situation are: (a) withholding information essential to the policymaking process; (b) maintaining poorly defined institutional roles in the EU policymaking cycle; (c) circumventing parliamentary input through the choice of Common Foreign and Security Policy as the legal basis for AFSJ initiatives; and (d) empowering EU agencies, which are creatures of the Member States, to exercise both executive and political functions.

1 Withholding Essential Information for the Policymaking Process

Information is essential for successful public policies, from conception to implementation. Unfortunately, in the AFSJ domain, the formal importance that has been acquired by EU institutions is not matched by a permanent and structured exchange of information between the Member States and the EU level. National ministries (interior and justice) still fail to share information among themselves and with EU institutions, undermining the development of the AFSJ.

The situation is variegated among AFSJ policies. Information exchange in Schengen cooperation on border controls, the longest-standing of the policy areas, is fairly well developed. As discussed in the previous section, asylum policy now has Regulation 862/2007 on European statistics on migration and international protection,[100] which has been quite successful. However, information exchange on issues related to police and security cooperation is disappointing. Even when EU legislation establishes a specific obligation for

---

visited November 1, 2018, www.consilium.europa.eu/en/policies/eu-fight-against-organised-crime-2018-2021.

[100] European Parliament and Council Regulation (EC) 862/2007.

Member State authorities to share data, the obligation is often not respected.[101] A clear example of specific duties on information exchange that go unheeded is the EU Directive against Terrorism, which directs Member State authorities to share information gathered in criminal proceedings connected to terrorist offenses. Without such information it is difficult for the European Commission to prepare impact evaluations for future legislation, and is near-impossible for the European Parliament – which lacks direct contact of any sort with national police authorities – to assess the need for legislation.

At the operational level, information sharing on criminal and security matters has also proven very difficult. Even though there is a basic framework for information exchange, there are many known instances in which national police and intelligence agencies, not to speak of the Council's Committee on Internal Security (COSI), have failed to share important information with the European Parliament and quite likely most national parliaments. Suffice it to note that according to Article 71 TFEU, the European Parliament and national parliaments should be regularly informed of Council activities linked with internal security; yet COSI does so with a single forty-page report circulated every eighteen months.[102] Even EU agencies such as Europol and Frontex, in which almost all the Member States are represented, including Denmark, the United Kingdom, and Ireland (which have a special status), have experienced considerable difficulties eliciting the information needed to monitor the situation in the Member States.[103] These agencies have been forced to develop from scratch their own systems for collecting data to better understand the real scope, on the ground, of the criminal and security threats.

This lack of information has spurred the EU effort, currently underway, to syphon off the maximum information possible from existing AFSJ databases by

[101] European Parliament and Council Directive (EU) 2017/541, art. 22.
[102] Draft Report to the European Parliament and National Parliaments on the Proceedings of the Standing Committee on Operational Cooperation on Internal Security for the Period January 2016–June 2017, COSI meeting, Doc. No. 14108/1/17 (November 20, 2017).
[103] For an illustration of this shortcoming in the Europol context, see Emma Disley et al., "Evaluation of the Implementation of the Europol Council Decision and of Europol's Activities," Europol Management Board, RAND, 2012, chapter 4, www.rand.org/pubs/technical_reports/TR1264.html. The report stated that: "There was a consensus among interviewees across all stakeholder groups (including liaison officers and HENUs [Heads of Europol National Units]) that there was scope to improve information sharing by Member States."; "[W]hich is the biggest restraint for Europol to be successful? I think that is on the national level, because Europol depends on us, Member States, feeding the information system with information. (Interview 39, MB members) If we want to be more operational, we need to put in all the operational intelligence, and there's still a long way to go before we can say that we are doing this. (HENU, focus group 4)."

improving interoperability[104] and centralizing some of the data.[105] Needless to say, this effort has significant data protection ramifications and has been heavily criticized by the European Data Protection Supervisor as well as by civil society.[106] One result will be the creation of a central repository for reporting and statistics that will be hosted by eu-LISA. The reform includes the following: A single European search portal will enable simultaneous searches, rather than having to undertake individual searches in each system. There will be a shared biometric comparison service, to cross-check digital fingerprints and facial images from several systems. A joint index of identity data will be created, providing biographical information such as date of birth and passport numbers of third-country citizens, to enable more reliable identification. Finally, a system will be put into place to detect multiple identities, to verify whether a person is registered in different databases under more than one identity.

2 Poorly Defined Institutional Roles in the EU Policymaking Cycle

At the front end of the policymaking process, a number of EU institutions compete to set the overall agenda for the AFSJ. The Lisbon Treaty gives the power to the European Council to "define the strategic guidelines for legislative and operational planning within the area of freedom, security and justice" (Article 68 TFEU). So far, however, the European Council has been ineffective in this role. First off, the European Council operates based on consensus and this has been nearly impossible to achieve since enlargement to the EU-28. The Member States vary tremendously in interests, size, administrative culture, and political orientations. This may explain why the European Council has progressively lowered its ambitions in the AFSJ domain, most notably in its 2014–2019 Guidelines, where it simply reaffirmed earlier

---

[104] European Parliament and Commission, Regulation (EU) 2019/817, 2109 O.J. (L 135) 27; European Parliament and Commission, Regulation (EU) 2019/818, 2109 O.J. (L 135) 85. See Chapter 9 for a comprehensive discussion of the data initiatives in the AFSJ, as well as the associated data protection concerns.

[105] For a general perspective see Valsamis Mitsilegas and Niovi Vavoula, "European Union Criminal Law," in *Specialized Administrative Law of the European Union: A Sectoral Review*, eds. Herwig C. H. Hofmann, Gerard C. Rowe, and Alexander H. Turk (New York: Oxford University Press, 2018), 153–188.

[106] A very critical observatory of all the interoperability-related measures has been established by Statewatch. See "Statewatch Observatory. Creation of a Centralised Justice & Home Affairs Database is 'a Point of no Return'," Statewatch website, last visited November 1, 2018, www.statewatch.org/interoperability/eu-big-brother-database.htm.

Progress and Failure in the Area of Freedom, Security, and Justice   403

statements and called for better implementation.[107] It also accounts for the fairly disappointing assessment of AFSJ progress in the European Council's mid-term review.[108]

Not only is the European Council hampered by internal disagreements but externally there are tensions with both the European Parliament and the Commission. The European Council has no legislative powers and it is therefore problematic for the European Parliament, which does have such powers (together with the Council), to be bound by the European Council conclusions. It would be wise for the European Council to involve the European Parliament[109] with its deliberations but this occurred only with the Stockholm Programme,[110] adopted by the European Council immediately after the entry into force of the Lisbon Treaty and covering the period 2010–2014. On other occasions, the European Parliament has submitted recommendations to the European Council, notably on the Anti-Drugs Strategy and the 2008 Pact on Migration, but no real dialogue ever took place. In some instances, this lack of dialogue has resulted in extreme differences between the two institutions, for instance on the approach to be taken to migration and asylum polices.

The Commission too is often at odds with the European Council. The Commission can also give policy direction in the AFSJ, based on its general institutional prerogatives contained in Article 17 TEU. However, the relationship between the European Council President (an innovation of the Lisbon Treaty) and the President of the Commission (who is also member of the European Council) is not always easy. As a result, the Commission often adopts a separate set of political agendas for borders, migration, internal security, criminal law, and the other AFSJ domains. It is worthwhile noting that even within the Commission there can be conflicting policy directions. Since 2010, the Justice and Home Affairs portfolio within the Commission has been split and this has generated both problems of internal coordination between Justice and Home Affairs, as well as an imbalance in legislative initiatives, which have come disproportionately from Home Affairs. The undue weight given to security (as opposed to justice) was supposed to have

---

[107] European Council Conclusions, EUCO 79/14 (June 26–27, 2014).

[108] Council of the European Union, Mid-Term Review of the JHA Strategic Guidelines-Information from the Presidency, Doc. No. 15224/1/17 (December 1, 2017).

[109] European Parliament Resolution, On the Communication from the Commission to the European Parliament and the Council – An Area of Freedom, Security and Justice Serving the Citizen – Stockholm Programme, P7_TA(2009)0090 (November 25, 2009).

[110] The Stockholm Programme – An Open and Secure Europe Serving and Protecting Citizens, 2010 O.J. (C 115) 1.

been addressed in 2014, by according a supervisory role to the first Commission Vice-President, but as of yet there has not been a noticeable change.

The confusion of roles and responsibilities is particularly acute in the counter-terrorism domain. There exists a plethora of institutional actors at the EU level: Member State interior ministers, the Counter-Terrorism Coordinator, the Committee for Internal Security (COSI, established under Article 71 TFEU), three members of the Commission (namely the Vice President, the Home and Migration Commissioner, and the Commissioner for Security), the EU agencies Europol, Eurojust, and, in the future, the European Public Prosecutor.

Even more pronounced is the lack of a clear division of responsibility for implementation and execution in the AFSJ. Although Member States retain primary authority for the operation of their police, immigration, and border control agencies, the Commission and the Council also play a role. When delegated and implementing powers are delegated to committees (as anticipated in Articles 290 and 291 TFEU), the Member States seek to tightly control the process and keep check on each other and the Commission through their representatives.

Overall, the outcome of these ambiguities is permanent power-bickering between the Council, Parliament, and Commission, and the Member State administrations. There have been attempts to improve relations through several interinstitutional agreements on "better law making."[111] These agreements seek to create an institutional framework that operationalizes the principle of "sincere cooperation" set down in Articles 4(3) and 14 TEU, but without much success to date.

3 Common Foreign and Security Policy as a Legal Basis

A third device used by the Member States to curtail the European Parliament's involvement and preserve the intergovernmental method has been to rely on the Treaty articles dealing with Common Foreign and Security Policy (CFSP) to enact AFSJ measures. In CFSP, the Parliament is largely cut out, and the powers of the Commission and the Court of Justice are significantly reduced.

This strategy has been endorsed by the Court of Justice, which has allowed for legal measures with internal and external implications to be based

---

[111] The interinstitutional agreement currently in force is the Interinstitutional Agreement between the European Parliament, the Council of the European Union and the European Commission on Better Law-Making, 2016 O.J. (L 123) 1.

exclusively on the CFSP.[112] This trend is regrettable, especially in light of the mutual respect clause in Article 40 TEU, which states that the "implementation of the common foreign and security policy shall not affect the application of the procedures and the extent of the powers of the institutions laid down by the Treaties for the exercise of the Union competences referred to in Articles 3 to 6 of the Treaty on the Functioning of the European Union [including AFSJ]." Not only does the use of CFSP cut out the European Parliament but the resulting commitments are not codified in internal law, and are diplomatic and nonbinding in nature.

One illustration of how CFSP has been used for AFSJ measures is EU EUNAVFOR MED Operation Sophia.[113] The Council adopted a CFSP Decision as an EU implementing measure of United Nations Security Council Resolution 2240 (2015) of October 9, 2015. UNSC Resolution 2240 reinforces the authority of countries to inspect and seize vessels of suspected migrant smugglers and human traffickers off the coast of Libya. The purpose is to disrupt the smuggler business model, as well as to train the Libyan Coastguard and Navy and contribute to the implementation of the UN arms embargo on the high seas off the coast of Libya. Notwithstanding the undeniable links to UNSC Resolution 2240, these activities also come within the EU's competences in external borders protection (Article 77 TFEU) and migration policy (Article 79 TFEU) and overlap with EU policy on migrant smuggling. As EUNAVFOR involves coast guard operations and the intervention of Frontex, it would have been desirable to ground this operation on EU border and migration competences, which require co-decision of the European Parliament, a qualified majority in the Council, and the full respect of EU law on police and judicial cooperation.

4 Empowering EU Agencies

In recent decades, EU agencies have proliferated and this trend has been particularly evident in the AFSJ.[114] Today, the AFSJ agencies comprise the Fundamental Rights Agency (FRA), Frontex on border policy, EASO on

---

[112] See notably Case C-658/11, *European Parliament v. Council of the European Union*, ECLI:EU: C:2014:2025 (Agreement between the European Union and the Republic of Mauritius), and Case C-263/14, *European Parliament v. Council of the European Union*, ECLI:EU:C:2016:435 (Agreement between the European Union and the United Republic of Tanzania).

[113] Council Decision (CFSP) 2015/778, On a European Union Military Operation in the Southern Central Mediterranean (EUNAVFOR MED), 2015 O.J. (L 122) 31.

[114] Matthew Wood, "Mapping EU Agencies as Political Entrepreneurs," *European Journal of Political Research* 57, no. 2 (2018): 404–426; Miroslava Scholten, "Mind the Trend!

asylum, Europol for police cooperation, CEPOL for police training, Eurojust for judicial cooperation, eu-LISA for the management of large AFSJ information systems, and European Monitoring Centre for Drugs and Drug Addiction (EMCDDA) dealing with prevention of drug abuse. (Indeed, with their proliferation has come the risk of conflicting agendas, and there has been an effort to build closer inter-agency collaboration.)[115] EU agencies are overseen by management boards of Member State representatives and are staffed independently of the European Commission. Because of their structure, EU agencies tend to circumscribe the Commission's executive powers and to weaken the European Parliament's oversight powers. The flip side of the coin is that they improve the influence of the Member States. Since the powers of EU agencies can be quite extensive, and can even include policymaking functions, they can significantly distort the balance of powers set down in the Treaties.

The case of Frontex illustrates this phenomenon, which results in less effective oversight and lawmaking powers of the European Parliament. Frontex plays a pivotal role in the new European Integrated Border Management.[116] It is not only vested with operational functions but also helps define the EU's strategy for policing the external borders and protecting against irregular migration. In principle, the "common strategy" to be adopted by the management board, as envisioned in Articles 3 and 4 of the Regulation, is technical. Yet, as recent events have shown, migration is a politically contentious policy area on which it has been difficult to reach agreement, and legislative reform on asylum and other aspects of the system are stalemated. Thus, in the absence of an overarching strategy adopted by the EU institutions, Frontex's common strategy will be the only one guiding EU action. Needless to say, this outcome is problematic from a democratic point of view. Can an EU agency define and, at the same time, implement an overarching political objective of the Treaty?

Under new legislation that is expected to be officially adopted in fall 2019, Frontex will become even more powerful.[117] The proposal will create a

---

Enforcement of EU Law Has Been Moving to 'Brussels'," *Journal of European Public Policy* 24, no. 9 (2017): 1348–1366.

[115] For a description of this effort, see Council of the European Union, *EU Justice and Home Affairs Agencies' Cooperation in 2016 – Final Report*, Doc. No. 15579/16 (December 16, 2016).

[116] European Parliament and Council Regulation (EU) 2016/2024, On the European Border and Coast Guard, 2016 O.J. (L 251) 1.

[117] *Proposal for a Regulation of the European Parliament and of the Council on the European Border and Coast Guard*, COM (2018) 631, 2018/0330/COD. No. 12143/18 (September 13, 2018), http://data.consilium.europa.eu/doc/document/ST-12143-2018-ADD-1/en/pdf.

Progress and Failure in the Area of Freedom, Security, and Justice 407

European Border and Coast Guard standing corps of 10,000 operational staff. These officers will be vested with executive powers and will support Member States on the ground; they will have improved technical equipment at their disposal and increased ability to act in third countries. According to the Commission, the European Border and Coast Guard standing corps will ensure that the EU collectively has the capabilities necessary to protect the EU external borders, prevent secondary movements, and effectively implement returns of irregular migrants. All of these changes will transform Frontex into a quasi-federal agency, and will require more democratic input into the strategic priorities for European Integrated Border Management, as well as democratic oversight of the functioning of Frontex.

V CONCLUSION

The transformation of the AFSJ in the Lisbon Treaty has produced a number of concrete legislative achievements. Overall, however, the intrinsic contentiousness of security, borders, and migration policy, which has been exacerbated by the refugee crisis of recent years, has stalled the development of a coherent, actual AFSJ. Indeed, given the political sensitivity of these core areas of state sovereignty, even the limited measures that have been adopted by the EU have been highly controversial. Setting aside Brexit, there has been resistance from Member States to implementing some of the essential EU measures on borders, migration, and asylum. In particular, the countries of the so-called Visegrad Group (Poland, Hungary, the Czech Republic, and Slovakia) and in the Baltic Region have been reluctant to cooperate on the relocation of refugees and other solidary measures. Even more worryingly, founding Member States such as the Netherlands and Germany, under the pressure of increasingly skeptical national public opinion, have become resistant to a bolder EU role in the AFSJ. The consequence of these national developments has been to undermine further policy coherence at the EU level: to avoid confrontation with the Member States, the latest European Council, Council, and Commission strategy documents have become a compilation of disparate measures in the same domain rather than a consistent toolbox addressed at well-understood internal and external threats.

The politics behind these AFSJ trends are not likely to disappear anytime soon. From a purely policy stance, however, there are a number of improvements that could be made to the European Council's strategic guidelines for the upcoming 2019–2024 legislature. Let me conclude this chapter with one possible agenda for the future:

1. Establish a transparent dialogue between the European Council and the European Parliament on the priorities to be implemented at the legislative, financial, and operational levels in the AFSJ. These priorities should take into account the shortcomings of the EU measures adopted in the previous legislature.

2. Promote at the national level data collection policies designed to generate comparable data and establish clear figures on the general financial impact of the implementation of the common EU policies foreseen by Title V TFEU (AFSJ).

3. For each AFSJ common policy (borders, asylum, migration, and police and judicial cooperation in criminal matters) enact a framework law with a clear strategy, assessment of priorities, solidarity mechanisms, and operational intervention as well as a clear link with national strategies in the same domains.

4. Revive the currently stalled EU legislative proposals dealing with the rights of citizens in the AFSJ, namely proposals on procedural rights in criminal law, anti-discrimination, transparency, and principles of good administration and accountability for EU agencies in the AFSJ.

5. Assess the compatibility of Third Pillar measures adopted before Lisbon and still in force with the Charter of Fundamental Rights and post-Lisbon CJEU jurisprudence. Establish a general independent evaluation mechanism of the adequacy of national implementation of AFSJ policies as required by Article 70 TFEU (as a complement to the specific evaluation mechanisms included in each EU legislative measure).

6. Develop a consistent wide-ranging policy for human mobility and regular migration by adopting an EU Migration Code dealing with skilled migrants, single permits, seasonal workers, and researchers.

7. Set aside the state-of-first-entry system for allocating asylum applications in the Dublin Regime and empower the European Asylum Support Office to process asylum requests for the whole EU. De-criminalize humanitarian protection for people in need by amending the current EU legislation that criminalizes the facilitation of irregular entry and transit irrespective of whether it is conducted for the purpose of a financial or material benefit.[118]

---

[118] The EU legislation in force is deemed to implement the Protocol against the Smuggling of Migrants by Land, Sea, and Air, supplementing the United Nations Convention against Transnational Organized Crime ("Palermo Convention" adopted by the UN General Assembly on November 15, 2000, by resolution 55/25). At the time, EU competences were still

Progress and Failure in the Area of Freedom, Security, and Justice   409

8. Extend the competences of the European Public Prosecutor to the fight against terrorism and serious crime (as foreseen by Article 86 TFEU) and create a specific section competent for criminal law in the CJEU. Adopt a new legal framework for freezing terrorist assets under Article 75 TFEU.

split into the First and the Third pillars, resulting in the adoption of two EU legislative measures: Council Directive 2002/90/EC, Defining the Facilitation of Unauthorised Entry, Transit and Residence, 2002 O.J. (L 328) 17, art. 1(1)(b) and Council Framework Decision 2002/946/JHA. According to these texts, any person who intentionally assists unauthorized entry, transit, or residence of a non-EU national in the EU is to be sanctioned. However, the Member States can decide not to criminalise people helping migrants for humanitarian reasons. Even the Commission has recently recognized that "this provision was criticised for its optional character, entailing a lack of clarity and legal certainty. Perceived risks of criminalisation of actions by civil society organisations or individuals assisting and/or working with irregular migrants were raised." However, quite strangely, the Commission has also concluded "there is no sufficient evidence to draw firm conclusions against the evaluation criteria about the need for a revision of the Facilitators Package at this point in time." See, Commission Staff Working Document, Executive Summary of the Refit Evaluation of the EU Legal Framework against Facilitation of Unauthorised Entry, Transit and Residence: The Facilitators Package (Directive 2002/90/EC and Framework Decision 2002/946/JHA), SWD (2017) 120 final (March 23, 2017).

IV

Constitutional Fundamentals

15

Defending Democracy in EU Member States
Beyond Article 7 TEU

KIM LANE SCHEPPELE AND R. DANIEL KELEMEN[*]

I INTRODUCTION

Founded on post-war optimism that a Europe of united democracies could provide both peace and prosperity, the European Union is slowly waking up to the fact that not all of its Member States are committed to democratic principles. Article 2 TEU pronounces (as fact) that "[t]he Union is founded on the values of respect for human dignity, freedom, democracy, equality, the rule of law and respect for human rights, including the rights of persons belonging to minorities." And Article 2 goes on to assert (as fact) that "[t]hese values are common to the Member States in a society in which pluralism, non-discrimination, tolerance, justice, solidarity and equality between women and men prevail." But for some EU member governments, these values no longer define the aspirational horizon. The requirements of Article 2 are simply no longer met in all Member States.

The Hungarian Fidesz government elected in 2010 started the march toward "illiberal" government, and the Polish Law and Justice (PiS) government elected in 2015 has joined the parade. The two governments have used their election mandates to undermine the rule of law by bringing their respective judiciaries under political tutelage, by exercising partisan control over the media, by undermining the independence of the civil service, by

---

[*] This chapter was originally prepared for the conference at The George Washington University Law School: The EU at a Crossroads: From Technocracy to High Politics? March 2018. Our analysis is limited to the Juncker Commission's tenure. We thank Petra Bárd, Gábor Halmai, Tomasz Koncewicz, Dimitry Kochenov, Laurent Pech, and Wojciech Sadurski plus the attendees at the GWU conference for helpful conversations about these issues. We are particularly grateful to Francesca Bignami for detailed comments on the draft and much patience as we kept revising up until the last possible minute. We are also grateful to Cassandra Emmons for footnote wrangling.

attacking human rights NGOs as alien, and by treating opposition parties as national enemies. They have railed against migrants, issued dog-whistle denigrations of Jews as disloyal and explicitly attacked Muslim refugees as invaders, rewritten their national histories to airbrush inconvenient episodes, and flaunted a sort of nationalism that valorizes ethnic purity. Government leaders in both Poland and Hungary regularly produce angry denunciations of the EU while taking in some of the largest per capita streams of EU funding.[1]

It has taken European institutions too long to recognize that these threats are serious, persistent, and damaging to the democratic infrastructure of the European Union. Failure to address democratic backsliding and attacks on rule of law by member governments not only undermines the EU's legitimacy as a community dedicated to such values but it also threatens the very functioning of the Union.[2] The EU relies for its basic operation on all of its Member States sharing a common commitment to liberal democracy, comprising the rule of law, democracy, and human rights. When a Member State fails to adhere to these basic principles, the constitutional structure of the EU is decisively weakened. EU governance relies heavily on the "sincere cooperation" (Article 4(3) TEU) of national courts and governments acting as agents of EU law.[3] If a government systematically undermines the rule of law at the national level, EU governance may effectively cease to function within that state.

European Commission Vice-President Frans Timmermans captured the essence of the problem in a July 2017 speech about the threat to the independent judiciary in Poland, explaining:

> Polish courts like the courts of all Member States are called upon to provide an effective remedy in case of violations of EU law, in which case they act as the 'judges of the European Union'. This matters potentially to anybody doing business in and with Poland, or even anybody visiting the country. I think every single citizen wants to have this, if they need a day in court,

---

[1] On Hungary: FIDH, "Hungary: Democracy under Threat: Six Years of Attacks against the Rule of Law," November 2016, www.fidh.org/IMG/pdf/hungary_democracy_under_threat.pdf. On Poland: Wojciech Sadurski, "How Democracy Dies (in Poland): A Case Study of Anti-constitutional Populist Backsliding," Sydney Law School Research Paper No. 18/01 (2018), https://papers.ssrn.com/sol3/papers.cfm?abstract_id=3103491.

[2] Vivien A. Schmidt, "Democracy and Legitimacy in the European Union," in *Oxford Handbook of the European Union*, eds. Erik Jones, Anand Menon, and Stephen Weatherill (Oxford: Oxford University Press, 2012), 661–675.

[3] Marcus Klamert, *The Principle of Loyalty in EU Law* (Oxford: Oxford University Press, 2014); Andreas Føllesdal, "Legitimacy Theories of the European Union," Center for European Studies, ARENA Working Paper 04/15 (2015), www.sv.uio.no/arena/english/research/publications/arena-working-papers/2001-2010/2004/wp04_15.pdf.

Defending Democracy in EU Member States 415

without having to think: "Hmm, is this judge going to get a call from the Minister telling him or her what to do." That is not how independent judiciary works ... This is no matter only for the Polish people. What is happening in Poland affects the Union as a whole. All of us, every single Member State, every citizen of the Union.[4]

As Timmermans emphasized, the damaging effects of the erosion of rule of law are not limited to the jurisdiction where they occur; rather, they radiate across the Union. The EU cannot be strong when some Member States are not committed to the basic premises of the EU's normative project; in fact, it may be unable to function at all.

That said, the European constitutional framework was not built to robustly address the problem of Member States retreating from their commitment to European values. Rather the reverse. The EU was built with many avenues for Member States to check the power of the Union institutions (above all through the powerful role of the intergovernmental Council in EU decision-making), but without many tools for EU institutions to check the Member States' commitment to the basic values of the EU once they entered the Union. Member States were admitted with the assumption that all were part of the democratic family of nations, and as such were firmly committed to the rule of law. The development of the EU's supranational legal order in the post-war decades was only possible because all Member States in fact remained committed to rule-of-law principles and were ultimately willing to accept the European Court of Justice's assertions of judicial authority.[5]

As we discuss in more detail later in this chapter, as the EU prepared to take in new Member States from East Central Europe, it introduced a procedure in Article F.1 of the Amsterdam Treaty (now Article 7 of the TEU) – designed to sanction Member States that persistently violated the EU's fundamental values. The procedure was reformed subsequently, supposedly in an effort to strengthen it, and yet it has thus far failed to prevent democratic backsliding and attacks on the rule of law in the two most egregious cases the EU has faced – in Hungary and Poland. The failure of Article 7 has left many commentators lamenting that the EU simply lacks the tools necessary to defend its fundamental values. We disagree. EU leaders in fact have a rich arsenal of tools at their disposal with which to defend democracy; the problem

---

[4] Frans Timmermans, First Vice-President European Commission, Opening Remarks of College Readout on Grave Concerns about the Clear Risks for Independence of the Judiciary in Poland, July 19, 2017, http://europa.eu/rapid/press-release_SPEECH-17-2084_en.htm.

[5] R. Daniel Kelemen, "The Court of Justice of the European Union in the Twenty-First Century," *Law and Contemporary Problems* 79, no. 1 (2016): 129.

to date has been that they have lacked the political will to act. As our colleague Laurent Pech notes, the bad workman always blames his tools.[6]

We recognize that Article 7 has significant weaknesses, above all its reliance on unanimous agreement at one critical stage. This does not mean that European institutions should not try to use the first part of Article 7, which does not require unanimity, if consensus is not complete.[7] But while recognizing the limits of Article 7, we argue that the EU could deploy a range of other strategies, from infringement actions concerning violations of the EU's fundamental values (as listed in Article 2 TEU) to the suspension of EU funding under existing financial regulations in order to sanction and discourage democratic backsliding. The European Court of Justice (ECJ) too can play a role, pressing EU leaders to act when they might otherwise prove too weak or beholden to the Member States to do so. Rather than focusing on new tools that might be introduced through Treaty change or even through secondary legislation, we focus here on the tools the EU can already deploy – should it choose to do so.[8] Of course, Treaty change could always build in new mechanisms for disciplining wayward Member States now that the problem has become clear. But Treaty change (like Article 7 itself) requires unanimous agreement, and it is clear that any approach requiring unanimity is bound to fail once one or more Member States have gone rogue, as is already the case in the EU today. We therefore limit ourselves to discussing how the EU might put existing tools to new uses.

The remainder of this chapter is divided into five sections. Section II outlines the development of the Article 7 procedure and describes how EU leaders failed for a long time to invoke it in the face of brazen attacks on democracy and the rule of law by elected autocrats in Hungary and have only moved to do so very late in the case of Poland. Section III provides a partisan political explanation for the failure of Article 7 and suggests why – though it might act as a deterrent to the most extreme forms of dictatorship – it is unlikely to ever provide an effective remedy against the rise of soft-authoritarian member governments in the EU. Section IV considers a series of alternative mechanisms the EU could use to defend its core values including: (a) systemic infringement proceedings brought by the Commission,

---

[6] Laurent Pech interview by Anna Wójcik, "'A Bad Workman Always Blames His Tools': An Interview with Laurent Pech," *Verfassungsblog*, May 28, 2018, https://verfassungsblog.de/a-bad-workman-always-blames-his-tools-an-interview-with-laurent-pech/.

[7] Laurent Pech and Kim Lane Scheppele, "Illiberalism Within: Rule of Law Backsliding in the EU," *Cambridge Yearbook of European Legal Studies* 19 (2017): 3–47.

[8] For a discussion of democratic backsliding and populism that considers the implications for EU economic and fiscal policy, see Chapter 17.

(b) the suspension of EU funds through various mechanisms, and (c) rulings by the ECJ to establish that some national judiciaries have been captured by autocratic governments and therefore may not be accorded the presumptions required to establish mutual trust. Section V concludes.

II DEMOCRATIC BACKSLIDING AND THE PROMISE OF ARTICLE 7 TEU

When the countries from post-communist Europe queued for admission to the EU after 1989, a formal assessment framework was developed for the first time that required accession states to pass muster as both consolidated democracies and robust market economies. These accession assessments had political, legal, and economic components. But the "Copenhagen criteria" that formed the bases for these tests were remarkably vague. As Dimitry Kochenov demonstrated in his sober analysis of the accession process, accession countries' progress in meeting the standards for entering the EU was measured by apparently detailed assessments of economic readiness for the single market, but the analysis of whether democracy, human rights, and the rule of law were firmly in place was left to observers whose impressionistic reports were considered good enough.[9]

As accession states competed to demonstrate that they met the Copenhagen criteria, however, some existing Member States worried about the possibility that the new Members would fail to keep up their commitments to European values. Pointing to the general lack of democratic experience on the part of the post-communist accession states, these established Member States raised the question of whether the Treaties should include a mechanism for disciplining any EU members if they experienced backsliding on core EU values.[10] The result was the insertion into the Treaty of Amsterdam of the precursor of the present-day Article 7 TEU, a mechanism through which wayward Member States could be sanctioned on the unanimous judgment of their peers by having their voting rights suspended in the Council.

From the start, it was clear that the Council, and therefore the Member States, were in charge of disciplining their fellow states. The sanctioning

[9] Dimitry Kochenov, *EU Enlargement and the Failure of Conditionality: Pre-Accession Conditionality in the Fields of Democracy and the Rule of Law* (Alphen aan den Rijn: Kluwer, 2008); Dimitry Kochenov, "Behind the Copenhagen Façade: The Meaning and Structure of the Copenhagen Political Criterion of Democracy and the Rule of Law," *European Integration Online Papers* 8, no. 10 (2004): 1–24.

[10] Wojciech Sadurski, "Adding Bark to a Bite: The Story of Article 7, E.U. Enlargement, and Jörg Haider," *Columbia Journal of European Law* 16, no. 3 (2009): 385–427.

Kim Lane Scheppele and R. Daniel Kelemen

mechanism was designed to prohibit Union institutions from scrutinizing too closely the internal workings of the Member States, leaving the checks to intergovernmental processes. As Wojciech Sadurski explained:

> Indeed, the evolution of the dominant opinion, from the early Reflection Group to the actual drafting of Article 7, shows a steady tendency to reinforce the control of Member States, through the Council, over the imposition of sanctions. This reinforcement is seen through a combination of factors such as the requirement for unanimity in the Council (minus the Member State in question), reduction of the role of the European Parliament, and suppression of any role for the Court of Justice. The Member States, while clearly seeing the new mechanism in the context of the impending enlargement of the Union, were at the same time careful not to extend, in any way, the scope of EU competences to the area of human rights within their own borders, and to restrict the possible control by the Union of their own behaviour towards their own citizens.[11]

Member States made themselves the central institution in the sanctioning process, leaving only a small role for the Commission and none for the Court of Justice. They also made the mechanism hard to use. The imposition of sanctions on a Member State would require unanimous agreement of other governments in the Council – a notoriously high bar in EU politics.[12] Even when there were far fewer Member States than there are now (only fifteen then) and on the one occasion when they were in agreement that something had to be done (concerning the rise of the far-right in Austria in 2000), Member States still lost their nerve when the opportunity arose to use this mechanism.

The inclusion of the far-right Freedom Party in Austria's government for the first time, occurring just one year after the sanctions mechanism took effect in EU law, provoked a rare unanimous reaction that nonetheless bypassed this new provision. Instead, Member States coordinated a set of bilateral sanctions against Austria outside the EU Treaty framework.[13] When it turned out that the Austrian government actually did nothing terribly objectionable, the

---

[11] Sadurski, 396 [footnotes omitted].

[12] For a contrasting view, which emphasizes the "prevention and ... prior monitoring powers" in Article 7 that do not require unanimous agreement, see Leonard Besselink, "The Bite, the Bark and the Howl: Article 7 TEU and the Rule of Law Initiatives," in *The Enforcement of EU Law and Values: Ensuring Member States' Compliance*, eds. András Jakab and Dimitry Kochenov (Oxford: Oxford University Press, 2017): 128–144.

[13] Heather Berit Freeman, "Austria: The 1999 Parliamentary Elections and the European Union Members' Sanctions," *Boston College International and Comparative Law Review* 25, no. 1 (2002): 109–124.

Member States lifted the sanctions but took away the lesson that they needed a mechanism for warning a Member State that it was at risk of violating basic principles before it actually did so. Shortly afterwards, Article 7 was amended by the Treaty of Nice to include a warning mechanism (now Article 7(1) TEU) that would give EU institutions the ability, based on a four-fifths vote in the Council, to put a Member State on notice that its conduct was violating EU values and risked triggering sanctions (under what is now Article 7(3) TEU) after a unanimous vote of the Council established a breach of values (under what is now Article 7(2) TEU). The EU's first opportunity to use the sanctioning mechanism inserted into the Treaties to deal with democratic backsliding was therefore met not by the actual imposition of sanctions, but instead by the revision of the mechanism itself, so that the EU had a legal way to bark first before biting.[14] Though the introduction of a pre-sanctions warning stage has typically been depicted as a means to strengthen Article 7, arguably the reform did more to weaken it. By adding a warning stage before a breach could be found and sanctions could be imposed, including an extensive process of dialogue with the state in question, the new warning mechanism made the process of sanctioning a state for violating the EU's fundamental values more lengthy and onerous.[15]

When the Fidesz government in Hungary moved rapidly after 2010 to capture all independent institutions (including the judiciary) and to remove all checks on the discretion of the Prime Minster, EU institutions again balked at using any part of Article 7 – not just its actual sanctions, but even its warning mechanism. Instead, in the State of the Union address given in September 2013, then-President of the European Commission José Manuel Barroso highlighted the increasing "challenges to the rule of law in our own member states" and referred to Article 7 TEU as the EU's "nuclear option,"[16] an option simply unthinkable.

Rather than activating Article 7, the Commission responded to developments in Hungary by introducing yet another procedural reform. In 2014, right before the European elections, the Commission announced a Rule of Law Framework, creating a process through which the Commission could enter

---

[14] Besselink, "The Bite, the Bark and the Howl," 128.

[15] Actually, the two procedures – warning in Article 7(1) and sanctioning in Articles 7(2) and (3) – are logically separate. The Council could go straight to Article 7(2) without passing through Article 7(1), but the two are often read as a sequence, which simply serves to slow down the whole sanctioning process and make it more cumbersome.

[16] José Manuel Durão Barroso, President of the European Commission, State of the Union Address 2013, September 11, 2013, http://europa.eu/rapid/press-release_SPEECH-13-684_en.htm.

into a dialogue with a Member State before deciding to recommend that the Council trigger Article 7(1). Essentially, the Commission created yet another antechamber to the Article 7(1), which itself had been created as antechamber to the sanctions mechanisms of Article 7(2–3).[17] If Article 7(1) was the bark before the bite of Article 7(2–3) sanctions, then the Rule of Law Framework was the growl, before the bark, before the bite. Notably, though the Rule of Law Framework was developed in response to the Hungarian situation, it has never to this day been used for Hungary.[18]

The Rule of Law Framework creates a process[19] very similar to the one that the Commission uses for infringement actions under Article 258 TFEU, which have existed in EU law since the 1950s, which allow the Commission to sue the Member States for breaches of EU law. The Commission first notifies a Member State that the Commission believes that the Member State may be at risk of violating European law – or, in this case, European values. Then, if the Member State does not respond by changing its ways, the Commission can issue an Opinion outlining specific action that the Member State must take to bring itself into line. Should that fail to achieve the desired result, the Commission can issue a Recommendation as a final warning – and, when all of those stages fail, it can recommend to the Council that Article 7 be triggered, much as it refers an action to the Court of Justice when the steps to negotiate an end to an infringement have failed. Though the Rule of Law Framework was justified as a mechanism that would strengthen the EU's hand in dealing with backsliding member governments, it is hard to escape the conclusion that it has had precisely the opposite effect. As with the introduction of Article 7(1), the Rule of Law Framework has introduced, de facto if not de jure, a lengthy new procedure that must be completed before the Commission can launch even the first warning stage of Article 7. It has rendered the prospect of actual sanctions ever more remote, with consequences that are evident in the one case where the procedure was actually deployed – vis-à-vis Poland.

In 2015, successive elections for the presidency and parliament in Poland set the stage for the EU's values crisis to spread beyond Hungary. Poland's PiS Party won an absolute majority of seats in both houses of the Polish parliament

---

[17] Communication from the Commission, *A New EU Framework to Strengthen the Rule of Law*, COM (2014) 158 final/2 (March 19, 2014).

[18] Dimitry Kochenov and Laurent Pech, "Better Late than Never? On the European Commission's Rule of Law Framework and Its First Activation," *Journal of Common Market Studies* 54, no. 5 (2016): 1062–1074.

[19] For a more detailed discussion of the Rule of Law Framework's procedures, see Kochenov and Pech, "Better Late than Never?"

and a PiS-affiliated candidate was elected to the presidency, allowing PiS to completely control the lawmaking process without having to rely on any votes save its own. PiS did not, however, have the supermajority required to amend the constitution, so it undertook to disable the key institution that could say that its actions were unconstitutional: the Constitutional Tribunal. After neutralizing the Constitutional Tribunal by illegally appointing judges to that body and then by refusing to publish its rulings that said that these appointments were unconstitutional, the Polish government then took aim at the general judiciary, capturing control of the courts and violating its own constitution as it consolidated power in the hands of one party.[20]

Even though the Commission had never invoked the Rule of Law Framework in the case of Hungary, which was much farther along in the process of democratic deconsolidation than Poland, the Commission sprang into action quite quickly with Poland.[21] In January 2016, the Commission activated the Rule of Law Framework against the government in Warsaw. After giving the Polish government many opportunities to correct its ways, the Commission escalated the dialogue with Poland through all of the stages of the Rule of Law Framework, culminating in multiple Recommendations issued throughout 2016 and 2017.[22] Poland not only did not back down but became more belligerent with each move of the Commission. Finally, in December 2017, the Commission finally recommended to the Council that Article 7(1) be triggered for Poland.[23] For the duration of the Juncker Commission, however, the Council never acted on the Commission's recommendation and taken a vote under Article 7(1) as to whether there is a "clear risk of a serious breach"

---

[20] Kriszta Kovács and Kim Lane Scheppele, "The Fragility of an Independent Judiciary: Lessons from Hungary and Poland – and the European Union," *Communist and Post-Communist Studies* 51 (2018): 189–200.

[21] Kochenov and Pech, "Better Late than Never?"

[22] For a detailed account of the Commission's reaction to attacks on the rule of law in Poland in 2016 and 2017, see the three part series by Laurent Pech and Kim Scheppele on "Poland and the European Commission" – "Part I: A Dialogue of the Deaf?" *Verfassungsblog*, January 3, 2017, https://verfassungsblog.de/poland-and-the-european-commission-part-i-a-dialogue-of-the-deaf/; "Part II: Hearing the Siren Song of the Rule of Law," *Verfassungsblog*, January 6, 2017, https://verfassungsblog.de/poland-and-the-european-commission-part-ii-hearing-the-siren-song-of-the-rule-of-law/; "Part III: Requiem for the Rule of Law," *Verfassungsblog*, March 3, 2017, https://verfassungsblog.de/poland-and-the-european-commission-part-iii-requiem-for-the-rule-of-law/. Also see R. Daniel Kelemen, "The Assault on Poland's Judiciary," *Foreign Affairs*, July 26, 2017, www.foreignaffairs.com/articles/poland/2017-07-26/assault-polands-judiciary.

[23] *European Commission Reasoned Proposal in Accordance with Article 7(1) of the Treaty on European Union Regarding the Rule of Law in Poland. Proposal for a Council Decision on the Determination of a Clear Risk of a Serious Breach by the Republic of Poland of the Rule of Law,* COM (2017) 835 final (December 20, 2017).

of the EU's fundamental values in Poland. The Council, instead, has urged more dialogue.

The Council, where Member States could sit in judgment of their fellow Member States, has therefore been largely missing in action throughout the rule-of-law crisis.[24] It bestirred itself to enact a Rule of Law Dialogue, a sort of "peer review" process in which each Member State would report once per year on its own progress in observing the rule of law.[25] Through eight long years of the Fidesz consolidation of power in Hungary, the Council has said and done nothing. And though the Commission's Reasoned Proposal to trigger Article 7(1) has been in gestation on its agenda for longer than a human pregnancy, the Council has yet to act on that either.

The European Parliament has been more active, passing resolution after resolution, starting with criticism of the Hungarian government's worrisome media law in 2011[26] and then expressing more concerted concern over the new constitution in 2012,[27] culminating in a comprehensive condemnation of the Hungarian government's constitutional capture in July 2013 after passage of the new Hungarian constitution's Fourth Amendment. This amendment inserted back into the constitution nearly all of the laws that the Constitutional Court had found unconstitutional and then disabled the Court by nullifying its past case law and preventing judicial review of constitutional amendments.[28] Finally, in May 2017, following attacks on the Central European University and foreign-funded civil society groups, the European Parliament sent to its Civil Liberties Committee (LIBE) a request to prepare a comprehensive report on Hungary that would allow the Parliament to vote on triggering Article 7(1) against Hungary.[29] After passing the Civil Liberties Committee of the Parliament, with the strong support of four other committees, the report was finally endorsed by the Parliament with the requisite two-

---

[24] Peter Oliver and Justine Stefanelli, "Strengthening the Rule of Law in the EU: The Council's Inaction," *Journal of Common Market Studies* 54, no. 5 (2016): 1075–1084.

[25] Ernst Hirsch Ballin, "Mutual Trust: The Virtue of Reciprocity – Strengthening the Acceptance of the Rule of Law through Peer Review," in *Reinforcing Rule of Law Oversight in the European Union*, eds. Carlos Closa and Dimitry Kochenov (Cambridge: Cambridge University Press, 2016): 133–146.

[26] European Parliament Resolution, On Media Law in Hungary, P7_TA(2011)0094 (March 10, 2011).

[27] European Parliament Resolution, On the Recent Political Developments in Hungary, P7_TA (2012)0053 (February 16, 2012).

[28] European Parliament Resolution, On the Situation of Fundamental Rights: Standards and Practices in Hungary (Pursuant to the European Parliament Resolution of 16 February 2012), P7_TA(2013)0315 (July 3, 2013) [hereinafter Tavares Report].

[29] European Parliament Resolution, On the Situation in Hungary, P8_TA(2017)0216 (May 17, 2017).

thirds majority on September 12, 2018 – thus triggering Article 7 against the Hungarian government and calling for the Council to vote on whether there is now a clear risk of a serious breach of EU values.[30]

From different quarters within the EU, then, Article 7(1) TEU is finally now being armed for use against Poland and Hungary. The Commission has pushed the Council to act on Poland and the Parliament has pushed the Council to act on Hungary. But Article 7 – even Article 7(1) – is still a heavy lift, for all of the reasons we have adduced. Member States run the show and Member States have been the least active partners among the European institutions in addressing democratic backsliding over the last eight years. Will they rise to the challenge once other European institutions have collected the evidence and presented them with a request for action? In the next section, we explain why we have reason to doubt the will of the Council to act, even when faced with overwhelming evidence.

III WHY MEMBER STATES FAIL THE EU

The tendency to sacrifice principles in the name of partisanship is an all-too-common feature of democratic politics around the world. Scholars of comparative politics have identified a particular set of effects that partisan politics can have in the context of multi-level, federal-type systems like the EU's. In such settings, partisanship can help sustain autocratic regimes at the state level within otherwise democratic federations.[31] Among other things, democratic leaders at the federal level may come to rely on authoritarian leaders at the state level to deliver votes to their federal level coalitions. As Gibson explains, "Authoritarian provincial political elites, with their abundant supplies of voters and legislators, can be important members of national [*aka federal level*]

---

[30] European Parliament, Committee on Civil Liberties, Justice and Home Affairs, *Draft Report On a Proposal Calling on the Council to Determine, Pursuant to Article 7(1) of the Treaty on European Union, the Existence of a Clear Risk of a Serious Breach by Hungary of the Values on which the Union Is Founded*, 2017/2131(INL), April 11, 2018, www.europarl.europa.eu/resources/library/media/20180411RES01553/20180411RES01553.pdf [hereinafter Sargentini Report]. For a more detailed description of this sequence of events, see Kovács and Scheppele, "The Fragility of an Independent Judiciary." On the Parliament's September 2018 denunciation of the Hungarian government, see Maïa de la Baume and Ryan Heath, "Parliament Denounces Hungary's Illiberalism," *Politico Europe*, September 12, 2018, www.politico.eu/article/european-parliament-approves-hungary-censure-motion/.

[31] As these scholars examine this phenomenon in states within national federations, they refer to it as "subnational authoritarianism." In the EU's supranational context, the equivalent is "national authoritarianism" within a supranational polity.

governing coalitions."[32] So long as the local autocrat can deliver needed votes, federal leaders of their party or coalition will be inclined to overlook their authoritarian practices and to defend them against any federal interventions in the name of democracy that might threaten to dislodge them.

This phenomenon has been commonplace in democratic federations across Latin America including Argentina and Mexico, as well as in the United States. In the US case, because the national Democratic Party needed the votes of Southern Democrats (Dixiecrats) to secure majorities in Congress and to elect Presidents, they shielded Dixiecrats against federal intervention, allowing them to maintain authoritarian enclaves in Southern States by "disenfranchise[ing] blacks and many poorer white voters, repress[ing] opposition parties, and impos[ing] racially separate – and significantly unfree – civic spheres."[33] Something very similar is happening in the EU.

As one of us has detailed elsewhere,[34] these sorts of political incentives help explain why the EU has so consistently failed to act as Viktor Orbán has brazenly defied the EU's democratic values and consolidated one-party rule in what political scientists would label a competitive authoritarian regime.[35] These dynamics also help explain why the EU has at least undertaken a somewhat more aggressive response to similar developments in Poland. Ultimately, these partisan political considerations – coupled with other intergovernmental political considerations discussed later – explain why Article 7 is almost certainly doomed to fail as a mechanism to safeguard democracy and the rule of law in the EU.

The sordid partisan political story behind the rise of autocracy in the EU can be summarized as follows: Fidesz, the political party that Viktor Orbán cofounded in 1988 and has controlled ever since, is a member at European

[32] Edward L. Gibson "Boundary Control: Subnational Authoritarianism in Democratic Countries," *World Politics* 58, no. 1 (2005): 107.

[33] Robert Mickey, Steven Levitsky, and Lucan Way, "Is America Still Safe for Democracy?" *Foreign Affairs* 96, no. 3 (2017): 22. More generally, see Robert Mickey, *Paths Out of Dixie: The Democratization of Authoritarian Enclaves in America's Deep South, 1944–1972* (Princeton, NJ: Princeton University Press, 2015); Edward L. Gibson, *Boundary Control: Subnational Authoritarianism in Federal Democracies* (New York: Cambridge University Press, 2012).

[34] R. Daniel Kelemen, "Europe's Other Democratic Deficit: National Authoritarianism in Europe's Democratic Union," *Government and Opposition* 52, no. 2 (2017): 211–238; R. Daniel Kelemen, "Europe's Authoritarian Equilibrium," *Foreign Affairs*, December 22, 2017, www.foreignaffairs.com/articles/hungary/2017-12-22/europes-authoritarian-equilibrium. For a contrary view, challenging the argument that partisanship has played a central role in explaining the EU's reaction to democratic backsliding, see Carlos Closa, "The Politics of Guarding the Treaties," *Journal of European Public Policy* 26, no. 5 (2019): 696–716.

[35] Steven Levitsky and Lucan A. Way, *Competitive Authoritarianism: Hybrid Regimes after the Cold War* (New York: Cambridge University Press, 2010).

level of the European People's Party (EPP), which is the largest pan-European political party. Traditionally, the EPP has been the party group of the center right, bringing together national parties such as Germany's Christian Democrats, France's Republicans, Spain's Popular Party, and Poland's Civic Platform. Through the term of the Juncker Commission, Orbán's Fidesz party delivered 12 out of the EPP's 217 seats in the European Parliament, helping it sustain its narrow lead over the second largest party, the Progressive Alliance of Socialists and Democrats (S&D) – the grouping of social democratic parties (which held 190 seats). Being the largest party in the European Parliament gives the EPP a decisive role in shaping EU legislation. Also, with the advent of the so-called *Spitzenkandidaten* process in the 2014 European election, the largest party in the Parliament won the right to name the European Commission President and thus to put its stamp on the policy direction of the EU's executive. The influence of these Europarties also extends into the Council where heads of government from the same Europarties regularly (though not always) cooperate. Members of the European Parliament (MEPs) have generally been loyal EPP members, and the Orbán government has been duly rewarded for its service to the EPP cause at European level even as it undermines the EPP's stated values when its component parties go back home.

Until 2018, EPP leaders consistently defended Hungary's autocratic leader against EU intervention. With the exception of a few words of concern (long since forgotten) expressed over the Orbán government's 2017 attack on the Central European University (which attracted great international attention), leaders of the EPP did not criticize Orbán as his government compromised the independent judiciary, the free press, and civil society organizations and – ultimately – consolidated one-party, semi-authoritarian rule. Instead, when EU leaders affiliated with other political parties called for EU action in reaction to the comprehensive assault on the rule of law and democratic norms in Hungary, EPP leaders blocked them.[36] Quite to the contrary, some EPP leaders routinely praised Orbán. For instance, EPP President Joseph Daul endorsed Orbán's reelection in 2014 and later declared, "I would put my hand in the fire for my friend Viktor Orbán." But the most full-throated Orbán defender over the past several years was the then-EPP Chair Manfred Weber.

---

[36] To be fair, some EPP MEPs – from the Commission's former Justice Commissioner and current MEP Viviane Reding to outspoken MEP Frank Engel – repeatedly denounced Orbán's actions. But, crucially, the Party leaders and the majority of EPP MEPs repeatedly blocked proposals for action against Orbán's regime, until a shift in position finally took place in 2018 as discussed later.

Weber repeatedly dismissed critiques of Orbán as politically motivated attacks by leftists and has continued to heap praise on him, even as the Hungarian leader has descended deeper into xenophobia, anti-Semitism, and autocracy. For instance, on November 12, 2017, well after Orbán had consolidated his soft-authoritarian regime and in the midst of an anti-Semitic mass campaign to demonize George Soros, Weber congratulated Orbán on his reelection as Fidesz chairman with a tweet that read, "Congratulations to Viktor#Orban, re-elected Chairman of #FIDESZ. Let's keep on our cooperation for a strong Hungary in a strong Europe. #FideszCongress @EPPGroup."

Against the wishes of the EPP, which voted by two-thirds *against* the proposal, the European Parliament's Civil Liberties Committee (LIBE) was instructed by the plenary in 2017 to prepare a report assessing whether the Parliament should trigger Article 7(1) against Hungary. It appeared as Rapporteur Judith Sargentini prepared her report that the EPP would still try to block it. But in September 2018, when the Parliament had to vote on whether to endorse the Sargentini Report, the EPP's position shifted. Though the party was divided, fully 58 percent of EPP MEPs voted at that point to endorse the Report and launch Article 7(1) against Hungary. In fact, EPP votes proved crucial to its passage, which required two-thirds of the votes cast overall.[37]

The turnaround of the EPP on Fidesz was politically advantageous at that particular moment. Surprisingly, after having defended Orbán for so long, the EPP's faction leader in the European Parliament, Manfred Weber, announced on the eve of the vote that he would be endorsing the Report.[38] The timing of the vote coincided with the start of the *Spitzenkandidaten* process, with candidates stepping forward to compete to be named their Europarty's candidate for the position of European Commission president. With Angela Merkel's blessing, Weber had announced his candidacy just a week before. He must have realized that his consistent support of Orbán might lead many EPP members to oppose his candidacy and some have speculated that it was a condition of Merkel's support for Weber that Weber agree to

---

[37] For a breakdown of the parties' votes on the initial vote in the plenary to charge the LIBE committee with assessing whether Article 7(1) should be triggered against Hungary and the final votes for the Sargentini Report, see Péter Krekó, "The Vote on the Sargentini Report: Good News for Europe, Bad News for Orbán, No News for Hungary," *Heinrich Böll Stiftung*, September 21, 2018, https://eu.boell.org/en/2018/09/21/vote-sargentini-report-good-news-europe-bad-news-orban-no-news-hungary. Only 32 percent of EPP MEPs had voted initially to refer the issue to committee.

[38] Patrick Kingsley, "E.U.'s Leadership Seeks to Contain Hungary's Orban," *New York Times*, September 11, 2018, www.nytimes.com/2018/09/11/world/europe/viktor-orban-european-peoples-party.html.

discipline Orbán. Thus, Weber's sudden decision to break with Orbán to endorse the Sargentini Report can be understood best as a political move designed to bolster his candidacy for the Commission presidency. Party politics again seemed to dominate European principles. Public awareness of the EPP's role in supporting the Orbán regime was increasing while Orbán's regime was hardening its policies and rhetoric, so other EPP members had started to see their association with Orbán as a political liability and voted for the Report as well.

In the end, however, the drive of the EPP for power dominated its temporary interest in principle. Even though many in the EPP said they would vote to expel Fidesz if the Sargentini Report passed the European Parliament and despite the fact that 58 percent of EPP MEPs voted for the Report themselves, the EPP announced just a week later that it would not be ejecting Fidesz from the party after all.[39] Other EPP MEPs have provided a cover for voting for the Report and yet keeping Orbán in the party by saying that the Article 7(1) process just opens a dialogue with Hungary, nothing more.[40] Until the *Council* votes, Article 7(1) is not even fully triggered! Tensions concerning the Orbán regime mounted within the EPP in early 2019, with some national member parties calling for a vote on Fidesz' expulsion. To avoid outright conflict, in March 2019 EPP leaders permitted Orbán to remove himself from party meetings as a sort of "self-suspension" pending an internal party investigation, of Orbán's alleged offenses. At the same time, however, Fidesz MEPs remained active in the EPP's group in the European Parliament, where they could support whomever the EPP eventually backed for the Commission Presidency.[41]

Partisan considerations also help explain why the EU has been somewhat more vigorous in its response to democratic backsliding and attacks on the rule of law in Poland since 2015. Poland's governing PiS party is a member of the nationalist, Eurosceptic "European Conservatives and Reformists (ECR)" group in the European Parliament, which is much weaker than the EPP

---

[39] Maïa de la Baume, David Herzenhorn, and Lili Bayer, "Europe's Center Right Won't Expel Orbán, Leader Says," *Politico Europe*, September 19, 2018, www.politico.eu/article/europes-center-right-wont-expel-hungarian-prime-minister-viktor-orban-leader-says-joseph-daul-epp/.

[40] After the passage of the Article 7(1) report Manfred Weber, for example, said, "The dialogue should begin, not end, in the upcoming weeks and months." Michael Peel, Mehreen Khanand, and Valerie Hopkins, "Orbán Heads into EU Showdown after Centre-Right Allies Desert Him," *Financial Times*, September 13, 2018, www.ft.com/content/d05646fa-b6b5-11e8-bbc3-ccd7de085ffe.

[41] Kim Lane Scheppele, "Europe's Largest Party Suspends Its Resident Autocrat- for Now," *Foreign Affairs*, March 28, 2019, www.foreignaffairs.com/articles/hungary/2019-03-28/europes-largest-party-suspends-its-resident-autocrat-now.

and hence less able to protect PiS against EU action.[42] This helps explain why the Commission has been willing to launch the Rule of Law Framework against Poland and to eventually recommend to the Council triggering Article 7(1) in reaction to the continued belligerence of the Polish government. It also explains why many EPP MEPs, who until recently opposed EU action against Hungary's government, have supported action against Poland's. However, the fact that the EPP leadership continues to shield Orbán for its own partisan reasons will enable him (in a showing of the cross-party solidarity of autocrats) to veto sanctions against Poland under Article 7(2) unless, as one of us has argued,[43] the Commission were to invoke Article 7 proceedings against both states simultaneously and eliminate the fellow-traveler veto.

The partisan dynamics described in this section closely resemble those that sustain subnational authoritarian enclaves in federal systems around the world, but in fact, the situation in the EU is even worse for two reasons. First, the EU's party system is trapped in a mid-range "authoritarian equilibrium." In polities with more fully developed party systems, federal parties may eventually pay a political price for supporting a brazen autocrat at the local level, as his actions can tarnish their party's "brand." There is almost no such price to be paid in the EU's half-baked party system. Few voters are even aware of the existence of Europarties, because national parties align with the Europarties at European level but the only thing that voters see when they go to vote are the national parties. The Europarties are not options on any ballot and therefore are not a popular brand in any meaningful sense. As a result, the misdeeds of a national autocrat who leads a member party would do no political damage to his Europarty or to other national member parties. Quite simply, Angela Merkel's Christian Democrats' consistent support for the autocratic Orbán has likely imposed absolutely no electoral cost on her party in national elections, in part because few of her voters really knew she was aligned with Orbán at European level. As the Hungarian problem rose through the European institutions to the point where EPP intransigence would be visible for all to see in the vote on the Sargentini Report, it appears that Merkel and Weber decided that the party had to take a stand against Hungary, if only for one day. But the general problem of Europarty unaccountability leaves the EU mired

[42] Kelemen, "Europe's Other Democratic Deficit," 229–230; R. Daniel Kelemen and Mitchell Orenstein, "Europe's Autocracy Problem," *Foreign Affairs*, January 7, 2016, www.foreignaffairs.com/articles/poland/2016-01-07/europes-autocracy-problem; and Kelemen, "Europe's Authoritarian Equilibrium."

[43] Kim Lane Scheppele, "EU Can Still Block Hungary's Veto on Polish Sanctions," *Politico Europe*, January 11, 2016, www.politico.eu/article/eu-can-still-block-hungarys- orban-veto-on-polish-pis-sanctions/.

in an authoritarian equilibrium where there are great incentives for Europarties to protect national autocrats who belong to their party groups, and absolutely no political price to be paid for doing so.[44]

Political dynamics in the EU shield autocrats in a second way, through the enduring power of intergovernmentalism in EU decision-making. While partisan politics may be sufficient to explain the coddling of autocrats within the EU, it is not strictly necessary. National leaders may block action against autocratic governments out of a sense of self-preservation (fearing that if the EU acts against the Polish or Hungarian governments now perhaps they could act against their government in the future) or out of a sense of reciprocal deference (with an implicit understanding that they will stay out of each other's internal affairs). The statement in spring 2018 by the heads of government of the three Baltic states – none of whom are affiliated with the PiS' ECR party group – that they would oppose any EU censure of Poland under Article 7 certainly reflects these dynamics.[45] Likewise the stalwart opposition of the governments in Bulgaria and Romania to suggestions – made in response to developments in Poland and Hungary – of strengthening rule-of-law conditionality attached to EU funding reflects the fact that they worry these same rules might one day affect them.[46] More generally, it is striking how few heads of government in the EU – regardless of party group – have denounced the rollback of liberal democracy in Hungary or Poland.[47] French

---

[44] As Kelemen points out, the incentives for Europarties to protect local autocrats have increased with efforts to democratize the EU, by empowering the European Parliament and by linking the selection of the Commission President to winning a plurality of seats in the European Parliament. Thus, ironically, democratizing the EU may have made the survival of Member State autocracies more likely. Kelemen, "Europe's Other Democratic Deficit," 217–218.

[45] Barbara Bodalska, "Baltic States against EU Sanctions on Poland," *Euractiv*, March 13, 2018, www.euractiv.com/section/justice-home-affairs/news/baltic-states-against-eu-sanctions-on-poland/.

[46] On Bulgaria: Georgi Gotev, "Bulgaria dislikes Commission Plan to Link EU Funding to Rule of Law," *Euractiv*, May 3, 2018, www.euractiv.com/section/future-eu/news/bulgaria-dislikes-commission-plan-to-link-eu-funding-to-rule-of-law/. On Romania: AFP, "Romania Backs Poland in Rejecting EU Funding Conditionality," *Euractiv*, February 2, 2018, www.euractiv.com/section/eu-priorities-2020/news/romania-backs-poland-in-rejecting-eu-funding-conditionality/.

[47] For instance, the toughest words the German Chancellor ever uttered about the regime Orbán was constructing came during a visit to Budapest (itself a victory for Orbán) in February 2015 when she said, "Personally, I can't do anything with the word 'illiberal' in connection with democracy." (*Mit dem Wort illiberal kann ich persönlich in Zusammenhang mit Demokratie nichts anfangen*). See "Merkel weist Orbán zurecht," *Zeit Online*, February 2, 2015, www.zeit.de/politik/ausland/2015-02/ungarn-besuch-angela-merkel-orban. A firm denunciation of nascent authoritarianism this was not. France's President Emmanuel Macron has spoken out more decisively than other leaders, emphasizing that Member States who do not respect the

President Emmanuel Macron's strong statements before the European Parliament concerning a looming civil war between liberal democracy and authoritarianism in Europe and the risks of a generation of "sleepwalkers" oblivious to this threat were all the more remarkable as so few other leaders have made such statements.[48] The EU's supranational, quasi-federal legal order has been constructed very much on the understanding that EU institutions – the Commission and the Court of Justice – would enforce the Union's legal norms, instead of national governments enforcing them against one another as would happen in more traditional international legal regimes.[49] Quite simply, for any legal norms the EU is serious about enforcing, the European Commission – and quite often private actors – are provided with firm legal bases for bringing enforcement litigation. The fact that Article 7 was put in the hands of the European Council provides *prima facie* evidence that it was never really intended to be used.

Yet, perhaps there is some silver lining on the dark shadow that the Council casts over the enforcement of the principles of European law. The literature on subnational authoritarianism teaches us that membership in an overarching democratic federation tends to soften the form of authoritarianism practiced at the state level. The possibility (however remote) of higher-level intervention gives lower-level state leaders "strong reasons to avoid blatantly authoritarian practices, which ... increase the likelihood of a federal intervention."[50] In other words, the EU may not be able to guarantee that its members remain democracies or adhere to the rule of law, but it at least prevents soft-authoritarian regimes from becoming full dictatorships. Newspapers may be bought by regime allies and shut down, but journalists will not systematically be jailed. Judges will be fired under the guise of changing the retirement age, but they won't be the victims of show trials. The electoral system and campaign advertising may be rigged in favor of the governing party, but opposition politicians will not routinely be arrested or die in mysterious circumstances. Seen in this light, we might understand Article 7 as providing an ultimate failsafe that could be deployed if a Member State descended into

---

EU's democratic values should have to face political consequences. See Esther King, "Europe is not a Supermarket," *Politico Europe*, June 22, 2017, www.politico.eu/article/emmanuel-macron-europe-is-not-a-supermarket/.

[48] "France's Macron Urges EU to Shun Nationalism," *BBC*, April 17, 2018, www.bbc.com/news/world-europe-43794856.

[49] William Phelan, *In Place of Inter-State Retaliation: The European Union's Rejection of WTO-style Trade Sanctions and Trade Remedies* (Oxford: Oxford University Press, 2015).

[50] Carlos Gervasoni, "A Rentier Theory of Subnational Regimes," *World Politics* 62, no. 2 (2010): 314.

outright dictatorship, and that should discourage soft-autocrats at the national level from hardening their rule. Comparing what is happening now in Hungary and Poland to the unraveling of nascent democracies in Europe's neighbors such as Turkey and Russia, one might consider this some consolation.

IV ALTERNATIVES TO ARTICLE 7 TEU: TOOLS READY FOR USE

Article 2 goes to the heart of the organization of the European Union and Article 7 is designed to enforce Article 2. However, because the procedure (Article 7(2) specifically) allows any single Member State to block the imposition of sanctions on a fellow Member State, such sanctions are unlikely to ever be imposed.[51] Even if the Council can muster the four-fifths vote necessary to trigger Article 7(1), this is simply a bark without a bite. If the offending Member State knows that the risks of actual sanctions are minimal due to the unanimity requirement in Article 7(2), then this Member State can blithely ignore the Article 7(1) warning. Worse yet, some Member States seem to revel in overt challenges to the EU, as long as there are no consequences for them. So, even if European institutions manage to generate an Article 7(1) warning, Member States determined to challenge the EU will fail to be deterred. Worse yet, having appeared to act, EU institutions may turn away from the problem before it is actually solved.

The values of Article 2 TEU are so crucial to the EU's own internal operation that they should not be entrusted only to the political enforcement mechanism of Article 7. They should also be enforceable in law.[52] Member States must actually be in compliance with the principles of Article 2 in order for the European legal order to work.[53] Adherence to the values announced in Article 2 is precisely what permits European Member States to trust each other's governments – and, in particular, their judiciaries – to apply EU law fairly and evenly.[54] It is also what allows EU citizens to take advantage of their

---

[51] To be fair, the Council might achieve unanimity in favor of sanctioning a regime that had established a hard-core dictatorship, but – as we have already seen – unanimity in favor of sanctioning more mild authoritarian regimes of the sort already established in Hungary is unlikely to be forthcoming.

[52] Dimitry Kochenov, "On Policing Article 2 TEU Compliance: Reverse *Solange* and Systemic Infringements Analyzed," *Polish Yearbook of International Law* 33 (2013): 145–170.

[53] Gianluigi Palombella, "Beyond Legality – Before Democracy: Rule of Law Caveats in the EU Two-Level System," in *Reinforcing Rule of Law Oversight in the European Union*, eds. Carlos Closa and Dimitry Kochenov (Cambridge: Cambridge University Press, 2016), 36–58.

[54] On the relationship between enforcement of general principles and the obligation of mutual trust, see Daniel Halberstam, "'It's the Autonomy, Stupid!' A Modest Defense of *Opinion 2/13*

EU citizenship rights both inside their own Member State and throughout the Union.[55] Much of the legal doctrine built up around the Treaties that unite the EU as a common legal space cannot possibly function as announced if the assumptions underlying the EU legal system are shattered. This suggests that Article 7 should be supplemented by other mechanisms for enforcing Article 2.

The sheer variety and vagueness of values specified in Article 2, however, has led a number of commentators to argue that Article 2 can *only* be enforced through Article 7, a distinctly political procedure in which the united outrage of fellow Member States is the only measure that can be effectively used to address noncompliance.[56] But some Article 2 values do have well understood contours, which lend them to legal enforcement as well. The rule of law, in particular, requires at a minimum the protection of politically independent judicial institutions and the even-handed enforcement of the law, both standards that are clear enough to be enforced legally within the EU and in Member States. The rule of law is also a particularly important value in the set listed in Article 2 because an independent judiciary and the even-handed enforcement of the law are themselves guarantors of other values like the enforcement of human rights. Without the rule of law, it is even impossible to ensure democratic governance since democratic elections require neutral referees enforcing election law and the "rules of the game."[57] Rule of law, then, might be thought of as the value that stands behind many of the other values in Article 2. While the rule of law is notoriously capable of many definitions, a core commitment to the independence of judicial institutions and nondiscriminatory enforcement of law are central elements in any conception.[58]

The dependence of EU Member States on each other's judiciaries is perhaps most crucial in the Area of Freedom, Security, and Justice, in which Member States are required to turn over individuals to other Member States under the nearly automatic procedure triggered by a European arrest warrant,

---

on EU Accession to the ECHR, and the Way Forward," *German Law Journal* 16, no. 1 (2015): 130–131.

[55] Jane Jenson, "The European Union's Citizenship Regime: Creating Norms and Building Practices," *Comparative European Politics* 5, no. 1 (2007): 53–60.

[56] Matej Avbelj, "The Inherent Limits of Law—The Case of Slovenia," *Verfassungsblog*, December 6, 2013, www.verfassungsblog.de/en/the-inherent-limits-of-law-the-case-of-slovenia-2/, and Paul Blokker, "Systemic Infringement Action: An Effective Solution or Rather Part of the Problem?" *Verfassungsblog*, December 5, 2013, www.verfassungsblog.de/en/systemic-infringement-action-an-effective-solution-or-rather-part-of-the-problem-2/.

[57] Daniel Ziblatt and Steven Levitsky, *How Democracies Die* (New York: Crown, 2018).

[58] Brian Tamanaha, *On the Rule of Law* (Cambridge: Cambridge University Press, 2004).

which requires states to arrest and transfer criminal suspects to the requesting Member State for trial or to complete a period of detention.[59] It is also a factor in enforcement of the Dublin Regulation, in which Member States can return asylum applicants to their first state of entry into the EU.[60] In fact, the same worry applies in differing ways to nearly all applications of EU law, including in the fields of civil, commercial, and family law touched by the Brussels Regulations on the mutual recognition and enforcement of judgments.[61] Member States of the EU hold out to their fellow Member States and to the EU the promise that EU law will be enforced in an even-handed way by an independent judiciary. With the broadening of topics that the EU governs as well as the deepening over decades of the interdependence of Member States within the European Union, Member States, their nationals and businesses operating across borders have built a community of fate that relies on the commitment of every Member State to operate as a democratic, rule-of-law-based, human-rights-protecting order.

It is therefore a matter of serious concern that Article 7 is unlikely to succeed because the only part of Article 7 that one can imagine ever being used is the part that only warns without carrying any practical effect. For the Union to survive and thrive, there must be other mechanisms for protecting the principled core of the European project. In this section, we will review the major alternatives to Article 7 that we believe that European institutions can already use without the need for further Treaty change.

1 *Bringing Systemic Infringement Actions*

The Commission already has a powerful tool for requiring Member States to follow EU law outside the parameters of Article 7 TEU: infringement procedures. But infringement procedures under Article 258 TFEU are typically brought by the Commission to challenge a specific and concrete violation of the EU *acquis* by a Member State. Infringement procedures carry the assumption that these violations occur in a Member State that is otherwise

---

[59] Libor Klimek, *European Arrest Warrant* (Zurich: Springer Publishing, 2015).

[60] Giulia Vicini, "The Dublin Regulation between Strasbourg and Luxembourg: Reshaping *Non-Refoulement* in the Name of Mutual Trust?" *European Journal of Legal Studies* 8, no. 2 (2015): 50–72.

[61] European Parliament and Council Regulation (EU) 1215/2012, On Jurisdiction and the Recognition and Enforcement of Judgments in Civil and Commercial Matters, 2012 O. J. (L 351) 1 [Brussels I], and Council Regulation (EC) 2201/2003, Concerning Jurisdiction and the Recognition and Enforcement of Judgments in Matrimonial Matters and Matters of Parental Responsibility, Repealing Regulation (EC) No. 1347/2000, 2003 O.J. (L 338) 1 [Brussels II].

generally compliant. What should the Commission do if a Member State's conduct raises serious questions about its more general willingness to observe EU law, particularly when a Member State threatens basic EU principles of democracy, rule of law, and protection of human rights or when it persistently undermines the enforcement of EU law within its jurisdiction?

If a Member State is threatening the basic values of the Treaties or putting the legal guarantees presumed by EU law in doubt, that Member State is probably violating more than one precise slice of EU law. Under present practice, the Commission picks its battles, so it currently fails to bring many infringement actions that it might otherwise be justified in launching. As Wennerås notes, the Commission lacks the resources to monitor application of all EU law across the twenty-eight Member States. But, as he also points out, the Commission has a tendency to see problems as individual trees rather than as larger forests and to bring very specific one-off cases rather than more systemic challenges.[62] For example, when the European Commission decided to bring Hungary's dismissal of its data protection ombudsman to the ECJ in 2012, the Commission limited the infringement to that one issue. Had it asked why the data protection ombudsman had been dismissed, the Commission might have learned that he was fired because he took action against the Hungarian government's routine collection of data in violation of EU law[63] and that the government has also created a new secret police force that had the power to carry out unlimited surveillance against the entire Hungarian population.[64] The unlimited surveillance was eventually found to be a violation of the European Convention of Human Rights,[65] but it was never raised as a matter of EU law. Surely the larger problem for EU law was that the Hungarian government was trying to do an end-run around data protection more generally. If so, the firing of the national official charged with ensuring enforcement of EU law was a symptom of a larger problem. But bringing an infringement only for the firing without considering the reasons

---

[62] Pål Wennerås, "Making Effective Use of Article 260 TFEU," in *The Enforcement of EU Law and Values: Ensuring Member States' Compliance*, eds. András Jakab and Dimitry Kochenov (Oxford: Oxford University Press, 2017), 79–98.

[63] Kim Lane Scheppele, "Making Infringement Procedures More Effective: A Comment on Commission v. Hungary, Case C-288/12 (8 April 2014) (Grand Chamber)," *Eutopia Law*, April 29, 2014, https://eutopialaw.com/2014/04/29/making-infringement-procedures-more-effective-a-comment-on-commission-v-hungary-case-c-28812-8-april-2014-grand-chamber/.

[64] Kim Lane Scheppele, "The New Hungarian Secret Police," *The Conscience of a Liberal* (blog), April 19, 2012, http://krugman.blogs.nytimes.com/2012/04/19/the-new-hungarian-secret-police/.

[65] *Szabó and Vissy v. Hungary*, App. no. 37138/14, ECLI:CE:ECHR:2016:0112JUD003713814.

missed an opportunity. When the Commission taps only a small part of a larger field, it invites legalistic responses (compensating the fired ombudsman) that do not address the underlying norm violation (which might have been better achieved by reinstating him, relaunching the cases he had started, or changing the government's data collection practices).

The Commission could simply increase the number of individual infringement actions against persistently violating states.[66] But even if the Commission were to bring more individual infringements to signal greater concern about a particular Member State, the ECJ is not institutionally able to see the patterns at issue if the cases are filed as they presently are: one by one, in isolation from each other and without the requirement of a national judge on every case to link the cases together. First, the ECJ has no way to assess how a Member State is behaving overall, since each separate violation will typically be taken up by a different panel that will not know about all of the other, different, cases coming from that one Member State. Second, even if a particular panel sees the connection with another case before another panel, merging cases on different points of law is not envisioned under the Court's rules of procedure, which limits joinder to cases on the same point of law.[67]

A different strategy of framing cases seems called for, a strategy that puts specific violations in a broader view and that sets the stage for the sort of remedies that would be necessary to bring a Member State back into line with basic values. For that, the Commission needs the option of the "systemic infringement procedure."[68] A systemic infringement procedure could be launched when the Commission recognizes that a Member State is engaging in a systemic violation of EU principles and is not just violating a particular narrow provision of EU law. A systemic infringement action would aim directly at the systemic nature of the violation by compiling a single legal action from a set of laws, decisions, and actions that together form a more troubling whole. Bundling together a *pattern of violations that adds up to more than the sum of the parts* would allow the Commission to capture how multiple violations of EU law intersect to raise larger issues about a Member

---

[66] See R. Daniel Kelemen and Michael Blauberger, "Can Courts Rescue National Democracy? Judicial Safeguards against Democratic Backsliding in the EU," *Journal of European Public Policy* 24, no. 3 (2017): 321–336 (for suggestions along these lines).

[67] European Court of Justice, Consolidated Version of the Rules of Procedure of the Court of Justice (September 25, 2012), art. 54 Joinder, https://curia.europa.eu/jcms/upload/docs/application/pdf/2012-10/rp_en.pdf.

[68] Kim Lane Scheppele, "Enforcing the Basic Principles of EU Law through Systemic Infringement Procedures," in *Reinforcing the Rule of Law Oversight in the European Union*, eds. Carlos Closa and Dimitry Kochenov (Cambridge University Press, 2016), 104–132.

State's compliance with European law, as we could see with the Hungarian data protection example. That said, the systemic infringement action needs to be more than simply a bundle of unrelated complaints, joined only by the fact that they come from a single Member State. The case should be tied together with an overarching legal theory that links the allegations together, making the systemic violation clear and pointing to a systemic remedy.

Bundling together a set of violations to demonstrate a larger pattern is hardly radical; in fact, the Commission has already tried it and the Court has confirmed the practice.[69] "General and persistent" violations have been found in a number of cases where the Commission has brought together evidence of a pattern of violations as in the flagship Irish Waste Directive case, where twelve different problematic waste disposal sites were found to be evidence of systemic nonenforcement.[70] The systemic quality of the violations matters because it allows the Commission to craft a more systemic remedy. In the environmental cases where "general and persistent" violations have been found, the remedy has been for the Member State to change the way it enforces the law and not just to clean up a particular site.[71] These structural remedies make a bigger difference than the small bore remedies available if only one stand-alone problem is alleged, which is precisely why systemic infringement actions are more effective tools than the narrow and technical infringements that are more typical uses of the Commission's practice.

As these examples indicate, bundling together a series of specific violations to demonstrate a larger pattern is no longer a radically novel idea in the Court's jurisprudence. But the use we propose is different from the other cases brought so far in one respect. Instead of simply documenting a pattern that shows EU law has been violated repeatedly on the same point by a single Member State, the systemic infringement procedure would focus on claims that raise questions of a more fundamental sort, where the Member State's commitment to European values would be raised by the set of violations alleged.

---

[69] See the discussion of this issue in Koen Lenaerts, Ignace Maselis, and Kathleen Gutman, *EU Procedural Law* (Oxford: Oxford University Press, 2014), 166–167, sec. 5.11 (with many examples in the notes).

[70] Case C-494/01, *Commission v. Ireland*, ECLI:EU:C:2005:250. See also Case C-135/05, *Commission v. Italy*, ECLI:EU:C:2007:250, and Case C-88/07, *Commission v. Spain*, ECLI: EU:C:2009:123.

[71] Pål Wennerås, "A New Dawn for Commission Enforcement under Articles 226 and 228 EC: General and Persistent (Gap) Infringements, Lump Sums and Penalty Payments," *Common Market Law Review* 43, no. 1 (2006): 31.

Systemic infringement procedures before the Court could be structured doctrinally in one of three ways:

First, and perhaps most ambitiously, systemic infringement actions could directly allege that a pattern of Member State conduct directly violates one or more of the basic principles outlined in Article 2. This used to seem a radical and novel suggestion, but the Court of Justice's 2018 decisions in the *Portuguese Judges* and *Celmer* cases (discussed *infra*) indicate that the Court is now ready to enforce Article 2 directly by linking it with Article 19(1) TEU, which guarantees effective remedies in national courts for violations of EU law.[72] In the run-up to these decisions, a number of commentators had argued that Article 2 could only be enforced through Article 7, as *lex specialis* designed to exclude ECJ action in this area.[73] But a growing number of commentators had urged the Court to consider Article 2 as enforceable EU *law*.[74] Now it seems that the ECJ has sided with those who believe that Article 2 is legal as well as political. As we will argue at greater length below, this could provide a major new tool for enforcing Article 2 values.

But legally enforcing the broad principles of Article 2 TEU, even by way of Article 19(1), is not the only theory under which a systemic infringement action could be framed. A systemic infringement procedure could argue, second, that a systemic violation of the basic principles of EU law puts a Member State in violation of Article 4(3) TEU. This is familiar ground to the ECJ, which has already developed an extensive jurisprudence of "sincere cooperation" or loyalty.[75] Using this rubric, the Commission would argue that the challenged laws and practices of a Member State systematically interfere with the operation of EU law in the Member State's jurisdiction and thus violate the Member State's loyalty obligations. The *Portuguese Judges* case used this strategy by invoking Article 4(3) TEU in conjunction with Article 2 TEU to provide a systemic reading of both together.[76] In fact, it would

---

[72] Case C-64/16, *Associação Sindical dos Juízes Portugueses* v. *Tribunal de Contas*, ECLI:EU:C:2018:117 [hereinafter *Portuguese Judges*], and Reference for a Preliminary Ruling from the High Court (Ireland), Case C-216/18 PPU, ECLI:EU:C:2018:586 [hereinafter *Celmer*] (discussed further later).

[73] Avbelj, "The Inherent Limits of Law," and Blokker, "Systemic Infringement Action."

[74] Christophe Hillion "Overseeing the Rule of Law in the EU: Legal Mandate and Means," in *Reinforcing Rule of Law Oversight in the European Union*, eds. Carlos Closa and Dimitry Kochenov (Cambridge: Cambridge University Press, 2016), 59–81; Editorial Comments, "Safeguarding EU Values in the Member States: Is Something Finally Happening?" *Common Market Law Review* 52, no. 3 (2015): 622.

[75] For a comprehensive account of the loyalty principle in EU law, see Klamert, *The Principle of Loyalty in EU Law*.

[76] *Portuguese Judges*, paras. 30–36.

almost appear as if the ECJ is begging the Commission to be more adventurous in the way it frames its infringement actions, offering Article 4(3) as an easy way to make the systemic argument, in addition to offering Article 2 as a legal ground.

In a third variant of the systemic infringement procedure, the Commission could allege that a Member State has engaged in a violation of rights under the Charter of Fundamental Rights (Charter or CFR). If the Commission is the guardian of the Treaty – all Treaties, including the Charter – then it has an obligation to ensure that fundamental rights are protected when violated by Member States implementing EU law. Here, the Commission would not be bringing a case against a Member State that infringed a particular individual's right, but would instead bring an Article 258 TFEU action for situations in which the regular misapplication of EU law itself generated a practice of widespread rights violations. A legal finding of systemic rights violations by the ECJ could be effective at teeing up the political invocation of Article 7 on the basis that the ECJ has certified violation of rights guaranteed by Article 2.

Given Article 51 CFR, which limits the scope of Charter rights to those violated while a Member State is engaged in enforcing EU law, not all cases of rights violations can be the subject of an infringement action. But the Commission, however gingerly, has started to use this third strategy of adding rights violations to *acquis* violations in infringement actions involving both Hungary and Poland. In its 2015 infringement action against Hungary for violating various directives and regulations connected to the migration crisis, the Commission threw in an additional charge: that Hungary had also violated Article 47 of the Charter, which guarantees the right to a fair trial, through the procedures Hungary used to hear asylum claims.[77] Afterwards, the Commission supplemented this first infringement action with another over the matter of asylum law, alleging additional fundamental rights violations.[78] In 2017, the Commission brought an action against Hungary for violating freedom of association as well as the right of data privacy with a sweeping NGO law that requires disclosure of foreign funding. The infringement action addressed the scope problem posed by Article 51 CFR by grounding its rights claims in restrictions on the free movement of capital.[79] And in the case that the Commission brought to the ECJ against Hungary in the matter of "Lex

---

[77] European Commission Press Release IP/15/6228, Commission Opens Infringement Procedure against Hungary Concerning Its Asylum Law (December 10, 2015).

[78] European Commission Press Release IP/17/5023, Migration: Commission Steps Up Infringement against Hungary Concerning Its Asylum Law (December 7, 2017).

[79] European Commission Press Release IP/17/1982, Infringements – Hungary: Commission Launches Infringement Procedure for Law on Foreign-Funded NGOs (July 13, 2017).

CEU," a law of apparently general application that had the effect of specifically targeting Central European University, the Commission alleged that the law violated "the right of academic freedom, the right to education and the freedom to conduct a business as provided by the Charter of Fundamental Rights of the European Union (Articles 13, 14, 16, respectively)."[80]

In confronting the Polish government's assault on judicial independence, the Commission has also started laying the ground for arguing that systemic violations of Member State obligations must be met with systemic compliance. In its first infringement action against Poland for assaulting the judiciary, launched at the same time as it issued its Reasoned Proposal to the Council advocating the invocation of Article 7(1) for Poland, the Commission took a very legalistic approach to infringements, primarily calling out the five-year difference in the retirement ages of male and female judges, though it also called attention to the ability of the Justice Minister to discretionarily suspend the retirement age for any specific judge.[81] At the same time, however, in its Reasoned Proposal to the Council, the Commission argued that a bonfire of the rule of law was occurring in Poland, showing that the Commission still strongly separated what it could do with infringements compared to what it could do in the Article 7 framework.

Since then, however, the Commission appears to have changed tack. In July 2018, the Commission filed another infringement action against Poland for its assaults on the Supreme Court, this time grounding the action in "the principle of judicial independence, including the irremovability of judges ... [through which] Poland fails to fulfil its obligations under Article 19(1) of the Treaty on European Union read in connection with Article 47 of the Charter of Fundamental Rights of the European Union."[82] But this new approach occurred only after the ECJ practically invited this line of argument in the

---

[80] European Commission Press Release IP/17/5004, Commission refers Hungary to the European Court of Justice of the EU over the Higher Education Law (December 7, 2017). The EU does not have direct authority in the area of higher education but because CEU is a private university, it is considered a service under EU law (Case C-109/92, *Stephan Max Wirth v. Landeshauptstadt Hannover*, ECLI:EU:C:1993:916). By itself, however, operating in the common market did not give the EU jurisdiction, because CEU is incorporated in the United States, so the General Agreement on Trade in Services was invoked. Both the EU and Hungary are signatories and the EU was claiming its right to enforce the measures agreed in that Treaty including, among other things, the freedom to conduct a business. This was an usually creative infringement action.

[81] European Commission Press Release IP/17/5367, Rule of Law. European Commission acts to Defend Judicial Independence in Poland (December 20, 2017).

[82] European Commission Press Release IP/18/4341, Rule of Law. Commission Launches Infringement Procedure to Protect the Independence of the Polish Supreme Court (July 2, 2018).

Portuguese Judges case, about which more later. By making the more general case about the rule of law, independence of the judiciary and the state of human rights in a Member State, the Commission has now finally laid the ground for arguing that systemic violations of Member State obligations must be met with systemic compliance and for using infringement actions to act.

Regardless of the way that it is ultimately grounded in EU law, a systemic infringement procedure enables the Commission to signal to the Court of Justice a more general concern about deviation from core principles than the Commission's more narrowly tailored infringement actions had permitted. A systemic infringement procedure has the advantage of putting before the ECJ evidence of a *pattern* of violation so that the overall situation in a particular Member State is not lost in a flurry of individual or comparatively trivial complaints, each of which would be judged on its own, never providing full documentation of the pattern that should cause even more concern. Until very recently, the Commission has been using its power to bring infringements much less effectively than it might, though under tutelage from the ECJ, the Commission might be learning to think bigger.

2 Halting the Funding of Autocracies

The EU finds itself in the perverse situation of providing some of the largest transfers of funds precisely to those governments who most prominently thumb their nose at its democratic and rule-of-law norms. In short, the EU subsidizes autocracy. Scholars of comparative politics show us that in fact this perverse circumstance is not uncommon, as autocratic states often take root in less-developed regions and are thus recipients of fiscal transfers in federal-type systems. In the EU, as in these other cases, local authoritarians can use federal transfers to support clientelistic networks that perpetuate their rule.[83]

These dynamics will sound familiar to anyone who has followed recent developments in Hungary and Poland, both huge beneficiaries of EU fiscal transfers. Poland is the largest overall recipient, taking in €86 billion from various European Structural and Investment Funds (ESIFs) in the current funding period (2014–2020).[84] Hungary meanwhile is the largest recipient of EU funds on a per capita basis, and more than 95 percent of all public

[83] Gervasoni, "A Rentier Theory of Subnational Regimes."
[84] European Commission, European Structural and Investment Funds 2014–2020: Official Texts and Commentaries (November 2015), 45, http://ec.europa.eu/regional_policy/sources/docgener/guides/blue_book/blueguide_en.pdf.

investments in Hungary in recent years have been co-financed by the EU.[85] A significant chunk of this EU largesse has found its way into the pockets of a set of new oligarchs created by the current governing party, helping sustain Orbán's sprawling, corrupt patronage network.[86] Ultimately, many of the other sanctions discussed for democratic backsliders – such as the suspension of voting rights under Article 7 – may matter very little to leaders of these regimes so long as the money keeps flowing.[87]

Many observers recognize the irony of this situation, but have concluded that there is little the EU can do because, in their view, the EU either lacks the legal grounds to suspend the flow of ESIFs in response to democratic backsliding[88] or would target the wrong actors by withholding funds[89] or would "poison" broader EU relations if it went down this path.[90] More recently, with an eye to the EU's next multi-annual budget that will run from 2021 to 2027, politicians and academics have advanced a series of proposals[91] (such as ones from the European Parliament,[92] the German government,[93] and European Commissioner for Justice Vera Jourová[94]) to strengthen the rule-of-law conditionality attached to EU funding.[95] A heated debate has ensued, with

[85] Christian Keszthely, "Hungary's Economy Heavily Depends on EU Funds, Study Finds," *Budapest Business Journal*, March 30, 2017, https://bbj.hu/economy/hungarys-economy-heavily-depends-on-eu-funds-study-finds_130880.

[86] Bálint Magyar, *The Post-Communist Mafia State: The Case of Hungary* (Budapest: CEU Press, 2016).

[87] Gábor Halmai, "The Possibility and Desirability of Economic Sanction: Rule of Law Conditionality Requirements against Illiberal EU Member States." EUI Working Paper law 2018/06, http://cadmus.eui.eu/bitstream/handle/1814/51644/LAW_2018_06.pdf?sequence=1.

[88] Hubert Heinelt and Wolfgang Petzold, "The Structural Funds and EU Cohesion Policy," in *Handbook of European Politics: Interpretive Approaches to the EU*, eds. Hubert Heinelt and Sybille Münch (Northampton, MA: Edward Elgar Publishing, 2018), 134–154.

[89] Marjorie Jouen, "The Macro-Economic Conditionality, the Story of a Triple Penalty for Regions," *Jacques Delors Institute*, Policy Paper 131 (March 2015).

[90] Florian Eder, "Juncker: German Plan to Link Funds and Rules Would Be 'Poison'," *Politico Europe*, June 1, 2017, www.politico.eu/article/juncker-german-plan-to-link-funds-and-rules-would-be-poison/.

[91] For a detailed review of the range of proposals regarding funding conditionality made to date, see Halmai, "The Possibility and Desirability of Economic Sanction."

[92] European Parliament Resolution, On an EU mechanism on Democracy, the Rule of Law and Fundamental Rights, P8_TA(2016)0409 (October 25, 2016).

[93] Guy Chazan and Duncan Robinson, "Juncker Rejects German Plan to Tie EU Funding to Democracy," *Financial Times*, June 1, 2017, www.ft.com/content/d1b69d8a-46cf-11e7-8519-9f94ee97d996.

[94] Eszter Zalan, "Justice Commissioner Links EU Funds to 'Rule of Law'," *EUobserver*, October 31, 2017, https://euobserver.com/political/139720.

[95] For more on these proposals, see Jasna Selih, Ian Bond, and Carol Dolan, "Can EU Funds Promote the Rule of Law in Europe?" Center for European Reform Policy Brief, November 2017, www.cer.eu/sites/default/files/pbrief_structural_funds_nov17.pdf.

442 Kim Lane Scheppele and R. Daniel Kelemen

governments who see themselves as the potential targets of such conditionality – not only Poland and Hungary, but other states with problematic judicial systems such as Romania and Bulgaria – adamantly denouncing these proposals. Likewise, the debate has raged within the Commission, with some EU leaders such as Justice Commissioner Jourová defending such plans, while others such as Commission President Jean-Claude Juncker adamantly oppose them.[96] But these proposals and the entire debate surrounding them misses the fact that, as we will show, the EU already has a sufficient legal basis to suspend the flow of funds to states in which rule-of-law norms are systematically violated. The real problem to date has not been the lack of adequate legal tools, but the lack of political will on the part of the European Commission to use the tools that already exist.

The Common Provisions Regulation (CPR) enacted in 2013 regulates the administration of ESIFs.[97] As Israel Butler of the Civil Liberties Union for Europe argued in a recent report, "the CPR, read in light of the Charter of Fundamental Rights and the case law of the Court of Justice, already allows the Commission to suspend ESIFs where a Member State does not uphold the rule of law."[98] We agree. Article 142(a) of the CPR provides that payments of ESIFs may be suspended if, "there is a serious deficiency in the effective functioning of the management and control system of the operational programme, which has put at risk the Union contribution to the operational programme and for which corrective measures have not been taken."[99] That requisite management and control system must "ensure that effective arrangements for the examination of complaints concerning the ESI Funds are in place" (Article 74(3), CPR), and must ensure that natural and legal persons have the right to an effective remedy from an independent and impartial

---

[96] Zalan, "Justice Commissioner Links EU Funds to 'Rule of Law'"; Chazan and Robinson, "Juncker Rejects German Plan to Tie EU Funding to Democracy."

[97] European Parliament and Council Regulation (EU)1303/2013, Laying Down Common Provisions on the European Regional Development Fund, the European Social Fund, the Cohesion Fund, the European Agricultural Fund for Rural Development and the European Maritime and Fisheries Fund and Laying Down General Provisions on the European Regional Development Fund, the European Social Fund, the Cohesion Fund and the European Maritime and Fisheries Fund and repealing Council Regulation (EC) No 1083/ 2006, 2013 O.J. (L 347) 320 [hereinafter CPR].

[98] Israel Butler, "Two Proposals to Promote and Protect European Values through the Multiannual Financial Framework," Civil Liberties Union for Europe, March 2018, www.liberties.eu/en/news/european-vaues-fund-two-proposals-mff/14471.

[99] CPR, art. 142(a).

tribunal as required under Article 47 of the Charter of Fundamental Rights.[100] The European Court of Justice has affirmed these principles, and emphasized that the framework for remedies must meet the requirements of Article 19(1) TEU for effective legal protection in fields covered by Union law.[101]

The procedure that the Commission must follow to claw back funds or refuse to pay on schedule under the CPR occurs in a dialogue between the Member State in question and the Commission, a dialogue that is not made public. Therefore, the Commission may have already been using the CPR to restrict funds for rule-of-law reasons more than is visible. In fact, the Commission in the European parliamentary debate over the Sargentini Report seems to have said as much. In that session, Commission Vice-President Frans Timmermans publicly noted that on his watch, "[t]he Hungarian operational programmes for EU structural and investment funds have been the subject of the highest amount of financial corrections in 2016 and 2017 among all EU Member States, as a result of the supervisory role of the Commission."[102] Later reporting indicated that the Commission had withheld $1.8 billion from Hungary due to irregularities.[103] Perhaps, then, the Commission may already be using the CPR to police the rule of law in Member States, but it just may not have announced that it is doing so. If part of the point of insisting on rule of law in the Member States is to dissuade others from going down that path, however, a silent procedure may not be as effective as one that is publicly documented.

Although the Commission has not yet been willing to use the CPR overtly to cut off funds to offending Member States, there are some signs that the Commission has attempted to use other available mechanisms to send warning signals to Member States that do not play by the rules. For example, shortly after the Hungarian government rammed through its worrisome new constitution on the strength of votes of the governing party alone, the Barroso Commission recommended that Hungary be fined under the Excessive

---

[100] Commission Notice, Guidance on Ensuring the Respect for the Charter of Fundamental Rights of the European Union when Implementing the European Structural and Investment Funds (ESI Funds), 2016 O.J. (C 269) 1.

[101] Case C-562/12, *Liivimaa Lihaveis MTÜ v. Eesti-Läti programmi*, ECLI:EU:C:2014:2229, paras. 67–75.

[102] Frans Timmermans, European Commission Vice-President, Opening Remarks in the European Parliament Plenary debate on the situation in Hungary (September 11, 2018), https:// ec.europa.eu/commission/commissioners/2014-2019/timmermans/announcements/opening-and-closing-remarks-european-parliament-plenary-debate-situation-hungary_en.

[103] "EU Funds Worth $1.8 Billion at Risk for Hungary due to Irregularities: Report," *Reuters*, September 25, 2018, www.reuters.com/article/us-eu-hungary-budget/eu-funds-worth-18-billion-at-risk-for-hungary-due-to-irregularities-report-idUSKCN1M521H.

Deficit Procedure (EDP) for its persistent violation of the EU deficit rules. The fines were huge: The Commission "proposed to suspend €495,184,000 of Cohesion Fund commitments taking effect on 1 January 2013, representing 0.5 % of GDP and 29% of the country's cohesion fund allocations for 2013."[104] And the grounds for suspending funds were solid: Hungary had clearly overshot EU deficit targets ever since it had entered the EU and therefore was an appropriate target for the EDP's sanctions. But many other countries were also in violation of the EDP's targets at that time and were not the subject of recommended sanctions, leading some (not least the Hungarian government) to argue that the Commission was singling Hungary out for special treatment. In the end, the Orbán government ramped up its revenue-generating measures to bring its budget deficit into line and ECO-FIN (the Council configuration for economic matters charged with confirming the Commission's assessment before it could be finalized) ultimately refused to support the sanctions,[105] so the threat fizzled out. But many observers at the time could not help but make the link between the measures that the Commission directed at Hungary and the rapid consolidation of power in the hands of Orbán that was taking effect during that time.

Given that the Commission has not felt comfortable making apparent that rule-of-law concerns affect its distribution of EU funds to offending Member States already, it may have wanted more explicit permission to use its power to suspend or claw back ESI funds flowing to Member States by inventing new mechanisms with this precise purpose. This might be behind the Commission proposal for a European Public Prosecutor in recognition of the fact that the EU's current anti-corruption mechanism was not working.[106] At the moment, European Anti-Fraud Office (OLAF) has the power to investigate corruption in the use of EU funds, but on conclusion of its investigations, it hands over the results to the Member States for further action, prosecution if necessary.

---

[104] European Commission Press Release IP/12/161, Commission Proposes to Suspend €495 million of Cohesion Fund for Hungary for 2013 for Failure to Address Excessive Deficit (February 22, 2012).

[105] For an overview of Hungary under the Excessive Deficit Procedure, see "Hungary and the European Union Excessive Deficit Procedure," *The Orange Files*, June 11, 2016, https://theorangefiles.hu/hungary-and-the-european-union-excessive-deficit-procedure/.

[106] Carlos Gómez-Jara Díez and Ester Herlin-Karnell, "Prosecuting EU Financial Crimes: The European Public Prosecutor's Office in Comparison to the US Federal Regime," *German Law Journal* 19, no. 5 (2018): 1191–1220; Willem Geelhoed, Leendert H. Erkelens, and Arjen W.H. Meij eds., *Shifting Perspectives on the European Public Prosecutor's Office* (Groningen: Asser Press/Springer, 2017).

Defending Democracy in EU Member States

Not surprisingly, these files often go nowhere.[107] The Member States most likely to abuse EU funds often have governments implicated in these corruption schemes at the highest levels[108] and, not surprisingly, these governments are not likely to prosecute themselves when OLAF hands them the evidence to do so. Some tougher mechanism, not dependent on the Member States themselves, was called for.

The creation of a European Public Prosecutor to scrutinize and prosecute corrupt uses of EU funds was authorized in June 2017,[109] when twenty Member States in the Council agreed to set up this new institution under the enhanced cooperation mechanism, which permits a substantial subset of Member States to agree to increased integration without waiting for all Member States to join. The regulation establishing this new office was passed in October 2017.[110] Not surprisingly, neither Hungary nor Poland decided to sign up as one of the founding states, nor did other Member States that are considered among the most thoroughly corrupt.

Proposals are now circulating to tie EU funding to the agreement by Member States to the acceptance of the jurisdiction of the European Public Prosecutor. If a Member State will not allow its uses of funds to be scrutinized, then, the theory goes, that Member State should not be entrusted with such funds. Justice Commissioner Vera Jourová first made the proposal to link allocations of EU funds to acceptance of the European Public Prosecutor,[111] and the call has since been picked up by critics of the Orbán government as a way for the EU to avoid subsidizing Member States that do not play by the rules.

Beyond the Public Prosecutor, there is also an attempt to make the distribution of ESIFs explicitly conditional on a Member State's commitment to

---

[107] Commission Staff Working Document Executive Summary of the Impact Assessment Accompanying the Document Proposal for a Council Regulation on the Establishment of the European Public Prosecutor's Office, SWD (2013) 274 final (July 17, 2013), para. 11.

[108] Corruption was an important element of the Sargentini Report, emphasized often in the plenary debate. The plenary debate can be viewed online at www.youtube.com/watch?v=ARfcG2FFi04.

[109] European Council Press Release 333/17, 20 Member States Agree on Details on Creating the European Public Prosecutor's Office (EPPO) (June 8, 2017).

[110] Council Regulation (EU) 2017/1939, Implementing Enhanced Cooperation on the Establishment of the European Public Prosecutor's Office ('the EPPO'), 2017 O.J. (L 283) 1. Since that time, all of the Member States that do not have opt-outs from the Area of Freedom Security and Justice have taken steps to join, save Hungary and Poland.

[111] Harry Cooper, "EU's Jourová Wants Funds Linked to New Prosecutor's Office," *Politico Europe*, June 8, 2017, www.politico.eu/article/eus-jourova-wants-funds-linked-to-new-prosecutors-office/.

the rule of law. As the Juncker Commission wound down, it proposed a regulation that would explicitly create rule-of-law conditionality in the use of ESIFs.[112] Butler has supported the idea that these legal bases for the suspension of EU funds on rule-of-law grounds should be spelled out in the regulations governing the next multi-annual financial framework.[113] But even though these new proposals would certainly be desirable and explicit recognition of this conditionality would be a step in the right direction, the more crucial point is that the legal bases for action already exist in the CPR but somehow the Commission has not yet had the will to aggressively and publicly use the power already in its hands.

Why then has the EU so far (now in Orbán's third consecutive government and far into PiS's first) refused to suspend the flow of funds to its nascent autocracies and to do so explicitly in the name of the rule of law? Again, as with its failure to impose Article 7 sanctions, all indications point to a lack of political will as the principal explanation. It would fall to the European Commission to lead the charge in suspending the flow of EU funds to Hungary or Poland, and though some Commissioners have supported the idea of rule-of-law conditionality as a future remedy, to date the Commission has simply refused to move in this direction.[114] This is hardly surprising given that Commission President Jean-Claude Juncker, when asked during a conference in Berlin if he supported what had started as Germany's proposals to attach rule of law and democracy conditions to EU funds, said: "I am of the opinion that one should not do that." He added that the proposal would be "poison for the continent."[115] In arguing this, he joins other critics who say that suspending funds to the poorer Member States will simply drive them into the arms of other powers with no interest in democracy or the rule of law, like China.[116] Whether Juncker's refusal to support funding conditionality stems

---

[112] *Commission Proposal for a Regulation of the European Parliament and of the Council on the Protection of the Union's Budget in Case of Generalized Deficiencies as Regards the Rule of Law in the Member States*, COM (2018) 324 final (May 2, 2018).

[113] Butler, "Two Proposals to Promote and Protect European Values."

[114] As Gabor Halmai notes, on one occasion when the EU did temporarily suspend some EU funds to Hungary just on the heels of the Orbán regime's dismantlement of the Constitutional Court, it claimed that this suspension was not due to general attacks on the rule of law in Hungary, but due to some technical irregularities in management of the funds (Halmai, "The Possibility and Desirability of Economic Sanction.") Also see Kester Eddy and James Fontanella-Khan, "Brussels Suspends Funding to Hungary over Alleged Irregularities," *Financial Times*, August 14, 2013, www.ft.com/content/9b85c228-04f1-11e3-9e71-00144feab7de.

[115] Chazan and Robinson, "Juncker Rejects German Plan to Tie EU Funding to Democracy."

[116] Thorsten Benner and Jan Weidenfeld, "Europe, Don't Let China Divide and Conquer: Cutting Funds to Countries that Disregard EU Values will Push Them into China's Arms," *Politico Europe*, April 20, 2018, www.politico.eu/article/europe-china-divide-and-conquer/.

from his partisan loyalty to EPP ally Viktor Orbán[117] – a sure target of any such sanctions – or from a sincere belief that sanctions would prompt destructive fissures within the EU, the fact remains that so long as the Commission lacks the political will to deploy the tools it has, arming it with an ever larger toolkit by itself would have less effect than its advocates might hope.

3 Adjusting the Principle of Mutual Trust and Suspending the Recognition of National Judiciaries

If the EU's political leaders in the Council, European Parliament, and Commission fail to take action to address the rule-of-law crisis in Poland and Hungary, the ECJ and national courts may be called on to address the situation. Indeed, this has already started to occur. As noted previously, the EU legal order is founded on an assumption of mutual trust between national judiciaries, which, in addition to their purely national functions, also serve as EU courts and are required to recognize one another's judgments. Attacks on judicial independence and the rule of law in any Member State will inevitably ripple across this interdependent legal order and generate litigation before national courts as well as before the ECJ itself, questioning whether this assumption of mutual trust can be sustained.

In February 2018, the ECJ helped set the stage for such litigation in its ruling in the *Portuguese Judges* case.[118] The case involved a reference from a Portuguese court asking if the austerity measures taken by the Portuguese government during the euro crisis infringed the independence of the judiciary. The ECJ said no, but went on to hold that there is a general obligation for Member States to guarantee judicial independence of their national courts; the decision also suggested that the Court would closely scrutinize the independence of Member State courts going forward. The Court's reasoning was truly path breaking for several reasons.

First, the Court grounded its decision in Articles 2, 4(3), and 19 TEU without reference to other provisions of the *acquis*. It therefore established that Member States must ensure the independence of their courts as a direct obligation under the Treaties, not dependent on any particular area of EU

---

[117] The 2014 European Parliament elections promised to strengthen democracy and voter engagement in the EU in part through the *Spitzenkandidaten* process, which was designed to inject partisan competition into the selection of the Commission President. Ever since he was selected through this process as the EPP's candidate, Jean Claude Juncker repeatedly promised that his would be a more political European Commission. Advocates of this politicization may rue their success.

[118] *Portuguese Judges.*

law. Second, the Court overtly interpreted Article 2 TEU together with Article 19(1) TEU as establishing that the EU's basic values require that Member States guarantee certain legal protections in their domestic systems. In short, Article 2 was used as a basis for the Court's legal interpretation, even though some commentators had previously argued that *only* the political process set out in Article 7 could be used to determine when Article 2 values had been violated.[119] Third, the ECJ established the standards it would use in assessing whether a Member State's judiciary was independent. According to the Court, judicial independence requires that courts operate autonomously without being subordinated to any other body and without taking instruction from elsewhere. An independent court must be protected against all external pressures, including protection for judges against removal from office.

By laying out the Treaty basis for judicial independence in this relatively uncontroversial case, the ECJ has given itself a weapon loaded for use when it examines what the Polish government has done to its courts. Laurent Pech and Sébastian Platon have quite rightly interpreted the judgment as a kind of shot across the bow of the Polish government in reaction to its attack on judicial independence.[120] Judges across Europe heard the shot, and a judge of the Irish High Court was the first to respond.

Just two weeks after the *Portuguese Judges* decision, on March 12, 2018, Justice Aileen Donnelly of the High Court in Ireland sent a historic reference for a preliminary ruling to the ECJ concerning the state of the rule of law in Poland.[121] The case involved a European Arrest Warrant (EAW) issued for a suspect, Artur Celmer, who faced charges for drug trafficking in his native Poland. Mr. Celmer's lawyers opposed surrendering him to Polish authorities under the EAW on the grounds that the rule of law was no longer functioning there. Justice Donnelly relied heavily on the Commission's Reasoned Proposal to the Council to trigger Article 7(1) TEU against Poland, and

---

[119] "There is no role mentioned for the Court of Justice in [Article 7 TEU] – no requirement that the Court must first have found an infringement of Article 2 TEU. The absence of the Court from this process clearly confirms the difference between legal mechanisms and purely political mechanisms." Lawrence Gormley, "Infringement Proceedings," in *The Enforcement of EU Law and Values: Ensuring Member States' Compliance*, András Jakab and Dimitry Kochenov, eds. (Oxford: Oxford University Press, 2017), 74.

[120] Laurent Pech and Sébastian Platon, "Rule of Law Backsliding in the EU: The Court of Justice to the Rescue? Some Thoughts on the ECJ Ruling in Associação Sindical dos Juízes Portugueses," *EU Law Analysis* (blog), March 13, 2018, http://eulawanalysis.blogspot.com/search?q=64%2F16.

[121] Ruaidhrí Giblin, "High Court Judge Seeks EU Ruling on Effect of Polish Law Changes," *Irish Times*, March 12, 2018, www.irishtimes.com/news/crime-and-law/courts/high-court/high-court-judge-seeks-eu-ruling-on-effect-of-polish-law-changes-1.3424530.

concluded that, "the rule of law in Poland has been systematically damaged by the cumulative impact of all the legislative changes that have taken place over the last two years."[122] Before rendering a final decision on whether Mr. Celmer could be returned to Poland, however, Justice Donnelly referred two related questions of EU law to the ECJ. She asked whether the lack of judicial independence in Poland was a sufficient ground for refusing an EAW request, and whether she needed to assess whether Mr. Celmer in particular would be subject to a violation of his rights if he were sent to Poland.

The relevant standard before *Celmer* was given in the Court's *Aranyosi*[123] judgment, which originated in references from the Higher Regional Court of Bremen asking whether it could refuse European arrest warrant requests from Hungary and Romania. In those cases, the detention conditions in the issuing Member States had been found by the European Court of Human Rights to have infringed the fundamental rights of the persons detained there. The ECJ ruled in *Aranyosi* that national judges must apply a two-pronged test to determine if requests made under EAWs could be refused. The national judge must assess (i) whether there are systemic deficiencies in rights protections in the country in question and, if so, (ii) whether there are substantial grounds to believe that the individual in question would be likely to have his or her rights violated because of the systemic deficiencies. Information to assess the second prong would result from an exchange of information between the judicial authority that issued the warrant and the one being requested to execute it.

In her *Celmer* reference, Justice Donnelly noted that applying the individualized assessment (the second prong) called for in *Aranyosi* was problematic in a situation where judicial independence itself had been undermined as a structural matter because

> [t]hese tests have been predicated on mutual trust and mutual recognition. A problem with adopting that [two-pronged] approach in the present case is that the deficiencies identified are to the edifices of a democracy governed by the rule of law. In those circumstances, it is difficult to see how individual guarantees can be given by the issuing judicial authority as to fair trial when it is the system of justice itself that is no longer operating under the rule of law.[124]

---

[122] *Celmer*, para. 124.
[123] Joined Cases C-404/15 and C-659/15, *Pál Aranyosi and Robert Căldăraru v. Generalstaatsanwaltschaft Bremen*, ECLI:EU:C:2016:198.
[124] *Celmer*, para. 142.

In other words, structural deficiencies in the rule of law would make the individualized assessment impossible because nonindependent judges in the issuing jurisdiction could not certify credibly that the person to be returned would receive a fair trial.

In expedited proceedings, the ECJ answered the reference with a judgment[125] that held that national judges were still bound by the two-pronged test. First, judges receiving an EAW request must consider the overall independence of the judiciary as they assess whether to send someone to another Member State to stand trial. The Court approvingly cited the Commission's Reasoned Proposal with regard to Poland as evidence that could be used by a national judge, which meant in practice that it would be easy to find that the Polish judiciary lacked the requisite independence. However, the Court refused to abandon the second prong of the *Aranyosi* test requiring individualized assessment. The existence of a structural deficiency, no matter how serious or pervasive, could not automatically answer the question of whether any specific EAW should be honored. Instead, the judge must still "assess specifically and precisely whether, in the particular circumstances of the case, there are substantial grounds for believing that, following his surrender to the issuing Member State, the requested person will run that risk [of breach of the essence of the fundamental right to a fair trial]."[126]

This judgment was a disappointment to those who had hoped the ECJ would make a more structural ruling. Once the independence of the judiciary was compromised in a particular state, then enforcement of EAWs should be suspended across the board because no credible representations can be made by judges that they are independent enough to guarantee the relevant conditions.[127] But even without going that far, the *Celmer* ruling will nonetheless allow judges all over the EU who wish to do so to refuse to honor EAW requests from Poland, relying on the Commission's Article 7(1) Reasoned Proposal. In addition, we might expect additional references to arrive before the ECJ asking related questions on whether there is a duty to recognize the judgments of the compromised Polish judiciary in civil and commercial matters. The ECJ's approach, despite insisting on a case-by-case assessment of the independence of particular courts within a system that has been broadly compromised, will open a new mechanism for national courts to play a role in

---

[125] *Celmer.*

[126] *Celmer*, para. 68.

[127] Indeed one of us has argued that the decision constitutes a catastrophic missed opportunity. Kim Lane Scheppele, "Rule of Law Retail and Rule of Law Wholesale: The ECJ's (Alarming) 'Celmer' Decision," *Verfassungsblog*, July 28, 2018, https://verfassungsblog.de/rule-of-law-retail-and-rule-of-law-wholesale-the-ecjs-alarming-celmer-decision/.

Defending Democracy in EU Member States

addressing attacks on the rule of law.[128] But this also risks legal chaos, as judges in some Member States (such as Ireland, Germany, or Spain) might regularly refuse to recognize judgments from Polish courts but judges in other Member States (like Hungary) may be content to continue recognizing the independence of Polish courts. While the ECJ's approach in *Celmer* may impose some costs on the Polish government for its attack on judicial independence, clearly a more structural remedy is needed to actually fix the Polish judiciary or to create a common approach across the EU. These open questions mean that *Celmer* will not be the last chapter in the ECJ's response to attacks on the rule of law at the national level.

Indeed, both the Commission and the national courts of Poland and Hungary have filed cases with the Court of Justice seeking to apply the new principle of judicial independence to their governments' judicial reforms. And the Court of Justice has responded with an uncompromising defense of rule-of-law norms.

First, the Commission began an infringement action against Poland for its judicial reforms in December 2017.[129] After the Commission made no headway with the Polish government on this first infringement, the Commission sent it to the Court of Justice[130] and launched a broader infringement action against Poland for its attacks on the Supreme Court. This case was sent to the ECJ in September 2018,[131] using the *Portuguese Judges* decision and its invocation of Article 19(1) TEU as the basis for the claim that Poland was infringing EU law on judicial independence with its measures that would have removed about one-third of the judges from the Supreme Court.[132] Perhaps most radically, the Commission expedited the matter and asked for interim measures so that the Polish government would be required to reinstate the judges affected by the lowered judicial retirement age.

---

[128] It is clear that the ECJ's decision in *Celmer* is having ripple effects across the EU. The Central Court of Madrid almost immediately sent questions to a Polish district court clearly meant to determine whether the judiciary in Poland is independent enough to permit the Spanish court to honor an EAW. Magdalena Gałczyńska, "Sąd w Madrycie pyta o niezawisłość sędziowską w Polsce. W tle tzw. sprawa Celmera," *Wiadomosci Onet*, October 1, 2018, https://wiadomosci .onet.pl/tylko-w-onecie/sad-w-madrycie-pyta-o-niezawislosc-sedziowska-w-polsce-w-tzw-sprawa-celmera/9vh20ef.

[129] European Commission Press Release IP/17/5367, Rule of Law: European Commission Acts to Defend Judicial Independence in Poland (December 20, 2017).

[130] Case C-192/18, *Commission v. Poland*, 2018 O.J. (C 182) 14.

[131] Case C-619/18, *Commission v. Poland*, ECLI:EU:C:2019:531.

[132] European Commission Press Release IP/18/5830, Rule of Law: European Commission Refers Poland to the European Court of Justice to Protect the Independence of the Polish Supreme Court (September 24, 2018).

To the surprise of many, the Court of Justice awarded interim measures in December 2018, and required that judges who were already retired be reinstalled.[133] The Court also expedited the decision on the merits. The government of Poland then repealed the challenged law in January 2019 in an attempt to moot out the case at the ECJ. But the Court of Justice pressed on, issuing a firm and stinging judgment against Poland in June 2019,[134] condemning its judicial reform measures and making clear that the Court of Justice stood ready to defend the independence of national judiciaries.

The Court held that the immediate lowering of the judicial retirement age had the effect of permanently ending judges' careers, and could not be justified by any of the explanations that the government of Poland put forward. The irremovability of judges, save in rare and exceptional cases, was essential to the rule of law protected in Article 2 TEU. Moreover, the provisions of the law that allowed the Justice Minister, at his discretion, to exempt some of the judges from the new retirement age did not dispel the concern that the measure was designed simply to remove judges from the bench whom the government no longer wanted. Rather the opposite: Leaving the extension of a judge's career to the discretion of the Justice Minister opened up the possibility for the judge facing early retirement to attempt to curry favor with the Justice Minister who held the key to the judge's continued career.

With this decision, the Court of Justice made clear that it will defend the independence of national judiciaries when their national governments attempt to place them under political pressure. It did so, however, in the context of an infringement action in which a general structural question could be better posed and answered than was the case in *Celmer*, a preliminary reference.

But judges who are the focus of the attempts by national governments to interfere with the independence of national judiciaries can also access the Court of Justice by sending preliminary references to the Court. And they are doing so in large numbers.

For example, as negotiations wore on in the Commission's infringement action on the judicial retirement age and its effects on the Polish Supreme Court, the Supreme Court decided it could wait no longer and filed a reference for a preliminary ruling with the ECJ in August 2018.[135] Sent at

---

[133] Case C-619/18 R, *Commission v. Poland*, ECLI:EU:C:2018:1021.

[134] Case C-619/18, *Commission v. Poland*, ECLI:EU:C:2019:531.

[135] Case C-522/18, Request for a preliminary ruling from the Sąd Najwyższy (Poland) lodged on 9 August 2018, 2018 O.J. (C 427) 8; see Jan Cienski, "Polish Supreme Court turns to ECJ for Help," *Politico Europe*, August 2, 2018, www.politico.eu/article/polish-supreme-court-turns-to-ecj-for-help-older-judges-retirement-eu-rule/; Robert Grzeszczak and Ireneusz Pawel, "The

Defending Democracy in EU Member States

the height of the crisis as the government attempted to force the judges to leave the Court, it was a cry for help from the president of the Court and another twenty-seven judges whom the government had moved to fire. Their argument largely overlapped the infringement action that the Commission filed a month later (as we have seen above) – so much so perhaps that one might wonder whether the Commission filed the action it did in order to back the affected judges.

In fact, the Polish Supreme Court filed a number of cases as it was being attacked and the Commission has played catch up as the Polish Court leads the way. For example, the Court sent another preliminary reference to Luxembourg in late summer 2018 asking whether judicial reassignments and dismissals of judges made by the newly packed National Judicial Council (KRS) breached Article 47 CFR, which requires an "effective remedy" for breaches of rights guaranteed by Union law to be available in a hearing before an "independent and impartial tribunal."[136] Under the Polish judicial reform, decisions of the KRS, which crucially shape judges' careers, could not be appealed to any court. As if to support the claim that the KRS was no longer independent, the European Network of Councils for the Judiciary (ENCJ) suspended the KRS from membership in the network in September 2018, noting that "[i]t is a condition of ENCJ membership that institutions are independent of the executive and legislature and ensure the final responsibility for the support of the judiciary in the independent delivery of justice," but that "as a result of the recent reforms in Poland the KRS no longer fulfill[s] this requirement."[137]

Here, too, the Commission sprang to the rescue and filed an infringement action against Poland, alleging almost exactly what the Polish Supreme Court had argued – but expanding the reach of the case to new reforms that did in fact create a system for appealing decisions of the KRS, but to a newly established chamber at the Supreme Court filled entirely with judges appointed by the very same, and politically tainted, KRS.[138] Here, too, the Commission's actions might allow the Court of Justice to get out ahead of the

---

Rule of Law Crisis in Poland: A New Chapter," *Verfassungsblog*, August 8, 2018, https://verfassungsblog.de/the-rule-of-law-crisis-in-poland-a-new-chapter/.

[136] Case C-585/18, Request for a preliminary ruling from the Sąd Najwyższy (Poland) lodged on 20 September 2018 – A. K. v. *Krajowa Rada Sądownictwa*.

[137] European Network of Councils for the Judiciary Press Release, ECNJ Suspends Polish National Judicial Council (KRS) (September 17, 2018), www.encj.eu/node/495.

[138] European Commission Press Release, IP/19/1957, Rule of Law: European Commission Launches Infringement Procedure to Protect Judges in Poland from Political Control (April 3, 2019).

preliminary references and resolve the matter in a way that does not require the national judges to be judges in their own case when their preliminary reference comes back to them for application. Perhaps seeing that one way to encourage the Commission to file infringement actions is to send preliminary references to the ECJ, the Polish Supreme Court, the Polish Supreme Administrative Court, and several Polish district courts have all sent additional references to the ECJ challenging other aspects of the Polish judicial reforms.[139] Seeing their success so far, the Hungarian judges have now joined in, questioning their ability to maintain their own independence given the pressures imposed on them.[140]

With the ECJ now clearly on the side of the national judiciaries and even acting to roll back measures that interfere with judicial independence, a powerful EU body has taken a strong stand against backsliding governments. So far, while the governments of Poland and Hungary have vigorously challenged every new infringement action brought against them and while both governments have attempted to discipline the judges who file preliminary references with the ECJ,[141] both Hungary and Poland have complied with ECJ judgments against them. If Poland or Hungary were to refuse to comply

---

[139] From the Polish Supreme Court: Joined Cases C-585/18, 2019 O.J. (C 44) 9, C-624/18, 2019 O.J. (C 44) 10, and C-625/18, 2019 O.J. C (44) 10 (lodged on September 29, 2018 and October 3, 2018) challenge different aspects of the new disciplinary chamber in the Court as its rulings apply to judges; Case C-668/18, 2019 O.J. (C 44) 12 (lodged on October 26, 2018) raises new questions about the application of the judicial retirement age; preliminary reference requests adopted on May 21, 2019, and June 12, 2019, raise further questions about the disciplinary chamber of the Supreme Court and appointments to the Supreme Court, but these cases have not yet been given case numbers. From the Polish Supreme Administrative Court: Case C-824/18, 2019 O.J. (C 164) 5 (lodged on December 28, 2018) raises questions about the composition of the National Council of the Judiciary and remedies against the Council's decisions. From Polish District Courts: Joined Cases C-558/18, 2019 O.J. (C 44) 8, and C-563/18, 2019 O.J. (C 44) 12 (lodged on September 3 and 5, 2018), challenge the new disciplinary regime for judges and Case C-623/18 (lodged on October 3, 2019) raises additional questions about this disciplinary regime.

[140] Marianna Biró, "Hungarian Judge Requests European Court of Justice to Examine His Own Independence," *Index*, July 17, 2019, https://index.hu/english/2019/07/17/hungary_judicial_independence_european_court_of_justice_suspended_case/.

[141] A few days after the Hungarian judge filed the preliminary reference with the ECJ on judicial independence, the Hungarian public prosecutor appealed to the Hungarian Supreme Court to have the stay of the proceedings quashed. Hungarian Public Prosecutor, Legfőbb ügyészi jogorvoslati indítvány a kerületi bíróság végzésével szemben (Chief Prosecutor's Appeal against the Order of the District Court), July 19, 2019, http://ugyeszseg.hu/legfobb-ugyeszi-jogorvoslati-inditvany-a-keruleti-birosag-vegzesevel-szemben/. The Commission has already launched an infringement action against Poland for this practice. European Commission Press Release, IP/19/4189, Rule of Law: European Commission Takes New Step to Protect Judges in Poland Against Political Control (July 17, 2019).

with an ECJ judgment, however, the Commission could seek a large fine under Article 260 TFEU.[142] No case has needed to go that far, but everyone can see that threat on the horizon, and perhaps it is precisely the prospect of serious financial sanctions that has generated the compliance we have observed thus far.

Whatever the reason, though, we can see that while the Member State governments in the Council have lacked the political will to act, the Court of Justice has stood up to defend the rule of law values in the EU Treaties.

V CONCLUSIONS

Article 7 TEU provides an avenue through which Member States that violate the fundamental principles of the European Union can be warned, and then sanctioned. But given the way that this mechanism is constructed, it can almost never be used. Already we have seen in two very serious cases – Hungary and Poland – that the rule of law can be destroyed and democracy gravely imperiled before European institutions even issue a warning under Article 7. And it is not clear that the politics of the European Union – both party politics and the self-interest of Member States – will allow even a warning to be uttered.

The problems posed by rogue states within the EU are immense. The EU is a web of legal obligations that relies on all Member States honoring their legal commitments under the Treaties. If a Member State rejects European values without leaving its formal membership in the European Union, the law that holds the whole European project together bends and will eventually break. Even as it has become apparent that the EU cannot function without the rule of law being guaranteed in every Member State, EU institutions have failed to halt the slide into illiberalism or even to defend themselves from the corrupting influence of states that have fallen from grace. One after another, European institutions have had the opportunity to use the tools at their disposal to intervene, and one after another, European institutions have failed, except, so far, the ECJ.

It is not too late, though substantial damage has already been done. So far, the Commission and the Court, working together, have shown that they possess robust tools to remedy the worst elements of illiberalism and autocracy. Even as the Commission and the Court have started using these tools more effectively, however, the process has begun late and we worry that they may be

---

[142] Wennerås, "Making Effective Use of Article 260 TFEU," 79–98.

reluctant to maintain a strong posture without more support from the Council, which we suspect will never act. We hope that the catalogue of existing tools that we have provided can and will be used to good effect. Perhaps most crucially, we hope to have convinced our readers that something can be done. In addition, we hope to persuade EU institutions that they have the power, the ability, the mandate, and the responsibility to safeguard the values of the European Union.

16

The Politics of Resentment and First Principles in the European Court of Justice

TOMASZ TADEUSZ KONCEWICZ[*]

I INTRODUCTION

Although the European Union has faced many crises in recent years, including Brexit and the euro crisis, the current trend of democratic backsliding in Hungary, Poland, and perhaps other Member States is the most serious of all. These governments have trampled upon the values of democracy, rule of law, and human rights. In doing so, they have called into question the very foundations of European integration and have undermined the European project from within. The governments of Hungary and Poland have openly challenged liberal democracy, one of the core constitutional features of the European Union.[1]

This chapter contributes to the growing literature on combating democratic backsliding[2] by focusing on the Polish case and the European Court of Justice's response. As used here, the term "democratic backsliding" means "the process through which elected public authorities deliberately implement governmental blueprints which aim to systematically weaken, annihilate or capture internal checks on power with the view of dismantling the liberal democratic state and entrenching the long-term rule of the dominant party."[3]

---

[*] I dedicate this chapter to Sir Professor David Edward. When it comes to my journey with, and in, EU law, it all started with him back in December 1998 in the Court of Justice. I will forever appreciate his kindness, generosity, and sense of direction he was always subtly sharing with me. I would also like to acknowledge the funding received from the European Union's Horizon 2020 Research & Innovation programme under Grant Agreement no. 770142, project RECONNECT – Reconciling Europe With its Citizens through Democracy and Rule of Law.

[1] For detailed analysis and further references Kim Lane Scheppele and Laurent Pech, "Illiberalism Within: Rule of Law Backsliding in the EU," *Cambridge Yearbook of European Legal Studies* 17 (2017): 3–47.

[2] See, e.g., Chapter 15.

[3] This is the definition adopted by Kim Lane Scheppele and Laurent Pech, "What is Rule of Law Backsliding?" *Verfassungsblog*, March 2, 2018, https://verfassungsblog.de/what-is-rule-of-

The chapter first analyzes that politics of resentment and the backsliding phenomenon that has been triggered. It continues by setting out the basis, in political theory, for positing the rule of law as the foundational value of the EU. The chapter then turns to the Commission's enforcement action against Poland for illegal logging in the Białowieża Forest, the Court of Justice's rulings in the case, and the implications for future efforts at turning the illiberal tide in Poland and elsewhere. The conclusion considers an important recent development in rule-of-law litigation, namely the Irish preliminary reference in the *Celmer* case and the possibility of other preliminary references involving the question of the mutual trust owed to the judiciary in places such as Poland.

II THE POLITICS OF RESENTMENT

1 *The Concept*

Resentment is crucial for understanding the rise of illiberal narratives in Europe. Although the role of emotion in politics has traditionally been under-theorized as compared to reason and the rational side of human beings, there is no doubt that in contemporary politics, emotion has become equally or, indeed, more important. Emotions are not the only driving force behind the political struggle; they are also a prize to be won. Crucially, emotions play a performative and constitutive function. They not only express but help bring subjects into being and constitute identities.[4] And one particularly potent combination of emotions has become salient in recent times – resentment. Populist leaders have tapped into a reservoir of anxiety about "the other," anger at the liberal establishment and the imposition of one correct world view, fear of exclusion, and uncertainty of one's place in the contemporary world. In short, resentment is driving many of the contemporary political developments.

To be sure, emotions are a legitimate part of the democratic process and anger and fear are not to be removed from the realm of political discourse as

---

law-backsliding/; see also Scheppele and Pech, "Illiberalism Within: Rule of Law Backsliding in the EU," 3. According to Nancy Bermeo, democratic backsliding means the state-led debilitation or elimination of the political institutions sustaining an existing democracy. Nancy Bermeo, "On Democratic Backsliding," *Journal of Democracy* 27, no. 1 (2016): 5–19; see also Staffan Lindberg, "The Nature of Democratic Backsliding in Europe," *Carnegie Europe*, July 24, 2018, https://carnegieeurope.eu/2018/07/24/nature-of-democratic-backsliding-in-europe-pub76868%20The%20Nature%20of%20Democratic%20Backsliding%20in%20Europe%20Source:%20Getty%20STAFFAN%20I.%20LINDBERG.

[4] Mary Holmes, "Feeling beyond Rules: Politicizing the Sociology of Emotion and Anger in Feminist Politics," *European Journal of Social Theory* 7, no. 2 (2004): 212–213.

any such attempt would be counterfactual. When, however, populist politicians tap into resentment and create political movements that have distinct implications for the existing institutional order, they take emotion to another level. Resentment is no longer a *feeling* but is *utterance* and *performance*, and it is transformed into the "the politics of resentment." Resentment is anchored within mainstream politics and is articulated in the public sphere.[5]

The politics of resentment transform our traditional understanding of political conflict. While politicians and political parties in democracies routinely put forward competing visions for society and politics, they always stick to the language of probability in setting out their alternatives to the existing government. They are prepared to test their alternatives through procedures and elections and accept that the constitution is the stage that frames political contestation.[6] As liberal democrats, they share a commitment to the core values of freedom and equality and the formal acknowledgment that their political adversaries have as valid a claim to represent the people as they do. By contrast, resentment-driven populist politicians see their claims as settling most fundamental issues once and for all, and they do not allow room for dissent. Because of the moral dimension of resentment, they do not acknowledge that their claims can be judged as true or false. Rather, their claims are always the best, and not open to further contestation.[7] The emotions of fear, anger, and rejection, all under the umbrella of resentment, do not allow for pluralism and the multiplicity of representation and undermine the normative and institutional framework through which populist leaders initially express and advance these sentiments. "The other" is no longer seen as a legitimate adversary. He becomes an enemy and, as a delegitimized political actor, is hounded and persecuted with the full strength of the law.

A core concept of the politics of resentment and populism is constitutional capture.[8] Gaining power does not soften populist animus. Quite the contrary, once elected, populist leaders are ready to deliver on their promises and they do so through a constitutional doctrine that competes with the dominant

---

[5] For general discussion, see Sara Ahmed, *The Cultural Politics of Emotion*, 2nd ed. (Edinburgh: Edinburgh University Press, 2014).

[6] I draw here on Jan-Werner Müller, "Populist Constitutionalism: A Contradiction in Terms?" Draft Paper, NYU Colloquium (on file with the author); see also Jan-Werner Müller, "Populist Constitutions: A Contradiction in Terms?" *Verfassungsblog*, April 23, 2017, https://verfassungsblog.de/populist-constitutions-a-contradiction-in-terms/.

[7] Müller, "Populist Constitutionalism."

[8] Core concept is defined as referring to the basic unit without which ideologies cannot exist. Michael Freeden, *Ideologies and Political Theory: A Conceptual Approach* (New York: Oxford, 1996), 77–80.

liberal constitutionalism.[9] This doctrine includes the following, often inter-related, elements: (i) a new understanding of the role of the constitution, no longer as protecting against the state, but as safeguarding the uniqueness of the state; (ii) the constitution ceases to be the supreme law of the land; (iii) the constitutional court is not only incapacitated but also "weaponized" to be used as a tool against political enemies; (iv) the political dominates the legal; (v) the rule of law is seen as an obstacle to protecting the collectivity; (vi) the rule of law is to facilitate the expression of the will of the people; (vii) political power is no longer subject to the checks and balances; (viii) supranational insti-tutions are dismissed as enemies of the people; (ix) the collectivity is trum-peted above individual citizens; (x) human rights evolve from the dignitary conception to that of community.

2 Delivering on the Politics of Resentment: The Case of Poland

The Polish case illustrates the trajectory from resentment to populism to the politics of resentment. While resentment fuels populism, the politics of resentment translate populism into constitutional doctrine. While populism uses resentment as a rhetoric and might even (begrudgingly) tolerate the system, the transformation of resentment into the mode of governance signals a break with the *status quo* in favor of constitutional revolution. The case of Poland illuminates the vulnerabilities of democratic government, the rule of law, and constitutionalism when confronted with the sweeping politics of resentment and its new constitutional doctrine.[10] As so eloquently summar-ized by Kornel Morawiecki (Honorary Marshall of the Sejm and father of the Polish Prime Minister), this doctrine stipulates: "The will of the people is above the law. Law is to serve the people. If it does not it is no longer law."[11]

It all started with the destruction of the Polish Constitutional Court in 2015–2016. After thirty years of building an impressive resume as one of the most influential and successful constitutional courts in Europe and living

---

[9] For important clarifications also Paul Blokker, "Populist Constitutionalism," *Verfassungsblog*, May 4, 2017, http://verfassungsblog.de/populist-constitutionalism/.

[10] Jan-Werner Müller, "Defending Democracy within the EU," *Journal of Democracy* 24, no. 2 (2013): 138–149 and Jan-Werner Müller, "Should the EU Protect Democracy and the Rule of Law Inside Member States?" *European Law Journal* 21, no. 2 (2015): 141–160.

[11] "Kornel Morawiecki: 'Nad Prawem Jest Dobro Narodu!' Prawo, Które nie Służy Narodowi to Bezprawie," *Kresy*, November 26, 2015, https://kresy.pl/wydarzenia/kornel-morawiecki-nad-prawem-jest-dobro-narodu-prawo-ktore-nie-sluzy-narodowi-to-bezprawie-video/. For constitutional ramifications of such a change see Tomasz T. Koncewicz, "Understanding Polish Counter Revolution Two and a Half Years Later," *Verfassungsblog*, July 7, 2018, https://verfassungsblog.de/the-polish-counter-revolution-two-and-a-half-years-later-where-are-we-today/.

proof of the rule of law in action, the Court fell under the relentless attack of a right-wing populist government and succumbed. It was transformed into an enabler for the political majority.[12] The constitutional debacle in Poland must be but a starting point for more general analysis of the processes of the politics of resentment and constitutional capture that strike at the core European principles of the rule of law, separation of powers, and judicial independence.[13] With the benefit of hindsight, we now know that the destruction of the Polish Constitutional Court (and earlier, the Hungarian Constitutional Court) was an opening act in the total subjugation of all independent institutions of the state. With no independent constitutional court left to guarantee effective compliance with the national constitution, the Polish ruling party has been busy completing a multi-pronged takeover of the whole of the national judiciary to enable the executive and legislative branches of the government to systematically interfere in the structure, composition, and daily functioning of the judicial branch.[14] In its reasoned proposal under Article 7 of the Treaty on European Union (TEU),[15] the European Commission succinctly pointed out that Polish authorities have adopted over a period of two years no less than thirteen laws affecting the entire structure of the justice system in Poland, impacting the Constitutional Tribunal, Supreme Court, ordinary courts, National Council for the Judiciary, prosecution service, and National School of Judiciary.[16] The capture

---

[12] Tomasz T. Koncewicz, "'Existential Judicial Review' in Retrospect and 'Subversive Jurisprudence' in Prospect: The Polish Constitutional Court Then, Now and...Tomorrow," *Verfassungsblog*, October 7, 2018, https://verfassungsblog.de/existential-judicial-review-in-retrospect-subversive-jurisprudence-in-prospect-the-polish-constitutional-court-then-now-and-tomorrow/.

[13] Pech and Scheppele, "Illiberalism Within: Rule of Law Backsliding in the EU"; Laurent Pech and Sébastien Platon, "Menace Systémique Envers l'Etat de Droit en Pologne: Entre Action et Procrastination," Fondation Robert Schuman, Question d'Europe no. 451, November 13, 2017.

[14] For more detailed analysis consult: Wojciech Sadurski and Maximilian Steinbeis, "What Is Going on in Poland Is an Attack against Democracy?" *Verfassungsblog*, July 15, 2016, http://verfassungsblog.de/what-is-going-on-in-poland-is-an-attack-against-democracy/; Wojciech Sadurski, "How Democracy Dies (in Poland): A Case Study of Anti-constitutional Populist Backsliding." Sydney Law School Research Paper 18/01, 2018. http://ssrn.com/abstract=3103491; Anna Śledzińska-Simon, "The Polish Revolution 2015–2017," *Iconnect* (blog), July 25, 2017, www.iconnectblog.com/2017/07/the-polish-revolution-2015-2017/; Tomasz T. Koncewicz, "Capture of the Polish Constitutional Tribunal and Beyond: Of Institution(s), Fidelities and the Rule of Law in Flux," *Review of Central and East European Law* 43, no. 2 (2018): 116–173.

[15] For a detailed account of Article 7 TEU and the procedures that have been initiated so far, see Chapter 15.

[16] *Reasoned Proposal in Accordance with Article 7(1) of the Treaty on European Union regarding the Rule of Law in Poland, Proposal for a Council Decision on the Determination of a Clear*

of the state and its institutions has continued.[17] The Polish government, as is typical of the politics of resentment, claims that it respects the rule of law and, consequently, that the criticism directed at it is not justified. But note that there are two important caveats: First, the Polish government insists that the rule of law should be interpreted differently from what was hitherto accepted; second, that there is no agreement on what the rule of law entails in practice (application).[18] Those two caveats transform the rule of law – one of the paradigms of the post-1989 transition – from the rule *of* law to rule *by* law,[19] and underpin a new constitutional doctrine now on the rise in Poland.

III THE EUROPEAN OVERLAPPING CONSENSUS AND THE POLITICS OF RESENTMENT

Mutual trust between the Member States has defined the European project ever since its inception.[20] Trust has been built on convergence between the fundamental values of Member States and their legal orders on the one hand, and the foundations of the Union legal order, on the other. Indeed, as Pierre Pescatore, one of the founding fathers of the Treaties, emphasized, the existence of European supranationality is predicated on the idea of "an order

---

Risk of a Serious Breach by the Republic of Poland of the Rule of Law, COM (2017) 835 final (December 20, 2017). For insightful analysis see Jan-Werner Müller, "If You're Not a Democracy, You're Not European Anymore," *Foreign Policy*, December 22, 2017, http://foreignpolicy.com/2017/12/22/if-youre-not-a-democracy-youre-not-european-anymore/.

[17] See Chapter 15 on developments through July 2019.

[18] See also Blokker, "Populist Constitutionalism"; James Traub, "The Party That Wants to Make Poland Great Again," *New York Times Magazine*, November 2, 2016, www.nytimes.com/2016/11/06/magazine/the-party-that-wants-to-make-poland-great-again.html; Phillip S. Swallow, "Explaining the Rise of Populism in Poland: The Post-Communist Transition as a Critical Juncture and Origin of Political Decay in Poland," *Inquiries Journal* 10, no.7 (2018): 1; Slawomir Sierakowski, "The Five Lessons of Populist Rule," *Project Syndicate*, January 2, 2017, www.project-syndicate.org/commentary/lesson-of-populist-rule-in-poland-by-slawomir-sierakowski-2017-01?barrier=accesspaylog; Tomasz T. Koncewicz, "Understanding the Politics of Resentment," *Verfassungsblog*, September 28, 2017, https://verfassungsblog.de/understanding-the-politics-of-resentment/.

[19] Wojciech Sadurski, "Prof. Wojciech Sadurski: 300 lat temu Monteskiusz rozgryzł Obecną Sytuację w Polsce [Wykład Warszawski: Relacja]," *Archiwum Osiatynskiego*, October 3, 2018, https://archiwumosiatynskiego.pl/wpis-w-debacie/sadurski-monteskiusz-rozgryzl-obecna-sytuacje-w-polsce/.

[20] Editorial Comments, "Union Membership in Times of Crisis," *Common Market Law Review* 51, no. 1 (2014): 1–11.

determined by the existence of common values and interests."[21] At the heart of this European order is a fundamental commitment to a set of first principles[22] that the Member States, institutions, and civil society actors bound by the Treaties expect and trust that others will uphold. The rule of law is among the most essential of these first principles, essential to the post-war consensus as it transformed political power into political power constrained by law.[23] It has been now put in jeopardy by the rise of the politics of resentment in Poland and elsewhere. The following section explores the importance of the first principles for the European political community through a discussion of Rawls' theory of overlapping consensus. Through this discussion, the threat and danger of Poland's new constitutional doctrine of the politics of resentment is revealed.

One important point of reference in political theory for understanding the possibility of a European, post-national political community is Rawls' overlapping consensus.[24] His overlapping consensus requires agreement on fundamental commitments of principle.[25] It is these essentials that I require others to respect as the condition of my own deference to decisions taken by others.[26] There will not be perfect agreement on these essentials as persistent differences between citizens living together in a constitutional regime – differences that are especially pertinent in the EU's post-national political order – create disagreement over the final shape of these constitutional essentials. Rawls, however, claimed that many disagreements among citizens in their understanding of justice can nevertheless lead to similar political judgments and these similar political judgments can then lead to "overlapping rather than

---

[21] See Pierre Pescatore, *The Law of Integration: Emergence of a New Phenomenon in International Relations Based on the Experience of the European Communities* (Leiden: Sijthoff, 1974).

[22] I borrow the term from David Edward's *An Appeal to First Principles* (on file with the author).

[23] "Constrained political power" might be said to be the driving force behind the European consensus and one of the paradigms of post-war constitutional settlement in Europe. Insistence on the element of constraint was in turn driven by distrust of popular sovereignty, and fear of backsliding into authoritarianism. On this see Jan-Werner Müller, "Beyond Militant Democracy," *New Left Review* 73 (January/February 2012): 39–47. On democracy and the rule of law as driving the European project see also Chapter 15.

[24] See, e.g., Charles F. Sabel and Oliver Gerstenberg, "Constitutionalising an Overlapping Consensus: The ECJ and the Emergence of a Coordinate Constitutional Order," *European Law Journal* 16, no. 5 (2010): 513.

[25] John Rawls, "The Idea of an Overlapping Consensus," *Oxford Journal of Legal Studies* 7, no. 1 (1987): 1–25; John Rawls, *Political Liberalism* (New York: Columbia University Press, 1993). On overlapping consensus also Jon Garthoff, "The Idea of an Overlapping Consensus Revisited," *Journal of Value and Inquiry* 46, no. 2 (2012): 183–196.

[26] Sabel and Gerstenberg, "Constitutionalising an Overlapping Consensus," 513.

strict consensus." What matters is that parties to the consensus agree that these disagreements will be ironed out, and spelled out within the discursive framework. Excluding actors with unreasonable and irrational doctrines is not only justified but necessary to achieve the overlapping consensus.

In navigating disagreement and settling on constitutional essentials, the time factor is important: overlapping consensus is subject to never-ending adjustment and mutual learning. In the words of Sabel and Gerstenberg, consensus arises from "an ongoing historical interaction between the emergent, common political view and the comprehensive views underlying it."[27] "We," in the shape of the peoples of Europe, have agreed to respect others' way of life, provided that their lives and decisions respect mutually agreed-upon essentials and fundamental values. The essence of the consensus is procedural and institutional. Seen through the lens of the overlapping consensus, and in the words of the European Court of Justice, EU law evolves through dialogue among all parties to the consensus, within "the institutional framework" that is integral to the consensus.[28] This dialogue ensures that every party to the consensus sees himself as an actor in, and architect of, the constitutional narrative; it is inclusive and reinforces diversity. At the same time, dialogue relies on a commonality of core values and only lasts as long as there is a *bona fide* desire to strike the reasonable balance between European unity and national diversity.

The rule of law should be understood as a fundamental principle with a clear nonnegotiable minimum, as it is critical to the institutional framework of the overlapping consensus. Modern constitutionalism accepts that in the absence of the rule of law, contemporary constitutional democracy would be impossible.[29] At a minimum, the rule of law requires the following elements: fairly generalized rule through law; a substantial amount of predictability; a significant separation between the legislative and the adjudicative function; widespread adherence to the principle that no one is above the law; and, implicit in all of this, independent and impartial courts. The rule of law is the principle that underpinned the original Treaties in 1951 and 1957, and that continues to do so more than sixty years afterwards. Without the commitment to the rule of law and the continuing confidence that parties to the consensus

---

[27] Sabel and Gerstenberg, "Constitutionalising an Overlapping Consensus," 544.

[28] Opinion 2/13 of the Court (Full Court), December 18, 2014, ECLI:EU:C:2014:2454 (on the accession of the EU to the European Convention of Human Rights).

[29] Michel Rosenfeld, "The Rule of Law and the Legitimacy of Constitutional Democracy," Cardozo Law School Public Law Research Paper no. 36/2001, https://papers.ssrn.com/sol3/papers.cfm?abstract_id=262350.

Politics of Resentment & First Principles in ECJ

will guarantee the independence of their courts, parties would have never been able to come together, and defer to each other, in the first place.

Having set the theoretical groundwork, it should be clear that the politics of resentment poses an existential challenge to the European project. In the politics of resentment, the overlapping consensus' commonality of values is replaced with unbridgeable difference. The original design of European integration, built on first principles including the all-important rule of law, is called into question by a competing constitutional vision – that of fundamental disagreements over values, which are considered ephemeral and far from crystalized, and the demotion and relativization of the rule of law.[30] Given the fundamental and persistent disagreements over basic (not just any) values brought to the fore by the politics of resentment, the pressing question arises whether the "we" of the European political community exists at all. With different conceptions of the rule of law – no independent judiciary, checks and balances, and judicial review in countries like Poland – the consensus is coming apart at the seams. These concepts were thought of as the basic minimum that all the parties to the consensus agreed to respect when they decided to join the European Union, but they are becoming increasingly tenuous with democratic backsliding in Poland and elsewhere.

IV THE WINDS OF THE POLITICS OF RESENTMENT START BLOWING ON KIRCHBERG

1 *The* Białowieża Forest *Case*

In view of the direct conflict between the Polish politics of resentment and the fundamental principles of the European overlapping consensus, a constitutional showdown between Poland and the European Court of Justice was only a matter of time. True to the Polish constitutional doctrine of rule *by* law – not a check on the political branches, but at the service of "the people" and populist politics – the Polish ruling party has repeatedly denounced the jurisdiction of the European Court of Justice.[31] This rejection of the Court

---

[30] Tomasz T. Koncewicz, "Understanding the Politics of Resentment: Of the Principles, Institutions, Counter-Strategies and ... the Habits of Heart," *Indiana Journal of Global Legal Studies* "Understanding the Politics of Resentment: of the Principles, Institutions, Counter-Strategies, Normative Change, and the Habits of Heart," *Indiana Journal of Global Legal Studies* 26, no. 2 (2019): 501–630.

[31] As per the Deputy Prime Minister and Minister for Higher Education Jarosław Gowin, the government may ignore the ruling of the Court of Justice, "Wicepremier Jarosław Gowin Powiedział, że Polski rząd może Zignorować Orzeczenie Trybunału Sprawiedliwości Unii

466 *Tomasz Tadeusz Koncewicz*

of Justice and the First Principle of the rule *of* law came to a head in the *Białowieża Forest* case.

The case concerned one of the most environmentally unique places in Europe: Unesco World Heritage Site – Białowieza Forest.[32] The Forest is an area of ancient woodland straddling the border between Belarus and Poland and is the only remaining example of the original forests that once covered much of Europe.[33] It is one of the best preserved natural forests in Europe, characterized by large quantities of dead wood and ancient trees, some of which are centuries old. In 2007, the Commission designated the Natura 2000 Puszcza Białowieska site in accordance with the Habitats Directive as a site of "Community importance" due to the presence of natural habitats and the habitats of certain animal and bird species. That site is also a special protection area for birds under the Birds Directive. In 2016, in response to an outbreak of Spruce Bark Beetle, the Polish Minister for the Environment authorized an increase in logging in the Forest District of Białowieża, as well as active forest management operations in areas previously outside the scope of such activity, such as "sanitary pruning," reforestation, and restoration. Work thus began on the removal of dead trees and trees affected by the Spruce Bark Beetle over an area of approximately 34,000 hectares of the Natura 2000 Puszcza Białowieska site, which has a total surface area of 63,147 hectares.

Taking the view that those active forest management operations have a negative impact on the conservation of natural habitats and the habitats of the animal and bird species, the Commission, on July 20, 2017, brought an enforcement action against Poland for failure to fulfill its obligations under the Habitats Directive and the Birds Directive.[34] The Commission also asked

---

Europejskiej w Sprawie Pytań Prejudycjalnych, Które Skierowali Sędziowie SN," *Rzeczpospolita*, August 27, 2018, www.rp.pl/Sadownictwo/180829478-Jaroslaw-Gowin-Rzad-moze-zignorowac-orzeczenie-TSUE.html. More recently, President A. Duda personally attacked Marek Safjan, the current Polish judge on the European Court of Justice. See Anna Wójcik, "'To Twierdzenie Bez Zadnych Podstaw': Prof. Safjan Kategorycznie Odpowiada Dudzie," *Oko Press*, October 11, 2018, at https://oko.press/to-twierdzenie-bez-zadnych-podstaw-prof-safjan-kategorycznie-odpowiada-dudzie/ ("These allegations are completely baseless: Prof. Safjan responds to Duda"). This exchange highlights how, now, the politics of resentment have moved from the domestic to the supranational arena, and the very authority of the European Court of Justice is on the line.

[32] David Levene, Damian Carrington, and Eric Hilaire, "Białowieża, Europe's Last Primeval Forest: In Pictures," *The Guardian*, April 6, 2011, www.theguardian.com/environment/gallery/2011/apr/06/bialowieza-europe-forest-in-pictures.

[33] On the Forest see "Białowieża Forest: The Last Primeval Forest in Lowland Europe," *Wildpoland* website, last visited October 26, 2018, https://wildpoland.com/bialowieza-forest/.

[34] Case C-441/17, *Commission v. Poland*, ECLI:EU:C:2018:255. In accordance of Article 258 TFEU: "If the Commission considers that a Member State has failed to fulfil an obligation under the Treaties, it shall deliver a reasoned opinion on the matter after giving the State concerned the opportunity to submit its observations. If the State concerned does not comply

the European Court of Justice, pending the judgment in the main proceedings, to order interim measures against Poland: to cease, except where there is a threat to public safety, the active forest management operations, including the removal of centuries-old dead spruces and the felling of trees as part of increased logging in the Białowieża Forest.

By order of July 27, 2017, the Vice-President of the Court provisionally granted that request, pending the adoption of an order terminating the proceedings for interim measures.[35] Despite the order, logging not only continued but intensified. Poland, in an unprecedented act of defiance in the history of European integration, refused to stop logging[36] and, as a result, huge chunks of the Forest are gone forever.[37]

On November 20, 2017, the Court sitting as the full, Grand Chamber of fifteen judges (which is unheard of in interim proceedings and indicates the importance of the case) decided the Commission's request for interim measures.[38] It first set down the applicable legal standard: The Court noted that it may order interim measures only if such an order is justified, *prima facie*, in fact and in law. Moreover, the order must be considered urgent in so far as, to avoid serious and irreparable damage to the EU's interests, it must be made and produce its effects before a final decision in the case is reached. Last, where necessary, the interests involved must be weighed up. With regard to the requirement of a *prima facie* case, the Court had no doubt that the condition was satisfied, since there was a major legal and factual disagreement whose resolution was not immediately obvious. As for urgency, the Court found that Poland's active forest management operations involved the removal of old, dying, or dead trees, including both those affected and unaffected by the Spruce Bark Beetle, and therefore it seemed very likely that the operations would have an impact on the relevant habitats. This point was reinforced by the fact that, until 2016, one of the measures for conserving those habitats was a prohibition on precisely that type of forest management operation. The Court noted that if the Commission's allegations of Poland's violation of the Directives were ultimately

---

with the opinion within the period laid down by the Commission, the latter may bring the matter before the Court of Justice of the European Union."

[35] Case C-441/17R, *Commission v. Poland*, EU:C:2017:622.

[36] Joanna Berendt, "Defying E.U. Court, Poland Is Cutting Trees in an Ancient Forest," *New York Times*, July 31, 2017, www.nytimes.com/2017/07/31/world/europe/poland-bialowieza-forest-bison-logging.html.

[37] Indeed, in this instance, the politics of resentment reached beyond Europe to the global level. Poland asked for the removal of Białowieża from the Unesco World Heritage list. "Poland Says Primeval Forest Should Not be UNESCO Natural Heritage Site," *Phys Org*, June 21, 2017, https://phys.org/news/2017-06-poland-primeval-forest-unesco-natural.html.

[38] Case C-441/17R, *Commission v. Poland*, ECLI:EU:C:2017:877 [hereinafter *Order for Interim Measures*].

established, the damage caused by the felling and removal of those trees would be impossible to rectify. Consequently, the Court found that the urgency of the interim measures requested by the Commission has been established.

Last, the Court weighed up the interests concerned. The Court noted that the interests were, on the one hand, the protection of the habitats and species of the Białowieża Forest from logging and, on the other hand, the prevention of damage to the natural habitats of the Białowieża Forest resulting from the Spruce Bark Beetle. The Court found that Poland had failed to provide information on the harm likely to be caused in the short term by the Spruce Bark Beetle and to explain why the cessation of forest management operations for the few months that would be required to give judgment in the main proceedings was likely to cause serious and irreparable damage to the Białowieża Forest habitat. As a result, the Court concluded that it was more urgent to protect the habitat from the harm caused by the forest management operations and it granted the application for interim measures. The Court, however, did permit a small exception to its prohibition on logging: if forest management operations were strictly necessary and proportionate to ensure, directly and immediately, the public safety of persons in the immediate vicinity of transport routes or other significant infrastructure; and if other less radical measures such as signposting were impossible for objective reasons.

The interim prohibition of logging, however, was not the end of the case. In view of Poland's disregard of the Court's earlier July order, the Commission had requested that Poland be ordered to pay a periodic penalty if it failed to respect the directions set out in the interim order. The Court granted the Commission's request. Specifically, the Court ordered Poland to send to the Commission, within fifteen days of notification of the order, details of all measures that it has adopted in order to comply fully, detailing, with justifications, the active forest management operations at issue that it intended to continue because necessary to ensure public safety. If the Commission came to the view that Poland had failed to comply fully with the order, it would be able to request that proceedings be resumed. The Court would then decide, by way of a new order, whether the interim order had been infringed. If so, the Court could order Poland to make a penalty payment of at least €100,000 per day, from the date of notification of the interim order to Poland until Poland complied with the Court's order, or until final judgment in the case was delivered, whichever came first.[39]

---

[39] The Advocate General Bot delivered his opinion in the case on February 20, 2018, and, not surprisingly, found Poland guilty of violating EU environmental law. Unfortunately, his opinion is silent on the constitutional dimension of the case. His only referral to the interim

From the perspective of the earlier discussion of first principles and the rule of law, the Court's holding on penalty payments is the most significant part of the judgment. In that part of the November 17 judgment, the Court revealed that it would go beyond the strict letter of EU law to vigorously enforce the rule of law principle against Member States set on flouting judicial authority and separation of powers. The Court noted that the purpose of the procedure for interim relief is to guarantee the full effectiveness of the future final decision, in order to avoid a lacuna in the legal protection afforded by the Court. Therefore, even though Article 279 TFEU on interim relief does not explicitly mention periodic penalties, the Court found that Article 279 TFEU confers on the Court the power to prescribe any interim measures that it deems necessary to ensure that the final decision is fully effective. Such a measure may entail, *inter alia*, provision for a penalty payment to be imposed should that order not be respected by the relevant party. Since the prospect of a penalty payment induces compliance with the interim measures ordered, it strengthens the effectiveness of those measures and guarantees the full effectiveness of the final decision, thus furthering the objective of Article 279 TFEU. In the words of the Court:

> *once the matter is before it,* the Court hearing the application for interim measures must satisfy itself that the measures that it is minded to order are sufficiently *effective* to achieve their aim. *It is specifically for that purpose that Article 279 TFEU grants the Court a broad discretion,* in the exercise of which it is empowered, inter alia, having regard to the circumstances of each case, to specify the subject matter and the scope of the interim measures requested, and also, if it deems appropriate, to adopt, where necessary of its own motion, any ancillary measure intended to guarantee the effectiveness of the interim measures that it orders [emphasis added].[40]

The phrase "once the matter is before the Court" is both a powerful reminder of the logic of the courtroom where law reigns supreme, and a message sent to the politics of resentment.

Then, in the two most consequential paragraphs of the judgment, the Court finally met the politics of resentment head on. In the first (101), the Court presented the Polish government's argument that only Article 260 TFEU empowered the Court to impose sanctions on Member States, since

order of the Court is contained in the factual part of the opinion. Opinion of Advocate General Bot, Case-441/71, *Commission v. Poland*, ECLI:EU:C:2018:80, para. 69.

[40] *Order for Interim Measures,* para. 99.

only Article 260 specifically contemplates a "penalty payment."[41] According to Poland, the Commission had to first bring an enforcement action pursuant to Article 258 TFEU and only if the Court holds against Poland and Poland fails to comply with the Court's decision can the Commission pursue penalties under Article 260. Clearly, the Court was not impressed. In the second paragraph (102), the Court stressed that, first, a periodic penalty payment cannot, in the circumstances of the present case, be seen as a punishment and, second, the Republic of Poland's interpretation of the system of legal remedies under EU law in general, and of proceedings for interim measures in particular, would have the effect of considerably reducing the likelihood of those proceedings achieving their objective in the event of the Member State concerned failing to comply with the interim measures ordered against it. Allowing Poland's argument to stand would be tantamount to sanctioning the impunity and letting the rogue government dictate the rules of the game. Instead, it is the courtroom that dictates the rule of the game. As the Court emphatically stated:

> The purpose of seeking to ensure that a Member State complies with interim measures adopted by the Court hearing an application for such measures by providing for the imposition of a periodic penalty payment in the event of non-compliance with those measures is to guarantee the effective application of EU law, such application being an essential component of the rule of law, a value enshrined in Article 2 TEU and on which the European Union is founded.

At first glance, this case might not appear remarkable, one of the hundreds of infringement cases heard and decided by the Court every year. But this deceptively simple case belongs to the annals of the European jurisprudence.[42] The case stands out for three reasons: (1) the Court issued for the first time an interim order imposing a periodic penalty on a Member State; (2) the authority of the Court was challenged in a principled way by the Polish government; (3) the Court responded firmly and definitively.[43] For the first time in two years, Poland's flouting of the rule of law was stopped in its tracks.

---

[41] The relevant text in Article 260(2) TFEU says: "If the Commission considers that the Member State concerned has not taken the necessary measures to comply with the judgment of the Court, it may bring the case before the Court after giving that State the opportunity to submit its observations. It shall specify the amount of the lump sum or penalty payment to be paid by the Member State concerned which it considers appropriate in the circumstances."

[42] For one of the first analyses see Daniel Sarmiento, "Provisional (and Extraordinary) Measures in the Name of the Rule of Law," *Verfassungsblog*, November 24, 2017, http://verfassungsblog .de/provisional-and-extraordinary-measures-in-the-name-of-the-rule-of-law/

[43] See also Chapter 15.

Right up until the *Białowieża Forest* case, Poland seemed to dictate the rules of the game by stonewalling the Commission and faking a dialogue in the Rule of Law Framework and the Article 7 TEU procedure, all the while completing the capture of the independent institutions and disabling the checks and balances.[44] At long last, the Court got its first opportunity to rule directly on the politics of resentment and say "enough is enough."

At the same time, it is important to be clear that imaginative judicial interpretation is not enough. There also must be the political will to stand up for the first principles and the rule of law, and, from that perspective, the follow-up to the Court's judgment in the logging case must be considered the most disappointing. Unsurprisingly, in the final judgment, which followed just over four months later, the Court ruled that by carrying on logging activities on the Natura 2000 site and the UNESCO-protected Białowieża Forest, Poland has failed to fulfil its obligations under EU law.[45] Yet, at no point in time did the Commission use the possibility to apply for penalties for noncompliance with the interim order, or later, under Article 260, for penalties for noncompliance with the final order.[46] The Commission never delivered on the constitutional promises of the Court's interim order. The lack of the political will to enforce the text has been deafening. The Commission failed to follow up on the interim order and reverted to fruitless

---

[44] For a description of how this law has been used, so far unsuccessfully, against Hungary and Poland, see Chapters 15 and 17. For the detailed reconstruction of the vast array of strategies deployed by Poland as part of its "dialogue of the deaf" with the Commission see Laurent Pech and Kim L. Scheppele, "Poland and the European Commission: Part I: A Dialogue of the Deaf?" *Verfassungsblog*, January 3, 2017, https://verfassungsblog.de/poland-and-the-european-commission-part-i-a-dialogue-of-the-deaf/; "Part II: Hearing the Siren Song of the Rule of Law," *Verfassungsblog*, January 6, 2017, https://verfassungsblog.de/poland-and-the-european-commission-part-ii-hearing-the-siren-song-of-the-rule-of-law/; "Part III: Requiem for the Rule of Law," *Verfassungsblog*, March 3, 2017, https://verfassungsblog.de/poland-and-the-european-commission-part-iii-requiem-for-the-rule-of-law/. For critique of the Commission in the follow-up to the logging case see Tomasz T. Koncewicz, "The Polish Crisis as a European Crisis: A Letter to Mr Jean-Claude Juncker," *Verfassungsblog*, October 16, 2017, https://verfassungsblog.de/the-polish-crisis-as-a-european-crisis-a-letter-to-mr-jean-claude-juncker/.

[45] *Commission* v. *Poland*. While the judgment endorsed the Commission's action and ruled against Poland, the constitutional issue raised by the interim order was lost and forgotten.

[46] Although the interim order of November 20, 2017 prescribing penalties had some effect (parts of the heavy equipment were removed and the logging gradually brought to a temporary halt) it took a full five months for the logging to formally and fully stop. See https://tvn24bis.pl/z-kraju,74/minister-srodowiska-chce-uchylenia-decyzji-ws-usuwania-drzew,837224.html. Moreover, it appears from the most recent reports that logging might soon start again in the Białowieża Forest, corroborating that Polish compliance was half-hearted at best. See https://oko.press/nadchodzi-kolejna-wycinka-w-puszczy-bialowieskiej/. In sum, the precedent laid down by the Court in its November 20, 2017 order remains highly relevant.

negotiations with the Polish government. We can only speculate that the Commission failed to apply for penalties because it believed that by going light on the interim injunction it might induce Poland to backtrack on some of its domestic reforms designed to undermine judicial independence and the court system. If this was indeed the reason for the Commission's inaction, then it would be yet another example of an ill-thought out compromise that sacrifices the constitutional essentials for short-term (and hypothetical to say the least) political gains. The destruction of the Białowieża Forest remains the lasting image of the failure of European governance.

2 Enforcing the Rule of Law and First Principles beyond the Białowieża Forest Case

The "exit from values" that has already occurred in Poland has now been complemented by an "exit from legality" at both the national and supranational levels. No longer is the government seeking to remove itself from liberal values and norms. It is now also seeking to separate itself legally from the institutions that supervise the respect for these values and norms. At the domestic level, legal control was removed when the Constitutional Court was destroyed. Now Poland is seeking to break free of the EU's supranational machinery of control and enforcement. All legal institutions, domestic and supranational, are seen to stand in the way of the popular will and their rejection is part of a comprehensive constitutional doctrine – the politics of resentment.

The broader significance of the *Białowieża Forest* case is that it shows that the Treaties do contain legal tools to respond to recalcitrant Member States riding roughshod over the core values and principles of the EU legal order and that the Court of Justice is increasingly willing to use them. From the early days of the Treaty of Rome, the mission of the Court of Justice has been to "ensure observance of law and justice in the interpretation and application" of EU law (now Article 19 TEU).[47] The evolution of what is often called the

---

[47] Article 19(1) TEU (formerly Article 220 of the Treaty Establishing the European Community [hereinafter TEC]) reads: "The Court of Justice of the European Union shall include the Court of Justice, the General Court and specialised courts. It shall ensure that in the interpretation and application of the Treaties the law is observed." On the interpretation and (often creative) uses of Article 19 TEU (Article 220 TEC) see classics: Pierre Pescatore, "La carence du législateur communautaire et le devoir du juge," in *Rechtsvergleihung, Europarecht und Staatenintegration: Gedächtnisschrift für Léontin-Jean Constantinesco*, eds. Gerhard Lüke, Georg Ress, and Michael R. Will (Cologne: Carl Heymanns Verlag, 1983), 559–580; Pierre Pescatore, "Commentaire français du Traité CEE, Article 164," Manuscript available at the library of the Court of Justice, 1988; Pierre Pescatore, "Une révolution juridique: Le rôle de la Cour de justice européenne," *Commentaire* 59, no. 3 (1992): 569–574; Pierre Pescatore, "Jusqu'où le juge peut–il aller trop loin?," in *Festskrift til Ole Due*, eds. Jens Rosenløv and

constitutional jurisprudence of the Court has been an exercise in developing an increasingly robust and thick notion of "law" to be observed by the Member States and the EU institutions. As is well known, this constitutional jurisprudence includes supremacy and direct effect of EU law and the Simmenthal duty to give effect to EU law in the domestic legal order by setting aside conflicting provisions of domestic law.[48] The Court of Justice's reasoning in the *Białowieża Forest* case shows that it is now willing to import the principles and values announced in Article 2 TEU into the definition of the law that Member States are bound to observe.

In the *Białowieża Forest* case, the rule of law was at issue. In future cases, those first principles should also embrace separation of powers and independence of the judiciary, together with the enforceability of these principles as part of the ever-evolving overlapping consensus. In its opinion on EU accession to the European Convention on Human Rights, the Court imaginatively called these essential characteristics of EU law "a structured network of principles, rules and mutually interdependent legal relations linking the EU and its Member States, and its Member States with each other, which are now engaged, as is recalled in the second paragraph of Article 1 TEU, in a 'process of creating an ever closer union among the peoples of Europe.'" The Court added that:

> This legal structure is based on the fundamental premise that each Member State shares with all the other Member States, and recognises that they share with it, a set of common values on which the EU is founded, as stated in Article 2 TEU. That premise implies and justifies the existence of mutual trust between the Member States that those values will be recognised and, therefore, that the law of the EU that implements them will be respected.[49]

When it comes to fundamentals, there is no place for bargaining. The Commission should start pleading enforcement cases against the background of this robust conception of "the law" and what I call the Court of Justice's existential jurisprudence – existential because it aims at defending the integrity of the EU legal system. The EU legal order must be ready to respond

---

Kirsten Thorup (Copenhagen: Gad, 1994): 299–338; André Potocki, "Le rôle de la Cour de Justice des Communautés Européennes dans l'unification du droit," *Palestra*, no. 7–8 (2000): 166–173 (on file with the author); Fernand Schockweiler, "La Cour de Justice des Communautés Européennes dépasse-t-elle les limites de ses attributions?," *Journal des tribunaux* 4 (1995): 73. For the remedial relevance of Article 19 TEU see also analysis *infra* and Chapter 15.

[48] Herwig Hofmann, "Conflicts and Integration: Revisiting Costa v Enel and Simmenthal II," in *The Past and Future of EU Law: The Classics of EU Law Revisited on the 50th Anniversary of the Rome Treaty*, eds. Miguel P. Maduro and Loïc Azoulai (Oxford: Hart, 2010). On Simmenthal analogies see also analysis in this volume.

[49] Opinion 2/13 of the Court (Full Court), para. 168.

whenever its basics are called into question. For the EU to have a chance against the rising politics of resentment, the conceptual lens through which the EU looks at the Member States must be challenged and changed.

V CONCLUSION: MOVING FORWARD

Maximizing the remedial framework here and now is the EU's most fundamental challenge, as evidenced by the ever-increasing number of rule-of-law cases that have begun making their way to the European Court of Justice.[50] No doubt, the Court will have plenty of opportunities to shape the contours of its emerging existential jurisprudence. However, the *Białowieża Forest* case teaches us that no matter how many creative legal tools and techniques are put on the table, their full effectiveness will in the end hang on the most elusive and important component of the process of rethinking the Treaty's constitutional design: the political will to enforce the EU rule of law against the new breed of European authoritarians. The Commission's vanishing act in the *Białowieża Forest* case stands out as a painful reminder of the limits of law when faced with hesitant and passive enforcers.

One possible antidote to this lack of political will has surfaced recently. With the concerns raised about the systemic damage done to the Polish justice system, an Irish High Court judge referred the question of whether she is bound, in her capacity as EU judge of general jurisdiction, to automatically execute a European Arrest Warrant issued by the Polish authorities. With this preliminary reference, we are now moving away from the political arena marred by cynicism and rotten compromises to the courtroom with its own logic and principles. Judges owe their loyalties to the Treaties and the law that they are supposed to uphold. The constitutional stakes could not be higher. Yet to fully grasp the constitutional importance of what happened in the Irish High Court, the referral must be placed in more systemic and temporal context.

---

[50] Case C-64/16, *Associação Sindical dos Juízes Portugueses* v. *Tribunal de Contas*, ECLI:EU: C:2018:117, and analysis Michal Ovádek, "Has the CJEU Just Reconfigured the EU Constitutional Order?" *Verfassungsblog*, February 28, 2018, https://verfassungsblog.de/has-the-cjeu-just-reconfigured-the-eu-constitutional-order/; Maciej Taborowski, "CJEU Opens the Door for the Commission to Reconsider Charges against Poland," *Verfassungsblog*, March 13, 2018, https://verfassungsblog.de/cjeu-opens-the-door-for-the-commission-to-reconsider-charges-against-poland/; Laurent Pech and Sébastien Platon, "Rule of Law Backsliding in the EU: The Court of Justice to the Rescue? Some Thoughts on the ECJ Ruling in Associação Sindical dos Juízes Portugueses," *EU Law Analysis* (blog), March 13, 2018, http://eulawanalysis.blogspot.fr/2018/03/rule-of-law-backsliding-in-eu-court-of.html.

The imagination and courage that the European Court of Justice showed in the *Białowieża Forest* case reminds us of what Niamh N. Shuibhne aptly called the "responsibilities of constitutional courts."[51] She argues that one of these is to protect and further the objectives and values enshrined in the court's *constitution* (emphasis in the original). Building on the spirit of what former ECJ Judge Constantinos N. Kakouris called "the mission of the Court,"[52] the current turn of events might signal that the Court of Justice is assuming its responsibility as a constitutional court. There is hope that with the referral by the Irish High Court,[53] the landscape will change in favor of enforcing the first principles that are being progressively recognized by the Court of Justice and that are essential to the survival of Europe's overlapping consensus.[54]

With national judges stepping into the breach now, a new legal channel is being opened through which the Polish rule-of-law crisis might be addressed. This is crucial given the ineffectiveness and misguided calculations of the political institutions of the EU. With the concerns about the systemic damage done to the Polish justice system brought to the fore by the Irish High Court, the dynamics have shifted dramatically. We are moving away from the political arena marred by cynicism and rotten compromises to the courtroom with its own logic and principles. A switch is taking place: the paradigm is shifting from judges asking judges (dialogue via preliminary rulings) to judges monitoring judges. The judges (those sitting in Luxembourg and domestic judges) owe their loyalties to the Treaties and the law that they are supposed to uphold (Article 19 TEU). As the Court of Justice has articulated, the effective application of EU law is an essential component of the rule of law;[55] effective judicial review is the essence of the rule of law;[56] the guarantee of judicial independence is inherent to adjudication and is a prerequisite for ensuring

---

[51] Niamh Nic Shuibhne, *The Coherence of EU Free Movement Law: Constitutional Responsibility and the Court of Justice* (Oxford: Oxford University Press, 2013).

[52] Constantinos N. Kakouris, "La mission de la Cour de Justice des Communautés Européennes et l'ethos du juge," *Revue des affaires européennes* 4 (1994): 35–41.

[53] The ruling of March, 12, 2018 is available at High Court of Ireland, *Minister for Justice and Equality* v. *Celmer* (No. 3), [2018] IEHC 153, www.courts.ie/Judgments.nsf/0/FD843302847F2E228025825D00457F19.

[54] Christian Davies, "Ireland Refuses Extradition over Concern at Polish Justice Reforms," *The Guardian*, March 13, 2018, www.theguardian.com/world/2018/mar/13/ireland-refuses-artur-celmer-extradition-poland-justice-reforms-ecj.

[55] *Order for Interim Measures.*

[56] Case C-72/15 (Grand Chamber), *PJSC Rosneft Oil Company* v. *Her Majesty's Treasury and Others*, ECLI:EU:C:2017:236.

effective judicial protection;[57] and now, since the Irish High Court reference, mutual trust in the performance and status of the courts in the Member States is of fundamental importance. These are all European first principles. The moment these principles start to crumble, so will the consensus. At long last, the politics of resentment face a powerful enemy: European courts with their own fidelities and loyalties.[58] From the way that Poland has rejected the European Court of Justice's order in the *Białowieża Forest* case, has ridiculed the Court's judges, and has continued to defy the authority of the Court, it is clear that the constitutional stakes could not be higher. On the line are the survival of Europe's first principles and the long-term viability of its overlapping consensus.

---

[57] *Associação Sindical dos Juízes Portugueses.*

[58] This optimism must be guarded though, in light of the ECJ's ruling on the Irish High Court's preliminary reference in Case C-216/18 PPU, Request for a Preliminary Ruling under Article 267 TFEU from the High Court (Ireland) (*Celmer* case). The Court seems to have failed to deliver on the promise of *Associação Sindical dos Juízes Portugueses.* For further analysis see Chapter 15. On the case also papers published at the online symposium organized by *Verfassungsblog* at https://verfassungsblog.de/category/themen/after-celmer/.

17

The Populist Backlash against Europe

Why Only Alternative Economic and Social Policies Can Stop the Rise of Populism in Europe

BOJAN BUGARIČ[*]

I INTRODUCTION

The European Union is facing an unprecedented political crisis. This club of liberal and democratic countries has been confronted by a nationalist and populist backlash that threatens the core principles at the very heart of the EU.[1] Capitalizing on the European sovereign debt crisis, the backlash against refugees streaming in from the Middle East, public angst over the growing terror threat, and Brexit, previously fringe populist political parties are growing with alarming speed. Populists not only attack policies that are based on core institutional pillars of the European integration project, but quite often they also challenge the very foundations of the project as such.

Populism is an ideology or political movement that "considers society to be ultimately separated into two homogeneous and antagonistic groups, the pure people versus the corrupt elite, and which argues that politics should be an expression of the *volonté générale* of the people."[2] Populism seeks to speak in the name of the common people. Its distinctive features are the prioritization of popular sovereignty, direct democracy, and a strong emphasis on anti-elitism. Beyond these shared common features, populism emerges in a variety of forms. While populism is hostile to elites, it is also vague and moralistic and as such quite easily instrumentalized by almost any type of ideology, both left and right. Hence, there exist several rather different varieties of populism:

---

[*] For their comments and suggestions, I would like to thank Francesca Bignami, Fernanda Nicola, Peter Lindseth, Philomila Tsoukala, and other participants at the GWU conference.

[1] Desmond Dinan, Neil Nugent, and William Paterson, eds., *The European Union in Crisis* (London: Palgrave, 2017); James Kirchick, *The End of Europe: Dictators, Demagogues, and the Coming Dark Age* (New Haven, CT: Yale University Press, 2017).

[2] Cass Mudde, "The Populist Zeitgeist," *Government and Opposition* 39, no. 4 (2004): 543.

478 *Bojan Bugarič*

agrarian, socioeconomic, xenophobic, reactionary, authoritarian, and progressive populism.[3]

Part of the blame for the populist upsurge falls on both center-right and center-left party leaders who have failed to respond effectively to the European debt crisis. This fact is often obscured by the current focus on the migrant crisis as the single most important contributor to the populist surge. As Vivien Schmidt correctly argues, it is "neo-liberalism gone too far"[4] that is the major contributor to the anger fueling the rise of populism in Europe. There are also other rival theories attempting to explain the current rise of populism, which point to a variety of structural factors, ranging from the effects of globalization and global trade on income distribution,[5] to a decline in the subjective social status of white men,[6] and, last but not least, to culture – where populism is a reaction against progressive cultural change.[7]

Although the roots of populism are complex, austerity and neoliberal structural reforms are undoubtedly among the most important underlying factors. The ruling parties' obsession with fiscal austerity, and with supply-side policies of privatization, deregulation, and liberalization, effectively triggered a "lost decade" of economic stagnation, rising unemployment, increasing poverty, and dwindling EU solidarity that paved the way for the poisonous ultra-nationalism now on the rise.[8] All this has driven trust in the

---

[3]   Margaret Canovan, *Populism* (New York: Harcourt Brace Jovanovich, 1981); Noam Gidron and Bart Bonikowski, "Varieties of Populism: Literature Review and Research Agenda," Working Paper Series, No.13-0004, Weatherhead Center for International Affairs, Harvard University, 2013, https://scholar.harvard.edu/files/gidron_bonikowski_populismlitreview_2013.pdf; Cass Mudde and Cristóbal Rovira Kaltwasser, "Populism," in *The Oxford Handbook of Political Ideologies*, eds. Michael Freeden and Marc Stears (Oxford: Oxford University Press, 2013), 495–498.

[4]   Vivien Schmidt, "Missing Topic in #EUref: Neo-Liberalism Gone Too Far," *Social Europe*, June 22, 2016, www.socialeurope.eu/missing-topic-euref-neo-liberalism-gone-far; see also Jürgen Habermas, "'New' Perspectives for Europe," *Social Europe*, October 22, 2018, www.socialeurope.eu/new-perspectives-for-europe.

[5]   Dani Rodrik, "Populism and the Economics of Globalization," *Journal of International Business Policy* (2018), https://drodrik.scholar.harvard.edu/files/dani-rodrik/files/populism_and_the_economics_of_globalization.pdf.

[6]   Noam Gidron and Peter A. Hall, "The Politics of Social Status: Economic and Cultural Roots of the Populist Right," *British Journal of Sociology* 68, no. 1 (2017): 57–84.

[7]   Ronald F. Inglehart and Pippa Norris, "Trump, Brexit, and the Rise of Populism: Economic Have-Nots and Cultural Backlash," Faculty Research Working Paper Series, *Harvard Kennedy School*, August 2016, www.hks.harvard.edu/publications/trump-brexit-and-rise-populism-economic-have-nots-and-cultural-backlash.

[8]   Barry Eichengreen, *The Populist Temptation: Economic Grievance and Political Reaction in the Modern Era* (New York: Oxford University Press, 2018), 163; Jason Beckfield, "European Integration and Income Inequality," *American Sociological Review* 71, no. 6 (2006): 964–985;

The Populist Backlash against Europe

EU to an all-time low and fueled pathologies not seen since the 1930s, placing the European integration project on truly precarious ground. The new populist "Zeitgeist" is best described by Jan Zielonka, who argues that "under attack is not just the EU but also other symbols of the current order: liberal democracy and neoliberal economics, migration and a multicultural society, historical 'truths' and political correctness, moderate political parties and mainstream media, cultural tolerance and religious neutrality."[9] Moreover, while populism comes in many versions, what almost all populists in Europe share is the rejection of "people and institutions that have governed Europe in the last three decades."[10]

In many countries, populist parties are the only ones to argue that there exists a real alternative. They protest against the "consensus at the center" – between the center-right and center-left – around the idea that there is no alternative to neoliberal globalization. In the eyes of populists, the European project is the embodiment of a ruthless process of globalization responsible for intolerable levels of inequality, declining trust in democracy, a rising danger of terrorism, and increasing fear of loss of one's "national" and "cultural" identity. Many major populist parties in Western Europe today are both anti-Eurozone and anti-European. On the left, only populists in Greece and Spain support both the euro and the European project. On the right, only two major populist parties (Germany's right-wing AfD and Italy's Five Star Movement) are not outright anti-European, but they are both against the euro.[11] The populists in the East have gone even farther in their confrontation with the EU. They frontally assault core EU values, contest the legitimacy of EU institutions and policies, and, at home, dismantle constitutional democracy.

The populist backlash in essence represents a delayed Polanyian response to the destructive forces of the unfettered logic of free markets.[12] As Karl Polanyi demonstrated in his *Great Transformation*,[13] when markets become

---

Jason Beckfield, *Unequal Europe: How Regional Integration Reshaped the Welfare State and Reversed the Egalitarian Turn* (New York: Oxford University Press, 2019).

[9] Jan Zielonka, *Counter-Revolution: Liberal Europe in Retreat* (New York: Oxford University Press, 2018), 2.

[10] Zielonka, *Counter-Revolution*, 3.

[11] Jeremy Ashkenas and Gregor Aisch, "European Populism in the Age of Donald Trump," *The New York Times*, December 5, 2016, www.nytimes.com/interactive/2016/12/05/world/europe/populism-in-age-of-trump.html.

[12] Robert Kuttner, *Can Democracy Survive Global Capitalism?* (New York: W.W Norton & Company, 2018), xx–xxii.

[13] Karl Polanyi, *The Great Transformation: The Political and Economic Origins of Our Time*, 2nd ed. (Boston: Beacon Press, 2001).

"dis-embedded" from their societies and create severe social dislocations, people eventually revolt. Despite important differences between the new populist forces in Europe, they have "more in common than we think. They are all pro-welfare (for some people, at least), anti-globalization, and most interestingly, pro-state, and although they say it *sotto voce* on the right, anti-finance."[14] As Chantal Mouffe argues, populists are not against the European project as such, but only against "the *neo-liberal* incarnation of the European project."[15]

Vindication of "the social"[16] by the populist forces does not mean only a defense of social rights but also a demand for greater autonomy of Member States on cultural (identity) and economic issues.[17] The populists do not seek to completely dismantle the EU. They do, however, demand that their national sovereignty be "restored" and oppose any further attempts toward an "ever closer union." Much like in the 1930s, the protagonists of "the social" appear in different political forms, ranging from the extreme right to the extreme left on the political spectrum. While populist forces often pose legitimate political questions about the current state of democracy in Europe, their solutions tend to be controversial.[18] Their visions of emancipating "the social" often bear an uncanny resemblance to illiberal and authoritarian ideals from the 1930s.

How did Europe get from the postwar ideal embodied in the Treaty of Rome that appeared to dislodge authoritarian nationalism to the situation where Member States feel threatened by the European project? Section II offers a brief overview of populism in the East, in particular the two most notorious cases of populist backlash, Poland and Hungary.

In Sections III and IV, I briefly examine how the EU deals with current populist backlash in cases where populists directly attack or undermine the

---

[14] Mark Blyth, "Global Trumpism: Why Trump's Victory Was 30 Years in the Making and Why It Won't Stop Here," *Foreign Affairs*, November 15, 2016, www.foreignaffairs.com/articles/2016-11-15/global-trumpism.

[15] Chantal Mouffe, "In Defence of Left-Wing Populism," *The Conversation*, April 29, 2016, http://theconversation.com/in-defence-of-left-wing-populism-55869; see also Chantal Mouffe, *For a Left Populism* (London: Verso, 2018).

[16] For a similar concept of the social, see Duncan Kennedy, "Three Globalizations of Law and Legal Thought: 1850–2000," in *The New Law and Economic Development: A Critical Appraisal*, eds. David M. Trubek and Alvaro Santos (Cambridge: Cambridge University Press, 2010), 19–73.

[17] For a legal analysis of these issues see Gráinne de Búrca, "Is EU Supranational Governance a Challenge to Liberal Constitutionalism?" *The University of Chicago Law Review* 85, no. 2 (March 2018): 337–368.

[18] Cristóbal Rowira Kaltwasser, "The Response of Populism to Dahl's Democratic Dilemmas," *Political Studies* 62, no. 3 (2014): 470–487.

authority of EU law. In Section V, I argue that what is needed is a different approach. Instead of focusing only on legal or economic sanctions, the EU should look to alternative economic and social policies that would speak directly to the anxieties of populist voters.[19] The good news is that this trend can be reversed – but only if European leaders, together with the Member States, articulate a coherent alternative to the failed economic and social policies of the last decade. An economic policy that promotes growth, better jobs and wages, and social inclusion can stem the nationalist-populist tide.

II THE POPULISTS AT THE GATE: THE HUNGARIAN AND POLISH CASES

In Europe, the main populist threat comes principally from the East. Fewer than fifteen years after accession to the European Union, Hungary, Poland, Slovakia, the Czech Republic, and Bulgaria have witnessed populists come to power. As a recent empirical study shows, the appeal of these populist parties has increased quite rapidly in the last two decades.[20] Since 2000, when populist parties took an average of 9.2 percent of the national vote, their vote share has tripled, reaching 31.6 percent in 2017.[21] An alarming finding of Freedom House's *Nations in Transit Report*[22] shows that for the first time since 1995, there are now more consolidated authoritarian regimes than consolidated democracies in the region. Hungary now has the lowest ranking in the Central European region. Poland's score reached its lowest point in the survey. Shortly after the global financial crisis in 2008, which served as a catalyst for change, alternative economic and political ideas emerged and spread through the region.[23] Neoliberal economic policies were gradually replaced with various statist models of development, combining economic

---

[19] For this point, see Fernanda Nicola, "Editorial: Another View of the Cathedral: What Does the Rule of Crisis Tell Us about Democratizing the EU?" *Maastricht Journal of European Law and Comparative Law* 25, no. 2 (2018): 133–138.

[20] Martin Eiermann, Yascha Mounk, and Limor Gultchin, *Report: European Populism: Trends, Threats, and Future Prospects,* Institute for Global Change, 2017, https://institute.global/insight/renewing-centre/european-populism-trends-threats-and-future-prospects.

[21] Eiermann, Mounk, and Gultchin, *Report. European Populism: Trends, Threats, and Future Prospects.*

[22] Freedom House, *Nations in Transit 2017 Report: The False Promise of Populism,* 2017, https://freedomhouse.org/report/nations-transit/nations-transit-2017.

[23] Tony Barber, "An Illiberal Streak Spreads Further across Central Europe," *Financial Times,* December 8, 2015, www.ft.com/content/e5f73e48-9cf4-11e5-b45d-4812f209f861.

protectionism with elements of leftist social welfare policies.[24] At the same time, political liberalism has been challenged by open flirtation with illiberal[25] and authoritarian forms of government.[26]

Despite sharing many of the core elements of populism, not all populists in Eastern and Central Europe are the same.[27] Authoritarian populism has so far emerged only in Hungary and Poland, the two former front-runners of democratic transition. Authoritarian populism combines the key features of populism with essential ingredients of illiberalism: opposition to pluralism, the rule of law, and rights of minorities.[28] Other countries in the region have yet to go down that road. In Slovakia, the nominally left-wing (social-democratic) populist Robert Fico lost his absolute majority in 2016 elections and quickly toned down his populist rhetoric. Later, in February 2018, the murder of the investigative journalist Jan Kuciak triggered one of the largest demonstrations in Bratislava in the post-communist era, resulting in the resignation of Prime Minister Fico. Although his Smer-SD (Direction-Social Democracy), a national-populist political formation that employs left-leaning socialist rhetoric, still remains the most powerful party in the current governing coalition, the position of Smer-SD has been seriously weakened. As a result, in comparison with Hungary and Poland, Slovakia in recent years has represented a less prominent case of the "illiberal turn," rarely earning a mention in discussions of "democratic backsliding."[29] Likewise, populists in the Czech Republic have not yet openly embraced illiberalism. The winner of the October 2017 elections in the Czech Republic was Andrej Babis, a billionaire populist impatient with the give-and-take of democratic politics, although not yet someone with a

---

[24] Anne Applebaum, "Europe's New Right Sounds Like the Old Left," *Financial Times*, January 27, 2016, www.ft.com/content/cffc9686-c393-11e5-808f-8231cd71622e; Mitchell Orenstein, "Reassessing the Neo-Liberal Development Model in Central and Eastern Europe," in *Resilient Liberalism in Europe's Political Economy*, eds. Vivien Schmidt and Mark Thatcher (New York: Cambridge University Press, 2013), 374–402.

[25] Illiberal democracies are understood here, following Fareed Zakaria, as: "democratically elected regimes, often ones that have been reelected or reaffirmed through referenda [that] are routinely ignoring constitutional limits on their power and depriving their citizens of basic rights and freedoms." See Fareed Zakaria, "The Rise of Illiberal Democracy," *Foreign Affairs* 76, no. 6 (1997): 22.

[26] Jan-Werner Müller, "Eastern Europe Goes South: Disappearing Democracy in the EU's Newest Member States," *Foreign Affairs* 93, no. 2 (2014): 14–19.

[27] Anna Grzymala Busse, "Global Populisms and Their Impact," *Slavic Review* 76, no. S1 (August 2017): S3–S8.

[28] Bart Bonikowski, "Ethno-Nationalist Populism and the Mobilization of Collective Resentment," *The British Journal of Sociology* 68, no. S1 (2017): 190.

[29] Grigorij Mesežnikov and Ol'ga Gyárfášová, "Slovakia's Conflicting Camps," *Journal of Democracy* 29, no. 3 (July 2018): 88.

clear illiberal nationalist program. His populist rhetoric is closer to the pluto-cratic version of populism espoused by figures like Donald Trump and the former Italian Prime minister Silvio Berlusconi, who promised to rid the country of corruption and run it like a business.[30]

In the Central European region, Hungary is the most visible example of authoritarian populism. Roughly a decade after Vladimir Putin steered his country toward "Putinism,"[31] a new ideology aspiring to represent a Russian alternative to the Western liberal order, Hungary followed in these footsteps. Hungary, a successful leader of transformation in the 1990s, had a current account deficit of €1.9 million in 2000, but €5.8 million by 2006; the country also became highly indebted and by 2009 its had debt reached 79 percent of GDP. Unemployment rose to 10 percent by 2010. Among the first countries in Europe to experience a bailout, Hungary received a rescue package from the International Monetary Fund (IMF) and the EU in 2008.[32] Because of the austerity measures introduced to reestablish financial order, a great part of the population suffered huge losses.[33] The crisis situation that characterized most of the country between 2008 and 2016 may be compared to waking up from a sweet dream to the gloomy reality for a great part of the population. All of a sudden, millions of people turned against obediently following Brussels. As Andrea Pirro explains, it was the deterioration of the Hungarian economy combined with the perception of the undemocratic nature of the European architecture, which boosted Fidesz's nationalism and Euroskepticism.[34]

When Orbán came to power in 2010, he inherited a spiraling deficit and a €20 billion IMF bailout program. The Fidesz agenda was to overturn

---

[30] Jiri Pehe, "Czech Democracy under Pressure," *Journal of Democracy* 29, no. 3 (July 2018): 71.

[31] Putinism represents a mixture of economic statism, political authoritarianism, and Russian Orthodox fundamentalism. Putin's economic nationalism is strongly embedded in his "conservative revolution," emphasizing the importance of Russian national "character" being at odds with traditional liberal values and principles. See Anne Applebaum, "Putinism: The Ideology," *LSE*, February 2013, www.lse.ac.uk/ideas/Assets/Documents/updates/LSE-IDEAS-Putinism-The-Ideology.pdf.

[32] Kate Connolly and Ian Traynor, "Hungary Receives Rescue Package, with Strings Attached," *The Guardian*, October 29, 2008, www.theguardian.com/business/2008/oct/29/hungary-economy-imf-eu-world-bank.

[33] As Claire Kilpatrick argues, "a key political priority of the newly elected Orbán government was to reduce public debt and deficit without resorting to typical austerity measures." Even though the Orbán government used atypical deficit reduction measures, they still had a dramatic effect on social rights. See Claire Kilpatrick, "Constitutions, Social Rights and Sovereign Debt States in Europe: A Challenging New Area of Constitutional Inquiry," Law 2015/34, EUI Working Papers.

[34] Andrea L. P. Pirro, *The Populist Radical Right in Central and Eastern Europe: Ideology, Impact, and Electoral Performance* (New York: Routledge, 2015), 149.

neoliberal economic policies. The government reshaped the country's taxation system, introducing, on the one hand, a flat-rate 16 percent income tax and imposing, on the other hand, crisis taxes on the telecom, energy, media, and financial sectors. The government also nationalized compulsory private pension funds, opening up a public revenue stream that has reduced the deficit. Since then, Orbán has forced utilities to reduce household bills and has required lossmaking banks to pay €3 billion in compensation to bank customers who took out foreign currency mortgages. Such populist measures helped his Fidesz party win another term in office in 2014.

Orbán has denounced the West as decadent and obsessed with money, and outlined a future Hungarian state – a "work based society." Orbán called his approach, adopted after his 2010 election victory, the "Eastern winds" approach to economic policy, to distinguish it from Western liberalism.[35] The key pillars of Orbán's new economic policy were re-nationalization of certain private companies, mostly in what he considered to be strategic sectors like oil (MOL), gas, utilities, and banks, punitive taxation of foreign banks and insurance companies, and economic protectionism. The Orbán government's "Eastern winds" approach, while officially an economic policy, has from the beginning been heavily imbued with the implication of political and social transformation away from Western liberalism and individualism toward Eastern authoritarianism and collectivism. After Viktor Orbán's speech in Tusnádfürdö, it became more than clear that he wants to create an illiberal state, a different kind of constitutional order from liberal democracy.[36] The Orbán government has transformed Hungary into a semi-authoritarian regime that limits freedom of speech and assembly, curtails media pluralism, and undermines protection of minorities. Orbán has also curbed the independence of the courts, the civil service, and other institutions essential to the rule of law.[37]

The novelty and irony of the Hungarian slide into authoritarianism is that it was achieved entirely through legal means. Due to its two-thirds majority in the Hungarian unicameral parliament (Diet), Fidesz faced few obstacles in

---

[35] "Orbán and the Wind from the East," *The Economist*, November 14, 2011, www.economist .com/eastern-approaches/2011/11/14/orban-and-the-wind-from-the-east.

[36] Kester Edy, "EU Urged to Monitor Hungary as Orbán Hits at 'Liberal Democracy'," *Financial Times*, July 30, 2014, www.ft.com/content/0574f7f2-17f3-11e4-b842-00144feabdc0.

[37] Miklós Bánkuti, Gábor Halmai, and Kim Lane Scheppele, "From Separation of Powers to a Government without Checks: Hungary's Old and New Constitution," in *Constitution for a Disunited Nation: On Hungary's 2011 Fundamental Law*, ed. Gábor Attila Tóth (Budapest: Central University Press, 2012), 268; Miklós Bánkuti, Gábor Halmai, and Kim Lane Scheppele, "Disabling the Constitution," *Journal of Democracy* 23, no. 3 (2012): 138–141.

achieving this "constitutional revolution."[38] When there arose a need to change the rules of the game, the Hungarian parliament was able to simply amend the Constitution. In Hungary, the new populist government managed with relative ease to render the courts toothless by packing them with loyalists and curtailing their independence. The populists understood very well that by displacing the Constitutional Court, the core of the rule of law, they removed the major obstacle to the fulfillment of their aspirations. The once powerful and highly respected Court for the moment disappeared from the political scene.[39] After neutralizing the Constitutional Court, the populist government continued its legal "revolution" with attacks on lower (regular) courts: It lowered the judicial retirement age, allowing Orbán to remove most of the presidents of the courts and replace them with judges more to his liking.

At the moment, the Hungarian version of authoritarian populism represents the most problematic example of this trend in the region. The Fidesz government achieved a fundamental revision of the rules of the constitutional and political order in Hungary. In a scant eight years, it managed to transform Hungary from one of the success stories of the transition from socialism to democracy into a semi-authoritarian regime, where the new constitutional structure vests so much power in the centralized executive that no real checks and balances exist to restrain this power. Despite the authoritarian turn, in 2018, Orbán secured his third successive election victory on the back of record turnout – and won another two-thirds majority, which will allow Fidesz to change the Constitution again and further entrench its power.

In Poland, the new right-wing and populist Law and Justice (PiS) government has also set out to exploit a mix of ethnic nationalism and anti-capitalism reminiscent of that present in the interwar period, when authoritarianism – masquerading as democracy – prevailed in Admiral Miklós Horthy's Hungary and Marshal Józef Piłsudski's Poland. After winning the majority of votes in 2015 elections, Poland joined Hungary on its path to authoritarian populism.[40]

In Poland, the best economic performer in the region, it was primarily the poor, old, and unemployed who helped to elect the new right-wing government. PiS promised a family allowance of $130 a month per child, funded through a tax on banks and big business; a minimum wage; and a return to a

---

[38] Kim Lane Scheppele, "Constitutional Coups and Judicial Review: How Transnational Institutions Can Strengthen Peak Courts at Times of Crisis," *Transnational Law and Contemporary Problems* 23 (2014): 51–117.

[39] Bánkuti, Halmai, and Scheppele, "Disabling the Constitution," 140.

[40] R. Daniel Kelemen, "Poland's Constitutional Crisis: How the Law and Justice Party Is Threatening Democracy," *Foreign Affairs*, August 25, 2016, www.foreignaffairs.com/articles/poland/2016-08-25/polands-constitutional-crisis.

retirement age of sixty for women and sixty-five for men. Despite the robust economic performance, the previous governing party, the neoliberal Civil Platform (PO) had left behind many regions like Silesia, as well as working people on so-called junk contracts earning less than $200 a month. The millions of Poles in the small towns and poorer regions of "Polska B" "felt themselves to be marginalized and left behind by the bulldozer of economic liberalism. They were also, it's important to add, alienated by the social liberalism, on issues such as abortion, gender, and sexual orientation, which came with the opening to Western Europe."[41] As Mitchell Orenstein and Bojan Bugarič observe, the new family allowance was a huge boon for many:

> For the many hundreds of thousands of working parents earning only 2,000–2,500 złotys a month, this meant a sudden untaxed pay raise of twenty or even forty percent. Within a year, children living in extreme poverty declined by a third. Single mothers found themselves able to quit overly exploitative jobs and seek other options. Though such individual largesse comes at the expense of long-term projects like improving child-care networks and pre-schools, it is clearly a social policy that has helped many and proved tremendously popular.[42]

Even the economically liberal Financial Times reports that these policies have "also earned Poland the top spot in Oxfam's latest index of social spending designed to reduce inequality." Moreover, the Financial Times also argues that "[o]n the issues that voters care about, most voters agree with Law and Justice – and Law and Justice has delivered on those issues."[43]

Like in Hungary, the first institutional target of the new Polish government was the Constitutional Tribunal. As a result of a series of changes, the Constitutional Tribunal, "as a mechanism of constitutional review has ceased to exist: a reliable aide of the government and parliamentary majority was born."[44] After neutralizing the Constitutional Tribunal, the Polish government prepared three bills, recently adopted by the Sejm, which aim to control

---

[41] Timothy Garton Ash, "Is Europe Disintegrating?" *The New York Review of Books*, January 19, 2017, www.nybooks.com/articles/2017/01/19/is-europe-disintegrating/.

[42] Mitchell Orenstein and Bojan Bugarič, "Economic Causes (and Policies) of Populism in Eastern Europe," European Consortium for Political Research, Hamburg, August 23, 2018, https://ecpr.eu/MyEcpr/MyEvent.aspx?EventID=115.

[43] James Shoter and Evon Huber, "Handouts Help Poland's Voters Look Past EU Fight," *The Financial Times*, October 18, 2018, www.ft.com/content/4805fd6c-d119-11e8-a9f2-7574db66bcd5.

[44] Wojciech Sadurski, "How Democracy Dies (in Poland): A Case Study of Anti-constitutional Populist Backsliding in Poland," Sydney Law School Research Paper No.18/1 (2018), https://papers.ssrn.com/sol3/papers.cfm?abstract_id=3103491.

The Populist Backlash against Europe 487

and capture the Supreme Court and the vast majority of other regular courts.[45] The new Law and Justice government also undermined Poland's independent civil service and adopted new legislation seeking to bring the media under direct government control.[46]

These legal and economic changes are part of a broader conservative political program founded on a set of moral values that purportedly serve the protection of the Polish nation.[47] As Leszek Koczanowicz argues, PiS "aims not only to transform certain external conditions, but also to accomplish a comprehensive re-invention of mentality and radically re-direct the trajectory of social thinking."[48] A combination of nationalism with social welfarism secures the extremely high popularity of the ruling PiS party in Poland. According to Aleks Szczerbiak, "many Poles feel that, while politicians have often promised to help the less well-off, Law and Justice is the first party to actually deliver on these pledges on such a scale."[49]

The new populism in Hungary and Poland differs from other populisms in Europe because it combines the elements of populism, ethno-nationalism, and authoritarianism. While ethno-nationalism is present in most Western European cases, it is the third element, authoritarianism, which sets the Hungarian and Polish type of populism apart from other European cases. Authoritarianism in the Hungarian and Polish context does not mean only the adoption of certain authoritarian values,[50] such as stringent security and intolerance of multiculturalism and pluralism, but also a "style of governance that attempts to circumvent the rule of law and democratic norms in favor of centralized authority and limited political freedom."[51] Authoritarian populists

---

[45] Sadurski, "How Democracy Dies."

[46] Jan-Werner Müller, "The Problem with Poland," *The New York Review of Books*, February 11, 2016, www.nybooks.com/daily/2016/02/11/kaczynski-eu-problem-with-poland/.

[47] Joanna Fomina and Jacek Kucharczyk, "Populism and Protest in Poland," *Journal of Democracy* 27, no. 4 (2016): 61.

[48] Leszek Koczanowicz, "The Polish Case. Community and Democracy under the PiS," *New Left Review* 102 (November/December 2016): 94.

[49] Aleks Szczerbiak, "Why Is Poland's Law and Justice Government So Popular?" *The Polish Politics Blog*, October 26, 2017, https://polishpoliticsblog.wordpress.com/2017/10/26/why-is-polands-law-and-justice-government-so-popular/; see also Remi Adekoya, "Why Poland's Law and Justice Party Remains So Popular?" *Foreign Affairs*, November 3, 2017, www.foreignaffairs.com/articles/central-europe/2017-11-03/why-polands-law-and-justice-party-remains-so-popular.

[50] Pippa Norris and Ronald Inglehart adopt such an approach in defining authoritarian populism, see Pippa Norris and Ronald Inglehart, *Cultural Backlash: Trump, Brexit and Authoritarian Populism* (New York: Cambridge University Press, 2018).

[51] Bart Bonikowski, "Ethno-Nationalist Populism and the Mobilization of Collective Resentment," *The British Journal of Sociology* 68, no. 1 (2017): 189–190.

488 *Bojan Bugarič*

in Hungary and Poland are explicitly anti-liberal but not necessarily anti-democratic.[52] They embrace the "form" of democracy and claim to speak for the people themselves, but, at the same time – by undermining its liberal constitutional foundations – they erode the substance of democracy and gradually transform it into various forms of illiberal and authoritarian regimes.[53]

What differentiates Orbán and Kaczynski from other populists in Europe is the extent to which they oppose liberal democracy. They have gone much further in subverting liberal democracy than most of the other populists in East-Central Europe. With a skillful invocation of conservative and authoritarian ideology, combined with the absence of a strong opposition, they mounted a successful crusade again liberalism. Irena Grudzinska-Gross writes about "the revival in Poland, Hungary and ... some other countries of the region, of the very old conservative style of government, including the resurrection of the extreme right wing movements and, in Poland, of religious fundamentalism."[54] Iván Szelényi and Tamás Csillag argue that this drift to illiberalism and authoritarianism also has a legitimating ideology, a traditionalist/neoconservative one, which emphasizes the value of patriotism, religion, and traditional family values. They maintain that a combination of political illiberalism, economic statism, and conservative ideology represents the building blocks of a new type of order in the post-communist world: A managed illiberal capitalism.[55] Because of these additional features, this form of populism has strong authoritarian inclinations.

III THE EU TO THE RESCUE?

Some observers argue that the existence of international organizations such as the European Union makes the backsliding currently underway in Poland and Hungary quite different from the "constitutional coups" of earlier eras.[56] One of the most crucial political questions facing Europe today is how well the EU is equipped, legally and politically, to defend democracy and the rule of law in its Member States. It is therefore necessary to examine how the EU is

---

[52] Anna Grzymala Busse, "Global Populisms and Their Impact," S3.

[53] Müller, "Eastern Europe Goes South," 15.

[54] Irena Grudzinska-Gross, "The Backsliding," *East European Politics and Societies and Cultures* 28, no. 4 (2014): 664.

[55] Tamás Csillag and Iván Szelényi, "Drifting from Liberal Democracy: Traditionalists/ Neoconservative Ideology of Managed Illiberal Democratic Capitalism in Post-Communist Europe," *Intersections: East European Journal of Society and Politics* 1, no. 1 (2015): 1–27.

[56] Kim Lane Scheppele, "Constitutional Coups and Judicial Review."

The Populist Backlash against Europe

managing its first real attempts at safeguarding democracy within Member States. A political club of democratic regimes established primarily to promote peace and prosperity in postwar Europe, the EU must now confront Member States that are turning away from liberal democracy. EU law currently offers three legal options for dealing with cases such as those of Hungary and Poland.

The first is to invoke Article 7 of the Treaty on European Union (TEU), the so-called nuclear option, which lays out a procedure for determining whether a Member State has violated the values stated in Article 2 and, if so, allows for the suspension of certain rights. This provision was first introduced in the 1997 Treaty of Amsterdam (amending the 1992 Maastricht Treaty), which states that in cases where there has been a "serious and persistent breach" of the "principles of liberty, democracy, respect for human rights and fundamental freedoms, and the rule of law," the Council of the European Union can "suspend certain . . . rights . . . including the voting rights of the representative of the government of that Member State in the Council." In December 2017, the European Commission launched Article 7 proceedings against Poland for breaching European common values and rule of law.[57] And, in September 2018, the European Parliament voted to trigger the EU's most serious disciplinary procedure against Hungary, saying the country's government poses a "systematic threat" to democracy and the rule of law. The vote was carried with the support of 448 MEPs, narrowly clearing the required two-thirds majority, after Hungary's prime minister, Viktor Orbán, was abandoned by many of his allies in the center-right European People's Party (EPP). The crucial problem of Article 7 is that in order to employ the preventing mechanism, Article 7 requires a majority of four-fifths of the Council and assent of the European Parliament. The sanctioning mechanism, on the other hand, requires an even higher threshold, i.e. unanimity in the Council and assent of the European Parliament. Hence, it is highly unlikely that Article 7 will ever be used against countries like Hungary or Poland.

The EU's second legal option for dealing with countries veering off the democratic path is detailed in Article 258 of the Treaty on the Functioning of the European Union (TFEU). Article 258 states that if the European Commission finds that a Member State has "failed to fulfil an obligation under the Treaties" and that State then fails to rectify the matter, the Commission "may bring the matter before the Court of Justice of the European Union [CJEU]." This is what has happened in the cases of Hungary and Poland.

---

[57] For a more comprehensive overview of the EU legal approaches to Poland and Hungary, see Laurent Pech and Kim Lane Scheppele, "Illiberalism Within: Rule of Law Backsliding in the EU," *Cambridge Yearbook of European Legal Studies*, 19 (2017): 3–47, and Chapter 15.

To focus on Hungary, the Commission has brought several separate suits against Hungary under Article 258 TFEU. The most interesting case involved a provision in Hungary's Transitional Act on the implementation of the 2012 Constitution, which lowered the retirement age of judges from seventy to sixty-two. This provision would have forced 274 judges and public prosecutors into retirement in a short period of time. The Commission considered the rule to be a violation of the independence of the judiciary. For strategic reasons, it decided to utilize very narrow legal grounds to deal with the case: It relied exclusively on Council Directive 2000/78/EC on equal treatment in employment, which prohibits discrimination on grounds of age. In November 2012, the European Court of Justice (ECJ) ruled that the radical lowering of the retirement age for Hungarian judges constituted age discrimination and violated Council Directive 2000/78/EC.[58]

Despite this legal victory, the retired judges were never comprehensively reinstated, and Fidesz loyalists basically stayed in place. As Jan-Werner Müller argues, in the end "Europe appeared impotent in getting at the real issue, which was political and had nothing to do with the discrimination [against] individuals."[59] Separate legal proceedings such as this discrimination suit may yield important legal victories, but they ultimately fail to address the broader institutional issues that threaten the foundations of the rule of law and liberal democracy in Hungary.

The final option in the EU's legal arsenal is the Rule of Law Framework. The Framework was adopted in 2014, mainly in response to the inability of the key EU actors to agree on invoking Article 7. Often called the "pre–Article 7 procedure," the Rule of Law Framework complements Article 7 by establishing a structured "preparatory" phase for taking Article 7 actions. The Commission first assesses whether there is a systemic threat to the rule of law in a specific country. It then sends a "rule-of-law opinion" to the Member State in question as a basis for dialogue to resolve the issue. If that Member State ignores the opinion, the Commission then issues a "rule-of-law recommendation" and monitors the country's follow-up. If it is ultimately unsatisfied with the country's response, the Commission may decide to activate Article 7.

The Framework's greatest shortcoming is that it offers little in the way of viable sanctions that can be used before the activation of Article 7. When Poland was investigated under the Framework in 2016, Prime Minister Szydło made it clear that her government was not worried about the inquiry.

---

[58] Case C-286/12, *Commission v. Hungary*, ECLI:EU:C:2012:687.

[59] Jan-Werner Müller, "Should the EU Protect Democracy and the Rule of Law Inside Member States," *European Law Journal* 21, no. 2 (March 2015): 148.

The Populist Backlash against Europe

Moreover, she did not shy away from expressing strong contempt toward Brussels' action, calling the investigation an "ideological threat" to Poland's national sovereignty.[60]

For now, it seems as though little can be expected from EU legal actions aimed at protecting the rule of law in Member States. Writing about "subnational authoritarianism," Daniel Kelemen argues that "legal levers alone are unlikely to safeguard democracy ... So long as political leaders are willing to put partisan interests above democratic values, they may allow ... autocracy to persist for decades within otherwise democratic political systems."[61] This holds true at the supranational (EU) and national (Member State) levels as well. It will take bold political action on the part of other EU Member States to defend core EU values more effectively.

IV FROM LEGAL TO ECONOMIC SANCTIONS?

Article 7 would likely be far more effective if it included the possibility of economic sanctions, which would weigh heavily on a country such as Hungary that is heavily dependent on EU structural funds. In 2012, Orbán declared that Hungary "will not be a colony" of the EU. But he had no qualms about signing a six-year budget agreement with the EU that will provide nearly $40 billion in aid for Hungary (whose annual GDP is $125 billion) between 2014 and 2020. Poland also benefits substantially from EU aid. On October 5, 2014, the *New York Times* reported that Poland (whose 2013 GDP was $518 billion), would receive a total of $318 billion in EU aid between 2008 and 2020. This is more than two times the present-day value of the Marshall Plan. The annual average accorded to each Marshall Plan recipient for four years was $2.5 billion. By 2020, Poland will be receiving $26.5 billion per year.

---

[60] Aleksandra Eriksson, "Poland Defies EU on Rule of Law," *EU Observer*, October 27, 2016, https://euobserver.com/news/135698. Afterwards, the Venice Commission – not an EU body, but a Council of Europe advisory group of constitutional experts – issued a draft opinion strongly criticizing the Polish government, and declaring that its actions "endanger not only the rule of law, but also the functioning of the democratic system." Council of Europe, Venice Commission, Opinion No. 833/2015, On Amendments to the Act of 25 June 2015 on the Constitutional Tribunal of Poland (March 11–12, 2016). But Szydło told the Polish media that the Venice Commission findings were not legally binding on Poland. See Jan Cienski and Maia de la Baume, "Poland's 'Rule of Law in Danger'," *Politico*, February 2, 2016, www.politico.eu/article/poland-kaczynski-szydlo-tribunal-constitution-crisis/.

[61] R. Daniel Kelemen, "Europe's Other Democratic Deficit: National Authoritarianism in a Democratic Union," *Government and Opposition* 52, no. 2 (April 2017): 211–238.

These aid deals should be a great source of leverage for the EU. Yet studies suggest that economic sanctions seldom work.[62] In the case of the EU, a big reason why "economic sanctions have fallen short in the past is that not all countries have complied. Indeed, significant differences of domestic opinion in the imposing country often undermine sanctions as well."[63] Therefore, future attempts at imposing economic sanctions should be backed by a strong regional consensus. In light of current events, however, achieving consensus is no small task. Even the EU institutions themselves have not agreed on a common language for the Hungarian and Polish cases. The EU's flawed approach to Hungary has already damaged the Union's political legitimacy, while the Eurozone crisis, the migration crisis, Brexit, and Russia's occupation of Crimea and other parts of Ukraine have left the EU more politically divided than ever before. Needless to say, in such a fragile union, consensus on sanctions may remain elusive.

Like other international organizations, the EU is more likely to exert pressure on a Member State when foreign interests are at stake; it is less likely to intervene over matters of domestic policy and "the internal functioning of democracy, such as curtailment of press freedoms, corruption in public administration, and the centralization of power in the hands of the ruling party,"[64] in part because it is in the EU's interest to maintain stability and also because the issue of national sovereignty is delicate. While the EU has made massive encroachments on the fiscal sovereignty of Member States (with the Fiscal Compact, the European Stability Mechanism, and the "Six Pack" and "Two Pack" legislation), it is more reluctant to impinge on national sovereignty when it comes to sensitive social or political matters. This contrast between fiscal and sociopolitical measures reflects the limits of EU integration toward a stronger political union. EU institutions and elites seem to lack the same enthusiasm and political will for protecting fundamental values such as democracy and the rule of law as they displayed for dealing with the Eurozone crisis.

---

[62] Gary Clyde Hufbauer, Jeffrey Schott, Kimberly Ann Elliott, and Barbara Oegg, *Economic Sanctions Reconsidered*, 3rd ed. (Washington, DC: Peterson Institute for International Economics, 2009).

[63] Kenneth Rogoff, "Do Economic Sanctions Work," *Project Syndicate*, January 2, 2015, www.project-syndicate.org/print/do-economic-sanctions-work-by-kenneth-rogoff-2015-1.

[64] Erin K. Jenne and Cass Mudde, "Hungary's Illiberal Turn: Can Outsiders Help?" *Journal of Democracy* 23, no. 3 (July 2012): 150.

V FROM SANCTIONS TO ALTERNATIVE ECONOMIC AND SOCIAL POLICIES

Instead of focusing only on sanctions, European political leaders should articulate a coherent alternative to the failed neoliberal economic policies of the last decade. What counts this time are sensible economic, social, and environmental policies promising to improve daily lives of European citizens. The EU needs to regain credibility by delivering simple and palpable benefits, such as good salaries, decent pensions, high-quality social services, and high environmental standards. In other words, it needs to improve what political theorists define as "output legitimacy."[65] Only an economic policy that promotes growth, better jobs, wages, and social inclusion can stem the nationalist tide. To prevent history from repeating itself, Europe must act now.

Since the beginning of the Eurozone crisis in 2009, governments across Europe have single-mindedly embraced fiscal austerity.[66] This has meant double-digit government spending cuts, and the elevation of the austerity paradigm spearheaded by German Chancellor Angela Merkel to an essentially "unbreakable law." The new Fiscal Compact, a treaty signed by all EU members except the United Kingdom and the Czech Republic, effectively outlaws the counter-cyclical economic policies espoused by Keynesianism, and establishes austerity and balanced budgets as the new fundamental principles of the EU constitutional order.[67] Lacking the unanimous support of all the Member States, the Fiscal Compact could not be adopted as an amendment to the EU Treaties. Instead, it took the form of a separate intergovernmental treaty, requiring ratification by at least twelve Eurozone members (Article 14 TSCG) to take effect. The Fiscal Compact was only the last in a series of constitutional and legislative measures adopted by EU political leaders with the intent to "solve" the Eurozone crisis.[68] As most of the other

---

[65] See Vivien Schmidt, "Democracy and Legitimacy in the European Union Revisited: Input, Output and Throughput," *Political Studies* 61, no. 1 (2013): 2-22.

[66] In this section I use a few parts from Bojan Bugarič and Matjaz Nahtigal, "The EU Fiscal Compact: Constitutionalization of Austerity and Preemption of Democracy in Europe," 2012, https://papers.ssrn.com/sol3/papers.cfm?abstract_id=2194475.

[67] Treaty on Stability, Coordination and Governance in the Economic and Monetary Union [hereinafter TSCG]. It was signed on March 2, 2012, and it entered into force on January 1, 2013, available at www.consilium.europa.eu/media/20399/st00tscg26_en12.pdf (not published in the OJEU). See Fintan O'Toole, "Treaty Seeks to Outlaw One Side of the Debate," *The Irish Times*, March, 6, 2012, www.irishtimes.com/opinion/treaty-seeks-to-outlaw-one-side-of-the-debate-1.476193.

[68] See contributions in Part I of this volume for a complete account of the legislative and constitutional changes enacted in response to the euro crisis.

measures initiated by the German-led, center-right coalition of political forces, the Fiscal Compact subscribed to a now-dominant economic "theory" of austerity that informs most of its rules. Namely, the main culprits for the euro crisis, according to this theory, are profligate governments and their public sectors. As a consequence, the only hope to discipline such "irresponsible" governments is to impose strict fiscal rules (balanced budgets) preventing the further increase of budget deficits and public debt.

The Fiscal Compact deviates from traditional EU values of democracy, institutional balance, and the equality of Member States.[69] It empowers European bureaucrats, judges, and bankers at the expense of European citizens. Instead of using an ordinary revision procedure for Treaty amendments (Article 48 TEU) or enhanced cooperation as provided for in Article 20 TEU and in Articles 326 to 334 TFEU, the Fiscal Compact was adopted outside the EU law, as a separate international treaty. As a consequence, it could bypass the more democratic and transparent procedure provided for in the EU law, in particular the participation of the European Parliament and national parliaments. Only Ireland put the Fiscal Compact to democratic debate, through a referendum, but it did so because of the requirements of the Irish constitution.[70] As an international treaty, the Fiscal Compact also side-stepped the independent judicial review, separation of powers, and respect for fundamental rights of EU law.[71] Furthermore, it entered into force when it was ratified only by twelve out of seventeen members of the Eurozone, which clearly deviates from the established consensual principles among the Member States. As Simon Hix, one of the leading experts on the EU political system, contends, any decision with significant redistributive consequences requires a strong sense of political legitimacy for the decision to be accepted by those to whom it applies. Given all of these flaws, therefore, it comes as no surprise that Hix concludes that the Fiscal Compact lacks

---

[69] Agustin Menendez, "Editorial: A European Union in Constitutional Mutation?." *European Law Journal* 20, no. 2 (March 2014): 127–41.

[70] Irish voters approved the Compact, but, as many commentators suggested, with a gun to their heads. Namely, Recital 25 of the Fiscal Compact makes access to financial assistance from the European Stability Mechanism, which Ireland needed at that time, conditional on the ratification of the Compact. As Andy Storey argues, in the Irish case the EU elites did almost everything to avoid a referendum in Ireland, including deliberately rewording the original text of the Compact. See Andy Storey, "The Vampire Treaty and the Irish Referendum," *Transnational Institute*, March 6, 2012, www.tni.org/en/article/vampire-treaty-and-irish-referendum.

[71] Lukas Oberndorfer, "The Fiscal Compact Bypasses Democracy and the Rule of Law," *Transnational Institute*, March 8, 2012, www.tni.org/en/article/the-fiscal-compact-bypasses-democracy-and-the-rule-of-law.

The Populist Backlash against Europe 495

political legitimacy.[72] Agustín José Menéndez, a prominent EU legal scholar, goes even further and argues that the Fiscal Compact is unconstitutional: "By taking fundamental decisions on the way European competences are organized and executed outside EU treaties, Member States are opting out of Union law. They are therefore undermining the integrity of EU law."[73]

Even more problematic are the substantive legal aspects of the Fiscal Compact. As recounted previously, the Compact, in essence, entrenches a certain economic theory at the level of constitutional law. Thus, for the first time in EU history, the EU constitution explicitly biases the content of decision-making in the direction of neoliberalism in the EU legal order; the new Austerity Union in the making does this in a more explicit and profound way, leaving almost no room for a discretionary fiscal policy to Member States.

While it is true that the Fiscal Compact mostly reproduces already existing provisions of EU law,[74] its importance should not be underestimated. The core provision of the Fiscal Compact (Article 3) contains a "structural budget deficit" rule that requires that the country's structural deficit not exceed 0.5 percent of GDP. To elaborate: Article 3 stipulates that the budgetary position of the general government of a Contracting Party shall be balanced or in

---

[72] "European Scrutiny Committee: Written Evidence Submitted by Simon Hix," UK Parliament website, last visited November 7, 2018, https://publications.parliament.uk/pa/cm201012/cmselect/cmeuleg/1817/1817we02.htm.

[73] Agustín José Menéndez, "The EU's Unconstitutional Treaties," *Politico*, June 27, 2012, www.politico.eu/article/the-eus-unconstitutional-treaties/.

[74] The legislative "Six Pack" and "Two Pack" preceded the adoption of the Fiscal Compact and were designed to enhance the surveillance of Member States' economic policies and to foster budgetary discipline. The Six Pack includes European Parliament and Council Regulation (EU) 1173/2011, On the Effective Enforcement of Budgetary Surveillance in the Euro Area, 2011 O.J. (L 306) 1; European Parliament and Council Regulation (EU) 1174/2011, On Enforcement Measures to Correct Excessive Macroeconomic Imbalances in the Euro Area, 2011 O.J. (L 306) 8; European Parliament and Council Regulation (EU) 1175/2011, Amending Council Regulation (EC) No 1466/97 on the Strengthening of the Surveillance of Budgetary Positions and the Surveillance and Coordination of Economic Policies, 2011 O.J. (L 306) 12; European Parliament and Council Regulation (EU) 1176/2011, On the Prevention and Correction of Macroeconomic Imbalances, 2011 O.J. (L 306) 25; Council Regulation (EU) 1177/2011, Amending Regulation (EC) No 1467/97 on Speeding up and Clarifying the Implementation of the Excessive Deficit Procedure, 2011 O.J. (L 306) 33; Council Directive 2011/85/EU, On Requirements for Budgetary Frameworks of the Member States, 2011 O.J. (L 306) 41. The Two Pack is composed of European Parliament and Council Regulation (EU) 472/2013, On the Strengthening of Economic and Budgetary Surveillance of Member States in the Euro Area Experiencing or Threatened with Serious Difficulties with Respect to Their Financial Stability, 2013 O.J. (L 140) 1; European Parliament and Council Regulation (EU) 473/2013, On Common Provisions for Monitoring and Assessing Draft Budgetary Plans and Ensuring the Correction of Excessive Deficit of the Member States in the Euro Area, 2013 O.J. (L 140) 11.

surplus. This is interpreted as the annual structural balance of the general government at its country-specific medium-term objective, as defined in the revised Stability and Growth Pact (SGP),[75] with a lower limit of a structural deficit (a deficit calculated using a cyclically adjusted budget balance corrected for one-off and temporary measures) of 0.5 percent of GDP at market prices (i.e. market price for sovereign debt). The aim of this "golden rule" of balanced budgets is to ensure stricter budgetary discipline among the EU governments. Another element of the Fiscal Compact is the so-called debt brake (*schuldenbremse*) contained in Article 4, modeled on the German constitutional provision that requires the federal government to reduce its structural deficit to 0.35 percent of GDP by 2016.[76] Under Article 4, Member States with government debt ratios in excess of 60 percent of GDP are to reduce their debt ratios in line with a numerical benchmark, which implies a decline of the amount by which their debt exceeds the threshold at a rate in the order of 1/20th per year over three years. Consequently, countries with a debt ratio exceeding 60 percent of GDP are subject to strict rules. The Fiscal Compact (following the Six Pack) makes it possible for the European Commission to open an excessive deficit procedure under Article 126 TFEU on the basis of the debt criterion. It also places compliance with its budgetary and other requirements under the jurisdiction of the European Court of Justice, which can fine countries up to 0.1 percent of their GDP if they do not transpose correctly the balanced budget rules. This jurisdiction represents an unprecedented constitutional intrusion, since the European Court of Justice has never had the power to interpret national constitutions of the Member States; the ECJ will be asked to decide on intricate issues of national constitutional law, which directly implicates the will of the people contained in national constitutions.[77]

---

[75] For a descriptive account of the original SGP rules and the subsequent reforms (2005–2011), see Antonio Estella, *Legal Foundations of EU Economic Governance* (Cambridge: Cambridge University Press, 2018), 134–157.

[76] No surprise then that one of the leading European legal journals, cynically referring to the statement of the CDU parliamentary leader Volker Kauder, entitled its editorial "The Fiscal Compact and the European Constitutions: Europe Speaking German," Leonard Besselink and Jan-Herman Reestman "Editorial: The Fiscal Compact and the European Constitutions: 'Europe Speaking German'," *European Constitutional Law Review* 8, no. 2 (2012): 1.

[77] Both Damian Chalmers and Agustin Menendez are highly critical of this new role for the European Court of Justice. See Damian Chalmers, "The ECJ Has Taken on Huge New Powers as Enforcer of Last Week's Treaty on Stability, Coordination and Governance. Yet Its Record as a Judicial Institution Has Been Little Scrutinized," *LSE European Blog*, March 7, 2012, http://blogs.lse.ac.uk/europpblog/2012/03/07/european-court-of-justice-enforcer/.

The Member State signatories are required to implement the Fiscal Compact with new provisions "of binding force and permanent character," preferably in their constitutions.[78] As a consequence, the economic theory of austerity will be constitutionalized on both the EU and national level; Keynesianism is ruled out precisely when it is most needed. Hence, the new Austerity Union will be almost impossible to change. The Fiscal Compact instrumentalizes national constitutional law for the benefit of the Union law "to a degree not seen before."[79] As Menéndez critically argues, national constitutions leave no room for the transfer of sovereignty to mere intergovernmental processes, yet this is precisely what has been accomplished through the Fiscal Compact and the introduction of constitutional amendments via the Fiscal Compact. The very choice of form is, according to Menéndez, a breach of national constitutional law,[80] and results in the amendment of the "pouvoir constituant" of the Member States.[81]

Beyond the form, as Antonio Estella argues, the new rules of EU economic governance (Fiscal Compact, Six Pack, and Two Pack) represent "an unprecedented turn to rigidity in the history of the evolution of the SGP."[82] The new rules restrict the fiscal policy of Member States even more so than the rules from before the euro crisis. The new rules strike "at the heart of the institutions of parliamentary democracy by dislocating as a matter of constitutional principle the budgetary autonomy of the Member States."[83] To put even more pressure on Member States, access to financial assistance under European Stability Mechanism (ESM)[84] is conditional on prior ratification of the Fiscal Compact. After the European Court of Justice ruling in the *Pringle* case,[85] where the Court basically constitutionalized the principle of strict conditionality contained in the ESM Treaty, countries seeking financial assistance from the ESM will be subjected to even more explicit forms of fiscal retrenchment imposed through the Memoranda of Understanding that struggling Member States have to "negotiate" with the Troika made up of the

---

[78] TSCG, art. 3, para. 2.
[79] Besselink and Reestman, "Editorial: The Fiscal Compact and the European Constitutions," 5.
[80] Menéndez, "The EU's Unconstitutional Treaties."
[81] Loïc Azoulai et al., "Another Legal Monster? An EUI Debate on the Fiscal Compact Treaty," Law 2012/09, EUI Working Papers, 12.
[82] Estella, *Legal Foundations of EU Economic Governance*, 170. For an overview of the implementation of the Fiscal Compact see Chapter 2.
[83] Besselink and Reestman, "Editorial: The Fiscal Compact and the European Constitutions," 1.
[84] ESM is the EU's major bailout mechanism, which was established in a separate international treaty and signed by the nineteen members of the Eurozone.
[85] Case C-370/12, *Pringle v. Ireland*, ECLI:EU:C:2012:756.

European Commission, the International Monetary Fund, and the European Central Bank.[86]

The Fiscal Compact has brought not only a deep intrusion into the fiscal maneuvering room of the Member States. It is also too rigid and too restrictive in terms of its budgetary and fiscal rules. Although many of its rules are ambiguous, that does not solve the problem of rigidity of its main "targets," i.e. rules on the allowed structural budget deficit and public debt. The European Macro Group – three European macroeconomic institutes: IMK from Düsseldorf, WIFO from Vienna, and OFCD from Paris – prepared a joint study on the impact of austerity measures reinforced by the Fiscal Compact. As the study shows,[87] few of the EU countries undergoing severe economic crisis are able to implement the rules without seriously undermining their prospects for future economic growth. Their detrimental effect can also be clearly seen from those countries that are used as role models for fiscal discipline. Switzerland, which first introduced the debt brake in 2003, today has indeed a very low debt-to-GDP ratio, but its levels of public investments are among the lowest in the developed world.[88] Germany, the main "exporter" of balanced budget rules and debt brakes also faces a critical lack of public investment in areas such as green energy and education.

It is no surprise that the EU's Austerity Union has been criticized from many quarters. At the height of the euro crisis, authors like Wolfgang Streeck, Fritz Scharpf, and Perry Anderson described the situation in bailout countries as sovereignty "on paper,"[89] an "occupation regime by the "Troika" [of the European Commission, International Monetary Fund, and European Central Bank],[90] and a Troika diktat regime "reminiscent of Austria in 1922, when the Entente, under League of Nations colors, posted a high commissioner to Vienna to run the economy."[91] Others have observed that both the management of the euro crisis and the Fiscal Compact have deepened the divide between the Union core and periphery in the Union. Damian Chalmers observes the differentiated impact of the Fiscal Compact on two different

---

[86] Estella, *Legal Foundations of EU Economic Governance*, 180.

[87] IMK, OFCE, and WIFO, "Fiscal Pact Deepens Euro Crisis – Joint Analysis of the Macro Group," March 2012, 20–23, www.boeckler.de/pdf/p_imk_report_71e_2012.pdf.

[88] Adam Tooze, "Germany's Unsustainable Growth; Austerity Now, Stagnation Later," *Foreign Affairs*, September/October 2012, www.foreignaffairs.com/articles/germany/2012-09-01/germany-s-unsustainable-growth.

[89] Wolfgang Streeck, "Markets and Peoples: Democratic Capitalism and European Integration," *New Left Review* 73 (January/February 2012): 63–71.

[90] Fritz Scharpf, "Monetary Union, Fiscal Crisis, and the Preemption of Democracy," LEQS Paper No. 36/2011, LSE Europe in Question Discussion Paper Series, May 2011.

[91] Perry Anderson, "After the Event," *New Left Review* 73 (January/February 2012): 49–61.

groups of countries: those few like Germany, Finland, Luxembourg, and Estonia who already have a balanced budget will not be particularly affected; and the overwhelming majority of others will face very demanding requirements.[92] Needless to say, countries like Greece, Portugal, and Spain may in fact, in the end, achieve their required deficit and debt targets but the costs are already prohibitively high. Greece, for example, a country ranked eighteenth according to the UN Human Development Index in 2008, is today on the verge of a humanitarian crisis. Even such pro-EU figures as Jacques Delors have fiercely criticized the Fiscal Compact. In a speech in the European Parliament, Delors referred to the Fiscal Compact as a gas factory ("usine a gaz").[93]

The problem is that this myopic austerity focus rests on a misdiagnosis of the euro crisis, has backfired economically, and has triggered grave social and economic repercussions in indebted countries.[94] Nevertheless, austerity remains the virtually unchallenged "official" EU economic doctrine. What Europe needs more than anything is a new anti-austerity coalition, focused on growth and social justice. Only a Europe willing to revert back to some basic Keynesian policies of economic stimulus, as the US government did at the outset of Barack Obama's presidency, combined with economic innovations that include much-needed investments in infrastructure, education, and social programs, can restore Europe to stability, and reverse its dangerous nationalist surge.

In order to achieve this objective, a fiscal and political Union might not be the best alternative. As Ashoka Mody convincingly explains, it is naïve to expect that only a further federalization of "incomplete" monetary Union could solve the accumulated problems of the Eurozone economies:

> Today many hope that, spurred by French President Emmanuel Macron's call for euro area reform, Merkel will work on repairing the euro area's architecture. Such a hope is illusory. Merkel is all too aware that any sign of financial generosity toward Europe will embolden the rebels within the CDU. Other northern nations have made clear that they will oppose calls on

---

[92] Damian Chalmers, "The European Redistributive State and a European Law of Struggle," *European Law Review* 18, no. 5 (2012): 678.

[93] Georgi Gotev, "Delors Points the Finger at Europe's 'Killers'," *EUROACTIV*, March 29, 2012, www.euractiv.com/section/elections/news/delors-points-the-finger-at-europe-s-killers.

[94] In an important study, three economists from the IMF argue that austerity policies can do more harm than good. Jonathan D. Ostry, Prakash Loungani, and Davide Furceri, "Neoliberalism Oversold?" *Finance and Development* 53, no. 2 (June 2016): 38–41; see also Paul de Grauwe and Yuemei Ji, "The Legacy of Austerity in the Eurozone," CEPS Commentary, October 4, 2013.

their taxpayers (Rutte 2018, Finance Ministers 2018). No euro area nation state is willing to cede its national parliament's sovereignty on fiscal matters. Policy decisions will remain disengaged from politics. Hence, even if new financial arrangements are engineered, it will be impossible to achieve accountability in euro area governance. Political tensions will continue to build.[95]

Instead of looking for "more Europe," Mody suggests, European leaders should shift their attention to domestic public rebellions.

For too long, euro area leaders have dismissed or denigrated the domestic public rebellions. This is a terrible mistake. However inchoate, and sometimes nationalistic and xenophobic, these rebellions have been, they convey an important message. In addition to the distress the euro directly inflicts, the single currency distracts European leaders' attention from where it ought to be directed: domestic priorities. Of special importance is strengthening human capital, a capability in which all southern euro area countries (and even some northern countries) are lagging behind world leaders. Investment in human capital is crucial to achieving greater equity and sense of fairness while helping to regain international competitiveness.

Put simply, European leaders must shift their efforts away from the ultimately impossible goal of making euro area governance more accountable and towards national domestic economic agendas that give hope to those who feel disenfranchised. If they fail to make this shift, domestic politics will continue to fragment, and as that happens, European politics will become ever more corrosive.[96]

Barry Eichengreen offers another economic explanation as to why only a renationalization of fiscal policy can stem the tide of European populism.[97] His core thesis is that the evidence for large cross-border spillovers of national fiscal policies is weak. At the same time, the core questions of fiscal policy – whom to tax, how to tax, and how much to tax – are one of the most sensitive political and social questions, which are quintessentially national prerogatives. When cross-country spillovers are small but national preferences differ, the

---

[95] Ashoka Mody, "The Euro Area's Deepening Political Divide," *Vox*, March 21, 2018, https://voxeu.org/article/euro-area-s-deepening-political-divide. Mody's arguments have been further elaborated in his magisterial study, Ashoka Mody, *Euro Tragedy: A Drama in Nine Acts* (New York: Oxford University Press, 2018). I would like to thank Peter Lindseth for this reference.

[96] Mody, "The Euro Area's Deepening Political Divide"; Mody, *Euro Tragedy*.

[97] Eichengreen, *The Populist Temptation*, 168–170. See also Barry Eichengreen, "The Euro's Narrow Path," *Project Syndicate*, September 11, 2017; Barry Eichengreen and Charles Wyplosz, "Minimal Conditions for the Survival of the Euro," *Vox*, March 14, 2016, https://voxeu.org/article/minimal-conditions-survival-euro.

best option is to leave the decision-making at the national level. He concludes: "For fiscal policy then, the appropriate reform is less Europe, not more Europe."[98]

Similarly, Vivien Schmidt notes that "the EU needs to give back to the member-states the flexibility they have had in the past to devise policies that work for them."[99] To this end, a more bottom-up and flexible reinterpretation of the rules of Eurozone governance is required: "[T]he Eurozone already has an amazing architecture of economic coordination, reaching into all the Eurozone ministries of finance and country economic experts. Why not use that coordination to ensure that countries themselves determine what works for their very specific economic growth models and varieties of capitalism?"[100] The existing framework of the European Semester,[101] redesigned in this way, could help Member States to get back on the path of sustainable growth. The fiscal councils could be supplemented by new competitiveness councils to act more as industrial policy councils rather than structural adjustment hawks; in Schmidt's words, "such a bottom-up approach is likely not only to promote better economic performance but also much more democratic legitimacy at the national level. This is because it would put responsibility for the country's economics back in national government's hands at the same time that it would encourage more legitimising deliberation at the EU level."[102] But in order to be redesigned in the suggested way, the European Semester would require simultaneous changes of SGP rules as well. As Mark Dawson argues, the European Semester "was envisaged as a measure to buttress and strengthen

[98] Eichengreen, *The Populist Temptation*, 169. An important precondition for such re-nationalization of fiscal policy is that banks be prevented from holding dangerous numbers of government bonds. However, for a critique of this argument see Dani Rodrik, "Does Europe Really Need Fiscal and Political Union," Project Syndicate, December 11, 2017, www.project-syndicate.org/commentary/separating-private-and-public-finance-in-europe-by-dani-rodrik-2017-12. See also Chapter 18, endorsing renationalization of fiscal policy.

[99] Vivien Schmidt, "How Should Progressives Respond to the EU's Many Crises and Challenges to Democracy?" *The Progressive Post*, April 3, 2017, https://progressivepost.eu/progressives-respond-eus-many-crises-challenges-democracy/.

[100] Schmidt, "How Should Progressives Respond to the EU's Many Crises and Challenges to Democracy?"

[101] The European Semester is a cycle of economic and fiscal policy coordination within the EU. It is part of the European Union's economic governance framework. Its focus is on the six-month period from the beginning of each year, hence its name – the "semester." During the European Semester, the Member States align their budgetary and economic policies with the objectives and rules agreed at the EU level. The legal basis for European Semester is the so-called Six Pack, European Parliament and Council Regulation 1175/2011. For a detailed analysis of the European Semester, see Chapter 3.

[102] Vivien Schmidt, "How Do Progressives Fight Back against Populism," *Social Europe*, April 4, 2017, www.socialeurope.eu/author/vivien-schmidt.

the Eurozone economy in particular and to recognise the need for heightened EU supervision of domestic budgets."[103] As a result, it is deeply embedded in the balanced budget fundamentalism of the SGP.[104]

However, none of these suggested reforms will work if the troubled countries remain overburdened by excessive debt and if they are left bereft of significant investment funds provided by banks or the state. For all this, the European Stability Mechanism is simply not enough. The EU needs to reinvent new forms of solidarity. As Schmidt suggests, new instruments such as Eurobonds, Europe-wide unemployment insurance, EU investment resources,[105] and an EU self–generated budget are needed. The first step in this direction was made in 2015 through the establishment of the European Fund for Strategic Investments (EFSI), part of the Investment Plan for Europe (the so-called Juncker Plan).[106] EFSI is an initiative launched jointly by the European Investment Bank and the European Commission to help overcome the current investment gap in the EU. However, as a recent study of the political economist Cornel Ban shows,[107] most EFSI loans and guarantees so far have gone to countries in a relatively strong economic position, with the exception of Italy and Spain, which at the time were undergoing steep recessions. In other words, Italy, Spain, France, Germany, and Poland received most of the loans, whereas the Baltic countries, Hungary, and Romania received dramatically less. As a result, "the countercyclical pattern looks quite patchy."[108]

One possible lesson to draw from this quite limited example of European "Keynesianism" is that the creation of a new anti-austerity coalition will not be an easy task. As Jeffrey Frieden and Stefanie Walter show, the outcome of the crisis has been quite unusual "because the costs of the crisis resolution have been borne almost exclusively by the debtor countries and taxpayers in the

---

[103] Mark Dawson, "New Governance and the Displacement of Social Europe: The Case of the European Semester," *European Constitutional Law Review* 14, no. 1 (2018): 196.

[104] For this point, see Dawson, "New Governance and the Displacement of Social Europe"; Francesco Costamagna, "National Social Spaces as Adjustment Variables in the EMU: A Critical Legal Appraisal," *European Law Journal* 24, no. 2–3 (May 2018): 163–190.

[105] For a critical assessment of the Juncker Plan (European Fund for Strategic Investments), see Cornel Ban, "Austerity Europe, Keynesian Europe: The Politics of Debt and Growth in Europe" (Unpublished, 2017).

[106] European Parliament and Council Regulation (EU) 2015/1017, On the European Fund for Strategic Investments, the European Investment Advisory Hub and the European Investment Project Portal and Amending Regulations (EU) No 1291/2013 and (EU) No 1316/2013, 2015 O.J. (169) 1.

[107] Ban, "Austerity Europe, Keynesian Europe: The Politics of Debt and Growth in Europe."

[108] Ban, "Austerity Europe, Keynesian Europe: The Politics of Debt and Growth in Europe."

Eurozone."[109] The rift between the debtor and creditor states that emerged as the consequence of this outcome implicates "powerful national interests and equally powerful particularistic special interests."[110] It is one thing to say that the survival of the Eurozone is in the interest of both groups of countries but quite another to persuade German, Dutch, Austrian, and other mostly Northern European surplus countries to agree to a more debtor-friendly version of adjustment policies.

What the EU needs is not only more financial resources but also new ideas about how to create more inclusive, diverse, and pluralistic European societies and economies. Here I agree with Aglietta, who argues:

> Integration in the absence of a Europe-wide development strategy succeeded only in concentrating industrial activity in the regions where it was already strong, while the periphery lost ground. To counter this slide into long-term stagnation will require a development project capable of relaunching innovation across the whole range of economic activities, driven by investment largely anchored at regional and local level, with a strong environmental component.[111]

If countless billions were found to prop up large European financial institutions, it is not implausible to think a small fraction of that sum could be devoted to such a development project. The future of the EU will be determined by the ability of European political forces and civil society to articulate and push forward alternative scenarios for such "possible Europes."[112]

Unfortunately, the politically weakened European mainstream parties – the traditional standard bearers of the post-World War II "embedded liberalism" consensus – are now on the defense. Instead of offering novel progressive solutions, the mainstream seems extremely vulnerable to the populist challenge coming both from the extreme right and extreme left. Instead of surrendering to the populists' false promises of quick fixes, the mainstream has to reinvent itself. It must respond to the social anxieties that are helping fuel nationalist populism. Populist leaders are promising better pensions, health care, and more jobs, an agenda that is winning over the abandoned working class communities that were once a stronghold of the European social democratic and other progressive parties. Leaders of socially oriented, pro-liberal parties can reverse the nationalist trend by returning the EU to its

---

[109] Jeffry Frieden and Stefanie Walter, "Understanding the Political Economy of the Eurozone Crisis," *Annual Review of Political Science* 20 (2017): 371–390.
[110] Frieden and Walter, "Understanding the Political Economy of the Eurozone Crisis," 386.
[111] Michel Aglietta, "The European Vortex," *New Left Review* 75 (May/June 2012): 36.
[112] Alain Supiot, "Possible Europes," *New Left Review* 57 (May/June 2009): 57–65.

initial role as the promoter of European solidarity and equality. Job training and "green" growth are just some of the possible public investments in this direction. As the Greece's humiliating defeat by the German-led austerity coalition illustrates, this will take a concerted, Europe-wide initiative.[113] If European democrats of various political colors do not start offering a more compelling agenda, Europe is on a dangerous political path.

[113] In summer 2015, the EU imposed harsh loan terms on Greece even though they were previously rejected by popular referendum.

18

The Democratic Disconnect, the Power-Legitimacy Nexus, and the Future of EU Governance

PETER L. LINDSETH

BY WAY OF INTRODUCTION, AN EFFORT AT "COMING TO TERMS" …

My assigned task with this contribution was to reflect on the democratic deficit as an aspect of EU governance. I feel compelled to begin, however, by suggesting, as I have elsewhere, that the very idea of a democratic deficit is a misnomer, and a deeply misleading one at that. Its wide usage reflects how difficult it has been for the standard discourse on the EU, even thoughtfully critical discourse, to 'come to terms' – both literally and figuratively – with the integration process as it actually is rather than as many hope it might be.[1]

The notion of a democratic deficit suggests that the EU's primary legitimacy challenge is supranational.[2] It purportedly results from a shortfall *within* EU institutions and processes, which are insufficiently democratic relative to the scope of power that the EU possesses. This deficit should therefore be

---

[1] For anyone who knows my work, shifting the conceptual vocabulary around European integration and its legitimation has long been a goal. See, e.g., Peter L. Lindseth, "Coming to Terms with Regulatory Power beyond the State," *Opinio Juris*, April 25, 2011, http://opiniojuris .org/2011/04/25/coming-to-terms-with-regulatory-power-beyond-the-state. My two best known interventions argue precisely along these lines: Peter L. Lindseth, *Power and Legitimacy: Reconciling Europe and the Nation-State* (Oxford: Oxford University Press, 2010) (arguing that the EU is "administrative, not constitutional"), and Peter L. Lindseth, "Democratic Legitimacy and the Administrative Character of Supranationalism: The Example of the European Community," *Columbia Law Review* 99, no. 3 (1999): 628–738. More recently, see Peter L. Lindseth, "The Perils of 'As If' European Constitutionalism," *European Law Journal* 22, no. 5 (2016): 696–718. This contribution builds on these and other of my writings cited in this chapter.

[2] The literature on the democratic deficit is obviously vast, and it also has a long history, typically being traced to David Marquand, *Parliament for Europe* (London: J. Cape, 1979), who is credited with coining the term. For more recent efforts to grapple with the question, see, e.g., Berthold Rittberger, *Building Europe's Parliament: Democratic Representation beyond the Nation-State* (Oxford: Oxford University Press, 2005); Daniel Innerarity, *Democracy in Europe: A Political Philosophy of the EU* (London: Palgrave Macmillan, 2018).

addressed through legal and institutional engineering at the supranational level (say, elections for the President of the European Commission, and powers over fiscal policy for the European Parliament). Reforms of this sort may be attractive for a whole range of instrumental and normative reasons. But the reality is that "deficit"-focused reforms of this type have consistently fallen short of providing genuinely democratic legitimation to the EU, at least in the proper sense of the term. Why is this so?

The reason is that the EU's specifically democratic challenge flows not from a "deficit" but from a "disconnect." The idea of disconnection better captures the dynamics at the heart of European governance, in which functional demands have compelled the delegation of regulatory power to supranational institutions even as the *experience* of democratic self-government has remained stubbornly national, or even subnational. The challenge from this perspective is to develop mechanisms to channel the more robust legitimacy of national institutions to the supranational level. European public law has come to rely on precisely this sort of mediated legitimacy, albeit often *sub silencio*, even as the dominant discourse has persistently, if wrongly, focused on fixes to the purported democratic deficit.

The sense of disconnection in European integration is actually quite typical of modern administrative governance, of which the EU is best understood as a supranational variant of the type. At its core, administrative governance (whether national or supranational) has involved the empowerment of technocratic regulatory institutions that operate beyond the confines of historically "constituted" bodies on the national level – legislative, executive, and judicial. Populists on both sides of the Atlantic seem to sense this feature intuitively; thus, when they target their ire against Washington or Brussels, they are in fact often expressing the same anti-elite, anti-technocratic animus.[3] But contrary to these increasingly vociferous critiques, the growth of modern administrative governance has in fact been a crucial innovation, creating relatively autonomous institutional capacities to address regulatory challenges that these same historically constituted bodies often proved ill-equipped to address on their own, whether within or beyond individual states. The core challenge has been to "maintain the connection" between the delegated regulatory power and

---

[3] And in turn they provide fertile ground for similarly inspired populist-political entrepreneurs. See, e.g., Philip Rucker and Robert Costa, "Bannon Vows a Daily Fight for 'Deconstruction of the Administrative State,'" *Washington Post*, February 23, 2017, www.washingtonpost.com/politics/top-wh-strategist-vows-a-daily-fight-for-deconstruction-of-the-administrative-state/2017/02/23/03f6b8da-f9ea-11e6-bf01-d47f8cf9b643_story.html; "Bannon Plan for Europe Populist 'Supergroup' Sparks Alarm," *BBC News*, July 23, 2018, sec. Europe, www.bbc.co.uk/news/world-europe-44926417.

national democratic and constitutional legitimacy in a historically recognizable sense.[4] Meeting that challenge has been essential to the sustainability of modern administrative governance, both national and supranational, over the long term.

From this perspective, the legitimacy challenge in the EU is best understood as a "new dimension to an old problem."[5] Despite the complexity of the resulting institutional apparatus, European integration in fact entails a classic agency-cost problem, to use the language of political economy.[6] This refers to the burden on the constitutional principal(s) to design mechanisms to ensure that the relatively autonomous administrative agent(s) exercise their delegated power consistent with the goals defined by the principal(s) rather than those preferred by the agent(s). This does not mean, of course, there are no *sui generis* dimensions in EU governance. Most importantly, European institutions must act as a peculiarly powerful kind of agent, whose core function is to overcome obstacles to effective coordination and cooperation among the principals themselves – i.e., the Member States. Whether in terms of rulemaking, enforcement, or adjudication, the EU exists to provide a set of supranational "pre-commitment" institutions (most prominently the Commission and the Court), whose purpose is to prevent "principal drift" among the Member States and thus to ensure the credibility of their mutual legal commitments to each other.

But therein lies the true rub with the EU as a form of supranational administrative governance. Policing the Member States' compliance with their legal commitments can often be intrusive and painful, in seeming derogation of sovereignty.[7] Normally, that intrusion can be justified in democratic terms if the supranational policing can reasonably be traced back to prior sovereign legal commitments. But if not – i.e., if the intrusion results from normative decisions made by the supranational institutions themselves – then the delegation is arguably being abused. In the worst case, what can occur is a full-blown "principal–agent inversion," in which the erstwhile agent

---

[4] On the need to "maintain the connection" in administrative governance, see Peter L. Strauss, "Formal and Functional Approaches to Separation-of-Powers Questions: A Foolish Inconsistency?" *Cornell Law Review* 72, no. 3 (1987): 493.

[5] Lindseth, "Democratic Legitimacy and the Administrative Character of Supranationalism," 630.

[6] See, e.g., Jonathan R. Macey, "Organizational Design and Political Control of Administrative Agencies," *Journal of Law, Economics, & Organization* 8, no. 1 (1992): 93–110.

[7] There is nothing, in principle, that excludes extending this policing function to a Member State's "rule of law" commitments under Article 2 TEU. That question, however, is not without complications, not least by virtue of the procedure specified in Article 7 TEU. In this regard, see Chapter 15.

claims the mantel of the principal in the system. This is the risk at the heart of what we might call the judicial analogue to the deficit mindset – the "as if" constitutionalism that has animated much of the jurisprudence of the European Court of Justice over several decades (a topic to which I will return at the end of this contribution).[8]

The EU's character as an agent of the Member States, as well as the democratic disconnect that inevitably flows from it, have had a direct bearing on a second overarching feature of EU governance that this contribution seeks to highlight: the "power-legitimacy nexus." This notion points to the fact that the nature of the EU's legitimacy (technocratic and administrative rather than robustly democratic and constitutional) also determines the scope of power that the EU can effectively exercise. There are, in other words, some things that an EU of a primarily technocratic and administrative character simply cannot do. This is not a normative claim (how the EU *should* be structured) but rather a sociological one (how the EU in fact *is*). The nexus helps us understand, most importantly, why the EU's supranational authority has remained almost entirely that of rule-setting and – to a lesser extent – enforcement, despite compelling demands for "more Europe" in numerous domains (and despite the "as if" constitutionalism of the European Court of Justice). The normative and regulatory powers of the EU are precisely what one finds allocated to technocratic and administrative bodies on the national level (even in the domain of fiscal discipline),[9] which in turn makes them amenable to delegation to technocratic and administrative bodies on the supranational level as well.

But there is one category of power that the EU, *qua* form of supranational administrative governance, has been unable to exercise consistent with the power-legitimacy nexus: the autonomous capacity to mobilize, in a compulsory and legitimate fashion, human and fiscal resources ("blood and treasure"). Even in an era of burgeoning administrative governance, genuinely constitutional bodies – most importantly national legislatures – have reserved compulsory mobilization powers to themselves in order to preserve the ultimately democratic character of the system. The transfer of such autonomous mobilization powers thus marks the democratic and constitutional Rubicon over which the EU has been unable to cross in a geopolitically or macroeconomically significant sense. It is for this reason that, in the crises of the last

---

[8] See Conclusion; see also Lindseth, "The Perils of 'As If' European Constitutionalism."

[9] See, e.g., Xavier Debrun, David Hauner, and Manmohan S. Kumar, "The Role for Fiscal Agencies," in *Promoting Fiscal Discipline*, eds. Manmohan S. Kumar and Teresa Ter-Minassian (Washington, DC: International Monetary Fund, 2007), 106–134.

decade, there has proven to be "a line in the sand beyond which only governments can set priorities and act."[10] Whatever the flaws and limitations of national forms of self-government (and there are many), they remain the focal points of democratic and constitutional legitimacy with regard to the crucial function of legitimate compulsory resource mobilization. Any effort to address the democratic legitimacy challenge in the EU must start from this basic reality.

The purpose of the remainder of this contribution is to offer some further thoughts on how the democratic disconnect and power-legitimacy nexus have shaped, and may continue to shape, the law and governance of European integration. Section I explores the role of democracy and identity in the evolution of European integration, offering a theoretical framework for why the lack of the latter has inhibited the development of the former. This discussion inevitably requires us to confront anew the "no-demos" problem in the EU,[11] which, when viewed in conjunction with a set of concepts drawn from the sociology of Pierre Bourdieu ("habitus" and "hysteresis"),[12] help us better appreciate the institutional consequences of the democratic disconnect and power-legitimacy nexus in the integration context. Section II then examines how the disconnect and nexus have made themselves felt in the development of European integration over the past decade of crisis. The focus here is on both the persistence of national resource mobilization and nationally mediated legitimacy in maintaining the connection between supranational regulatory power and national democratic and constitutional bodies in the process of European integration.

Section III then turns to more recent calls for reform. It considers whether, in view of the evident functional advantages of "Europeanizing" resource mobilization powers, the EU could be on the verge of a dramatic democratic and constitutional transformation. Such a transformation is never entirely out of the question, of course, but at this stage in integration skepticism still seems to be in order. Unless there is a rare confluence of functional, political, and cultural factors giving rise to what the historical-institutionalist literature calls a "critical juncture"[13] (also not out of the question), the more likely scenario is continued incremental changes that are nonetheless constrained by the democratic disconnect and power-legitimacy nexus. This reality also has a

---

[10] Jean Pisani-Ferry, "Whose Economic Reform?" *Project Syndicate*, July 30, 2013, www.project-syndicate.org/commentary/the-purpose-and-strategy-of-structural-reofrm-by-jean-pisani-ferry.

[11] See Notes 16–27 and accompanying text.

[12] See Notes 28–29 and accompanying text.

[13] See Notes 58–59 and accompanying text.

510   *Peter L. Lindseth*

bearing, moreover, on the "as if" constitutionalism that animates the jurisprudence of the European Court of Justice. The Conclusion argues that, even as the Court must fulfil a crucial role in upholding the rule of law, it too should take cognizance of the democratic disconnect and the power-legitimacy nexus. As such, it should avoid overly entrenched readings of the Member State commitments in the Treaties, striving instead to create a greater space for national and intergovernmental politics in defining the ultimate contours of the integration project going forward.

I DEMOCRACY AND IDENTITY IN THE EVOLUTION OF EUROPEAN INTEGRATION

With every episode of Euroskepticism, beginning with the difficult ratification of the Maastricht Treaty in 1992–1993, and continuing through the rise of anti-EU political parties over the last decade, a typical response has been to try to "democratize" the EU. In recent years, efforts along these lines have included giving the European Parliament more powers in fiscal matters and institutionalizing the so-called *Spitzenkandidaten* process, through which parties run in elections for the European Parliament based on a candidate for the presidency of the European Commission.[14] I would suggest, however, that the question we really need to be asking ourselves is whether, and in what way, reforms of this nature are in fact "democratizing." It is not hard to see how they could be democratizing *in form*, in that they would establish an electoral linkage between EU institutions and a European electorate. But should we automatically equate this kind of electoral legitimacy with specifically democratic legitimacy? Put another way, would these reforms also be democratizing *in substance*?

There is considerable room for doubt on this last question, although the issue is a deeply delicate one, precisely because of some of the more objectionable features of the populist resurgence in Europe in recent years.[15] To get a sense of why this is so (both in terms of "doubt" and "delicateness"), it is necessary to return to the longstanding debate on whether there exists a European identity and what is in fact its relationship to "democratic" reform.

Democracy, as Robert Dahl long ago reminded us, is not just a question of constructing mechanisms of representation through which an electorate

---

[14] For an account of the emergence of the *Spitzenkandidaten* process, see Chapter 6.
[15] For a succinct overview as well as proposed policy responses, see Chapter 17.

(however randomly defined) is allowed to select those elected to govern the polity.[16] The more difficult, and antecedent, question is always whether and to what extent that electorate *experiences itself* as a "demos" (as in *demos-kratia*, or "rule by the people"). It is only within the confines of such a demos-legitimate polity, Dahl suggested, that the power of the majority to rule over the minority can operate without that rule being resisted as domination by an "other."

This issue of self-rule versus rule by an "other" should not, in other words, be seen as solely a populist concern. Populists abuse the idea of democracy by infecting it with an anti-pluralist virus, according to which only a subset of the population is genuinely representative of the demos (which is itself narrowly defined). But even for those of us who try live by a much more pluralist and inclusive conception of representation, the challenge of demos-legitimacy remains unavoidable. Dahl rightly stressed that, for representative institutions to be experienced as demos-legitimate, neither the electorate nor the broader polity can be some random assemblage. Neil MacCormick, for example, in a manner quite consistent with Dahl, also recognized that democratic legitimacy is tied to the sense that a particular political community, as a collectivity, sees itself as *"entitled* to effective organs of political self-government"[17] through institutions that the community constitutionally established for this purpose. As MacCormick further taught us, a demos need not be grounded in exclusionary ethnic, religious, or linguistic affinities; indeed, a demos-legitimacy can also be "civic" even as it still must be grounded in a "historical" and indeed "cultural" experience for a particular community.[18]

We can at this point usefully turn to Lincoln, focusing on the threshold criterion of democracy as defined in *The Gettysburg Address*: *"of* the people." The EU governance literature has long focused on *"by* the people" (input legitimacy) and *"for* the people" (output legitimacy)[19] but has arguably paid

---

[16] Robert Dahl, "Can International Organizations Be Democratic? A Skeptic's View," in *Democracy's Edges*, eds. Ian Shapiro and Casiano Hacker-Cordón (London; New York: Cambridge University Press, 1999), 19–36. For the classic effort to translate this concern into the European context, see J. H. H. Weiler, "Does Europe Need a Constitution? Demos, Telos and the German Maastricht Decision," *European Law Journal* 1, no. 3 (1995): 219–258.

[17] Neil MacCormick, *Questioning Sovereignty: Law, State, and Nation in the European Commonwealth* (New York: Oxford University Press, 1999), 173.

[18] MacCormick, 169–174.

[19] See, e.g., Vivien A. Schmidt, *Democracy in Europe: The EU and National Polities* (New York: Oxford University Press, 2006), 21–22; Fritz W. Scharpf, *Governing in Europe: Effective and Democratic?* (New York: Oxford University Press, 1999).

insufficient attention to "*of* the people" (demos legitimacy) and its ramifications.[20] As Dahl's work suggests, the representatives emerging out of a putatively democratic electorate and polity must themselves be seen as "of" a people/demos. The existence of some common form of identity, even if civic in a MacCormick sense, is necessary both as to the *formation* of a demos-legitimate polity as well as to the sense of *connection* between the elected and the electorate that gives the governing institutions a specific sense of democratic legitimacy.

Of course, one could fairly point out at this stage that the EU is not just some random assemblage. The process of European integration emerged out of a terrible and shared experience of violence and destruction between 1914 and 1945 (and, of course, tracing further back as well). This in turn led postwar Europeans to seek ways of governance in common that might transcend the pathologies of nationalism. Over the last nearly seventy years, one could say, European society has made great strides along the specifically democratic dimension of polity and identity formation, at least to the point of forging a strong secondary European identity on top of a primary national identity. (Brexit has arguably helped in this process, by demonstrating to the European public the overall benefits of the integration project, given the serious costs Britain is incurring by departing.) From this perspective, one might fairly dismiss my analysis to this point as simply trying to tee up just another "no-demos" argument for why there can *never* be European integration, something defied by the progress in integration to date.

That reaction would be understandable, if clearly misdirected in this instance. The claim that there exists a broad-based European identity, even a "secondary" one, sufficient to sustain democratic legitimacy at the EU level is unfortunately belied by detailed studies in economic and political sociology.[21] These strongly suggest that European identity is stronger among the more mobile upper-middle echelons of society rather than the left-behinds who have provided the foot soldiers for the populist resurgence. It is no doubt true that the so-called no-demos thesis has often been used to support some of the most rejectionist and retrograde positions on integration, not merely populist but also extreme nationalist and illiberal, which all share a fundamental anti-pluralism.[22] But the mere fact that such positions have gained

---

[20] Peter L. Lindseth, "Of the People: Democracy, the Eurozone, and Lincoln's Threshold Criterion," *Berlin Journal*, no. 22 (2012): 4–7.

[21] See, e.g., Neil Fligstein, *Euroclash: The EU, European Identity, and the Future of Europe* (New York: Oxford University Press, 2008).

[22] See Jan-Werner Müller, *What Is Populism?* (Philadelphia: University of Pennsylvania Press, 2016).

greater political traction over the past decade raises serious concerns regarding the state of European identity and its capacity to support greater integration.[23]

In any case, rejectionism – the "never" version of no-demos – is not my position. As my own early intervention into the no-demos debates of the 1990s tried to make clear,[24] just because the EU as yet lacks demos-legitimacy (and hence democratic and constitutional legitimacy in its own right) does not mean that it is *illegitimate*. Rather, it means that it is *differently* legitimate (i.e. as a supranational extension of administrative governance), with a different set of powers commensurate with its ultimately administrative character. The EU is more a 'demoi-cracy' – an assemblage of multiple demoi seeking to achieve goals in common through supranational institutions functionally established for this purpose.[25] A demoi-cratic EU may be useful for certain things but not others, just as the power-legitimacy nexus suggests. Such a Europe remains "a community of projects, not a community of identity," as Kalypso Nicolaïdis once succinctly put it.[26] This reality compels us to take cognizance of how the EU (as yet) lacks its own democratic and constitutional legitimacy, and that *at this stage* such legitimacy is still distributed primarily *among* the several Member States, which is something "deeply rooted in the history of [the European] continent."[27]

We must therefore recognize that the lack of a European democratic identity poses a barrier to the sort of "deficit"-focused institutional engineering that one might see as essential to the evolution of integration in response to crisis. Identity – regardless of its normative content – operates as a kind of "habitus" in the way Bourdieu developed that concept.[28] That is, it serves as a historically constructed (and hence evolving) interpretive framework through which the legitimacy of polities and their corresponding forms of rule are judged and perhaps even resisted. Like Bourdieu, we can call this resistance effect "hysteresis,"[29] borrowing a concept from the natural sciences, where it is

---

[23] Even before the onset of crisis, as two leading commentators had noted, Europe had seemed to enter a period of "constraining dissensus." See Liesbet Hooghe and Gary Marks, "A Postfunctionalist Theory of European Integration: From Permissive Consensus to Constraining Dissensus," *British Journal of Political Science* 39, no. 1 (2009): 1.

[24] Lindseth, "Democratic Legitimacy and the Administrative Character of Supranationalism."

[25] Peter L. Lindseth, "Equilibrium, Demoi-cracy, and Delegation in the Crisis of European Integration," *German Law Journal* 15, no. 4 (2014): 529–567.

[26] Kalypso Nicolaïdis, "We, the Peoples of Europe . . .," *Foreign Affairs* 83, no. 6 (2004): 102.

[27] Giandomenico Majone, *Dilemmas of European Integration: The Ambiguities and Pitfalls of Integration by Stealth* (New York: Oxford University Press, 2005), 173.

[28] See generally Pierre Bourdieu, *The Logic of Practice* (Cambridge: Polity Press, 1990).

[29] See generally Cheryl Hardy, "Hysteresis," in *Pierre Bourdieu: Key Concepts*, ed. Michael James Grenfell, 2nd ed. (New York: Routledge, 2014), 131–148.

514 *Peter L. Lindseth*

used to describe dynamic systems whose outputs are time-dependent on present and past inputs.[30] Or we could describe it as a collective analogue to "reactance" in individuals,[31] the term used by social psychologists to refer to the refusal to accept what is perceived as domination by an "other."

Integration may well overcome these effects eventually: that is, when or if Europeans develop the necessary demos-legitimacy and begin to experience democratic self-government in supranational terms. But until that time, Europeans will likely need to "reconcile" (i.e. interpret) shifts in forms of rule consistent with conceptions of legitimacy inherited from the past.[32] It is within this historical dynamic of reconciliation, operating against the complex background of democracy and identity, that the democratic disconnect and the power-legitimacy nexus show their effects in the process of institutional change. Even as functional pressures seem to have persistently favored "more Europe," robust legitimacy tied to national institutions has acted as a clear counterweight to these functional pressures. This still-robust national legitimacy (particularly over the last decade of crisis, as we shall see in Section II) has both defined political interests and shaped discourses in favor of a more incremental approach.

II THE DISCONNECT, NEXUS, AND MOBILIZATION CONSTRAINTS IN THE EU'S DECADE OF CRISIS

In the period of multiple crises over the last ten years, the democratic disconnect and power-legitimacy nexus have manifested themselves, most importantly, in the persistence of national resource mobilization as a cornerstone of EU governance. Although there are increasingly insistent calls for change (which Section III explores), this essential reality has shown itself to be remarkably resilient. That hardly means, of course, that the last decade has been without incremental steps in reinforcing the integration process. There have been numerous strides made in terms of either deeper coordination (e.g. in defense and security), legislative and regulatory harmonization (e.g. in asylum policy), supranational capacity building (e.g. in controlling external

---

[30] The concept now has a wide range of applications across several scientific fields (notably physics) as well as engineering and economics. See generally Mark A. Krasnosel'skii and Aleksei V. Pokrovskii, *Systems with Hysteresis* (Berlin: Springer, 1989).

[31] See Sharon S. Brehm and Jack W. Brehm, *Psychological Reactance: A Theory of Freedom and Control* (New York: Academic Press, 1981).

[32] For more on this historical dynamic of reconciliation, see, e.g., Peter L. Lindseth, "Reconciling with the Past: John Willis and the Question of Judicial Review in Inter-War and Post-War England," *The University of Toronto Law Journal* 55, no. 3 (2005): 657–689.

Democratic Disconnect, Power-Legitimacy Nexus & the Future   515

frontiers), as well as, perhaps most importantly, in intensified supranational surveillance of Member State action (e.g. in the fiscal domain). Even if these strides are significant, however, none entails any major shift in legitimate compulsory mobilization powers to the EU, consistent with what the power-legitimacy nexus predicts.

Let's begin with fiscal capacity. The EU budget remains roughly 1 percent of the Member States' aggregated Gross National Income (GNI), and only a small portion of that is derived from the EU's "own resources" (and even those "own resources" are in fact collected nationally, via customs duties as well as a small percentage of the VAT). In other words, there is no EU tax collection service that "wears the EU badge," so to speak, operating on the basis of the EU's own autonomous tax-collection legitimacy rather than that of the Member States. As for the remainder of the EU's budget, it is based almost entirely on politically negotiated Member State contributions in the seven-year framework, which are obviously derived from resources mobilized nationally.

Given these limited (or, perhaps more accurately, nonexistent) mobilization capacities at the EU level, the various crises of the last ten years have forced European elites to be creative in leveraging the EU's budget toward more ambitious goals, generally by way of loan guarantees.[33] At the outset of the Eurozone crisis, the EU used the guarantee model to support the European Financial Stabilisation Mechanism (EFSM), the initial emergency lending program of up to €60 billion, which was backed by an implicit guarantee in the EU budget.[34] The EU later used the same approach in the European Fund for Strategic Investment (EFSI) – the cornerstone of the so-called Juncker Plan in 2015 to stimulate spending on infrastructure projects – which built on an explicit €16 billion guarantee fund in the EU budget to support lending via the European Investment Bank (EIB).[35]

Beyond the EU's own budget, the historic model has been for the Member States, on an intergovernmental basis, to mobilize any needed fiscal resources to provide capital, e.g., for such institutions as the EIB, a body collectively owned by the Member States. This same model was used to establish the

---

[33] For further discussion of these EU budgetary developments, see Chapter 2; and Chapter 4.

[34] The actual mechanics of the guarantee is explained in the Communication from the Commission, *On the European Financial Stabilisation Mechanism*, COM (2010) 713 final (November 30, 2010).

[35] European Parliament and Council Regulation 2015/1017, On the European Fund for Strategic Investments, the European Investment Advisory Hub and the European Investment Project Portal and Amending Regulations (EU) No 1291/2013 and (EU) No 1316/2013, 2015 O.J. (L 169) 1.

European Stability Mechanism (ESM), perhaps the most important institutional innovation in the context of the Eurozone crisis. The ESM uses the combined capital contributions from the Member States as backing for issuing its bonds, the proceeds of which are then loaned at politically determined interest rates, subject to strict conditionality, to Member States that otherwise lack access to the credit markets.

In a similar vein, nationally mobilized resources have also provided the necessary start-up funding to the Single Resolution Fund (SRF), a key component of the Single Resolution Mechanism (SRM) within the European Banking Union. The SRF is being gradually built up over eight years, based on contributions from financial institutions. But in the interim, participating Member States are providing the necessary bridge financing for bank resolution under the terms of an intergovernmental agreement,[36] augmented more recently by the ESM as a further "backstop."[37] Along similar lines, the Member States are working toward a Cooperative Financial Mechanism, or CFM, to provide funding for joint military projects (this is distinct from the much smaller "European Defence Fund" established by the Commission within the EU budget to support Member State coordination efforts).[38] The CFM is expected to be funded by voluntary contributions from the participating Member States, which will remain joint owners of the fund themselves.[39]

Beyond these recent initiatives (all of which show continued dependence on national mobilization of fiscal resources), there continues to be the near total absence of any autonomous mobilization of human resources in the EU

---

[36] See generally "Single Resolution Mechanism- Consilium," European Council website, last visited March 17, 2018, www.consilium.europa.eu/en/policies/banking-union/single-resolution-mechanism/. One commentator has criticized the choice of an intergovernmental agreement as being based on a flawed legal argument that EU regulations cannot impose financial obligations on the states. See Federico Fabbrini, "On Banks, Courts and International Law: The Intergovernmental Agreement on the Single Resolution Fund in Context," *Maastricht Journal of European and Comparative Law* 21, no. 3 (2014): 444–463. However, regardless of whether flawed or not, the fact that the argument was deemed adequate to the Member States to justify their approach is *itself* a manifestation of the power-legitimacy nexus in action.

[37] The use of the ESM to further supplement the SRF, if needed, was made at the Euro Summit Meeting of June 29, 2018; see www.consilium.europa.eu/media/35999/29-euro-summit-statement-en.pdf. However, "the leaders backed the German view that the ESM can only play that role from 2020 and only if risks in the banking sector fall so much that ESM help would not be needed." "EU Leaders See Bigger ESM Role, but Budget, Deposit Insurance on Hold," *Reuters*, June 29, 2018, www.reuters.com/article/us-eu-summit-euro/eu-leaders-see-bigger-esm-role-but-budget-deposit-insurance-on-hold-idUSKBN1JP2CY.

[38] European Commission Press Release IP/17/1508, A European Defence Fund: €5.5 Billion per Year to Boost Europe's Defence Capabilities (June 7, 2017).

[39] See Robin Emmott, "As Britain Steps Aside, EU States to Negotiate Joint Defence Fund," *Reuters*, May 18, 2017, http://uk.reuters.com/article/uk-eu-defence-idUKKCN18E1Y6.

Democratic Disconnect, Power-Legitimacy Nexus & the Future 517

in policing or defense. For example, Europol[40] and the European Defence Agency (EDA) have relatively limited, albeit growing, staffs, and both institutions play important coordinating roles (and the latter, working with the EIB, will also play a supportive role in getting the CFM off the ground).[41] But in terms of actual policing or defense, neither body exercises coercive power directly, whether internally or externally; rather, this authority – and legitimacy – still resides almost entirely at the Member State level (an analogue to the lack of an EU tax collection service in the fiscal domain).

Frontex, which was re-established in 2015 as the European Border and Coast Guard Agency in response to the migration crisis, may prove to be a modest exception to this rule.[42] Its expanding powers include, *inter alia*, deployment of teams for joint operations with Member States as well as rapid interventions where a Member State's border control proves deficient and an urgent need for EU assistance exists. This is an important if small step in the development of the EU's coercive policing powers, leading the agency's chief to say in a recent interview: "I would not object if you define us as a law enforcement agency at EU level."[43]

Falling short of powers of fiscal and human mobilization but still crucial to European governance are the core regulatory powers of supranational authority – i.e., setting rules of general and prospective application, as well as adjudication. Here, too, the power-legitimacy nexus makes itself felt, reflected in the dependence of this supranational regulatory power on mechanisms of national oversight and intermediation that channel the Member States' more robust democratic and constitutional legitimacy to the EU level.[44] Most importantly, the EU has long depended on the involvement of national executives – whether via the Council of Ministers in its various formations or the European Council assembling heads of state or government themselves – in order to establish a connection between supranational action and historically constituted representative government on the national level. These intergovernmental fora have been especially important during the crises of the last decade, along with the so-called Eurogroup, comprised of Eurozone

---

[40] For a detailed description of Europol's functions, see Chapter 10.
[41] See "European Defence Agency and European Investment Bank Sign Cooperation Agreement," February 28, 2018, www.eda.europa.eu/info-hub/press-centre/latest-news/2018/02/28/european-defence-agency-and-european-investment-bank-sign-cooperation-agreement.
[42] For a discussion of EU asylum policy and border control, including Frontex, see Chapter 8.
[43] Nikolaj Nielsen, "Frontex: Europe's New Law Enforcement Agency?" *EU Observer*, February 22, 2018, https://euobserver.com/justice/141062.
[44] On the historic evolution of this "mediated legitimacy" in the EU, see Lindseth, *Power and Legitimacy: Reconciling Europe and the Nation-State*.

finance ministers. Moreover, beyond national executives, national high courts have taken notice of expanding supranational regulatory powers, and this scrutiny has intensified in the decade of crisis. Several national high courts have asserted the right to engage in review of supranational action, even if a highly deferential one, in a way designed to balance integration's imperatives against the need to preserve the autonomous democratic and constitutional character of national institutions.[45] Similarly, national parliaments have become more assertive as well, whether as to scrutiny of actions of their own governments at the EU level or of the action of the EU itself, including, most importantly, in monitoring the implementation of the principle of subsidiarity.[46]

If we understand EU public law to encompass its foundations at the national level (as we certainly must), then we can perceive in these developments the continuing convergence of EU public law around the legitimating structures and normative principles of the "postwar constitutional settlement of administrative governance."[47] The point of such mechanisms is, as noted, to maintain the connection between supranational regulatory power and national democratic and constitutional legitimacy. The aim is also, as noted, reconciliation; that is, they are designed to allow supranational delegation to proceed while seeking to preserve some semblance of national democracy in a historically recognizable sense.[48]

My own work has termed this "mediated legitimacy" but one could just as well call it, as another commentator has aptly put it, the EU's "parasitic legitimacy" on the democratic and constitutional orders of the Member States.[49] Regardless of the term we use, these two elements in combination – nationally grounded resource mobilization and nationally mediated legitimacy – point to the character of EU governance as ultimately derivative

---

[45] See, most famously, but hardly exclusively, the decisions of the German Federal Constitutional Court; most recently, Bundesverfassungsgericht, Judgment 2 BvR 2728/13 of June 21, 2016, www.bverfg.de/e/rs20160621_2bvr272813.html. As the German Court further noted, a "large majority of constitutional and supreme courts of the other Member States" shares its understanding of the need, in extremis, for some form of national judicial review of supranational action as a means of reconciling European integration with national democracy. See Judgment 2 BvR 2728/13, para. 142 (surveying the case-law).

[46] For an overview, Peter L. Lindseth, "National Parliaments and Mediated Legitimacy in the EU: Theory and History," in *National Parliaments after the Lisbon Treaty and the Euro Crisis: Resilience or Resignation?* ed. Davor Jančić (Oxford: Oxford University Press, 2017), 37–57.

[47] Lindseth, *Power and Legitimacy: Reconciling Europe and the Nation-State.*

[48] See Note 32 and accompanying text.

[49] Kaarlo Tuori, *European Constitutionalism* (Cambridge: Cambridge University Press, 2015), 3–4, 42.

and delegated (i.e. administrative), operating on behalf of multiple constitutional principals in the various Member States. That character is not – or at least is not yet – autonomously democratic and constitutional in its own right, precisely in line with what the democratic disconnect and the power-legitimacy nexus would predict.

Nowhere have the disconnect and nexus manifested themselves more clearly than in the EU's role in responding to the Eurozone crisis. It is no doubt true that the adoption of the Six Pack, Two Pack, and Fiscal Compact seemingly curtailed the power of national parliaments in their core legislative prerogatives – taxing, spending, and borrowing. These powers are now subject to fiscal and macroeconomic surveillance enforced by supranational institutions, most importantly the European Commission, via the so-called European Semester. In this way, the traditional pre-commitment method of integration has cut ever closer to the rights of national parliaments in the mobilization of fiscal resources. Nonetheless, this surveillance has not really altered the nature of the EU's pre-commitment system in any fundamental respect. The EU has remained almost entirely dependent on national parliaments to exercise powers of legitimate compulsory mobilization in order to give the necessary material backing to the regulatory system that integration creates. This is true even in Greece, where the perpetual drama over the last decade has been whether the EU or the Troika could persuade or compel the Greek parliament to take decisions that only a national parliament has the power and legitimacy ultimately to take.

This is the paradox of conditionality as a mode of supranational governance. The EU and the other Member States have been able to set conditions on assistance but they could not displace national bodies; they must still depend on the power and legitimacy of the particular national parliament in question, even in an atmosphere of extreme crisis. The reason for this ultimate dependence, I would suggest, is that the management of the many crises confronting the EU this past decade, at a micro level, has required not simply regulatory power but, more importantly, capacities of legitimate compulsory mobilization that only the Member States possess. The EU has been forced to rely on a strategy whereby nearly all essential costs – political and economic – have been borne internally, by the individual states. This is especially true of so-called bailout programs, a misnomer to be sure. While the Member States have financed mechanisms to make loans on favorable terms, those loans have been subject to strict conditionality and have also remained on the books of the debtor country, becoming part of the debtor country's debt burden going forward.

Undoubtedly, the crises of the past decade have required a good deal of cross-border coordination. But that coordination has, more often than not, been intergovernmental, via the Eurogroup or the Council, rather than supranational, via the EU's two pre-commitment institutions *par excellence*: the Commission and the Court of Justice. Among the main exceptions has, of course, been the crucial role played by the European Central Bank (ECB); however, the ECB's sometimes heroic role in monetary policy (for example, in the programs collectively known as "Quantitative Easing") has been driven by *the incapacity* of the EU, combined with the *unwillingness* of the Member States, to mobilize *fiscal* resources on a coordinated, supranational scale commensurate with the demands of the crisis.[50] This has been true even as Member States have tried to intensify supranational surveillance of national actors, whether in imposing fiscal discipline in the Eurozone, compelling creditor bail-ins in bank resolutions, or attempting to force compliance with the Common European Asylum System during the refugee crisis, just to name a few examples (several of which are dealt with elsewhere in this volume). Supranational institutions have provided useful means of implementing mobilization decisions among the Member States, but the key drivers of decision-making have necessarily been the Member States themselves, because that is where the locus of power and legitimacy ultimately lies.

In this sense, the decade of crisis has forced advocates of intensified European integration to recognize the limits of technocracy and also see the essential role of a kind of "high politics." But before we begin to think that this is a new phenomenon, we should take a look back at other key junctures in the history of European integration to realize that it has arguably been "ever thus." This key national role was true even at the outset of the integration process itself. Postwar functionalists had hoped that supranational technocratic bodies could effectively operate without "some over-all *political authority*" above them.[51] In keeping with this aspiration, the Schuman Declaration originally envisioned a similar autonomous model for the High Authority, only to see the Member States insist (successfully) on the creation of a Council of Ministers in the negotiations leading to the Treaty of Paris.[52] As Alan Milward's magisterial historical work has demonstrated, European

---

[50] Peter L. Lindseth, "Power and Legitimacy in the Eurozone: Can Integration and Democracy Be Reconciled?" in *The Constitutionalization of European Budgetary Constraints*, eds. Maurice Adams, Federico Fabbrini, and Pierre Larouche (Oxford: Hart Publishing, 2016), 379–398.

[51] David Mitrany, *A Working Peace System: An Argument for the Functional Development of International Organization*, 4th ed. (London: National Peace Council, 1946), 45 [emphasis in original].

[52] See Peter L. Lindseth, "Transatlantic Functionalism: New Deal Models and European Integration," *Critical Analysis of Law* 2, no. 1 (2015): 83–105.

integration emerged as it did – i.e. with national executives providing essential political leadership within the Council – as "a total rejection of integration within [this autonomous technocratic] political framework."[53]

Similarly, in the midst of the oil crisis of 1974, European leaders established the European Council as a regular assembly of the heads of state or government to guide the integration process, albeit outside the formal structure of European institutions. In its seemingly blatant intergovernmentalism and lack of basis in the Treaties, this new body appeared to federalists and other pro-Europeans as a fundamental reversal of the progress toward integration. But Milward again, this time writing with Vibeke Sørensen, provided the more persuasive, historically informed assessment: "[R]ather than reversing the process of European integration," the establishment of the European Council "actually signifie[d] a wish to extend Community decision-making to new areas in response to changes in national policy objectives arising from the fundamental change in economic circumstances of the western European countries after 1974."[54]

In other words, the delegation of more power to the level of EU governance has consistently required, beyond fixes to the purported democratic deficit, the development of mechanisms of legitimacy mediated through national bodies in order to overcome the democratic disconnect. The initial establishment of the European Council suggested that, for the process of European integration to have any hope of continued development with the end of the three decades of steady postwar expansion (the *"trentes glorieuses"*), clear *political* backing by the national chief executives would be needed. Technocratic policy development in the Commission (the "Community model"), even under ministerial supervision in the Council of Ministers, would not be enough. It should thus not surprise us that, with its formalization in the Treaty of Lisbon in 2009, the European Council emerged in the Eurozone crisis as the EU's "principal decisionmaker," clearly eclipsing the Commission, which "no longer [served] as agenda setter and initiator of legislation."[55] As the last decade has demonstrated, that crucial combination of power and legitimacy still remains with the Member

---

[53] Alan S. Milward, *The Reconstruction of Western Europe, 1945–51* (Berkeley: University of California Press, 1984), 207.

[54] Alan S. Milward and Vibeke Sørensen, "Interdependence or Integration? A National Choice," in *The Frontier of National Sovereignty: History and Theory, 1945–1992*, eds. Alan S. Milward et al. (New York: Routledge, 1993), 24–25.

[55] Stefano Micossi, "The Eurozone Crisis and EU Institutional Change: A New CEPR Policy Insight," *VoxEU.Org* (blog), April 15, 2013, www.voxeu.org/article/eurozone-crisis-and-eu-institutional-change-new-cepr-policy-insight.

522 — Peter L. Lindseth

States, exercised via the European Council. The EU, whether in the form of the Commission, the Court, or even the European Parliament, serves primarily as an implementation mechanism – an "agent" – exercising delegated powers from the Member States – collectively, the "principal."

III LOOKING AHEAD: CRITICAL JUNCTURE OR CONTINUED INCREMENTALISM?

It is against this backdrop that we must reflect on the likely contours of European governance in the years to come. This section will necessarily be briefer than the last, not least because any discussion of the future, no matter how well informed by history, is always speculative. The task before us is to evaluate the likelihood of further reform emerging out of the decade of crisis, including additional empowerments of supranational institutions in terms of resource mobilization powers. Might any such empowerments mark a transcendence of the democratic disconnect and the power-legitimacy nexus by transferring real mobilization powers to the EU level? And if so, will they, in a deeper sense, mark a principal–agent inversion, turning the EU into an autonomous level of democratic and constitutional government in its own right, thus fundamentally transforming the character of European integration going forward?

It should be clearly stated at the outset of this discussion that there is nothing inherently objectionable in such an inversion, as long as it is supported by the necessary demos-legitimate underpinnings. Indeed, if so supported, the resulting principal–agent inversion might be just what European integration functionally requires to move forward. In such a world, the EU would overcome its central contradiction, in which it has power to make regulatory norms but otherwise lacks the legitimacy to mobilize the fiscal and human resources essential to give muscle to the resulting supranational regulatory regime. Rather, a transformed EU would come to possess genuine fiscal capacities, along with the autonomous legitimacy to exercise them, which in turn could lead to all sorts of net-positives. For example, Eurobonds – a European "safe-asset" – could complement new forms of EU taxing authority, giving the EU macroeconomically salient borrowing capacities while also reinforcing the EU's fragile banking system and perhaps advancing the status of the euro as a potential reserve currency to rival the US dollar. Armed with taxing and borrowing powers at the EU level, Europe-wide redistributive mechanisms would then become possible, allowing for a genuine recycling of surpluses from wealthier regions to the poorer (perhaps via unemployment insurance or some other solidaristic welfare mechanism), which in turn would help to address regionally asymmetric economic shocks. The Eurozone could then become the genuine "optimal currency area" that it is far from being today. It could also then begin to mobilize human resources to project coercive and deterrent power both internally (through policing) and externally (through defense), crucial to the EU becoming a full-fledged geopolitical player. Most importantly for our purposes, the EU could then construct real democratic and constitutional bodies (legislative, executive, and judicial) capable of autonomously legitimating the EU's exercise of its various mobilization powers.

Alas, the likelihood of European integration achieving such a radical transformation any time soon remains low, although it is hardly out of the question. As the historical-institutionalist literature teaches, inherited institutional settlements (as well as the political practices and cultural habits of mind they embody) are generally "sticky";[56] that is, they show remarkable resilience in the face of functional, political, or cultural pressures for change. Such change, therefore, is much more often evolutionary than revolutionary, a manifestation of the phenomenon of hysteresis in action.[57] Revolutionary transformations usually require a "critical juncture," as the literature puts it;[58] that is, a rare confluence of functional, political, and cultural shifts that radically undermine existing institutional settlements, thus overcoming hysteresis and thereby opening the way for genuinely new institutional configurations.[59]

However, when we speak of critical junctures, at least on a scale adequate to transform European governance in the fundamental ways we are discussing, we should not mince words. What we are in fact talking about are the peculiar possibilities that arise from existential and often violent upheavals – the French Revolution, the US Civil War, the catastrophic events of 1914–1945, to name just three historical episodes. Indeed, with regard to integration, this last episode was obviously crucial to opening the way in Western Europe for new structures of public governance beyond the state in the immediate

---

[56] See, e.g., Peter J. Boettke, Christopher J. Coyne, and Peter T. Leeson, "Institutional Stickiness and the New Development Economics," *American Journal of Economics and Sociology* 67, no. 2 (2008): 331–358.

[57] See Notes 29–30 and accompanying text.

[58] Giovanni Capoccia, "Critical Junctures and Institutional Change," in *Advances in Comparative-Historical Analysis*, eds. James Mahoney and Kathleen Thelen (Cambridge: Cambridge University Press, 2015), 147–179.

[59] Peter L. Lindseth, "Between the 'Real' and the 'Right': Explorations along the Institutional-Constitutional Frontier," in *Constitutionalism and the Rule of Law: Bridging Idealism and Realism*, eds. Maurice Adams, Ernst Hirsch Ballin, and Anne Meuwese (Cambridge: Cambridge University Press, 2017), 60–93.

postwar years. But even that process, it should be remembered, was marked by its own form of hysteresis, turning out to be as much about the "rescue of the nation-state" as its transcendence.[60] And this more limited process of integration was made possible by the unique historical context of the Cold War and the shield provided "by a hegemon's security umbrella."[61]

The Cold War has now passed, and so too has the peculiar interim moment of (temporary) unipolar geopolitical, economic, and epistemic dominance of the United States (the "Washington consensus"). That atmosphere of neoliberal consensus, for good and ill, arguably provided the context within which the EU could conceive and launch the euro on such hopeful (if ultimately illusory) terms. The period *since* the 1990s, however, has been one of steady disruption, contestation, and increasingly violent conflict, expressed both as war and terrorism. In this period, Europe has found itself buffeted from multiple sides, not least by the previously reliable hegemon, the United States. However, not even the geopolitical recklessness of the Bush administration (the Iraq war in the wake of 9/11) or its economic mismanagement leading to the global financial crisis (dramatically testing the euro), or even the sometimes-seeming indifference of a "pivoting-to-Asia" Obama administration, could have prepared the EU for what has followed: the open hostility of Donald Trump, both as to Europe's security and its economic well-being.

The Trump presidency reflects the confluence of numerous other dynamics buffeting Europe, not least the rise of a deeply illiberal populism visible both at Europe's core as well as its edges, feeding into developments (hostility to immigration, Brexit, ongoing Hungarian and Polish challenges to the rule of law, the M5S-Lega victory in Italy) that threaten the EU's coherence directly. And it is not just Donald Trump who is cheering on these developments; rather, there is also the overtly and covertly disruptive Russia of Vladimir Putin, on whose energy supplies major Member States (i.e. Germany) happen to dangerously rely. And further destabilizing the situation is the emergence of a revisionist China as a major economic and geopolitical force. Whether the pace of China's rise can be sustained over the intermediate or long term remains to be seen, but its emergence is nonetheless a harbinger of future revisions to the global order in which the relative weight of Europe will almost certainly diminish.

---

[60] Alan S. Milward, *The European Rescue of the Nation-State*, 2nd ed. (London: Routledge, 2000).

[61] Kalypso Nicolaïdis, "European Demoicracy and Its Crisis," *Journal of Common Market Studies* 51, no. 2 (2013): 360.

All these factors are well known, so my recounting them here will hardly surprise anyone. I do so simply to stress that, in such an unstable atmosphere, increasing political tensions and the dangers of miscalculation could well precipitate a genuine (and potentially transformative) critical juncture. I frankly hope not, because there is simply no telling what kind of Europe might emerge out of such an upheaval. Existential threats might lead to a net-beneficial breakthrough in EU governance of the type described earlier, marked by robust democratic and constitutional legitimacy at the EU level, as well as the array of powers to go with it. Or the threats might lead to dramatic weakening or even collapse of the integration project as we have come to know it over the last seven decades.

Given those imponderables, I choose instead to think about a still difficult but somewhat less distressing scenario. It is one in which EU governance is given the space to evolve, incrementally but still more ambitiously, albeit taking cognizance of the constraints posed by the democratic disconnect and the power-legitimacy nexus.

Consider, for instance, the fate of the agenda set out by French President Emmanuel Macron in his famous Sorbonne speech in September 2017,[62] which included new EU-level taxes and law-enforcement initiatives, a Euro-zone budget, as well as a new range of security initiatives, among many other things. He made a compelling case that the future of European integration functionally demanded these sorts of institutional shifts. However, as we know from history, functional demand alone, without concomitant changes in political interests or cultural understandings of legitimate governance, will not precipitate the needed changes. This is in fact proving to be the case with the EU. The policies actually adopted at the Euro Summit in June 2018 in response to Macron's push, perhaps unsurprisingly, actually were quite limited.[63] The headwinds facing Macron's agenda were well anticipated by the speech of Dutch Prime Minister Mark Rutte in Berlin in early March 2018.[64] The EU is not "an unstoppable train speeding towards federalism," Rutte asserted. Rather, "[i]t is up to each country to maintain and develop its own financial, socio-economic, legal and democratic assets, within the parameters set by the EU." Rutte was all in favor of cooperation that "added

---

[62] "Sorbonne Speech of Emmanuel Macron- Full text /English Version," *Ouest France*, September 26, 2017, http://international.blogs.ouest-france.fr/archive/2017/09/29/macron-sorbonne-verbatim-europe-18583.html.

[63] See Note 37 and sources cited.

[64] Speech by the Prime Minister of the Netherlands, Mark Rutte, at the Bertelsmann Stiftung, Berlin, March 2, 2018, www.government.nl/documents/speeches/2018/03/02/speech-by-the-prime-minister-of-the-netherlands-mark-rutte-at-the-bertelsmann-stiftung-berlin.

value" but any new initiatives must allow the Member States to remain "strong and able to maintain their own identity."[65]

Looking ahead, it is certain that the question of control over resource mobilization, both human and fiscal, will continue to loom large in the ongoing debates about "more Europe." The Member States in the north, at least at this stage, are still deeply reluctant to make open-ended commitments to resource sharing with what they still see as their inadequately self-disciplined neighbors to the south. This explains, for example, the continuing opposition, led by Germany, to the adoption of a jointly funded "European Deposit Insurance Scheme" (EDIS) as part of the Banking Union, despite pleas from the European Central Bank.[66] If Europe is unable to adopt an EDIS, despite the seemingly compelling case,[67] it is difficult to imagine the Member States reaching agreement over other reforms that would imply an even greater autonomous fiscal capacity at the supranational level (e.g. a Europeanized unemployment insurance scheme). If anything, just as likely would be a continuing erosion of the EU-level fiscal surveillance mechanisms adopted during the crisis, led perhaps by a newly assertive Italy in the role of self-styled antagonist toward German hegemony. The result could be a de facto renationalization of fiscal policy autonomy at the Member State level, which would not necessarily be a bad thing.[68]

The one domain most likely to see a more immediate augmentation of EU-level resource mobilization (human, if not fiscal) is in border control. It is already not outlandish, as noted earlier, to view the reconstituted Frontex as "a law enforcement agency at EU level."[69] It is not just that the functional case for an autonomous European capacity in this space is overwhelming (and overwhelmingly fair to the front-line states, who have born the particular burdens to date). It is also that the politics of the question uniquely align

---

[65] In this sense, Rutte's speech echoed the "demoi-cratic" interpretation of EU governance. See Notes 26–27 and accompanying text.

[66] "ECB's Draghi Renews Plea for Euro Area Deposit Insurance," *Reuters*, July 9, 2018, https://uk .reuters.com/article/us-ecb-policy-draghi/ecbs-draghi-pleads-with-parliament-for-euro-area-deposit-insurance-idUKKBN1JZ1KW.

[67] Jacopo Carmassi et al., "Completing the Banking Union with a European Deposit Insurance Scheme: Who Is Afraid of Cross-Subsidisation?" Occasional Paper Series, European Central Bank, April 2018.

[68] See Barry Eichengreen and Charles Wyplosz, "Minimal Conditions for the Survival of the Euro," *VoxEU.Org* (blog), March 14, 2016, https://voxeu.org/article/minimal-conditions-survival-euro ("The fiction that fiscal policy can be centralised should be abandoned, and the Eurozone should acknowledge that, having forsaken national monetary policies, national control of fiscal policy is all the more important for stabilization"). See also Bugarič, "The Populist Backlash against Europe."

[69] See Note 43 and accompanying text.

anti-EU populists like Matteo Salvini and Viktor Orbán with their more Europhilic *confrères* to the north and west, who have needed to respond to the increasingly anti-immigration mood. Thus, in charting an otherwise incrementalist course for the future, the joint Macron–Merkel "Meseberg Declaration" of June 2018 called for "improved protection of European external borders through an ambitious strengthening in terms of staff and mandate of Frontex," leading to the creation of "a genuine European border police."[70]

The irony is that some of integration's most hostile internal opponents like Salvini and Orbán – playing on an issue in deep tension with the cosmopolitan ethos of EU elites – are actually the ones driving this shift in capacities to the EU level. They have become the unexpected (and certainly inadvertent) agents of Europeanization – those who some commentators currently see as "calling the shots."[71] Whether this emerges as a sustainable pattern over time remains to be seen. However, if so, a similar dynamic could well take hold in the security and defense space, this time driven by external opponents. The role of Russia in promoting European divisions, particularly in supporting Euroskeptic parties and fomenting disruptive cultural currents on social media, has also crystallized the sense of Putin's regime as a strategic threat (even as the populists look more kindly on Russia's role). And given the extent to which Donald Trump has undermined confidence in the United States, there is a realization that Europe will no longer be able to rely, as in the past, on its security hegemon of the last seventy years. Whether and how Europe responds – perhaps through the creation of genuinely autonomous military capabilities – will be another test. This could then demand the Europeanization of human as well as even fiscal resources – the true mark of an autonomously "constitutionalized" European Union.

BY WAY OF CONCLUSION, SOME REFLECTIONS ON THE EUROPEAN COURT OF JUSTICE

Allow me to close by focusing on one additional irony, this one relating to the role of the European Court of Justice in EU governance. The Court has long been a key driver in the process of integration; nonetheless, it may now be time for the ECJ to reflect on its role in perhaps surprising and (for some)

---

[70] See German Federal Government, "Meseberg Declaration," June 19, 2018, www .bundesregierung.de/Content/EN/Pressemitteilungen/BPA/2018/2018-06-19-meseberg-declaration.html.

[71] Mark Leonard, "Are Europe's Populists Calling the Shots?," *Project Syndicate*, June 28, 2018, www.project-syndicate.org/commentary/merkel-migration-and-the-populist-siege-by-mark-leonard-2018-06.

counterintuitive ways. I have explored this argument in detail elsewhere,[72] so I will only briefly review it here in closing.

Despite the fact that the EU operates primarily as a pre-commitment agency of the Member States, EU judges have long insisted on interpreting the integration process "as if" it already had an autonomous democratic and constitutional character in its own right. The problem, as I noted earlier, is that the Court's approach amounts to a kind of principal–agent inversion.[73] For example, as Gareth Davies has shown,[74] the Court has effectively taken on the role of principal in how it interprets the contours of the internal market. Not in the sense of legislative initiative, of course, but rather in the decisional constraints that the Court's often-maximalist interpretations of the Treaties have imposed on the range of substantive policy choices open to political actors. "Examination of the major legislative internal market acts," Davies concludes, shows that "they are an exercise in codifying case law. The Commission, Council and Parliament display collective legislative subservience to the Court"; hence "to be an agent of the Treaties is, in substance, to be an agent of the Court."[75] Dieter Grimm has rightly called this the "over-constitutionalisation" of EU law.[76] The Court has exploited its peculiarly powerful role in policing the Member States' policy commitments in the Treaties and secondary legislation by entrenching its own maximalist preferences as to what integration should be.

The problem is that the Court's approach ignores the fundamental contradiction in EU governance: National institutions, the true sources of democratic and constitutional legitimacy in the EU system, are increasingly constrained in the exercise of their own constitutional authority but supranational institutions are unable to fill the void because Europeans refuse to endow them with the *sine qua non* of genuine constitutionalism: the autonomous capacity to mobilize fiscal and human resources in a legitimate and compulsory fashion. The Court's approach, by providing a kind of interpretive *lingua franca*, has socialized generations of European elites into overlooking the EU's lack of the necessary sociopolitical underpinnings for genuine constitutionalism (hence the persistent discussions of the "democratic deficit" as opposed to the "democratic disconnect"). And in this way, the Court's "as

---

[72] Lindseth, "The Perils of 'As If' European Constitutionalism."

[73] See Notes 5–8 and accompanying text.

[74] Gareth Davies, "The European Union Legislature as an Agent of the European Court of Justice," *Journal of Common Market Studies* 54, no. 4 (2016): 846–861.

[75] Davies, European Union Legislature, 847.

[76] Dieter Grimm, "The Democratic Costs of Constitutionalisation: The European Case," *European Law Journal* 21, no. 4 (2015): 460–473.

if' constitutionalism may well have contributed to deeply flawed institutional and policy choices by political actors that led to the crises of the last decade. The adoption of the common currency, for example, presupposed a degree of centralized political power and legitimacy, most importantly relating to shared taxing and borrowing authority, which the EU obviously lacks and does not seem much closer to attaining. The still tenuous border-free zone in Schengen ultimately presupposed a degree of centralized political power and legitimacy to mobilize human resources (policing, defense, and border control) that the EU has been struggling to develop, albeit slowly.

To restore some semblance of balance between the political and legal dimensions of integration, the Court of Justice needs to reflect carefully on the balance between supranational pre-commitment and national prerogatives. The Court should continue the effort to develop a robust role in guaranteeing the rule of law, the prerequisite for any European project (notably in response to the current *dérives* in Poland and Hungary).[77] But it also must guard against a hypertrophy of the judicial sphere, avoiding the temptation of an outright juristocratic principal–agent inversion, however seemingly well intentioned. The Court must seek a sense of balance between politics and law, allowing room for political actors – not just through intergovernmental negotiation but also at the national level – to define the contours of the integration project. Adequate space for integration-through-politics as opposed to the more traditional integration-through-law will be crucial, for example, in a successful conclusion of Brexit (one way or another) as well as in disincentivizing other reluctant Member States from looking for the door. Creating such a space will be an important part of future efforts to combat the democratic disconnect, and it will also be consistent with the demands of the power-legitimacy nexus that ultimately defines the EU's character.

---

[77] See Chapter 15 and Chapter 16 for a discussion of the Court's role in promoting the rule of law.

Conclusion

19

Conclusion

The Rule of Law, Rights, and Democracy in Sovereignty-Sensitive Domains

FRANCESCA BIGNAMI

The expansion of EU law over the past quarter-century beyond market regulation and into domains of classic state sovereignty has been breathtaking. In the 1990s, it might have been possible to dismiss some of the developments as paper phenomena, but with the introduction of the euro, the Lisbon Treaty's provisions on immigration and internal security law, the dizzying succession of institutional transformations provoked by the euro crisis, and the pressure to develop a role in monitoring constitutional fundamentals, it is fair to say that the EU looks more state-like today than it has at any other point in its history. Yet it is difficult to find any latter-day Jean Monnets celebrating. The EU's exercise of such powers has been contentious, and the rise of populism is the most telling sign. The politics of policymaking have become more complex than ever, characterized by a variety of ideological and regional cleavages. But even though the populist voices in favor of disintegration might be the loudest, there are also steady and substantial efforts being made to improve the EU's capacity to overcome divisions and govern legitimately.

As a joint project of mostly legal scholars, this book and concluding chapter cannot opine on how to render the politics more stable. This chapter can, however, scrutinize the legal edifice that has been built in sovereignty-sensitive domains, uncover where that edifice falls short of the ideals and normative standards of the law, and suggest improvements. The European project has always relied heavily on cooperation with and acceptance by the legal establishments of the Member States.[1] Even though the dynamics have shifted over time, and it is no longer possible to speak of integration through law sheltered from politics, the legitimacy of integration continues to turn in

---

[1] Joseph H. H. Weiler, "A Quiet Revolution: The European Court of Justice and Its Interlocutors," *Comparative Political Studies* 26, no. 4 (1994): 510–534.

534   *Francesca Bignami*

no small measure on how the law that is generated measures up against classic notions of law in a liberal and social democratic constitutional order.

Drawing on the subject-specific contributions in this volume, this concluding chapter assesses the overall legal architecture that has emerged across the gamut of economic policy, human migration, internal security, and constitutional fundamentals.[2] It takes as its metric what for the European legal tradition is by now the commonplace trio of rule of law, fundamental rights, and democracy – prominent in both the European Convention on Human Rights and the EU Treaties.[3] Thanks to the cross-cutting perspective offered by this book's coverage of sovereignty-sensitive law it is possible to identify important characteristics and flaws of that law – flaws that can get buried or minimized in the subject-specific literature driven more by the details and concerns of the individual policy areas. For each parameter of rule of law, fundamental rights, and democracy, the discussion focuses on a shortcoming of sovereignty-sensitive law, in particular as that law has developed since 2009 under the influence of the euro crisis and the new powers conferred in the Lisbon Treaty. The analysis is broken out by the subject areas covered in this book, with the exception of constitutional fundamentals, which is less central than the other areas to the sections on rights and democracy. As highlighted in the next section, there are no specific EU lawmaking competences for constitutional fundamentals and the emerging law is being developed in ECJ jurisprudence. Since this chapter's analysis of rights and democracy focuses on the legitimacy of the EU's lawmaking activity, it is less relevant to what for the moment is the largely jurisprudential domain of constitutional fundamentals. The discussion of each of the three parameters concludes with constructive proposals for improving the law.

[2]   The use of these terms is the same as in the introductory chapter and in the organizing scheme of the book. To refresh the reader's memory: economic policy refers to fiscal policy, general programs affecting the economy, and banking regulation connected to the economic stability of the Eurozone; human migration refers to intra-EU migration under the law of free movement of persons, to third-country immigration (both economic immigration and asylum seekers), and to border control; internal security refers to police and judicial cooperation; and constitutional fundamentals (at the national level) covers the list of values in Article 2 Treaty on European Union, encapsulated in the rule of law, rights, and democracy.

[3]   There is an extensive literature that analyzes how the rule of law, democracy, and rights apply in the EU context. For one important, and critical, discussion of the experience of these values in EU governance, see Andrew Williams, *The Ethos of Europe: Values, Law and Justice in the EU* (Cambridge: Cambridge University Press, 2010). For purposes of the analysis in this chapter, as explained later, it suffices to take the legal and institutional settlement contained in the Lisbon Treaty as the baseline.

Conclusion 535

As explained in the introduction to this book, the EU has come to govern and make law in the sovereignty-sensitive domains that have raised populist hackles through the historical process of spillover. Legal prerogatives over economic policy, human migration, internal security, and constitutional fundamentals have expanded in piecemeal fashion. There is no grand constitutional declaration of political and legal authority. But that should not be an obstacle to developing a structurally coherent legal architecture that abides by the standards common to the European legal tradition.

I LEGAL COMPLEXITY AND THE RULE OF LAW

European integration through spillover has given rise to legal complexity that bypasses the ordinary complexity of law in developed economies and plural societies and that makes it difficult for citizens and even, in certain cases, legal professionals to know what rules govern individuals in their dealings with other individuals and their public authorities. This complexity has obvious, negative implications for the rule of law – law must be knowable for it to count as law.[4] The crux of the problem is the use of two very different types of legal norms in the process of European integration – international and supranational.[5] International norms are applicable between Member States and subject to treaty-based dispute resolution and, in some cases, centralized enforcement. Since they are conceived as operating in the international realm, as between states, and not applicable to the

[4] This element of the rule of law has a long pedigree, going back at least as far as Jeremy Bentham's writings on codification, see Philip Schofield, "The Legal and Political Legacy of Jeremy Bentham," *Annual Review of Law and Social Science* 9 (2013): 51–70, and is very much alive and well today, with ongoing efforts at simplification and improving the quality of law in various jurisdictions. See, e.g., Conseil d'État, "Étude annuelle 2016: Simplification et qualité du droit," 2016.

[5] These labels are used in line with classic debates in analytical philosophy on the nature of law and the distinction between borderline cases (international law) and core cases (domestic law, which I call supranational law in the EU case). H. L. A. Hart, *The Concept of Law* (Oxford: Oxford University Press, 1994), 15. I use the term "supranational norms" instead of "domestic norms," since the latter has traditionally been used to refer to the legal norms of nation states and causes confusion in the EU context. It should also be noted that my use of the labels "international" and "supranational" in this discussion of legal complexity is designed to capture only the nature of the rules, not the status of the legal system. The latter, of course, is a highly contested matter and I am not suggesting that the EU is akin to the legal system of a federal nation state nor am I taking sides in the debate. For an introduction to the legal philosophy of EU Law, see Julie Dickson and Pavlos Eleftheriadis, eds., *Philosophical Foundations of EU Law* (Oxford: Oxford University Press, 2012).

citizens of those states, they are often not published and made widely available. Likewise, citizens cannot rely on international rules and cannot go to court to enforce and challenge those rules. These rules tend to be used for contentious, sovereignty-sensitive issues because Member States can retain more control over the future evolution of intergovernmental cooperation. By contrast, supranational norms are akin to classic domestic law: They are binding on public authorities and citizens in their dealings with one another and are subject, in the courts, to enforcement, interpretation, and judicial review for compliance with higher-law principles. Those courts, in the EU's judicial system, include both the European Court of Justice (ECJ) and the courts of the Member States. Supranational norms are generally used when the EU institutions deal directly with individuals, when the issue benefits from a high degree of Member State consensus, or when the policy requires uniform implementation. For individuals to know what is law they must be able to distinguish between rules in the international category – not law – and those in the supranational category – law.

In light of the quantity of EU norms, parsing them into the international and supranational categories is no small hurdle to the knowability of law. The difficulty is compounded, however, by the fact that the distinction between the two categories has been a moving target. That is because as spillover occurs, and intergovernmental cooperation through international instruments intensifies, the reality of policymaking often belies the international label given to the norms. As a result, the legal establishment, whether through the European Court of Justice's jurisprudence or through legal reform, has sought to transform international into supranational norms. This impetus comes in large measure from the moral implications of failing to hold such norms to the standards of domestic legal norms. If most of the substance of public action affecting individuals is being driven by the European level, not the national level, then the rights and obligations created at the European level should meet the standards of law in a rule-of-law system: they should be published and widely available so that European citizens know what conduct is expected of them and their public authorities; in line with the liberty function of law in classic liberalism, individuals should be able to rely on the rules in court, thus guaranteeing private rights and curbing arbitrary state action; and those same rules should be challengeable in court based on the higher-law principles of the system, in accordance with the post-war consensus on administrative and constitutional law.

Even though the jurisprudence and legal reform that has transformed international norms into supranational ones has generally had beneficial consequences for the rule of law, it has also had negative ones, which in

Conclusion

European legal scholarship comes under the heading of "legal certainty."[6] The essential problem is that as rules move from the international to the supranational categories, there is confusion, albeit generally only for a certain transitional period — confusion as to whether those rules can be relied upon by individuals in their dealings with other individuals and their public officials, and as to whether those rules can be litigated in their Member State courts. This uncertainty is particularly problematic when, as is often the case, there is an alternative Member State law that sets out different, possibly conflicting, rights and obligations. Although the primacy of EU law over Member State law is well established[7] and therefore there is no confusion as to the ranking of legal norms, there is confusion as to what counts as a legal norm. This uncertainty, for any given class of legal rules, generally only persists for a limited period, until the jurisprudential change has been consolidated or the transitional period set down in the legal reform has expired. Therefore, for purposes of this discussion, the legal certainty issue is grouped together with the more general problem of legal complexity.

Because of their impact on national sovereignty, European integration in the policy areas covered in this volume has proceeded, as an initial matter, through international norms and instruments and has then come under pressure to migrate to the supranational category. As a result, legal complexity has undermined the knowability of law. The rest of this section briefly narrates this legal trajectory, which maps onto the historical spillover process described in the introductory chapter of initially cautious intergovernmental cooperation followed by more intense integration. It concludes with recommendations for the EU's ongoing efforts at legal simplification.

1 Early Forms of Cooperation on Economic Policy and Human Migration through Directives

Under the original Treaty of Rome, there was one type of legal instrument available for interstate cooperation that was squarely international –

---

[6] For a discussion of this concern in recent scholarship and jurisprudence, see Mikael Rask Madsen, Henrik Palmer Olsne, and Urška Šadl, "Competing Supremacies and Clashing Institutional Rationalities: The Danish Supreme Court's Decision in the *Ajos* Case and the National Limits on Judicial Cooperation," *European Law Journal* 32, no. 1-2 (2017): 140–150.

[7] Given the focus on EU law, this discussion omits the issue of primacy from the perspective of Member State legal systems and the voluminous debate on constitutional pluralism. See, e.g., Neil Walker, "Constitutional Pluralism Revisited," *European Law Journal* 22, no. 3 (2016): 333–355.

538   *Francesca Bignami*

directives.[8] They were "binding, as to the result to be achieved, upon each
Member State to which [they are] addressed, but shall leave to national
authorities the choice of form and methods."[9] Since directives were thought
to operate in the international realm, as between states, and not to apply
broadly to the citizens of those states, publication was not required. Relatedly,
it was generally believed that directive provisions could not be invoked by
individuals in their domestic courts and through the preliminary reference
system, except for the rare instances when Member States explicitly relied on
their provisions to impose liabilities on individuals. Many of the early efforts at
coordinating economic policy and regulating intra-EU travel and residence
rights were conducted through directives.

As has been amply chronicled in legal and historical scholarship, the
distinction between directives and instruments of the supranational ilk, i.e.
regulations, has been progressively eroded by the European Court of Justice so
that the rules contained in directives can, for the most part, be relied on by
individuals in their Member State courts.[10] In the standard account of
the expansion of direct effect – the doctrinal test used to vet norms and to
recognize the supranational as opposed to international status of certain legal
rules – the emphasis has been on the Court's federalizing mission to create an
effective and uniform legal order. In the facts and the rhetoric of the early
cases, however, the rule-of-law considerations discussed previously were also
on full display: the robust cooperation occurring under the legal rubric of
directives made it difficult to treat directives as categorically different from the
squarely supranational instrument of the regulation and denying directives
direct effect would undermine the liberty function of law (in the reasoning of

[8]   Early views of the legal status of directives can be found in Benedetto Conforti, "Mécanismes
      juridiques assurant la mise en œuvre de la législation communautaire par les autorités
      législatives ou exécutives nationales (Rapport general)," 1965 FIDE Congress 25 (1966);
      "Rapports nationaux de la 1ème commission," 1965 FIDE Congress 25–26 (1966); "Troisième
      FIDE Colloque, 25, 26, 27 novembre 1965," *Revue trimestrielle de droit européen* 1 (1965): 618;
      "Troisième colloque de droit européen," *Revue internationale de droit comparé* 18, no. 1 (1966):
      152–60.
[9]   Article 288 TFEU.
[10] For a general legal discussion of directives and their direct effect, see Sacha Prechal, *Directives
      in EC Law*, 2nd ed. (Oxford: Oxford University Press, 2005); for a legal history account, see
      Morten Rasmussen, "How to Enforce European Law: A New History of the Battle over the
      Direct Effect of Directives, 1958–1987," *European Law Journal* 23, no. 3-4 (2017): 290–308. As
      the debate has evolved, the view put forward here of the doctrine of direct effect has become
      more controversial, see Elise Muir, "Of Ages in – and Edges of – EU Law," *Common Market
      Law Review* 48, no. 1 (2011): 39–62, but it is consistent with the early usage of the doctrine and
      also brings out the legal parallels to more recent episodes of integration in sovereignty-sensitive
      policy areas.

Conclusion 539

the Court, "rights" and "equality") in a rule-of-law system.[11] At the same time, there has been pushback from elements of the legal establishment and national courts drawing on the legal certainty concern. This was true in the 1970s, when the Court faced opposition from high courts in France and Germany for recognizing that Directive 64/221 (on limitations on the free movement of persons) and Directive 77/338 (on calculation of value-added tax) could have direct effect;[12] and it is still true today, as the Court continues to close gaps in the supranational status of directives, as evidenced by the recent opposition from the Danish Supreme Court to the use of general principles of law to give horizontal direct effect to provisions of Directive 2000/78 (on equal treatment in employment).[13]

2 Economic Policy

In part because the Court has significantly reduced the possibility of cooperation through international legal norms within the original Treaty of Rome, the more recent efforts at cooperating in sovereignty-sensitive policy areas have all begun outside the Treaty of Rome, in newly negotiated international treaties not subject to the jurisdiction and case law of the Court.[14] As discussed in the introductory chapter and the economic policy section of this book, Economic and Monetary Union (EMU) was originally placed in the mainstream Treaty of Rome (which at the time was referred to as the "First Pillar" and is now called the Treaty on the Functioning of the European Union [TFEU]), and there have been a number of important measures adopted

---

[11] The possibility of direct effect for directives was established in a line of cases beginning with decisions (another instrument initially believed to be of the international ilk when addressed to Member States) and ending with directives. These cases all focus on the robust practice of European governance and the corresponding need to give individuals rights. See Opinion of Advocate General Roemer, Case 9/70, *Grad v. Finanzamt Traunstein*, ECLI:EU:C:1970:76, p. 847; Opinion of Advocate General Roemer, Case 33/70, *SACE v. Italian Ministry for Finance*, ECLI:EU:C:1970:107, p. 1228; Opinion of Advocate General Mayras, Case 41/74, *Van Duyn v. Home Office*, ECLI:EU:C:1974:123, p. 1355; L. J. Brinkhorst, "S.A.C.E. v. Ministry of Finance of the Italian Republic, Case 33/70," *Common Market Law Review* 8, no. 3 (1971): 384–92.

[12] See Gerhard Bebr, "The Rambling Ghost of Cohn-Bendit: *Acte Clair* and the Court of Justice," *Common Market Law Review* 20, no. 3 (1983): 439–72.

[13] Madsen, Olsne, and Šadl, "Competing Supremacies and Clashing Institutional Rationalities."

[14] Another important, and related, reason, is that cooperation in these sovereignty-sensitive areas has proceeded without all the Member States and therefore, especially before the Amsterdam Treaty introduced the concept of "variable geometry" and the possibility of moving forward with just a subset of Member States under the rubric of the EU Treaties, it was necessary to use separate international agreements covering a separate set of signatory states.

under those provisions, i.e. the surveillance system set out under the Six Pack and the Two Pack, as well as an amendment to the TFEU's no-bailout provision. However, the most significant law on fiscal transfers has been adopted outside the TFEU. Although the situation of the Eurozone bailouts and conditionality is complex, the bulk of the loans came from the European Financial Stability Facility (EFSF), established by international agreement, and shortly thereafter the European Stability Mechanism (ESM), also created by international agreement and the current organization for financial assistance to Eurozone states facing economic difficulties.[15] In line with the international status of the norms, the various loan agreements setting out the financial terms of the loans and the accompanying memoranda of understanding (MoU) on the conditions that had to be met for the successive tranches of the loans to be released were not systematically published and were generally not made available to the public. Moreover, even though the ESM carves out a role for the European Court of Justice, its jurisdiction is limited to adjudicating disputes between the contracting state parties or between the state parties and the international organization; there is no possibility for individuals to access the ECJ, either directly or through the preliminary reference procedure. The other Eurozone fiscal mechanism that has been created in response to the euro crisis – the fund for creditors and shareholders of failed banks in resolution – is also being funded by an international agreement.[16] There too, the jurisdiction of the ECJ is limited to disputes between the contracting parties. It also bears recalling that the ratcheting up of the balanced-budget rule for the Member States was accomplished by international treaty (the Fiscal Compact).

There have been a number of legal challenges to the MoUs under EU fundamental rights law, but the cases involving MoUs connected to the EFSF and ESM loans (as opposed to the smaller loans that were made under TFEU facilities) have not been successful so far since those MoUs are considered international instruments – not EU acts subject to the jurisdiction of the ECJ.[17] At the same time, however, there has been jurisprudential movement toward

---

[15] Some of the loan facilities were established under the TFEU. For a discussion of the complexity generated by the multiple sources of loans, as well as rule-of-law issues related to the EFSF and ESM loans, see Claire Kilpatrick, "On the Rule of Law and Economic Emergency: The Degradation of Basic Legal Values in Europe's Bailouts," *Oxford Journal of Legal Studies* 35, no. 2 (2015): 325–353; Claire Kilpatrick, "The EU and Its Sovereign Debt Programmes: The Challenges of Liminal Legality," *Current Legal Problems* 70, no. 1 (2017): 337–363.

[16] Intergovernmental Agreement on the Transfer and Mutualisation of Contributions to the Single Resolution Fund. Available at Council Doc. 8457/14 (May 14, 2014).

[17] See, e.g., Joined Cases C-105/15 P to 109/105 P, *Mallis and Malli* v. *Commission and ECB*, ECLI:EU:C:2016:702.

recognizing that the substance of economic policymaking for bailout countries is driven in large part by the European level, not by discretionary decisions made in Athens, Madrid, or any of the other recipient governments. Not only can the terms of MoUs be quite precise, but they rely on the EU institutional system for enforcement, i.e. European Commission surveillance under the Six Pack and Two Pack. Thus, in one recent judgment, the litigants were allowed to proceed against the MoU on the theory that the Commission, which was one of the parties responsible for negotiating the MoU, could be held responsible under the principles of government liability.[18] Legal commentators have also proposed that these MoUs be brought within the TFEU's system of legal rights and remedies by recognizing their role in the Six Pack, and especially the Two Pack (one piece of which applies exclusively to bailout countries), a budgetary surveillance system that is squarely conducted under the TFEU.[19]

There have also been law reform proposals to eliminate the international status of the ESM and bring it within the EU Treaties. The Commission's proposal on establishing a "European Monetary Fund" (EMF) would be the most far-reaching.[20] For present purposes, the most important elements are the provisions requiring publication of MoUs and decisions of the Board of Governors and the establishment of the EMF as a Union body, which would bring it under the jurisdiction of the ECJ and its jurisprudence on the legal status of norms. What might be called the "domestication" of ESM law is one important reason why the Commission's proposal has faced significant opposition, the other being the creation of direct lines of accountability to the Council and the European Parliament. Although the future evolution of the law governing bailouts and conditionality is an open question, it is evident that it is in a period of flux as various legal actors are seeking to push that law toward a supranational legal framework more in line with rule-of-law principles.

3 Human Migration

Cooperation on the borders and immigration aspects of human migration began earlier than economic policy, but it too started in international

---

[18] Joined Cases C-8/15 P to C-10/15 P, *Ledra Advertising* v. *Commission and ECB*, ECLI:EU: C:2016:701.

[19] Kilpatrick, "The EU and Its Sovereign Debt Programmes," 340–53; Menelaos Markakis and Paul Dermine, "Bailouts, the Legal Status of Memoranda of Understanding and the Scope of Application of the EU Charter: *Florescu*," *Common Market Law Review* 55, no. 2 (2018): 643–671.

[20] *Commission Proposal for a Council Regulation on the Establishment of the European Monetary Fund*, COM (2017) 827 final (December 6, 2017).

agreements – the Schengen Agreement, soon followed by the Schengen Convention; and specifically for asylum, the Dublin Convention.[21] Soon thereafter came the Maastricht Treaty, which introduced border control and immigration as policy areas under the EU umbrella. However, this was done by creating the so-called pillar system, and placing these issues outside the mainstream "First Pillar" Treaty (concerning the single market, what is now called the TFEU) and into the special new intergovernmental Treaty (the Treaty on European Union [TEU]) containing the "Third Pillar" for Justice and Home Affairs. The instruments set out for cooperation and policymaking in the Third Pillar were squarely international: conventions, under public international law; and so-called joint actions, whose legal effects between the Member States were never settled.[22] The question of ECJ jurisdiction was left to be negotiated in the individual conventions, and a complicated set of arrangements was adopted.

Then came the Amsterdam Treaty, which remedied most of the rule-of-law defects of cooperation through norms of the international variety by transitioning them into the supranational category.[23] Border control and immigration were removed from the Third Pillar and placed in the mainstream First Pillar Treaty. The legal instruments to be used for policymaking were the standard, supranational ones. Moreover, for the first time, individuals were given the right to rely on, and bring challenges to, the measures taken in the field through the EU judicial system, i.e. through the preliminary reference procedure involving Member State courts and the ECJ. The Amsterdam Treaty, however, did place restrictions on the preliminary reference procedure by only contemplating references from courts of last resort and by excluding from the procedure issues relating to law and order and the protection of security. These restrictions were only removed in the Lisbon Treaty.

The last important move made in the Amsterdam Treaty was to integrate what, until then, had been the free-standing organization and law under the international Schengen Convention (the so-called Schengen *acquis*) into the EU legal order. Cooperation on external borders through the Schengen

---

[21] The discussion in this concluding chapter largely excludes the intra-EU dimension of human migration, since the law (on free movement of persons) developed much earlier and has been squarely supranational since the 1980s. However, it should be recalled that the decision to abolish internal borders and establish a common external border in the Schengen Agreement had the effect of facilitating the rights enjoyed under the law of free movement of persons.

[22] Steve Peers, *EU Justice and Home Affairs Law* (Harlow: Longman, 1999), 25–29. This discussion only covers JHA instruments for internal cooperation, not for cooperation on external affairs.

[23] Peers, *EU Justice*, 39–62.

Conclusion

Convention involved mostly border control and immigration issues but there were also aspects related to apprehending criminals and enforcing customs law. Since, as explained in the next section, the Amsterdam Treaty left internal security in the Third Pillar even as it placed border control and immigration in the First Pillar, the integration of the Schengen *acquis* into the EU legal order was not straightforward. Ultimately, the Schengen Convention (and the related *acquis*) was divided into border control and immigration provisions, which were allocated to the First Pillar; police and customs cooperation provisions, which were allocated to the Third Pillar; and the Schengen Information System, which since it was used for multiple purposes was left to the default solution of the Third Pillar.[24]

In contrast with economic policy, the shift from international to supranational in the field of human migration is complete. Since the Amsterdam Treaty has been in force for twenty years now, there is no hang over of international rules adopted in the era of the Schengen and Dublin Conventions or under the Maastricht Treaty. All of the legal norms that currently exist for border control and immigration have been enacted under the First Pillar and fit the supranational mold. In addition, since the Lisbon Treaty, the ordinary rules on ECJ jurisdiction apply, most importantly for preliminary references. In sum, the variety in types of legal norms used for human migration policy has been reduced considerably now that they are all clearly of the supranational ilk and the change (and prejudice to legal certainty) associated with the transition from international to supranational has now been completed. At the end of this historical process, the knowability of law and the related respect for the rule of law have improved considerably.

4 *Internal Security*

As with border control and immigration, European cooperation on internal security began in the international Schengen Convention and then was brought into the EU framework in the Maastricht Treaty. Like border control and immigration, the drafters of the Maastricht Treaty placed internal security in the Third Pillar and stipulated that policymaking was to proceed through international "conventions" and "joint actions" and with *ad hoc*, not guaranteed, ECJ jurisdiction. At the time of the Amsterdam Treaty, however, the two policy trajectories diverged. While border control and immigration policy were transferred to the supranational First Pillar, internal security remained

---

[24] Peers, *EU Justice*, 56–60.

in the Third Pillar. The Amsterdam Treaty retained conventions (and eliminated joint actions) and stipulated two new types of instruments for cooperating on internal security, still of the international ilk: an instrument called "framework decisions" for harmonizing Member State law related to internal security, which were binding on the Member States but where "direct effect" was expressly excluded; and another new instrument called "decisions" for all other purposes, which again were to be binding but where "direct effect" was expressly excluded. Although ECJ jurisdiction over preliminary references was not mandatory, Member States had the option of signing up to a modified form of the procedure and the vast majority did. Through the preliminary reference procedure, the ECJ was soon called upon to rule on the interpretation and effect of Third Pillar measures: it held that framework decisions, like directives (in so-called horizontal situations), could have "indirect effect," i.e. were legal instruments of the supranational ilk;[25] somewhat later, the ECJ also found that framework decisions were subject to interpretation and validity challenges based on EU fundamental rights.[26] Thus we can observe law reform and jurisprudential pressure pushing legal norms from the international to the supranational categories in the domain of internal security.

The final step in this legal trajectory was the Lisbon Treaty. The Third Pillar, where internal security had been placed, was eliminated and internal security is now to be found in the mainstream TFEU. These powers are to be exercised through the standard set of supranational EU legal instruments – no longer are there conventions, framework decisions, and decisions for internal security matters. With one exception, the limitations on preliminary reference jurisdiction have been removed and the general provisions on ECJ jurisdiction now apply. That exception is for review, in the context of EU police and judicial cooperation, of the "validity or proportionality of operations carried out by the police or other law-enforcement services of a Member State or the exercise of the responsibilities incumbent upon Member States with regard to the maintenance of law and order and the safeguarding of internal security."[27] This is a significant limitation on judicial review of police action linked to EU law and illustrates the continuing reluctance to move away from international-style norms in sovereignty-sensitive policy areas.

The historical trajectory of EU law in the domain of internal security vividly demonstrates the legal complexity connected to the spillover process. Interstate cooperation began through international norms. In successive

---

[25] Case C-105/03, *Maria Pupino*, ECLI: EU:C:2005:386.
[26] Case C-399/11, *Stefano Melloni v. Ministerio Fiscal*, ECLI:EU:C:2013:107.
[27] Article 276 TFEU.

treaties, to remedy their rule-of-law deficiencies, European legal reformers replaced them with norms that were public, binding, and amenable to individual enforcement and challenge (based on higher law) in the EU court system; the ECJ's jurisprudence also contributed to the shift from international to supranational. But the switch was incremental, leading to an immense variety of instruments and judicial frameworks, as well as uncertainty, along the way. Indeed, the process was more complex than conveyed in this account because the Lisbon Treaty subjected the application of the ECJ's TFEU preliminary reference jurisdiction (for Third Pillar internal security measures that had been adopted prior to Lisbon's elimination of the Third Pillar) to a five-year transitional period during which the Third Pillar procedure continued to operate.

The shift from international to supranational legal norms in internal security policy is largely – but not entirely – complete. There are two remnants of the international approach and hence sources of complexity: the carve out for judicial review of police action; and the continuing existence of acts adopted under the Third Pillar during the Maastricht and Amsterdam Treaty years, whose legal effects, i.e. international character, are expressly preserved under the Lisbon Treaty. With respect to Third Pillar acts, their number has been reduced over the years (because they have been repealed or rendered obsolete by subsequent TFEU measures) but there are bits and pieces that linger: implementing measures left over from the Schengen *acquis* that were transferred into the Third Pillar by the Amsterdam Treaty; three Conventions and a number of Joint Actions related to internal security and adopted under the Maastricht Treaty; and a number of Decisions and Framework Decisions left over from the Amsterdam Treaty, including the European Arrest Warrant, which is of great practical importance in light of how much it is used by Member State authorities.[28]

5 Constitutional Fundamentals

Turning to the constitutional fundamentals of the Member States, the legal norms were originally of the international variety. As explained earlier in this book, they were introduced in the Amsterdam Treaty and inserted into the historically intergovernmental TEU.[29] The rules on constitutional

[28] Steve Peers, *EU Criminal Law, Policing, and Civil Law*, vol. II of *EU Justice and Home Affairs Law*, 4th ed. (Oxford: Oxford University Press, 2016), app. II.

[29] They were originally numbered Articles 6 and 7 TEU and since the Lisbon Treaty are numbered Articles 2 and 7 TEU.

fundamentals were styled as a general declaration of common principles, were not accompanied by lawmaking competences, and were exempted from the ordinary system of ECJ jurisdiction. Instead, a special enforcement mechanism was created under Article 7 TEU. That procedure ultimately turns on the willingness of the European Council (the most intergovernmental of EU institutions) to determine by unanimity vote (excluding the offending Member State) that there has been a serious breach of constitutional fundamentals. The ECJ's jurisdiction is limited – much more so than in the fiscal treaties and the Maastricht-era conventions that were agreed on internal security. It can intervene only at the behest of the Member State found to be in serious breach and only on the issue of whether the procedural requirements were respected.

In the Nice and Lisbon Treaties relatively little changed as a matter of formal treaty text. As Kim Lane Scheppele and R. Daniel Kelemen explain in Chapter 15, in the Nice Treaty, the Article 7 TEU enforcement mechanism was amended to include a warning mechanism for offending Member States. In the Lisbon Treaty, the constitutional fundamentals to be respected by the Member States were restyled as "values" and the list was expanded somewhat. Moreover, in line with the Lisbon Treaty's ambition to incorporate the advances made in the ill-fated Constitutional Treaty, the legal provisions are now included in a revamped TEU that sets down the essential constitutional principles of the EU. As a matter of legal doctrine, this has facilitated the main novelty in this policy domain – as explained in this volume's introductory chapter, spillover in the form of a robust, supranational system of enforcement through the ECJ's ordinary jurisdiction in the TFEU and free of the intergovernmental constraints of Article 7 TEU.

In a number of recent cases, the ECJ has been called upon to assess the independence of the Polish judiciary and Poland's compliance with the rule of law. These include both Commission infringement actions and preliminary references.[30] Since the movement from international to supranational is unfolding not through the changing status of legislative instruments but the operation of what might gradually become oversight by a human rights court, it has a smaller impact on legal complexity and legal certainty; judicial oversight is relatively familiar from the European Court of Human Rights (ECtHR) and the quantity and specificity of the norms is less significant.

---

[30] Case C-619/18, *Commission v. Poland*, ECLI:EU:C:2019:531 [hereinafter *Polish Supreme Court*]; Case C-216/18 PPU, *Minister for Justice and Equality v. LM*, ECLI:EU:C:2018:586 [hereinafter *Celmer*]. For a summary of the many preliminary references and infringement actions against Poland that are pending in the ECJ, see Opinion of Advocate General Tanchev, Joined Cases C-585/18, C-624/18 and C-625, A.K. v. *Krajowa Rada Sądownictwa* and *CP DO v. Sąd Najwyższy*, ECLI:EU:C:2019:551.

Nevertheless, there are two important sources of uncertainty: First, so far, the case law has tied surveillance of constitutional fundamentals to Member State application and implementation of EU law. However, it has been suggested that the Court should unmoor the rule of law, rights, and democracy from the specific obligations of EU law and police Member States *tout court*, as a direct obligation of Member States under Article 2 TEU to govern with respect for constitutional fundamentals.[31] This change could potentially allow the Court to cover elements of domestic constitutional orders that still today are omitted from the scope of EU law but nonetheless are central to a functioning liberal democracy. The second and related source of uncertainty is the question of which rights and duties will be monitored by the ECJ in light of the vagueness of the Article 2 TEU values. At present, the focus has been judicial independence, but that is only one of the important elements of liberal democratic morality. The Court will undoubtedly draw from the EU Charter of Fundamental Rights, in a process that might eventually come to resemble the US Supreme Court's incorporation of the US Bill of Rights, which originally only applied to the federal government but beginning in the early twentieth century was gradually and selectively applied to the states.

The chart below summarizes, chronologically, the evolution of the different policy areas with attention to the type of legal norms used at each stage. It shows a clear trajectory from the international to supranational category for human migration and internal security, and to a lesser extent for constitutional fundamentals. With respect to economic policy, the legal norms are both international and supranational and the situation is still in flux.

6 Reducing Legal Complexity and Bolstering the Rule of Law in the EU

Reducing complexity and improving the knowability of law through simplification is a perennial item on the EU agenda and this discussion highlights a

---

[31] See Scheppele and Kelemen's analysis in this volume of Case C-64/16, *Associação Sindical dos Juízes Portugueses* v. *Tribunal de Contas*, ECLI:EU:C:2018:117; Laurent Pech and Sébastien Platon, "Judicial Independence under Threat: The Court of Justice to the Rescue in the ASJP Case," *Common Market Law Review* 55, no. 6 (2018): 1827–1854; Carlos Closa, "Reinforcing EU Monitoring of the Rule of Law: Normative Arguments, Institutional Proposals and the Procedural Limitations," in *Reinforcing Rule of Law Oversight in the European Union*, eds. Carlos Closa and Dimitry Kochenov (Cambridge: Cambridge University Press, 2016); Christophe Hillion, "Overseeing the Rule of Law in the EU: Legal Mandate and Means," in *Reinforcing Rule of Law Oversight in the European Union*, eds. Carlos Closa and Dimitry Kochenov (Cambridge: Cambridge University Press, 2016).

TABLE 1 *Mapping Type of Legal Norms in Sovereignty-Sensitive Policy Areas: International and Supranational*

POLICY AREA	PRE-MAASTRICHT	MAASTRICHT (1992)	AMSTERDAM (1997)	CONTEMPORARY DEVELOPMENTS: POST-LISBON/EURO CRISIS
ECONOMIC POLICY		1st Pillar (EMU)		**TFEU** -**Art. 136(3) TFEU on bailouts** (2011) -**Six Pack** (2011) -**Two Pack** (2013) -**C-8/15 P to C-10/15 P**, *Ledra Advertising* (2016) *International:* *-EFSF (2010); ESM (2012)* *-Fiscal Compact (2012)* *-IGA on bank resolution (2014)*
HUMAN MIGRATION (BORDER CONTROL AND IMMIGRATION)	*Schengen Convention; Dublin Convention*	*3rd Pillar (conventions, joint actions)*	1st Pillar But: limited preliminary reference jurisdiction	**TFEU**
INTERNAL SECURITY	*Schengen Convention*	*3rd Pillar (conventions, joint actions)*	*3rd Pillar (conventions, framework decisions [FD], decisions)* But: optional preliminary reference jurisdiction and indirect effect for FD	**TFEU** But: 3rd Pillar measures still in force with same legal effects as before; exception for preliminary reference review of police action
CONSTITUTIONAL FUNDAMENTALS			*Arts. 6 & 7 TEU (renumbered as Arts. 2 & 7 TEU in Lisbon Treaty)*	**Jurisprudential developments under TFEU:** -**Commission infringement action (C-619/18,** *Polish Supreme Court***)** -**Preliminary reference (C-216/18 PPU,** *Celmer***)**

Key: International instruments and legal norms are in *italics*; supranational instruments and legal norms are in **bold**. Aspects of the norms that are not captured by the international/supranational categorization are in plain font.

Conclusion 549

number of areas where progress could still be made.[32] First, even though as discussed earlier, directives have largely become supranational instruments, there is one circumstance in which directives still cannot officially be invoked by individuals in their Member State courts – in horizontal situations between individuals. In light of the substantial doctrinal evolution that has occurred since *Van Duyn* and the other early directive cases from the 1970s and 1980s, it seems that the time is ripe to discard this rule.[33] The test for direct effect, which is based on the precision of the norms, could still be applied to the individual provisions of directives (and, of course, all other types of legal instruments), but establishing that the norms are precise enough to allow for claims to be litigated would now effectively operate as just one of many conditions that individuals must satisfy to succeed in court – conditions that are central to virtually all legal systems. By discarding the special rule on horizontal direct effect, the doctrine would no longer operate to categorically exclude certain types of EU law from being litigated in Member State courts as under the original doctrine of direct effect.[34] With respect to bailouts, irrespective of which proposal for ESM reform is adopted, MoUs should be integrated with the system of legal instruments in the TFEU and should be subject to the ordinary jurisdiction of the ECJ. Based on an inventory of the remaining Third Pillar measures for internal security, the ones of any significance should be identified; they should either be readopted as TFEU measures or, if not politically feasible, any pertinent differences with respect to their TFEU counterparts should be highlighted.[35]

One objection to reducing the scope for international-style instruments by curtailing the doctrine of direct effect and consolidating everything within the TFEU is that it reduces the flexibility of norms in a political system where state sovereignty is still critical. But there are many other tools available to lawmakers to signal that legal norms are open-textured and cannot give relief

---

[32] For instance, legal simplification was one of the four mandates given to the drafters of the Constitutional Treaty. See Jean-Claude Piris, *The Lisbon Treaty: A Legal and Political Analysis* (Cambridge: Cambridge University Press, 2010), 11.

[33] This is certainly not a novel suggestion, since the prejudice to legal certainty caused by doctrinal innovations that expand the effect of directives in horizontal situations can be said to be as great or greater than the prejudice to legal certainty that would be caused by a wholesale doctrinal shift to direct effect. See Opinion of Advocate General Jacobs, Case C-316/93, *Nicole Vaneetveld* v. *Le Foyer*, ECLI:EU:1994:32, para. 31.

[34] *Deuxième colloque internationale de droit européen organisé par l'Association néerlandaise pour le droit européen, The Hague, October 24–26, 1963* (Zwolle: N.V. Uitgeversmaatschappij W.E.J. Tjeenk Willink, 1966), 49–63.

[35] In this sense, see Steve Peers, *EU Immigration and Asylum Law*, vol. I of *EU Justice and Home Affairs Law*, 4th ed. (Oxford: Oxford University Press, 2016), 72.

550   Francesca Bignami

to affected individuals in court, without having to resort to the legal fiction
that those norms do not exist in court. Most straightforward, the legal norm
can be written in such a way that it does not dictate specific outcomes for
individuals when they go to court, even though it does oblige state authorities
to take steps to implement common policies. Another possibility is the use of
labels to signal how rigid or flexible the instrument is intended to be – on the
flexible end of the spectrum Article 288 TFEU already includes "recommendations" but there could also be "guidelines" or "guidance."

II ACCESS TO JUSTICE AND FIRST- AND SECOND-GENERATION RIGHTS

One of the remarkable things about the current politics is that the essential
dilemmas of public law that marked the development of the nation state in the
nineteenth and twentieth centuries are today front and center of the EU legal
stage. As EU policymaking has expanded to core state prerogatives, the
fundamental rights mission of the ECJ has mushroomed. The ECJ has issued
numerous judgments on the rights of criminal suspects in cases involving the
European Arrest Warrant[36] and in fraud prosecutions.[37] It has heard and, so
far, rejected claims that cuts in public sector salaries and pensions, designed to
satisfy the conditions attached to EU bailouts, violate the property and social
rights of those public employees.[38] These are first- and second-generation
constitutional rights that are enshrined in national constitutions, that are
elaborated in national criminal procedure, criminal law, and labor and social
security law, and that go to the heart of the liberal and social democratic
constitutional tradition.[39]

Developing a jurisprudence of first- and second-generation rights is not
categorically different from earlier forms of ECJ fundamental rights litigation.
The right to certain forms of public income together with the associated
equality and legitimate expectations guarantees have been litigated in the
context of the common agricultural policy and other market sectors since

---

[36] See, e.g., *Melloni; Celmer.*

[37] C-42/17, *Criminal proceedings against M.A.S. and M.B.*, ECLI:EU:2017:936.

[38] C-258/14, *Florescu*, ECLI:EU:C:2017:448.

[39] For a discussion of the difference between first- and second-generation rights in the French
tradition, see Diane Roman, "Les droit sociaux, entre 'injusticiabilité' et 'conditionnalité':
éléments pour une comparaison," *Revue international de droit comparé* 61, no. 2(1) (2009):
285–313. For a comparative law survey of social rights, see Krzysztof Wojtyczek, ed., *Social
Rights as Fundamental Rights: XIXth International Congress of Comparative Law* (The Hague:
Eleven International Publishing, 2016).

Conclusion 551

the 1960s.[40] Due process rights have been established in the context of administrative enforcement of competition law, again since the 1960s.[41] There are good reasons to believe that the Court's jurisprudential method for developing rights based on the "constitutional traditions common to the Member States" can be transferred relatively seamlessly from the market arena to economic policy, internal security, and other sovereignty-sensitive areas.

Where the current phase of fundamental rights adjudication gives pause is in the mechanisms available for bringing claims against EU measures before the ECJ. Access to justice for individuals is based on the so-called subjective rights model of public law litigation. When the Court was first established in the 1950s, it was largely conceived as a judicial forum for hearing claims of illegal behavior by public administration. The drafters of the Treaty of Rome adopted the German model of subjective rights in property and liberty, as opposed to the French model of objective interests in lawful government, as the test for obtaining standing and getting individual claims heard by the Court.[42] This had the effect of dramatically limiting access to the Court, and channeling most litigation, including litigation challenging the validity and fundamental rights compliance of EU measures, through the system of preliminary references from domestic courts to the ECJ. Notwithstanding the considerable critique of this system over the years,[43] it was changed only marginally in the Lisbon Treaty and standing doctrine remains largely the same as it was in 1957.

Now that the EU governs in the areas of economic policy, human migration, and internal security, the preliminary reference mechanism as the vehicle for testing the validity of EU legislation and other legal acts of general application is coming under strain. There are at least two reasons to think that preliminary references are ill suited to the current governance landscape. First, and most straightforward, the fundamental rights at stake now are more central to individual well-being and liberal and social democratic morality than the economic rights vindicated by the relatively sophisticated market

---

[40] See Eleanor Sharpston, "Legitimate Expectations and Economic Reality," *European Law Review* 15, no.2 (1990): 103–160.

[41] See Francesca Bignami, "Creating European Rights: National Values and Supranational Interests," *Columbia Journal of European Law* 11, no. 2 (2005): 259–272.

[42] Michel Fromont, "L'influence du droit français et du droit allemand sur les conditions de recevabilité du recours en annulation devant la Cour de Justice des Communautés Européennes," *Revue trimestrielle de droit européen* 2, no. 1 (1966): 47–65.

[43] See, e.g., Erik Petersen, "L'influence possible du droit anglais sur le recours en annulation auprès de la Cour de Justice des Communautés Européennes," *Revue trimestrielle de droit européen* 2, no. 1 (1966): 31.

actors of the previous generation of litigation. Preliminary references always involve delay and uncertainty, both because of the complex national systems that exist for litigating against public authorities and because of resistance of domestic courts to making preliminary references on the validity issue – out of deference to the external imperatives of enforcing EU law, reluctance to delay the resolution of the case, aversion to losing control of the case to Luxembourg, and other reasons. Although the structural benefits of the preliminary reference system might have outweighed the disadvantages in the common market days, the calculus changes once the policy prerogatives and rights shift.

Acknowledging this qualitative difference between litigation in the new and old policy areas, the Lisbon Treaty modified the preliminary reference procedure so that if the question is "with regard to a person in custody, the Court of Justice of the European Union shall act with the minimum of delay."[44] But the actual deprivation of physical liberty is not the only reason why public powers in the areas of human migration and internal security are more central to liberal democratic morality than market regulation. Arbitrary state action in these areas can oppress and deter democratic participation without having to incarcerate individuals. Similarly, the budgetary constraints imposed by EU economic law have important effects on public sector pay and the availability of social services and social security programs, as well as the equal treatment of beneficiaries and respect for their legitimate expectations. These are considered property and social rights in the European constitutional tradition and it is important for citizens to be able to test EU policies based on these rights. In sum, there is good reason to think that it should be easier to litigate in Luxembourg now that the EU acts in domains of classic state sovereignty that have significant impacts on the civil, political, and social rights of EU citizens.

The second development, also connected to the EU's contemporary policy agenda, is that in sovereignty-sensitive areas the allocation of responsibility between the different levels of government can be complex, which, in turn, can prevent cases from being heard in Luxembourg. Even as Member States are driven by the spillover logic to govern through the EU, they seek to retain as much control as possible to preserve their distinctive national approaches and bureaucratic organizations. Therefore, EU legislation in sovereignty-sensitive policy areas typically grants Member States considerable discretion. There is a stark contrast between these new arrangements – broadly sketched conditionality attached to the various bailout funds, minimum harmonization

---

[44] Article 267 TFEU.

Conclusion

of immigration and criminal law, optional law enforcement cooperation through EU agencies, to name just a few – and the administration of the customs and common agricultural policy (CAP) of the first decades of European integration. In the celebrated string of fundamental rights cases that were brought through the preliminary reference system in the 1970s, all of which involved a combination of CAP and customs law, there was no question that the German authorities were acting in a ministerial fashion by executing the commands of CAP regulations and that the challenge should be aimed at the European legal sources, not the German administrative acts.[45] Today, when a retiree's pension is cut, an individual is stopped at the external border, or a suspect is put on trial for terrorism, it is far less clear what part of that state action is attributable to EU law, what part to Member State law.

In principle, it is not necessary to be able to scientifically parse which authority is responsible for what to challenge the fundamental rights *bona fides* of a Member State act taken in the context of an EU legislative scheme. The doctrinal test is that all Member State actions taken to implement EU law or that come within the scope of EU law can be reviewed by the ECJ for fundamental rights; a wide array of Member State determinations have been swept up under this test. In practice, however, the test has not proven as generous as it might seem on its face. In certain cases, the EU layer can be unclear to litigants and national courts and therefore they may not refer the issue to the ECJ; or, if they do refer the issue, they may fail to establish to the satisfaction of the ECJ the requisite link between the national measure and the EU law. Besides the legal confusion, there are also strategic reasons for not referring the validity issue to the ECJ. National courts, by training their fundamental rights scrutiny on the domestic policies adopted to implement EU law, can avoid head-on conflicts with the EU and can retain control over the case and the fundamental rights determination.

Putting together the two pieces of the puzzle, the risk is that EU law will not be reviewed for compliance with fundamental rights, and for compliance with fundamental rights that are central to the liberal and social democratic identity kit. In the past, so-called privileged parties that always have standing, in particular the European Parliament, might have served as surrogates for individuals in fundamental rights litigation. However, as the Parliament becomes

---

[45] C-29/69, *Stauder v. Stadt Ulm*, ECLI:EU:C:1969:57; C-11/60, *Internationale Handelsgesellschaft*, ECLI: EU:C:1970:114; C-44/79, *Hauer v. Land Rheinland-Pflaz*, ECLI: EU:C:1979:290.

more politicized, a phenomenon that is discussed in Renaud Dehousse's contribution to this book (Chapter 6), and is more directly connected to the political forces in the Commission and the Council involved in passing laws, it can be expected to behave more like a standard legislature and less like a fundamental rights advocate. In sum, the traditional system of access to justice for individuals, based on the subjective rights model of litigation, is increasingly out of sync with the political realities and the formal powers of the EU. The inadequacies of the preliminary reference system in sovereignty-sensitive domains are illustrated below with examples from the areas of economic policy, human migration, and internal security.

1 Economic Policy

As explained earlier, in absolute figures, the most important bailouts were conducted under international agreements and their loan terms were treated as international legal norms. However, there were smaller loans made under programs established under the TFEU, namely Article 143 TFEU balance of payments assistance and Article 122 (2) TFEU on granting Union financial assistance to Member States (limited to the Union's relatively meager budget). These smaller loans also came with MoUs and yet even though the MoUs were based on the TFEU and therefore clearly legal norms of the supra-national variety, subject to the jurisdiction of the ECJ, there is only one case to date that has tested, through the preliminary reference procedure, the funda-mental rights compliance of MoU-related austerity measures.[46] By contrast, there has been extensive litigation on the constitutionality of such programs under national constitutional law in national courts, in particular in Latvia, Portugal, and Romania.

Even though access to domestic courts has been relatively straightforward, access to the ECJ has been far more difficult, in large measure because of the Member State discretionality characteristic of sovereignty-sensitive legal frameworks more generally speaking. The legal scholar Claire Kilpatrick has extensively documented and analyzed this phenomenon in her writings.[47]

---

[46] Florescu.
[47] See Kilpatrick, "The EU and Its Sovereign Debt Programmes"; Claire Kilpatrick, "Constitutions, Social Rights and Sovereign Debt States in Europe: A Challenging New Area of Constitutional Inquiry," in Constitutional Change through Euro-Crisis Law, eds. Thomas Beukers, Bruno de Witte, and Claire Kilpatrick (Cambridge: Cambridge University Press, 2017), 279–326.

In most of the cases brought to the constitutional courts of Latvia, Portugal, and Romania, there were no preliminary references made on the validity of the national austerity measures under EU law. Part of the reason was that the relationship between the EU bailout sources and the national laws cutting pensions, public sector pay, and other forms of public spending was unclear; fiscal law is complex as a general matter, and the EU layer of legal sources was particularly complex and lacking in transparency. Another reason for the dearth of preliminary references was the desire of national constitutional courts to avoid confrontation with, and interference by, EU institutions. In those cases where preliminary references were made, most were summarily rejected by the ECJ because the national court had not adequately articulated the relationship between the national austerity legislation and the EU bailout sources, as necessary to invoke social and property rights under the EU Charter of Fundamental Rights. The upshot of this procedural obstacle course is that there is copious national jurisprudence on the social and property rights that must be considered in designing austerity measures but hardly any ECJ jurisprudence on those same rights when European leaders devise the bailout terms that drive austerity measures.

2 Human Migration

Even though EU law on border controls and third-country nationals has expanded considerably, the Member States continue to enjoy extensive autonomy with respect to the substantive and procedural criteria for entry and residence and with respect to the administrative apparatus, which remains overwhelmingly national. At the same time, the borderless Schengen Area and the variegated set of travel and residence entitlements that apply when third-country nationals move between the Member States require extensive cooperation among national authorities. Information exchange on third-country nationals has emerged as the EU's principal tool for managing border control and immigration policy in this context of pervasive decentralization. As explained in Niovi Vavoula's contribution to this volume (Chapter 9), national authorities now enter information into and extract information from a number of EU databases on third-country nationals – SIS II, Eurodac, VIS, EES, and ETIAS.

Although some of these EU databases have been operational for quite some time, none have been challenged before the ECJ, through the preliminary reference system or any other procedural avenue. Yet there are clearly possible fundamental rights objections that can be made, as elaborated in Vavoula's data protection and privacy analysis, and in Valsamis Mitsilegas's rule-of-law analysis in Chapter 11 of this volume. The reason for the dearth of challenges again rests in the discretion built into this sovereignty-sensitive area of law. Any determination that affects the liberty or property interests of an individual, which is what in the EU's subjective rights model is necessary to bring a challenge to the EU regulations establishing the databases, is at least one step removed from the information contained in the database at issue. Even when, as a matter of EU law, national authorities are compelled to consult the database and to deport individuals based on the information contained in the database, the result is never automatic because of the application of discretionary factors to the removal decision. Moreover, this chain of events is quite uncommon in the operation of EU databases. Many of their features are designed as convenient tools for national authorities to assist them with different functions, not mandatory duties. It may never be clear to the individuals concerned whether their information in the EU database was consulted or was used to make an adverse determination. In these types of administrative arrangements, it is difficult to peel away the different levels of government action and attack what plausibly is at the source of the alleged injustice – the EU legislation establishing the database. To put the problem as concretely as possible, what route would an EU citizen take to obtain a judgment on the right to personal data protection in the revamped database on asylum seekers (Eurodac) or the Schengen database (SIS II), similar to the judgments that have been rendered by the German Constitutional Court on functionally similar German databases?[48]

3 Internal Security

If anything, protection of internal security touches even more directly upon state sovereignty than control over human migration, and the EU legislative schemes in this domain build in extensive flexibility at the national level. As explained in the internal security part of this book, information exchange is an important type of EU policy instrument for enabling national police and judicial authorities to combat cross-border criminal activities. Most of the EU databases on third-country nationals discussed previously can also be consulted by law enforcement actors in the context of criminal investigations. Moreover, there are a number of EU information systems that are specifically directed at detecting and investigating criminal activity and obtaining

---

[48] See, e.g., Bundesverfassungsgericht, Judgment 1 BvR 518/02 of April 4, 2006 (police counterterrorism data mining); Judgment 1 BvR 1215/07 of April 24, 2013 (counterterrorism database).

information on previous convictions, including among others: the Europol Information System; the decentralized Prüm system for exchanging fingerprints, DNA, and vehicle registrations; the decentralized European Criminal Records Information System; and the newly established European Criminal Records Information System for Third-Country Nationals.

None of these internal security databases have been the target of fundamental rights challenges in the EU court system. The reasons are similar to those analyzed in the context of border control and immigration since the discretionary logic evident there applies with even greater force to law enforcement bodies. For the most part, EU information systems are crafted as attractive tools for national police and judicial authorities and do not include mandatory duties on inputting data, extracting data, or taking follow-up measures to pursue the alleged criminal activity. This characteristic of EU information systems can sometimes get lost in the operation of European Arrest Warrants, which do create specific duties – they are registered in SIS II, they are subject to a mutual recognition system that creates a quasi-automatic duty to return the suspect to the home Member State, and they have generated copious litigation in domestic courts and the ECJ. European Arrest Warrants, however, represent only one of the many EU schemes involving information exchange designed to assist law enforcement actors; most do not operate with quasi-automatic triggers and instead vest national bodies with considerable discretion. As a result, the EU layer can be invisible to those who would have standing to challenge EU legislation in the subjective rights model – the individuals placed under surveillance or prosecuted by their national authorities who defend against police and prosecutorial action in their domestic courts.

The EU has also enacted a number of minimum harmonization directives designed to facilitate evidence gathering and to create a common baseline for the criminal proceedings of national authorities, both the procedural and substantive aspects. At the same time, precisely because of the contentiousness and sovereignty implications of EU internal security policy, these directives allow for considerable discretion when they are transposed into national law.[49] Here too, the difficulty of allocating responsibility for state action in the EU's multi-level system has impeded fundamental rights challenges to the EU portion of the legislative framework. So far, the most vivid illustration of this phenomenon is the litigation generated by the EU Data Retention Directive.[50]

---

[49] Part of the reason for this discretion was the old split between the First and the Third Pillars, but that split itself reflected the national sensitivities of internal security policy.
[50] European Parliament and Council Directive 2006/24/EC, O.J. (L 105) 54.

The Directive sought to improve the investigative capacities of national police authorities by requiring national telecommunications providers to retain the telecommunications data of their clients. However, the Directive also gave extensive leeway to Member State legislatures at the transposition phase to define the length of the retention period and the conditions that had to be satisfied for the police to obtain access to the data.

When data retention came under fire for violating data protection and privacy rights, a number of national constitutional courts preferred to review the national component alone, rather than refer the question of the validity of the EU Directive to the ECJ.[51] It is reasonable to suspect that some of the motives mimicked those evident in economic policy and judicial review of austerity measures – a desire to retain control of the issue and to avoid direct confrontation with EU institutions, including the ECJ. Of course, ultimately, the Directive did come before the ECJ in preliminary references made by an Irish court and the Austrian Constitutional Court, and the ECJ found that it was invalid on fundamental rights grounds.[52] That judgment, however, was handed down almost seven years after the Member State duty to transpose the Directive had taken effect and after a number of national constitutional courts had issued their own judgments.

The discretionary logic of minimum harmonization very likely serves as an obstacle to fundamental rights scrutiny with respect to other pieces of EU criminal law. For instance, as Valsamis Mitsilegas observes in Chapter 11, the EU legislation setting down a common set of terrorist offenses adopts a preventive justice model that criminalizes travel and speech activities – activities that in a classic, backward-looking system of criminal justice are generally treated as legitimate.[53] So far, however, there has not been a fundamental rights challenge to this EU legislation. Part of the reason may very well be that EU law only establishes a common core for the terrorist offenses and, at the time of transposition, the Member States can leave a heavy national footprint, making it difficult to separate the EU from the national components.

---

[51] Curtea Constituțională Decision No. 1258, October 8, 2009 (Romania); Bundesverfassungsgericht, Judgment 1 BvR 256/08 of March 2, 2010 (Germany); Cyprus Supreme Court, Civil Applications 65/2009, 78/2009, 82/3009 and 15/2010-22/2010, February 1, 2011; Constitutional Court of the Czech Republic, Pl. ÚS 24/10, March 22, 2011.

[52] Joined Cases C-293/12 and C-594/12, *Digital Rights Ireland*, ECLI:EU:C:2014:238.

[53] See European Parliament and Council Directive (EU) 2017/541, On Combating Terrorism, 2017 O.J. (L 88) 6 (replacing Council Framework Decision 2002/475/JHA).

Conclusion

4 *Expanding Individual Standing in the European Court of Justice and Reinforcing Rights in EU Legislation*

It is certainly not the case that all law must be tested in court for adherence to fundamental rights. There is undoubtedly a place for the political branches to interpret and apply higher-law requirements. Moreover, it is intrinsic to the multi-level system of European governance and the subsidiarity principle that there will be differences in the fundamental rights enjoyed by the citizens of the many Member States. At the same time, it should not be possible for national governments to evade constitutional requirements and rights by shifting important policy determinations from the domestic to the EU level. To do so would quite obviously undermine the legitimacy and credibility of the EU. The preliminary reference system, which forms the backbone of the EU judiciary by linking domestic courts with the ECJ, has quite rightly been celebrated as one of the motors of European integration.[54] At the same time, as this discussion has suggested, the preliminary reference system does not always allow for adequate fundamental rights scrutiny of EU legal acts.

The obvious solution to this dilemma would be to take up once again the proposals for loosening conditions of individual standing in the ECJ. The last time there was extensive debate on the issue was during the Convention on the Future of Europe, which was responsible for drafting the Constitutional Treaty of 2004. The various subgroups included one on the European Court of Justice, where a number of options were put forward for expanding direct access.[55] Two in particular would address the shortcomings reviewed earlier. First, it was proposed that individuals could be given the right to file fundamental rights complaints against EU legal acts directly with the ECJ. Second, it was suggested that the criteria be relaxed for individual standing before the Court, as specified in Article 263 TFEU. The most generous version of this shift would have enabled individuals affected by EU legal acts of general application, including what this chapter has been referring to as EU legislation, to be challenged in the ECJ based on all the legal grounds typically

---

[54] See, e.g., Joseph H. H. Weiler, The Transformation of Europe, *Yale Law Journal* 100, no. 8 (1991): 2413–2415; Karen J. Alter, *Establishing the Supremacy of European Law: The Making of an International Rule of Law in Europe* (Oxford: Oxford University Press, 2001); Alec Stone Sweet and Thomas L. Brunell, "Constructing a Supranational Constitution: Dispute Resolution and Governance in the European Community," *American Political Science Review* 92, no.1 (1998): 63–81.

[55] European Convention, Chairman of the Discussion Circle on the Court of Justice, Final Report of the Discussion Circle on the Court of Justice, CONV 636/03, CERCLE I 1 (March 25, 2003).

available under Article 263 TFEU, which includes rights. Although this is not the place for discussing the specifics of the different proposals, the growing power of the EU in areas that heavily implicate fundamental rights strongly suggests that it is time to revise the clunky procedural system for challenging EU laws and other legal acts of general application.

III INTERGOVERNMENTALISM AND SUPRANATIONAL DEMOCRACY

It is common ground in the European constitutional tradition that it is not enough to have legal rules that are clear and that can be enforced in a judicial forum; and not enough to have legal rules that can be challenged based on the higher law of the system. Those legal rules must also be generated through processes that are considered democratic. Since the Maastricht Treaty's paradigm shift from single market to political union, the question of whether the European Union is capable of operating as a true democracy has been a constant preoccupation for politicians and scholars alike. The perplexities of overcoming the democratic deficit and creating the institutional and societal underpinnings for a supranational democracy have been recurring themes over the past twenty-five years.[56]

With the Lisbon Treaty, it appeared that there would be a pause in the debate on the democratic deficit. Although the rejection of the Constitutional Treaty made it clear that the public did not have the stomach for a true Europe-wide constitution, the Lisbon Treaty that followed included many of the same democratizing institutional innovations, just stripped of constitutional symbolism.[57] The Lisbon Treaty consolidated what had come to be known as the Community method for lawmaking and entrenched a hierarchical model of legislative and administrative power that replicated in many ways the institutional arrangements of national democracies. Significantly, the Community method of Commission legislative proposal and co-decision by Parliament and Council was relabeled the "ordinary legislative procedure."[58] The Parliament (together with the Council) was formally tasked with the "legislative and budgetary" function and was also given the "political control" function.[59] The Treaty provided that the acts enacted through this legislative procedure could confer "delegated" and "implementing" powers to the

---

[56] See Chapter 18 for references to the literature on the EU's democratic deficit and Peter L. Lindseth's contribution to the debate.

[57] See generally Piris, *The Lisbon Treaty*.

[58] Article 289 TFEU.

[59] Article 14 TEU.

Conclusion 561

Commission[60] and left standing the existing ECJ jurisprudence under which it was permissible to delegate powers to bodies not established under the Treaties, e.g. EU agencies, as long as they were not "discretionary powers implying a wide margin of discretion."[61] This core institutional template was applied even to the sovereignty-sensitive policy areas covered in this book – human migration and internal security,[62] and certain aspects of economic policy.[63] This Lisbon template represented one attempt to reconcile the pragmatic politics of the supranational realm with the normative and ideal understandings of a democratic polity.

As it turns out, the entry into force of the Lisbon Treaty coincided with the onset of the European sovereign debt crisis and was followed, six years later, by the Syrian refugee crisis and several high-profile terrorist attacks in France and Belgium. To understand the democratic credentials of law in the economic policy, human migration, and internal security domains, it is important to ask what happened to the Lisbon template in the aftermath, in the various institutional responses to these crises. Looking broadly, it is apparent that the European Parliament and the allocation of responsibilities between legislation and administration tended to recede into the background and instead the intergovernmental model of bargaining among states and conferral of authority to administrative bodies that could be trusted to carry out those bargains took center stage.[64]

1 *Economic Policy*

As brought out in the economic policy section of this volume, intergovernmental tendencies have been on display in economic governance. The massive government bailouts that occurred during the euro crisis and the

---

[60] Articles 290 and 291 TFEU.

[61] C-9/56, *Meroni v. High Authority*, ECLI:EU:C:1958:7. For an up-to-date discussion of the jurisprudence, see Johannes Saurer, "EU Agencies 2.0: The New Constitution of Supranational Administration beyond the EU Commission," in *Comparative Administrative Law*, 2nd ed., eds. Susan Rose-Ackerman, Peter L. Lindseth, and Blake Emerson (Cheltenham: Edward Elgar, 2017), 619–631.

[62] In the interest of accuracy, it should be noted that there are a few exceptions, for instance the regulation of conditions under which law enforcement of one Member State may operate on the territory of another Member State (Article 89 TFEU).

[63] Article 121 TFEU on the adoption of regulations on the multilateral surveillance procedure.

[64] On the intergovernmental model generally, see Andrew Moravcsik, *The Choice for Europe: Social Purpose and State Power from Messina to Maastricht* (Ithaca, NY: Cornell University Press, 1998); more specifically on the role of administrative and judicial bodies in this model, see Mark A. Pollack, *The Engines of European Integration: Delegation, Agency, and Agenda Setting in the EU* (Oxford: Oxford University Press, 2003).

new fiscal apparatus that resulted, namely the ESM, have been driven by an intergovernmental coalition built around a Franco-German alliance.[65] The bargain that was reached was bailouts and an improved capacity for budgetary intervention, in return for austerity and fiscal stability. To credibly commit to this bargain, independent bodies have been given significant oversight and sanctioning powers over Member State fiscal policy. These delegations to independent bodies include the balanced budget rule in the Fiscal Compact, to be enforced by national constitutional courts and fiscal councils; and the reinforced Stability and Growth Pact, which confers significant surveillance and sanctioning powers over national budgets to the European Commission.[66]

In the area of banking regulation, which also revealed itself to be critical for the stability of the Eurozone, there also has been conferral of power to an independent body – the European Central Bank (ECB). In light of the tight relationship between banks and their Member States, in particular as a result of their government debt holdings, it was felt that national banking authorities did not adequately enforce the rules on minimum capital requirements and other issues central to bank solvency. Lax national regulators, and potential bank insolvencies, could risk destabilizing the entire Eurozone. To credibly commit to strict banking regulation, the Member States have taken away oversight and enforcement powers from national regulators and have given them to the independent ECB, which now has exclusive licensing and supervision powers over large banks, as well as a central role in winding up failed banks.[67]

It should be noted that these delegations stand out in the extent to which the Commission and the ECB operate independently of the political actors in the system and outside of ordinary accountability relationships. It is for this reason that the institutional schemes that have been created in economic policy fit more closely the pattern of credible commitments to facilitate interstate bargains than they do delegations of power to administrative authorities to improve the expertise and efficiency of policymaking – delegations that generally can be modified if the political actors in the system disagree. This enhanced independence is evident in a number of elements of economic governance. In surveilling national budgets and economic policies, if the Commission recommends sanctions against Member States for excessive budget deficits or for macroeconomic imbalances, those sanctions apply automatically unless vetoed by a qualified majority vote in the

---

[65] Chapter 4.
[66] Chapter 3; Chapter 6.
[67] Chapter 6.

Conclusion

563

Council.[68] This stands in contrast with the previous system by which the Council had to affirmatively adopt the recommended sanction for it to take effect. Although the European Parliament may request the Commission, Council, and other institutions to appear and give information on any aspect of the surveillance occurring in the European Semester, including potential sanctions (so-called Economic Dialogues), there are very few reporting requirements or other forms of direct parliamentary oversight.[69] With respect to bank regulation, it is generally agreed that the ECB is one of the most independent of all the institutions established under the EU Treaties.[70] Among other things, the ECB is constituted by national central banks, which themselves have constitutional guarantees of independence; it is governed by a President and members of an Executive Board that hold office for a fixed, eight-year term; and its operations are not subject to the same transparency regime as other institutions, at least in part to protect its independence.

2 *Human Migration*

In the domain of human migration, the EU's most developed scheme on the right of entry and residence for third-country nationals applies to asylum seekers. In asylum governance, the Syrian refugee crisis provoked unilateralism, followed by a certain amount of intergovernmentalism.[71] At the time of the crisis, a new generation of EU asylum legislation had just been adopted following the ordinary legislative procedure. Even though this legislation and the associated TFEU provisions contain mechanisms for dealing with migratory pressures, the political leaders of Austria, Hungary, Germany, and other Member States acted outside of this framework when confronted with large-scale secondary movements in 2015–2016; they unilaterally closed their borders using the emergency exception to border-free travel in the Schengen Border Code. Later on, there were two EU measures passed on emergency relocation of asylum seekers. However, they were not implemented by the countries of the Visegrad Group (Poland, Hungary, the Czech Republic, and Slovakia), leading to Commission infringement actions.

---

[68] Chapter 6.

[69] European Parliament Briefing, Economic Dialogue with the Other EU Institutions under the European Semester Cycles (2014–2019), PE 528.782 (January 2019).

[70] Antonio Estella, *Legal Foundations of EU Economic Governance* (Cambridge: Cambridge University Press, 2018), 76–87.

[71] See Chapter 8 for more detailed description and analysis of these developments in the asylum field, as well as references to the broader literature.

564 Francesca Bignami

So far, the most robust EU response to the refugee crisis has been the empowerment of EU agencies, most notably the European Border and Coast Guard (Frontex) and, to a lesser extent, the European Asylum Support Office (EASO). During the crisis, both Frontex and EASO assumed unprecedented operational responsibilities at hotspots in Greece and Italy. There is new legislation expanding Frontex's mandate, and a legislative proposal that would do the same for EASO. There is also the possibility that, *de facto*, these EU agencies might assume policymaking responsibilities. As Emilio De Capitani argues in his contribution to this book (Chapter 14), even though there is a legislative proposal on the table that seeks to improve what is broadly acknowledged to be a dysfunctional asylum system, the process remains deadlocked by intergovernmental disagreements; the risk is that Frontex will step into the void, thus exercising not simply operational but also policymaking functions.

This combination of unilateralism, legislative deadlock, and empowerment of EU agencies is another example of intergovernmentalism taking over from the Lisbon template. Action through the ordinary legislative procedure and the emergency mechanisms set out under the TFEU have proven difficult. Instead, Member States have either acted alone or through EU agencies, which, unlike the Commission and the ECB, are generally cast not as independent authorities but as more akin to creatures of the Member States.[72] They are headed by management boards comprised of Member State representatives; their permanent staff is not hired as part of the EU civil service system; and they rely heavily on personnel from Member State administrations, in the case of Frontex and EASO as seconded national officers charged with assisting the Member State under migratory pressure with border policing and asylum applications.[73] To be sure, as Evangelia (Lilian) Tsourdi argues in Chapter 8, it is vital to develop an administrative component to the Common European Asylum System. Moreover, the integrated administration that is spearheaded by EU agencies often reflects and develops common technocratic and supranational world views rather than serving as proxies for intergovernmental

---

[72] See R. Daniel Kelemen, "The Politics of 'Eurocratic' Structure and the New European Agencies," *West European Politics* 25, no. 4 (2002): 93–118; Ariadna Ripoll Servent, "A New Form of Delegation in EU Asylum: Agencies as Proxies of Strong Regulations," *Journal of Common Market Studies* 56, no. 1 (2018): 83–100.

[73] However, Frontex's autonomous administrative capacity has been enhanced with the recent adoption of EU legislation that will increase the number of Frontex employees from 1,500 to 10,000.

Conclusion 565

bargaining.[74] Nonetheless, it remains the case that in the asylum field, EU agencies have the potential for short-circuiting the European Parliament and the supranational dimension of legislation and administrative oversight.

3 *Internal Security*

With respect to internal security, there has been an acceleration of legislative activity since the Lisbon Treaty extended the ordinary legislative procedure, including qualified majority voting in the Council, to the policy field. There are now legislative measures facilitating mutual recognition in cross-border criminal investigations and prosecutions, setting down minimum standards for criminal offenses, and setting down minimum standards for rights of the defense and victims.[75] Among the most significant developments has been the legislation strengthening EU agencies involved in coordinating cross-border police investigations and criminal prosecutions – Europol, Eurojust, and now, for fraud involving the EU budget, the European Public Prosecutor.

In this field, the impact of crisis, which has taken the form of high-profile terrorist attacks, has been quite different from what has been observed in economic policy and human migration. Internal security is less integrated than the other two policy fields. It is characterized by national autonomy and unilateralism, but with ever-increasing efforts at cooperation under the EU umbrella. In this domain, Member State resistance to cooperation appears to have bureaucratic roots, not political ones as in the case of economic policy and bailouts or human migration and asylum burden-sharing. Police and prosecutors fear that disclosing information to authorities in other jurisdictions will compromise their sources and investigations and therefore they are reluctant to exchange strategic and operational information across borders and feed the relevant information on criminal activity into EU databases. There are many EU laws that seek to overcome this bureaucratic foot-dragging by creating and improving technical systems for information-sharing among Member State authorities; establishing freestanding EU databases that can be useful tools for national law enforcement actors; and imposing duties on national authorities to assist one another with evidence-gathering and prosecutions.

---

[74] Morten Egeberg and Jarle Trondal, "Researching European Union Agencies: What Have We Learnt (and Where Do We Go from Here)?" *Journal of Common Market Studies* 4, no. 55 (2017): 675–690.

[75] See Chapters 10 and 14; see also, with particular attention to the criminal law dimension, Valsamis Mitsilegas, *EU Criminal Law after Lisbon: Rights, Trust and the Transformation of Justice in Europe* (Oxford: Hart Publishing, 2016).

As highlighted in the internal security part of this volume, the EU legislative and administrative effort to counteract bureaucratic resistance to cooperation has been accelerated—not hindered—by high-profile terrorist attacks and other criminal events with cross-border dimensions. The new initiative announced by Commission President Juncker in April 2016, called the EU Security Union, includes a heavy emphasis on further expanding information-sharing and creating more EU information tools that can be attractive to national law enforcement authorities.[76] For instance, the new EU Passenger Name Record (PNR) System requires the exchange of PNR data to enable national authorities to identify terrorist suspects; Europol's newly established European Counter-Terrorism Centre pools already existing information and data analysis capacity to assist national counter-terrorism investigations; and the recently adopted EU legislation on making existing EU databases interoperable would effectively create a new resource for national police authorities.

Yet even as progress has been made on the operational aspects of cross-border investigations and prosecutions, the failure of national interior ministries and other government actors to communicate information continues to undermine the quality of EU legislation.[77] Many of the measures that have been enacted by the European Parliament and Council have been passed without comprehensive information on the shortcomings of national criminal law and law enforcement that would justify an EU layer of law and governance. In the same vein, the Commission has had difficulties obtaining the national data necessary to conduct periodic reviews of the effectiveness of EU legislation.

Internal security is marked by less integration than economic policy and human migration but recent terrorist attacks and other salient examples of cross-border criminal activity have led to the intensification of EU-level initiatives. Among the most significant advances in European integration has been information-sharing coordinated by Europol and Eurojust. However, these are EU agencies, which, as explained earlier, have a distinct intergovernmental bent. They are governed by management boards of Member State representatives, have relatively small permanent staffs that are recruited outside of the general civil service framework, and rely on domestic police and judicial officers seconded for limited periods for many of their personnel needs. By contrast, legislation and oversight by the supranational European Parliament and Commission have been hampered by

---

[76] Chapter 11.
[77] Chapter 14.

Conclusion 567

traditional state reluctance to disclose information and cooperate on issues related to territorial security.

4 *The European Parliament, the European Court of Justice, and Forging Supranational Deliberation and Democracy*

Beyond recognizing the intergovernmental tendencies in sovereignty-sensitive areas and the factual and political limits on the Lisbon Treaty's version of supranational democracy, this experience brings out what is missing from the current set up and what should be advanced in the future governance of sovereignty-sensitive policy fields – a pan-European perspective, which in the Lisbon template is to be supplied by the European Parliament. Even though intergovernmentalism can achieve results, as illustrated by the salvaging of the Eurozone, it comes up short on the construction of a European political identity. Bargains struck in Brussels are sold by European leaders at home because they are advantageous to national interest. The relationship between Brussels and national capitals is transactional rather than pitched as part of a wider scheme of governing in the common European interest.[78] National politicians are notorious for taking the credit when things are going well, and blaming Brussels when economic and other policy outputs stumble. Although there are of course exceptions, it is rare to hear European political leaders making the case for Europe to their voters, especially if the EU policy in question appears, on balance, to entail more burdens than benefits for the particular Member State.

The *European Parliament* is the one Europe-wide public forum where public policies and their effects on all Europeans can be debated and where elected representatives and their voters are confronted with the consequences of nationally driven conceptions of the public interest. The absence of social justice – both rights and solidarity – is cited by many as the principal flaw of EMU and the asylum system.[79] In the European Parliament, the moral implications of this absence can be confronted head on. It is a forum where it is difficult to avoid the question of whether EMU is sustainable or desirable when it imposes through its policies such regionally differentiated benefits and

---

[78] See Helen Wallace, "The JCMS Annual Review Lecture: In the Name of Europe," *Journal of Common Market Studies* 55, no. S1 (2017): 13. Although Wallace refers specifically to the UK relationship to the EU, it is also evident in the narratives and politics of other Member States.

[79] See, e.g., Agustín J. Menéndez, "The Crisis of Law and the European Crises: From the Social and Democratic *Rechtsstaat* to the Consolidating State of (Pseudo-)Technocratic Governance," *Journal of Law and Society* 44, no. 1 (2017): 56–78 (Eurozone); Chapter 8 (asylum).

burdens, and is complicit in generating vastly different life chances and circumstances. If the answer is no, then the European Parliament is also the place where the solutions to this hard question can be put forward and debated – whether it be to include EU citizens from other Member States within certain commitments to social rights and solidarity, to scale back on the European project, or some other route. Likewise, the Parliament offers a setting for scrutinizing the inequities of how the Schengen Area and the asylum system have played out – the attraction of Schengen Area border-free movement compounding the migratory pressures on Member States on the geographic frontline while at the same time the Dublin System assigning all responsibility for those asylum seekers to those same Member States.

Similarly, the European Parliament is an important forum for airing the civil and political rights dimensions of the EU's policies on human migration, internal security, and constitutional fundamentals. There are many material benefits to be gained from safeguarding the Schengen Area of borderless travel and ratcheting up the border control, immigration, and internal security policies that are central to governance of the Schengen Area. The risk, however, is that the implications for civil and political rights will be overlooked. A parliamentary body like the European Parliament is the natural venue for deliberating upfront and hardwiring these rights into human migration and internal security policy. In enforcing constitutional fundamentals against the Member States, there is also a temptation to overlook violations of civil and political rights in favor of economic, geopolitical, and other realpolitik considerations; the Parliament is a public forum for exposing the hypocrisy of EU approaches that privilege convenience over liberal democracy and turn a blind eye to democratic backsliding. In sum, the European Parliament and the surrounding politics and media can be said to represent the closest thing Europe has at the moment to Habermas's public sphere. It offers an important arena for developing a European identity and perspective on the critical areas of EU governance that have come to the fore over the past decade – an identity and perspective that are necessary for the legitimate governance of these areas in the long run.

By no means is this discussion intended to be starry-eyed about the European Parliament (EP). It is a well-established fact that turnout for EP elections is low and has declined over time.[80] For most of its history, voters have used EP elections to express their attitudes toward their national governments and

---

[80] Chapter 6 discusses politicization and voter behavior in national and EP elections; see also Julie Hassing Nielsen and Mark N. Franklin, eds., *The Euro-sceptic 2014 European Parliament Elections: Second Order or Second Rate?* (London: Palgrave, 2017).

Conclusion 569

parties, not their preferences on EU issues. Even with the rise of Euroskepticism and the many legal and political developments narrated in this book, EP elections have served more as an opportunity to express anti-EU sentiment than to take sides over the direction of important EU policies. At the level of parliamentary politics, it should come as no surprise that the workings of the European Parliament fall short of the democratic deliberation ideal. This volume offers two prominent examples of the grittier side of EP politics. As Kim Lane Scheppele and R. Daniel Kelemen explain in Chapter 15, the European People's Party (EPP), the largest pan-European political party in the EP and the party group of the center right, has been one of the biggest defenders of Hungary's Fidesz and Viktor Orbán. Since Fidesz is a member of the EPP and delivers the votes necessary for the EPP to sustain its lead over the other parties in the European Parliament, the EPP has stalled efforts to sanction Hungary for democratic backsliding. On a separate note, Emilio De Capitani (Chapter 14) explains that the European Parliament has opposed moves to improve transparency in the legislative process, and the progress that has been made can largely be attributed to litigation and the ECJ's jurisprudence. Nevertheless, the question of how to foster the pan-European perspectives and debates that are critical for supranational democracy remains. Even taking into account the Parliament's many flaws, it is better placed to foster such perspectives and debates than the intergovernmental Council and European Council or any of the EU's other institutions.

The upshot of this discussion is that even though the governance of sovereignty-sensitive policy areas often takes an intergovernmental turn, the European Parliament should still be kept in the loop. In the debates on Eurozone governance, there is an important proposal that has been advanced for a Eurozone parliament as a means of counteracting the inequities that have arisen from EU economic policy.[81] Although it is not politically viable to give the Parliament decisional powers over bailouts and fiscal surveillance at this point in European history, it is important for the Parliament to have oversight powers in the area. This requires greater transparency than is currently the case: The Commission's surveillance of Member State budgets and economic policies and the national measures taken in response should be made public and accessible, in layman's terms, to the Parliament and the public. Likewise, in border control, immigration, and internal security, the transparency of the relevant EU agencies (Frontex, EASO, Europol, Eurojust) could be enhanced and the Parliament's scrutiny powers improved. Currently

---

[81] Stéphanie Hennette, Thomas Piketty, Guillaume Sacriste, and Antoine Vauchez, *Pour un traité de démocratisation de l'Europe* (Paris: Éditions du Seuil, 2017).

these agencies submit their annual agency work programs to Parliament and consult Parliament on their multi-annual programs but there is the potential for more regular parliamentary involvement, debate, and input through routine agency reporting and oversight.[82] The European Parliament could also take a more proactive role in fostering pan-European civic education and public debate. For instance, it could publish and distribute a weekly or biweekly magazine for the general public, following examples such as the German Bundestag's *Das Parliament*. The publication could report on topical issues from the Parliament's perspective, and could also include an insert explaining in very straightforward language important aspects of EU policies and EU governance. In sum, the experience of European governance of sovereignty-sensitive policy areas demonstrates a penchant for intergovernmentalism, even in cases where the Lisbon Treaty provides otherwise. But it is possible to craft forms of parliamentary participation that have the potential for fostering pan-European debate and that might, in the future, overcome national fault lines and pave the way for an important decisional role for the Parliament.

It is fitting to conclude this discussion of EU law's democratic credentials with the *judicial branch*. In the Lisbon template, the *European Court of Justice* is tasked with the classic functions of a constitutional and administrative court and a court of last resort on EU legal sources. As is to be expected, the Court is not to exercise negative or positive legislative powers. However, a number of scholars argue that the Court has assumed such powers by giving overly expansive interpretations to the market freedoms in the TFEU and thereby illegitimately narrowing the space for legislative action and democratic choice.[83] In essence, the claim is that the Court has constitutionalized the market freedoms at the expense of the other objectives of the Treaties and European integration. More recently, a similar argument has been made with respect to EMU and its commitment to fiscal stability and a balanced

---

[82] European Parliamentary Research Service, *EU Agencies, Common Approach and Parliamentary Scrutiny: European Implementation Assessment* (Brussels: European Union, 2018), 57–67; 82–87.

[83] Dieter Grimm, "The Democratic Costs of Constitutionalisation: The European Case," *European Law Journal* 21, no. 4 (2015): 460–473; Gareth Davies, "The European Union Legislature as an Agent of the European Court of Justice," *Journal of Common Market Studies* 54, no. 4 (2016): 846–861; Fritz W. Scharpf, "De-Constitutionalisation and Majority Rule: A Democratic Vision for Europe," *European Law Journal* 23, no. 5 (2017): 315–334; Agustín José Menéndez, "Constitutional Review, Luxembourg Style: A Structural Critique of the Way in which the European Court of Justice Reviews the Constitutionality of the Laws of the Member States of the European Union," *Contemporary Readings in Law and Social Justice* 9, no. 2 (2017): 116–145.

Conclusion 571

budget.[84] The overall effect in the eyes of the critics is to have imposed a neoliberal mold on EU law and governance that is extremely difficult to shake.

The claim of judicial interference with the legislative process through over-constitutionalization is indeed a serious challenge for the democratic credentials of EU law. It also has special relevance for my analysis in this concluding chapter, since I argue for more supranational legal norms and expanded individual standing to reduce legal complexity and improve the protection of rights. Both proposals would, on their face, lead to an even greater role for the ECJ—with the potential for even more matters to be taken out of the hands of the EP and national parliaments.

On closer examination, however, these proposals would not necessarily empower the judicial branch more. As explained earlier, legal simplification by integrating the norms generated through ESM bailouts and the old Third Pillar with the TFEU and curtailing the doctrine of direct effect would not necessarily affect the flexibility of law, since there are many other techniques for signaling the flexibility of legal rules. The prospect of more fundamental rights challenges to EU measures by expanding individual standing in the ECJ likewise does not automatically imply greater constitutionalization. In light of the extensive array of rights protected by the EU Charter of Fundamental Rights (CFR), the Court will be called upon to balance fundamental rights of equal status, far more than in the previous generation of internal market litigation. Such multi-polar rights-balancing often produces indeterminate outcomes and allows the legislature's choices to stand. Similar considerations can be made with respect to the ECJ's potential future role in guaranteeing the constitutional fundamentals of the Member States. There is no reason why the margin of appreciation doctrine, used by ECtHR, cannot also be used by the ECJ when it scrutinizes Member State practices based on the guarantees of certain essential CFR provisions.

Turning to the terrain of judicial and political practice, there is evidence in the contributions to this volume that the TFEU provisions on market freedoms and fiscal stability are less rigid, more flexible than is sometimes presumed in the critical academic literature. The chapter by Ulf Öberg and Nathalie Leyns on intra-EU migration and the law of free movement of persons demonstrates that the Court has moved away from the neoliberal approach that it took in the *Laval*, *Rüffert*, and *Viking* line of cases.[85]

---

[84] See Chapter 17 and the literature cited therein.

[85] For other examples of less categorical application of the market freedoms, see Jan Zglinski, "The Rise of Deference: The Margin of Appreciation and Decentralized Judicial Review in EU Free Movement Law," *Common Market Law Review* 55, no. 5 (2018):1341–1385.

Moreover, they show that the EU legislature was able to mobilize in response to the ECJ's neoliberal jurisprudence and to enact new legislation giving Member States greater power to regulate the pay and working conditions of posted workers from other Member States.[86] In a similar vein, the chapters on economic policy by Nicolas Jabko and Renaud Dehousse separately bring out aspects of flexibility in EMU governance. Most straightforward, Jabko narrates how the no-bailout provision in the TFEU was amended when it proved necessary to save the euro. Dehousse argues that Commission enforcement of the rules on fiscal stability in the context of the Six Pack and Two Pack surveillance system is not automatic but allows for a fair bit of Commission discretion. In sum, the EU Treaties and the jurisprudence of the Court of Justice have not consistently operated as straightjacket and recent experience with market and economic governance furnishes a number of examples of where the political process has prevailed.

Hence there is good reason to believe that more litigation in the ECJ will not cut off legislative politics. In fact, in line with an important strand of legal theory, expanding individual standing to allow for more fundamental rights claims against EU legislation might spawn more vigorous democratic debate in the EU polity. Sociolegal scholarship has demonstrated that under certain circumstances rights can operate as a powerful discursive resource in politics and can serve as an important lightning rod for organized, collective challenges to the *status quo*.[87] This insight is particularly apt for the social rights that were written into many European constitutions after the Second World War, which require positive state action and the mobilization of material resources. Because of the spillover logic of European integration, democracy must play catch up with the policy and legal apparatus that has been built for economic policy, human migration, and internal security. Affirming, in the public and prestigious forum of the EU courtroom, not only liberal market rights but also the full array of civil, political, and social rights that are part of the European constitutional tradition can lend discursive resources to those political actors that seek to promote such rights in EP elections and debates.

---

[86] This is a counter-example to the "join decision trap," which magnifies the counter-majoritarian effect of an activist supreme court. Fritz W. Scharpf, "De-Constitutionalisation and Majority Rule: A Democratic Vision for Europe," *European Law Journal* 23, no. 5 (2017): 315–334; Fritz W. Scharpf, "The Joint Decision Trap: Lessons from German Federalism and European Integration," *Public Administration Review* 66, no. 3 (1988): 239–278.

[87] See Stuart A. Scheingold, *The Politics of Rights: Lawyers, Public Policy, and Social Change* (New Haven, CT: Yale University Press, 1974) and discussion of this and other sociolegal theories of rights in Michael McCann, "The Unbearable Lightness of Rights: On Sociolegal Inquiry in the Global Era," *Law and Society Review* 48, no. 2 (2014): 245–273.

A multi-faceted judicial practice of fundamental rights might contribute to more balanced political contestation over the appropriate direction for sovereignty-sensitive policy areas. To return to the populism with which this chapter began, it might help channel some of the outright opposition to the project of European integration into a plural and democratic debate over the content of the many policies of European integration.

IV CONCLUSION

The rule of law, rights, and democracy is not a tired idiom but a set of foundational legal values to be continuously revisited and assessed in the changing landscape of EU law. Over the past decade, the EU has become increasingly implicated in core areas of traditional state prerogatives, and the emerging legal architecture reveals a number of flaws. The excessive complexity of today's EU law undermines the ordering and liberty qualities of law. Simplification, by curtailing the doctrine of direct effect and integrating ESM law and old Third Pillar law with the TFEU, is critical. The laborious preliminary reference system is inadequate for calling to task EU lawmakers when they legislate on economic policy, human migration, and internal security and potentially breach fundamental civil, political, and social rights. Standing should be expanded so that it is easier for individuals to go to the European Court of Justice to obtain a hearing on potential legislative infringements of their fundamental rights. The intergovernmental politics of sovereignty-sensitive areas shortchanges the future development of Europe-wide debate and perspectives on the right direction for policymaking. There should be extensive reporting and disclosure in each of the policy areas to the European Parliament to keep alive pan-European debate and pave the way, eventually, for a living and breathing practice of supranational democracy. The Parliament could also take greater responsibility for routinely informing the lay public on important aspects of EU policy and governance. The trio of rule of law, rights, and democracy underscores the importance of the emerging law on Member State constitutional fundamentals and highlights the desirability of the ECJ's emerging role as a human-rights court.

Among pro-EU forces, thinking on legal reform is divided. On the one hand, there is little appetite for Treaty reform among European political leaders. Especially in the current political environment of populism and Euroskepticism, there is apprehension that any attempt to pick at, and improve, small pieces of the Treaties might embolden some to push for the wholesale unraveling of other parts of the Treaties. Treaty amendments also require Member State ratification, and that raises the prospect of national referenda, again something that is feared in the current political climate. On the other hand, as canvassed in the economic policy section of this book, the fallout from the euro crisis and austerity have led others to call for far-reaching Treaty reform, in particular to EMU – either the full-fledged transformation and federalization of economic policy or the dismantling of the common currency. To save Europe, the thinking goes, it is necessary to radically change her.

The analysis and proposals put forward here avoid this all-or-nothing schism in the debate on how to move forward. Significant Treaty changes present considerable political risks, which are not worth taking at this historical moment. The rule of law, rights, and democracy are undoubtedly better off with than without the EU construct and its central building blocks. In countless ways, EU citizens have been emboldened by the EU to exercise personal liberties and to freely define and pursue life projects – liberties and life projects that are hard to imagine in the absence of the EU's legal framework and geopolitical status. Historical counterfactuals are always tricky, but there is a good case to be made that pursued within the confines of the European nation state, or on a regional and world stage where EU citizenship meant little, these freedoms would be stunted. In responding to the current politics of anti-globalization and populist backlash, many have blamed well-heeled cosmopolitan elites and the inequitable distribution of the benefits and burdens of globalization that has created a large class of left-behinds. However fitting this diagnosis might be for other parts of the world, it has limited purchase over the EU. Even though neoliberalism and austerity have increased inequality over the past quarter-century, European societies are still marked by policies with significant redistributive and social insurance aims. Because of the continuing prominence of the social justice aspects of democracy, the educational, professional, employment, and cultural opportunities afforded by Europeanization have been quite broadly available. It is not only that goods have been able to move freely and generate new consumption habits. People have also had the means and the material safety net important for experimenting with educational, cultural, and employment opportunities in other European jurisdictions. The availability of public education, at both the secondary and post-secondary levels, and the social democratic aspects of labor markets and social security systems have enabled great numbers of EU citizens to take advantage of free movement.

Just because it is worthwhile asserting the virtues of the EU and appreciating the risks of tinkering too much with its legal construct does not mean that we should doff our critical caps and eschew constructive changes. Many of the

Conclusion 575

proposals advanced in this concluding chapter are modest and could be accomplished through changes in EU institutional practices. Improving the role of the European Parliament in economic policy, human migration, and internal security would simply require greater transparency and reporting by the European Commission and EU agencies, which could occur informally and eventually through an interinstitutional agreement. The European Parliament's publication activities are already significant and a weekly or bi-weekly magazine targeted at the lay public and distributed broadly should fit comfortably within that existing mission. The integration of old Third Pillar internal security measures into the TFEU would ideally include new legislative measures, but could also stop short; it could entail cataloging and explanation, akin to the preparatory work done by the European Commission's Legal Service when it consolidates or codifies EU law in specific policy areas. Some of the other proposals that emerge from this volume's survey of sovereignty-sensitive domains are targeted at the ECJ and could be accomplished through jurisprudential changes. This is particularly so for the doctrine of direct effect, which has been created by the ECJ and can be modified by the ECJ.

The only two elements of this chapter's constructive analysis that might require Treaty amendments are those concerning the integration of ESM law into the TFEU and the expansion of individual standing in the ECJ. Reform of the ESM that is focused on legal simplification (and not the more politically contentious issue of giving the EU institutions a direct decisional role in country bailouts) could require a Treaty amendment. That is because such a move would confer upon the ESM a special status like that of the ECB, which is established under the TFEU and is not an EU body created by legislative act. Under this special status, the ESM would have the power to issue decisions on its own authority, independent of the normal institutional constellation set out in the TFEU, while at the same time its decisions would have supranational – not international – legal status. As for individual standing, in the sixty years since the TFEU's jurisdictional system was first set down, the Court has been steadfast in giving the provision on individual standing a narrow interpretation. The last time the issue was extensively debated, during the Convention on the Future of Europe responsible for drafting the Constitutional Treaty, most of the participating scholars and jurists took the view that any change would require an express Treaty amendment. Although the merits of this position can be disputed, it is true that the specific kind of individual standing advocated here – some form of direct access to contest the fundamental rights compliance of all legal measures, including legislative acts – would be a dramatic departure from the current system. Thus, even though there might be room for expanding standing through doctrinal evolution in the case law, the path would be slow, and a Treaty amendment would be the surest vehicle for making the changes.

In short, limited Treaty amendments bringing the ESM into the EU legal order and allowing direct access for fundamental rights challenges to legislative acts and other legal acts of general application would be significant improvements to the EU legal order. Even if the political environment and calculus are not favorable currently, there are steps that could be taken to pave the way for future Treaty reform. In the case of any future bailouts, as briefly sketched in the introduction to this volume, the European Commission could systematically incorporate the MoU terms in the Two Pack fiscal surveillance regulation, which would place them in the TFEU's supranational system of legal norms and ECJ jurisdiction. Over the years, the many calls that have been made for reforming individual standing have been resisted with the assertion that between direct access for individual acts and preliminary references for everything else, the EU's system of access to justice is complete. In light of the legal developments covered in this book, the completeness claim should be carefully scrutinized by the EU institutions. However the particularities of these and the many other questions raised by this book are resolved, one thing is sure. The uncharted path of European integration is served best not by dogmas and orthodoxies but by the open-minded evaluation and re-evaluation of how to advance core European constitutional values in the EU's evolving legal, social, and political order.

Index

1951 Refugee Convention, 194, 196–197, 199

access to justice, 550–560
accession
   Article 7 TEU, 417
   Copenhagen criteria, 16–17, 417
   free movement of persons, 168–169
Adler-Nissen, Rebecca, 97
Aglietta, Michel, 503
Alternative für Deutschland (AfD), 3, 107, 479
Amsterdam Treaty, 548
   AFSJ, 377
   Article 7 TEU, introduction of, 16, 415, 417, 489, 545
   asylum policy, 197, 199, 375
   border control, 12, 236, 375, 377, 390, 542–543
   immigration, 12, 375, 377, 542–543
   internal security, 543
Anderson, Perry, 498
ANEL. *See* Independent Greeks
Area of Freedom Security and Justice (AFSJ)
   agenda 2019-2024, 407–409
   circumvention through CFSP, 404–405
   EU agencies, 396–398, 405–407
   European Parliament, 385
   intergovernmentalism, 404
   judicial independence, centrality of, 432–433
   legislative output post-Lisbon, 387–399
   Lisbon Treaty innovations, 375–387
   national parliaments, 385–386
   policymaking process, flaws of, 375–402
Article 2 TEU, 17, *see also* European values
   Article 7 TEU, 431–432
   Białowieża Forest case, 470, 473
   systemic infringement actions, 437–438

Article 7 TEU, 17, *see also* Rule of Law Framework
   ECJ jurisdiction, 545–546
   history of, 417
   Hungary, 419, 422–423, 426
   ineffectiveness, reasons for, 416, 418, 424–430
   intergovernmentalism, 17, 417–419, 429–430, 545
   Poland, 422–423, 428, 461
   procedure, 17, 417–419
   subnational authoritarianism, 430–431
Asylum Package, 391–393
asylum policy, 194–226, 391–393
Asylum Procedure Regulation (proposed), 392
Asylum, Migration and Integration Fund (AMIF), 218–222, 224
austerity, 499, 554–555
   Europeanization of politics, 22, 143–144
   Fiscal Compact, 56, 493–494, 497
   Greece, in, 106, 143–144
   populism, stoked by, 3–9, 478
Austerity Union, 495, 497–498

Babiš, Andrej, 482–483
bailouts
   conditionality, 9, 21, 40, 48, 50–51, 56, 61–62, 72, 83–85, 497, 516, 519, 552
   Cyprus, 57, 103
   enhanced surveillance (Two Pack), 10, 38, 108, 138, 540
   ESM, 9–10, 33, 48, 51, 58, 72, 102–103, 497, 516, 540, 571
   IMF, 37, 40, 72, 103, 143, 483
   Ireland, 82, 101, 103
   legal challenges (fundamental rights), 56–58
   MoU, 83–84, 497, 540, 549

577

578   *Index*

bailouts (cont.)
  permanent mechanism for, 9, 106–107
  sovereignty, impact on, 103–107
balanced budget rule
  Fiscal Compact, 10, 38, 70, 493, 495–496, 562
Ban, Cornel, 502
Bank Recovery and Resolution Directive
  (BRRD), 126
Banking Union, 38–39, 92
  ECB's role in, 39, 128–129
  political ramifications of, 99–100, 129, 141
  UK and, 22, 129
Barroso Commission, 153, 443
Barroso, José Manuel, 419
Basel Committee on Banking Supervision
  (BCBS), 111, 117–118, 123, 125, 131–133
Berlusconi, Silvio, 38, 483
Bigo, Didier, 230, 304
Blue Card Directive, 394
Bonditti, Philippe, 229
border control, 5, 11–13, 192, 196, 232–237, 275,
  277, 288–290, 294, 302–306, 375–390,
  526–527, 542–544, 548, 555
Bourdieu, Pierre, 509, 513–514
Brexit, 3, 98, 109, 492, 512, 524
  EU financial regulation, impact on, 112,
  133–134
  free movement as factor in, 13, 187–188
Broeders, Dennis, 230
Brown, Gordon, 127
Bugarič, Bojan, 486

Calliess, Christian, 62
Cameron, David, 148, 151
Central and Eastern European countries, 157,
  166–169, 185, *see also* Eastern Europe
Chalmers, Damian, 498–499
Charter of Fundamental Rights of the EU
  (EUCFR), 57, 274, 332, 334, 340, 376, 378,
  408, 438, 442, 547, 555, 571
  Article 4, 207
  Article 7, 253, 284
  Article 8, 388
  Article 13, 439
  Article 14, 439
  Article 16, 439
  Article 42, 388
  Article 47, 439, 443, 453
  Article 51, 58, 438
  Article 52, 253
  Article 53, 379

civil and political rights, 557–558
  access to justice for, 29, 535–558, 573
  as first-generation rights, 550
  in sovereignty-sensitive policy areas, 568
Civil Liberties, Justice and Home Affairs
  (LIBE) Committee, 295, 299, 422, 426
CLOUD Act, 286, 319, 324–328, 335–341
coalition building, 22, 46, 50, 65, 93, 106–108,
  150, 423–424, 562
collective action. *See* industrial action
collective bargaining, 174
  Ohlin Report, 159–160
Committee on Internal Security (COSI), 401,
  404
Common European Asylum System (CEAS),
  193, 392
  AFSJ, 195–196
  executive federalism, 204–205
  externalization, 200, 224–226
  funding, 217–223
  history of, 191, 194–196
  implementation, 201, 205–206, 212–217
  integrated administration, 201, 205–206, 223,
  226
  legislative harmonization, 193, 200
  refugee status, 197, 217
  responsibility assignation, 203, 206
  subsidiary protection, 197–198
  temporary protection, 198–199
  unilateralism, 225–226
Common Foreign and Security Policy (CFSP)
  EUNAVFOR MED Operation Sophia,
  306–308, 405
  internal/external security, 308
  legal basis AFSJ measures, 404
Common Provisions Regulation (CPR),
  442–443
Computer Emergency Response Teams
  (CERTs), 296
Conference of INGOs to the Council of
  Europe, 342–371, 374
conferral, principle of, 43, 379–380
constitutional fundamentals, 548, *see also*
  Article 2 TEU; Article 7 TEU; European
  values; judicial independence
  accession, 16–17
  Article 2 TEU, 547
  Article 7 TEU, 19–20, 545–546
  Council of Europe System, 16
  defintion of, 5
  ECJ as human rights court, 546–547, 571

Index

intergovernmentalism, 17, 545–546
legal complexity, 545–548
populism, 19–20
spillover from integrated administration, 15
values, 546
Constitutional Treaty, 168–169, 546, 559–560, 575
Cooley, Alexander, 94
Cooperative Financial Mechanism (CFM), 516
Council Decision 2000/596/EC, 217
Council Decision 2004/512/EC, 237
Council Decision 2005/211/JHA, 239
Council Decision 2005/671/JHA, 292
Council Decision 2007/533/JHA, 239
Council Decision 2008/633/JHA, 237
Council Decision (CFSP) 2015/778, 306
Council Decision (CFSP) 2016/2314, 307
Council Decision (EU) 2015/1523, 209
Council Decision (EU) 2015/1601, 209
Council of Europe, 273, 344
　Additional Protocol to Council of Europe
　　Convention on the Prevention of
　　Terrorism, 276, 309–310, 396
　Budapest Convention on Cybercrime, 341
　civil society and, 368–369, 371–374
　constitutional fundamentals and, 15,
　　368–374
　Convention on the Prevention of Terrorism,
　　395
Council of the EU, 198, 328, 330, 489
counter-terrorism
　CFSP, 270–278
　Counter-Terrorism Group, 277, 293–294
　databases, 15, 282–284, 289–290
　EU-US cooperation, 271
　history of, 269–270, 272–273
　institutional framework of, 274, 278–281, 404
　JHA, 274
　law enforcement and judicial cooperation,
　　274, 290–294
　national security excluded, 277–278
　terrorist threat, 270–272
Counter-Terrorism Group (CTG), 277,
　293–294
Country Specific Recommendations (CSRs)
　competitiveness, 74–75
　compliance with, 85–88
　enforcement MIP, 86–87
　flexicurity, 77
　judicial system, 85
　know-how from bailouts, 71, 80–85

labor market reforms, 77–78
recurrent property tax, 81–82
social and welfare policy, 80–85, 88
structural reforms, 84
Structural Reforms Support Service, 78
country-of-origin principle
　ECJ cases, 171–181
　lex loci laboris principle contra, 170
　Services Directive, 169–170
　social dumping, 170, 178
Csillag, Tamás, 488
Czech Republic
　populism, 481–483
　rejection relocation asylum seekers, 20, 225,
　　407, 563

Dahl, Robert, 510–512
data protection. *See* right to personal data
　protection
data retention, 303, 557
　ECJ, 284–285, 317
　German FCC, 316–317, 558
　Romanian Constitutional Court, 317, 558
databases, 227–231
　9/11 impact on, 236–237
　biometrics in, 238, 240–241, 252, 255,
　　260–261, 264, 283, 286–287, 294–295
　counter-terrorism purposes, 273, 282–297,
　　305–306
　first wave, 24, 231–235
　immigration control, 232–233, 236–238,
　　248–249, 256–260, 289–290
　interoperability of, 241, 251–253, 263–265,
　　294–296, 305–306
　law enforcement, 232, 238–239, 241–243,
　　252–253, 262–265
　legal challenges, lack of, 555, 557–558
　privacy assessment of, 253–265
　second wave, 24, 235–243
　surveillance of movement, 245, 247–248,
　　258, 303–304
　terrorism impact on, 243, 246, 236–237
　third wave, 24, 243–253
　third-country nationals in, 243–265,
　　283
Daul, Joseph, 425
Davies, Gareth, 528
Dawson, Mark, 89, 501
de Búrca, Gráinne, 121
De Vries, Catherine E., 143
Deauville Agreement, 106

580   Index

Decision 575/2007/EC, 218
Delors, Jacques, 147, 499
democracy
   AFSJ, 385–386
   European Parliament, 58–64, 135, 385–386,
     510, 567–570
   Europeanization domestic politics, 136,
     143–146
   Spitzenkandidaten, 147–152, 188–190
democratic backsliding, 413–431
democratic deficit. *See also* democratic
    disconnect
   euro crisis, aggravated by, 142–143, 152
   European Semester, in, 142, 563
   no-demos problem, 509, 512–513
   technocracy, 21, 89, 97, 127, 313–315, 506,
     508, 520–521
democratic disconnect, 27
   demos-legitimacy, 511–512
   fiscal capacity, 515–516
   mobilization fiscal resources, 514–516
   mobilization human resources, 516–517
   power-legitimacy nexus, 508–509, 517–519,
     521–522
direct effect in criminal law, 378–379
Direction-Social Democracy (Slovakia), 482
Directive 64/221/EEC, 539
Directive 77/338/EEC, 539
Directive 96/71/EC, 164
Directive 2000/78/EC, 490, 539
Directive 2004/58/EC, 13
Directive 2005/71/EC, 394
Directive 2006/123/EC, 169
Directive 2008/115/EC, 393
Directive 2009/50/EC, 394
Directive(EU) 2011/85, 37, 495
Directive(EU) 2011/98, 394
Directive(EU) 2014/67, 179, 181
Directive(EU) 2016/680, 388
Directive(EU) 2016/681, 274, 310
Directive(EU) 2017/541, 310, 400
Directive(EU) 2018/957, 185
Directive Against Terrorism, 401
directive on equal treatment (proposed), 375–390
directives (generally)
   direct effect, 538–539
   from international to supranational, 537–539
   horizontal direct effect, lack of, 549
   indirect effect, 544
   legal complexity, 537–539
distortion of competition, 159, 163–164, 172, 178

Dombrovskis, Valdis, 77, 150
Draghi, Mario, 107, 141
Dublin Convention, 193–194, 234, 542,
   548
   refugees in orbit, 12, 206
Dublin system, 24, 193
   Dublin III Regulation, 215, 225, 257
   Dublin III System, 206–208
   Dublin IV proposal, 210–212
   Eurodac, 234–235, 241, 256–258

Eastern Europe, 4, 13, 209, *see also* Central and
   Eastern Europen Countries
ECOFIN Council, 58–59, 139
Economic and Monetary Union (EMU)
   diagnosis of flaws, 34–35, 74
   euro crisis, impact of, 36–39, 98–108
   history, 34–39
   politicized integration, 92–93, 98–108
   politics, 40–41, 44–47
economic migration, 219, 394
economic policy, 548
   access to justice, 540, 554–555
   credible commitments, 562
   democracy in, 569
   ECJ jurisdiction, 539–540, 554
   European Parliament, oversight, 563
   European Semester, 67–78, 519
   fiscal discipline, 8–9
   fiscal transfers, 9, 540
   independent institutions, 562–563
   intergovernmentalism, 561–563
   international treaties, basis in, 539–540
   legal challenges (fundamental rights),
     540–541
   legal complexity, 539–541
   national parliaments, oversight, 59–60,
     519
   North-South cleavage, 9, 154
   populism, 9
   quantitative easing, 9
   reform of, 541
   sanctions, 10, 561–563
   spillover from monetary policy, 3–8
   surveillance, 10, 540–541, 562
e-evidence proposals. *See* European
   Production and Preservation Orders,
   proposal for
Eichengreen, Barry, 500
Electronic Travel Authorisation System
   (ESTA), 246, 260, 283

EMU. *See* Economic and Monetary Union
Entry/Exit System (EES), 230, 394, 553
  information contained in, 245
  purposes of, 244–245
equality in free movement law
  equal pay for equal work, 23, 157–158, 160,
    163, 165, 169, 172, 175–176, 180–181,
    185–188
Esping-Andersen, Gøsta, 84
EU Agency for Network and Information
    Security (ENISA), 296, 384
EU budget, 100, 217, 222, 397, 515
  proposals to expand, 49–51, 65
EU citizenship, 13, 161, 305, 432, 574
  right to privacy, 316–317, 323, 556
  surveillance of mobility, 266
EU Counter-Terrorism Coordinator, 274, 279
EU criminal law, 18, 276, 302–303, 309–310,
    375–378, 394, 558
EU financial regulation
  financial crisis, after, 22, 111–112, 123–134
  financial crisis, before, 22, 111, 113–123
  Germany's role, 113–114
  public salience as factor, 127
  transnational standards, reliance on, 118
  UK's role, 22, 111, 113–116, 128–130
EU Intelligence and Situation Centre
    (INTCEN), 279
eu-LISA, 211, 224, 281, 314, 384, 402, 406
EUNAVFOR MED Operation Sophia,
    306–308, 405
euro crisis
  Banking Union, 88, 92, 99
  causes of, 33–34, 53, 70, 74
  democratic deficit, aggravation of, 60,
    137–142, 152
  ECB powers, 9, 38–39, 48, 59–60, 92, 99, 141
  EMU, impact on, 36–39, 48
  ESM, 37, 48, 59, 72, 92, 99, 102–103, 105
  European Commission politicization, 46
  European Commission powers, 138–139, 153
  Europeanization domestic politics, 22–23,
    143–146
  Euroskepticism and, 142–143, 146
  Fiscal Compact, 38, 53
  reconstituting sovereignty practices,
    98–108
  supranational bodies, 59–60, 141–142
Eurobonds, 51, 105, 502, 522
Eurodac, 261, 263–264, 555
  Dublin System, in, 234–235, 256–258

information contained in, 235, 248–249
law enforcement tool, 241–243, 294, 306, 392
reform of, 242, 248–249, 392
Eurogroup, 45, 64, 517, 520
Eurojust, 239, 280, 292–293, 375–397, 406,
    565–566
European Anti-Fraud Office (OLAF),
    397–398, 444–445
European arrest warrant, 273, 280, 432
  Aranyosi, 449
  Celmer, 19, 448–451
  Melloni, 379
European Asylum Support Office (EASO), 24,
    210, 383, 405
  Asylum Support Teams, 213–214, 223–224
  EASO Regulation, 214–215
  EU Agency on Asylum, proposed, 216–217,
    224, 564
  integrated administration, 212–213, 216,
    223–224
  joint-processing, 214–215, 224
European Banking Authority (EBA), 128–129
European Border and Coast Guard Agency.
    See Frontex
European Central Bank (ECB)
  asset-buying programmes, 38, 53
  Gauweiler, 42–44
  independence, 100, 141, 562–563
  monetary policy, 9, 43, 48, 53, 100, 520
  OMT programme, 38, 53
  QE programmes, 38, 43, 53, 520
  SSM, 39, 141
  Weiss, 43
European Civil Protection and Humanitarian
    Aid Operations (ECHO), 383
European Commission, 72, 328, 330
  Article 7 TEU, 16, 430, 489
  European Semester, 67–68, 73–90
  parliamentary model, 23, 147–148, 188–189
  Rule of Law Framework, 419–420
  technocracy, 21, 68, 521
  trusteeship model, 23, 153
European Conservatives and Reformists, 427
European Convention on Human Rights
    (ECHR)
  Article 15, 344–349, 357–367, 374
  Article 8, 253, 342–343, 349–350, 357–358,
    368–369, 374
European Council, 70, 107, 188, 190, 243, 274,
    294, 307, 385, 400, 402–404, 408, 430, 517,
    521–522, 546

582   *Index*

European Counter-Terrorism Centre
(ECTC), 279–280, 566
European Court of Human Rights (ECtHR)
A. v. United Kingdom, 346–347, 362
Brannigan v. United Kingdom, 348, 366
Lawless v. Ireland, 345, 360–362
S and Marper v. United Kingdom, 255
Sakis v. Turkey, 349
Zakharov v. Russia, 365
European Court of Justice (ECJ)
access to justice in, 540, 551, 554
Article 7 TEU, 418, 546
databases, examination of, 253–256, 284–285,
317, 555
democracy, effect on, 570–573
democratic disconnect, 510, 527–529
direct access to, 559–560, 571, 575–576
directives, 538–539
fundamental rights, 550–551, 553–554
human rights court, as, 546–547, 560,
571
infringement actions, rule-of-law, 434–435,
437–438
jurisdiction, 544, 546
jurisdiction over AFSJ, 274, 375–377
MoU, examination of, 540–541, 554
over-constitutionalization, 570–571
preliminary reference system, 18, 29, 452,
454, 542, 544, 551–552, 559, 573
standing, 551, 559–560, 573, 575–576
transparency and access to documents,
389
European Court of Justice (ECJ) cases
Alpenrind, 161–183
Altun, 182–183
Aranyosi, 449–450
Arblade and Others, 167
A-Rosa Flussschiff, 182
Białowieża Forest case, 27, 465–472
Celmer, 18, 437, 448–451, 548
Commission v. Germany (C-244/04), 167
Commission v. Hungary (C-286/12), 490
Commission v. Hungary (C-288/12), 434
Commission v. Poland (C-619/18), 451
Defrenne v. Sabena, 163
Digital Rights Ireland, 254–255, 263, 317
Finalarte, 166–167
French Merchant Seamen, 162–163
Gauweiler, 39, 42–43
Kadi litigation, 315
Laval, 173, 176–177, 180

Ledra Advertising, 57–58, 548
Melloni, 379
*Opinion 1/15 on EU-Canada PNR
Agreement*, 254–256, 261, 263, 311
Opinion 2/13 on ECHR accession, 378, 464, 473
Portuguese Judges, 437–438, 440, 447–448,
451
Pringle, 39, 51, 58, 497
RegioPost, 179–180
Rüffert, 175–177, 180
Rush Portuguesa, 165–166, 176
Schwarz, 255, 260
Taricco I and II, 379
Tele2, 254–255, 263, 284–285, 312, 317
Viking, 177–178
Weiss, 43
European Criminal Records Information
System (ECRIS), 283, 557
European Criminal Records Information
System for Third-Country Nationals
(ECRIS-TCN), 230, 250–252, 262, 266,
557
inclusion dual nationals, 251
European Cybercrime Centre (EC3), 280, 285
European Deposit Insurance Scheme
(proposed), 526
European Economic Community, 16, 158,
160–161, *see also* Treaty of Rome
European elections, 23, 135–136, 147–152,
188–190, 425
European External Action Service (EEAS),
279
European Financial Stability Facility (EFSF),
33, 37, 103
as international treaty, 540
European Fund for Strategic Investments
(EFSI), 502, 515
European governance, models of
administrative governance, 506–510
Community Method, 29, 59, 152, 375, 377,
390, 400, 560
intergovernmentalism, 29–30, 59–60, 92,
137–143, 194, 272, 278, 375, 377, 400, 404,
415, 418, 429–430, 515, 521, 536, 545,
561–567
parliamentarism, 23, 147–154, 188–190
principal-agent delegation, 94–95, 507,
522–523, 528–529
supranationalism. *See* Community method
European Integration Fund, 218
European Investigation Order, 273, 280, 329

Index

European Macro Group, 498
European Monetary Fund, 49, 61–62
politics of, 541
European Monitoring Centre for Drugs and
Drug Addiction (EMCDDA), 406
European Observatory of Drugs, 384
European Parliament
AFSJ legislation, 385
economic dialogue, 60
economic policy, 563, 569
EU agencies, oversight of, 397, 400, 406,
563, 569–570
European elections, 23, 135–136, 147–152,
188–190
internal security, 299, 401, 568–570
LIBE Committee, 295, 299, 422, 426
rule-of-law crisis, 422–423
Spitzenkandidaten, 46, 147–152, 188–190
subnational authoritarianism, 428
supranational democracy, 29, 60, 63, 385,
400–407, 505–506, 510–514, 567–573
European People's Party (EPP), 148, 151, 189,
425–428, 489, 569
European Pillar of Social Rights, 90, 184–185
European Police College (CEPOL), 280–281,
297, 406
European Production and Preservation Orders,
proposal for, 319–320, 329–335
European Public Prosecutor (EPPO),
384–385, 396–398, 404, 409, 444–445, 565
Hungary, 445
Poland, 445
European Refugee Fund, 217–218, 220
European Return Fund, 218
European Semester, 71
Annual Growth Survey, 70–71
CSRs, 77–78
economic coordination through, 70, 72,
75–76, 79
economic dialogue, 60, 563
effectiveness of, 71–72, 85–88
flexibility in, 80–81
macroeconomic imbalance, 71
redesign of, 73–80
Six Pack, 70–71
Social Europe, 79–80, 88–90
structural reforms, 67–68, 71–72, 75–85
Two Pack, 70–71
European Social Contract, 157–158
European Social Pillar. *See* European Pillar of
Social Rights

European Socialist Party (PES), 147–148,
151
European Stability Mechanism (ESM), 72, 92,
102–104, 497, 516, 540
Article 136(3) TFEU, 37
democratic accountability, 61–62
international treaty, as, 37
proposed reform, 541
European Strategic Communications
Network, 275
European Structural and Investment Funds
(ESIFs)
CPR, 442–443
CSR-compliance conditionality, 76
rule-of-law conditionality, 440, 443,
445–446
European Supervisory Authorities (ESAs),
128–129
European System of Financial Supervision,
128
European Travel Information and
Authorisation System (ETIAS), 394, 555
information contained in, 260
purposes of, 246
scope, 246–248
European values. *See also* Article 2 TEU
independent judiciary, 432
non-discriminatory enforcement law, 157,
160, 162–163, 413
rule of law, 414–415, 417, 432, 458, 463
Europol, 290–291, 293, 383, 396–397, 401, 406,
566
analytical work files, 290
cooperation third countries, 291
Focal Point Travellers Initiative, 296
Joint Investigation Teams (JITs), 291
Europol Information System, 282, 290, 298,
557
Euroskepticism, 137–142, 146
populism, 154
Eurozone
courts, impact on, 39–44
democratic accountability, 21, 61–62
fiscal control, 36–39, 53–54
institutional framework, 58–60
Eurozone Council, 59, 65
Eurozone European Council, 59
Eurozone reforms (proposed), 49–50
budget, 48–51
constitutionality of, 51–53, 55–58, 61–64
democratic accountability, 58–64

Eurozone reforms (proposed) (cont.)
European Investment Protection Scheme, 49
European Minister of Economy and Finance, 61
European Monetary Fund, 49, 61
European Unemployment Reinsurance Scheme, 49
Fiscal Compact, 54–55
fiscal flexibility, 55
Five Presidents' Report, 45, 49, 60–61
Glienicke Group, 47
politics of, 46–47, 50–51, 65–66
T-Dem, 47, 60
White Paper on the Future of Europe, 45
EU-US cooperation
counter-terrorism, 271, 282, 300
law enforcement, 327–329, 332–334, 336–341
EU-US Passenger Name Record (PNR) Agreement, 271
EU-US Terrorist Financing Tracking Programme, 271, 282
Excessive Deficit Procedure (EDP), 10, 69, 444, 496
Exit/Entry System (EES), 247–248
External Borders Fund, 218

Fabbrini, Federico, 47
Fico, Robert, 482
Fidesz, 3–4, 413, 419, 422, 424–427, 483–485, 490, 569
Financial Stability Board (FSB), 126, 132
financial transaction tax (proposed), 124
fines. *See also* sanctions
CSRs, non-compliance, 69
EDP, 10, 443–444
Fiscal Compact, 71
MIP, 10
First Pillar, 376–377, 539, 542–544, 548
Fiscal Compact
Article 16, 54
Article 3, 495–496
Article 4, 496
austerity and, 56, 493–494
balanced budget rule, 10, 494–496, 562
compliance with, 54–55
constitutional law, 38, 51–53, 56, 495, 497
debt brake, 496
democratic deficit, 142
euro crisis, 53, 498–499
flexibility, 55, 498

international treaty, as, 38, 54, 494, 540
proposed reforms to, 54–55
SGP, 139
Six Pack, 10, 139
sovereignty, impact on, 142, 492, 497–498, 519
fiscal discipline, 8–9, 22, 99, 101–108, 493–499, 508, 520, *see also* fiscal stability
fiscal stability, 21, 37, 53–58, 65, 561–563, 570–572, *see also* fiscal discipline
Five Presidents' Report, 45, 49, 60–61, 108
Five Star Movement, 3, 479
flexibility clause
AFSJ, 376–384
Focal Point Travellers initiative, 296
foreign fighters. *See foreign terrorist fighters*
foreign terrorist fighters
Additional Protocol to Council of Europe Convention on the Prevention of Terrorism, 276, 309–310, 396
Council of Europe Counter-terrorism Convention, 309
UN Security Council Resolution 2178, 276, 309
France, 153
EDP, 36, 69, 138, 140
Law 55-385, 350–353
Law 2015-1501, 351–353, 360
Law 2017-1510, 353
state of emergency, 343, 350–352, 372
validity Article 15 ECHR derogation, 358–362, 367
Franklin, Mark N., 136
free movement of persons, 12–13
East-West split, 154, 168–170
Ohlin Report, 159–160
Spaak Report, 158–159
freedom of establishment
Viking, 177–178
Freedom Party (Austria), 418–419
freedom to provide services. *See also* posting of workers
Arblade and Others, 167
Commission v. Germany (C-244/04), 167
Finalarte, 166–167
regulatory competition model, 158, 172–173, 176, 186
regulatory neutrality model, 172–173, 176, 186
Rush Portuguesa, 165–166
social dumping, 158, 167–168, 172

Front de gauche, 136
Front National, 3
Frontex, 192, 213, 281, 313, 383–384, 401,
    405–406
    expansion of, 289, 391, 406–407, 517, 527, 564
Froud, Julie, 107
fundamental rights. *See also* civil and political
    rights; social rights
    access to justice (ECJ), 551
    interoperability, 263–265, 305–306
    preventive justice, 311–313, 316–317
    privatization, 311–313
    Security Union, 301, 305–306
Fundamental Rights Agency (FRA), 281, 295,
    384, 405

Gammeltoft-Hansen, Thomas, 97, 230
Garben, Sacha, 90
Genschel, Philipp, 93
German Federal Constitutional Court
    (Bundesverfassungsgericht or FCC)
    Gauweiler, 42–43, 52–53
    Lisbon Treaty judgment, 41
    Maastricht Treaty judgment, 35–36
    standing doctrine, 43–44
Germany
    CSRs, 83
    EDP, 36, 69, 138
    ESM, 41
    European Semester, 72
    exporter balanced budget rule, 498
    no bailout rule, 100–102, 105, 107
    politics of, 65, 105, 107, 150, 494
    SGP, 68
    unilateralism asylum policy, 225
Global Counter-Terrorism Forum (GCTF),
    271, 288
Global Systemically Important Banks (G-SIBs),
    125
Greece, 101, 289, 499
    CSRs, 71–74
    EASO in, 210, 216, 224, 564
    euro crisis, 70
    Europeanization of politics, 143–146
    Mediterranean style welfarism, 82
    MoU, 83
    relocation asylum seekers, 209
    sovereignty impact of bailouts, 37, 103–104,
    106
    structural reforms, 81
    welfare-regime reform, 83–84

Grimm, Dieter, 528
Grudzinska-Gross, Irena, 488
Gülen Movement, 355–356, 363, 366

Hague Programme, 241, 243, 304
Hix, Simon, 494–495
Hollande, François, 351
horizontal differentiation
    AFSJ, in, 206, 228, 386–387
Horizontal Regulation, 219, 223
hotspots, 24, 216, 289, 391, 564
human migration. *See also* border control;
    Common European Asylum System;
    free movement of persons; freedom to
    provide services; visa policy, economic
    migration
    access to justice, 555–556
    Brexit, 13
    definition of, 5
    democracy in, 563–565
    ECJ jurisdiction, 555–556, 559–560
    European Parliament, oversight agencies,
    569–570
    intergovernmentalism, 563–565
    international treaties, basis in, 541–542
    legal challenges (fundamental rights),
    555–556, 559–560
    legal complexity, 541–543
    populism, 15
    reform of, 559–560, 567–573
    spillover from abolition internal borders,
    10–13
    Third Pillar, 541–543
Hungary
    Article 258 TFEU, 490
    Article 7 TEU, 419, 422–423, 426
    austerity, 483
    authoritarian populism, 483–485,
    487–488
    constitutional capture, 422
    data protection ombudsman, 434–435
    democratic backsliding, 413–415, 422–426,
    457, 483–485, 488
    EDP, 443–444
    infringement actions against, 438–439
    legal challenge to relocation asylum seekers,
    209–210
    Putinism, 483
    rejection relocation asylum seekers, 20, 225,
    407, 563
    Rule of Law Framework, 419–420

immigration. *See* Amsterdam Treaty; asylum policy; Common European Asylum System; economic migration; Lisbon Treaty; Maastricht Treaty; visa policy

Independent Greeks (ANEL), 136, 144

indirect administration, 383–384, *see also* Common European Asylum System, executive federalism

industrial action, 159, 169, 172, 174–177

information sharing. *See also* information sharing environment
barriers to, 401
Member State duty, 400–401

information sharing environment
battlefield information, 287–288
biometric technologies, 286–287
border controls, in, 283–284
cloud as challenge to, 285–286
cybersecurity, 270–296
data protection, 284, 295, 298–300
data retention, 284–285
digitalization of security, 298
encryption as challenge to, 285
European Intelligence Academy, 297
interoperability, 294–296
law enforcement and judicial cooperation, in, 292–293
obstacles to, 285–286
security and intelligence services, among, 293–294
third countries, 291

infringement actions
rule-of-law, 451

infringement actions, systemic, 26, 433–440

integrated administration, 17–18, 205–206, 223, 384, 564, *see also* Common European Asylum System, integrated administration; EASO, integrated administration

Intergovernmental Agreement (IGA) on the Transfer and Mutualisation of Contributions to the Single Resolution Fund, 516
international treaty, as, 39

interim measures, 451, 466–468
penalty for non-compliance, 27, 468

internal market, 10, 90, 157, 161–162, 173, 185, 187, 195, 199, 528

internal security. *See also* counter-terrorism
access to justice, 557
definition of, 5, 276

democracy in, 399
ECJ jurisdiction, 544
European Parliament, oversight agencies, 569–570
intergovernmentalism, 559–565
international treaties, basis in, 543–544
legal challenges (fundamental rights), 558
legal complexity, 544–545
populism, 15
reform of, 535–565, 575
spillover from abolition internal borders, 14
Third Pillar, 377, 543–545

internal security strategy (ISS), 398–399, *see also* Security Union

International Accounting Standards Board (IASB), 111, 114, 123

International Monetary Fund (IMF), 37, 72, 81, 103, 483, 498

International Organization of Securities Commissions (IOSCO), 111

Internet Referral Unit, 280, 285

interoperability, 251–253
data protection, 263–265, 402
fundamental rights, 313–315

Italy, 33, 38, 53, 109, 141, 153, 192, 289, 526
EASO in, 210, 213, 224, 564
relocation asylum seekers, 209

Jachtenfuchs, Markus, 93, 95

Jones, Erik, 92, 95, 100

Jourová, Vera, 441–442, 445

judicial independence, 18, 475
Hungary, 485
Poland, 439–440, 449, 451
Portuguese Judges, 447–448

Juncker Commission, 79, 140, 153, 270

Juncker, Jean-Claude, 45–47, 88, 103, 148, 150–151, 189, 270, 442, 446–447, 566

Justice and Home Affairs (JHA), 228, 270, 273–274, 304, 376–377, 542
availability of information, 273, 286–287, 292–294, 375–400
mutual recognition judicial decisions, 273–274, 394–396, 433

Kagan, Robert, 121

Kakouris, Constantinos N., 475

Katsanidou, Alexia, 144

Kattainen, Jyrky, 150

Kelemen, Daniel, 88, 92, 95, 100, 491, 546, 569

Keohane, Robert O., 94

Kilpatrick, Claire, 554
Kochenov, Dimitry, 417
Koczanowicz, Leszek, 487
Krasner, Stephen D., 94
Kuciak, Jan, 482
Kurdistan Workers' Party, 358

Lagarde, Christine, 36
Lamfalussy Process, 114–115, 128
Law and Justice (PiS), 4, 413, 420–421, 427, 444, 485–487
legal certainty, 28, 181, 536–537, 539, 546
legal complexity, 28, 536–537
   changing status norms, 535–545
   variety legal norms, 535–545
legal norms, types of, 535–537, 539–540
   international, 28, 535–537, 539–546
   supranational, 28, 535–542, 544, 546
legal simplification, 547–550
Lisbon template, 560–561, 564, 567, 570
Lisbon Treaty, 390, 393, 546
   AFSJ, 375–387, 402
   asylum policy, 195–201, 391
   Community method, 29, 375–376, 560
   criminal justice, 375–394
   internal security, 14, 276–277, 380, 544
   preliminary reference system, 542–545, 552
   supranational democracy, 385–386, 560–561
London, City of, 112, 114–115, 118, 123, 134

Maastricht Treaty, 4–5, 147, 228, 548, see also Third Pillar
   border control, 542–543
   EMU, 8, 35–36
   immigration, 542–543
   internal security, 14, 543
   Third Pillar, 377, 542–543
MacCormick, Neil, 511–512
Macroeconomic Imbalance Procedure (MIP), 10, 86, 108, 138–139
Macron, Emmanuel, 46, 49–50, 65, 297, 430, 499, 525–526
Mair, Peter, 135–136
Medium-Term Budgetary Objective (MTBO), 49, 54–55, 496
Memorandum of Understanding (MoU) 497
   legal challenges, 57–58, 540–541, 554
Menéndez, Augustín José, 495, 497

Mengozzi, Paolo, 174–175
Merkel, Angela, 99, 101, 105–107, 138, 142, 148, 426, 428, 493, 499
Meunier, Sophie, 92, 95, 100
Milward, Alan S., 520–521
Mody, Ashoka, 499–500
monetary policy, 8–10, 34–36, 42–43, 53, 75, 100, 520
monetary union, 34–36
Monti, Mario, 146
Moscovici, Pierre, 65, 76–77, 150
Mouffe, Chantal, 480
Multi-Annual Financial Framework, 219, 446
mutual legal assistance (MLA), 25, 271, 273, 280, 286, 321–323, 327–328
mutual recognition
   AFSJ, 382, 384
   criminal law, 329, 394, 565
   databases, 557
   European Arrest Warrant, 273, 557
   free movement of establishment, 178
   free movement of services, 170–171
   social security certificates, 161–182
mutual trust, suspension of, 382, 447–451, see also European Arrest Warrant

national budgets
   EDP, 562–563
   European Semester cycle of, 70–71
   sovereignty, 71
   timing of, 71
   Two Pack, 108
national security, 277–278, 380–381
New Democracy (Greece), 144
no bailout rule (Article 125(1) TFEU), 35–36, 48, 61, 100, 102–103, 540, 572
   Germany, 100–102, 105, 107
   Pringle, 51
non-discrimination, 157, 160–161, 188, see also equality in free movement law
   ECJ case law, early, 162–163
   nationality, 162–163
   sex, 163

Orbán, Viktor, 424–428, 441, 444, 447, 483–485, 488–489, 491, 526–527, 569
Orenstein, Mitchell, 486
Otjes, Simon, 144
Outright Monetary Transactions (OMT)
   Programme, 38, 42, 53

overlapping consensus. *See also* Rawls, J.
  rule of law as fundamental to, 464–465
over-the-counter (OTC) derivatives, 118, 123, 127

Pagliari, Stefano, 127
Panhellenic Socialist Movement (PASOK), 144
Papandreou, George, 143
parliamentarism, 147–154, 188–190
Party for Freedom (Netherlands), 3
Passenger Name Record (PNR) Directive, 274, 282–283, 566
Pech, Laurent, 416, 448
Pescatore, Pierre, 462–463
Piketty, Thomas, 47
Pirro, Andrea, 483
Platon, Sébastien, 448
Podemos, 3, 154
Poland
  Article 7 TEU, 422–423, 428, 461
  authoritarian populism, 458–462, 485–488
  Białowieża Forest case, 465–472
  Commission v. Poland (C-619/18), 451, 546
  democratic backsliding, 413–415, 420–421, 457, 460–462, 485–488
  independence of judiciary, 414–415, 420–421, 439–440, 448–449, 451–455, 461, 486–487
  infringement actions against, 439–440, 451, 453, 546
  Polska B, 486
  rejection relocation asylum seekers, 20, 407, 563
  Rule of Law Framework, activated against, 421–422, 427–428, 490–491
Polanyi, Karl, 479–480
Polish Constitutional Tribunal, capture of, 421, 486–487
Polish National Judicial Council, packing of, 453
Polish Supreme Court, capture of, 451
politicization, 97–98
  effect on European integration, 91–93, 109
  European elections, 147–152
  Europeanization domestic politics, 22–23, 136–137
politics of resentment, 457–476
populism, 102, 148, 506, 511–512, 524–525
  austerity as contributor to, 9–10, 478–479
  authoritarian, 3, 19–20, 458–462, 481–488
  causes of, 3–9, 13, 158, 187–188, 190, 478–479

ethno-nationalism, 3, 13, 487–488
  ideology of, 4, 19–20, 458–462, 477–478
  left-wing, 3, 102, 148, 154
  right-wing, 3–4, 13, 102, 148, 154
  social, vindication of, 158, 187–188, 479–480
Portugal, 40, 499, 554
  CSRs, 85
posting of workers. *See also* freedom to provide services
  amendments to Posting of Workers Directive, 185–186
  country-of-origin principle, 169–173, 178–179, 185
  Enforcement Directive, 179
  Laval, 173–177
  Posting of Workers Directive, 164–165, 172, 175, 179–180
  RegioPost, 179–180
  Rüffert, 175–177
  Sähköalojen, 180–181
preventive justice, 302–304, 308–309, 311–313, 315–318, 558
price stability, 48, 53
primacy, 114, 537
  police and judicial cooperation in criminal law, 375–378
Privacy Shield, 340–341
Progressive Alliance of Socialists and Democrats, 425
Prüm, 283, 295, 557
Putin, Vladimir, 483, 524, 527

Qualification Regulation (proposed), 392
quantitative easing (QE) programmes, 38, 43, 48, 52–53, 130, 520

Radicalization Awareness Network, 275
Rajoy, Mariano, 105
Rawls, John, 463–464
Reception Conditions Directive (proposed), 391
refugee crisis, 20, 208–209, 216, 221–224, 407, 520, 561, 564
Regulation 173/2011, 37
Regulation 407/2002, 234
Regulation 439/2010, 212, 216–217
Regulation 472/2013, 38
Regulation 473/2013, 38
Regulation 514/2014, 219
Regulation 516/2014, 218
Regulation 603/2013, 235, 242–243

Index

Regulation 604/2013, 206–208, 225, 257
Regulation 767/2008, 237
Regulation 862/2007, 381–382, 400
Regulation 871/2004, 239
Regulation 883/2004, 181–183
Regulation 1049/01, 389
Regulation 1173/2011, 139
Regulation 1174/2011, 37, 139
Regulation 1175/2011, 37, 60
Regulation 1176/2011, 37
Regulation 1177/2011, 37
Regulation 1260/2013, 382
Regulation 1303/2013, 86–87
Regulation 1466/97, 36, 68
Regulation 1467/97, 36, 68
Regulation 1986/2006, 239
Regulation 1987/2006, 239, 241
Regulation 2016/1624, 281, 289
Regulation 2016/679, 232, 388
Regulation 2017/1939, 396–397, 445
Regulation 2018/1860, 249
Regulation 2018/1861, 249
Regulation 2725/2000, 234
relocation (asylum seekers), 24, 225, 407
    Emergency Decisions, 20, 195–208, 216, 225,
        563
    infringement actions, 209
    legal challenges, 209–210
Renzi, Matteo, 146
Researchers Directive, 394
Return Directive, 393
reverse qualified majority voting (RQMV),
    138–139
right of access to documents, 388, 397
right to personal data protection
    Article 8 EUCFR, 253, 388
    Digital Rights Ireland, 254–255, 263, 317
    e-privacy regulation, draft, 299, 388
    General Data Protection Regulation
        (GDPR), 299, 323, 336, 388
    Opinion 1/15 on EU-Canada PNR
        Agreement, 254–256, 263
    privacy by design, 299–300
    Schwarz, 255, 260
    Tele2, 254–255, 263, 284–285, 312, 317
right to privacy. *See also* right to personal data
    protection
    Article 7 EUCFR, 253
    Article 8 ECHR, 253, 342–343, 349–350, 353,
        356–358, 362, 364–365, 368–369, 371,
        373–374

S and Marper v. UK, 255
Zakharov v. Russia, 255, 365
Rule of Law Dialogue, 422
Rule of Law Framework, 420, 490
    Hungary, 419–420
    Poland, 421–422, 427–428, 471
rule of law, undermining. *See also* Article 2
    TEU; Article 7 TEU; European values;
    judicial independence
    legal complexity, 535–537
    preventive justice, 315–317
    Security Union, 315–317
    technical, 313–315
Rutte, Mark, 500, 525–526

Salvini, Matteo, 526–527
sanctions. *See also* Article 7 TEU; fines;
    infringement actions, rule of law;
    infringement actions, systemic
    EDP, in, 36, 69, 100–101, 138, 444,
        562–563
    MIP, in, 139, 562–563
    rule-of-law violations, 415, 417–420, 431, 446,
        455, 489, 491–492
    Six Pack reinforcing, 108
Santer Commission, 147
Santer, Jacques, 147
Sargentini Report, 426–428, 443
Sarkozy, Nicolas, 106, 127, 142–143, 146
Saydé, Alexandre, 172–173
Scharpf, Fritz, 498
Schattschneider, Elmer Eric, 102, 109
Schäuble, Wolfgang, 153
Schelkle, Waltraud, 103
Schengen *acquis*, 193, 228, 260, 384, 542–543,
    545
Schengen Agreement, 11, 227, 391, 399,
    542
Schengen Area, 387
Schengen Borders Code, 193, 244–245,
    289–290, 390–391, 563
Schengen Convention, 14, 228, 542–543,
    548
    spillover from, 11
Schengen Information System (SIS I), 231–232
    alerts, 232–233
    criminal law instrument, as, 232–233
    immigration instrument, as, 232–233
Schengen Information System (SIS II), 555
    alerts, grounds for, 258–259
    biometric identifiers, 240–241, 252, 286–287

Schengen Information System (SIS II) (cont.)
  data protection, 259, 556
  interlinking alerts, 240
  reform of, 240–241, 249
Schengen Information System, generally,
  11–12, 14, 273, 289–290, 543
Schmidt, Vivien, 96, 478, 501–502
Schulz, Martin, 46–47, 51, 148
Schwartz, Paul, 324
Securities Market Programme (SMP), 38, 53
Security Union, 243, 260, 270, 278, 301–302,
  304, 306, 315, 566, see also Internal
  Security Strategy
Services Directive, 169
  country-of-origin principle, rejection of,
    169–170
  mutual recognition, 170–171
shared competence, 276–277
  AFSJ, over, 199, 379–380
sincere cooperation, principle of, 375–382, 404,
  see also mutual trust, suspension of
  democratic backsliding, 414, 437
  Social Security Regulation, in, 182
Single European Act, 10–11, 161
Single Permit Directive, 394
Single Resolution Fund (SRF), 39, 48, 129, 516
Single Resolution Mechanism (SRM), 9, 39,
  516
Single Supervisory Mechanism (SSM), 9, 39,
  141
Six Pack, 53, 492, 519, 548
  fines, 71
  reverse qualified majority voting, 138–139
  sanctions, 108
  SGP modified by, 70, 108, 138–139, 497
  surveillance, 3–10, 37–38, 138, 540–541, 572
Slovakia
  legal challenge to relocation asylum seekers,
    209–210
  populism, 481–482
Social Democratic Party (Germany), 46
social dumping, 178
  Polish plumber controversy, 170
  populism, 158
social justice, 567, 574
social rights
  access to justice for, 29, 551–554, 572–573
  bailouts, in, 56–58
  equal treatment, 170, 185–186, 552
  legitimate expectations, 550, 552
  as second-generation rights, 550

Social Security Regulation, 181
  Alpenrind, 183–184
  Altun, 182–183
  A-Rosa Flussschiff, 182
  sincere cooperation, principle of, 182
  social security certificates, 182–184
solidarity, 189, 270, 478
  AFSJ, 375–383, 408
  alert and intervention mechanisms, 383
  asylum policy, 191, 193, 196, 199, 201–203,
    209–210, 212, 391, 567
  economic policy, 102–103, 502, 567
Solove, Daniel, 312
Sørensen, Vibeke, 521
sovereignty, 101, 141, 146, 170, 173, 187, 378, 407,
  477, 480, 492, 497, 500, 507, 533–537, 539,
  549, 552, 556, 567, 569
sovereignty practices, 22, 93, 95–109
Spain, 101, 141, 479, 499
  CSRs, 71, 81, 86–87
  EDP fine, 71, 86–87
  ESM, 105–106
spillover, 6–30, 262, 272, 500–501, 535–537, 544,
  546, 552, 572
Spitzenkandidaten, 23, 188–190, 425–426, 510
  effect on turnout 2014 elections, 148–150
  European Commission, politicization, 46,
    147, 153–154
  history of, 147–148
  political support for, 147–148, 151
Spruyt, Hendrik, 94
Stability and Growth Pact (SGP)
  corrective arm, 8, 69
  EDP, 10, 69
  Fiscal Compact, 139, 496, 562
  flexibility in, 69–70, 139
  history of, 36
  preventive arm, 8, 69
  Six Pack modifying, 70, 108
state of emergency.
  France, 343, 350–352, 358–362
  Turkey, 350, 353–367, 370
Stored Communications Act (SCA), 319, 324,
  332
Streeck, Wolfgang, 498
structural reforms, 67–81, 83, 88, 140
subsidiarity, 186, 518, 559
  AFSJ, in, 199, 381, 385–386
supremacy. See primacy
surveillance
  digital, 311–313, 350, 353, 356–357, 365–366

fiscal, 21, 59, 69, 515, 519–520, 526, 562–563, 569

movement, of, 230–231, 243–248, 258, 266

Six Pack reinforcing, 10, 37–38, 108, 138, 540–541

Two Pack, enhanced in, 10, 37–38, 108, 138, 540–541

Sweden, 63, 213

CSRs, 81–82

trade unions, 169, 173–175

Sweden Democrats, 3

Syriza, 3, 144, 154

Szczerbiak, Aleks, 487

Szelényi, Iván, 488

Szydło, Beata, 490

Tampere European Council, 195

TEU and TFEU, Protocol 2, 386

TEU and TFEU, Protocol 25, 380

Third Pillar, 376–377, 542, 548

border control, 542

conventions, 542, 544–545

decisions, 544

framework decisions, 544

immigration, 542

internal security, 543–545

joint actions, 542, 544–545

Tillman, Erik R., 143

Timmermans, Frans, 151, 414–415, 443

Transatlantic Financial Market Regulatory Dialogue, 119, 132

transnational financial standards

EU as internationalist, 120–123, 130–133

EU financial regulation, in, 111–114, 116–118

neoliberalism, 116–118

standard setting bodies, 111, 131

US hegemony, 111, 114, 118–119

Treaty of Nice

revision Article 7 TEU, 419

Treaty of Rome, 20, 174, 472, 539

common market, 158–161

directives, 537–538

non-discrimination, 160–163

standing, 551

Treaty on European Union (TEU), 14, 161, 194, 201, 446, 542

Article 1, 473

Article 2, 17, 26, 413, 416, 431–432, 437–438, 448, 452, 470, 473, 489, 547–548

Article 3, 63

Article 4(2), 277, 380

Article 4(3), 382–408, 414, 437–438, 447

Article 5(1), 43

Article 5(3), 381

Article 7, 17–20, 26, 415–424, 426–433, 437–439, 441, 448, 450, 455, 461, 471, 489–491, 546, 548

Article 10, 61

Article 12, 386

Article 13(2), 382

Article 14, 404, 560

Article 15, 59

Article 17, 188, 403

Article 19(1), 437, 439, 443, 447–448, 451

Article 20, 242, 494

Article 40, 405

Article 48, 102, 494

Treaty on Stability, Coordination, and Governance. *See* Fiscal Compact

Treaty on the Functioning of the European Union (TFEU), 12, 54, 539

Article 2(2), 380

Article 4(2), 380

Article 15, 388–389

Article 16, 253, 388

Article 45, 162

Article 56, 163–167, 174–177

Article 67, 196, 199, 380

Article 68, 402

Article 69, 386

Article 70, 384, 386, 408

Article 71, 380, 386, 401, 404

Article 74, 209

Article 75, 386, 409

Article 76, 385

Article 77, 196, 383, 405

Article 78, 196–197, 199–200, 205, 212, 383, 386, 391

Article 79, 196, 383, 393, 405

Article 80, 202–203, 383

Article 82, 394

Article 83, 385, 394, 398

Article 85, 380, 384, 386, 394

Article 86, 384–385, 394, 397, 409

Article 88, 380, 384, 386, 397

Article 119, 35

Article 120, 35, 100

Article 121, 54, 60, 100

Article 122, 554

Article 123, 35, 43, 52

Article 125, 35, 48, 51, 61

Article 126, 35–36, 496

Treaty on the Functioning of the European Union (TFEU) (cont.)
  Article 130, 43
  Article 136(1) and (2), 58
  Article 136(3), 37, 51, 548
  Article 143, 554
  Article 157, 163
  Article 218, 378
  Article 222, 383
  Article 258, 26, 420, 433–435, 438, 470, 489–490
  Article 260, 455, 469, 471
  Article 263, 559–560
  Article 267, 552
  Article 279, 469
  Article 288, 538, 550
  Article 290, 404
  Article 291, 383, 404
  Article 326-334, 494
  Article 352, 384
Troika, 81, 103–104, 106, 497–498, 519
Trump, Donald, 483, 524, 527
Tsipras, Alexis, 106, 144, 150
Turkey
  decree no. 670, 356, 365
  decree no. 671, 356–367
  state of emergency, 343–374
  validity Article 15 ECHR derogation, 362–367
Tusk, Donald, 270
Two Pack, 53, 70–71, 492, 497, 519, 548
  enhanced surveillance in, 10, 37–38, 108, 138, 540–541, 572, 576

UN Security Council, 306, 308
  Resolution 2178 (2014), 276, 309
  Resolution 2240 (2015), 307, 405
  Resolution 2292 (2016), 307
United Kingdom (UK)
  Banking Union, 22, 129
  EFSM, 129–130
  ESAs, 128–129
  EU financial regulation, 110–111, 113, 133–134

Financial Services Act 1986, 118
Financial Services and Market Act 2000, 118
London, city of, 112, 114–115, 118, 123, 134
transnational standard-setting bodies, 110, 112, 114–115, 118, 130, 133
United States (US), 335–341
  CLOUD Act, 319, 324–328
  counter-terrorism and, 271, 298, 304
  EU-US Terrorist Financing Tracking Programme, 271, 282
  Joint Investigation Teams (JITs), 280, 291
  Stored Communications Act (SCA), 319, 324, 332
  transnational financial standards, 111, 118–119
US Supreme Court, 547
  Microsoft Ireland, 324–325

Van der Eijk, Cees, 136
Van Rompuy, Herman, 101, 108, 142, 148
Vanhercke, Bart, 88
Venice Commission (Council of Europe), 363, 365
  NGOs in, 369–371
Verdun, Amy, 89
Véron, Nicolas, 112, 119, 123, 130
Visa Code, 237
Visa Information System (VIS), 555
  access to data, 238–239
  personal data contained in, 237–238
  reform of, 236–237
visa policy, 393
  short-stay visas (Schengen visa), 236–237
  VIS, 236–237
Visegrad Group, 407, 563
von der Leyen, Ursula, 152, 190

Weber, Manfred, 151, 425–428
Weidmann, Jens, 140
White Paper on the Future of Europe, 45

Zeitlin, Jonathan, 88–89
Zielonka, Jan, 479